Ten Cool Things To Do w[...] Fedora Linux 14

Just because Fedora is a serious operating system doesn't mean it can't be fun too. Here is a list of ten fun and useful things to do with Fedora:

1. **Launch Fedora 14 live on your PC:** Insert the live CD that comes with this book, reboot, and start using Fedora from nearly any PC. Fedora won't touch the contents of your computer unless you tell it to. If you like Fedora, click the Install button to install Fedora to your hard disk. (See Chapter 2.)

2. **Customize your Desktop:** Not only does Linux support multiple desktop environments, including GNOME, KDE, Xfce, and Moblin, you can customize the look and feel of each desktop environment. (See Chapter 3.)

3. **Run thousands of applications:** From the offical Fedora repository to a boatload of other repositories, you can choose from literally thousands of free applications, including hundreds of games. (See Chapter 5.)

4. **Get online:** Get on the Internet using the Network Manager and then browse the Web, send e-mail, chat, and even video conference. Share files using FTP or BitTorrent swarming network transfer software. (See Chapter 8.)

5. **Manage music collections:** Launch Rhythmbox to gather, organize, and play music from your hard disk, CDs, or network file systems. Try new ways for streaming audio and video. (See Chapter 7.)

6. **Publish your ideas:** Choose from dozens of publishing tools to create documents (OpenOffice.org Writer), hard-copy page layouts (Scribus), and vector graphics (Inkscape). (See Chapter 6.)

7. **Share an Internet connection, securely:** Fedora can be set up as a router and a firewall. With a home or small office LAN setup, you can use Fedora to share an Internet connection among multiple Linux, Windows, or Mac systems. Then set up a firewall in Fedora to protect your LAN from intruders. (See Chapters 13, 14, and 15.)

8. **Run Windows applications, or Windows itself:** By adding the wine software packages, you can run many Windows applications right from a Fedora desktop. (See Chapter 5.) Use virtualization to run Windows, Unix, or other versions of Linux on your same PC. (See Chapter 23.)

9. **Create a home server:** Learn to configure a mail server (Chapter 18), FTP server (Chapter 19), and Web server (Chapter 20). You can share printers, disks, and other resources to all your home computers.

10. **Create presentations:** Start up OpenOffice.org Impress to create presentations from scratch or using templates. Tailor presentations to display as slide shows, view on screen, or print on paper. (See Chapter 6.)

Fedora® Bible

2011 Edition

Featuring Fedora® Linux® 14

Christopher Negus

Eric Foster-Johnson

Wiley Publishing, Inc.

Fedora® Bible 2011 Edition: Featuring Fedora® Linux® 14

Published by
Wiley Publishing, Inc.
10475 Crosspoint Boulevard
Indianapolis, IN 46256
www.wiley.com

Copyright © 2011 by Wiley Publishing, Inc., Indianapolis, Indiana

Published simultaneously in Canada

ISBN: 978-0-470-94496-7
ISBN: 978-1-118-08569-1 (ebk)
ISBN: 978-1-118-08573-8 (ebk)
ISBN: 978-1-118-08570-7 (ebk)

Manufactured in the United States of America

10 9 8 7 6 5 4 3 2 1

For general information on our other products and services please contact our Customer Care Department within the United States at (877) 762-2974, outside the United States at (317) 572-3993 or fax (317) 572-4002.

Wiley also publishes its books in a variety of electronic formats. Some content that appears in print may not be available in electronic books.

Library of Congress Control Number: 2011921771

About the Authors

Christopher Negus has been working with Unix systems, the Internet, and (most recently) Linux systems for more than two decades. During that time, Chris worked at AT&T Bell Laboratories, Unix System Laboratories, and Novell, helping to develop the Unix operating system. Features from many of the Unix projects Chris worked on at AT&T have found their way into Red Hat Enterprise Linux, Fedora, and other Linux systems.

Chris is the author of all editions of what started out as the *Red Hat Linux Bible*, which because of the name changes of Red Hat's Linux projects has evolved into the book you are holding. Most recently, Chris co-authored multiple books in the Linux Toolbox series: *Fedora Linux Toolbox, Ubuntu Linux Toolbox, Mac OS X UNIX Toolbox, SUSE Linux Toolbox,* and *BSD UNIX Toolbox* (Wiley Publishing). Besides that, Chris authored the *Linux Bible 2009 Edition* and co-wrote the *Fedora Bible 2010 Edition, CentOS Bible, Linux Troubleshooting Bible,* and *Linux Toys II* for Wiley Publishing. Chris also authored *Live Linux CDs* and co-authored the *Official Damn Small Linux Book,* as part of the Negus Software Solutions Series.

Today, Chris works as a Linux instructor for Red Hat, Inc. and has achieved certification as a Red Hat Certified Engineer (RHCE) and Red Hat Certified Examiner (RHCX). At home, Chris enjoys spending time with his wife, Sheree, and his boys, Caleb and Seth. His hobbies include soccer, singing, and exercising with Sheree.

Eric Foster-Johnson is a veteran programmer who works daily with Linux, Mac OS X, Unix, Windows and other operating systems. By day, he writes enterprise Grails and Java software for ObjectPartners, a Minnesota consulting firm. He has authored and co-authored a number of Linux and Unix titles, including the *Fedora Bible 2010 Edition, Red Hat RPM Guide, Teach Yourself Linux, Teach Yourself Unix,* and *Perl Modules.*

About the Technical Editor

John Kennedy has worked as a Linux and/or Unix System Administrator since 1997. He has experience with Red Hat, SUSE, Debian, and Solaris. John's life is almost 100% free of proprietary operating systems. He currently lives near Oxford, England with his wife, Michele, and son, Kieran. His daughter, Denise, lives in the United States.

Credits

Acquisitions Editor
Mary James

Project Editor
Linda Harrison

Technical Editor
John Kennedy

Production Editor
Rebecca Anderson

Copy Editor
Luann Rouff

Editorial Director
Robyn B. Siesky

Editorial Manager
Mary Beth Wakefield

Freelancer Editorial Manager
Rosemarie Graham

Marketing Manager
Ashley Zurcher

Production Manager
Tim Tate

Vice President and Executive Group Publisher
Richard Swadley

Vice President and Executive Publisher
Barry Pruett

Associate Publisher
Jim Minatel

Project Coordinator, Cover
Katie Crocker

Compositor
Jeff Wilson, Happenstance Type-O-Rama

Proofreaders
Scott Klemp, Word One New York
Carrie Hunter, Word One New York

Indexer
J & J Indexing

Cover Designer
Michael E. Trent

Cover Image
Joyce Haughey

Acknowledgments

A special acknowledgment goes to the people at Red Hat, Inc. and members of the Fedora Project. Each version of Fedora gets better and better, becoming easier and easier to install. With Fedora 13 and 14 (new since the last edition of this book), the easy printer set up stands out as one of the best features in Fedora for a long time.

Tasks that used to be hard, such as graphics configuration, virtualization, and package management, have now, for the most part anyway, become ancient history. This is due to the work of thousands all over the world improving Fedora in particular and Linux in general.

At Wiley, we'd like to thank Linda Harrison, Mary James, Carol Long, Luann Rouff, and Rebecca Anderson. A special shout-out goes to Sara Shlaer, who helped in so many ways on this book for many years.

John Kennedy provided a thorough technical editing pass and came up with many great suggestions to improve this book.

Finally, a special thanks goes to those of you who bought this and earlier editions of the *Fedora* and *Red Hat Linux Bibles*. Go out and become a force for Linux in your work, home, and community.

Contents at a Glance

Contents

Contents

Contents

Contents

Contents

Contents

Contents

Contents

Contents

Contents

Contents

Contents

Chapter 16: Setting Up Printers and Printing 607

Chapter 17: Setting Up a File Server 619

Contents

Contents

Contents

Preface

With the Fedora Linux operating system and the instructions in this book, you can transform your PC into a safe, powerful, and free computer system. Starting with Fedora, you can easily replace (or coexist with) Microsoft Windows on your everyday desktop computer. You can also configure your computer to share your files, printers, Web pages, or directory services with other computers. Then, if you choose, you can transition your skills to manage anything from a small office to a large, corporate Red Hat Enterprise Linux computer installation.

Who Are You?

You're someone who needs, or wants, to run Linux, and you desire to get up and productive as quickly as possible. This book covers what you need to know to get Fedora Linux up and running with a minimum of fuss on your existing PCs. From there, you'll learn how to get Linux on a network, from a local network to the world-wide Internet. You'll also learn how to lock down Linux, making it secure, and how to perform daily administrative functions such as backups.

You don't need to be a programmer to use this book. You may be someone who just wants to use Linux (to run programs, access the Internet, and so on); or you may simply want to know how to administer a Linux system in a workgroup or on a network.

It is assumed that you are somewhat computer literate but have little or no experience with Linux (or Unix). You may need to use Linux at work, typically as a server or software development platform.

You may be migrating from Microsoft operating systems to Linux because of its networking and multiuser features. You may be looking to start a career as a computer technician or network administrator and think that spending a few dollars for an entire operating system and book is more economical than taking technical classes offered on late-night television. Or you might just think a "free" operating system is cool.

This Book's Learn-Through-Tasks Approach

The best way to learn a computer system is to get your hands on it. To help you learn Linux, this book takes a task-oriented approach. Where possible, this book will step you through the process of working with a feature, such as setting up a network or configuring your desktop.

When you are done with a task, you should have a good, basic setup of the feature that it covers. After that, I often provide pointers to further information on tweaking and tuning the feature.

Instead of assuming that you already know about cryptic topics such as troff, FTP, and TCP/IP, I ease you into those features with headings such as "Publishing with Fedora," "Setting Up a File Server," and "Connecting to the Internet." Heck, if you already knew what all those things were and how to get them working, you wouldn't need this book, would you?

When many tools can be used to achieve the same results, I usually present one or two examples. In other words, I don't describe six different Web browsers, twelve different text editors, and three different news servers. I tell you how to get one or two similar tools really working and then note the others that are available.

What You Need

This book covers Fedora Linux. However, because Fedora technology feeds into distributions such as Red Hat Enterprise Linux (RHEL), CentOS (www.centos.org), StartCom (www.startcom.org), White Box Enterprise Linux (www.whiteboxlinux.org), and Oracle's Unbreakable Linux (www.oracle.com/us/technologies/linux/index.html), you can use this book to learn about those distributions as well.

To follow along with this book, you can install the official Fedora 14 software found on the accompanying DVD. If you don't have a DVD drive, you can use the CD that comes with this book to try out Fedora and install a desktop Fedora system to your hard disk. Or you can follow along with your CentOS system (which is free) or Red Hat Enterprise Linux system, (which you can obtain with a subscription from Red Hat, Inc.).

To install Fedora 14 with the media that come with this book, you need a PC with the following general configuration:

- An Intel Pentium or compatible CPU, 200MHz Pentium Pro or better (for text mode); 400MHz Pentium Pro or better (for GUI mode). Fedora 14 has been optimized for Pentium 4 processors. (Intel 486 computers will not work with Fedora 14.)

- At least 256MB of RAM (text-based install) or 384MB of RAM (graphical install). To run the GNOME or KDE desktop 512MB are needed, although the Fedora Project recommends having more. (For low-RAM systems, try the Xfce desktop described in Chapter 3.)

- At least 620MB of hard disk space (you have to select a minimal install). You need 2.3GB of hard disk space for a personal desktop install, 3.0GB for a typical workstation installation, or at least 1.1GB of space for a server installation. For the live CD, you need at least 3.0GB of disk space.

- A DVD or CD drive. This is recommended for installation (because we give you the installation DVD), although you can install from CD (we provide a live CD that can also be installed to hard disk), over a network, or from a local hard disk instead. For network and hard disk installs, booting installation from a 3.5-inch floppy disk drive is no longer supported. Chapter 2 describes methods of launching installation if you don't have a bootable DVD drive: Once the install is started, you need either an extra hard disk partition or another computer (that can be reached over the network) that has packages or images of the Fedora distribution on it. (Chapter 2 describes how to do that, in case you're interested.)

Not every piece of PC hardware works with Fedora, but most mainstream modern hardware should work just fine. While there is no official hardware compatibility list as there is for Red Hat Enterprise Linux (available at https://hardware.redhat.com), overall hardware support should be improved in Fedora 14. There are versions of Fedora available for other computer architectures as well. You can download official install and live CDs and DVDs from the Fedora project (http://fedoraproject.org/en/get-fedora.html). Likewise, you can get X86 and X86 64-bit versions of CentOS from that project's site (http://mirror.centos.org/).

Fedora Bible 2011 Edition: Featuring Fedora 14 Improvements

Fedora® Bible 2011 Edition: Featuring Fedora® Linux® 14 (talk about a mouthful) represents the continuing development of the *Red Hat Linux Bible*, which made its debut in 1999. Periodically since Red Hat Linux 6.1, revisions of this book have followed new versions of Red Hat.

Red Hat, Inc. split its Red Hat Linux development efforts into two tracks: the Fedora Project and the Red Hat Enterprise Linux (RHEL) product. This book now covers the latest of the Fedora Linux distributions: Fedora 14. In addition, since the 2010 Edition covered Fedora 12, you'll see new features in Fedora 13 as well. By learning the features in Fedora 14, you will also be preparing yourself for future releases of RHEL.

The foundation for Fedora, RHEL, and this book rests on the tradition begun with Red Hat Linux. The enhancements included in this edition reflect that foundation, plus some bold new cutting-edge Linux technology.

This edition covers a wide range of features in Fedora 14. The following list describes new features of this book compared to the previous edition:

- **Fedora 14 Official Install DVD** — We provide Fedora 14 on DVD with this edition. This is the exact DVD produced by the Fedora Project, offering a wide range of desktop, workstation, and server software.

- **Fedora 14 Desktop Edition Live CD** — Before you install Fedora, you can try out a desktop-oriented live version of Fedora 14 by booting the CD that comes with this book. For this edition, we decided to use the GNOME live CD (there is also a KDE live CD available for download). While that CD is running, you can use it to prepare your computer to do a permanent installation. The contents of that CD can also be installed directly to your hard disk.

- **Productivity, productivity, productivity** — Much of this book has been changed, sometimes subtly, to focus on getting you up to speed and productive as quickly as possible. Some of the older features are gone, replaced by newer features. In addition, the goal is to cover enough to get you started and then point you in the right direction should you need more information. I've continued focusing on productivity since the 2010 Edition.

- **Virtualization** — Virtualization, the capability to run other operating systems on top of your Fedora system, forms a major focus for Fedora 13 and 14. This release adds numerous changes and improvements across the board relating to virtualization, from improved performance with large memory virtualizations to virtual storage management.

- **GNOME 2.32.0 Desktop** — GNOME 2.32.0 includes hundreds of improvements across the board, including organizing your contacts, such as for instant messaging, and much better support for displaying PDF files.

- **KDE 4.5 Desktop** — The KDE Plasma Desktop includes a number of workspace improvements aimed at helping you focus on your tasks. The new Activity Manager helps you switch between activities, such as reading e-mail and other tasks. KDE also improved support for netbooks and other small devices. (KDE is not on the CD that comes with this book, but you can install it from the DVD.)

- **MeeGo and Moblin desktops** — Aimed at netbooks and other smaller systems with limited processing power, these desktops provide a productive user interface. MeeGo is a new effort, bringing together the Moblin environment with Nokia's Maemo (used in mobile phones and Internet tablets).

- **Automatic print driver installation** — As covered in Chapter 16, in most cases, you can simply plug your printer to your Fedora Linux system and Fedora will take care of the rest, automatically installing the proper print driver. If you have ever struggled with printers and Linux in the past, you'll greatly appreciate this new feature.

- `systemd` — Fedora 14 replaces `upstart` for launching system tasks. Just a few short releases ago, `upstart` replaced the old system `init` task. Now with `systemd`, Fedora offers faster and more efficient system start-up and a more robust system better able to handle restarting processes that fail.

In addition to the new features just described, procedures throughout the book have been tested and corrected to match changes that have been made to Fedora 14 software in this version.

Conventions Used in This Book

Throughout the book, special typography indicates code and commands. Commands and code are shown in a monospaced font:

```
This is how code looks.
```

In the event that an example includes both input and output, the monospaced font is still used, but input is presented in bold type to distinguish the two. Here's an example:

```
$ ftp ftp.handsonhistory.com
```

```
Name (home:jake): jake
Password: ******
```

In a number of examples, you'll see a variable in italics. The previous command might be displayed as the following:

```
$ ftp hostname
```

In this case, you should replace *hostname* with the name of a particular host on your network.

The following boxes are used to call your attention to points that are particularly important.

Note
A note box provides extra information to which you need to pay special attention. ■

Tip
A tip box shows a special way of performing a particular task. ■

Caution
A caution box alerts you to take special care when executing a procedure, or damage to your computer hardware or software could result. ■

Cross-Reference
A cross-reference box refers you to further information, outside the existing chapter, about a subject. ■

How This Book Is Organized

The book is organized into four parts.

Part I: Getting Started in Fedora

Part I consists of Chapters 1 through 4. Chapter 1 serves as an introduction to the Linux operating system and to Fedora in particular. Chapter 2 discusses what you need to install Fedora and how to make the decisions you'll be faced with during installation. It includes procedures for installing from DVD, CD-ROM, hard disk, or network connection (NFS, FTP, or HTTP servers).

In Chapter 3, you learn about the GNOME, KDE, and Xfce desktop environments, as well as the X Window system. These GUIs provide graphical means of using Fedora. Chapter 4 describes ways of exploring and understanding Fedora, primarily from the Linux shell command interpreter. You learn how to use the bash shell, the vi text editor, and the commands for moving around the Linux file system.

Part II: Using Fedora

Part II consists of Chapters 5 through 8, which include information for the typical user who wants to use Linux to run applications and access the Internet.

Chapter 5 contains information on obtaining, installing, and running Linux applications. It also helps you run applications from other operating systems in Linux. Chapter 6 describes Linux productivity applications such as the Openoffice.org suite for word processing, spreadsheets, and presentations. I cover both old-time publishing tools and new, graphical word processors that are available with Fedora.

Chapter 7 covers some of the more fun areas of Linux, delving into music, video, and images. It describes how to use audio and video players, and how to configure sound cards and CD burners, as well as play games. Chapter 8 describes tools for browsing the Web (such as the Firefox browser) and related tools (such as e-mail clients and newsreaders).

Part III: Administering Fedora

Part III consists of Chapters 9 through 13, which cover general setup and system maintenance tasks, including how to set up user accounts, automate system tasks, and back up your data. Chapter 9, in which you learn what you need to know about basic system administration, describes the root login, administrative commands, configuration files, SELinux (security-enhanced Linux), and log files. Chapter 10 describes how to set up and provide support for multiple users on your Fedora system.

In Chapter 11 you learn how to create shell scripts and use the cron facility to automate a variety of tasks on your Fedora system. Techniques for backing up your system and restoring files from backup are described in Chapter 12. Chapter 13 describes issues related to securing your computing assets in Fedora.

Part IV: Fedora Network and Server Setup

Part IV consists of Chapters 14 through 23, which describe step-by-step procedures for setting up a variety of server types. Simple configurations for what might otherwise be complex tasks are contained in each chapter. Learn to arrange, address, and connect your Linux computers to a local area network (LAN) in Chapter 14. Chapter 15 describes techniques for connecting your Linux computer and LAN to the Internet, using features such as IP forwarding, IP masquerading, routing, and proxy servers.

Chapter 16 describes how to set up different types of print server interfaces, including Samba (to share with Windows systems) and native Linux CUPS printing. Chapter 17 describes file servers, such as Network File System (NFS) servers and Samba file servers. Chapter 18 describes how to configure the sendmail e-mail server.

Chapter 19 describes how to configure and secure an FTP server, as well as how to access the server using FTP client programs. Chapter 20 teaches you how to set up Fedora as a Web server, focusing on the popular Apache server software. Chapter 21 describes how to set up a DHCP server to distribute information to client workstations on the network.

Chapter 22 describes how to set up and use a MySQL database server in Linux. Chapter 23 takes you through the process of hosting other operating systems through virtualization.

Appendix

This book contains one appendix. The appendix describes the contents of the companion media.

About the Companion Media

The Fedora 14 DVD that accompanies this book provides the software you need for a complete working Fedora system. With this software, you can install sets of software packages that result in an installation from a few hundred megabytes to up to well over 9GB of software.

We also include a Fedora 14 Desktop Edition Live/Install CD. That CD can be booted to run a live Fedora GNOME desktop system, without touching the contents of your hard disk. You can install the contents of the live CD to your hard disk, enabling you to use that desktop system permanently from your hard disk.

This book describes how to configure and use the software for those different media. See the appendix for specifics on the media.

Part I

Getting Started in Fedora

An Overview of Fedora

Linux was a phenomenon waiting to happen. The computer industry was suffering from a rift. In the 1980s and 1990s, people had to choose between inexpensive, market-driven PC operating systems from Microsoft and expensive, technology-driven operating systems such as Unix. Free software was being created all over the world, but it lacked a common platform to rally around. Linux has become that common platform.

For several years, Red Hat Linux was the most popular commercial distribution of Linux. In 2003, Red Hat, Inc., changed the name of its distribution from Red Hat Linux to Fedora Core (later changing the name to simply Fedora) and moved its commercial efforts toward its Red Hat Enterprise Linux products. It then set up Fedora to be the following:

- Sponsored by Red Hat
- Supported by the Linux community
- Inclusive of high-quality, cutting-edge open-source technology
- A proving ground for software slated for commercial Red Hat deployment and support

Red Hat Enterprise Linux, conversely, has become the basis for Red Hat's fully supported product line, geared toward big companies with the need to set up and manage many Linux systems. After taking its software through a year or two of Fedora releases, which occur about once every six to nine months, Red Hat releases a new version of its commercial product, Red Hat Enterprise Linux (RHEL), which includes the following:

- Subscription service to RHEL that offers stable, tested software (much of the same software in Fedora that has gone through rigorous testing).

- Multiple support programs, ranging from an online knowledge base to assistance with custom deployment, engineering, and software development to full 24/7 onsite support.
- Official documentation, training, and certification programs.

Fedora itself has become a respected and active Linux distribution that thousands of people use worldwide as a desktop, server, or programming workstation. It is the best way to get the latest Linux software that is being built on a foundation for enterprise-quality systems.

Using Fedora is a great way to get a head start learning the features of upcoming RHEL releases. The latest Fedora Linux operating system (referred to as Fedora 14) is included on the DVD that comes with this book. The book also includes a Fedora Live CD with a desktop Linux system that you can use to try out Fedora, and then install directly to your hard disk when you are ready.

Introducing Fedora 14

With the split between community (Fedora) and commercial (Red Hat Enterprise Linux) versions of what was Red Hat Linux, Red Hat has created a model that can suit the fast-paced changes in the open-source software world while still meeting the demands for a well-supported commercial Linux distribution.

Many technology professionals choose Red Hat Enterprise Linux because of its reputation for solid performance. With the Fedora Project, Red Hat has created an environment where open-source developers can bring high-quality software packages to a freely distributed, community-oriented Linux system.

More than 15,000 individual software packages (compared to just over 600 in Red Hat Linux 6.2) are included in the single, massive Fedora 14 software repository. These packages contain features that would cost you thousands of dollars to duplicate if you bought them as separate commercial products. These features enable you to do all of the following:

- Connect your computers to a LAN or the Internet
- Create documents and publish your work on paper or on the Web
- Work with multimedia content to manipulate images, play music files, view video, and even master and burn your own CDs and DVDs
- Play games individually or over a network
- Communicate over the Internet using a variety of Web tools for browsing, chatting, transferring files, participating in newsgroups, and sending and receiving e-mail
- Protect your computing resources by having Fedora act as a firewall or a router to protect against intruders coming in through public networks
- Configure a computer to act as a network server, such as a print server, Web server, file server, mail server, news server, and database server

This is just a partial list of what you can do with Fedora. Using this book as your guide, you will find that many more features are built into Fedora as well.

Remember that old Pentium computer in your closet? Don't throw it away! Just because a new release of Fedora is out doesn't mean that you need all new hardware for it to run. Support for many old computer components is carried from one release to the next. With a minimal install, you could use Fedora as a router (to route data between your LAN and the Internet), firewall (to protect your network from outside intrusion), or file server (to store shared files on your LAN) — with maybe an Ethernet card or an extra hard disk added.

At this point, you may feel that Linux is something you want to try out. This brings us to the basic question: What is Linux?

What Is Linux?

Linux is a free operating system that was created by Linus Torvalds when he was a student at the University of Helsinki in 1991. Torvalds started Linux by writing a *kernel* — the heart of the operating system — partly from scratch and partly by using publicly available software. (For the definition of an operating system and a kernel, see the sidebar "What Is an Operating System?" later in this chapter.) Torvalds then released the system to his friends and to a community of "hackers" on the Internet and asked them to work with it, fix it, and enhance it. It took off.

Note

I make the distinction here between hackers (who just like to play with computers) and crackers (who break into computer systems and cause damage). ■

Today, thousands of software developers around the world are contributing software to the free and open-source software (FOSS) community that feeds the Linux initiative. Because the source code for the software is freely available, anyone can work on it, change it, or enhance it. Developers are encouraged to pass their fixes and improvements back into the community so that Linux can continue to grow and improve.

On top of the Linux kernel effort, the creators of Linux also drew on a great deal of system software and applications that are now bundled with Linux distributions from the GNU project (GNU stands for "GNU is Not Unix"), which is directed by the Free Software Foundation (www .gnu.org). A vast amount of software can be used with Linux, making it an operating system that can compete with or surpass features available in any other operating system in the world.

If you have heard Linux described as a free version of Unix, there is good reason for it. Although much of the code for Linux started from scratch, the blueprint for what the code would do was created to follow POSIX (Portable Operating System Interface for Unix) standards. POSIX is a computer industry operating system standard that every major version of Unix complied with. In other words, if your operating system was POSIX-compliant, it was Unix. Today, Linux has formed its own standards and services organizations to help interoperability among Linux systems, including the Linux Foundation, which supports such efforts as the Linux Standard Base (www.linuxfoundation.org).

Linux's Roots in Unix

Linux grew within a culture of free exchange of ideas and software. Like Unix — the operating system on which Linux is based — the focus was on keeping communications open among software developers. Getting the code to work was the goal, and the Internet was the primary communications medium. Keeping the software free and redistributable was a means to that goal. What, then, were the conditions that made the world ripe for a computer system such as Linux?

In the 1980s and 1990s, while Microsoft flooded the world with personal computers running DOS (Disk Operating System) and Windows operating systems, power users demanded more from an operating system. They ached for systems that could run on networks, support many users at once (multiuser), and run many programs at once (multitasking). DOS and Windows didn't cut it. Unix, on the other hand, grew out of a culture where technology was king and marketing people were, well, hard to find at Bell Laboratories in Murray Hill, New Jersey. A quote from Dennis Ritchie, co-creator of Unix and designer of the C programming language, in a 1980 lecture on the evolution of Unix, sums up the spirit that started Unix. He was commenting on both his hopes and those of his colleagues for the Unix project after a similar project called Multics had just failed:

> What we wanted to preserve was not just a good environment in which to do programming, but a system around which a fellowship could form. We knew from experience that the essence of communal computing as supplied by remote-access, time-shared machines, is not just to type programs into a terminal instead of a keypunch, but to encourage close communication.

In that spirit, the first source code of Unix was distributed free to universities. Like Linux, the availability of Unix source code made it possible for a diverse population of software developers to make their own enhancements to Unix and share them with others.

What Is an Operating System?

An operating system is made up of software instructions that lie between the computer hardware (disks, memory, ports, etc.) and the application programs (word processors, Web browsers, spreadsheets, etc.). At the center is the kernel, which provides the most basic computing functions (managing system memory, sharing the processor, opening and closing devices, etc.). Associated with the kernel are a variety of basic services needed to operate the computer, including the following:

- **File systems** — The file system provides the structure in which information is stored on the computer. Information is stored in files, primarily on hard disks inside the computer, but also on removable media such as CDs and DVDs. Files are organized within a hierarchy of directories.

- **Device drivers** — These provide the interfaces to each of the hardware devices connected to your computer. A device driver enables a program to write to a device without needing to know details about how each piece of hardware is implemented. The program opens a device, sends and receives data, and closes the device.

- **User interfaces** — An operating system needs to provide a way for users to run programs and access the file system. Linux has both graphical and text-based user interfaces. GNOME and KDE provide graphical user interfaces, whereas shell command interpreters (such as bash) run programs by accepting typed commands and options.

- **System services** — An operating system provides system services, many of which can be started automatically when the computer boots. In Linux, many services run continuously, enabling users to access printers, Web pages, files, databases, and other computing assets over a network.

Without an operating system, an application program would have to know the details of each piece of hardware, instead of just being able to say "open that device and write a file there."

By the early 1980s, major computer hardware vendors licensed the Unix source code to run on their computers. To try to create an environment of fairness and community to its OEMs (original equipment manufacturers), AT&T began standardizing what these different ports of Unix had to be able to do in order to still be called Unix. To that end, POSIX standards and the AT&T Unix System V Interface Definition (SVID) were created, specifications Unix vendors could use to create compliant Unix systems. Those same documents also served as road maps for the creation of Linux.

Elsewhere, the Unix source code previously distributed to universities had taken on a life of its own. The Berkeley Software Distribution (BSD) began life in the late 1970s as patches to the AT&T Unix source code from students and staff at the University of California at Berkeley. Over the years, the AT&T code was rewritten, and BSD became freely distributed, with offshoot projects such as FreeBSD, OpenBSD, and NetBSD still available.

Linux has been described as a Unix-like operating system that reflects a combination of SVID, POSIX, and BSD compliance. Linux continues to aim toward POSIX compliance, as well as compliance with standards set by the new owner of the Unix trademark, The Open Group (www.unix.org). Much of the direction of Linux today comes from the Linux Foundation (www.linuxfoundation.org), which was founded in 2007 by a merger of the Free Standards Group and the Open Source Development Labs.

Common Linux Features

No matter what distribution of Linux you use, the piece of code common to all is the Linux kernel. Although the kernel can be modified to include support for the features you want, every Linux kernel can offer the following features:

- **Multiuser** — Not only can you have many user accounts available on a Linux system, you can also have multiple users logged in and working on the system at the same time. Users can have their own environments arranged the way they want: their own home directory for storing files and their own desktop interface (with icons, menus, and applications arranged to suit them). User accounts can be password-protected, so users can control who has access to their applications and data.

- **Multitasking** — In Linux, it is possible to have many programs running at the same time, which also means that the Linux operating system can itself have programs running in the background. Many of these system processes make it possible for Linux to work as a server, with these background processes listening to the network for requests to log in to your system, view a Web page, print a document, or copy a file. These background processes are referred to as *daemons*.

- **Hardware support** — You can configure support for almost every type of hardware that can be connected to a computer. There is support for floppy drives, CDs, removable disks (such as DVDs and USB flash drives), sound cards, tape devices, video cards, and most anything else you can think of.

  In order to support a hardware device, Linux needs a *driver*, a piece of software that interfaces between the Linux kernel and the device. Drivers are available in the Linux kernel to support hundreds of computer hardware components that can be added or removed as needed.

Note

Most hardware manufacturers don't provide Linux drivers with their peripheral devices and adapter cards. Although most popular hardware will be supported eventually in Linux, it can sometimes take a while for a member of the Linux community to write a driver. Also, some outdated hardware may not be updated to work with the latest Linux kernels. Some manufacturers that do provide Linux drivers for their hardware provide binary-only, proprietary drivers. On occasion, those drivers, such as ones to use VMware or NVidia video cards, can cause compatibility issues with other Linux software and become a problem when you upgrade to later Linux kernels. ∎

- **Networking connectivity** — To connect your Linux system to a network, Linux offers support for a variety of local area network (LAN), network interface cards (NICs), modems, and serial devices. In addition to LAN protocols, such as Ethernet (both wired and wireless), all of the most popular upper-level networking protocols can be built in. The most popular of these protocols is TCP/IP (used to connect to the Internet). Other protocols, such as IPX (for Novell networks) and X.25 (a packet-switching network type that is popular in Europe) are also available.

- **Network servers** — Providing networking services to the client computers on the LAN or to the entire Internet is what Linux does best. A variety of software packages are available that enable you to use Linux as a print server, file server, FTP server, mail server, Web server, news server, or workgroup (DHCP or NIS) server.

To make a Linux distribution useful, components need to be added on top of the Linux kernel. For humans to access a Linux system, they can enter commands to a shell or use graphical interfaces to open menus, windows, and icons. Then you need actual applications to run. In particular, a useful Linux desktop system includes the following:

- **Graphical user interface (X Window System)** — The powerful framework for working with graphical applications in Linux is referred to as the X Window System (or simply X). X handles the functions of opening X-based graphical user interface (GUI) applications and displaying them on an X server process (the process that manages your screen, mouse, and keyboard).

On top of X, you use an X-based desktop environment to provide a desktop metaphor and window manager to provide the look-and-feel of your GUI (icons, window frames, menus, and colors, or a combination of those items called *themes*). Fedora focuses on the GNOME and KDE desktop environments but also has several other desktop environments, such as Xfce, and window managers, such as Blackbox and AfterStep, available.

- **Application support** — Because of compatibility with POSIX and several different application programming interfaces (APIs), a wide range of free and open-source software is available for Linux systems. Compatibility with the GNU C libraries is a major reason for the wide-ranging application support. Often, making an open-source application available to a particular version of Linux can be done by simply recompiling the source code to run on that Linux version.

Primary Advantages of Linux

Compared to various commercially available operating systems, Linux's best assets are its price, its reliability, and the freedom it gives you. With the latest 2.6 Linux kernel, you can also argue that scalability is one of its greatest assets. Today, Linux is used in the New York Stock Exchange, banks, highly secure U.S. government installations, and many other institutions for which uptime, security, and performance are critical. It's also used in handheld devices, netbooks, and commercial TV video recorders.

Most people know that its initial price is free (or at least under $50 when it comes in a box or with a book). However, when people talk about Linux's affordability, they usually mean its total cost, which includes no (or low) licensing fees, the ability to reuse any of the code as you choose, and the capability of using inexpensive hardware and compatible add-on applications that are free to download and use. Although commercial operating systems tend to encourage upgrading to more powerful hardware, Linux doesn't require that (although faster hardware and larger disks are nice to have).

In terms of reliability, the general consensus is that Linux is comparable to many commercial Unix systems but more reliable than most desktop-oriented operating systems. This is especially true if you rely on your computer system because it is a Web server or a file server. (You don't have to reboot every time you change something, unless you've replaced the kernel itself.)

This reliability also extends into the realm of safety. While exploits have been aimed at Linux software, Linux users are for the most part safe from the culture of malware and viruses that plague Windows users. With so many people peering at the Linux source code, a benefit of its freedom, mistakes are often fixed in record time. Large-scale Linux deployments don't need to install anti-virus software, a situation you would never allow with Windows in a corporate setting. Furthermore, when people install anti-virus software on Linux, it is usually to scan files and e-mail messages for Windows viruses, to help the distraught users of Windows.

Because you can get the source code, you are free to change any part of the Linux system, along with any open-source software that comes with it, in any way that you choose. Unlike many self-contained commercial products, open-source software tends to be built in pieces that are meant to interact with other pieces, so you are free to mix and match components to suit your tastes. As mentioned earlier, Linux is a culture that encourages interoperability. For example, if you don't like a window manager, you can plug in a different one because so many were built to operate within the same framework.

Another advantage of using Linux is that help is always just a click away on the Internet. There is probably someone out there in a Linux newsgroup or mailing list willing to help you solve your problem, especially since the culture of Linux thrives on people helping other people. Because the source code is available, if you need something fixed you can even patch the code yourself! Conversely, I've seen commercial operating system vendors sit on reported problems for months without fixing them.

What Is Fedora?

Having directories of source code floating around the Internet was not a bad way for hackers to share software. However, for Linux to be acceptable to a less technical population of computer users, it needed to be simple to install and use. Likewise, businesses that were thinking about committing their mission-critical applications to a computer system would want to know that this system had been carefully tested and well supported.

To those ends, several companies and organizations began gathering and packaging Linux software together into usable forms called *distributions*. The main goal of a Linux distribution is to make the hundreds (or even thousands) of unrelated software packages that make up Linux work together as a cohesive whole. Popular Linux distributions include Debian, Ubuntu, openSUSE, SUSE Linux Enterprise, Slackware, Damn Small Linux, and Gentoo. One of the most popular commercial distributions is Red Hat Linux. Red Hat, in turn, sponsors the Fedora Project, which brings us Fedora Linux.

Red Hat forms the Fedora Project

In 2003, Red Hat split its work on Linux into two paths: Red Hat supports the Fedora Project along with offering a commercial version of Linux, called Red Hat Enterprise Linux:

- **Fedora Project** (www.fedoraproject.org) — An open-source project, beginning from a Red Hat Linux 9 base, that produces its own Linux distribution. While the project is sponsored by Red Hat, Inc., there is no official support for the Linux distribution (simply called Fedora) that the project produces.

- **Red Hat Enterprise Linux** (www.redhat.com/rhel) — An official set of commercial Linux products from Red Hat, Inc., that are offered on an annual subscription basis. Red Hat backs up its Enterprise product line with technical support, training, and documentation.

The primary results of the Fedora Project are sets of binary and source code packages (distributed as DVD or CD images) containing the Linux distribution referred to as Fedora. Before its name was changed to Fedora, that distribution was being tested simply as the next in the series of Red Hat Linux distributions (presumably, Red Hat Linux 10). The software packages included on the DVD and CD that come with this book are distributed as the official fourteenth release of that software: Fedora 14.

The name change from Red Hat Linux to Fedora Core (and later to just Fedora) wasn't the only difference between Fedora and Red Hat Enterprise Linux, however. Red Hat, Inc. also changed its association with Fedora in the following ways:

- **No boxed sets** — Red Hat decided to not sell Fedora through retail channels.

- **Short guaranteed update cycle** — Critical fixes and security patches will be available for each Fedora release for a much shorter period of time than RHEL products. As a result, users will have to upgrade or reinstall the system more often.

- **No technical support offerings** — No technical support programs are available from Red Hat for Fedora, but by sponsoring the Fedora project you get a form of free support because Red Hat staffers fix bugs and integrate the latest Linux technology.

- **No Red Hat documentation** — The set of manuals that came with the previous Red Hat Linux product was not brought over to Fedora. Instead, a series of small task-oriented documents are being collected for the project in article format. The Fedora Documentation project (`http://docs.fedoraproject.org`) is, however, following a path to release Red Hat documentation under an open-source license so that the Fedora Project can develop and distribute that documentation.

By not creating a whole support industry around Fedora, the project is free to produce software releases on a much shorter schedule (usually a six-month release cycle). This enables Fedora users to always have the latest software features and fixes included with a recent version of the operating system. The Fedora Project is more than just the Fedora Linux release, however; it is really a collection of projects (`http://fedoraproject.org/wiki/Projects`) that also includes the following:

- **One Laptop Per Child (OLPC)** — The Fedora Project is working with Red Hat, Inc., and the OLPC project (`www.laptop.org`) to provide laptops to children around the world. Fedora software is being used as the foundation for the software part of OLPC.

- **Fedora Ambassadors and Marketing** — This focuses on spreading the word about Fedora to the world. Ambassadors have been assigned to different parts of the U.S. and to countries around the world to represent Fedora in their areas. The marketing project is helping to encourage presentations, developer conferences, and other initiatives to publicize Fedora.

- **Fedora Live CD Tools** — The Fedora Live CD initiative centers on a set of tools under the name `livecd-creator`. Using `livecd-creator`, the Fedora Project produces its own official Fedora live CDs. A live CD provides a means of running a Linux system on a computer without installing it to hard disk. It offers a great way to try out Fedora without disturbing anything installed on your hard disk. Because `livecd-creator` is itself an open-source project, you can use the tools to create your own live CDs.

- **Fedora Artwork** — Creates the graphics used with Fedora (backgrounds, logos, login screens, and so on), primarily using tools that are distributed with Fedora.

- **Fedora Documentation** — Besides seeking to release Red Hat documentation under an open-source license and maintaining it publicly with the Fedora Project, the Fedora Documentation Project is pursuing other initiatives, including assigning writers (to cover various software topics) and editors (to clean up and manage documentation contributions).

For information on the status of these and other Fedora projects, you can refer to the Fedora Weekly News (`http://fedoraproject.org/wiki/FWN`). If you are interested in contributing to any of the Fedora projects, the Fedora Projects page mentioned earlier is a good place to start.

Third-party repositories for Fedora containing software packages that Red Hat won't distribute due to licensing or patent issues have also grown and stabilized lately. (See the descriptions of software repositories in Chapter 5.)

As the end-user forum of choice for Fedora users, Red Hat has endorsed the FedoraForum.org site (`www.fedoraforum.org`), which already has more than 149,000 members and over 1,260,000 posts you can search for answers to your questions.

Red Hat shifts to Red Hat Enterprise Linux

The major shift of attention to Red Hat Enterprise Linux as the focus of Red Hat, Inc.'s commercial efforts has been on the horizon for some time. Some characteristics of Red Hat Enterprise Linux are as follows:

- **Longer release intervals** — Instead of offering releases every six months or so, Enterprise software has closer to an 18-month to two-year update cycle. Customers can be assured of a longer support cycle without having to upgrade to a later release.

- **Multiple support options** — Customers will have the option to purchase different levels of support. All subscriptions will include the Update Module, which allows easy access to updates for Red Hat Enterprise Linux systems. The Management Module enables customers to develop custom channels and automate management of multiple systems. The Monitoring Module enables customers to monitor and maintain an entire infrastructure of systems.

- **Documentation and training** — Manuals and training courses will center on the Red Hat Enterprise Linux distribution.

Choosing between Fedora and Enterprise

If you bought this book to try out Linux for the first time, rest assured that what you have on the DVD and CD included with this book is a solid, battle-tested operating system. There is still a lot of overlap between Fedora and Red Hat Enterprise Linux, but many of the newest features of Fedora 14 provide a way to test much of the software that is slated to go in later editions of Red Hat Enterprise Linux.

Although Fedora may not be right for everyone, it is great for students, home users, most small businesses, and anyone just wanting to try out the latest Linux technology. Larger businesses should seriously consider the implications for support, training, and future upgrade paths before choosing whether to go the Fedora route or sign on with Red Hat Enterprise Linux. Also, businesses should be willing to deal with more frequent upgrades, because release and support cycles are much shorter with Fedora than with RHEL.

Despite its lack of formal support, however, Fedora is being used today in many businesses, schools, and homes around the world. In whatever way you plan to ultimately use Fedora, it is without a doubt a good way to learn and use the latest Linux technology as it is released to the Linux community and before it makes its way to Red Hat Enterprise Linux.

Many companies and organizations don't choose between Fedora and RHEL, but instead offer a mixed environment. The most critical servers may run Red Hat Enterprise Linux, with a full support contract with Red Hat. In the same location, Fedora may be used for desktop systems or office-based file and print servers. Organizations that need features similar to those in RHEL without the cost can use CentOS (which is a rebuild of RHEL source code). As someone learning to use Fedora with this book, you can likewise scale your use of this technology as far as you want to go.

Why Choose Fedora?

To distinguish itself from other versions of Linux, each distribution adds some extra features. Because many power features included in most Linux distributions come from established open-source projects (such as Apache, Samba, KDE, and so on), enhancements for a particular distribution often make it easier to install, configure, and use Linux. Also, because you can find different software packages to do the same jobs (such as window managers or a particular server type), a distribution can distinguish itself by which packages it chooses to include and feature with its default installations.

Fedora is continuing the Red Hat Linux tradition by offering many features that set it apart from other Linux distributions, including the following:

- **Cutting-edge Linux technology** — In Fedora 14, major features include the GNOME 2.32 and KDE 4.5 desktops, Firefox 3.6, OpenOffice.org 3.3, Ext4 file system support, and the latest Linux kernel.

- **Software packaging** — Red Hat, Inc. created the RPM Package Manager (RPM) method of packaging Linux. RPMs enable less technically savvy users to easily install, search, manage, and verify Linux software. With RPM tools, you can install from CD, hard disk, over your LAN, or over the Internet. It's easy to track which packages are installed or to look at the contents of a package. Because RPM is available to the Linux community, it has become one of the de facto standards for packaging Linux software.

Tools such as yum and PackageKit, which are built to take advantage of RPM technology, have been added to Fedora to extend your ability to install and update packages. Those tools can point to online repositories, so the latest software packages are often only a click away.

Cross-Reference

Chapter 5 describes how to install RPM packages and use yum repositories. ■

- **Easy installation** — The Fedora installation software (called *anaconda*) provides easy steps for installing Linux. During installation, anaconda also helps you take the first few steps toward configuring Linux. You can choose which packages to install and how to partition your hard disk. You can even get your desktop GUI ready to go by configuring user accounts, the keyboard, the mouse, and even your network connection. With Fedora 14, you can install directly from a running live CD or choose from several different install-only media.

Cross-Reference

Chapter 2 covers Fedora installation. ■

- **Desktop environments (GNOME and KDE)** — To make it easier to use Linux, Fedora is packaged with the GNOME and KDE desktop environments. GNOME is installed by default and offers some nice features that include drag-and-drop protocols and tools for configuring the desktop look and feel. KDE is another popular desktop manager that includes a wide range of tools tailored for the KDE environment, such as the Konqueror Web browser. You can try out separate Fedora live CDs for GNOME and KDE, and then install software from those CDs directly to your hard disk. (This book includes the GNOME live CD.)

- **GUI Administration tools** — There are some helpful configuration tools for setting up some of the trickier tasks in Linux. Several different GUI tools provide a graphical, form-driven interface for configuring networking, users, file systems, security, and initialization services. Instead of creating obtuse command lines or having to create tricky configuration files, these graphical tools can set up those files automatically.

Note

There are advantages and disadvantages to using a GUI-based program to manipulate text-based configuration files. GUI-based configuration tools can lead you through a setup procedure and error-check the information you enter. However, some features can't be accessed through the GUI; and if something goes wrong, it can be trickier to debug. With Linux, you have the command-line options available as well as the GUI administration tools. The book *Fedora Linux Toolbox*, by Christopher Negus and Francois Caen (Wiley, 2008) is a good way to learn more Linux commands. ■

- Testing — The exact configuration that you get on the Fedora distribution has been thoroughly tested by experts around the world. Because Fedora is now represented by a single huge software repository, the most intensely tested software will be that which is offered in official CD and DVD versions of Fedora.

- **Automatic updates** — The software packages that make up Fedora are constantly being fixed in various ways. To provide a mechanism for the automatic selection, download, and installation of updated software packages, Fedora relies primarily on the yum facility.

  With the addition of yum software repositories on the Internet that include Fedora packages, whole sets of RPM software packages can be updated with a single yum update command. The PackageKit facility provides graphical tools with Fedora to install from multiple software repositories on the Internet (as opposed to local CD or DVD media.) A desktop applet automatically alerts you when updated packages are available to download and install. See Chapter 5 for descriptions of these tools.

New Features in Fedora 13 and 14

Since the last edition of this book, there have been two Fedora releases, 13 and 14. When it comes to versions of different software projects that come with Fedora, the major components in Fedora 14 include (with version numbers) the following:

- Linux kernel: version 2.6.35
- GNOME (desktop environment): version 2.32.0
- KDE (desktop environment): version 4.5.2
- X Window System (X.org graphical windowing system): version 11, Release 1.9.1
- OpenOffice.org (office suite): version 3.3.0
- GIMP (image manipulation application): version 2.6.11
- GCC (GNU C language compilation system): version 4.5.1
- Apache (Web server): version 2.2.16
- Samba (Windows SMB file/print sharing): version 3.5.6
- CUPS (print services): version 1.4.4
- Sendmail (Mail Transport Agent): version 8.14.4
- vsFTPd (secure FTP server): version 2.2.2
- MySQL (database server): version 5.1.51
- BIND (Domain Name System server): version 9.7.2

Tip
These features are being continuously updated. Fedora ships with tools to help keep your system up-to-date with the latest versions of software. ∎

The following sections describe additional major new features of Fedora 13 and 14.

Automatic print driver installation

Printers have never been easy on Linux, and installing printers has historically been a pain. Starting with Fedora 13, though, most USB printers will work right out of the box. Fedora detects the printer and automatically downloads the appropriate driver. In addition to USB, Fedora can detect most Bluetooth, network, or parallel printers as well. See Chapter 16 for more information about printers and printing.

NetworkManager improvements

In Fedora 13, NetworkManager was revised to support a command-line interface. This means that you can take advantage of NetworkManager when logging into remote systems. In addition, you can now script NetworkManager actions using the command-line interface.

Better support for small devices

Fedora 14 includes improved support for small devices such as netbooks, especially in the area of user interfaces and graphical desktops for small, low-powered systems. Fedora 14 includes the Sugar desktop version 0.90. Sugar drives the XO laptop from the One Laptop Per Child project and aims to provide a very simple interface for children to collaborate on low-end portable computers.

In addition, Fedora 14 includes version 1.0 of the MeeGo desktop for netbooks. MeeGo unifies two prior desktops for small Linux systems, Nokia's Maemo and Intel's Moblin project for tablet and netbook devices. Fedora 13 includes the open-source edition of the Zarafa mail server. Designed as a drop-in Web replacement for Microsoft Exchange, Zarafa supports e-mail, calendars, and tasks, along with a number of standards such as iCal and CalDAV, designed to make it easy to share your data.

Getting Fedora Software and Spins

In addition to the main download site at `http://fedoraproject.org/en/get-fedora`, there are a number of other useful places to get Fedora software and variant distributions.

Cross-Reference
See Chapter 5 for more on getting Fedora software. ∎

RPMfusion.org third-party software repository

Although not specifically a Fedora or RHEL feature, several of the most popular third-party software repositories for these two distributions have banded together into a single RPM Fusion (rpmfusion.org) repository. By most accounts, this has reduced a lot of the conflicts that existed between those repositories, and provided a single access point for grabbing many software packages that are not in Fedora or RHEL due to challenges such as license restrictions.

Getting custom Fedora spins

Fedora used to be released as a set of CDs or a DVD containing all the Fedora packages that could be installed from those media. The results of new tools first added in Fedora 7 for creating custom software repositories (Pungi) and custom live CDs (livecd-creator) have continued to improve in the form of a growing set of *custom spins*.

A custom spin of Fedora is a CD, DVD, or USB flash drive image that can be run as a live CD and/or Fedora installer. Official Fedora spins include the following:

- **Fedora DVD** — Contains nearly 4GB with a cross-section of desktop, server, and software development software packages that you can install to hard disk. The contents of this disk are similar to what used to be in Fedora Core.

- **Fedora CD Set** — This six-CD set contains everything from the Fedora install DVD. This is for those who don't have a DVD drive on their computer.

- **Fedora Desktop Edition Live CD (GNOME)** — From this single, 700MB live CD you can run a GNOME desktop Fedora 14 system. An install icon on the desktop enables you to install that desktop system to your hard disk. (This CD is included with this book.)

- **Fedora Desktop Edition Live CD (KDE)** — Fedora is showing KDE some love by offering a KDE desktop live/install CD of Fedora 14. As with the GNOME desktop, you can select the install icon to install the KDE desktop system to your hard disk.

The official Fedora 14 GNOME desktop CD and Installation DVD included with this book are for standard 32-bit PCs (i386). If you need media to install Fedora on 64-bit PC (X86_64) computer architectures, you can download ISO images for those media using either BitTorrent (`http://spins.fedoraproject.org`) or an official Fedora public mirror site (`http://mirrors.fedoraproject.org`). Refer to Chapter 2 for information on using and installing Fedora from these different media.

Unofficial custom spins are also available from Fedora. The term *spin* means a compilation of software from the Fedora software repository, combined into the form of one or more bootable images, typically, to fit on a CD or DVD that enables you to either run live or install that set of software or both. Already available are Fedora Live Developer, Games, Art, Xfce Desktop, Education, and Electronic Lab spins.

Creating your own spins

The same tools that the Fedora Project uses to build packages and create live CDs and installation CDs are themselves distributed with Fedora. That means anyone can use those tools to create their own installation package sets, and then turn those package sets into their own repositories. Using those repositories, you could then create your own CD or DVD images to later install or run live.

The Pungi project (`http://fedorahosted.org/pungi`) was created for Fedora to build the Fedora system itself. The pungi package contains the `pungi` command and related configuration files. You can use the `pungi` command to fashion your own installation trees that result in installable ISO images.

The Fedora Live CD project (`http://fedoraproject.org/wiki/FedoraLiveCD`) has produced tools for building your own live CDs from Fedora software repositories. The primary tool for creating those live CDs is called livecd-creator. Refer to the Live CD HOWTO (`http://fedoraproject.org/wiki/FedoraLiveCD/LiveCDHowTo`) for information on using livecd-creator.

The Culture of Free Software

Fedora was born from a culture of free software development and continues to thrive from that culture. The copyright for software included in Fedora systems is covered primarily under the GNU public license. That license, which most free software falls under, provides the following:

- **Author rights** — The original author retains the rights to his or her software.
- **Free distribution** — People can use the GNU software in their own software, changing and redistributing it as they please. They do, however, have to include the source code with their distribution (or make it easily available).
- **Copyright maintained** — Even if you were to repackage and resell the software, the original GNU agreement must be maintained with the software. That means all future recipients of the software must have the opportunity to change the source code, just as you did.

Remember that there is no warranty on GNU software. If something goes wrong, the original developer of the software has no obligation to fix the problem. However, the Linux culture has resources for that event. Experts on the Internet can help you iron out your problems, or you can access one of the many Linux newsgroups or forums to read how others have dealt with their problems and to post your own questions about how to fix yours. Chances are good that someone will know what to do — and may even provide the software or configuration file you need.

If you need reliable support for your Linux system, commercial Linux support is available from a variety of companies; and many of the software projects that go into Linux offer their own support features, which enables you to get help directly from those who are building the code.

Note

The GNU project uses the term *free software* to describe the software that is covered by the GNU license, where free stands for free speech as opposed to free beer. Many Linux proponents tend to use the term *open-source software* to describe software. Although source code availability is part of the GNU license, the GNU project claims that software defined as open source is not the same as free software because it can encompass semi-free programs and even some proprietary programs. See `www.opensource.org` for a description of open-source software. ∎

Summary

Linux is a free computer operating system that was created by Linus Torvalds in 1991 and has grown from contributions from software developers all over the world. Fedora and Red Hat Enterprise versions of Red Hat Linux are distributions of Linux that package together the software needed to run Linux and make it easier to install and use.

This book specifically describes Fedora 13 and 14, and a complete version of Fedora 14 is included on the DVD that comes with this book. In addition, this book includes the Fedora 14 Desktop Edition Live CD to allow you to try out Fedora on your computers prior to installing the operating system to your hard disk. Fedora includes cutting-edge Linux technology that is slated for inclusion in commercial Red Hat Linux systems. You can get different "spins" of Fedora (both live and install CDs) from the Internet or from distributions that come with books such as this one.

Linux is based on a culture of free exchange of software. Linux's roots are based in the Unix operating system, which provided most of the framework that was used to create Linux. That framework came from the POSIX standard, the AT&T System V Interface Definition, and the Berkeley Software Distribution (BSD), pieces of which have all found their way into Linux. Now the Linux Standard Base creates the standards to provide consistency among Linux distributions.

Installing Fedora

2

A simplified installation procedure is one of the best reasons for using a Linux distribution such as Fedora. In many cases, for a computer dedicated to using Fedora, you can just pop in the DVD or CD that comes with this book, choose the default settings, and be up and running with Linux in less than an hour.

If you want to share your computer with both Linux and Microsoft Windows, Fedora offers several ways to go about doing that. A Fedora Desktop Edition Live CD is included with this book and will help prepare your computer before installation. If your computer doesn't have a DVD or CD drive, network and hard disk installs are available. To preconfigure Fedora for installation on multiple, similar computers, you can use a kickstart installation, covered in "Performing a kickstart installation" later in this chapter.

In the past few releases of Fedora, the project has made some great improvements to the installation process. Most notably, a recent feature in anaconda (the Fedora installer) enables you to install software from multiple online repositories during the initial Fedora install.

Although this procedure focuses on installing Fedora on a standard PC (i386 32-bit architecture), the Fedora Project also produces installable versions of Fedora for the 64-bit PC Intel architecture (x86_64). Because the latest Apple Mac computers are based on Intel architecture, Fedora can be installed on those machines as well (see the section "Installing Fedora on an Intel-based Mac" later in this chapter).

Starting with Fedora 13, the Fedora Project dropped support for the PowerPC architecture. With both Sony dropping Linux support on the PlayStation 3 and Apple migrating its users to the Intel architecture, PowerPC usage has dropped dramatically. See `https://fedoraproject.org/wiki/Architectures/PowerPC` for more on PowerPC and Fedora.

IN THIS CHAPTER

Choosing installation media

Quick installation

Detailed installation instructions

Special installation procedures

Special installation topics

Troubleshooting installation

Spinning your own Fedora

Note

This chapter follows the install procedure for Fedora 14, which comes with this book. The procedure is very similar to the Red Hat Enterprise Linux installation process. For details on installing RHEL, refer to the Red Hat Enterprise Linux 6 Installation Guide at `http://docs.redhat.com/docs/en-US/Red_Hat_ Enterprise_Linux/6/html/Installation_Guide/index.html.` ∎

Understanding Fedora Installation Media

The Fedora Project provides a lot of software to help you get started installing the release, as well as creating your own releases if you desire:

- **Fedora Repository** — This repository, maintained by the Fedora Project, includes all the software.

- **Installation Media** — The Fedora repository contains too much software for the average person to download. Therefore, the Fedora Project offers more reasonable-sized installation media that include a single 3.5G installation DVD, a GNOME Desktop Live CD, and a KDE Desktop Live CD. Either of the live CDs can also be used to install the Fedora desktop system contained on that CD to hard drive. You can also download the equivalent of the installation DVD as a set of five CDs if you don't have a writable DVD drive. See `http://fedoraproject.org/en/get-fedora-all` to download Fedora or use the media included with this book.

- **Spins** — After the release, look for Fedora *spins* that include custom releases of Fedora, typically aimed at special interests such as games, education, or electronic design (`http://spins.fedoraproject.org/`). A *spin* is just a selected grouping of Fedora software into a live or install CD or DVD image. Other spins include special desktop integration such as the Xfce desktop spin.

- **Build Tools** — To help people put together the massive amount of available Fedora software into a form that is useful to them, the Fedora Project created several software tool projects. With Fedora and optionally other software repositories, Pungi can be used to create a new set of installation media, while livecd-creator can build a live CD or live DVD. (See descriptions of these tools at the end of this chapter.)

With this book, we have included the official Fedora 14 Desktop Edition Live CD and the official Fedora 14 Installation DVD.

Using the Fedora 14 Live CD

The official Fedora 14 Desktop Edition Live CD that comes with this book is a great way to try out Fedora before you commit to installing it. In addition to answering the obvious question of "does Fedora run on my PC at all?" the CD itself contains useful tools for examining your hardware and preparing your computer for installation.

A live CD is a bootable medium (usually a CD, but other removable media, such as DVDs or USB flash drives can be used the same way) that contains an entire operating system. In most cases, you can boot the live CD without touching the contents of your hard drive.

With the Fedora 14 Desktop Edition Live CD, you can boot up to a working GNOME desktop that works like most desktop computer systems installed to hard disk. If you don't like the system, then reboot, remove the CD, and your computer will return to the way it was. If you like it, you can click a single button and install the same desktop system to your hard disk.

Here's a quick set of steps to try out the Fedora 14 Desktop Edition Live CD (included with this book):

Note
The live CD will not run well on less than 256MB of RAM. Also, if you find that the live CD hangs at some point in the boot process, refer to boot options later in this chapter. With the boot label highlighted on the boot menu, press the Tab key to be able to add boot options to the boot command. Keep in mind that the performance of a CD is not comparable to that of a hard disk. Once you have installed Fedora on your hard disk it should be much faster and more responsive. ■

1. Insert the Live CD into your CD drive and reboot.

2. From the boot screen, either let the CD timeout and boot or press any key to see other selections. From the boot menu, highlight either Boot or Verify and Boot, and then press Enter. (The verify step ensures that the medium isn't corrupted.) You can also choose to skip the Live CD and boot from the local drive or perform a memory test. In most cases, you'll want to boot from the Live CD to see how well Fedora runs on your computer.

3. When you see the login screen, you can select a language or just let the login prompt timeout. (No password is required because this is a live CD.) The GNOME desktop starts up.

4. From the GNOME desktop, here are a few things you can try from the live CD:

   - **Run applications** — Try any of the applications you choose from menus in the top panel. If you have an Internet connection (Fedora automatically configures most wired Ethernet cards), you can try Web browsing and other Internet applications. You can even add more applications. Select System ⇨ Administration ⇨ Add/Remove Software to select applications to install over the Internet. (Because the live CD is a read-only medium, software you add will disappear when you reboot.)

   - **Check hardware** — Refer to the section "Preparing for installation using the live CD" later in this chapter for suggestions on how to check out your computer hardware.

   - **Prepare for dual booting** — If you want to keep an installed Windows system that is already on your computer's hard disk, you can prepare your computer to be able to dual boot both Windows and a new install of Fedora. Refer to the section "Setting up to dual-boot Linux and Windows" later in this chapter for information on resizing your computer's hard disk partitions to make room for Fedora.

If you like the live CD, and your computer is prepared for you to install to it, you can immediately install the contents of the live CD to your computer's hard drive. Select the Install to Hard Drive icon from the desktop, and then follow the installation procedure in the next sections.

Note

If you prefer the KDE Desktop Environment over GNOME, Fedora offers a live CD spin based on the KDE desktop. You can download that live CD from any Fedora mirror site. ∎

Quick Installation

It can be a little intimidating to see a thick chapter on installation; but if you have a little bit of experience with computers and a computer with common hardware, you can probably install Fedora pretty easily. The procedure in this section will get you going quickly if you have the following:

- **Media** — The Fedora installation DVD or live/install CD, both of which come with this book.

- **PC** — A Pentium-class PC (at least 200 MHz for text mode; 400 MHz Pentium II for GUI) with a built-in, bootable DVD or CD drive, at least 256MB of RAM (for text mode) or 384MB of RAM (for GUI mode). With demanding applications such as the OpenOffice.org suite, you really should have at least 512MB of RAM for running a Linux desktop.

- **Disk space** — If you are installing from the live CD, you need at least 3GB of disk space. Keep in mind that the live CD install only copies the live CD files to your hard disk. You can't select individual packages, as you do when installing from the DVD. (The fact that files are compressed on the CD accounts for the need for more hard disk space than the 700MB CD image would indicate.)

  With the DVD, depending on which packages you choose to install, the disk space you need can range from about 600MB (for a minimal server with no GUI install) to 10GB (to install all packages). I recommend from 2GB to 3GB minimum if you are installing a desktop system. (The Fedora Project recommends at least 5 percent of additional free space, plus any disk space you require for user data.)

For this quick procedure, you must either be dedicating your entire hard disk to Linux, have a preconfigured Linux partition, or have sufficient free space on your hard disk outside any existing Windows partition.

Caution

If you are not dedicating your whole hard disk to Fedora and you don't understand partitioning, skip to the section "Detailed Installation Instructions" later in this chapter. That section describes options for having both Linux and Windows on the same computer. ∎

Here's how you get started:

1. Insert the Fedora 14 installation DVD or live CD into your computer's drive.

2. Reboot your computer.

3. The next step depends on whether you are using the live CD or DVD included with this book:

   - For the DVD, choose whether you want to install or upgrade an existing system.

   - For the install/live CD, let the boot screen time out. When the CD boots up to a GNOME desktop, double-click the Install to Hard Drive icon to begin the installation.

During installation, you are asked questions about your computer hardware and the network connections. After you have completed each answer, click Next. The following list describes the information you will need to enter. (If you need help, all of these topics are explained later in this chapter.)

- **Install or Upgrade** — If you are installing from DVD and have an earlier version of Fedora installed, you can choose Upgrade to upgrade your system without losing data files. Otherwise, you can continue with a new installation by selecting Install Fedora. (Upgrades are not supported when you are installing from the live CD.)

- **Media Check** — If you are installing from the DVD, you can optionally check the DVD to ensure that it is not damaged or corrupted. This option is not on the live CD.

- **Language Selection** — Choose the language used during the install (you can add other languages later). This option is not on the live CD.

- **Keyboard Configuration** — Choose your keyboard type from a list of international keyboard types.

- **Type of installation** — Choose whether you have a basic storage device, such as a normal hard disk, or a specialized storage device such as FCoE (Fiber Channel over Ethernet), a storage area network (SAN), or ISCSI (Internet Small Computer System Interface) device. See the detailed instructions for more information on these.

- **Select Hostname** — Choose a hostname for your system. You can also configure your network.

- **Time Zone Selection** — Identify the time zone in which you are located. Uncheck the System Clock uses UTC box if you are booting multiple operating systems from this machine, because most operating systems expect the BIOS clock to match local time.

- **Set Root Password** — Add the root user account password.

- **Disk Partitioning Setup** — Choose to remove Linux partitions, all partitions, or no partitions (and use existing free space) to have space to install Fedora. Because repartitioning can result in lost data, I recommend that you refer to descriptions on repartitioning your hard disk later in this chapter.

- **Boot Loader Configuration** — Add the GRUB boot manager to control the boot process. (GRUB is described later in this chapter.) With multiple operating systems on the computer, select which one to boot by default.

- **Choose Software** — If you are installing from DVD, choose from several preset installation classes, such as Office and Productivity (for laptop, home, or desktop use), Software Development (desktop plus software development), or Web Server (file, print, Web, and other server software). I suggest you also select Customize now so that you can see exactly which packages you have selected (and add others if you want). If you are installing from the live CD, you won't be able to choose the software to install (in this or the next step) because the entire contents of the CD are installed to hard disk.

- **Installation Categories** — If you are installing from DVD, select each category that appears to see which groups of software packages are installed. Then select the Optional packages button to add or subtract packages from each group.

- **Installation** — Up to this point, you can quit the install process without having written anything to disk. When you select Next from the installation categories, the selected packages are installed.

Note

After answering the questions, the actual installation of packages from the DVD takes between 20 and 60 minutes, depending on the number of packages and the speed of the computer hardware. For the live CD, the installation process is typically much faster because the contents of the CD are simply copied to hard disk. Upgrades can take much longer. ■

When installation is done, remove the Fedora DVD and click Exit to reboot your computer. If you installed from the live CD, reboot your computer and remove the live CD before it's time for the installed system to boot. Linux should boot by default. After Linux boots for the first time, Firstboot runs to let you read the license information, set the system date and time, add a user account, and optionally send the Fedora Project details of your system hardware. On subsequent reboots, you will see a login prompt. You can log in and begin using your Linux system.

If you need more information than this procedure provides, continue to the Detailed Installation Instructions.

Detailed Installation Instructions

This section provides more details on installation using the DVD that accompanies the book, as well as other more obscure ways to install Fedora. Besides expanding on the installation procedure, this section also provides information on different installation types and choosing computer hardware.

If anything goes wrong during installation and you get stuck, go to the section "Troubleshooting Installation" at the end of this chapter. It offers suggestions for solving common installation problems.

Caution

If, when installing Windows or Fedora, you find that the other operating system is no longer available on your boot screen, don't panic and don't immediately reinstall. You can usually recover from the problem by booting the live CD that comes with this book, and then using the `grub-install` **command to reinsert the proper master boot record. Refer to the section "Using the GRUB boot loader" later in this chapter. If you are uncomfortable working in emergency mode, seek out an expert to help you. ■**

Choosing an installation method

Fedora offers very flexible ways of installing the operating system. This book comes with the following installation media (described in Appendix A):

- **Fedora 14 DVD** — Contains the entire Fedora 14 operating system, including all binary packages that are associated with a software group.

- **Fedora 14 Desktop Edition Live CD** — If you don't have a DVD drive, you can install from the included official Fedora 14 Desktop Edition Live/Install CD. The CD enables you to run a live version of Fedora 14 that includes the GNOME desktop environment. From the running live CD system, you can launch an install process that copies the entire contents of the live CD to your hard disk. Once you have Fedora installed, you can download any missing packages later.

If your computer has a DVD drive, I recommend installing Fedora from the DVD that comes with this book after testing your computer with the live CD. However, if you don't have a DVD drive, you also have the option of installing a desktop Fedora system from the CD with this book or from any of several different types of media. Several special types of installation are described fully in the section "Special Installation Procedures."

Install or upgrade?

First you should determine if you are doing a new install or an upgrade. If you are upgrading an existing Fedora system to the latest version, the installation process tries to leave your data files and configuration files intact as much as possible. You need to do an upgrade from the DVD because upgrades are not available from the Fedora live CD.

An upgrade installation takes longer than a new install. A new install simply erases all data on the Linux partitions (or entire hard disk) that you choose. (You can optionally select which partitions to format.)

If you choose to upgrade, you can save yourself some time (and disk space) by removing software packages you don't need. An upgrade will just skip packages that are not installed and not try to upgrade them. Here are a few other tips related to upgrades:

- **Conflicting packages** — If you upgrade a system on which you installed packages from sources outside of the Fedora project and they conflict with Fedora packages, those features may no longer work. It's probably best to remove those packages before upgrading, and then apply them again later if you like.

- **Third-party packages** — If you have installed packages from third-party repositories that are specific to your current kernel (such as drivers for NVidia video cards or wireless LAN cards) you need to get new versions of those packages that match your upgraded kernel.

- **Kernel requirements** — To upgrade, you must have at least a Linux 2.0 kernel installed on the system you are upgrading.

- **Configuration files** — With an upgrade, your configuration files that are replaced are saved as `filename.rpmsave` (for example, the hosts file is saved as `hosts.rpmsave`). More often, however, your old configuration files will remain in place, while the system copies new configuration files to `filename.rpmnew`. The locations of those files, as well as other upgrade information, is written to `/root/upgrade.log`. The upgrade installs the new kernel, any changed software packages, and any packages that the installed packages depend on being there. Your data files and configuration information should remain intact.

- **Digital certificates** — If you are using digital certificates on your system, you must relocate them to the `/etc/pki` directory after the upgrade. (See Chapter 13 for information on setting up digital certificates.)

- **Java** — If you used the Java RPM from Oracle to provide Java support, conflicts with that package may cause it to be erased during an upgrade. If that occurs, you can install the Java RPM from `jpackage.org` or install the Java tarball from Oracle into your `/opt` directory.

A feature that is available when you are upgrading to Fedora 14 is the `preupgrade` package. By installing preupgrade on a Fedora 13 system (`yum install preupgrade`), you can prepare your system to upgrade to Fedora 14 by launching a single application to do the following:

- Determine which packages need to be downloaded to upgrade to Fedora 14.

- Download the packages needed to complete the upgrade (while Fedora 13 is still running)

- Download the boot images needed for the upgrade.

The advantage to using preupgrade is that you can continue using your system while you do most of the time-consuming work (such as downloading packages) that needs to be done to complete an upgrade. Also, before you get into running the installer, you will be able to see if there are any package dependencies you should deal with (before committing to the actual upgrade).

With the `preupgrade` package installed, you can start the GUI version of `preupgrade` by typing **preupgrade** from a terminal window as root user. Files needed for the upgrade are copied to the `/var/cache/yum/preupgrade*` directories. Once preupgrade is complete, you can reboot to begin the upgrade.

From DVD, network, or hard disk?

When you install Fedora, the distribution doesn't have to come from the installation DVD or CD. After booting the installation DVD, press Tab with the Install selection highlighted. Then type the word **askmethod** at the end of the boot command line displayed and press Enter. You are offered the choice of installing Fedora from the following locations:

- **Local DVD or CDROM** — This is the most common method of installing Fedora and the one you get by simply pressing Enter from the installation boot prompt. All packages needed to complete the installation are on the DVD that comes with this book.

- **Hard drive** — If you can place a copy of the Fedora distribution on your hard drive, you can install it from there. (Presumably, the distribution is on a hard drive partition to which you are *not* installing.)

- **NFS directory** — Enables you to install from any shared directory on another computer on your network using the Network File System (NFS) facility.

- **HTTP** — Enables you to install from a Web page address (http://) or FTP site (ftp://).

If your computer doesn't have a DVD drive, you can use the boot.iso CD image from http://download.fedoraproject.org/. Navigate to releases/14/Fedora/i386/os/images/ to get the boot.iso CD image file. Make a CD from this file and use that CD to start a network install (HTTP, FTP, or NFS). Just type **linux askmethod** at the boot prompt to begin the installation process.

If you don't have a bootable DVD or CD drive, there are other ways to start the Fedora installation from another medium such as a USB device, PXE server, or hard drive, as described later in this chapter.

The following specialty installation types also may be of interest to you:

- **Boot CD** — You can create a boot CD from the location mentioned above. Copy and burn the file boot.iso from the images directory. You can use the CD you create from that image to begin the install process if you have a DVD drive that is not bootable or if you have the Fedora 14 software available on any of the media described in the linux askmethod section.

- **USB or other bootable media** — If your computer can be configured to boot from alternative bootable media, such as a USB pen drive that is larger than a floppy disk, you can use the livecd-tools package to build an installable image for your USB device from one of the Live CD or minimal boot images.

- **Kickstart installation** — This enables you to create a set of answers to the questions Fedora asks during installation. This can be a time-saving method if you are installing Fedora on many computers with similar configurations.

A Fedora Installation Guide is now available from the Fedora Project if you need further information. You can access the guide here:

    http://docs.fedoraproject.org/en-US/Fedora/14/html/Installation_
    Guide/index.html

Installing Fedora on a Laptop

Because laptops can contain nonstandard equipment, before you begin installing on a laptop you should check out other people's experiences installing Linux on your model. To do that, visit the Linux on Laptops site (www.linux-on-laptops.com).

Most laptops contain bootable CD-ROM (or DVD) drives. If yours doesn't, you probably need to install from a device connected to a USB or PCMCIA slot on your laptop. PCMCIA slots enable you to connect a variety of devices to your laptop using credit card-size cards (sometimes called PC Cards). Linux supports hundreds of PCMCIA devices. You can use your laptop's PCMCIA slot to install Fedora from several different types of PCMCIA devices, including the following:

- A DVD drive
- A CD-ROM drive
- A LAN adapter

See Chapter 9 for further information on using Linux on laptops.

Preparing for installation using the live CD

Before you begin installing Fedora 14, you should check your computer hardware and prepare your computer to install Linux. By booting a live CD, you can ensure the following:

- The Linux kernel (the heart of the operating system) will boot.
- Device drivers are available for the hardware on your computer.
- Your hard disk has enough free space to install Fedora (and if not, you can use tools on the live CD to resize your hard disk partitions to make space).

You can try out Fedora using the Fedora 14 Desktop Edition Live CD that comes with this book without making any changes to your existing setup. You can identify your hardware drivers and disk partitions. Then, if you need to, you can change your hard disk to prepare it to install Fedora (primarily if you need to retain an existing operating system, such as Windows, to dual boot with Linux).

To use Fedora live, insert the Fedora 14 Desktop Edition Live CD that comes with this book, and then reboot your computer. After a 10-second timeout period, the live CD begins booting Fedora.

After taking a few moments to detect your hardware and start up services, Fedora should present you with a graphical (GNOME) desktop. With the live CD running on the PC on which you want to install Fedora, there are several ways to check your computer's hardware. You can also take additional steps to configure and debug any hardware problems before you begin installing Fedora. The following procedures describe what you can do with the live CD to prepare to install Fedora.

Displaying hardware information

To display information about your computer's hardware from the Fedora live CD, open a terminal window (from the main menu, select Applications ⇨ System Tools ⇨ Terminal). Then, from the terminal window, type the following command:

```
$ /sbin/lspci -vv | less
```

Press the spacebar to page through the list of PCI devices on your computer (press q to exit). Note the model names and numbers of any hardware that doesn't seem to be working. Next, plug in any USB devices you want to use (USB flash drives, cameras, webcams, and so on) and type the following:

```
$ /usr/sbin/lsusb
```

To get more in-depth information from Fedora's Hardware Abstraction Layer, the part of Fedora that handles all the messy details of interfacing with a variety of devices and shields those details from the rest of the operating system, you can install the gnome-device-manager tool (the GUI equivalent to the hal-device command-line tool). To install gnome-device-manager, type the following:

```
$ su -
# yum install gnome-device-manager
```

You can open Gnome Device Manager from the main menu (search for the Device Manager application on the Applications ⇨ System Tools menu) or type **gnome-device-manager**.

To check out information about your computer's memory, open the System Monitor by selecting Applications ⇨ System Tools ⇨ System Monitor from the Applications menu. Then select the Resources tab. The following information about your computer's available memory is displayed:

- **Physical Memory** — Shows how much RAM is available on your computer and how much is being used currently.

- **Swap Memory** — If there is a swap partition (which there won't be if you are starting with a Windows-only PC), this shows the amount of space available on that partition, as well as how much is being used. (If you already have a Linux system installed on the machine, you may need to turn on the swap partition manually. For example, if the swap partition were located at /dev/sda2, you could type **swapon /dev/sda2** from a terminal window as root user to turn on that swap partition.)

Writing down the information about your hardware and memory will be helpful later if something goes wrong. For example, if you use Google to search for an answer or ask a question at a forum, you will know exactly what hardware is not working.

Note

The list of hardware supported by Red Hat Enterprise Linux is available on the Internet at https://hardware.redhat.com/. This hardware should also work with Fedora. ■

Testing your hardware

Although most configuration you do disappears when you reboot your computer after using the live CD, running through some tests and a bit of setup can help when you configure the same equipment on the installed Fedora. Here are a few ways to test useful hardware devices from the Fedora Live CD:

- **Sound card** — To test your sound card, select System ➪ Preferences ➪ Sound to open the Sound Preferences window. This window displays information associated with the sound card.

- **Network/Internet** — To test your network connection, you can simply open a Web browser to see if you have an active connection. If you don't, select System ➪ Preferences ➪ Network Connections. From the Network Connections window that appears, select the tab for the type of connection, such as Wired or Wireless. Use the Add button to configure your Ethernet, ISDN, modem, token ring, wireless card, or xDSL connection (as described in Chapters 14 and 15).

- **Monitor and video card** — To check your monitor, open the Display Settings window (select System ➪ Preferences ➪ Monitors). You can get information about the video card from the gnome-device-manager application described previously. If you prefer to use the command line to check what video card was detected, type the following from a terminal window:

```
# grep Chipset /var/log/Xorg.0.log
```

You can try other hardware devices as well by opening whatever applications you need to access the device (a Web browser, a file manager, etc.). Many USB devices (digital cameras, pen drives, etc.) will be detected and are often displayed on the desktop. Running the `lsmod` and `modinfo` commands can help you determine which devices were loaded for those modules. Here are a few other quick commands for checking out your computer:

- `cat /proc/interrupts` — Shows what interrupts are in use
- `cat /proc/cpuinfo` — Shows CPU information
- `cat /proc/bus/usb/devices` — Shows attached and detected USB devices
- `/sbin/lspci` — Shows list of PCI devices found (`-vv` for more verbose info)
- `cat /proc/cmdline` — See command-line options the system booted with
- `cat /proc/ioports` — Shows ioports in use and the devices using them
- `less /var/log/messages` — Page through the log of system start-up messages

For any hardware that is not working properly, write down as much information as you can about it (name, model number, version, driver, etc.). Check Fedora mailing lists or use a search engine to find that hardware, adding keywords such as Linux or Fedora.

If your computer has an existing Windows operating system installed, you can use the live CD to set up your computer to dual boot Linux and Windows. See the section "Setting up to dual-boot Linux and Windows" later in this chapter for details. Besides describing how to resize your hard disk to fit Linux on it, the section also describes how you can later mount and access Windows (VFAT and NTFS file systems) from Linux.

Beginning the installation

If you think you have properly prepared to install Fedora, you can begin the installation procedure. Throughout most of the procedure, you can click Back to make changes to earlier screens. However, once you go forward after being warned that packages are about to be written to hard disk, there's no turning back. Most items that you configure can be changed after Fedora is installed.

Caution

If your computer contains any data that you want to keep, be sure to back it up now. Even if you have multiple disk partitions, and don't expect to overwrite the partitions you want, a backup is a good precaution in case something goes wrong. ■

1. **Insert the DVD or live CD.** This procedure assumes you are booting and installing from either the DVD or CD that comes with this book. (If you are not able to boot from either of those media, refer to the section "Alternatives for starting installation." If you are booting from DVD or CD but installing the software packages from a network or hard disk, refer to the section "Installing from other Media.")

   The DVD can be used for any type of install; the CD with this book can only be used to copy the Fedora 14 desktop system running on the CD to hard disk.

2. **Start your computer**. If you see the Fedora boot screen, continue to the next step.

Tip

If you don't see the boot screen, your DVD or CD-ROM drive may not be bootable. You may have the option to make your DVD or CD-ROM drive bootable or copy a boot image to a bootable USB device (such as a pen drive). Here's how: Restart the computer. Immediately, you should see a message telling you how to go into setup, such as by pressing the F1, F2, F12, or Del key. Enter setup and look for an option such as "Boot Options" or "Boot from." If the value is "A: First, Then C:," change it to "CD-ROM First, Then C:" or something similar. Save the changes and try to install again.

If installation succeeds, you may want to restore the boot settings. If your DVD or CD drive still won't boot, you may need to use an alternative method to boot Fedora installation (described in "Alternatives for starting installation" later in this chapter). ■

3. **Start the boot procedure**. At the boot screen, do one of the following, depending on whether you are installing from the DVD or CD:

   - **Fedora 14 Install DVD** — With "Install or upgrade" highlighted on the boot menu, press Enter to begin the installation.

- **Fedora 14 Desktop Edition Live CD** — Either wait for the boot screen to time out or with Boot highlighted on the boot menu, press Enter to start the live CD. When the CD boots up to a GNOME desktop, double-click the Install to Hard Drive icon to begin the installation.

The boot screen is menu-driven, so if you want to change any of the boot options for a menu selection, highlight that selection and press the Tab key. You can then remove or add options before pressing Enter to continue. For example, to install from a different medium (such as over the network), add the askmethod boot option. See the sidebar "Choosing Different Install Modes" for more boot options.

Although many of the steps are the same, the DVD and CD installs are different in a few key ways. In particular, the DVD install lets you select which packages to install. The CD install simply copies what is essentially an installed system from the live CD to your hard disk. Therefore, some of the steps that follow won't apply to the live CD install.

4. The previous section on "Quick Installation" covers the basic options and decisions you need to make when installing. The following sections add details to the selections you need to make for the Fedora Install DVD.

- **Media check** — At this point, you may be asked to check your installation media. If so, press Enter to confirm that the DVD is in working order. If a disk is damaged, this step saves you the trouble of getting deep into the install before failing. After the DVD is checked, select Skip to continue.

- **Continue** — When the welcome screen appears, click Next when you're ready to continue.

- **Choose a language** — When prompted, indicate the language you want to use during the installation procedure by moving the arrow keys. Then select Next. (Later, you will be able to add additional languages.).

- **Choose a keyboard** — Select the correct keyboard layout (U.S. English, with Generic 101-key PC keyboard by default). Some layouts enable dead keys (on by default). Dead keys enable you to use characters with special markings (such as circumflexes and umlauts).

Choosing Different Install Modes

Although most computers automatically install Fedora in the default mode (graphical), sometimes your video card does not support that mode. Also, although the install process detects most computer hardware, sometimes your hard disk, Ethernet card, or other critical piece of hardware cannot be detected and you'll need to enter special information at boot time.

The following list describes different installation options you can use to start the Fedora install process. You would typically try these modes only if the default mode failed (that is, if the screen was garbled or installation failed at some point). For a list of other supported modes, refer to `http://fedoraproject.org/wiki/Anaconda/Options` (if you have a running Fedora system somewhere with the anaconda package installed) or press F1 through F5 keys to see short descriptions of some of these types.

To use these boot options, highlight the first entry on the boot menu and press Tab. When the boot command appears at the bottom of the screen, type the options you want at the end of that line and press Enter to boot the install process.

- **text** — Type **text** to run installation in a text-based mode. Do this if installation doesn't seem to recognize your graphics card. The installation screens aren't as pretty, but they work just as well.

- **ks** — Type **ks** to run a Fedora installation using a kickstart file. A kickstart file provides some or all of the installation option answers you would otherwise have to select manually. (A section on creating and using kickstart files is contained later in this chapter.)

- **resolution** — To choose a particular resolution, use the **resolution** option. For example: **resolution=1024x768**.

- **noprobe** — Typically, the installation process tries to determine what hardware you have on your computer. In `noprobe` mode, installation will not probe to determine your hardware; you will be asked to load any special drivers that might be needed to install it.

- **mediacheck** — Type **mediacheck** to check your DVD before installing. Because media checking is done next in the normal installation process, you should do this only to test the media on a computer you are not installing on. For Fedora Live CDs, select the Verify and Boot option to check the CD before booting.

- **rescue** — The `rescue` mode is not really an installation mode. This mode boots from DVD or CD, mounts your hard disk, and lets you access useful utilities to correct problems preventing your Linux system from operating properly.

- **dd** — Type **dd** if you have a driver disk you want to use to install.

- **askmethod** — Type **askmethod** to have the installation process ask where to install from (local DVD/CD, NFS image, FTP, HTTP, or hard disk).

- **updates** — Type **updates** to install from an update disk.

5. **Choose the type of installation you want to perform**. Choose Basic Storage Devices if you have a normal hard disk or solid-state disk. Choose Specialized Storage Devices for storage area networks (SANs), Firmware RAID, Multipath, FCoE fiber channel, or ISCSI devices.

6. **Choose a fresh install or upgrade**. If the installer detects a version of Linux on your hard disk, you will be prompted to choose between Fresh Installation and Upgrade an Existing Installation.

7. **Enter a hostname for your system**. This name identifies the computer within your domain. For example, if your computer were named "baskets" in the handsonhistory.com domain, your full hostname would be baskets.handsonhistory.com. You can enter the domain name, or have it assigned automatically if your network uses DHCP.

Cross-Reference

Refer to Chapter 14 for descriptions of IP addresses, netmasks, and other information you need to set up your LAN. See Chapter 15 for information related to domain names. ■

8. **Select the time zone**. Either click a spot on the map or choose from the drop-down box. Before you click your exact location on the map, click on the area of the map that includes your continent or move the slider to zoom in. Then select the specific city. You may need to select a major city in your time zone, such as Chicago for US Central time, if your town isn't listed. You can click "System clock uses UTC" to have your computer use Coordinated Universal Time (also known as Greenwich Mean Time). With multiple operating systems installed, especially Windows, do not check this box because some operating systems expect the BIOS to be set to local time.

9. **Set the root password**. You must choose a password for your root user at this point. The root password provides complete control of your Fedora system. Without it, and before you add other users, you will have no access to your own system. Enter the Root Password, and then type it again in the Confirm box. (Remember the root user's password and keep it confidential! Don't lose it!) Click Next to continue.

Tip

Use the passwd command to change your password later. See Chapter 13 for suggestions on how to choose a good password. See Chapter 10 for information on setting up user accounts. ■

10. **Choose your partitioning strategy**. You have the following options related to how your disk is partitioned for a Fedora installation:

Note

Instead of installing to a local hard disk, you can identify an ISCSI initiator as the storage device by selecting the Advanced Storage Configuration button and entering the IP address and ISCSI Initiator Name of the SCSI device. You can also specify a Fibre Channel over Ethernet, or FCoE SAN storage device. Once that is identified, you can use that device for installing Fedora. ■

- **Use All Space** — This erases the entire contents of the hard disks you select.
- **Replace Existing Linux System(s)** — This erases all Linux partitions but leaves Windows partitions intact.
- **Shrink Current System** — This option allows you to resize your existing partitions so you can install Fedora in the space freed.
- **Use Free Space** — This works only if you have enough free space on your hard disk that is not currently assigned to any partition. (You can choose this option if you resized your Windows partition to make space for Linux, as described in the section "Setting up to dual-boot Linux and Windows" later in this chapter.)
- **Create Custom Layout** — Select this if you want to create your own custom partitioning.

Note

If you chose to create a custom layout, refer to the section "Partitioning your disk" later in this chapter for details on using those tools. ■

If you have multiple hard disks, you can select which of those disks should be used for your Fedora installation. Check the Review and Modify Partitioning Layout check box to see how Linux is choosing to partition your hard disk. Click Next to continue.

11. **Review and modify partitioning layout**. If you chose to review or customize your partitioning, you will see the Disk Setup tool with your current partitioning layout displayed. You can change any of the partitions you choose, provided that you have at least one root (/) partition that can hold the entire installation and one swap partition. A small /boot partition (about 500MB) is also recommended.

Caution

Partitioning your disk improperly can cause loss of data. Refer to the section "Partitioning your disks" later in this chapter for further information on disk partitioning. ■

The swap partition is often set to twice the size of the amount of RAM on your computer (e.g., for 512MB RAM you could use 1024MB of swap). Linux uses swap space when active processes have filled up your system's RAM. At that point, an inactive process is moved to swap space. You get a performance hit when the inactive process is moved to swap, and another hit when that process restarts (moves back to RAM). For example, you might notice a delay on a busy system when you reopen a window that has been minimized for a long time.

You need to have enough swap space because when RAM and swap fill up, no other processes can start until something closes. Bottom line: add RAM to get better performance; add swap space if processes are failing to start. The Fedora Project suggests a minimum of 32MB and a maximum of 2GB plus the amount of RAM of swap space. For example, if you have 4GB of RAM, make the swap size 6GB.

Click the Next button (review partitions that are being reformatted and select Write changes to disk if the changes are acceptable) to continue.

12. **Configure the boot loader**. All bootable partitions and default boot loader options that are detected are displayed. By default, the install process uses the GRUB boot loader, installs the boot loader in the master boot record of the computer, and chooses Fedora as your default operating system to boot.

Note

If you keep the GRUB boot loader, you have the option of adding a GRUB password. The password protects your system from having potentially dangerous kernel options sent to the kernel by someone without that password. This password can and should be different from the root password you are asked to enter during installation. The GRUB boot loader is described later in this chapter. ■

The names shown for each bootable partition will appear on the boot loader screen when the system starts. Change a bootable partition name by clicking it and selecting Edit. To change the location of the boot loader, click "Change device" and select where to install the boot loader. If you don't want to install a boot loader (because you don't want to change the current boot loader), click "No boot loader will be installed." (If the defaults are OK, skip the next step.)

13. **Change the device**. If you selected to configure advanced boot loader options, you can now choose where to store the boot loader. Select one of the following:

    - **Master Boot Record (MBR)** — This is the preferred place for GRUB. It causes GRUB to control the boot process for all operating systems installed on the hard disk.

    - **First Sector of Boot Partition** — If another boot loader is being used on your computer, you can have GRUB installed on your Linux partition (first sector). This enables you to have the other boot loader refer to your GRUB boot loader to boot Fedora. If you use this option, you need to modify your other boot loader to point to your Fedora partition (otherwise, you won't be able to boot the Fedora you are installing).

14. **Choose install classes**. For a new install, the installer automatically selects a set of basic software to install. In addition to that set, you can choose one or more of the following groups of software. For each of these installation groups, you have the opportunity to install a set of preset packages or customize that set:

    - **Graphical Desktop** — Installs software appropriate for a home or office personal computer or laptop computer. This includes the GNOME desktop (no KDE) and various desktop-related tools (word processors, Internet tools, etc.). Server tools, software development tools, and many system administration tools are not installed.

    - **Software Development** — Similar to a Graphical Desktop installation but adds tools for system administration and software development. (Server software is not installed.)

    - **Web Server** — Installs the software packages that you would typically need for a Linux Web server (in particular, Apache Web server and print server). It does not include many other server types by default (FTP, DHCP, mail, DNS, FTP, SQL, or news servers). The default server install also includes a GUI (GNOME only).

    - **Minimal** — Installs just the basics needed to run Fedora.

    You can also select software repositories outside of Fedora, from which you can select packages to install during the initial Fedora installation. Use the check box in order to install from other software repositories. Select Add additional software repositories to add other repositories (such as RPMFusion.org, described in Chapter 5). Then, select the Customize Now button if you want to specifically select which packages in the selected tasks are installed. This enables you to see which categories from each task and which packages within those categories are selected to be installed. It also lets you add or remove package selections. Note that packages from multiple repositories can appear in the same category (e.g., games from both Fedora and RPMFusion packages would appear in the Games category if the RPMFusion repository were enabled).

15. **Customize categories**. If you selected Customize Now, you are presented with software categories on the left side of the screen and package groups on the right side.

    Select a category to see which groups it contains. Select a group and click Optional packages to see which optional packages are available in that group and which are selected to be installed. Categories include the following:

    - **Desktop Environments** — The GNOME desktop environment is selected by default. KDE is the other main option.

- **Applications** — This category includes packages of office applications, games, sound and video players, Internet tools, and other applications. (Many of these applications are described in Chapters 5 through 8.)

- **Development** — General and specialized software development tools are included in packages in this category.

- **Servers** — Packages in this category are for Web, mail, FTP, database, and a variety of other network server types.

- **Base System** — This contains basic system administration tools, many common utilities, and support for basic system features (such as X Window System, Java, and Legacy software support).

- **Languages** — Packages containing support for multiple languages are contained in this category.

- **Uncategorized** — These are packages that don't easily fit into other categories.

After you have chosen the packages you want to install, select Next to continue. The installer takes some time to check for dependencies among the packages you selected.

16. **Installation**. A screen indicates that Fedora is being installed. Installing the packages typically takes from 20 to 60 minutes to complete, although it can take much longer on older computers.

    For live CD installation, the live CD image is simply copied to your hard disk.

17. **Finish installing**. When you see the Congratulations screen, you are done. Eject the DVD or CD and click Reboot.

Your computer will restart. If you installed GRUB, you will see a graphical boot screen that gives you several seconds to press a key to view and/or change the bootable partitions. After that, your Fedora installation should boot.

The first time your system boots after installation, Fedora Firstboot runs to do some initial configuration of your system. The next section explains how Fedora Firstboot works.

Note
Firstboot runs automatically only if you have configured Fedora to boot to a graphical login prompt. To start it from a text login, log in as root and type the following from a terminal window:

```
# rm /etc/sysconfig/firstboot
# /usr/sbin/firstboot ■
```

Running Fedora Firstboot

The first screen you see is the Welcome screen. Click Forward to step through each procedure as follows:

- **License Information** — Read the Fedora License information about the GPL.

- **Create User** — For your daily use of Fedora, you should have your own user account; and typically log in with this user name (of your choosing), using only the root user to perform administrative tasks. In the first of the four text boxes on the screen, type a user name (something such as jparker or alanb). Next, type your full name (such as John W. Parker or Alan Bourne). Then type your password in the Password text box and again in the Confirm Password text box. Click Forward. Firstboot will warn you if your password is considered too weak and therefore easier to break.

  If some form of network authentication is used, such as LDAP, Kerberos, or Winbind authentication, you can click the Use Network Login button. See the "Enabling Authentication" sidebar for information on choosing different authentication types.

- **Date and Time** — Set the date and time, or click to synchronize date and time over the network to enable the network time protocol to keep your system clock properly set. Click Forward when you are done.

- **Hardware Profile** — The Smolt hardware profiler runs to gather and display all kinds of information about your hardware. Select Send Profile if you agree to have this information sent to the Fedora Project. Firstboot is now complete. Click Finish to continue (you may need to reboot). See Chapter 3 for a description of how to log in to Fedora and start learning how to use Linux.

When Fedora starts up the next time, it will boot up normally to a login prompt. A graphical boot screen is displayed (instead of a scrolling list of services starting up).

Enabling Authentication

In most situations, you enable shadow passwords and SHA512 passwords (as selected by default) to authenticate users who log in to your computer from local passwd and shadow password files. To change that behavior, you can select the Use Network Login button during the Create User setup during Firstboot.

The shadow password file prevents access to encrypted passwords. SHA512 is an algorithm used to encrypt passwords in Linux and other Unix systems. It replaces an algorithm called crypt, which was used with early Unix systems. When you enable SHA512 passwords, your users can have longer passwords that are harder to break than those encrypted with crypt. You can also use MD5 or SHA256 for encrypting passwords, although these methods are less secure.

If you are on a network that supports one of several different forms of network-wide authentication, you may choose one of the following features (on the Identity & Authentication tab):

- **User Account Database** — You can choose local accounts only (the default), in addition to LDAP, FreeIPA, NIS, or Winbind. Once you have chosen, you can select the authentication method, such as LDAP or Kerberos passwords for LDAP. For LDAP, you can enter the LDAP Server name and optionally an LDAP distinguished name to look up the user information your system needs.

- **Authentication Method** — Depending on your choice for the user account database, you can configure the authentication method, such as LDAP or Kerberos passwords for LDAP. For LDAP, you enter the LDAP Server name and optionally an LDAP distinguished name to look up the user information your system needs. For Kerberos, you can add information about a Kerberos Realm (a group of Kerberos servers and clients), KDC (a computer that issues Kerberos tickets), and Admin server (a server running the Kerberos kadmind daemon). For Winbind, you can configure active directory or domain controllers.

On the Advanced Options tab, you can control the password hashing algorithm, but you should probably leave the default SHA512 alone. You can also do the following:

- **Enable Smart Card Support** — Tick this check box to allow users to log in using a certificate and key associated with a smart card.

- **Fingerprint Reader** — Tick this check box to allow users to authenticate using a fingerprint reader.

Going forward after installation

If your Fedora system installed successfully, you are ready to start using it. Before you head off in your chosen direction, however, I strongly recommend you do a few things:

- **Get updates** — As bugs and security vulnerabilities are discovered in Fedora, updates to your software packages are made available. Look for a desktop applet that alerts you that updates are available. Select that icon to see available updates, then select to download and install them when you are ready. Alternatively, you can run `yum update` from a terminal window (as root user) to get available updates downloaded and installed on your computer. (See Chapter 5 for further information on getting software updates.)

- **Check your security** — Chapter 13 contains a security checklist that steps you through different levels of security built into your Linux system. I suggest you go through that checklist. Sometimes a feature won't work because of the way permissions, firewalls, SELinux, and other security facilities are set on your system.

- **Learn the desktop and the shell** — Go through Chapter 3 to learn your way around the GNOME and KDE desktops that are available with Fedora. After that, learn about the shell in Chapter 4. If something goes wrong with your system, the help you can get from forums and mailing lists will almost always include commands to run from the shell.

- **Check nonworking hardware** — If a printer, network card, or other hardware component isn't working immediately, try tools for configuring those items under the System ➪ Administration menu (described throughout this book). If that doesn't work, there are a few standard places to look for information. Review the Fedora Release Notes. From the Release Notes page, look for a link to Help and Support. Visit the Bugzilla page (`https://bugzilla.redhat.com`) and search for the name or model number of hardware that is giving you trouble or check Red Hat's Certified Hardware List at `https://hardware.redhat.com/`.

After you have examined these topics, you can go anywhere else in the book that interests and excites you.

The rest of this chapter is devoted to special topics relating to installing Fedora. If you're happy with the way your Fedora system installed, you can skip to the next chapter.

Special Installation Procedures

If you don't want to, or can't, use the procedure to install Fedora from DVD or CD, the procedures in the following sections give you alternatives. The first subsection describes alternative ways of booting the installation, such as PXE or USB flash drives (if your computer doesn't have a bootable DVD or CD drive).

After the install procedure boots, use the "Installing from other media" section that follows to learn how to install Fedora from media other than DVD or CD-ROM (using FTP, HTTP, NFS, or hard disk installs). If you want the installation screens to appear on another computer as you install, refer to the section "Starting a VNC install." The subsection following that describes how to do kickstart installations.

Alternatives for starting installation

If your computer has no DVD or CD drive or the one it has is unbootable, you need an alternative way to boot the install process:

- Boot installation from hard disk.
- Boot from a USB flash drive or other USB device.
- Do a PXE install using a preboot execution environment install server.
- Use boot.fedoraproject.org's set of boot images to start booting and then download the rest from a server, similar to PXE.

Procedures for starting installation in those ways are described in the following sections.

Booting installation from hard disk

Booting the install process is similar to booting a regular Linux system. Starting an install from your hard disk is basically two steps:

1. Put the files needed to boot installation on your hard disk.
2. Configure your boot loader to tell your computer's master boot record about those installation files.

This procedure presumes that a Fedora or Red Hat Enterprise Linux system is already running on the computer (so you are doing an upgrade or a fresh install of Fedora). It also presumes that you can get those files onto the hard disk (I describe how to do that from a DVD or CD that can be mounted even if it can't be booted).

Note

See the section later in this chapter "Setting up an HTTP, FTP, or NFS install server," because presumably you need the contents of the Fedora installation DVD accessible from somewhere other than the DVD itself. ∎

1. Insert the Fedora DVD into the DVD drive while Fedora is running.

2. If the DVD isn't automatically mounted, as root user type the following to mount it:

```
# mount /media/disk
```

3. Note that the mount point for the DVD may be in a different location, such as /media/ Fedora 14 i386 DVD. Another option if the DVD doesn't mount is to create a mount point and mount the DVD there. For example, you could type **mkdir /mnt/dvd ; mount /dev/dvd /mnt/dvd**.

4. Copy the vmlinuz and initrd.img files from the installation DVD to your boot directory:

```
# cd /media/disk/isolinux
# cp initrd.img /boot/initrd-boot.img
# cp vmlinuz /boot/vmlinuz-boot
```

Note

If you are unable to mount a DVD or CD on the machine, you could copy the files from another machine on the network using scp. Alternately, you could download those files to your /boot directory from a Fedora FTP site that contains the Fedora distribution. ∎

5. Change your local /boot/grub/grub.conf file to include an entry for the vmlinux and initrd files you just added to your boot directory. For example:

```
title Fedora 14 installation
        root (hd0,0)
        kernel /vmlinuz-boot
        initrd /initrd-boot.img
```

6. This example assumes that your /boot partition exists on the first partition of your first IDE hard drive (hd0,0 which is /dev/sda1). You can type **df** to see where your /boot partition is located.

7. Reboot your computer.

8. When the boot countdown message appears, press any key to display the GRUB boot screen. From there, press the down arrow key to move to the entry titled "Fedora 14 installation" and press Enter. From here you should be able to start installation normally.

Booting installation from a USB device

Most newer computer motherboards can boot from USB devices, enabling you to copy boot disk images to something like a USB flash drive to start the installation. To add the software needed to boot a flash drive or other USB device to start the Fedora install process, you can do the following:

1. Install either the liveusb-creator graphical package, or the livecd-tools package. Either package enables you to work with the live CD images.

2. Download the Fedora Desktop Edition Live CD (which uses the GNOME desktop) or the KDE Desktop Edition Live CD.

3. Insert the live CD into the drive while Fedora is running. The CD should be automatically mounted in the /media directory.

4. If the CD isn't automatically mounted, as root user type the following to mount it:

```
# mount /media/disk
```

5. If you don't know the mount point directory for your CD drive, check the /etc/fstab file to see if it's listed there. If it's not listed, create your own mount point.

6. Insert the pen drive or other USB storage device into a USB port. The device should be automatically mounted under the /media directory under a name such as usbdisk.

7. Run the tool you downloaded to copy the .iso file from the live CD to your USB drive. For example, you can use a command like the following, replacing the /path/to/live.iso with the path to the .iso file on your live CD:

```
# /usr/bin/livecd-iso-to-disk /path/to/live.iso /dev/sdb1
```

8. To start the installation process from the USB drive to which you just copied the image, remove the USB drive and insert it into the computer where you want to install Fedora. Then reboot that computer. It should boot to the Fedora installation boot screen.

9. If the installation boot screen doesn't appear, your computer may not be set to boot USB devices. Go into setup mode when the computer first boots and try to change the boot order in the computer BIOS so that USB devices are booted first.

10. If the installation boot screen does appear, you will use the linux askmethod way of installing. Refer to the section "Installing from other media" later in this chapter for information on how to proceed.

Booting installation using PXE

Another method to begin Fedora installation is to use Pre-eXecution Environment (PXE). With PXE, the installation process begins by setting the BIOS of your computer to look on the network for a PXE server from which to boot.

For information on how to do a PXE install, refer to /usr/share/doc/syslinux-*/pxelinux .txt (provided that the syslinux package is installed). For the PXE install server, you can use the kernel and initrd images from the images/pxeboot directory on the Fedora DVD. You need to be able to set up a DHCP server and Tftp server to complete this procedure. Then you can get the Fedora installation files from any of the media types described in the section "Installing from other media."

Booting installation using boot.fedoraproject.org

Starting with Fedora 13, you can use the images located at `http://boot.fedoraproject.org`. Pre-built boot images are available for DVDs, USB devices, boot floppies, and from GRUB using the lkrn image.

Follow these simple steps:

1. Download the desired boot image.
2. Boot from the image. When it starts, it should configure your network and download the boot menus and installation information. Then, the installation proceeds similarly to the normal method from an install DVD, but using HTTP instead.

Installing from other media

Once the installation process has booted (from DVD, as described in the previous section), Fedora will let you get the actual packages to be installed from a Web server (HTTP), an FTP server, a shared NFS directory, or local hard disk.

Note

To use HTTP, FTP, or NFS installations, your computer must be connected via an Ethernet connection to a network that can reach the computer containing the Fedora distribution. You cannot use a direct dial-up connection. For a local hard-disk install, the distribution must have been copied to a local disk (or separate disk partition) that is not being used for installation. See the section "Setting up an HTTP, FTP, or NFS install server" for details on copying the distribution and making it available. ■

Beginning installation

You can use the DVD that comes with this book (or an alternative method described in the previous section) to start a network or hard-disk install:

1. **Insert the Fedora installation DVD into the drive**.
2. **Reboot the computer**. You should see the Fedora boot screen.
3. **Start askmethod**. Press Tab with the first entry on the boot screen highlighted and add the following to the end of the boot prompt:

   `askmethod`

4. **Select the language.**
5. **Select your keyboard type.**
6. **Choose the installation method**. Select any of the following installation methods: Local CDROM, NFS image, FTP, HTTP, or Hard drive.
7. **Configure the network card**. For any of the network installs, you are asked to select whether to allow for dynamic configuration using DHCP or enter the information manually. (This may be detected automatically.) If your card is not automatically detected, you need to obtain a driver disk that contains the driver needed by your network card.

Note

The Fedora project does not currently offer a driver disk, so you need to obtain the appropriate driver on your own. ■

8. **Configure TCP/IP.** For any of the network install types (NFS, FTP, and HTTP), you are prompted to configure TCP/IP for your computer.

9. **Identify the location of the Fedora distribution.** You must identify the NFS server name, FTP site name, or website name that contains the Fedora directory holding the distribution. If you are installing from hard disk, you must identify the partition containing the distribution and the directory that actually contains the Fedora directory.

Note

For an FTP install, if you are not downloading from a public FTP site that allows anonymous login, you must select the "Use non-anonymous FTP" check box when you identify the server and directory. You need a user name and password that has access to the shared directory. ■

10. **Continue with installation.** If the distribution is found in the location you indicated, continue the installation as described in the previous section.

The next section describes how to set up your own server for installing Fedora.

Setting up an HTTP, FTP, or NFS install server

If you have a LAN connection from your computer to a computer that has at least 2.5GB of disk space and offers NFS, FTP, or Web services, you can install Fedora from that server. Likewise, you can install from a spare disk partition by using a hard disk install. The following procedures enable you to set up a Linux install server by copying all files from the DVD or by copying the entire DVD image.

Configuring an install server using files

To do an FTP or HTTP install, you must copy the files from the installation DVD to a directory that you make available to the network. For example, you could do the following:

```
# mkdir /f14install/fedora
# mount /media/disk           # With DVD inserted
# cp -r /media/disk/* /f14install/fedora/
# umount /media/disk; eject /media/disk
```

In this example, all files were copied. Setting up an NFS install server or hard disk install requires copying the DVD image to the shared NFS directory.

Configuring an install server using disk images

Instead of copying all files from the installation DVD, you can copy the entire DVD image to your hard disk for NFS or hard disk installs. To install the DVD, type the following:

```
# mkdir /f14install/fedora
```

```
# dd if=/dev/cdrom of=/f14install/fedora/disk1.iso # With DVD inserted
# umount /media/disk ; eject /media/disk
```

See the "Hard disk install" section later in this chapter for the next steps for this type of installation.

NFS server

Add an entry to the /etc/exports file to share the distribution directory you created. Remember that for NFS installs, this directory must contain the DVD ISO image. The following entry makes the directory available in read-only form to any computer:

```
/f14install/fedora    *(ro)
```

Next, restart NFS by typing the following as root user:

```
# service nfs restart
```

To set the NFS service to be on permanently (it is off by default), type the following as root:

```
# chkconfig nfs on
```

Web server

If your computer is configured as a Web server, you need to simply make the distribution directory available. For example, with just the ISO image (or images) in the current directory, you could type the following:

```
# mkdir /var/www/html/fedora/
# cp *.iso /var/www/html/fedora
```

Then simply start the Web server as you would normally (service httpd start). If, for example, your computer were named pine.handsonhistory.com, you would identify the install server as pine.handsonhistory.com and the directory as fedora.

FTP server

If your computer is configured as an FTP server, you need to make the distribution directory available in much the same way you did with the Web server. For example, after creating the distribution directory as described, type the following:

```
# ln -s /f14install/fedora /var/ftp/pub/fedora
```

If your computer were named pine.handsonhistory.com, you would identify the install server as pine.handsonhistory.com and the directory as pub/fedora.

Hard disk install

With the ISO images of the DVD copied to a disk partition that is not being used for your Fedora install, you can use the hard disk install. If the ISO images exist in the /f14install/fedora directory of the first partition of your IDE hard disk, you could identify the device as /dev/sda1 and the directory holding the images as /f14install/fedora.

Starting a VNC install

With a VNC install, you can boot up the installation process on the machine you want to install Fedora to, and then step through the installation screens on another computer (running a VNC server). This can be convenient if you want to sit at your own desk while you install Fedora on a computer down the hall. Start a VNC client on the system you want to work at. (Install the tigervnc package, if needed, with the `yum install tigervnc` command).

Then, enter the following boot options:

```
vnc vncconnect=10.0.0.1 vncpassword=myF14pass
```

This sets up the address of your workstation (not the system being installed) as having an IP address of `10.0.0.1` and a password of `myF14pass`.

Note

If you are not able to connect to the vncviewer, make sure that port 5500 is open and accepting connections on your desktop system. Check the descriptions of iptables in Chapter 13 for further information on opening ports in your firewall. ■

Performing a kickstart installation

If you are installing Fedora on multiple computers, you can save yourself some trouble by preconfiguring the answers to questions asked during installation. The method of automating the installation process is referred to as a *kickstart* installation. A kickstart file can drive a regular Fedora installation, and can also be used to create Fedora Live CDs.

Caution

Based on the information you provide in your `ks.cfg` file, kickstart will silently go through and install Fedora without intervention. If this file is not correct, you could easily remove your master boot record and erase everything on your hard disk. Check the `ks.cfg` file carefully and test it on a noncritical computer before trying it on a computer holding critical data. ■

The general steps of performing a kickstart installation are as follows:

1. **Create a kickstart file.** The kickstart file, named `ks.cfg`, contains the responses to questions that are fed to the installation process.
2. **Install the kickstart file.** You have to place the `ks.cfg` file on a USB drive or CD, on a local hard disk, or in an accessible location on the network.
3. **Start the kickstart installation.** When you boot the installation procedure, you need to identify the location of the `ks.cfg` file.

In the example in this chapter, you create your kickstart file directly with a text editor. If you prefer, you can use the Kickstart Configurator (`system-config-kickstart` command, from the package of the same name), which is a graphical tool for creating kickstart files.

Creating the kickstart file

A good way to begin creating your kickstart file is from a sample `ks.cfg` file. When you install Fedora, the installation process places a file called `anaconda-ks.cfg` into the `/root` directory. You can use this file as the basis for the `ks.cfg` file that you will use for your kickstart installs.

The particular `/root/anaconda-ks.cfg` file you get is based on the information you entered during a regular installation (CD, NFS, and so on). Presumably, if you are installing Fedora on other computers for the same organization, multiple computers may have a lot of the same hardware and configuration information. That makes this a great file from which to create your `ks.cfg` file.

To start, log in as the root user. Then make a copy of the `anaconda-ks.cfg` file to work on:

```
# cp anaconda-ks.cfg ks.cfg
```

Use any text editor to edit the `ks.cfg` file. Remember that required items should be in order and that anytime you omit an item, users will be prompted for an answer. Entries from a `ks.cfg` file that was created from a regular DVD installation of Fedora are used as a model for the descriptions that follow. You should start with your own `anaconda-ks.cfg` file, so your file will start out somewhat differently. Commented lines begin with a pound sign (#).

The first uncommented line in the `ks.cfg` file should indicate whether the installation is an upgrade or an install. The `install` option runs a new installation. You can use the `upgrade` keyword instead to upgrade an existing system. (For an upgrade, the only requirements are a language, an install method, an install device, a keyboard, and a boot loader.)

```
install
```

The method of installation is indicated on the next line. Possible locations for the installation media include NFS (`nfs --server=servername --dir=installdir`), FTP (`url --url ftp://user:passwd@server/dir`), HTTP (`url --url http://server/dir`), or hard drive (`harddrive --dir=/dir --partition=/dev/partition`). For the default DVD or CD install, you may see the following:

```
cdrom
```

Because the DVD or CD installation is the default, you may also see no method of installation.

The required `lang` command sets the language (and to be more specific, the country as well) in which Fedora is installed. The default value is U.S. English (`en_US.UTF-8`):

```
lang en_US.UTF-8
```

You can install multiple languages to be supported in Fedora. Here is an example of the default being set to U.S. English:

```
langsupport --default en_US.UTF-8 en_US.UTF-8
```

The required `keyboard` command identifies a United States (us) keyboard by default. More than 70 other keyboard types are supported. (Run `system-config-keyboard` to see a list of available keyboard types.)

```
keyboard us
```

The optional `xconfig` command can be used to configure your monitor and video card. If you use the `skipx` command instead, no X configuration is done. When you use the `xconfig` command, you can identify the type of X server to use based on your video card driver (`--driver`). A handful of other options enable you to set the color depth in bits (`--depth`), whether the default desktop is GNOME or KDE (`--defaultdesktop`), whether the login screen is graphical (`--startxonboot`), and the amount of RAM on your video card (`--videoram`). (All the information after `xconfig` should appear on one line.)

With most modern hardware, you don't need to set up either of these commands, as Fedora will automatically configure the video card and monitor in most cases.

The optional `network` command enables you to configure your Fedora system's interface to your network. The following example tells your computer to get its IP address and related network information from a DHCP server (`--bootproto=dhcp`). If you want to assign a particular IP address, use the `-bootproto=static` option. Then change the IP address (`--ip`), netmask (`--netmask`), IP address of the gateway (`--gateway`), and IP address of the DNS server (`--nameserver`) to suit your system. You can also add a hostname (`--hostname`).

Note

Although the `network` **values appear to be on three lines, all values must be on the same line.**

```
network --device eth0 --bootproto dhcp
```

or

```
network --device=eth0 -bootproto=static --ip=192.168.0.1
    --netmask 255.255.255.0 --gateway 192.168.0.1
    --nameserver 192.168.0.254 --hostname duck.example.com
```

You can also use the --bootproto=query option, which will ask for the network information at installation time. ■

Again, with most modern hardware, you normally don't need the `network` command.

The `timezone` command sets the time zone for your Linux system. The default, shown here, is United States, New York (`America/New_York`). The --utc option indicates that the computer's hardware clock is set to UTC time. If you don't set a time zone, `US/Eastern` is used.

```
timezone --utc America/New_York
```

The `rootpw` command sets the password to whatever word follows (in the following example, paSSword). It is a security risk to leave this password hanging around, so you should change this password (with the `passwd` command) after Linux is installed. You also have the option to add an encrypted password instead (`--iscrypted`).

```
rootpw paSSword
```

or

```
rootpw --iscrypted                         (line continues...)
$6$NBg.5O2gfd64i269$GFCcHJdEbPgdc3.T/e3hQnqmiWR/PYsdGrfIRJd/.
dpGnOA9QLj6nvbA7PHjN.OUHZV3Ect.X3N8d9BJjjYjB.
```

The `selinux` command indicates whether or not Security Enhanced Linux is enabled. The following line shows it as enabled and enforcing:

```
selinux --enforcing
```

The required `authconfig` command sets the type of authentication used to protect your user passwords. The `--enableshadow` option enables the `/etc/shadow` file to store your passwords. The `--passalgo=sha512` option enables SHA512-based encryption for the passwords. (You would typically use both.)

```
authconfig --enableshadow --passalgo=sha512
```

The `firewall` command enables you to set the default firewall used by your Fedora system. The default value is `enabled` (if the firewall is turned on). You can also set `firewall` to `disabled` (no firewall). As you can see in the example, you can optionally indicate that there be no restrictions from host computers on a particular interface (`--trust eth0`). You can also allow an individual service (`--service=ssh`) or a particular *port:protocol* pair (`--port 1234:udp`).

```
firewall --enabled --trust=eth0 -service=ssh --port=1234:udp
```

Cross-Reference
See Chapter 13 for more on firewalls. ■

The `bootloader` command sets the location of the boot loader (GRUB, by default). For example, `--location=mbr` adds GRUB to the master boot record. (Use `--location=none` to not add GRUB.) The `driveorder=` option describes which hard disk to look on first for the master boot record. You can also add kernel options to be read at boot time using the `append` option (`--append hdd=ide-scsi`) or an optional password for GRUB (`--password=`*GRUBpassword*).

```
bootloader --location=mbr --driveorder=sda --append="rghb quiet"
password=GRUBpassword
```

Partitioning is required for a new install, optional for an upgrade. The code that follows is from the sample `ks.cfg` file. The `clearpart --linux` value removes existing Linux partitions (or use `--all` to clear all partitions) on the first hard drive (`--drives=sda`). The `part /boot`, `/`, and `swap` set the file system type (`--fstype`) and partition name (`onpart`) for each partition assignment. You can also set sizes of the partitions (`--size`) to however many megabytes you want. You can also create logical volume group (volgroup) and individual logical volume (logvol) entries for your partitioning. Uncomment the last four lines if you want these commands to be used.

```
# The following is the partition information you requested
# Note that any partitions you deleted are not expressed
# here so unless you clear all partitions first, this is
# not guaranteed to work
#clearpart --linux --drives=sda
#part /boot --fstype ext4 --size=500
#part / --fstype ext4 --size=700 --grow --ondisk=sda
#part swap --size=128 --grow --maxsize=256 --ondisk=sda
```

To indicate which packages to install, begin a section with the %packages command. (A few examples follow.) Designate whole installation groups, individual groups, or individual packages. On the %packages line, you can indicate whether or not to resolve dependencies by installing those packages needed by the ones you selected (--resolvedeps). After %packages, start an entry with an @ sign for a group of packages, and add each individual package by placing its name on a line by itself. Here is an example:

Tip
You can find a listing of package groups and individual packages on the Fedora installation DVD. Find the *comps.xml file in the repodata directory. However, if you start with the anaconda-ks.cfg file that resulted from installing Fedora, you might already have a set of packages that you want to install. ■

```
%packages --resolvdeps
@base
@editors
@games
@graphical-internet
@kde-desktop
@office
@sound-and-video
    .
    .
    .
xfsprogs
mtools
samba*
-nano
gpgme
gnupg2
%end
```

Note
The %packages command is not supported for upgrades. The best alternative to install new packages during an upgrade is to add the necessary commands to the %post section. This exactly emulates what you would do manually after an upgrade, but automatically. ■

The `%post` command starts the post-installation section. After it, you can add any shell commands you want to run after installation is completed. It's useful to add `useradd` commands for users you want to add during installation. You can also use the `usermod` command to add the user's password. (See Chapter 21 for information on creating an encrypted password.) Note that there is no `%post` section by default.

```
%post
/usr/sbin/useradd jake
chfn -f 'John W. Jones' jake
/usr/sbin/usermod -p '$1kQUMYbFOh79wECxnTuaH.' jake
```

At this point you should have a working `ks.cfg` file.

Installing the kickstart file

Once the `ks.cfg` file is created, you need to put it somewhere accessible to the computer doing the installation. Typically, you will place the file on a computer that is reachable on the network or on a hard disk. You can also place the file on a floppy disk, CD, or NFS drive.

Being able to place the `ks.cfg` file on a computer on the network requires a bit more configuration. You can set up a DHCP or a BOOTP server configured to provide network information to the new install computer. You can also set the network information from the installation boot prompt. An NFS server containing the `ks.cfg` file must export the file so that it is accessible to the computer installing Linux. To use a `ks.cfg` file from the local hard disk, you can place the file on any partition that is a Windows (VFAT) or Linux (ext4) partition.

Booting a kickstart installation

If the kickstart file (`ks.cfg`) has been created and installed in an accessible location, you can start the kickstart installation. Here is an example of how you can do a kickstart installation using the Fedora DVD and a `ks.cfg` file located on an HTTP server. Note that you'll need to have your network set up with a DHCP server for this example.

1. Insert the Fedora DVD and restart the computer.

2. When you see the boot screen, insert the floppy containing the `ks.cfg` file, highlight the first boot entry, and press the Tab key. When the boot command line appears, modify it to add the following text, replacing *hostname/path* with the Web location to use:

   ```
   ks=http://hostname/path/ks.cfg
   ```

3. You should see messages about formatting the file system and reading the package list. The packages should install without any intervention. Next you should see a post-install message. Finally, you should see the Complete message.

4. Press the spacebar to restart your computer (the DVD should eject automatically).

Tip
You can install using kickstart over NFS (`ks:nfs:server:path/ks.cfg`**), from a Web server (**`ks=http://server/path/ks.cfg`**), or from your hard drive (**`ks=hd:device:/ks.cfg`**).** ∎

For more on Kickstart, see http://fedoraproject.org/wiki/Anaconda/Kickstart.

Special Installation Topics

Some things that you run into during installation merit whole discussions by themselves. Rather than bog down the procedures with details that not everyone needs, I have included in this section instructions to address issues such as setting up a dual-boot Linux and Windows system, disk partitioning, and boot loaders.

Setting up to dual-boot Linux and Windows

It is possible to set up your computer so that you can have two (or more) complete operating systems installed on it. When you power up the computer, you can choose which operating system you want to boot. This setup is referred to as a *dual-boot* computer.

If a Microsoft Windows operating system was installed when you got your PC, it's likely that the entire hard disk is devoted to Windows. Fedora installation procedures retain existing Windows partitions by default, but they don't let you take space from existing disk partitions without destroying them. If you want to be able to run Linux on that machine, you need to do one of the following:

- **Erase the disk** — If you never wanted Windows in the first place (or if Windows is badly broken or infected), you may decide to completely erase it from your hard disk. In this case, you won't have a dual-boot system, but you can jump right to the Fedora install procedure and start installing — by telling the install process to just use (erase) the whole disk.

- **Add a second disk** — This lets you maintain your Windows installation on the computer without having to do the potentially dangerous resizing of your Windows partitions. (Refer to Chapter 9 for information on adding a second disk; then go right to the Fedora installation section.)

- **Resize your Windows partition(s)** — Many people choose this route for dual-booting Windows and Linux. When done successfully, you don't have to add hardware and you can keep your whole Windows system.

The rest of this section is devoted to a discussion and procedure for resizing your Windows partitions to create a dual-boot computer with Windows and Linux.

Resizing your Windows partitions

By resizing your Windows partitions you can free up disk space that can be used for your Fedora installation. Because there is some danger in resizing your disk partitions and changing how your computer boots, however, you should carefully read the Caution that follows.

Caution

Setting up a dual-boot system is discouraged by people who write Linux books (like me) because if something goes wrong you can lose all your data or make your computer unbootable (usually temporarily). New users often won't have a backup and will simply erase their hard disk if the computer won't boot after a procedure like the following. Then they complain a lot. Therefore, I am officially recommending that you *not* set up a dual-boot system, and then telling you how to do it.

If, after resizing your Windows partitions and installing Fedora, your computer becomes unbootable, refer to the section "Troubleshooting Installation" later in this chapter for advice about what to do. ∎

Before you begin resizing your Windows system, boot Windows and do the following:

- **Back up your data!** — Of course, you should always have a current backup of your important data. However, now is a particularly good time to do a backup, just in case one of those disk catastrophes I warned you about actually happens.

- **Defragment your disk** — Before you resize your hard disk, you should use a defragmenting utility in Windows to have all files stored contiguously on the disk. That way, when you reassign free space to Linux partitions, you have a continuous area of the disk to work with.

Despite the fact that I have successfully resized several NTFS partitions using the GParted utility, I still recommend caution (and a good backup of your data) before proceeding. You may also want to look at a commercial Windows tool such as the Acronis Disk Director suite (www.acronis.com).

Microsoft Windows 7 comes with tools for resizing your disk partitions. From the Start menu, search for partitions to find the Disk Management utility. Open this application. Then right-click on the volume you want to resize and select either Extend Volume or Shrink Volume to change its size.

The open-source tool I describe here for resizing your disk is called GParted. It can be used to resize partitions that contain a variety of file system types.

If your Windows system is backed up and your disk defragmented, you can begin the process of resizing your NTFS or VFAT disk partition with GParted using the Fedora 14 Desktop Edition Live CD included with this book. Here's how to resize your NTFS partitions using that CD:

1. Insert the Fedora 14 Desktop Edition Live CD and reboot your computer.

2. At the boot prompt, with the first entry highlighted, press Enter.

3. When the Desktop Live CD boots to a GNOME desktop, to begin resizing your hard disk you need to install the gparted package. Assuming you have an Internet connection, type the following from a terminal window:

```
$ su -
# yum install gparted
```

4. From the System Tools submenu of the Applications menu, search for the GParted Partition Editor application and select it. The GParted graphical partitioning tool opens, displaying your current disk partitions.

5. Select the disk (probably /dev/sda) and partition (probably NTFS or VFAT for a Windows partition) you want to resize. The Resize/Move button should become available.

6. Select the Resize/Move button to open a Resize/Move pop-up window.

7. Grab the slider bar from the right and move it to select how much you want to resize your partition. The New Size box shows the new size of your partition. The Free Space Following box shows how much free space you will have after you are done.

8. Click Resize/Move to begin resizing your partition. When it is done, you will see the resized partition and a new entry showing the free space.

Caution

The resize is committed in the next step. You can quit now without making any changes if you are nervous. In any case, make sure that the partition you are resizing is not mounted. (In this example, I'd type umount /dev/sda1 **as root user from a shell before running the next step. ■**

9. If the new partition sizes look OK, click Apply to commit the changes.

10. At this point, you can close the GParted window and begin the regular installation procedure for Fedora, using the disk space that you just freed up.

After you have installed Fedora, there are a few other useful things you might want to do so you can use files from your Windows partitions in Linux.

Using Windows partitions from Linux

With some space available on your disk, when you go to install Linux, consider adding a small FAT16 or FAT32 partition (maybe 2GB) on your disk. Every x86 operating system, including Windows and Linux, supports those types. With that added, you will be able to freely exchange files between your Linux and Windows system on the FAT16 partition.

With FAT partitions, however, keep in mind that there are limitations. FAT is limited to between 2GB and 4GB file sizes. Also, FAT16 doesn't support filenames longer than the classic eight characters with a three-character extension. Total partition size for FAT file systems is 32GB.

After you have installed Linux in the space freed up by the previous procedure, you should be able to choose between Linux and Windows when the Fedora boot screen appears during boot time. Press any key to go to the GRUB boot screen. Then move the arrow key to choose to boot Linux or Windows.

The first time you boot Windows, you might be asked to check your disk (because your Windows partition will be a different size than expected). After that, there should be no change in how you use your Windows system. Your disk space will just be smaller.

When you boot up Linux, if you have a lot of documents, digital images, music, or other content on your Windows partition, you probably want to be able to use that content from Linux. To do that, you need to do the following:

- Determine which partition is your Windows partition.

- Mount the Windows partition on your Linux file system.

The following procedure describes how to do those things:

1. Check partitions. To determine which partition contains your Windows file system, use the fdisk command as follows:

```
# fdisk -1
Disk /dev/sda: 60.0 GB, 60011642880 bytes
16 heads, 63 sectors/track, 116280 cylinders
Units = cylinders of 1008 * 512 = 516096 bytes

   Device Boot    Start        End      Blocks   Id   System
/dev/sda1     *       1      41725    21029053+   7   HPFS/NTFS
/dev/sda2         106741     116280     4808160   12  Compaq↵
 diagnostics
/dev/sda3          41725      41932     104422+   83  Linux
/dev/sda4          41932     106734    32660145    5  Extended
/dev/sda5          41932     106718    32652081   8e  Linux LVM
```

In this example, the Windows partition is on device /dev/sda1 and is an NTFS file system. (The other common type of Windows file system is VFAT.)

2. Mount the Windows file system. You can access your Windows file system from Linux using the mount command. Assuming your Windows partition is an NTFS file system on /dev/sda1 (as in the preceding example), you could type the following to create the Windows mount point and mount the file system there:

```
# mkdir /mnt/win
# chmod 755 /mnt/win
# mount -oro -t ntfs /dev/sda1 /mnt/win
# chmod 755 /mnt/win
# ls /mnt/win
```

3. The -oro option to mount will mount the file system as read-only. Remove the -oro option to mount read/write. Replace the ntfs with vfat if your Windows partition is a VFAT file system. The ls command is just to find out if you can see the contents of your Windows partition.

4. You can have the mount occur permanently by adding an entry to the /etc/fstab file. Here's an example of the line you could add to /etc/fstab to have the partition mounted every time the system reboots:

```
/dev/sda1     /mnt/win     ntfs     ro     0 0
```

At this point, you can use the files from your Windows partition as you would any other files on your system. You can open a folder or change directories to the /mnt/win directory to see the contents. Then use any applications you choose to open your documents (OpenOffice.org), music (Rhythmbox), images (GIMP), or any other content type you want to use from your Windows partition in Linux.

Note

If your Linux system uses an ext2 or ext3 file system (but not the default ext4 file system), you can do the reverse of what was just described as well: access your Linux partition from Windows. For information on how to do this, see the Ext2 Installable File System for Windows (www.fs-driver.org). ∎

Partitioning your disks

The hard disk (or disks) on your computer provide the permanent storage area for your data files, applications programs, and the operating system (such as Fedora). Partitioning is the act of dividing a disk into logical areas that can be worked with separately. There are several reasons you may want to do partitioning:

- **Multiple operating systems** — If you install Fedora on a PC that already has a Windows operating system, you may want to keep both operating systems on the computer. To run efficiently, they must exist on completely separate partitions. When your computer boots, you can choose which system to run. Note that you are limited in the number of partitions you can have (with IDE drives you can have 63 partitions; with SCSI devices, you are limited to 15 partitions per device).

- **Multiple partitions within an operating system** — To avoid having their entire operating system run out of disk space, people often assign separate partitions to different areas of the Linux file system. For example, if /home and /var were assigned to separate partitions, then a gluttonous user who fills up the /home partition wouldn't prevent logging daemons from continuing to write to log files in the /var/log directory.

- **Different file system types, quotas, or mount options** — Different kinds of file systems have different structures. File systems of different types must be on their own partitions. In Fedora, you need at least one file system type for / (typically ext4) and one for your swap area. File systems on CD-ROM use the iso9660 file system type. You may also want to mount particular file systems, like /home, with mount options like noatime (don't record the time when a file is accessed) that would be detrimental to other file systems like /tmp, where common clean-up strategies look for files not recently used.

During installation, Fedora enables you to partition your hard disk using the Disk Setup utility (a graphical partitioning tool). The following sections describe how to use Disk Setup (during installation) or fdisk (when Fedora is up and running or by switching virtual terminals while the install is running). See the section "Tips for creating partitions" for some ideas for creating disk partitions.

Partitioning with Disk Setup during installation

During installation, you are given the opportunity to change how your hard disk is partitioned. Fedora recommends using Disk Setup. The Disk Setup screen is divided into two sections. The top shows general information about each hard disk. The bottom shows details of each partition.

For each of the hard disk partitions, you can see the following:

- **Device** — The device name is the name representing the hard disk partition in the /dev directory. Each disk partition device begins with two letters: sd for IDE disks or

SCSI disks, ed for ESDI disks, or xd for XT disks. After that is a single letter representing the number of the disk (disk 1 is a, disk 2 is b, disk 3 is c, etc.). The partition number for that disk (1, 2, 3, etc.) follows that.

- **Mount Point/Raid/Volume** — The directory where the partition is connected into the Linux file system (if it is). You must assign the root partition (/) to a native Linux partition before you can proceed. If you are using RAID or LVM, the name of the RAID device or LVM volume appears here.

- **Type** — The type of file system that is installed on the disk partition. In most cases, the file system will be Linux (ext4), Win NTFS (ntfs) or VFAT (vfat), or Linux swap. However, you can also use the previous Linux file system (ext3), physical volume (LVM), or software RAID. In fact, LVM is used by default for your root file system when you install Fedora. This enables you to add more disk space later to that partition, if needed, without having to create a new partition.

- **Format** — Indicates whether (checkmark) or not (no checkmark) the installation process should format the hard disk partition. Double-check which partitions you want to format, so that you do not lose data.

Caution

Partitions marked with a check are erased (!), so on a multiboot system, be sure your Windows partitions, as well as other partitions containing data, are not checked! ■

- **Size (MB)** — The amount of disk space allocated for the partition. If you chose to let the partition grow to fill the existing space, this number may be much larger than the requested amount.

- **Start/End** — Represents the partition's starting and ending cylinders on the hard disk.

In the top section, you can see each of the hard disks connected to your computer. The drive name is shown first, followed by the disk's model name. The total amount of disk space, the amount used, and the amount free are shown in megabytes.

Reasons for partitioning

There are different opinions about how to divide up a hard disk. Here are some issues to consider:

- **Do you want to install another operating system?** If you want Windows on your computer along with Linux, you need at least one Windows, one Linux, and one Linux swap partition.

- **Is it a multiuser system?** If you are using the system yourself, you probably don't need many partitions. One reason for partitioning an operating system is to keep the entire system from running out of disk space at once. That also serves to put limitations on what an individual can use up in his or her home directory (although disk quotas are good for that as well).

- **Do you have multiple hard disks?** You need at least one partition per hard disk. If your system has two hard disks, you may assign one to / and one to /home (if you have a lot of users) or /var (if the computer is a server sharing a lot of data).

- **Do you upgrade often?** I've found it works well to put /home on a separate partition, which makes it easier to preserve my files even if I install new versions of Fedora. (In this case, be sure to not check the box for formatting the /home partition, as you want to leave these files alone).

Deleting, adding, and editing partitions

Before you can add a partition, some free space must be available on your hard disk. If all your hard disk space is currently assigned to one partition (as it often is in DOS or Windows), you must delete or resize that partition before you can claim space on another partition. The section "Resizing your Windows partitions" earlier in this chapter discusses how to take disk space from an existing Windows partition to use later for Linux partitions, without losing information in your existing single-partition system.

Caution

Make sure that any data you want to keep is backed up before you delete the partition. When you delete a partition, all its data is gone. ■

Disk Setup is less flexible, but more intuitive, than the fdisk utility. Disk Setup lets you delete, add, and edit partitions.

Tip

If you create multiple partitions, make sure that there is enough room in the right places to complete the installation. For example, most of the Linux software is installed in the /usr directory (and subdirectories), whereas most user data is eventually added to the /tmp, /home or /var directories. It's a good idea to have separate partitions for every directory structure users can write to. Likewise, NFS shares also are often put on separate partitions. ■

To delete a partition in Disk Setup, do the following:

1. Select a partition from the list of Current Disk Partitions on the main Disk Setup window (click it or use the arrow keys).

2. To delete the partition, click Delete.

3. When asked to confirm the deletion, click Delete.

4. If you made a mistake, click Reset to return to the partitioning as it was when you started Disk Setup.

To add a partition in Disk Setup, follow these steps from the main Disk Setup window:

1. Select New. A window appears, enabling you to create a new partition.

2. Type the name of the mount point (the directory where this partition will connect to the Linux file system). You need at least a root (/) partition and a swap partition.

3. Select the type of file system to be used on the partition. You can select from Linux native (ext3 or preferably ext4), software RAID, Linux swap (swap), physical volume (LVM), or Windows FAT (vfat).

Tip

To create a file system type other than those shown, leave the space you want to use free for now. After installation is complete, use `fdisk` to create a partition of the type you want. ■

4. Type the number of megabytes to be used for the partition (in the Size field). If you want this partition to grow to fill the rest of the hard disk, you can put any number in this field (1 will do fine).

5. If you have more than one hard disk, select the disk on which you want to put the partition from the Allowable Drives box.

6. Type the size of the partition (in megabytes) into the Size (MB) box or select one of the additional size options.

7. Optionally, select Force to Be a Primary Partition if you want to ensure that you can boot the partition, or Check for Bad Blocks if you want to have the partition checked for errors.

8. Optionally, choose to encrypt the partition.

9. Select OK if everything is correct. (The changes don't take effect until several steps later when you are asked to begin installing the packages.)

To edit a partition in Disk Setup, from the main Disk Setup window follow these steps:

1. Click the partition you want to edit.

2. Click the Edit button. A window appears, ready to let you edit the partition definition.

3. Change any of the attributes (as described in the add partition procedure). For a new install, you may need to add the mount point (/) for your primary Linux partition.

4. Select OK. (The changes don't take effect until several steps later, when you are asked to begin installing the packages.)

Note

If you want to create a RAID device, you need to first create at least two RAID partitions. Then click the RAID button to make the two partitions into a RAID device. For more information on RAID, refer to Chapter 9 or the Fedora Installation guide. The latter is available at `http://docs.fedoraproject.org/en-US/Fedora/14/html/Installation_Guide/index.html`. To create an LVM volume group, you must create at least one partition of type "physical volume (LVM)." ■

Partitioning with fdisk

The fdisk utility does the same job as Disk Setup, but it's no longer offered as an option during Fedora installation. (If you are old school, however, you can press Ctrl+Alt+F2 during the installation process and run fdisk from the shell to partition your disk.)

The following procedures are performed from the command line as root user.

Caution

Remember that any partition commands can easily erase your disk or make it inaccessible. Back up critical data before using any tool to change partitions! Then be very careful about the changes you do make. Keeping an emergency boot disk handy is a good idea, too. ■

The fdisk command is one that is available on many different operating systems (although it looks and behaves differently on each). In Linux, fdisk is a menu-based command. To use fdisk to list all your partitions, type the following (as root user):

```
# fdisk -l

Disk /dev/sda: 40.0 GB, 40020664320 bytes
255 heads, 63 sectors/track, 4865 cylinders
Units = cylinders of 16065 * 512 = 8225280 bytes

   Device Boot    Start      End    Blocks   Id  System
/dev/sda1    *        1       13    104391   83  Linux
/dev/sda2            14     4833  38716650   83  Linux
/dev/sda3          4834     4865    257040   82  Linux swap
```

To see how each partition is being used on your current system, type the following:

```
# df -h
Filesystem       Size  Used  Avail  Use%  Mounted on
/dev/sda2        37G   5.4G   30G   16%   /
/dev/sda1        99M   8.6M   86M   10%   /boot
none             61M      0   61M    0%   /dev/shm
```

From the output of df, you can see that the root of your Linux system (/) is on the /dev/sda2 partition and that the /dev/sda1 partition is used for /boot.

Caution

Before using fdisk to change your partitions, I strongly recommend running the df -h command to see how your partitions are currently being defined. This helps reduce the risk of changing or deleting the wrong partition. ■

To use fdisk to change your partitions, begin (as root user) by typing

```
# fdisk device
```

where *device* is replaced by the name of the device you want to work with. For example, here are some of your options:

- /dev/sda — For the first IDE or SCSI hard disk; sdb, sdc, and so on for other SCSI disks. (Beginning with Fedora 10, IDE hard drives no longer appear as hda, hdb, and so on.)
- /dev/md0 — For a RAID device.

After you have started fdisk, type **m** to see the options. Here is what you can do with fdisk:

- **Delete a partition** — Type **d** and you are asked to enter a partition number on the current hard disk. Type the partition number and press Enter. For example, /dev/sda2 would be partition number 2. (The deletion won't take effect until you write the change. Until then, it's not too late to back out.)

- **Create a partition** — If you have free space, you can add a new partition. Type **n** and you are asked to enter 1 for a logical partition (5 or higher) or p for a primary partition (1–4). Enter a partition number from the available range. Then choose the first cylinder number from those available. (The output from fdisk -l shown earlier displays cylinders being used under the Start and End columns.)

  Next, enter the cylinder number the partition will end with (or type the specific number of megabytes or kilobytes you want: for example, +50M or +1024K). You just created an ext3 Linux partition. Again, this change isn't permanent until you write the changes.

- **Change the partition type** — Press **t** to choose the type of file system. Enter the partition number of the partition you want to change. Type the number representing the file system type you want to use in hexadecimal code. (Type **L** at this point to see a list of file system types and codes.) For a Linux file system, use the number 83; use 82 for a Linux swap partition. For a Windows FAT32 file system, you can use the letter b.

- **Display the partition table** — Throughout this process, feel free to type **p** to display (print on the screen) the partition table as it now stands.

- **Saving and quitting** — If you don't like a change you make to your partitions, press **q** to exit without saving. Nothing will have changed on your partition table.

  Before you write your changes, display the partition table again and ensure that it is the way you want it. To write your changes to the partition table, press **w**. You are warned about how dangerous it is to change partitions and asked to confirm the change.

Tips for creating partitions

Changing your disk partitions to handle multiple operating systems can be very tricky, in part because each operating system handles partitioning information differently, and provides different tools for doing it. Here are some tips to help you get it right:

- If you are creating a dual-boot system that includes Windows, try to install the Windows operating system first. Otherwise, the Windows installation may make the Linux partitions inaccessible.

- The `fdisk` man page recommends that you use the partitioning tools that come with an operating system to create partitions for that operating system. For example, the DOS `fdisk` knows how to create partitions that DOS will like, and the Fedora `fdisk` will happily make your Linux partitions. Once your hard disk is set up for dual boot, however, you should probably not go back to Windows-only partitioning tools. Use Linux `fdisk` or a product made for multiboot systems (such as GParted).

- You can have up to 63 partitions on an IDE hard disk. A SCSI hard disk can have up to 15 partitions. You probably won't need nearly that many, however.

If you are using Fedora as a desktop system, you probably don't need a lot of different partitions within your Linux system. There are, however, some very good reasons to have multiple partitions for Linux systems that are shared by a lot of users or are public Web servers or file servers. Multiple partitions within Fedora offer these advantages:

- **Protection from attacks** — Denial-of-service attacks sometimes attempt to fill up your hard disk. If public areas, such as `/var`, are on separate partitions, a successful attack can fill up a partition without shutting down the whole computer. Because `/var` is the default location for Web and FTP servers, and therefore might hold a lot of data, often entire hard disks are assigned to the `/var` file system alone.

- **Protection from corrupted file systems** — If you have only one file system (`/`), corruption of that file system can cause the whole Fedora system to be damaged. Corruption of a smaller partition can be easier to correct and often enables the computer to stay in service while the corruption is fixed.

Here are some directories that you may want to consider making into separate file system partitions:

- `/boot` — Sometimes the BIOS in older PCs can access only the first 1,024 cylinders of your hard disk. To ensure that the information in your `/boot` directory is accessible to the BIOS, create a separate disk partition (at least 500MB) for `/boot` and make sure it exists below cylinder 1,024. Then, the rest of your Linux system can exist outside of that 1,024-cylinder boundary if you like. For newer hard disks, you can sometimes avoid this problem by enabling the Linear Mode check box during installation. Then the boot partition can be anywhere on the disk.

- `/usr` — This directory structure contains most of the applications and utilities available to Fedora users. Having `/usr` on a separate partition enables you to mount that file system as read-only after the operating system has been installed. This prevents attackers from replacing or removing important system applications with their own versions that may cause security problems. A separate `/usr` partition is also useful if you have diskless workstations on your local network. Using NFS, you can share `/usr` over the network with those workstations.

- `/var` — Your FTP (`/var/ftp`) and Web server (`/var/www`) directories are, by default, stored under `/var`. Having a separate `/var` partition can prevent an attack on those facilities from corrupting or filling up your entire hard disk. Often this partition is highly utilized and grows in size over time.

- /home — Because your user account directories are located in this directory, having a separate /home account can prevent an indiscriminate user from filling up the entire hard disk. (Disk quotas are another way to control disk use; see Chapter 9.) Also, some people have a separate /home partition so they can reinstall the operating system, erasing the root (/) partition, and simply remounting the /home partition.

- /tmp — Protecting /tmp from the rest of the hard disk by placing it on a separate partition can ensure that applications that need to write to temporary files in /tmp are able to complete their processing, even if the rest of the disk fills up.

Although casual Fedora users rarely have a need for a lot of partitions, those who maintain and have to recover large systems are thankful when the system they need to fix has several partitions. Multiple partitions can localize deliberate damage (such as denial-of-service attacks), problems from errant users, and accidental file system corruption.

Installing Fedora on an Intel-based Mac

The latest Apple computers feature Intel-based computer architecture. The Fedora Project has enhanced Fedora so that it can be installed (either by itself or dual-booting with Mac OS X) on recent Apple hardware. Reasons you might want to install Fedora on one of these "Mactel" computers include the following:

- **Dual booting** — You might like the Mac OS X desktop (Aqua) and proprietary applications (such as iPhoto or iTunes) for yourself or family members some of the time. However, you might sometimes want access to server applications, administration tools, the development environment, or thousands of free applications you can get with Fedora.

- **Fedora only** — You might like the form, features, and performance of Apple Mac computers enough to pay a bit extra to have it as your primary desktop Fedora computer.

This section describes how to start with an Intel-based Apple Mac computer (I used a Mac Mini for this example) and configure it to either dual boot with Mac OS X or run Fedora alone.

Caution
Installing Fedora on Intel-based hardware is still an experimental technology in the Fedora community. Some hardware components require extra tweaking or won't work at all. I recommend that you skip this procedure if you can't risk the chance that your disk may be blown away and will have to be reinstalled from scratch. ■

Before installing Fedora on your Mac
Let's start with a reminder that this procedure is only for Apple Mac computers that are based on Intel architecture. I ran this procedure on a new Mac Mini 1.1 (Intel Core Duo CPU, 512MB RAM). However, the same procedure should work for Intel-based iMac, MacBook, MacBook Pro, or Mac Pro computers.

When you purchase your Mac, the entire hard disk is devoted to Mac OS X. To keep your Mac OS X installation on the computer (so you can boot either Mac OS X or Fedora), you need to reduce the amount of space devoted to Mac OS X. Then you use the space to create one or more partitions for installing Fedora.

Although the procedure for resizing and repartitioning your disk is fairly safe, there is some risk that you could corrupt your Mac OS X partition or make the machine (temporarily) unbootable. For that reason, before starting the procedure that follows, *please back up any important data!*

Installing Fedora

Mac OS X Leopard and higher versions offer software called Boot Camp that can be used to resize Mac hard disks (using the default HFS+ file system type). The following procedure describes how to update your firmware, resize your disk, and install Fedora:

1. **Check for firmware updates** — Update your Mac OS X system to the latest firmware. Refer to the Mac OS X Firmware Updates page for information on how to do that (`http://support.apple.com/kb/HT1237`). Then go to Apple Downloads (`www.apple.com/support/downloads`) to get the firmware update, if necessary. Also update the rest of your Mac system software to the latest version.

2. **Install Refit** — Refit (`http://refit.sourceforge.net/`) provides a boot menu to select Linux, Mac OS X, or other operating systems.

3. **Shrink your Mac partition** — By default, Mac OS X uses your entire hard disk. Use the Disk Utility application to shrink your partition. All you need for now is free space on which to install Fedora Linux.

4. **Insert the Fedora DVD** — Insert your Fedora live CD or installation DVD. Note that for Macintosh computers, you'll want the 64-bit Linux version, called X86_64. Reboot and select the Linux penguin at boot time.

5. **Install Fedora** — Begin a normal Fedora install (as described earlier in this chapter), noting the following:

   - **Partitioning** — Default partitioning by the Fedora installer should work properly (leaving your Mac HFS+ partition alone and creating a Fedora /boot and LVM partition using the rest of the space).

   - **Boot loader** — Again, the installer should do the correct thing and configure the boot loader to be installed on a Fedora partition and not in the master boot record, as would normally be the case. (The boot loader must not be installed in the master boot record of the whole disk or the disk will become unbootable.)

You may have issues after installation whereby Linux won't boot. It is common to see, for example, the error message "No bootable device – insert boot disk and press any key."

If you see this error message, try the Refit partition tool, which enables you to synchronize your partitions. On my system, Refit's partition tool indicated that it needed to update the MBR, or Master Boot Record. After choosing yes, I could boot the Mac system normally using Refit.

Remember that installing Fedora on an Intel-based Mac is still considered experimental. The less you stray from the defaults (partitioning, boot loaders, and so on), the better your chance of getting a workable Fedora system running on your Mac.

If you run into problems, I recommend you refer to the Fedora Project's Fedora On Mactel page (`http://fedoraproject.org/wiki/FedoraOnMactel`) or the Refit help page (`http://refit.sourceforge.net/help/`). Other Linux projects also offer resources for getting Linux to boot on Intel Mac architecture.

Using the GRUB boot loader

With multiple operating systems installed and several partitions set up, how does your computer know which operating system to start? A *boot loader* enables you to choose when and how to boot the bootable operating systems installed on your computer's hard disks. The boot loader that is installed by default with Fedora is called the Grand Unified Boot loader (GRUB).

GRUB is a GNU software package (`www.gnu.org/software/grub`) that replaced the older LILO as the only boot loader available in Fedora. GRUB offers the following features:

- Support for multiple executable formats.
- Support for multiboot operating systems (such as Fedora, FreeBSD, NetBSD, OpenBSD, and other Linux systems).
- Support for non-multiboot operating systems (such as Windows) via a chain-loading function. Chain-loading is the act of loading another boot loader (presumably one that is specific to the proprietary operating system) from GRUB to start the selected operating system.
- Support for multiple file system types.
- Support for automatic decompression of boot images.
- Support for downloading boot images from a network.

For more information on how GRUB works, type **man grub** or **info grub**. The `info` command returns more details about GRUB. Alternately, see the GRUB wiki at `http://grub.enbug.org`.

When you install Fedora, information needed to boot your computer (with one or more operating systems) is automatically set up and ready to go. Simply restart your computer. When you see the boot message, press the Enter key (quickly before it times out) and the GRUB boot screen appears (it says GRUB at the top and lists bootable partitions below it). Then you can do one of the following:

- **Default** — If you do nothing, the default operating system will boot automatically after a few seconds.

- **Select an operating system** — Use the up and down arrow keys to select any of the operating systems shown on the screen. Then press Enter to boot that operating system.

- **Edit the boot process** — If you want to change any of the options used during the boot process, use the arrow keys to select the operating system you want and type **e** to select it. Follow the procedure described in the next section to change your boot options temporarily.

If you want to change your boot options so that they take effect every time you boot your computer, see the section "Permanently changing boot options." Changing those options involves editing the /boot/grub/grub.conf file.

Temporarily changing boot options

From the GRUB boot screen, you can select to change or add boot options for the current boot session. First, quickly press any key before GRUB times out and boots the default system. From the GRUB selection screen that appears, select the operating system you want (using the arrow keys) and type **e** (as described earlier). You will see a graphical screen that contains textual information, including GRUB's root (the /boot partition), the kernel, and the initial RAM disk (initrd), which contains the minimum files and directories needed during the boot process.

If you are going to change any of the lines related to the boot process, you would probably change only the second line to add or remove boot options. Here is how you do that:

1. Position the cursor on the kernel line and type **e**.

2. Either add or remove options after the name of the boot image. You can use a minimal set of bash shell command-line editing features to edit the line. You can even use command completion (type part of a filename and press Tab to complete it). Here are a few options you may want to add or delete:

   - **Boot to a shell** — If you forgot your root password or if your boot process hangs, you can boot directly to a shell by adding init=/bin/sh to the boot line. (The file system is mounted read-only, so you can copy files out. You need to remount the file system with read/write permissions to be able to change files.)

   - **Turn off a service** — If your boot process is hanging on a particular service, you can often turn off that service from the boot prompt. For example, you could add the options noacpi (to turn off ACPI power management), nopcmcia (to turn off PCMCIA card slot support), or nodma (to turn off DMA, if you are getting disk errors). Add selinux=0 to temporarily turn off SELinux. Sometimes turning off a service at the boot prompt enables you to fix the problem after the system is up and running.

   - **Select a run level** — If you want to boot to a particular run level, add the number of the desired run level to the end of the kernel line. For example, to have Fedora boot to run level 3 (multiuser plus networking mode), add 3 to the end of the kernel line. You can also boot to single-user mode (1), multiuser mode (2), or X GUI mode (5). Level 3 is a good choice if your GUI is temporarily broken.

3. Press Enter to return to the editing screen.

4. Type **b** to boot the computer with the new options. The next time you boot your computer, the new options will not be saved. To add options permanently, see the next section.

Permanently changing boot options

You can change the options that take effect each time you boot your computer by changing the GRUB configuration file. In Fedora, GRUB configuration centers around the /boot/grub/grub. conf file.

This file is created when you install Fedora. Here is an example of a grub.conf file:

```
# grub.conf generated by anaconda
#
# Note that you do not have to rerun grub after making
# changes to this file
# NOTICE: You have a /boot partition.  This means that
#          all kernel and initrd paths are relative to /boot/, eg.
#          root (hd0,0)
#          kernel /vmlinuz-version ro root=/dev/sda7
#          initrd /initrd-version.img
#boot=/dev/sda
default=0
timeout=5
splashimage=(hd0,0)/grub/splash.xpm.gz
hiddenmenu
title Fedora (2.6.35.6-45.fc14.i686)
    root (hd0,0)
    kernel /vmlinuz- 2.6.35.6-45.fc14.i686ro ↵
root=UUID=866237bb-d845-4117-a1b2-e286d0f56f15 rhgb quiet
initrd /initramfs-2.6.35.6-45.fc14.i686.img
title Windows XP
     rootnoverify (hd1,0)
     chainloader +1
```

The default=0 line indicates that the first partition in this list (in this case Fedora) will be the one that is booted by default. The line timeout=5 causes GRUB to pause for five seconds before booting the default partition. The default timeout is zero seconds, but because more than one operating system is listed, I changed the setting to allow a few seconds in order to choose which operating system to boot. (Because of the hiddenmenu option, you won't even see the GRUB boot screen if you don't press Enter before five seconds.)

Note
GRUB indicates disk partitions using the following notation: (hd0,0). The first number represents the disk; the second is the partition on that disk. Therefore, (hd0,1) is the second partition (1) on the first disk (0). That would equate to /dev/sda2 in Linux. ∎

The `splashimage` line looks in the second partition on the first disk (`hd0,0`) for the boot partition (in this case `/dev/sda1`, which is the `/boot` partition). GRUB loads `splash.xpm.gz` as the image on the splash screen (`/boot/grub/splash.xpm.gz`). The splash screen appears as the background of the boot screen.

Note

You can replace the splash screen with any image you like, provided that it meets certain specifications. Using GIMP or another image editor, save the image to 640x480 pixels, 14 colors, and xpm format. Next, use gzip to compress the file. Then copy that file to the `/boot/grub` directory. The last step is to edit the `grub.conf` file to have the `splashimage` value point to the new file. ■

The two bootable partitions in this example are `Fedora` and `Windows XP`. The title line for each of those partitions is followed by the name that appears on the boot screen to represent each partition.

For the Fedora system, the `root` line indicates the location of the boot partition as the second partition on the first disk. Therefore, to find the bootable `kernel` and the `initrd` initial RAM disk boot image that is loaded, GRUB looks in the root of `hd0,0` (which is represented by `/dev/sda1` and is eventually mounted as `/boot`). Other options on the `kernel` line set the partition as read-only initially (`ro`) and set the root file system using a UUID label.

For the Windows XP partition, the `rootnoverify` line indicates that GRUB should not try to mount the partition. In this case, Windows XP is on the first partition of the second hard disk (`hd1,0`) or `/dev/sdb1`. Instead of mounting the partition, loading an operating system, and passing options to the new operating system, `chainloader +1` specifies to hand control of the booting of the operating system to another boot loader. The +1 indicates that the first sector of the partition is used as the boot loader.

Note

Microsoft operating systems require that you use the `chainloader` to boot them from GRUB. ■

If you make any changes to the `/boot/grub/grub.conf` file, you do *not* need to load those changes. They are automatically picked up by GRUB when you reboot your computer. If you are accustomed to using the older LILO boot loader, this may be confusing at first, as LILO requires you to rerun the `lilo` command for the changes to take effect.

Adding a new GRUB boot image

You may have different boot images for kernels that include different features. These days, as you get updated kernels for Fedora, you simply load an RPM containing the new kernel, and that new kernel is added to the `grub.conf` file as the default kernel to be booted. At boot time, you can choose which kernel you want to run.

Note

To avoid having dozens of entries on your boot screen and a lot of kernels hanging around, all but the two most recent kernels are removed when you install new kernels on your Fedora system. Likewise, instead of getting a lot of boot entries as you add new kernels, only the two most recent kernel entries are maintained in your `grub.conf` file. ■

If you build your own kernel, however, or get one to use from another source, you need to modify the grub.conf file yourself to tell Fedora to boot that kernel. Here is the procedure for modifying the grub.conf file:

1. Copy the new image from the directory in which it was created (such as /usr/src/kernels/linux-2.6.35.6-45/arch/i386/boot) to the /boot directory. Name the file something that reflects its contents, such as bz-2.6.35.6-45. For example:

```
# cp /usr/src/linux-2.6.35.6-45/arch/i386/boot/bzImage↵
/boot/bz-2.6.35.6-45
```

2. Add several lines to the /boot/grub/grub.conf file so that the image can be started at boot time if it is selected. For example:

```
title Fedora (My own IPV6 build)
    root (hd0,0)
    kernel /bz-2.6.35.6-45 ro root=/dev/sda2
    initrd /initrd-2.6.35.6-45.img
```

3. Reboot your computer.

4. Press Enter at the boot prompt. When the GRUB boot screen appears, move your cursor to the title representing the new kernel and press Enter.

The advantage to this approach, as opposed to copying the new boot image over the old one, is that if the kernel fails to boot, you can always go back and restart the old kernel. When you feel confident that the new kernel is working properly, you can use it to replace the old kernel or perhaps just make the new kernel the default boot definition.

Troubleshooting Installation

The following information on troubleshooting your Fedora installation covers three different areas: what to try if you fail to install Fedora; what to do if it installs but fails to boot up; and how to go forward if Fedora is basically working but selected features or hardware components are not.

Insert your Fedora boot media and reboot your computer. If your computer bypasses the DVD or CD completely and boots right from hard disk, you may need to change the boot disk order as stored in the BIOS. If the DVD or CD drive keeps blinking but doesn't install, you might have a bad DVD or CD or you might have an older drive that can't use DMA (in the latter case, try adding nodma to the boot command line). If it hangs at some point during the install, there are many boot options to try, if the install is hanging on a bad or unrecognized hardware item (see descriptions of boot options in the section on "Temporarily changing boot options").

If you were able to boot Fedora, you can see how the installation went by checking different aspects of your system. There are three log files to look at once the system comes up:

- `/root/upgrade.log` — When upgrading packages, output from each installed package is sent to this file. You can see what packages were installed and if any failed.

- `/var/log/dmesg` — This file contains the messages that are sent to the console terminal as the system boots up, including messages relating to the kernel being started and hardware being recognized. If a piece of hardware isn't working, you can check here to ensure that the kernel found the hardware and configured it properly.

- `/var/log/boot.log` — This file contains information about each service that is started up at boot time, so you can check whether each service started successfully. If a service doesn't start properly, this file may offer clues that will help you learn what went wrong.

If something was set wrong (such as your network setup) or just isn't working quite right (such as your video display), you can always go back after Fedora is running and correct the problem. Here is a list of utilities you can use to reconfigure different features that were set during installation:

- **Changing a keyboard language** — `system-config-keyboard`
- **Adding or deleting software packages** — `yum`, `PackageKit`, or `rpm`
- **Partitioning** — `fdisk`
- **Boot loader** — `/boot/grub/grub.conf`
- **Networking (Ethernet & TCP/IP)** — `system-config-network`
- **Time zone** — `system-config-date`
- **User accounts** — `useradd` or `system-config-users`
- **X Window System** — `gnome-display-properties`

Here are a few other miscellaneous tips that can help you during installation:

- If installation fails because the installation procedure is unable to detect your video card, try restarting installation in text mode. After Fedora is installed and running, use the `Xorg -configure` command to see what the X server has detected for your video card and monitor. (For some cards, such as those from NVIDIA, you need to get and install special drivers from the manufacturer's website or `http://rpmfusion.org`.)

Caution

Some video card drivers from NVIDIA and ATI will overwrite important Xorg driver files. If you later change to a different video card, features of the new card (such as DRI) might fail. The solution is to entirely remove the NVIDIA or ATI drivers and reinstall your xorg and mesa packages. ∎

- If installation completes successfully but your screen is garbled when you reboot, try to get Fedora to boot to a text-login prompt. To do this, add the number 3 to the end of the kernel boot line in GRUB. Linux will start with the GUI temporarily disabled. (See Chapter 3 for other advice related to fixing your GUI.)

- If installation improperly probes your hardware or turns on a feature that causes problems with your hardware, you might be able to solve the problem by disabling the offending feature at the install boot prompt. Try adding one or more of the following after the word linux at the installation boot prompt: ide=nodma (if your system hangs while downloading the image), apm=off or acpi=off (if you experience random failures during install), or nousb, nopcmcia, or nofirewire (if you suspect that install is hanging on devices of those types).

- If you are still having problems installing Fedora, try searching FedoraForum.org to see if they have an answer. Sign up for an account to ask a question yourself.

Spinning Your Own Fedora Install or Live Media

All software included in Fedora can be redistributed. Therefore, you can not only use the software as you please, but also repackage and redistribute it if you care to. Not only is the Fedora Project committed to protecting your rights to redistribute Fedora, but it has gone so far as to give you the tools to build your own brand-new Fedora-based distribution to suit your needs.

Fedora has created several tools that enable you to build your own install or live media images. Using these tools, you can pick the packages you want from the Fedora repository, add new repositories, and combine the content into ISO images that can be burned to CDs, DVDs, USB flash drives, or other media. In short, you can make your own custom Linux distribution.

The two major tools that Fedora produces (which the project itself currently uses to produce its own install and live CDs) are Pungi and livecd-creator:

- **Using Pungi for building install media** — Pungi is a distribution composition tool (https://fedorahosted.org/pungi) you can use to "spin" your own Linux distribution from Fedora software packages and, optionally, your own packages. You give Pungi the location of one or more software repositories (containing Fedora RPMs) and it will gather that software, along with the anaconda installer, and make ISO images that you can use to install that set of software. Because Pungi uses tools associated with the anaconda installer, you can use anaconda features, including kickstart files to list packages and other items you gather for your custom ISO images.

- **Using livecd-creator for building live media** — You can use the livecd-creator tool to make your own Fedora-based Live CDs from packages in one or more software repositories (http://fedoraproject.org/wiki/FedoraLiveCD/LiveCDHowTo). Besides gathering packages, like Pungi, livecd-creator can use kickstart files and the anaconda installer to make and recreate the Live ISO images that suit you.

While the practice of using Pungi and livecd-creator to create your own Linux derivative is beyond the scope of this book, as you gain experience with Fedora, you might find many interesting ways to use these tools. For example, people have used livecd-creator to make a live DVD focusing on games, a free digital artwork CD, and a software developer tools DVD. If you develop your own software, you can build live or install CDs that showcase your software in various ways.

Summary

Installing Linux has become as easy as installing any modern operating system. Precompiled binary software and preselected packaging and partitions make most Fedora installation a simple proposition. Improved installation and GUI configuration windows have made it easier for computer users who are not programmers to enter the Linux arena.

In addition to providing some step-by-step installation procedures, this chapter discussed some of the trickier aspects of Fedora installation. In particular, this chapter covered specialty installation procedures (such as dual-booting with Windows), ways to partition your hard disk, and how to change the boot procedure. The chapter also provided pointers about using tools such as Pungi and livecd-creator to create your own Fedora install and live CD media.

Getting Productive with the Desktop

## 3

The desktop is the most personal feature of your computer. The way that icons, menus, panels, and backgrounds are arranged and displayed should make it both easy and pleasant to do your work. With Fedora, you have an incredible amount of control over how your desktop is arranged and how it behaves.

From the initial login screen to the desktop background and screensaver, the latest version of Fedora sports distinctive looks for the GNOME, KDE, and Xfce desktops, as well as continuing efforts to provide a similar experience across all the desktop environments. GNOME and KDE form the main Linux desktops. Which one you should use is largely a matter of preference. For machines with less horsepower, the Xfce desktop can be an excellent choice. For low-end netbooks with small screens, you may want to try the Moblin or newer MeeGo desktops.

With each desktop environment, you can get a full set of desktop applications, features for launching applications, and tools for configuring preferences.

The basic desktop is provided by the X.Org X server. X is short for the X Window System, and the X server provides the framework on which GNOME, KDE, and other desktop applications and window managers rely. If you have used the XFree86 X server in other Linux distributions, special features of the X.Org server described later in this chapter might interest you.

Cross-Reference

See Chapter 1 for a description of the X Window System. ∎

This chapter takes you on a tour of your desktop — going through the process of logging in, trying out some features, and customizing how your

IN THIS CHAPTER

Logging in to Linux

Getting started with the desktop

Choosing GNOME, KDE, or Xfce desktops

Using the GNOME desktop environment

Switching desktop environments

Using the KDE desktop environment

Using the Xfce desktop environment

Using the Moblin desktop environment

Using the MeeGo desktop environment

Enabling 3D desktop effects

Getting your desktop to work

desktop looks and behaves. Sections on GNOME, KDE, and Xfce desktops cover how to navigate these desktops and be productive as quickly as possible. The last section describes how to trouble-shoot problems that may occur especially in the automatic detection of your graphics hardware.

Given the right video card and monitor, you can enable cool 3D desktop effects, such as windows that wobble when you move them or changing workspaces on a revolving cube.

Logging in to Fedora

Because Linux was created as a multiuser computer system, you start by logging in (even if you are the only person using the computer). Logging in accomplishes three functions:

- It identifies you as a particular user.
- It starts up your own shell and desktop (icons, panels, backgrounds, and so on) configurations.
- It gives you appropriate permissions to change files and run programs.

After the computer has been turned on and the operating system has started, you see either a graphical login screen (the default) or a text-based login prompt. The text-based prompt should look something like this:

```
Fedora release 14 (Laughlin)
Kernel 2.6.35.6-45.fc14.i686 on an i686
localhost login:
```

Note

If you see a text-based login prompt instead of the graphical login screen but you want to use the GUI, type your user name and password. When you see a command prompt, type `startx` to start up your desktop. You can also change run levels, covered in Chapter 11, to start in graphics mode permanently. ∎

The graphical login is typically your entry into the graphical user interface (GUI). On the graphical login screen, notice the several buttons and user names that appear on the login screen. Click on the entry for you and enter your password to log in. (This is called the *face browser*, as you can display a picture of your face — or anything else that you want — to represent yourself.) If you don't see the user name you want, simply select Other and type your user name and password as prompted. Users also can add an image (96 × 96 pixels by default) to represent themselves in the About Me window (select System ➪ Preferences ➪ About Me to add your own image).

You can log in as either a regular user or the root user:

- **A regular user** — As someone just using the Linux system, you probably have your own unique user name and password. Often, that name is associated with your real name (such as johnb, susanp, or djones). If you are still not sure why you need a user login, see the sidebar "Why Do I Need a User Login?" You probably have at least one user account available that was added the first time you booted Fedora.

- **The root user** — Every Linux system has a *root* user assigned when Linux is installed. The root user (literally type the user name **root**) can run programs, use files, and change the computer setup in any way. Because the root user has special powers, and can therefore do special damage, you usually log in as a regular user (which allows access only to that user's files and those that are open to everyone). Logging in as the root user isn't provided as an option on the graphical login screen. You need to select Other to manually log in as root.

Cross-Reference

See Chapter 9 for a description of the root user, and Chapter 10 for information on how to set up and use other user accounts. Refer to Chapter 13 for suggestions on how to choose a good password. For information on instances in which the root user doesn't have complete control over the system, refer to the descriptions of SELinux (Security-Enhanced Linux) in Chapter 9. ■

If your desktop did not start, refer to the "Troubleshooting Your Desktop" section at the end of this chapter. Otherwise, continue on to the next section.

Why Do I Need a User Login?

If you are working on a PC and you are the only one using your Linux computer, you may wonder why you need a user account and password. Unlike Windows, Linux (as its predecessor Unix) was designed from the ground up to be a multiuser system. Here are several good reasons why you should use separate user accounts:

- Even as the only person using Linux, you want a user name other than root for running applications and working with files so you don't change critical system files by mistake during everyday computer use.

- If several people are using a Linux system, separate user accounts protect your files from being accessed or changed by others.

- Networking is probably the best reason to use a Linux system. If you are on a network, a unique user name is useful in many ways. Your user name can be associated with resources on other computers: file systems, application programs, and mailboxes to name a few. Sometimes a root user is not allowed to share resources on remote Linux systems.

- Over time, you will probably change personal configuration information associated with your account. For example, you may add aliases, create your own utility programs, or set properties for the applications you use. By gathering this information in one place, it's easy to move your account or add a new account to another computer in the future.

- Keeping all your data files and settings under a home login directory (such as /home/chris) makes it easier to back up the data and restore it later if needed.

Getting Familiar with the Desktop

The term *desktop* refers to the presentation of windows, menus, panels, icons, and other graphical elements on your computer screen. Originally, computer systems such as Linux operated purely in text mode — no mouse, no colors, just commands typed on the screen. Desktops provide a more intuitive way to use your computer.

As with most things in Linux, the desktop is built from a set of building blocks. The building blocks of your desktop, to use a car analogy, are as follows:

- The X Window System (which is like the frame of the car)
- The GNOME, KDE, or Xfce desktop environment (which is like a blueprint of how the working parts fit together)
- The Metacity window manager (which provides the steering wheel, seat upholstery, and fuzzy dice on the mirror)
- The Fedora desktop theme (the paint job and the pin stripe)

Once Linux is installed (see Chapter 2) and you have logged in (see the previous section), you should see either the GNOME or the KDE desktop. At this point, I'll take you on a tour of the desktop and step you through some initial setup to get your desktop going.

Figure 3-1 shows an example of the Fedora GNOME desktop.

FIGURE 3-1

After login, Fedora starts you off with a GNOME desktop by default.

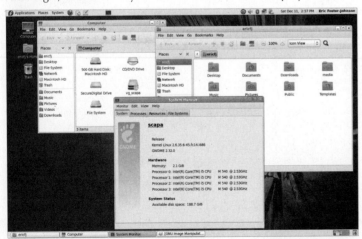

Because GNOME is the default desktop for Fedora when you install from the official DVD or GNOME live CD (both included with this book), I'll start by walking you around the GNOME desktop (with a few references to KDE applications, which can also be run from GNOME). The tour includes trying out your home folder, changing some preferences, and configuring your panel.

Touring your desktop

If you are unfamiliar with the GNOME desktop that comes with Fedora, I suggest you take this quick tour to familiarize yourself with the desktop features. If you are using the KDE desktop, refer to the KDE section later in this chapter for tips on using KDE.

- **The top bar** — Provides application menus (Applications, Places, and System), quick-launch icons, and desktop widgets such as the display of the time and date, or the power remaining on your laptop battery
- **The bottom bar** — Lists the applications you have launched, and controls which virtual workspace is visible
- **Icons** — Represent storage devices such as hard disks or folders, such as your home folder
- **The rest of the desktop** — Holds application windows, or just shows a pretty background picture

If you are familiar with Microsoft Windows or Mac OS X systems, then you won't have any problems figuring out the GNOME desktop. GNOME looks and acts a lot like Microsoft Windows, making it easy for newcomers to Linux to get started.

Furthermore, the Fedora project has gone to great lengths to make the various desktops look and act similarly. You will find similar menus and organization for applications in the KDE and GNOME desktops, and many applications appear virtually identical. You can also run KDE programs on a GNOME desktop and vice versa.

Getting more desktop space with virtual workspaces

Virtual workspaces provide a feature common to many desktops such as GNOME and KDE. With virtual workspaces, you can open a number of windows in one workspace and then quickly switch to another workspace.

To try this out, launch a few windows and then click in the lower right-hand workspace switching area next to the Trash icon in the bottom bar. Each rectangle in this area, shown in Figure 3-2, represents a separate virtual workspace. Inside each of these rectangles, you'll see a representation of the windows that appear in that virtual workspace.

FIGURE 3-2

Click to select a different virtual workspace.

Applications you launch will appear in this virtual workspace.

Tip

By default, GNOME starts with two virtual workspaces. To add more, right-click on the virtual Workspace Switcher and select Preferences from the pop-up menu. ■

With this feature, you can organize your work by project, based on your current work; by task, such as e-mail communication; and so on. Virtual workspaces are especially handy for people who are interrupted a lot. You can simply change to another virtual workspace to run the applications you need during the interruption, and then switch back to your previous work.

Using the GNOME Desktop

GNOME (pronounced *guh-nome*) provides the default desktop on Fedora and aims to make the transition from Windows as smooth as possible. The GNOME project has spent a lot of time trying to make the desktop easy to use, and it focuses on usability.

Launching applications from the top bar

Across the top of the display, you'll see three menus by default:

- **Applications** — Holds installed desktop applications split into submenus by category, such as Office, Graphics, and Internet. For the most part, these categories make sense, except for the Accessories and System Tools menus, which don't always reflect the applications you'd expect to appear in a given menu.

- **Places** — Contains shortcuts to disks, folders, and storage devices. This includes your home folder and prebuilt folders for Documents, Music, Pictures, Videos, and Downloads, along with shortcuts to hard disk and network browsing.

- **System** — Controls your user preferences and contains a set of Administration applications. Preferences enable you to select a picture for yourself (About Me), turn on Desktop Effects, and control which applications should be launched when you log in (Startup Applications). Most of the Administration applications require the root user password to control your system. You can also log out from the System menu, shut down the system, or reboot.

Tip

The Applications ⇨ System Tools menu also contains some administration tools, including the SELinix Policy Generation Tool and the Virtual Machine Manager. ■

As you install applications (see Chapter 5), they will appear under the Applications menu. One of the handiest applications is the Terminal application, shown in Figure 3-3, which provides a Linux shell. Launch Terminal from the Applications ⇨ System Tools menu.

FIGURE 3-3

The Terminal application provides a Linux command-line shell.

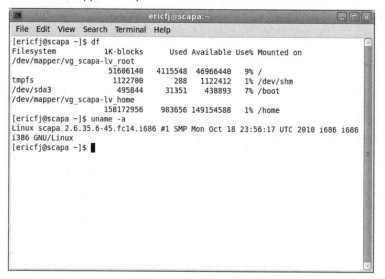

You can also launch applications from the quick-launch icons that appear by default to the right of the System menu. By default, you'll see icons for the Firefox web browser, the Evolution e-mail and calendaring client, and the gnote sticky note application.

Tip

If your system seems to be having problems with networking, left-click on the network applet on the top panel, especially if it shows any form of red *x* or other error or warning. You may need to enable networking. Select one of the available network interfaces such as System eth0 for the first (and likely only) wired Ethernet connection. See Chapters 14 and 15 if this does not solve the networking issue. ■

Switching windows from the bottom bar

The bottom bar is technically just another GNOME panel. By default, however, the bottom bar shows a tab for each open application. Click an application's tab to minimize it when visible, to restore an application you previously minimized, or to bring an application's windows to the front if they are hidden behind other windows. At the far-right end of the bottom panel is the virtual Workspace Switcher, as well as a Trash icon. (The Trash icon also appears on the upper-left portion of the screen under the icon for your home directory.)

Browsing files

The Nautilus file manager, which is the default GNOME file manager, provides a graphical way to browse disks, network shares, and other parts of your system.

When you open the Nautilus file manager window (from a GNOME menu or by opening the Home icon or other folder on your desktop), you see the name of the location you are viewing (such as the folder name) and what that location contains (files, folders, and applications). Figure 3-4 shows an example of the file manager window displaying the home directory of a user named ericfj (/home/ericfj).

FIGURE 3-4

From here you can move around the file system, open directories, launch applications, and open Samba folders.

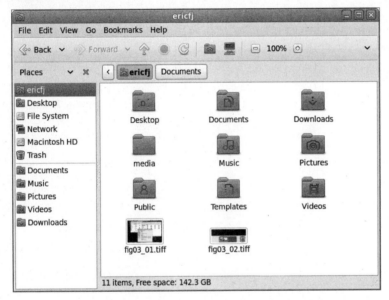

Icons on the toolbar of the Nautilus window let you move forward and back among the directories you visit. To move up the directory structure, click the up arrow. To refresh the view of the folder or Web page, click the Reload button. The Home folder button takes you to your home directory, also called a *personal folder*, and clicking the Computer button shows you see the same type of information you would see by clicking a My Computer icon on a Windows system (CD drive, floppy drive, hard disk file systems, and network folders).

Icons in Nautilus often indicate the type of data that a particular file contains. The contents or file extension of each file can determine which application is used to work with the file; or you can right-click an icon to open the file it represents with a particular application or viewer.

Some of the more interesting features of Nautilus include the following:

- **Sidebar** — From a Nautilus window, click View ⇨ Side Pane to enable/disable the appearance of the sidebar in the left column of the screen. From the sidebar, you can select from a drop-down list to display different types of information. The Tree option shows a tree view of the directory structure, so you can easily traverse your directories.

The Notes option enables you to add notes that become associated with the current directory or Web page. The History option displays a history of directories you have visited, and enables you to click those items to return to the sites they represent. Use the Emblems option to add small icons, or emblems, to the file icons. This can help you identify important files, show your current work, and more easily find particular files. Drag an emblem to the file you want.

- **Windows file sharing** — If your computer is connected to a LAN on which Windows computers are sharing files and printers, you can view those resources from Nautilus. Click File ➪ Connect to Server from a Nautilus window, and then select a service type of Windows share in the dialog that appears. Enter the information necessary to connect to the share.

- **MIME types and file types** — To handle different types of content that may be encountered in the Nautilus window, you can set applications to respond based on MIME type and file type. With a folder displayed, right-click a file for which you want to assign an application. Click Open With Other Application. If you want the application you pick to become the default for that type of file, select the Remember this application check box.

- **Drag and drop** — You can drag and drop files and folders within the Nautilus window, between the Nautilus window and the desktop, or between multiple Nautilus windows. Many GNOME-compliant applications also support the GNOME drag-and-drop feature. For example, you could drag an image file from Nautilus and drop it on an Eye of GNOME image viewer to work with that image. You can also drag and drop between KDE and GNOME applications, such as the KDE Dolphin file browser and Nautilus. Not all applications support this feature, though.

For more information on the Nautilus file manager, visit the GNOME website (`http://live.gnome.org/Nautilus`).

Nautilus also allows you to work with files on removable media such as CDs, DVDs, and USB drives. When you insert media, Nautilus tries to identify the type, such as audio CD or an SD card of photos. Nautilus will then either ask you what to do or launch an application such as a CD player to play music.

To change what Nautilus does with removable media, select Edit ➪ Preferences and choose the Media tab. You can then change which applications are launched when you insert audio CDs, DVD videos, Blu-ray discs, blank CDs, and other media.

Customizing the desktop

The System ➪ Preferences menu provides a number of options that enable you to customize your desktop. The Appearance window, for example, enables you to select fonts, colors, and desktop themes, and change the screen background. Fedora includes several background images, or you can select an image of your own.

Tip
You can also right-click on the desktop to change the desktop background. ■

Modifying the GNOME panels

By default, Fedora includes panels on the top and bottom of the GNOME desktop. From those panels you can start applications (from buttons or menus), see what programs are active, manage network interfaces, monitor power issues, adjust your audio volume, and switch workspaces. There are also many ways to change the top or bottom panel — by adding applications or monitors or by changing the placement or behavior of the panel, for example.

Click any open space on either panel to see the Panel menu. From the GNOME Panel menu, you can perform a variety of functions, including the following:

- **Add to panel** — Add an applet, menu, launcher, drawer, or button.
- **Properties** — Change the position, size, and background of the panel.
- **Delete This panel** — Delete the current panel.
- **New panel** — Add panels to your desktop in different styles and locations.

You can also work with items on a panel; for example, you can do the following:

- **Move items** — To move items on a panel, simply drag and drop them to a new position.
- **Set Preferences or Properties** — Right-click on an icon on the panel and select Preferences or Properties, depending on which is available. From the pop-up menu that appears, you can usually set properties specifying what is launched when the application is selected.

The following sections describe some things you can do with the GNOME panel.

Adding an application launcher

Icons on your panel represent a Web browser and productivity applications. You can add your own icons to launch applications from the panel as well. To add a new application launcher to the panel, do the following:

1. Right-click in an open space on the panel.
2. Select Add to Panel ⇨ Application Launcher ⇨ Forward from the menu. All application categories from your Applications menu appear.
3. Select the arrow next to the category of application you want, choose the application, and select Add. (Alternatively, you can simply drag and drop the applet item on to the panel.) An icon representing the application appears.

To launch the application you just added, single-click it.

If the application you want to launch is not on your Applications menu, you can build one yourself as follows:

1. Right-click in an open space on the panel.

2. Select Add to Panel ➪ Custom Application Launcher ➪ Add. The Create Launcher window appears.

3. Provide the following information for the application that you want to add:

   - **Type** — Select Application (to launch an application) or Application in Terminal (to launch an application within a terminal window). Another option is Location, to open a directory.

   - **Name** — A name to identify the application (this appears in the tooltip when your mouse is over the icon).

   - **Command** — The command line that is run when the application is launched. Use the full path name, plus any required options.

   - **Comment** — A comment describing the application. As with Name, this information appears when you later move your mouse over the launcher.

4. Click the Icon (it might say No Icon). Select one of the icons shown and click OK. Alternatively, you can browse the file system to choose an icon.

Note

Icons available to represent your application are contained in the /usr/share/icons directory. These icons are in either SVG, PNG, or XPM format. If the directory doesn't contain an icon you want to use, create your own and assign it to the application. ■

5. Click OK.

The application should now appear in the panel. Click it to start the application.

Adding an applet

There are dozens of small GNOME applications called *applets* that you can run directly on the GNOME panel. These applets can display information you want to see on an ongoing basis or they might just provide some amusement. To see what applets are available and to add applets to your panel, perform the following steps:

1. Right-click an open space in the panel so that the panel menu appears.

2. Select Add to Panel. An Add to Panel window appears.

3. Select from among several dozen applets, including a character palette for inserting characters not found on your keyboard, a clock, a remote desktop viewer, a dictionary lookup, a stock ticker called Invest, a weather report, a lock screen, log out, and many others. The applet appears on the panel, ready for you to use.

After an applet is installed, right-click it to see what options are available. For example, select Preferences for the stock ticker, and you can add or delete stocks whose prices you want to monitor. If you don't like the applet's location, right-click it, click Move, slide the mouse until the applet is where you want it (even to another panel), and click to set its location.

GNOME provides a lot of interesting applets that you can try out. Here are two examples of available applets (and the packages you need to install in order to use them):

- **CPU Temperature (gnome-applet-sensors)** — Watch the temperature of your CPU or hard disk from your panel in Fahrenheit or Celsius.
- **Network traffic (gnome-applet-netspeed)** — Display the amount of traffic traveling across your network interfaces (both incoming and outgoing).

Keep in mind that applets can be a drain on system resources. If you no longer want an applet to appear on the panel, right-click it, and then click Remove From Panel. The icon representing the applet will disappear. If you run out of room on your panel, you can add a new panel to another part of the screen, as described in the next section.

Adding another panel

You can have several panels on your GNOME desktop. For example, you can add panels that run along the sides of the screen, in addition to the ones already located along the top and bottom. To add a panel, do the following:

1. Right-click an open space in the panel so that the panel menu appears.
2. Select New Panel. A new panel appears at the right side of the screen.
3. Right-click an open space in the new panel and select Properties.
4. From Panel Properties, select where you want to place the panel from the Orientation box (Top, Bottom, Left or Right).

After you've added a panel, you can add applets or application launchers to it as you did to the default panel. To remove a panel, right-click it and select Delete This Panel.

Adding a drawer

By adding a *drawer* to your GNOME panel, you can add several applets and launchers that occupy only one slot on your panel. That way, you can use the drawer to display the available applets and launchers, pulling them out of the drawer icon on the panel.

To add a drawer to your panel, right-click the panel and then select Add to Panel ➪ Drawer. The drawer should appear on the panel. The drawer behaves just like a panel. Right-click the drawer area, and add applets or launchers to it as you would to a panel. Click the drawer icon to retract the drawer.

Changing panel properties

Properties you can change that relate to a panel are limited to the orientation, size, hiding policy, and background. To open the Panel properties window that applies to a specific panel, right-click an open space on the panel, and then choose Properties. The most useful setting is Autohide. With this set, the panel will be hidden until you move the mouse nearby, which gives you more space to work with on your desktop.

Using the Metacity window manager

The Metacity window manager provides a simple means to manage windows and acts as the default GNOME window manager.

Basic Metacity functions that might interest you are keyboard shortcuts and the Workspace Switcher. Table 3-1 shows keyboard shortcuts to get around the Metacity window manager.

Use the window menu, located in the upper-left corner of window title bars, to move a window to another workspace and control window visibility on various workspaces.

TABLE 3-1

Metacity Keyboard Shortcuts

Task	Keyboard Shortcut
Icon focus Cycle backward, with pop-up icons	Alt+Shift+Tab
Cycle forward, without pop-up icons	Alt+Esc
Cycle backward, without pop-up icons	Alt+Shift+Esc
Panel focus Cycle forward among panels	Alt+Ctrl+Tab
Cycle backward among panels	Alt+Ctrl+Shift+Tab
Workspace focus Move to workspace to the right	Ctrl+Alt+right arrow
Move to workspace to the left	Ctrl+Alt+left arrow
Move to upper workspace	Ctrl+Alt+up arrow
Move to lower workspace	Ctrl+Alt+down arrow
Minimize/restore **all windows**	Ctrl+Alt+D
Show window menu	Alt+Spacebar
Close menu	Esc

You can view and change information about Metacity controls and settings using the `gconf-editor` window (as root, type `yum install gconf-editor`, then `gconf-editor` as a regular user from a terminal window). As the window says, it is not the recommended way to change preferences. Therefore, when possible, you should change the desktop through GNOME preferences. However, `gconf-editor` is a good way to see descriptions of each Metacity feature.

From the `gconf-editor` window, select apps ⇨ metacity. Then choose from general, global_ keybindings, keybindings_commands, window_keybindings, and workspace_names. Click each key to see its value, along with short and long descriptions of the key.

Switching to another user

If you want to log in as another desktop user without closing your current desktop session, you can use the Fast User Switch feature of GNOME. Look for the User Switcher applet in your top panel (by default, it should display your name on the applet) or add the applet yourself (it's identified as User Switcher in the Add to Panel window).

To use Fast User Switch, click the User Switcher applet and select Quit. Choose Switch User to see a list of user names on your system. To log in as one of those users, click on the name and log in when the login screen appears. A desktop for the new user appears, while the previous desktop keeps running on a different virtual terminal.

After you have logged in and started a desktop for another user, you can use the same User Switcher applet to switch between the multiple user desktops. A check box appears next to the names of users who have desktops launched on the different virtual terminals accessible from your display.

Exiting GNOME

When you are done with your work, you can either log out from your current session or shut down your computer completely. If you have multiple user sessions open, you should log out of each of those first (to ensure that you don't lose any unsaved work.)

To exit from GNOME, click the System button from the panel. Then, choose Log out. You'll be prompted to confirm you want to log out.

If you are unable to get to the Log out button (if, for example, your Panel crashed), there are two other exit methods. Try one of these two ways, depending on how you started the desktop:

- If you started the desktop by typing **startx** from your login shell, press Ctrl+Alt+Backspace to kill X and return to your login shell. Or, you can press Ctrl+Alt+F1 to return to where you first ran **startx**, and then press Ctrl+C to kill the desktop.
- If you started the desktop from a graphical login screen (and Ctrl+Alt+Backspace doesn't work), first open a virtual text console by pressing Ctrl+ALT+F2. After logging in as the same user who logged into X, type **ps x | grep gnome-session** and determine the

process number (the leftmost number for the `gnome-session` application). Then type **kill -9 *PID***, where *PID* is replaced by the process ID number. You should see the graphical login screen.

Although these are not the most graceful ways to exit the desktop, they work. You should be able to log in again and restart the desktop.

Switching Desktop Environments

The GNOME display manager and login window no longer provide a means to switch desktop sessions to other desktops, such as KDE or Xfce. The KDE login window, however, does allow you to switch sessions.

If you decide you want to try a different desktop environment, the Desktop Switcher provides a graphical means of changing your desktop environment preferences between KDE, GNOME, Xfce, and other desktop software depending on what is installed. To open the Desktop Switcher, type **switchdesk** from a terminal window and select the new desktop you want to use.

Note

To use the Desktop Switcher window, you must have the `switchdesk-gui` package installed. Otherwise, you can use the `switchdesk` command, followed by the name of the desktop you want to switch to, from a terminal window to change your desktop. You also need to have at least one alternative window manager or desktop system installed. You can install KDE and XFCE by running `yum groupinstall KDE` or `yum groupinstall XFCE`, respectively.

After running `switchdesk` or `switchdesk-gui`, you need to perform one other task. As root, edit or create the file `/etc/sysconfig/desktop` and add the following lines to it:

```
DESKTOP="KDE"
DISPLAYMANAGER="KDE"
```

After saving the file, you need to reboot. You will see the KDE desktop manager.

To change your desktop environment temporarily, select Session from the KDE login screen and choose the desktop you want. You can choose it for the current session only or have it be your default desktop. From the KDE login window, you can also select other session types (desktops) you have installed, such as Xfce.

Using the KDE Desktop

The KDE desktop, also called the KDE Plasma Desktop, provides an enhanced desktop favored by many users. It provides a sparse interface compared to GNOME, one that often appeals to expert users (although many expert users run GNOME as well).

The KDE desktop was developed to provide an interface to Linux and other Unix systems that could compete with Mac OS or Microsoft Windows operating systems for ease of use. Integrated within KDE are tools for managing files, windows, multiple desktops, and applications. If you can work a mouse, you can learn to navigate the KDE desktop. Fedora 14 includes version 4.5 of KDE, as shown in Figure 3-5.

Note

KDE is not installed by default for Fedora. Therefore, to use the procedures in this section, you might have to install KDE. During installation, you could use a Custom install type to install KDE. Otherwise, run the `yum groupinstall KDE` **command. You can also download the KDE Desktop Spin of Fedora 14 from** `http://spins.fedoraproject.org/kde/.` ∎

FIGURE 3-5

KDE offers a sparse look with most of the controls on the bottom of the screen.

Each KDE release improves the overall desktop experience. With 4.5, the KDE Phonon sound server is integrated with the PulseAudio system used in Fedora. The following section describes how to get started with KDE.

Launching applications

Instead of the default top panel used in the GNOME desktop, KDE provides a small F (for Fedora) menu on the bottom left of the screen. From this menu, you can select Applications and then browse through the menus under Applications. These menus are similar by default, but not exactly the same as the GNOME menus. Figure 3-6 shows the Applications menus. Select the tabs on the bottom of this menu to change the available options.

- **Favorites** — Lists items you're likely to use most often
- **Applications** — Shows a hierarchy of menus based on categories such as Office and Utilities from which you can launch applications
- **Computer** — Provides shortcuts to directories, network file servers, and system information
- **Recently Used** — Shows items you've used recently, including files and applications
- **Leave** — Enables you to log out, restart the system, or shut it down

Tip
Launch a terminal window from the Applications ⇨ Utilities menu. ∎

FIGURE 3-6

Launch applications from the KDE Applications menus.

Switching windows from the bottom bar

From the bottom bar, called the taskbar, you can do the following:

- **Toggle windows** — Left-click any running task in the taskbar to toggle between opening the window and minimizing it.
- **Move windows** — Move a window from the current desktop to any other virtual desktop. Right-click any task in the taskbar, select To Desktop, and then select any desktop number. The window moves to that desktop.
- **Position windows** — Specify whether the selected window should be above or below other windows or displayed in full screen. Right-click the running task in the taskbar and select Advanced. Then choose Keep Above Others, Keep Below Others, or Fullscreen.

All the windows that are running, regardless of which virtual desktop you are on, appear in the taskbar.

Tip

If the window becomes stuck in a location where the title bar is off the screen, you can move it back to where you want it: Hold down the Alt key and press the left mouse button in the inner window. Then move the window where you want it and release. Alternatively, right-click anywhere on the window frame and select Move to move the window. ∎

Using virtual desktops

To provide more space to run applications than will fit on your physical screen, KDE gives you access to several virtual desktops at the same time. Using the Desktop 1, 2, 3, and 4 buttons on the Panel, you can easily move between the different desktops. Just click the one you want.

If you want to move an application from one desktop to another, you can do so from the window menu. Click the window menu button for the window you want to move, click To Desktop, and then select Desktop 1, 2, 3, or 4. The window will disappear from the current desktop and move to the one you selected.

Managing files with Dolphin and Konqueror

Dolphin is a streamlined file manager that is invoked by default when you open a folder in KDE. Konqueror, which is the old file manager, can handle a wider range of content — from local files and folders to remote Web content. For most usage, Konqueror provides the KDE Web browser.

Because both applications share common roots, many of the operations you can do are the same across both applications.

Note

For further information on Dolphin, refer to the Dolphin File Manager home page (`http://dolphin`
`.kde.org/`). ■

To launch Dolphin, click the Home icon that represents your home directory. Dolphin displays
an icon to represent each file. Choose Preview from the View menu to see a preview of the contents of each file. Choose Split from the View menu to split the display to show two folders at
once. This allows you to drag and drop files between the folders within the same window.

Tip

**Dolphin (as well as most of KDE) uses a single mouse click to launch applications, view files, and so on. If you
are familiar with the GNOME desktop or Windows, you may be used to double-clicking instead.** ■

Working with files

Because most of the ways of working with files in both Konqueror and Dolphin are quite intuitive
(by intention), I'll just give a brief rundown of how to do basic file manipulation:

- **Open a file** — Click a file. The file will open right in the Konqueror or Dolphin window, if possible, or in the default application set for the file type. You can also open a
  directory (to make it the current directory), application (to start the application), or link
  (to open the target of a link) in this way.

- **Choose an application** — Right-click to open a menu. When you right-click a data file,
  select the Open With menu. The menu that appears shows which applications are set up
  to open the file.

- **Delete a file** — Right-click and select Move to Trash. You are asked if you really want
  to delete the file. Click Trash to move the item to the Trash folder. (If you are brave, you
  can use Shift+Del to permanently delete a selected file. Just keep in mind that you won't
  be able to restore it from the Trash if you change your mind.)

- **Copy a file** — Right-click and select Copy. This copies the file to your clipboard. After that,
  you can paste it to another folder. Click the Klipper (clipboard) icon in the panel to see a list
  of copied files. (See the Move a file bullet item for a drag-and-drop method of copying.)

- **Paste a file** — Right-click (an open area of a folder) and select Paste. A copy of the file
  you copied previously is pasted in the current folder.

- **Move a file** — With the original folder and target folder both open on the desktop,
  press and hold the left mouse button on the file you want to move, drag the file to an
  open area of the new folder, and release the mouse button. From the menu that appears,
  click Move Here. (You can also copy or create a link to the file using this menu.)

- **Link a file** — Drag and drop a file from one folder to another. When the menu appears,
  click Link Here. (A linked file lets you access a file from a new location without having
  to make a copy of the original file. When you open the link, a pointer to the original file
  causes it to open.)

There are also several features for viewing information about the files and folders in your Konqueror and Dolphin windows. With the addition of Dolphin to KDE, some file manager features that were once available in Konqueror have been moved to the more streamlined Dolphin file manager. The following items include file management features supported by those two applications:

- **View quick file information** — Right-click a file in a Konqueror or Dolphin window and select Properties. A pop-up window appears with information about the item, including its filename, file size, modification times, and file type.

- **View hidden files** — In Konqueror or Dolphin, select View ➪ Show Hidden Files. This enables you to see files that begin with a dot (.). Dot files tend to be used for configuration and don't generally need to be viewed in your daily work.

- **Change icon size** — In Dolphin, select View ➪ Zoom In to make the file and folder icons bigger (or Zoom Out to make them smaller).

- **Change icon view** — In Konqueror or Dolphin, select View ➪ View Mode, and then select to view the folder contents as icons, details, or columns.

To act on a group of files at the same time, you can take a couple of actions. To select a group of files, click in an open area of the folder and drag the pointer across the files you want to select. All files within the box will be highlighted. In Dolphin, you can also select Edit ➪ Select All to select all files and folders in a folder. When files are highlighted, you can move, copy, or delete the files as described earlier.

Searching for files with Dolphin and kfind

If you are looking for a particular file or folder, the Find feature that was previously part of Konqueror can now be launched from Dolphin. To search for a file from the Dolphin file manager, choose Tools ➪ Find File and the window will appear. You could also start the Find/Folders window by typing **kfind** from a terminal window.

Simply type the name of the file you want to search for (in the Named text box) and the folder, including all subfolders, you want to search in (in the Look in text box). Then click the Find button. You can also use metacharacters with your search. For example, search for *.rpm to find all files that end in .rpm, or z*.doc to find all files that begin with z and end with .doc. You can also select to have the search be case sensitive or click the Help button to get more information on searching.

To further limit your search, click the Properties tab, and then enter a date range (between), a number of months before today (during the previous x months), or the number of days before today (during the previous x days). Select the Contents tab to choose to limit the search to files of a particular type (of Type), files that include text that you enter (Containing Text), or that are of a certain size (Size is) in kilobytes.

In Dolphin, you can change file manager settings by selecting Settings ➪ Configure Dolphin. The Dolphin Preferences window opens. From this window you can set how items in a folder are displayed by default, as well as a variety of other folder startup settings.

Using Konqueror

The features in the Konqueror file manager/Web browser rival those that are offered by other user-friendly desktop systems. Konqueror provides a full-featured Web browser like Firefox, along with a full-featured file manager.

Some of Konqueror's greatest strengths over earlier file managers include the following:

- **Network desktop** — If your computer is connected to the Internet or a LAN, features built into Konqueror enable you to create links to files (using FTP) and Web pages (using HTTP) on the network and open them within the Konqueror window. Those links can appear as file icons in a Konqueror window or on the desktop. When a link is opened (single-click), the contents of the FTP site or Web page appears right in the Konqueror window. Given proper folder permission, you could drag and drop files to your FTP server in this way.

- **Web browser interface** — The Konqueror interface works like Firefox, Internet Explorer, or another Web browser in the way you select files, directories, and Web content. You can open Web content by typing Web-style addresses in a Location box.

- **File Associations** — If you want a particular type of file to always be launched by a particular application, you can configure that file yourself. KDE already defines dozens of MIME types that can automatically detect particular file and data types and start the right application. There are MIME types defined for audio, image, text, video, and a variety of other content types. Click Settings ➪ Configure Konqueror to change the file associations.

Of course, you can also perform many standard file manager functions with Konqueror. For manipulating files, you can use features such as Select, Move, Cut, Paste, and Delete. You can search directories for files, create new items (files, folders, and links, to name a few), view histories of the files and websites you have opened, and create bookmarks.

Customizing the KDE desktop

If you want to change the look, feel, or behavior of your KDE desktop, the best place to start is the System Settings window. Using the System Settings window, you can configure dozens of attributes associated with colors, fonts, and screensavers used by KDE. It also contains options that enable you to do basic computer administration, such as changing date/time settings and modifying your display. To open the System Settings window, select the Fedora menu, then the Computer icon, and choose System Settings. The System Settings window appears. Click any item you want to configure, or type in the Search box to find a selection that matches what you type.

Adding widgets

You want to be able to quickly access the applications you use most often. One of the best ways to ensure that is possible is to add widgets to the panel or the desktop that can either run continuously (such as a clock or news ticker) or launch the applications you need with a single click. Procedures to add widgets to the panel and desktop are described in the following sections.

Adding widgets to the panel

You can add any KDE widgets to the KDE panel quite easily:

1. Right-click any place on the panel.
2. Select Panel Options ⇨ Add Widgets.
3. Double-click the widget you want to add.

An icon representing the widget should immediately appear on the panel. (If the panel seems a bit crowded, you can remove some widgets you don't use, or add a widget directly to the desktop.) At this point, you can change any properties associated with the widget by right-clicking the widget in the panel and then selecting to change its settings.

If you decide later that you no longer want the widget to be available on the panel, right-click it and click Remove.

Adding widgets to the desktop

To add a widget to the desktop, you can use the desktop menu as follows:

1. Right-click an open area of the desktop.
2. Select Add Widgets from the menu.
3. Double-click the widget you want from the list that appears.

If you decide later that you no longer want the widget to be available on the desktop, hover the mouse over it and click the X to delete it.

Using the Xfce Desktop Environment

The Xfce desktop environment provides a lightweight interface for using your Fedora system. Because it is designed to conserve system resources and load applications quickly, Xfce is usually the best choice if you are using Fedora on a less powerful computer (for example, if you have less than 512MB of RAM).

To meet its goals of running fast and efficiently, Xfce offers its own applications for doing many desktop operations. Here are some examples:

- **Thunar File Manager** — A fast and efficient way to manage your files and folders.
- **Xfce Application Finder** — A useful tool for finding every desktop-ready application on the system. (From the Xfce menu, select Accessories ⇨ Appfinder.)
- **Xfce Settings Manager** — Provides tools for changing desktop, display, file manager, keyboard, mouse, sound and various other desktop settings. (From the Xfce menu,

select Preferences ⇨ Xfce 4 Settings Manager at the top of the menu. You can select the other entries under the Preferences menu to set the default printer and control other aspects of your system.)

- **Items** — Dozens of items are available to add to the Xfce panel to monitor battery life, manage clipboards, display time, search dictionaries, watch system performance, and do many other tasks. Right-click on the panel and select Add New Items.

The version of Xfce for Fedora 14 is highly customized to fit in with the default Fedora themes and general look. The Fedora logo replaces the Xfce mouse logo on the main desktop menu, for example.

To use Xfce, you need to install the Xfce desktop packages (`yum groupinstall XFCE`). To launch an Xfce desktop, you can either select Xfce from the Sessions box on the KDE login screen or use the switchdesk feature (described earlier in this chapter) to make Xfce your default desktop. See `www.xfce.org` for more on XFCE.

Using the Moblin Desktop

The Moblin desktop provides a specialized desktop aimed at users of systems sporting small screens and limited resources, such as netbooks.

By default, Moblin takes over the entire screen and tries to show just one application at a time. Remember that this is intended for systems with small screens and limited RAM and processing power.

To use Moblin, you need to install the Moblin desktop packages (`yum install moblin*`). To launch this desktop, you can either select Moblin from the Sessions box on the KDE login screen or use the switchdesk feature (described earlier in this chapter) to make Moblin your default desktop.

Using the MeeGo Desktop

Designed to replace Moblin, MeeGo unites the mobile efforts of Nokia's Maemo project along with Moblin, creating a new desktop environment for small systems such as tablets and netbooks. As of Fedora 14, MeeGo is still experimental in Fedora.

To install MeeGo, run the `yum groupinstall "MeeGo NetBook UX Environment"` command. To run MeeGo, select MeeGo from the Sessions box on the KDE login screen as described earlier.

Go to `www.meego.com` for more information on the MeeGo desktop.

Running 3D Accelerated Desktop Effects

If your system has a supported graphics card, you can turn on fun 3D desktop effects. To turn on Desktop Effects from the GNOME desktop, select System ➪ Preferences ➪ Desktop Effects. When the Desktop Effects pop-up window appears, select Enable Desktop Effects. From the KDE desktop, open the System Settings window, then select Desktop ➪ Desktop Effects. Then choose Enable Desktop Effects.

Tip

If you have an nVidia graphics card that is not supported for desktop effects, you can try the alternate driver available from RPMFusion.org, in the xorg-x11-drv-nvidia package. See Chapter 5 for information about how to install software from the RPMFusion.org repository, and http://rpmfusion.org/Howto/nVidia for more on the RPMFusion drivers for nVidia cards. ■

Figure 3-7 shows an example of desktop workspaces rotating on a cube.

The following are some interesting effects:

- **Spin cube** — Hold the Ctrl+Alt keys and press the right and left arrow keys. The desktop cube spins to each successive workspace (forward or back).

- **Slowly rotate cube** — Hold the Ctrl+Alt keys, press and hold the left mouse button, and move the mouse around on the screen. The cube will move slowly with the mouse among the workspaces.

- **Tab through windows** — Hold the Alt key and press the Tab key. You will see reduced versions of all your windows in a strip in the middle of your screen, with the current window highlighted in the center. Still holding the Alt key, press Tab or Shift+Tab to move forward or backward through the windows. Release the keys when the one you want is highlighted.

- **Scale and separate workspaces** — Hold Ctrl+Alt and press the down arrow key to see reduced images of the workspace shown on a strip. Still holding Ctrl+Alt, use the right and left arrow keys to move among the different workspaces. Release the keys when the workspace you want is highlighted.

If you get tired of wobbling windows and spinning cubes, it's easy to turn off the desktop effects. Just select System ➪ Preferences ➪ Desktop Effects again and toggle to the Standard effects to turn off the feature.

To learn more about the Accelerated Indirect GL X (AIGLX) project, the project behind the desktop effects, refer to the following website:

    http://fedoraproject.org/wiki/RenderingProject/aiglx

FIGURE 3-7

With desktop effects enabled, windows wobble as you move them around on the desktop, and workspaces spin on a cube.

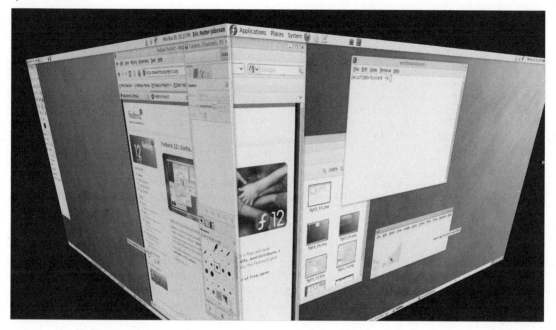

Troubleshooting Your Desktop

If your desktop is not functioning properly (or at all), your video card may not have been configured properly. This section helps you get your video card configured properly and your desktop up and running smoothly.

GUI doesn't work at startup

If Fedora has been successfully installed (along with the desired desktop environment) but the GUI wasn't set to start at boot time, you may see only a simple text-based login prompt when you start Fedora. This login prompt may look something like this:

```
Fedora release 14 (Laughlin)
Kernel 2.6.35.6-45.fc14.i686 on an i686

localhost login:
```

Log in as the root user. As noted earlier, you can check whether you have a GUI that is at least working well enough for you to correct it. Type the following command:

```
# startx
```

What Happens During Desktop Startup?

The X server and graphical login screen are started by the prefdm script. By default, the login screen is displayed by the GNOME display manager (gdm command), which handles both logging in and starting the desktop environment for your console monitor, as well as graphical logins from other computers and X terminals.

The prefdm script is launched only if the run level in the /etc/inittab file is set to 5, as follows:

```
id:5:initdefault:
```

If the initdefault state is 3, the system boots to a text-based login prompt. See Chapter 11 for information on Linux run states and startup processes.

Some processes started during every X session are launched from scripts in the /etc/X11/xinit/xinitrc.d directory. Check those scripts to see if any of the settings they include might be causing problems. (You can also use those scripts to launch applications of your own each time X starts.)

If you are unable to get the video card and monitor configured properly, or if you don't need a GUI, you can configure the computer to start up in text mode. To do this using any shell text editor (such as the vi command described in Chapter 4), change the initdefault line in the /etc/inittab file from id:5:initdefault: to id:3:initdefault.

If you prefer to have Fedora boot to a GUI, change the 3 to a 5.

If the desktop works fine when you type **startx**, you might want to change to a graphical login, so the GUI starts automatically every time. See the "What Happens During Desktop Startup" sidebar for information on booting to a GUI. If X crashes, check /var/log/Xorg.0.log for clues about what went wrong.

If your GUI is so distorted you can't even see how to correct it, switch to a virtual terminal to correct the problem. For example, hold the Ctrl and Alt keys, and press F2. You will see a plain-text login prompt. Log in as root user and type **init 3** to make the garbled GUI login screen go away. As an alternative, press Ctrl+Alt+Backspace to close the X session (this works only when running X via startx). Then you can try tuning your video card as described in the following section.

Tip

Switching virtual terminals is a great way to get out of a GUI that is broken or stuck and run the commands you need to fix a problem. You can use any function key from F1 through F8 with Ctrl+Alt to switch terminals. The GUI itself is probably on the F1 virtual terminal. Linux experts use virtual terminals during Fedora installation to debug a problem or during startup to view text startup messages. ∎

Tuning your video card and monitor

If your GUI starts up but needs some tuning (to get better resolution, more colors, or to fix flickering), you can use the Monitor Preferences window to adjust your desktop.

From the GNOME desktop menus, select System ⇨ Preferences ⇨ Monitors. From here you can control all the monitors connected to your system, adjust the screen resolution, and change the refresh rate. You no longer need the special xorg.conf configuration file to run the X Window System. For a number of Fedora releases, the Xorg server dynamically probes your system's hardware to determine all the configuration settings. In most cases, your system should just work; but if things aren't working properly, you can try to create an xorg.conf file manually.

With no GUI on as root user, type the following commands from a shell:

```
# Xorg -configure
# X -xf86config /root/xorg.conf.new
```

The first line creates xorg.conf.new in the /root directory. The second tries to start your GUI with that new config file. You should see the mouse cursor (an X) and a blank screen. If the GUI works, press Ctrl+Alt+Backspace to exit, and then copy /root/xorg.conf.new to /etc/X11/xorg.conf. You can also edit this file to see if anything doesn't quite match up with your system's hardware.

Getting more information

If you tried configuring X and you still have a server that crashes or has a garbled display, your video card may be unsupported or it may require special configuration. Here are several locations you can check for further information:

- **X.Org** (www.x.org) — The latest information about the X servers that come with Fedora is available from the X.Org website.
- **X documentation** — README files that are specific to different types of video cards are delivered with the X.Org X server. A lot of good information can also be found on the xorg.conf man page (type man **xorg.conf**).

Summary

The X Window System provides the basis for most graphical user interfaces available for Fedora and other Linux systems today. Although X provides the framework for running and sharing applications, the GNOME, KDE, Xfce, Moblin, and MeeGo desktop environments, along with a window manager and theme, provide the look-and-feel of your desktop.

Using various configuration files and commands, you can change nearly every aspect of your graphical environment. You can assign backgrounds a single color or fill them with single or tiled graphic images. You can use and manage multiple virtual workspaces.

Fedora's entry into the 3D hardware acceleration arena is represented by the AIGLX project and the Desktop Effects settings. By making a few simple selections, as described in this chapter, you can have desktops that rotate on a cube and windows that wobble and fade. Look for more 3D features in the future.

After reading this chapter, you should feel comfortable working with the GNOME and KDE desktops. The next chapter will help you work from the traditional command-line interface, referred to as the *shell*.

Using Linux Commands

This chapter presents a view of Linux from the shell. The *shell* is a command-line interpreter that enables you to access some of the most critical Linux tools. The shell is powerful, complex, and almost completely unintuitive.

The shell provides one of the most powerful tools for controlling and administering your Linux system. You can perform almost every task on Linux — from installing new software to configuring your network firewall — from the command line. In addition, many commands work best from the command line, providing you with the control and flexibility necessary to set up modern Linux systems. A command line that sports the power of the shell is one of the things that makes Linux stand out against Windows, with its anemic DOS command shell.

Although at first it isn't obvious how to use the shell, with the right help you can quickly learn many of the most important shell features. In Fedora, bash is the shell command interpreter used by default (and therefore the one used for most of the examples in this chapter). Other shells, such as csh, tcsh, ksh, sh, and others, are also available in Fedora and are therefore also noted in this chapter.

This chapter is your guide to working with the Linux system commands, processes, and file system from the shell. It describes the shell environment and helps you tailor it to your needs. It also describes how to use and move around the file system.

Understanding the Shell

Before icons and windows took over computer screens, you typed commands on a keyboard to interact with most computers. On Unix systems, from which Linux was derived, the program used to interpret and manage commands was referred to as the *shell*.

The shell provides a way to run programs, work with the file system, compile computer code, and manage the computer. Although the shell is less intuitive than common GUIs, most Linux experts consider the shell to be much more powerful than GUIs. Because shells have been around for so long, many advanced features have been built into them. Many old-school Linux administrators and programmers primarily use a GUI as a way to open a lot of shells.

The Linux shell illustrated in this chapter is called the bash shell, which stands for Bourne Again SHell. The name is derived from the fact that bash is compatible with the first Unix shell: the Bourne shell (represented by the sh command). Other popular shells include the C shell (csh), which is popular among BSD Unix users, and the Korn shell (ksh), which is popular among Unix System V users. Linux also has a tcsh shell (a C shell look-alike) and an ash shell (another Bourne shell look-alike). Bash is the default Linux shell. It is also the default on Mac OS X.

Note

While you can invoke the Bourne shell with /bin/sh, the command actually runs the bash shell in sh compatibility mode. Running /bin/sh produces a shell that behaves more like sh than bash, but you will probably be able to use bash scripting concepts that the real Bourne shell wouldn't recognize. The sh shell still exists primarily for compatibility with scripts that were written specifically for that shell. ∎

Although most Linux users have a preference for one shell or another, when you know how to use one shell, you can quickly learn any of the others by occasionally referring to the shell's man page (for example, type **man bash**). The bash shell is roughly compatible with the sh shell.

The Shell Interface

Throughout this book are procedures that require you to use a shell to run commands. How you first get to a shell depends on whether your computer is configured to have a graphical user interface (GUI) or not. A desktop system, by its nature, starts with a GUI. Server systems often are run entirely from the command line. Here are ways of reaching a shell, depending on whether you have a desktop GUI running or not:

- **No desktop** — If your Linux system has no GUI (or one that isn't working at the moment), you log in from a text-based prompt and immediately begin working from the shell.
- **With desktop** — With the GNOME desktop running, you can open a Terminal window (select Applications ➪ System Tools ➪ Terminal) to start a shell. You can begin typing commands into the Terminal window.

If you are using a shell interface, the first thing you see is the shell prompt. The default prompt for a normal user is simply a dollar sign:

```
$
```

The default prompt for the root user is a pound sign (also called a hash mark):

```
#
```

Note

If you use a shell other than the default bash **shell in Fedora, in some cases you may see a percent sign (%) as the user prompt instead of the dollar sign.** ■

For most Linux systems, the $ or # prompts are preceded by your user name, system name, and current directory name. So, for example, a login prompt for the user named jake on a computer named pine with /tmp as the current directory would appear as follows:

```
[jake@pine tmp]$
```

You can change the prompt to display any characters you like. You could use as your prompt the current directory, the date, the local computer name, or any string of characters. When you see a tilde (~) character as the current directory (instead of tmp as shown in the preceding code), it indicates that your home directory is the current directory. (To configure your prompt, see the section "Setting your prompt" later in this chapter.)

Although a tremendous number of features are available with the shell, it's easy to begin by just typing a few commands. Try some of the commands shown in the remainder of this section to become familiar with your current shell environment.

In the examples that follow, the $ or # symbols indicate a prompt. The prompt is followed by the command that you type and then by Enter or Return (depending on your keyboard). The lines that follow show the output that results from the command.

Checking your login session

When you log in to a Linux system, Linux views you as having a particular identity. That identity includes your user name, group name, user ID, and group ID. Linux also keeps track of your login session: it knows when you logged in, how long you have been idle, and where you logged in from.

To find out information about your identity, use the id command as follows:

```
$ id
uid=501(chris) gid=501(chris) groups=501(chris),4(adm),7(lp)
    context=unconfined _u:unconfined _r:unconfined_t:s0-s0:c0.c1023
```

This shows that the user name is chris, which is represented by the numeric user ID (uid) 501. Here, the primary group for chris is also called chris, which has a group ID (gid) of 501. Chris also belongs to other groups called adm (gid 4) and lp (gid 7). These names and numbers represent the permissions that chris has to access computer resources. (Permissions are described later in this chapter in the section on working with files.) Note that by default, Fedora creates a group for each user with the same name as the user name, such as chris in this case.

If your computer has SELinux enabled, the id command also shows context information. In this example, you see the following on id output:

```
context= unconfined _u:unconfined _r:unconfined_t:s0-s0:c0.c1023
```

Cross-Reference
See Chapter 9 of information on SELinux. ■

You can see information about your current login session by using the who command. In the following example, the -m option tells the who command to print information about the current user, -u says to add information about idle time and the process ID, and -H asks that a header be printed:

```
$ who -umH
NAME       LINE         TIME                  IDLE      PID    COMMENT
chris      tty1         2010-10-21 14:12       .        2013
```

The output from this who command shows that the user name is chris. Here, chris is logged in on tty1 (which typically is the monitor connected to the computer), and his login session began at 14:12 on October 21. The IDLE time shows how long the shell has been open without any command being typed (the dot indicates that it is currently active). COMMENT would show the name of the remote computer the user had logged in from, if that user logged in from another computer on the network, or the name of the local X display if you were using a Terminal window (such as :0.0).

Checking directories and permissions

Associated with each shell is a location in the Linux file system known as the *current directory* or *working directory*. As previously mentioned, each user has a directory that is identified as the user's home directory. When you first log in to Linux, you begin with your home directory as the current directory.

When you request to open or save a file, your shell uses the current directory as the point of reference. Simply give a filename when you save a file, and it will be placed in the current directory. Alternatively, you can identify a file by its relation to the current directory (*relative path*). As a third option, you can ignore the current directory and identify a file by the full directory hierarchy that locates it (*absolute path*). The structure and use of the file system is described in detail later in this chapter.

To find out what your current directory is, type the **pwd** command:

```
$ pwd
/usr/bin
```

In this example, the current, or working, directory is /usr/bin. To find out the name of your home directory, type the **echo** command, followed by the **$HOME** variable:

```
$ echo $HOME
/home/chris
```

In the preceding example, the home directory is /home/chris. To get back to your home directory, you can simply type the change directory (cd) command. Although cd, followed by a directory name, changes the current directory to the directory that you choose, simply typing **cd** (with no directory name) takes you to your home directory:

```
$ cd
```

You can also use the tilde (~) character to indicate the home directory, so cd ~ would have the same result as just cd. This is useful when changing to long paths in your home directory (such as ~/local/files, instead of /home/chris/local/files).

At this point, list the contents of your home directory, using the ls command. You can either type the full path to your home directory to list its contents or use the ls command without a directory name to list the contents of the current directory. Using the -a option to ls enables you to view the hidden files (files whose name starts with a period are hidden from normal listings) as well as all other files. With the -l option, you can see a long, detailed list of information about each file. (You can put multiple single-letter options together after a single dash, such as -la.)

```
$ ls -la /home/chris
total 158
drwx------.   2   chris   chris     1024  Sep 13 13:55 .
drwxr-xr-x.   3   root    root      1024  Sep 13 01:49 ..
-rw-------.   1   chris   chris     2204  Sep 13 21:30 .bash_history
-rw-r--r--.   1   chris   chris       24  Sep 13 01:50 .bash_logout
-rw-r--r--.   1   chris   chris      230  Sep 13 01:50 .bash_profile
-rw-r--r--.   1   chris   chris      124  Sep 13 01:50 .bashrc
drw-r--r--.   1   chris   chris     4096  Sep 13 01:50 .kde
-rw-rw-r--.   1   chris   chris   149872  Sep 13 22:49 letter
```

Displaying a long list (-l option) of the contents of your home directory shows you more about file sizes and directories. Directories such as the current directory (.) and the directory above the current directory (..) are noted as directories by the letter d at the beginning of each entry. In this case, dot (.) represents /home/chris, and two dots (..), which is also referred to as the *parent directory*, represent /home. The /home directory is owned by root. All other files are owned by the user chris (who belongs to the chris group).

The file or directory names shown on the right are mostly dot (.) files that are used to store GUI properties (.kde directory) or shell properties (.bash files). The only non-dot file shown in this example is the one named letter. The ls command places the permissions for the file at the beginning of each line. (Permissions and configuring shell property files are described later in this chapter.) Other information in the listing includes the number of hard links to the file (column 2), the size of each file in bytes (column 5), and the date and time each file was most recently modified (column 6).

Note

A symbolic link is a file that points to another file, effectively allowing you to have multiple filenames representing a single physical file. Permissions for a symbolic link appears as lrwxrwxrwx but are not interpreted as full read/write/execute permissions. If you try to open a symbolic link, the permissions on the file that link points to (the original file) determine whether you can access the file. ■

Checking system activity

In addition to being a multiuser operating system, Linux is also a multitasking system. *Multitasking* means that many programs can be running at the same time. An instance of a running program is referred to as a *process*. Linux provides tools for listing running processes, monitoring system usage, and stopping (or killing) processes when necessary.

The most common utility for checking running processes is the ps command. With ps, you can see which programs are running, the resources they are using, and who is running them. The following is an example of the ps command:

```
$ ps au
USER    PID %CPU %MEM  VSZ   RSS   TTY    STAT START  TIME COMMAND
root   2146 0.0  0.8 1908  1100  tty0   Ss+  14:50  0:00 login -- jake
jake   2147 0.0  0.7 1836  1020  tty0   Ss+  14:50  0:00 -bash
jake   2310 0.0  0.7 2592   912  tty0   R+   18:22  0:00 ps au
```

In this example, the a option asks to show processes of all users associated with the user's current terminal, and the u option asks that user names be shown, as well as other information such as the time the process started and memory and CPU usage. The concept of "terminal" comes from the old days, when people worked exclusively from character terminals, so a terminal typically represented a single person at a single screen. Now you can have many "terminals" on one screen by opening multiple terminal windows.

On this shell session, there isn't much happening. The first process shows that the user named jake logged in to the login process (which is controlled by the root user). The next process shows that jake is using a bash shell and has just run the ps au command. The terminal device tty0 is being used for the login session. The STAT column represents the state of the process, with R indicating a currently running process, and S representing a sleeping process. (A *sleeping* process is one that is still active but waiting for some event to complete before continuing. It may be waiting for someone to type something at a shell or for a process to send information it requested.) A small s indicates a session leader (a process that that controls a number of other processes), and + indicates the foreground process group (as opposed to a process running in the background).

The USER column shows the name of the user who started the process. Each process is represented by a unique ID number, referred to as a process ID (PID). (You can use the PID if you ever need to kill a runaway process.) The %CPU and %MEM columns show the percentage of the processor and random access memory, respectively, that the process is consuming. VSZ (virtual set size) shows the size of the image process (in kilobytes), and RSS (resident set size) shows the size of the program in memory. START shows the time the process began running, and TIME shows the cumulative system time used.

Many processes running on a computer are not associated with a terminal. A normal Linux system has many processes running in the background. Background system processes perform such tasks as logging system activity or listening for data coming in from the network. They are often started when Linux boots up and they run continuously until it shuts down. To see and thereby monitor all the processes running on your Linux system, type the following:

```
$ ps axu | less
```

Adding the pipe (|) and the less command to ps axu enables you to page through the many processes that will appear on your screen. A pipe enables you to direct the output of one command to be the input of the next command. Use the spacebar to page through, and type **q** to end the list. You can also use the arrow keys to move one line at a time through the output.

Exiting the shell

To exit the shell when you are done, type **exit** or press Ctrl+D.

This section demonstrated just a few commands in order to familiarize you quickly with your Linux system. Hundreds of other commands that you can try are contained in directories such as /bin and /usr/bin. There are also administrative commands in the /sbin or /usr/sbin directories. Many of these commands are described in the remainder of this chapter.

Using the Shell in Linux

When you type a command in a shell, you can also include other characters that change or add to how the command works. In addition to the command itself, these are some of the other items that you can type on a shell command line:

- **Options** — Most commands have one or more options you can add to change their behavior. Options typically consist of a single letter, preceded by a dash. You can also often combine several options after a single dash. For example, the command ls -la lists the contents of the current directory. The -l asks for a detailed (long) list of information, and the -a asks that files beginning with a dot (.) also be listed. When a single option consists of a word, it is usually preceded by a double dash (--). For example, to use the help option on many commands, you would enter --help on the command line. Here's an example of help information for the ls command (output is piped to the less command to page through it; type **q** to quit):

```
$ ls --help | less
Usage: ls [OPTION]... [FILE]...
List information about the FILEs (the current directory by default).
Sort entries alphabetically if none of the -cftuvSUX nor --sort.

Mandatory arguments to long options are mandatory for short options too
  -a, --all                  do not hide entries starting with .
```

```
        -A, --almost-all              do not list implied . and ..
        .
        .
        .
```

- **Arguments** — Many commands also accept arguments after any options are entered. An argument is an extra piece of information, such as a filename, that can be used by the command. For example, cat /etc/passwd displays the contents of the /etc/passwd file on your screen. In this case, /etc/passwd is the argument.

- **Environment variables** — The shell itself stores information that may be useful to the user's shell session in what are called *environment variables*. Examples of environment variables include $SHELL (which identifies the shell you are using), $PS1 (which defines your shell prompt), and $MAIL (which identifies the location of your mailbox).

Tip

You can check your environment variables at any time. Type declare to list the current environment variables. Or you can type echo $VALUE, where VALUE is replaced by the name of a particular environment variable you want to list. ■

- **Metacharacters** — These are characters that have special meaning to the shell. Metacharacters can be used to direct the output of a command to a file (>), pipe the output to another command (|), or run a command in the background (&), to name a few.

To save you some typing, there are shell features that store commands you want to reuse, recall previous commands, and edit commands. You can create aliases that enable you to type a short command to run a longer one. The shell stores previously entered commands in a history list, which you can display and from which you can recall commands.

Unless you specifically change to another shell, the bash shell is the one you use with Fedora. The bash shell contains most of the powerful features available in other shells. Although the description in this chapter steps you through many bash shell features, you can learn more about the bash shell by typing **man bash**. For other ways to learn about using the shell, refer to the sidebar "Getting Help with Using the Shell."

Locating commands

If you know the directory that contains the command you want to run, one way to run it is to type the full path to that command. For example, you run the date command from the /bin directory by typing the following:

```
$ /bin/date
```

Of course, this can be inconvenient, especially if the command resides in a directory with a long name. The better way is to have commands stored in well-known directories, and then add those directories to your shell's PATH environment variable. The path consists of a list of directories that are checked sequentially for the commands you enter. To see your current path, type the following:

```
$ echo $PATH
/usr/local/bin:/usr /bin:/ bin:/usr/local/sbin:/usr/sbin:/sbin:
/home/chris/bin
```

The results show the default path for a regular Linux user. Directories in the path list are separated by colons. Most user commands that come with Linux are stored in the /bin, /usr/bin, or /usr/local/bin directories. The last directory shown is the bin directory in the user's home directory.

Getting Help with Using the Shell

When you first start using the shell, it can be intimidating. All you see is a prompt. How do you know which commands are available, which options they use, or how to use more advanced features? Fortunately, a lot of help is available. Here are some places you can look to supplement what you learn in this chapter:

- **Check the** PATH — Type echo $PATH. This will return a list of the directories containing commands that are immediately accessible to you. Listing the contents of those directories (with the ls command) displays most standard Linux commands.

- **Use the** help **command** — Some commands are built into the shell, so they do not appear in a directory. The help command lists those commands and shows options available with each of them. (Type help | less to page through the list.) For help with a particular built-in command, type help *command*, replacing *command* with the name that interests you. The help command works with the bash shell only.

- **Use** --help **with the command** — Many commands include a --help option that you can use to get information about how the command is used. For example, type date --help | less. The output shows not only options, but also time formats you can use with the date command.

- **Use the** man **command** — To learn more about a particular command, type man command, replacing command with the command name you want. The command name man is short for manual. A description of the command and its options appears on the screen.

- **Use the** info **command** — Command descriptions that aren't available on man pages are often available for the info facility. Type info command to see a text-based interface for stepping through information about the command.

- **Look in** /usr/share/doc — Many commands come with extra documentation that appears under subdirectories here. For example, /usr/share/doc/xsane* contains extra information about XSane, a program that works with document scanners. (The * is used because each subdirectory includes the version number of the package, such as /usr/share/doc/xsane-0.997 in this case.)

Also note administrative commands are in your path. These directories include /sbin and /usr/sbin. In prior versions of Fedora, these directories were not part of the default path.

The path directory order is important. Directories are checked from left to right, so in this example, if there is a command called foo located in both the /bin and /usr/bin directories, the one in /bin is executed if /bin is first in your path. To have the other foo command run, either type the full path to the command or change your PATH variable. (Changing your PATH and adding directories to it are described later in this chapter in the section on "Adding environment variables.")

Tip

If you want to add your own commands or shell scripts, place them in the bin directory in your home directory (such as /home/chris/bin for the user named chris). This directory is automatically added to your path (although you must type mkdir $HOME/bin to create the directory). As long as you add the command to your bin with execute permission (described in the "Understanding file permissions" section), you can immediately begin using the command by simply typing its name at your shell prompt. Note there are always security concerns when adding new commands. This is in part why your local bin directory appears after the system bin directories in your PATH. Be careful when adding commands and read the section "Understanding file permissions" carefully. ∎

Not all the commands that you run are located in directories in your PATH. Some commands are built into the shell. Other commands can be overridden by creating aliases that define any commands and options that you want the command to run. There are also ways to define a function that consists of a stored series of commands. Here is the order in which the shell checks for the commands you type:

1. **Aliases** — Names set by the alias command that represent a particular command and a set of options. (Type **alias** to see what aliases are set.) Often, aliases enable you to define a short name for a long, complicated command. Some users use aliases to map a command name from another operating system to the similar utility in Linux.

2. **Shell reserved word** — Words that are reserved by the shell for special use. Many of these are words that you would use in programming-type functions, such as do, while, case, and else.

3. **Function** — A set of commands that are executed together within the current shell.

4. **Built-in command** — A command that is built into the shell.

5. **File system command** — This is a command that is stored in and executed from the computer's file system. (These are the commands that are indicated by the value of the PATH variable.)

To find out where a particular command is taken from, you can use the type command. (If you are using a shell other than bash, use the which command instead.) For example, to find out where the bash shell command is located, type the following:

```
$ type bash
bash is /bin/bash
```

Try these few words with the `type` command to see other locations of commands: `which`, `case`, and `return`. If a command resides in several locations, you can add the `-a` option to view all the known locations of the command.

Tip

Sometimes you may run a command and receive an error message that the command was not found or that permission to run the command was denied. In the first case, confirm that you spelled the command correctly and that it is located in your PATH. In the second case, the command may be in the PATH, but it may not be executable. Adding execute permissions to a command is described later in this chapter. ∎

Rerunning commands

It's annoying, after typing a long or complex command line, to learn that you mistyped something. Fortunately, some shell features enable you to recall previous command lines, edit those lines, or complete a partially typed command line.

The *shell history* is a list of the commands that you have entered before. Using the `history` command, you can view your previous commands. Then, using various shell features, you can recall individual command lines from that list and change them however you please.

The rest of this section describes how to do command-line editing, how to complete parts of command lines, and how to recall and work with the history list.

Command-line editing

If you type something wrong on a command line, the `bash` shell ensures that you don't have to delete the entire line and start over. Likewise, you can recall a previous command line and change the elements to make a new command.

By default, the bash shell uses command-line editing that is based on the `emacs` text editor, so if you are familiar with `emacs`, you probably already know most of the keystrokes described here.

Tip

If you prefer the `vi` command for editing shell command lines, you can easily make that happen. Add the line

> **set -o vi**

to the `.bashrc` file in your home directory. The next time you open a shell, you can use `vi` commands (as described in the tutorial later in this chapter) to edit your command lines. You can also use `set` from the command line, but it will apply to your current session only. ∎

To do the editing, you can use a combination of control keys, meta keys, and arrow keys. For example, Ctrl+f means to hold the Control key and type **f**. Alt+f means to hold the Alt key and type **f**. (Instead of the Alt key, your keyboard may use a meta key or the Esc key. On a Windows keyboard, you can sometimes use the Windows key.)

To try out a bit of command-line editing, type the following command:

```
$ ls /usr/bin | sort -f | less
```

This command lists the contents of the /usr/bin directory, sorts the contents in alphabetical order (regardless of uppercase and lowercase), and pipes the output to less (so you can page through the results). Now, suppose you want to change /usr/bin to /bin. You can use the following steps to change the command from the shell:

1. Press Ctrl+a. This moves the cursor to the beginning of the command line.
2. Press Ctrl+f or the right arrow (→) key. Repeat this command a few times to position the cursor under the first slash (/).
3. Press Ctrl+d. Type this command four times to delete /usr.
4. Press Enter. This executes the command line.

Caution

Typing Ctrl+d at the shell prompt typically causes the shell to stop (and to log you out if you logged in to a shell only). In general, you should use the Del or Backspace keys instead of Ctrl+d to edit the command line. ∎

As you edit a command line, at any point you can type regular characters to add those characters to the command line. The characters appear at the location of your cursor. You can use right (→) and left (←) arrows to move the cursor from one end to the other on the command line. You can also press the up (↑) and down (↓) arrow keys to step through previous commands in the history list to select a command line for editing. (See the section "Command-line recall" for details about how to recall commands from the history list.)

Table 4-1 lists the numerous keystrokes that you can use to move around the command line.

TABLE 4-1

Keystrokes for Navigating Command Lines

Keystroke	Full Name	Description
Ctrl+f	Character forward	Go forward one character.
Ctrl+b	Character backward	Go backward one character.
Ctrl+ right arrow (or Alt+f)	Word forward	Go forward one word.
Ctrl+ left arrow (or Alt+b)	Word backward	Go backward one word.
Ctrl+a (Home key)	Beginning of line	Go to the beginning of the current line.
Ctrl+e (End key)	End of line	Go to the end of the line.
Ctrl+l	Clear screen	Clear the screen and leave a line at the top of the screen.

Note

In a GNOME shell window, typing Alt+f will call down the File menu, not move forward in the command line. Alt+t will similarly pull down the Terminal menu. ∎

Table 4-2 lists the keystrokes for editing command lines.

TABLE 4-2

Keystrokes for Editing Command Lines

Keystroke	Full Name	Description
Ctrl+d	Delete current	Delete the current character.
Backspace or Rubout	Delete previous	Delete the previous character.
Ctrl+t	Transpose character	Switch the positions of the current and previous characters.
Alt+t	Transpose words	Switch the positions of the current and previous words.
Alt+u	Uppercase word	Change the current word to uppercase.
Alt+l	Lowercase word	Change the current word to lowercase.
Alt+c	Capitalize word	Change the current word to an initial capital.
Ctrl+v	Insert special character	Add a special character. For example, to add a Tab character, press Ctrl+v+Tab.

Table 4-3 lists the keystrokes for cutting and pasting text on a command line.

TABLE 4-3

Keystrokes for Cutting and Pasting Text in Command Lines

Keystroke	Description
Ctrl+k	Cut text to the end of the line.
Ctrl+u	Cut text to the beginning of the line.
Ctrl+w	Cut the word located behind the cursor.
Alt+d	Cut the word following the cursor.
Ctrl+y	Paste the most recently cut text.
Alt+y	Rotate back to previously cut text and paste it.
Ctrl+c	Cancel the entire command line.

Command-line completion

To save you a few keystrokes, the bash shell offers several different ways to complete partially typed values. To attempt to complete a value, type the first few characters and then press Tab. Here are some of the values you can type partially:

- **Environment variable** — If the text begins with a dollar sign ($), the shell completes the text with an environment variable from the current shell.

- **User name** — If the text begins with a tilde (~), the shell completes the text with a user name. (This is actually just a case of file or directory expansion. For example, ~chr might expand to ~chris/, which would identify the home directory /home/chris.)

- **Command, alias, or function** — If the text begins with regular characters, the shell tries to complete the text with a command, alias, or function name.

- **Filenames** — After a command has been typed, anything beginning with a / or regular characters is completed as a path to a directory or filename. This is one of the most common forms of command-line completion because it can help you traverse directory paths with long names or complete long filenames.

- **Hostname** — If the text begins with an at (@) sign, the shell completes the text with a hostname taken from the /etc/hosts file.

Tip

To add hostnames from an additional file, you can set the HOSTFILE variable to the name of that file. The file must be in the same format as /etc/hosts. ■

Here are a few examples of command completion. (Where you see <Tab>, it means to press the Tab key on your keyboard.) Type the following:

```
$ echo $OS<Tab>
$ cd ~ro<Tab>
$ fing<Tab>
$ cat /etc/fed<Tab>
$ mail root@loc<Tab>
```

The first example causes $OS to expand to the $OSTYPE variable. In the next example, ~ro expands to the root user's home directory (~root/). Next, fing expands to the finger command. After that, /etc/fed expands to /etc/fedora-release, which contains information on your current release of Fedora. Finally, the address of root@loc expands to the computer name localhost.

Of course, sometimes there are several possible completions for the string of characters you have entered. In that case, you can check the possible ways text can be expanded by pressing Tab twice at the point where you want the completion. The following code shows the result you would get if you checked for possible completions on $P:

```
$ echo $P<Tab><Tab>
$PATH $PIPESTATUS $PPID $PROMPT_COMMAND $PS1 $PS2 $PS4 $PWD
$ echo $P
```

In this case, there are eight possible variables that begin with $P. After the possibilities are displayed, the original command line returns, ready for you to complete it as you choose.

If the text you are trying to complete is not preceded by a $, ~, or @ (unlike the preceding example), you can still try to complete it with a variable, user name, or hostname. Press the following to complete your text:

- **Alt+~** — Completes the text before this point as a user name
- **Alt+$** — Completes the text before this point as a variable
- **Alt+@** — Completes the text before this point as a hostname
- **Ctrl+x+~** — Lists possible user name text completions
- **Ctrl+x+$** — Lists possible environment variable completions
- **Ctrl+x+!** — Lists possible command name completions

Note

You may find that only the Alt key on the left side of your keyboard works with the preceding examples. Also, remember that characters such as the tilde (~) and dollar sign ($) require the Shift key as well as the Alt or Ctrl keys.

Enter the Ctrl+x sequences as Ctrl+x and then the next character. For example, to enter Ctrl+x+$, hold down the Ctrl and x keys, release the Ctrl and x keys and then hold down the next key or key combination, such as Shift+4 to get $. ∎

Command-line recall

After you type a command line, that entire command line is saved in your shell's history list. The list is stored in a history file, from which any command can be recalled to run again. After it is recalled, you can modify the command line, as described earlier.

To view your history list, use the `history` command. Type the command without options or followed by a number to list that many of the most recent commands. For example:

```
$ history 8
382 date
383 ls /usr/bin | sort -a | more
384 man sort
385 cd /usr/local/bin
386 man more
387 useradd -m /home/chris -u 101 chris
388 passwd chris
389 history 8
```

There are several ways to run a command immediately from this list, including the following:

- **Run Command Number (!n)** — Replace the n with the number of the command line, and the command line indicated is run. For example, to repeat the `date` command shown as command number 382 from the previous history listing, you could type the following:

```
$ !382
date
Sat Oct 16 21:30:06 PDT 2010
```

- **Run Previous Command (!!)** — Runs the previous command line. To run that same date command again immediately, type the following:

```
$ !!
date
Fri Oct 16 21:30:39 PDT 2009
```

- **Run Command Containing String (!?string?)** — Runs the most recent command that contains a particular *string* of characters. For example, you could run the date command again by searching for part of that command line as follows:

```
$ !?dat?
date
Fri Oct 16 21:32:41 PDT 2009
```

Keep in mind that with an exclamation point, the command is run immediately, without giving you a chance to confirm.

Instead of just running a history command line immediately, you can recall a particular line and edit it. You can use these keys to do that:

- **Step (Arrow Keys)** — Press the up ( ) and down ( ) arrow keys to step through each command line in your history list to arrive at the one you want. (Ctrl+p and Ctrl+n do the same functions, respectively.)
- **Reverse Incremental Search (Ctrl+r)** — After you press these keys, you are asked to enter a search string to do a reverse search. As you type the string, a matching command line appears that you can run or edit.
- **Reverse Search (Alt+p)** — After you press these keys, you are asked to enter a string to do a reverse search. Type a string and press Enter to see the most recent command line that includes that string.
- **Forward Search (Alt+n)** — After you press these keys, you are asked to enter a string to do a forward search. Type a string and press Enter to see the most recent command line that includes that string.
- **Beginning of History List (Alt+<)** — This brings you to the first entry of the history list.

Another way to work with your history list is to use the fc command. If you type **fc** followed by a history line number, that command line is opened in a text editor. After making the changes you want and exiting the editor, the command runs. You can also enter a range of line numbers (for example, `fc 100 105`). All the commands open in your text editor, and then run one after the other when you exit the editor.

The history list is stored in the `.bash_history` file in your home directory. Up to 1,000 history commands are stored by default. Note that this list provides a history of your commands, something the root or other users may not want to expose.

Connecting and expanding commands

A truly powerful feature of the shell is the capability to redirect the input and output of commands to and from other commands and files. To allow commands to be strung together, the shell uses metacharacters. As noted earlier, a metacharacter is a typed character that has special meaning to the shell for connecting commands or requesting expansion.

Piping commands

The pipe (|) metacharacter connects the output from one command to the input of another command. This enables you to have one command work on some data, and then have the next command deal with the results. Here is an example of a command line that includes pipes:

```
$ cat /etc/passwd | sort | cut -f1,5 -d: | less
```

This command lists the contents of the /etc/passwd file and pipes the output to the sort command. The sort command takes the user names that begin each line of the /etc/passwd file, sorts them alphabetically, and pipes the output to the cut command. The cut command takes fields 1 and 5, with the fields delimited by a colon (:), and then pipes the output to the less command. The less command displays the output one page at a time, so that you can go through the output one line or page at a time (press **q** to quit at the end of the output).

Pipes are an excellent illustration of how Unix, the predecessor of Linux, was created as an operating system comprised of building blocks. A standard practice in Unix was to connect utilities in different ways to get different jobs done. For example, before the days of graphical word processors, users created plain-text files that included macros to indicate formatting. To see how the document actually looked, they used a command such as the following:

```
$ gunzip < /usr/share/man/man1/grep.1.gz | nroff -c -man | less
```

In this example, the contents of the grep man page (grep.1.gz) are directed as input to the gunzip command to be unzipped. The output from gunzip is piped to the nroff command to format the man page using the manual macro (-man) and disable color output (-c). That output is piped to the less command to display the output. Because the file being displayed is in plain text, you can substitute any number of options to work with the text before displaying it. You can sort the contents, change or delete some of the content, or bring in text from other documents. The key is that, instead of all those features being in one program, you get results from piping and redirecting input and output between multiple commands.

Sequential commands

Sometimes you may want a sequence of commands to run, with one command being completed before the next command begins. You can do this by typing several commands on the same command line and separating them with semicolons (;):

```
$ date ; troff -me verylargedocument | lpr ; date
```

In this example, I was formatting a huge document and wanted to know how long it would take. The first command (date) showed the date and time before the formatting started. The troff command formatted the document and then piped the output to the printer. When the formatting was done, the date and time was printed again (so I knew when the troff command completed).

Background commands

Some commands can take a while to complete, and you may not want to tie up your shell waiting for a command to finish. In those cases, you can have the commands run in the background by using the ampersand (&).

Text formatting commands (such as nroff and troff, described earlier) are examples of commands that are often run in the background to format a large document. You also might want to create your own shell scripts that run in the background to check continuously for certain events to occur, such as the hard disk filling up or particular users logging in.

Here is an example of how to run a command in the background:

```
$ troff -me verylargedocument | lpr &
```

Other ways to manage background and foreground processes are described in the "Managing background and foreground processes" section.

Expanding commands

With command substitution, you can have the output of a command interpreted by the shell, rather than by the command itself. This way, you can have the standard output of a command become an argument for another command. The two forms of command substitution are $(command) or `command`. (The first case is the preferred method. The second case uses back quotes, also called *back ticks*.)

The command in this case can include options, metacharacters, and arguments. Here is an example of using command substitution:

```
$ vi $(find /home | grep xyzzy)
```

In this command line, the shell performs command substitution before it runs the vi command. First, the find command starts at the /home directory and prints out all files and directories below that point in the file system. Next, this output is piped to the grep command, which filters out all files except for those that include the string xyzzy. Finally, the vi command opens for editing (one at a time) all filenames that include xyzzy.

This particular example might be useful if you knew that you wanted to edit a file for which you knew the name but not the location. As long as the string were uncommon, you could find and open every instance of a filename existing beneath a point you choose in the file system.

Expanding arithmetic expressions

There may be times when you want to pass arithmetic results to a command. You can use two forms to expand an arithmetic expression and pass it to the shell: $[expression] or $((expression)). Here is an example:

```
$ echo "I am $[2010 - 1957] years old."
I am 53 years old.
```

In this example, the shell interprets the arithmetic expression first (2010 - 1957), and then passes that information to the echo command. The echo command displays the text, with the results of the arithmetic (53) inserted.

Using shell environment variables

Every active shell stores pieces of information that it needs to use in what are called *environment variables*. An environment variable can store things such as locations of configuration files, mailboxes, and path directories. They can also store values for your shell prompts, the size of your history list, and the type of operating system.

To see the environment variables currently assigned to your shell, type the **declare** command. (It will probably fill more than one screen, so type **declare | less**.) You can refer to the value of any of those variables by preceding it with a dollar sign ($) and placing it anywhere on a command line. For example:

```
$ echo $USER
chris
```

This command prints the value of the USER variable, which holds your user name (chris). Substitute any other variable name for USER to print its value instead.

Common shell environment variables

When you start a shell (by logging in or opening a terminal window), a lot of environment variables are already set. Here are some variables that are either set when you use a bash shell or that you can set to use with different features:

- BASH — Contains the full path name of the bash command. This is usually /bin/bash.
- BASH_VERSION — Number of the current version of the bash command.
- EUID — Effective user ID number of the current user. It is assigned when the shell starts, based on the user's entry in the /etc/passwd file.

- **FCEDIT** — If set, this variable indicates the text editor used by the `fc` command to edit `history` commands. If this variable isn't set, the `vi` command is used. By default, this variable is not set.

- **HISTFILE** — Location of your history file. It is typically located at `$HOME/.bash_history`.

- **HISTFILESIZE** — Number of history entries that can be stored. After this number is reached, the oldest commands are discarded. The default value is 1,000.

- **HISTCMD** — Returns the number of the current command in the history list; that is, the number in the history where the next-entered command will go.

- **HOME** — This is your home directory. It is your current working directory each time you log in or type the `cd` command with any options.

- **HOSTTYPE** — A value that describes the computer architecture on which the Linux system is running. For Intel-compatible PCs, the value is i386, i486, i586, i686, or something like i386-linux. For AMD 64-bit and Intel EM64T machines, the value is x86_64. There is also ppc and ppc64, for older Apple computers (PowerPC 32-bit and 64-bit).

- **MAIL** — Location of your mailbox file. The file is typically your user name in the `/var/spool/mail` directory.

- **OLDPWD** — Directory that was the working directory before you changed to the current working directory.

- **OSTYPE** — A name identifying the current operating system. For Fedora, the `OSTYPE` value is either `linux` or `linux-gnu`, depending on the type of shell you are using. (Bash can run on other operating systems as well.)

- **PATH** — The colon-separated list of directories used to find commands that you type. The default value for regular users is

  ```
  /usr/kerberos/bin:/usr/local/bin:/usr/bin:/bin:/usr/local/sbin:↵
  /usr/sbin:/sbin:/home/chris/bin
  ```

- **PPID** — The process ID of the command that started the current shell (for example, its parent process).

- **PROMPT_COMMAND** — Can be set to a command name that is run each time before your shell prompt is displayed. Setting `PROMPT_COMMAND=date` lists the current date and time before the prompt appears.

- **PS1** — Sets the value of your shell prompt. There are many items that you can read into your prompt (date, time, user name, hostname, and so on). Sometimes a command requires additional prompts, which you can set with the variables `PS2`, `PS3`, and so on. (Setting your prompt is described later in this chapter.)

- **PWD** — The directory that is assigned as your current directory. This value changes each time you change directories using the `cd` command.

- **RANDOM** — Accessing this variable causes a random number to be generated. The number is between 0 and 32767.

- **SECONDS** — Number of seconds since the time the shell was started.

- **SHLVL** — Number of shell levels associated with the current shell session. When you log in to the shell, the SHLVL is 1. Each time you start a new bash command (by, for example, using su to become a new user, or by simply typing bash), this number is incremented.

- **TMOUT** — Can be set to a number representing the number of seconds the shell can be idle without receiving input. After the number of seconds is reached, the shell exits. This is a security feature that makes it less likely for unattended shells to be accessed by unauthorized people. (This must be set in the login shell for it to actually cause the shell to log out the user. You can use it in any terminal session to close the current shell after a set number of seconds, for example TMOUT=30.)

- **UID** — User ID number assigned to your user name. The UID number is stored in the /etc/password file.

Setting your own environment variables

Environment variables can provide a handy way of storing bits of information that you use often from the shell. You can create any variables that you want (avoiding those that are already in use) so that you can read in the values of those variables as you use the shell. (The bash man page lists variables already in use.)

To set an environment variable temporarily, you can simply type a variable name and assign it to a value. Here is an example:

```
$ AB=/usr/dog/contagious/ringbearer/grind/ ; export AB
```

This example causes a long directory path to be assigned to the AB variable. The export AB command says to export the value to the shell so that it can be propagated to other shells you may open. With AB set, you can go to the directory by typing the following:

```
$ cd $AB
```

Tip

You may have noticed that the environment variables shown here are in all caps. Although case does matter with these variables, setting them as uppercase is a convention, not a necessity. You could just as easily name a new variable xyz as XYZ (variables are case sensitive so they are not the same, but either will work if you use case consistently). System environment variables, such as PATH, are uppercase. ■

The problem with setting environment variables in this way is that as soon as you exit the shell in which you set the variable, the setting is lost. To set variables more permanently, you should add variable settings to a bash configuration file, as described later in this section.

If you want to have other text right up against the output from an environment variable, you can surround the variable in braces. This protects the variable name from being misunderstood. For example, if you want to add a command name to the AB variable shown earlier, you can type the following:

```
$ echo ${AB}adventure
/usr/dog/contagious/ringbearer/grind/adventure
```

Remember that you must export the variable so that it can be picked up by other shell commands beyond the current shell, especially outside of a shell script. You must add the export line to a shell configuration file for it to take effect the next time you log in. The export command is fairly flexible. Instead of running the export command after you set the variable, you can do it all in one step, as follows:

```
$ export XYZ=/home/xyz/bin
```

You can override the value of any environment variable. This can be temporary by simply typing the new value, or you can add the new export line to your $HOME/.bashrc file. One useful variable to update is PATH. Here is an example:

```
$ export PATH=$PATH:/home/xyz/bin
```

In this example, I added the /home/xyz/bin directory to the PATH, a useful technique if you want to run a bunch of commands from a directory that is not normally in your PATH, without typing the full or relative path each time. Remember that the order of the PATH is important. If /home/xyz/bin/ls preceded by $PATH and the /home/xyz/bin/ls command existed, typing **ls** would use that command instead of /bin/ls. As noted earlier, replacing common Linux commands can be a security issue.

If you decide that you no longer want a variable to be set, you can use the unset command to erase its value. For example, typing unset XYZ would cause XYZ to have no value set. (Remember to remove the export from the $HOME/.bashrc file — if you added it there — or it will return the next time you open a shell.)

Managing background and foreground processes

If you are using Linux over a network or from a *dumb* terminal (a monitor that allows only text input with no GUI support), your shell may be all that you have. You may be used to a windowing environment where you have a lot of programs active at the same time so that you can switch among them as needed. This shell thing can seem pretty limited.

Note

One way to overcome the limitations of a single shell is to use the screen command. Screen allows you to have multiple shells open at the same time, as well as disconnect and reconnect to different shell sessions without completely closing them. See the section "Switching terminals with the screen program" later in this chapter for more on the screen command. ∎

Although the bash shell doesn't include a GUI for running many programs, it does let you move active programs between the background and foreground. In this way, you can have a lot of programs running, while selectively choosing the one you want to deal with at the moment.

There are several ways to place an active program in the background. One mentioned earlier is to add an ampersand (&) to the end of a command line. Another way is to use the at command to run commands such that they are not connected to the shell. (See Chapter 11 for more information about the at command.)

To stop a command and put it in the background, press Ctrl+z. After the command is stopped, you can either bring it to the foreground to run (the fg command) or start it running in the background (the bg command).

Starting background processes

If you have programs that you want to run while you continue to work in the shell, you can place the programs in the background. To place a program in the background at the time you run the program, type an ampersand (&) at the end of the command line. For example:

```
$ find /usr > /tmp/allusrfiles &
```

This command finds all files on your Linux system (starting from /usr), prints those filenames, and puts those names in the file /tmp/allusrfiles. The ampersand (&) runs that command line in the background. To check which commands you have running in the background, use the jobs command, as follows:

```
$ jobs
[1]   Stopped (tty output)   vi /tmp/myfile
[2]   Running                find /usr -print > /tmp/allusrfiles &
[3]   Running                nroff -man /usr/man2/* >/tmp/man2 &
[4]-  Running                nroff -man /usr/man3/* >/tmp/man3 &
[5]+  Stopped                nroff -man /usr/man4/* >/tmp/man4
```

The first job shows a text-editing command (vi) that I placed in the background and stopped by pressing Ctrl+z while I was editing. Job 2 shows the find command I just ran. Jobs 3 and 4 show nroff commands currently running in the background. Job 5 had been running in the shell (foreground) until I decided too many processes were running and pressed Ctrl+z to stop job 5 until a few processes had completed.

The plus sign (+) next to number 5 shows that it was most recently placed in the background. The minus sign (-) next to number 4 shows that it was placed in the background just before the most recent background job. Because job 1 requires terminal input, it cannot run in the background. As a result, it is Stopped (preventing terminal output or input) until it is brought to the foreground again.

Tip

To see the process ID for the background job, add a -l option to the jobs command. If you type ps, you can use the process ID to figure out which command is for a particular background job. ■

Moving commands to the foreground and background

Continuing with the example, you can bring any of the commands on the jobs list to the foreground. For example, to edit myfile again, type the following:

```
$ fg %1
```

You can skip the percent sign (%) if you wish. As a result, the vi command opens again, with all text as it was when you stopped the vi job.

Caution

Before you put a text processor, word processor, or similar program in the background, make sure you save your file. It's easy to forget you have a program in the background, and you will lose your data if you log out or the computer reboots later. ■

To refer to a background job (to cancel it or bring it to the foreground), use a percent sign (%) followed by the job number. You can also use the following to refer to a background job:

- **%** — Used alone, a percent sign refers to the most recent command put into the background (indicated by the plus sign). This action brings the command to the foreground.

- **%string** — Refers to a job where the command begins with a particular string of characters. The string must be unambiguous. (In other words, typing %vi when there are two vi commands in the background results in an error message.)

- **%?string** — Refers to a job where the command line contains a string at any point. The string must be unambiguous or the match will fail.

- **%--** — Refers to the previous job stopped before the one most recently stopped.

If a command is stopped, you can start it running again in the background using the bg command. For example, take job number 5 from the jobs list in the previous example:

```
[5]+ Stopped              nroff -man man4/* >/tmp/man4
```

Type the following:

```
$ bg %5
```

After that, the job runs in the background. Its jobs entry appears as follows:

```
[5]  Running              nroff -man man4/* >/tmp/man4 &
```

If you want to run a job in the background and have it continue to run after you close the shell from which you ran it, you can run that command by preceding it with the nohup command. For example, to update your locate database (which store all files on your system so you can find them easily with the locate command) so it will keep running after you exit the shell, type the following command:

```
# nohup updatedb &
```

Caution

Output from the command is sent to the file `nohup.out`. **With a lot of output, this could fill your hard disk partition.** ■

Configuring your shell

You can tune your shell to help you work more efficiently. Your prompt can provide pertinent information each time you press Enter. You can set aliases to run longer commands with fewer keystrokes and permanently set environment variables to suit your needs. To make each change occur when you start a shell, you can add this information to your shell configuration files.

Several configuration files support how your shell behaves. Some of the files are executed for every user and every shell. Others are specific to the user who creates the configuration file. Here are the files that are of interest to anyone using the `bash` shell in Linux:

- `/etc/profile` — This file sets up user environment information for every user. It is executed when you first log in. This file provides values for your path, as well as setting environment variables for such things as the location of your mailbox and the size of your history files. Finally, `/etc/profile` gathers shell settings from configuration files in the `/etc/profile.d` directory. Note that you can override all of these settings in other startup files.

- `/etc/bashrc` — By default, this file is executed for every user who runs the `bash` shell, each time a `bash` shell is opened. It sets the default prompt and may add one or more aliases. Values in this file can be overridden by information in each user's `~/.bashrc` file.

- `~/.bash_profile` — This file is used by each user to enter information specific to his or her own use of the shell. It is executed only once, when the user logs in. By default, it sets a few environment variables and executes the user's `.bashrc` file. You can instead create a file named `~/.bash_login` to serve the same purpose as `~/.bash_profile`.

- `~/.bashrc` — This file contains information specific to your `bash` shells. It is read when you log in and each time you open a new `bash` shell. This is the best location to add environment variables and aliases so that your shell picks them up.

- `~/.bash_logout` — This file executes each time you log out (exit the last `bash` shell). By default, it simply clears your screen.

To change the `/etc/profile` or `/etc/bashrc` files, you must be the root user. Users can change the information in the `$HOME/.bash_profile`, `$HOME/.bashrc`, and `$HOME/.bash_logout` files in their own home directories.

The following sections provide ideas about items to add to your shell configuration files. In most cases, you add these values to the `.bashrc` file in your home directory. However, if you administer a system, you may want to set some of these values as defaults for all of your Linux system's users.

Setting your prompt

Your prompt consists of a set of characters that appear each time the shell is ready to accept a command. The PS1 environment variable sets what the prompt contains. If your shell requires additional input, it uses the values of PS2, PS3, and PS4.

When your Fedora system is installed, your prompt is set to include the following information: your user name, your hostname, and the base name of your current working directory. That information is surrounded by brackets and followed by a dollar sign (for regular users) or a pound sign (for the root user). Here's an example of that prompt:

```
[chris@myhost bin]$
```

If you change directories, the bin name would change to the name of the new directory. Likewise, if you were to log in as a different user or to a different host, that information would change.

You can use several special characters (indicated by adding a backslash to a variety of letters) to include different information in your prompt. These can include your terminal number, the date, and the time, as well as other pieces of information. Here are some examples:

- \! — Shows the current command history number. This includes all previous commands stored for your user name.

- \# — Shows the command number of the current command. This includes only the commands for the active shell.

- \$ — Shows the user prompt ($) or root prompt (#), depending on which user you are. Note that \$ is specially set up at login. After login, using \$ will result in a prompt with a dollar sign. The special support for # occurs only in the shell startup files.

- \W — Shows only the current working directory base name. For example, if the current working directory were /var/spool/mail, this value would simply appear as mail.

- \[— Precedes a sequence of nonprinting characters. This could be used to add a terminal control sequence to the prompt for such things as changing colors, adding blink effects, or making characters bold. (Your terminal determines the exact sequences available.)

- \] — Follows a sequence of nonprinting characters.

- \\ — Shows a backslash.

- \d — Displays the day, month, and number of the date. For example: Sat Jan 23.

- \h — Shows the hostname of the computer running the shell.

- \n — Causes a new line to occur.

- \nnn — Shows the character that relates to the octal number replacing *nnn*.

- \s — Displays the current shell name. For the bash shell, the value would be bash.

- \t — Prints the current time in hours, minutes, and seconds (for example, 10:14:39).

- \u — Prints your current user name.

- \w — Displays the full path to the current working directory.

Tip

If you are setting your prompt temporarily by typing at the shell, you should put the value of PS1 **in quotes. For example, you could type** export PS1="[\t \w]\$ " **to see a prompt that looks like this:** [20:26:32 /var/spool]$. ∎

To make a change to your prompt permanent, add the value of PS1 to your .bashrc file in your home directory (assuming that you are using the bash shell). There may already be a PS1 value in that file that you can modify. Refer to the Bash Prompt HOWTO (www.tldp.org/HOWTO/ Bash-Prompt-HOWTO) for information on changing colors, commands, and other features for your bash shell prompt.

Adding environment variables

You may consider adding a few environment variables to your .bashrc file. These can help make working with the shell more efficient and effective:

- TMOUT — Sets how long the shell can be inactive before bash automatically exits. The value is the number of seconds for which the shell has not received input. This can be a nice security feature, in case you leave your desk while you are still logged in to Linux. To avoid getting logged off while you are working, you may want to set the value to something like TMOUT=1800 (to allow 30 minutes of idle time), or simply don't set this variable to disable this feature.

- PATH — As described earlier, the PATH variable sets the directories that are searched for commands you use. If you often use directories of commands that are not in your PATH, you can permanently add them. To do this, add a PATH variable to your .bashrc file. For example, to add a directory called /getstuff/bin, add the following:

  PATH=$PATH:/getstuff/bin ; export PATH

  This example first reads all the current path directories into the new PATH ($PATH), adds the /getstuff/bin directory, and then exports the new PATH.

Caution

Some people add the current directory to their PATH **by adding a directory identified simply as a dot (.), as follows:**

  PATH=.:$PATH ; export PATH

This lets you always run commands in your current directory (which people may be used to if they have used DOS). However, the security risk with this procedure is that you could be in a directory that contains a command that you don't intend to run from that directory. For example, a malicious person could put an ls **command in a directory that, instead of listing the content of your directory, does something devious.**

- *WHATEVER* — You can create your own environment variables to provide shortcuts in your work. Choose any name that is not being used and assign a useful value to it. For example, if you do a lot of work with files in the `/work/time/files/info/memos` directory, you could set the following variable:

```
M=/work/time/files/info/memos ; export M
```

You can make that your current directory by typing `cd $M`. You can run a program called `hotdog` from that directory by typing **$M/hotdog**. You can edit a file called `bun` from there by typing **vi $M/bun**.

Adding aliases

Setting aliases can save you even more typing than setting environment variables. With aliases, you can have a string of characters execute an entire command line. You can add and list aliases with the `alias` command. Here are some examples:

```
alias p='pwd ; ls -CF'
alias rm='rm -i'
```

In the first example, the letter p is assigned to run the command `pwd`, and then to run `ls -CF` to print the current working directory and list its contents in column form. The second example runs the `rm` command with the `-i` option each time you simply type **rm**. (This is an alias that is often set automatically for the root user, so that instead of just removing files, you are prompted for each individual file removal. This prevents you from removing all the files in a directory by mistakenly typing something such as `rm *`.)

While you are in the shell, you can check which aliases are set by typing the `alias` command. If you want to remove an alias, you can type **unalias**. (Remember that if the `alias` is set in a configuration file, it will be set again when you open another shell.)

Working with the Linux File System

The Linux file system is the structure in which all the information on your computer is stored. Files are organized within a hierarchy of directories. Each directory can contain files, as well as other directories.

If you were to map out the files and directories in Linux, it would look like an upside-down tree. At the top is the root directory, which is represented by a single slash (/). Below that is a set of common directories in the Linux system, such as `bin`, `dev`, `home`, `lib`, and `tmp`, to name a few. Each of those directories, as well as directories added to the root, can contain subdirectories.

Figure 4-1 illustrates how the Linux file system is organized as a hierarchy. To illustrate how directories are connected, Figure 4-1 shows a `/home` directory that contains subdirectories for three users: `chris`, `mary`, and `tom`. Within the `chris` directory are subdirectories: `briefs`, `memos`, and `personal`. To refer to a file called `inventory` in the `chris/memos` directory, you could type the full path of /home/chris/memos/inventory. If your current directory were /home/chris/memos, you could refer to the file as simply inventory.

FIGURE 4-1

The Linux file system is organized as a hierarchy of directories.

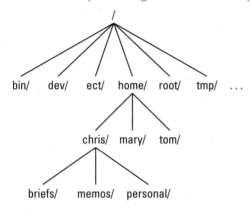

The following Linux directories may be of interest to you:

- /bin — Contains common Linux user commands, such as ls, sort, date, and chmod.
- /boot — Has the bootable Linux kernel and boot loader configuration files (GRUB).
- /dev — Contains files representing access points to devices on your systems. These include terminal devices (tty*), hard disks (hd* or sc*), RAM (ram*), and CD-ROM (cd*). (Applications normally access these devices directly through the device files, but end users rarely access them directly.)
- /etc — Contains administrative configuration files.
- /home — Contains directories assigned to each user with a login account.
- /media — Provides a location for mounting devices, such as remote file systems and removable media. In Fedora, many removable media are mounted automatically in this directory when the media is inserted (CD or DVD) or connected (USB pen drives or cameras).
- /proc — Provides a mechanism for the kernel to send information to processes.
- /root — Represents the root user's home directory.
- /sbin — Contains administrative commands and daemon processes.
- /sys — A /proc-like file system, added with the Linux 2.6 kernel and intended to contain files for getting hardware status and reflecting the system's device tree as it is seen by the kernel. It pulls many of its functions from /proc.
- /tmp — Contains temporary files used by applications.

- /usr — Contains user documentation, games, commands (bin), libraries (lib), and a variety of other user and administrative commands and files.

- /var — Contains directories of data used by various applications. In particular, this is where you would place files that you share as an FTP server (/var/ftp) or a Web server (/var/www). It also contains all system log files (/var/log). In time, FTP, HTTP, and similar services will move to the /srv directory to adhere to the Linux Standards Base (www.freestandards.org/spec).

The file systems in the DOS or Microsoft Windows operating systems differ from the Linux file structure. See the sidebar "Linux File Systems versus Windows-Based File Systems."

Creating files and directories

As a Fedora user, most of the files you save and work with will probably be in your home directory. Here are commands you use to create and use files and directories:

- cd — Change to another directory.

- pwd — Print the name of the current working directory.

- mkdir — Create a directory.

- chmod — Change the permission on a file or directory.

- ls — List the contents of a directory.

Linux File Systems versus Windows-Based File Systems

Although similar in many ways, the Linux file system has some striking differences from file systems used in MS-DOS and Windows operating systems. Here are a few:

- In MS-DOS and Microsoft Windows file systems, drive letters represent different storage devices (for example, A: is a floppy drive and C: is a hard disk). In Linux, all storage devices are fit into the file system hierarchy. Therefore, the fact that all of /usr may be on a separate hard disk or that /mnt/rem1 is a file system from another computer is invisible to the user.

- Slashes, rather than backslashes, are used to separate directory names in Linux. For example, C:\home\chris in an MS system is /home/chris in a Linux system.

- Filenames almost always have suffixes in DOS (such as .txt for text files or .doc for word-processing files). Although at times you can use that convention in Linux, three-character suffixes have no required meaning in Linux. They can be useful for identifying a file type.

- Every file and directory in a Linux system has permissions and ownership associated with it. Security varies among Microsoft systems. Because DOS and MS Windows began as single-user systems, file ownership was not built into those systems when they were designed. Later releases added features such as file and folder attributes to address this problem.

The following procedure steps you through the process of creating directories within your home directory, moving among your directories, and setting appropriate file permissions:

1. Go to your home directory. To do this, simply type **cd**. (For other ways of referring to your home directory, see the "Identifying Directories" sidebar.)

2. To ensure that you are in your home directory, type **pwd**. When I do this, I get the following response (yours will reflect your home directory, of course):

   ```
   $ pwd
   /home/chris
   ```

3. Create a new directory called test in your home directory, as follows:

   ```
   $ mkdir test
   ```

4. Check the permissions of the directory by typing the following:

   ```
   $ ls -ld test
   drwxrwxr-x. 2 chris  chris   1024  Oct 13 12:17 test
   ```

Note

The output of ls, especially the time and date output, is highly dependent on your locale. While this helps make Linux speak your language, it also makes it more difficult to write shell scripts to parse the output of ls. Furthermore, you'll even see differences in the output if your LANG environment variable (which sets the locale) is set to C (the old-fashioned Unix locale for English) or en_US.UTF-8 (the default for English in the U.S.A.). ■

Notice that this listing says that test is a directory (d), the owner is chris, the group is sales, and the file was most recently modified on October 13 at 12:17 p.m. Suppose that you want to prevent everyone else who uses this computer from using or viewing the files in this directory. The permissions for the directory are rwxrwxr-x. I explain what these permissions mean later in this section.

Note

When you add a new user in Fedora, the user is assigned to a group of the same name by default. For example, in the preceding text, the user chris would be assigned to the group chris. This approach to assigning groups is referred to as the *user private group scheme*. For more information on user private groups, refer to Chapter 10. ■

5. For now, type the following:

   ```
   $ chmod 700 test
   ```

   This step changes the permissions of the directory to give you complete access, and everyone else no access at all. (The new permissions should read like rwx------.)

See the "Understanding file permissions" section later in this chapter for more information on permissions.

6. Make the `test` directory your current directory as follows:

```
$ cd test
```

Using metacharacters and operators

To make more efficient use of your shell, the `bash` shell lets you use certain special characters, referred to as metacharacters and operators. A *metacharacter* can help you match one or more files without typing each filename completely. An *operator* lets you direct information from one command or file to another command or file.

Using file-matching metacharacters

To save you some keystrokes and enable you to refer easily to a group of files, the `bash` shell accepts metacharacters. Anytime you need to refer to a file or directory, such as to list it, open it, or remove it, you can use metacharacters to match the files you want. Here are some useful metacharacters for matching filenames:

- * — This matches any number of characters.
- ? — This matches any one character.
- [...] — This matches any one of the characters between the brackets, which can include a dash-separated range of letters or numbers.

Identifying Directories

When you need to identify your home directory on a shell command line, you can use the following:

- $HOME — This environment variable stores your home directory name.
- ~ — The tilde (~) represents your home directory on the command line.

You can also use the tilde to identify someone else's home directory. For example, ~chris would be expanded to the chris home directory (probably /home/chris).

Other special ways of identifying directories in the shell include the following:

- . — A single dot (.) refers to the current directory.
- .. — Two dots (..) refer to a directory directly above the current directory.
- $PWD — This environment variable refers to the current working directory.
- $OLDPWD — This environment variable refers to the previous working directory before you changed to the current one.

To try out some of these file-matching metacharacters, go to an empty directory (such as the test directory described in the previous section) and create some files. Here's an example of how to create some empty files (although the touch command is more commonly used to assign the current date and time to an existing file than to create a new one):

```
$ touch apple banana grape grapefruit watermelon
```

The next few commands show you how to use shell metacharacters to match filenames so they can be used as arguments to the ls command. Using the metacharacters shown in the code that follows, you can match the filenames you just created with the touch command. Type the following commands and see if you get the same responses:

```
$ ls a*
apple
$ ls g*
grape grapefruit
$ ls g*t
grapefruit
$ ls *e*
apple grape grapefruit watermelon
$ ls *n*
banana watermelon
```

The first example matches any file that begins with an a (apple). The next example matches any files that begin with g (grape, grapefruit). Next, files beginning with g and ending in t are matched (grapefruit). Next, any file that contains an e in the name is matched (apple, grape, grapefruit, watermelon). Finally, any file that contains an n is matched (banana, watermelon).

Here are a few examples of pattern matching with the question mark (?):

```
$ ls ????e
apple grape
$ ls g???e*
grape grapefruit
```

The first example matches any five-character file that ends in e (apple, grape). The second matches any file that begins with g and has e as its fifth character (grape, grapefruit).

Here are a few examples of using brackets to do pattern matching:

```
$ ls [abw]*
apple banana watermelon
$ ls [agw]*[ne]
apple grape watermelon
```

In the first example, any file beginning with a, b, or w is matched. In the second, any file that begins with a, g, or w and also ends with either n or e is matched. You can also include ranges within brackets. For example:

```
$ ls [a-g]*
apple banana grape grapefruit
```

Here, any filenames beginning with a letter from a through g are matched.

Using file-redirection metacharacters

Commands receive data from standard input and send it to standard output. Standard input is normally user input from the keyboard, and it is normally displayed on the screen. Using pipes (described earlier), you can direct standard output from one command to the standard input of another. With files, you can use less than (<) and greater than (>) signs to direct data to and from files. Here are the file redirection characters:

- < — Directs the contents of a file as input to the command (because many commands take a filename as an option, the < key is not usually needed)
- > — Directs the output of a command to a file, overwriting any existing file
- >> — Directs the output of a command to a file, adding the output to the end of the existing file

Here are some examples of command lines in which information is directed to and from files:

```
$ mail root < ~/.bashrc
$ man chmod | col -b > /tmp/chmod
$ echo "Finished project on $(date)" >> ~/projects
```

In the first example, the contents of the .bashrc file in the home directory are sent in a mail message to the computer's root user. The second command line formats the chmod man page (using the man command), removes extra back spaces (col -b), and sends the output to the file /tmp/chmod (erasing the previous /tmp/chmod file, if it exists). The final command results in the following text being added to the user's project file:

```
Finished project on Wed Oct 27 13:46:49 PST 2010
```

You could also pipe the output of the previous command to another command. For example, the following command line would send the line just shown in a mail message to the user boss@ example.com:

```
$ echo "Finished project on $(date)"|mail -s 'Done' boss@example.com
```

Understanding file permissions

After you've worked with Linux for a while, you are almost sure to get a Permission denied message. Permissions associated with files and directories in Linux were designed to keep users from accessing other users' private files and to protect important system files.

The nine bits assigned to each file for permissions define the access that you and others have to your file. Permission bits appear as rwxrwxrwx. The first three bits apply to the owner's permission, the next three apply to the group assigned to the file, and the last three apply to all others. The r stands for read, the w stands for write, and the x stands for execute permissions. If a dash appears instead of the letter, it means that permission is turned off for that associated read, write, or execute.

You can see the permission for any file or directory by typing the ls -ld command. The named file or directory appears as those shown in the following example:

```
$ ls -ld ch3 test
-rw-rw-r--.  1 chris   sales     4983  Dec 12 22:13 ch3
drwxr-xr-x.  2 chris   sales     1024  Dec 12 13:47 test
```

The first line shows a file (ch3) that has read and write permission for the owner and the group. All other users have read permission, which means they can view the file but cannot change its contents (although a user may be allowed to remove the file, as the permission to remove a file is based on directory permissions). The second line shows a directory (indicated by the letter d before the permission bits). The owner has read, write, and execute permissions, while the group and other users have only read and execute permissions, with a dash indicating write permission is turned off. As a result, only the owner can add, change, or delete files in that directory. Any other user, however, can only read the contents, change to that directory, and list the contents of the directory. (Note that by using the -d option, the test directory entry is listed without listing its contents.)

If you own a file, you can change the permissions on it as you please. You can do this with the chmod command. For each of the three sets of permission on a file (read, write, and execute), r is assigned to the number 4, w to 2, and x to 1. Therefore, to make permissions wide open for yourself as owner, you would set the first number to 7 (4 plus 2 plus 1). The same would be true for group and other permissions. Any combination of permissions can result — from 0 (no permission) through 7 (full permission).

Here are some examples of how to change permissions on a file and what the resulting permissions would be:

```
chmod 777 files  →   rwxrwxrwx.
chmod 755 files  →   rwxr-xr-x.
chmod 644 files  →   rw-r--r-.
chmod 000 files  →   ---------.
```

You can also turn file permissions on and off using plus (+) and minus (-) signs, respectively. This can be done for the owner user (u), owner group (g), others (o), and all users (a). For example, the following command removes the write permission for all users:

```
chmod a-w files
```

This example set changes the permissions for all users, including the owner of the file (a), and removes the write permission (-w). To add write permission instead, use a plus (+w).

The following examples show how the permission-changing commands work. To best demonstrate the effects of removing permissions, all these items assume you are starting fresh with a file that has all permissions open (rwxrwxrwx). Here are some chmod examples and resulting permissions after using a minus sign:

```
chmod a-w files   →   r-xr-xr-x

chmod go-rwx files   →   rwx------
```

Likewise, here are some examples, starting with all permissions closed (---------), where the plus sign is used with chmod to turn permissions on:

```
chmod u+rw files   →   rw-------
chmod a+x files   →   --x--x--x
chmod ug+rx files   →   r-xr-x---
```

When you try to create a file, by default it is given the permission rw-rw-r--. A directory is given the permission rwxrwxr-x. These default values are determined by the value of umask. Type **umask** to see what your umask value is. For example:

```
$ umask
0002
```

The umask value represents the permissions that are *not* given on a new file, with an extra leading digit relating to special modes. The umask value masks the permissions value of 666 for a file and 777 for a directory. The umask value of 002 (ignoring the special leading digit) results in permission for a directory of 775 (rwxrwxr-x). That same umask results in a file permission of 664 (rw-rw-r--). (Execute permissions are off by default for regular files.) The default umask value on Fedora is 0002, with the leading digit indicating no special modes for the sticky bit as well as set user and group ID flags.

Tip

Using the -R option of chmod, you can change the permissions for all files and directories within a directory structure at once. For example, if you want to open permissions completely to all files and directories in the /tmp/test directory, you can type the following:

```
$ chmod -R 777 /tmp/test
```

This command line runs chmod recursively (-R) for the /tmp/test directory, as well as any files or directories that exist below that point in the file system (for example, /tmp/test/hat, /tmp/test/hat/caps, and so on). All would be set to 777 (full read/write/execute permissions). ■

Moving, copying, and deleting files

Commands for moving, copying, and deleting files are fairly straightforward. To change the location of a file, use the mv command. To copy a file from one location to another, use the cp command. To remove a file, use the rm command. Here are some examples:

```
$ mv abc def
```

```
$ mv abc ~
$ cp abc def
$ cp abc ~
$ rm abc
$ rm *
```

Of the two move (mv) commands, the first moves the file abc to the file def in the same directory (essentially renaming it), whereas the second moves the file abc to your home directory (~). The first copy command (cp) copies abc to the file def, whereas the second copies abc to your home directory (~). The first remove command (rm) deletes the abc file; the second removes all the files in the current directory (except those that start with a dot).

Caution

Be sure to use the * and other wildcard characters wisely because you might match (and therefore remove) files you don't intend to match. There is no undelete command on Linux. ∎

For the root user, the mv, cp, and rm commands are aliased to each be run with the -i option. This causes a prompt to appear, asking you to confirm each copy and removal, one file at a time. For file moves, the -i option will prompt you if the move would overwrite a file, but you may still unintentionally move a file, so be careful. This is done to prevent the root user from messing up a large group of files by mistake. To temporarily get around an alias, type the full path to the command (for example, **/bin/rm -rf /tmp/junk/***).

Using Text Editors

Because many Linux commands tend to require long sets of command-line parameters, you may find yourself writing shell scripts — files of shell commands that you can run — or editing your commands inside text editors. Text editors make it much easier to edit commands than the bash or other shell command-line editing capabilities.

Cross-Reference

See Chapter 11 for more on shell scripts. ∎

It's almost impossible to use Linux for any period of time without needing to use a text editor. If you are using a GUI, you can run gedit, which is fairly intuitive for editing text. Most Linux shell users will use either the vi or emacs commands to edit text files. The advantage of vi or emacs over a graphical editor is that you can use it from any shell, a character terminal, or a character-based connection over a network (using telnet or ssh, for example). No GUI is required.

Because of its near-universal availability, vi has been the default text editor used on Linux, Unix, and many other systems over the decades. If you have access only to a terminal, it is a good idea to learn some vi commands.

Using the vi text editor

In modern versions of Linux, vi is provided by vim, the (Vi Improved) text editor that provides the features of the far older vi editor along with a host of newer features such as color highlighting of command and program syntax. In Linux, when you type in the vim or vi commands, you get vim. Vim is provided by the vim-minimal and vim-enhanced packages in Fedora.

Tip

The root user will see plain old vi **by default, instead of the enhanced** vim. **This is partly a result of security issues and partly an attempt to create a comfort zone for system administrators. Because** vim **is highly customizable and can run many tasks for you in the background, a security concern is that a small** vim **customization could, when run by the root user, introduce some form of security problem. In addition, root users may not be looking for** vim **customization files when checking for security holes. Also, as the root user, you should use simple tools that clearly show everything that is going on, especially when editing system configuration files. ■**

Anywhere in this book that I suggest you manually edit a configuration file, you can use vi to do that editing (from any shell). (If vi doesn't suit you, try some of the other text editors mentioned in this section for other options.)

The vi editor is difficult to learn at first; but when you know it, you will be able to edit and move around quickly and efficiently within files. Your fingers never have to leave the keyboard to pick up a mouse or press a function key. The following sections should show you enough to find your way around vi.

Starting with vi

Most often, you start vi to open a particular file. For example, to open a file called /tmp/test, type the following command:

```
$ vi /tmp/test
```

If this is a new file, you should see something similar to the following:

```
~
~
~
~
~
"/tmp/test" [New File]
```

A highlighted rectangle at the top represents where your cursor is. The bottom line keeps you informed about what is going on with your editing (here you just opened a new file). In between, there are tildes (~) as filler because there is no text in the file yet. Here's the intimidating part: There are no hints, menus, or icons to tell you what to do. On top of that, you can't just start typing. If you do, the computer is likely to beep at you. (And some people complain that Linux isn't friendly.)

Tip

If you use ssh to log in to other Linux computers on your network, you can use any editor to edit files. A GUI-based editor will pop up on your screen. With the -X option, ssh turns on X11 forwarding, which can make it more convenient to access remote systems. However, this bypasses file permissions on the remote host, so use this with care. When no GUI is available, you need a text editor that runs in the shell, such as vi, jed, or joe. ■

The first things you need to know are the different operating modes. The vi editor operates in either command mode or input mode. When you start vi, you are in command mode. Before you can add or change text in the file, you have to type a command to tell vi what you want to do. A command consists of one or two letters and an optional number. To get into input mode, you need to type an input command. To start out, type either of the following input commands:

- a — Add. After you type a, you can input text that starts to the right of the cursor.
- i — Insert. After you type i, you can input text that starts to the left of the cursor.

Type a few words and press Enter. Repeat that a few times until you have a few lines of text. When you are done typing, press Esc. You are now back in command mode. Now that you have a file with some text in it, try moving around in your text with the following keys or letters.

Tip

Remember the Esc key! It always places you back into command mode. ■

- **Arrow keys** — Use the arrow keys to move up, down, left, or right in the file one character at a time. To move left and right you can also use Backspace and the spacebar, respectively. If you prefer to keep your fingers on the keyboard, use h (left), l (right), j (down), or k (up) to move the cursor.
- **w** — Moves the cursor to the beginning of the next word
- **b** — Moves the cursor to the beginning of the previous word
- **0 (zero)** or **^** — Moves the cursor to the beginning of the current line
- **$** — Moves the cursor to the end of the current line
- **H** — Moves the cursor to the upper-left corner of the screen (first line on the screen)
- **M** — Moves the cursor to the first character of the middle line on the screen
- **L** — Moves the cursor to the lower-left corner of the screen (last line on the screen)

Now that you know how to input text and move around, the only other editing you need to know is how to delete text. Here are a few vi commands for deleting text:

- **x** — Deletes the character under the cursor
- **X** — Deletes the character directly before the cursor
- **dw** — Deletes from the current character to the end of the current word
- **d$** — Deletes from the current character to the end of the current line
- **d0** — Deletes from the previous character to the beginning of the current line

If you feel pretty good about creating text and moving around the file, you may want to wrap things up. Use the following keystrokes for saving and quitting the file:

- **ZZ** — Save the current changes to the file and exit from vi.
- **:w** — Save the current file but continue editing.
- **:wq** — Same as ZZ.
- **:q** — Quit the current file. This works only if you don't have any unsaved changes.
- **:q!** — Quit the current file and *don't* save the changes you just made to the file.

Tip

If you've really trashed a file by mistake, the :q! command is the best way to exit and abandon your changes. The file reverts to the most recently saved version. Therefore, if you just did a :w, you are stuck with the changes up to that point. If you just want to undo a few bad edits, press u to back out of changes. ∎

You have now learned a few vi editing commands. More commands are described in the following sections. First, however, are a few tips to smooth out your first trials with vi:

- **Esc** — Remember that Esc gets you back to command mode. (I've watched people press every key on the keyboard trying to get out of a file.) Esc followed by ZZ gets you out of input mode, saves the file, and exits.
- **u** — Press u to undo the previous change you made. Continue to press u to undo the change before that, and the one before that. (With the traditional vi editor, u undoes a single command and r returns what you just undid.) You can undo as many times as allowed by the undo level setting. Use the :set ul command in vi to see the undo level, and :set ul=*number* to set the undo level to the given number. The default is 1,000 levels.
- **Ctrl+r** — If you decide you didn't want to undo the previous edit, use Ctrl+r for redo. Essentially, this command undoes your undo.
- **Caps Lock** — Beware of pressing Caps Lock by mistake. Everything you type in vi has a different meaning when the letters are capitalized. You don't get a warning that you are typing capitals — things just start acting weirdly.
- **:! command** — You can run a shell command while you are in vi using :! followed by a command name. For example, type **:!date** to see the current date and time, type **:!pwd** to see what your current directory is, or type **:!jobs** to see if you have any jobs running in the background. When the command completes, press Enter and you are back to editing the file. You could even do that with a shell (:!bash) to run a few commands from the shell, and then type **exit** to return to vi. (I recommend doing a save before escaping to the shell, just in case you forget to go back to vi.)
- **-- INSERT --** — When you are in input mode, the word INSERT appears at the bottom of the screen. Other messages also appear at the line at the bottom of the screen.
- **Ctrl+g** — If you forget what you are editing, pressing these keys displays the name of the file you are editing and the current line that you are on. It also displays the total

number of lines in the file, the percentage of how far you are through the file, and the column number the cursor is on. This just helps you get your bearings after you've stopped for a cup of coffee at 3:00 a.m.

Moving around the file

Besides the few movement commands described earlier, there are other ways of moving around a vi file. To try these out, open a large file that you can't do much damage to. (Try copying /var/log/messages to /tmp and opening it in vi.) Here are some movement commands you can use:

- **Ctrl+f** — Pages ahead, one page at a time.
- **Ctrl+b** — Pages back, one page at a time.
- **Ctrl+d** — Pages ahead, one-half page at a time.
- **Ctrl+u** — Pages back, one-half page at a time.
- **G** — Goes to the last line of the file.
- **gg** or **1G** — Goes to the first line of the file. (Use any number with a G or gg to go to that line in the file.)

Searching for text

To search for the next occurrence of text in the file, use either the slash (/) or the question mark (?) character. Within the search, you can also use metacharacters. Here are some examples:

- **/hello** — Searches forward for the word hello.
- **?goodbye** — Searches backward for the word goodbye.
- **/The.*foot** — Searches forward for a line that has the word The in it and, after that at some point, the word foot.
- **?[pP]rint** — Searches backward for either print or Print. Remember that case matters in Linux, so using brackets enables a search for words with either case.

The vi editor was originally based on the ex editor, which did not let you work in full-screen mode. However, you could run commands that enabled you to find and change text on one or more lines at a time. When you type a colon and the cursor goes to the bottom of the screen, you are essentially in ex mode. Following are some examples of those ex commands for searching for and changing text. (These examples search the words Local and Remote, but you can use any appropriate words.)

- **:g/Local** — Searches for the word Local and prints every line with an occurrence of that word from the file. (If there is more than a screen-full, the output is piped to the more command.)
- **:g/Local/s//Remote** — Substitutes the first occurrence of the word Local on every line of the file with the word Remote.

- `:g/Local/s//Remote/g` — Substitutes every occurrence of the word `Local` with the word `Remote` in the entire file.

- `:g/Local/s//Remote/gp` — Substitutes every occurrence of the word `Local` with the word `Remote` in the entire file, and then prints each line so that you can see the changes (piping it through `more` if output fills more than one page). Another way to globally search and replace without printing every line that changes is to type **:%s/ Local/Remote/g**.

Using numbers with commands

You can precede most `vi` commands with numbers to have the command repeated that number of times. This is a handy way to deal with several lines, words, or characters at a time. Here are some examples:

- **3dw** — Deletes the next three words
- **5cl** — Changes the next five letters (that is, removes the letters and enters input mode)
- **12j** — Moves down 12 lines

Putting a number in front of most commands just repeats those commands. At this point, you should be fairly proficient at using the `vi` command. If you would like further instruction, try the VIM Tutor by running the `vimtutor` command.

Note

When you invoke `vi` on Fedora, you're actually invoking the `vim` text editor, which runs in `vi` compatibility mode. Those who do a lot of programming might prefer `vim`, because it shows different levels of code in different colors. `vim` has other useful features, such as the ability to open a document with the cursor at the same place it was located when you last exited that file. ■

Most experienced Linux and Unix users traditionally have used `vi` or `vi`'s main alternative, `emacs`, as their text editor. Many extensions are available with `emacs` to handle editing of many different file types. You'll find traces of `emacs` in the shell command-line editing commands.

Using graphical text editors and notepads

The old terminal-oriented text editors such as `vi` or `emacs` may not be your cup of tea. In addition to these old stalwarts, Linux offers a host of text editors that run within a graphical environment, including the following:

- **GNOME Text Editor (gedit)** — From the GNOME desktop, select Applications ➪ Accessories ➪ gedit Text Editor. With the gedit window that opens, you can type, cut, and paste, and use arrow keys to move around. Besides creating text documents, gedit has spell check and search tools. Highlight mode (select View ➪ Highlight Mode) causes different parts of the text you are writing as computer code (such as C or Java) or markup (such as HTML or XML) to be displayed in different colors.

- **KDE Text Editor (kwrite)** — From the KDE desktop, the KWrite application is the default text editor. KWrite includes many of the same text-editing features as gedit, but also has bookmark features and support for multiple language input.

- **Kate Text Editor (kate)** — Also from the KDE desktop, this editor offers enhanced features for programming and editing shell scripts, in addition to showing multiple views of your files.

- **Sticky Notes (gnote)** — Different note-taking applications include KNotes (for KDE) and Gnote (for GNOME). Gnote puts a notepad icon in your top panel, from which you can create and manage notes. (Launch Gnote from the Applications ⇨ Accessories menu if you do not see an icon on the top panel.) Create a new note that includes URLs (click to open in a browser) and links to other notes. Spelling is checked as you type. Organize notes in notebooks or do keyword searches to find the note you want. Gnote is similar to another GNOME note program called Tomboy.

Note
The `emacs` **editor, while originally intended only for the terminal, is also available in a number of graphical incarnations, including** `emacs` **(running under the X Window System on your desktop) and** `xemacs`. ■

Working with Virtual Terminals

After getting Linux to provide a high-resolution graphical display on your new widescreen monitor, you can kick Linux back into a text-only mode using virtual terminals. Enter Ctrl+Alt+F2 to switch to a virtual terminal. You'll see your whole display switch back into text mode and get a login prompt.

By default, Ctrl+Alt+F1 switches to the first virtual terminal, which is the terminal used to boot Linux. Ctrl+Alt+F7 switches back to the terminal used to run the X Window System — your graphical display. In between, with F2–F6, you get virtual terminals. These are especially useful if your graphical display appears to be hung.

If you find the X Window System hung, switch to another virtual terminal. Log in and run the following command:

```
$ ps -e | grep X
```

You should see a response with the command `Xorg`, such as the following:

```
2613 tty7      00:00:01 Xorg
```

The `tty7` tells you that X is running on the virtual terminal associated with Ctrl+Alt+F7.

Next, send a signal to this program using the program's process ID (2613 in this case) with the `kill` command.

Caution

Don't run this command unless you really need it. This forces all your desktop programs to stop, and any work you have not saved will likely be lost. ■

For example:

```
# kill -HUP 2613
```

You need to log in as the root user to run this command on the Xorg process.

This command causes the X server to restart. You should see the screen change, and a spinning arrow cursor will be displayed until the desktop restarts. You then need to log in again. In addition, the restarting process may switch to another virtual terminal, such as tty8 (accessible via Ctrl+Alt+F8).

You can also use Ctrl+Alt+Backspace to stop the X server; but if X is hung, this key sequence may not work.

Switching terminals with the screen program

A handy program called screen creates a form of text-based windowing on your terminal. You can use screen to get more than one virtual terminal inside a plain old Linux shell terminal.

Tip

Screen **is especially handy when you log onto remote systems using commands such as** ssh. **You can use** screen **to help you run multiple commands at the same time on the remote system, or to check on the progress of long-running remote commands.** ■

To start screen, use the screen command:

```
$ screen
```

You might miss the slight flash on the terminal as screen starts up. If you're running inside a shell window, you'll see that screen adds a notice to the title bar that you are on the first virtual screen: [screen 0: bash]. (You will notice that many programs in the Unix and Linux world start counting with zero.)

To control the virtual screens, you need to issue screen commands that start with Ctrl+a. To create another virtual terminal, type Ctrl+a, release the keys, and type **c**. You will then see [screen 1: bash] in the terminal window's title bar.

To switch to another virtual screen, press Ctrl+a and then the number of the other virtual screen, such as Ctrl+a, then 0, to switch back to the first virtual screen.

Each virtual screen offers a Linux shell into which you can enter commands. Press Ctrl+a, then press " to list the available virtual screens. (Note that this is Ctrl+a followed by Shift+" on U.S. keyboards.)

Press Ctrl+a, then k to kill the current virtual screen; and, if you need to enter the Ctrl+a into the running program, press Ctrl+a, then a, which tells screen to pass a Ctrl+a to the terminal, rather than interpret Ctrl+a as starting a screen command. For help, type Ctrl+a, then ?.

Press Ctrl+a, then \ to quit screen (and all the virtual screens it created), which returns you to the original shell.

Summary

Working from a shell command-line interpreter within Linux may not be as simple as using a GUI, but it offers many powerful and flexible features. This chapter described how to log in to Fedora and use shell commands. Features for running commands include recalling commands from a history list, completing commands, and joining commands.

You learned how shell environment variables can be used to store and recall important pieces of information and how to modify shell configuration files to tailor the shell to suit your needs. Finally, this chapter described how to use the Linux file system to create files and directories, use permissions, and work with files (moving, copying, and removing them), and how to edit text files from the shell using the vi command.

Part II

Using Fedora

Accessing and Running Applications

F edora comes with thousands of software applications, covering every major category of desktop, server, and programming software. By accessing some third-party, Fedora-specific software repositories on the Internet, you have access to many more software packages. Often, getting a new software package downloaded and installed is as simple as running a single yum command. As always, you should apply due diligence when choosing what to download. See the section "Downloading and installing applications with yum" for more on this.

Some of the same tools you use to get and install software packages in Fedora (such as yum and rpm commands) can also be used to manage your installed software and get updates or security patches when they become available. Options in those tools enable you to query which packages you installed, as well as list and verify the contents of those packages. Likewise, GUI tools such as PackageKit can be used to automatically grab and install new and updated packages as they become available.

Once an application is installed, launching it can be as easy as it is in any friendly desktop system: by clicking a few menus on the desktop. There are also some neat ways to launch applications from another computer so that you can work with them (securely) from your own desktop, as covered in the section "Running remote X applications" later in this chapter.

In cases for which you must have a specific application that isn't available for Linux (such as Microsoft Office or a particular media player), several emulators and compatibility software facilities enable you to run software made for Windows, DOS, or other operating systems. You can also build and install your own software packages for Fedora, starting with software available as source RPMs or packaged in a variety of archive formats, such as tarballs.

This chapter covers the tools and procedures for getting, installing, and managing software applications in Fedora.

IN THIS CHAPTER

Getting and installing software packages

Getting Fedora software updates

Managing RPM packages

Running desktop applications

Running Remote X applications

Using emulators to run applications from other operating systems

Running DOS applications

Running Windows applications with WINE

Getting and Installing Software Packages

Applications that are packaged specifically to run on Fedora systems are usually stored in RPM format. RPM is short for "RPM package manager." The rpm command provides low-level control over packages installed on your system. On top of rpm resides the yum command, short for the "Yellow Dog Updater, Modified," and named after the Yellow Dog Linux distribution. Both commands are shown in the following sections.

Except for a few components used to start the system, most of the Fedora operating system itself is packaged in RPM format. When you look for software to install in Fedora, you should start in the following locations:

- **Install DVD** — Any package you didn't install during the initial installation process can be installed later from the DVD that comes with this book or from third-party repositories. To do that, you can use the rpm command. After initial installation, however, provided you have an Internet connection, using online repositories to add packages using the yum utility or the PackageKit window is often the better method. That's because those tools can not only get and install the packages you request, but also find and get additional packages that can't fit on a single DVD, updated versions of the packages (if available), as well as any dependent packages required to install the packages you want.

- **Fedora repository** — When you install Fedora, your yum facility is automatically configured to use the online Fedora repository. Because there are multiple instances of the repository, yum points to mirror lists from the Fedora project (http://mirrors .fedoraproject.org) to choose a Fedora repository that is near you.

- **Third-party Fedora repositories** — Because of licensing issues and patent questions, some software that is popular for use with Fedora is not included in Fedora itself. For example, software for playing commercial DVD movies and MP3 audio files is not included in Fedora.

  In recent Fedora releases, several popular third-party repositories (Dribble, Freshrpms, and Livna) have joined to form the RPM Fusion Project (http://rpmfusion.org), to help eliminate inconsistencies among those popular repositories. Enable that repository first to check for packages you want that are not in Fedora. Another repository with a good reputation is the http://ATRPMs.net site.

  You can download packages directly from these sites or (preferably) set up yum so you can download and install packages more easily.

Caution

Security should be a concern when you access any repository. Yum does support https access to repositories and package signature verification. In addition, you should read up on the security concerns outlined at www .cs.arizona.edu/stork/packagemanagersecurity/attacks-on-package-managers.html. ■

- **Software project sites** — Often, individual software projects offer their own set of RPM packages for their own projects. This is particularly useful for projects under continuous development (such as the WINE project). If the project doesn't offer RPMs, it will typically offer code in what is called a *tarball*. The tarball may include binary code or, more often, source code you can build for your environment. (I describe how to install from source code tarballs later in this chapter.)

If you know what software package you want and it is available from more than one location, choose one from an official Fedora repository. A repository outside of Fedora that's committed to being compatible with the main Fedora repository is your next best choice because that will help take care of any dependency problems. (RPMFusion.org is a particularly good choice.)

Most Fedora repositories are light on descriptions of the packages they offer. The following list summarizes some other websites that you can browse to find detailed information about software that runs in Linux. Then you can search Fedora repositories (described later in this chapter) for Fedora-specific versions of those packages.

- **Freshmeat** (http://freshmeat.net) — This site maintains a massive index of Linux software. You can do keyword searches for software projects or browse for software by category.

- **SourceForge** (http://sourceforge.net) — This site hosts thousands of open-source software projects. You can download software and documentation from those projects through the SourceForge site.

- **Rpmfind** (www.rpmfind.net) — This site provides a way to search for open-source software that is packaged in the RPM Package Management (RPM) format across a variety of repositories. You can do a keyword search from this website.

- **Google** (www.google.com) — You can use Google (or another general-purpose search engine) to find information about the project you are interested in.

Often, you can't just download a single software package to get the software in that package to work. Many packages depend on other packages. For example, software packages for playing audio and video typically rely on other software packages for decoding different kinds of content. To handle software dependency issues (and because it includes many other valuable features), Fedora has based its packaging tools on the yum program.

Downloading and installing applications with yum

The yum command enables you to install and update selected software packages in RPM format from software repositories on the Web. Once you know the software package that you want, yum is probably the best way to download and install that package. Yum also includes features for listing and managing RPMs after they are installed.

Yum is the foundation for software updates in Fedora. Besides the yum command, the PackageKit facility and even the Fedora installer itself (anaconda) now use yum as the underlying mechanism for getting and updating software in Fedora.

The yum package is included on the Fedora DVD that comes with this book. To use yum to install RPM software packages, follow these basic steps:

1. Determine the software package you want. Yum is delivered with the current Fedora repository already configured. Use yum or PackageKit search tools (described later) to find packages you want; or add more repositories for yum to search to your /etc/ yum.conf file or /etc/yum.repos.d/ directory (also described later). Many software repositories offer RPM packages that automatically configure entries in the yum.repos.d directory to point to those repositories.

2. Configure yum. You have the option to configure the /etc/yum.conf file to set options that relate to how you use your yum repositories, as described in the next section. Then add any repositories, in addition to the Fedora repository, from which you want to get packages.

3. Run yum. The yum command can be used to download and install any package from the yum repository, including any packages on which the one you want depends.

Caution

The Fedora Project has gone to great lengths to ensure that software it provides is of good quality and unimpaired by legitimate patent claims. When you download packages that are not official packages for Fedora, you are on your own to check the quality and legality of that software. Some users refuse to configure yum to access non-official repositories. In addition, the yum command informs you from which repository it intends to download packages and lets you choose whether to go forward with downloading and installing. ■

In addition to downloading and installing new software packages, yum can also be used to check for available updates and to list various kinds of information about available packages.

Configuring yum (/etc/yum.conf)

The /etc/yum.conf file is already preconfigured to include options that affect how you download and use RPM packages with yum. All necessary, basic repository listings are contained in files in the /etc/yum.repos.d directory. Here is what the yum.conf file contains:

```
[main]
cachedir=/var/cache/yum/$basearch/$releasever
keepcache=0
debuglevel=2
logfile=/var/log/yum.log
exactarch=1
obsoletes=1
gpgcheck=1
plugins=1
installonly_limit=3
color=never

# PUT REPOS HERE OR IN separate file.repo files
# in /etc/yum.repos.d
```

The cachedir directory (/var/cache/yum/$basearch/$releasever) is where the RPM files are downloaded to by yum when you ask to install or upgrade packages. The $basearch variable is replaced by your system's computer architecture, and $releasever is replaced by the version number of your Fedora system.

The keepcache=0 option causes all downloaded packages and headers to be erased after they are installed. If you select to save the RPM files (which some people do if they want to share packages with multiple machines, without multiple downloads), you need to set keepcache=1 and ensure that the directory has enough disk space to handle it. During a testing cycle, I ended up with about 1GB of RPMs in my /var/cache/yum file system (of course, they can be deleted after they are installed).

Note
You can clean out a lot of the data cached by yum with the command yum clean all. ∎

Messages related to yum processing are sent to /var/log/yum.log by default, using a debug level of 2 (0 to 10 is legal, with 2 producing minimal success or failure messages). The exactarch setting of 1 indicates that you must match the name and release architecture exactly for yum to choose a given package instead of allowing yum to select fallback packages from similar architectures.

The obsoletes option lets yum determine obsolete packages during updates. The gpgcheck indicates whether or not a check of the package's GPG key is done (1 indicates the check is done). The value of metadata_expire determines when the metadata you have from a repository expires, after which Fedora will check to determine whether there is new metadata to download on the next invocation of yum. The default of metadata_expire=1.5h causes metadata to expire 1.5 hours after it is received. If you set this value, the number you use can be followed by an m (minutes), h (hours), or d (days). With no added letter, the number you enter is read as seconds. If you do not add this setting to the yum.conf file, then yum will use the default value.

Some packages can be installed but should not be updated. These packages include kernel, kernel-PAE and others, as set by the default installonlypkgs value in yum. Because kernel packages are stored separately, you can keep multiple kernel packages installed on your system. By default, the installonly_limit value of 3 in /etc/yum.conf keeps the latest three installonlypkgs on your system, but will delete older packages of the same name as new kernel packages are added.

Here are some tips relating to setting up yum.conf:

- **Getting metadata** — The metadata that describes the contents of a yum repository is downloaded to your computer when you run the yum command. If you run the command again after the metadata expires (1.5 hours by default, as described earlier), you will have to wait again while yum checks whether new metadata is available to download before yum proceeds. If available, yum downloads the new metadata.

  If yum is configured to access several repositories, it can take a long time to repeatedly check and update metadata. To get around this problem, you can extend the metadata_expire value or run yum with a -C on the command line (to use the exist-ing metadata). The downside is that if the repository data has changed, you might not be getting the latest packages.

- **Excluding repositories** — Excluding repositories on the yum command line is another way to save time by preventing unneeded metadata from being downloaded. For exam-ple, if you know a package you want is in Fedora, disable the free rpmfusion repository by adding --disablerepo=rpmfusion-free or -disablerepo=rpmfusion-* to the yum command line.

- **Enabling plugins** — Fedora comes with the plugins feature enabled. This causes plu-gins in the /usr/lib/yum-plugins directory to be enabled. When you start out, you may have only a few plugins.

For more information about the yum.conf file, type **man yum.conf** from a shell.

Adding yum repositories (/etc/yum.repos.d/)

When you use the yum command to request to install a software package, it checks repositories listed in the /etc/yum.conf file and in files in the /etc/yum.repos.d directory. By default, you begin with repository listings from the following:

- **Fedora (fedora.repo)** — This includes the same packages that are on the DVD included with this book. Using yum, you can install any of those packages, or updates to them, from the repositories. There are thousands of software packages in this repository.

- **Fedora updates (fedora-updates.repo)** — As updates become available from Fedora, you can automatically access those updates from mirror sites listed in fedora-updates. repo.

The following is a list of other repositories you might consider adding to your own /etc/yum .repos.d/ files. Several of these repositories have made it easy for you by offering an RPM that adds the GPG encryption key (used to verify the package's contents) and yum.repos.d file needed to access their repositories.

Keep in mind that these repositories change over time, as new ones are added, some are neglected, and others are consolidated. The locations of repository directories and GPG keys can change without notice.

Note

I recommend adding only repositories you need. Adding unnecessary repositories can slow down yum's per-formance. You might also consider setting enabled=0 in their respective ./etc/yum.repos.d/*.repo files to disable the repository from general usage. Then, invoke yum -enablerepo=reponame only dur-ing those instances you want to install or update from that particular repository. The -enablerepo option enables the repository just for the given command, enabling you to disable most repositories and only turn them on when needed. ∎

- **RPM Fusion** (`http://rpmfusion.org`) — This site has a good selection of audio and video players that are outside of the mainstream Fedora repositories, as well as a host of packages provided by merging the Dribble, Freshrpms, and Livna repositories.

- **RPMrepo.org** (`http://rpmrepo.org`) — This site contains a merger of separate repositories that offer Fedora RPM packages including `http://RPMforge.net`, `http://dag.wieers.com`, `http://freshrpms.net`, and `http://dries.ulyssis.org`.

- **Livna.org** (`http://rpm.livna.org`) — Most of the software previously hosted by the Livna.org repository has been moved to the RPM Fusion repository. However, the libdvdcss package (needed to play commercial DVD movies) is still hosted by Livna.org. If you want that package, you can enable this repository and install the package as follows:

```
# rpm -Uhv http://rpm.livna.org/livna-release.rpm
# yum install libdvdcss
```

- **Dag** (`http://dag.wieers.com/packages`) — This site contains more than 45,000 RPMs from more than 2,400 different projects. Although packages from this repository are now posted to RPMrepo.org, packages are still available from this site for older versions of Fedora.

- **ATRPMs** (`http://atrpms.net/dist/f12`) — This site has RPMs containing many drivers for video cards, wireless cards, and other hardware not included with Fedora. If you want to try out a personal video recorder, this site also has RPMs for the MythTV project. By installing the atrpms-repo RPM, `yum` is configured to access the ATRPMs.net repository. Look for the Fedora 14 atrpms-repo RPM at this URL: `http://atrpms.net/dist/f14`

Running yum to download and install RPMs

With the repositories identified, downloading and installing an RPM you want is as simple as running `yum` with the `install` option to request the RPM. With an active connection to the Internet, open a terminal window as root user.

The first thing `yum` does is download metadata and headers for all packages you might want from each repository. Then, after presenting you with the list of dependencies it thinks you need, it asks if you want to install the necessary packages. Here is an example of using the `yum` command to download the `mythtv` media player:

```
# yum install mythtv
Setting up Install Process
Parsing package install arguments
fedora        100% |============| 2.1 kB     00:00
atrpms        100% |============| 951  B     00:00
    .
    .
    .
```

```
Transaction Summary
================================================
Install    20  Package(s)
Update      0  Package(s)
Remove    113  Package(s)
Total download size: 17M
Is this ok [y/N]: y
Downloading Packages
   .
   .
   .
```

As you can see from this example, yum checked two different software repositories, Fedora and atrpms packages, for the current Fedora release. After listing the dependencies, yum asks if it is okay to install them. Type **y** and the package and all its dependencies will be installed. Note that the mythtv package comes from the atrpms site. You need to add that repository.

Some packages need to install packages that match the kernel you are running, so installing such a package might also bring an updated kernel package with it.

Using yum to install packages locally

If you want to install RPM packages with yum that are available from your local system (by inserting the Fedora DVD or copying an RPM to a local directory), you can use the localinstall option to yum. For example, if you were to insert the Fedora DVD that comes with this book (and it was mounted on /media/disk), you could type the following to install the joe package:

```
# yum localinstall /media/disk/Fedora/Packages/joe-*
   .
   .
   .

Examining joe-3.7-5.fc14.i686.rpm
Marking joe-3.7-5.fc14.i686.rpm to be installed
   .
   .
   .

Dependencies Resolved
=================================================================================
 Package Arch  Version       Repository        Size
=================================================================================
Installing:
 joe    i386  3.7-5-fc14 /media/disk/Fedora/Packages/joe-3.7-5.fc14.i686  1.1 M

Transaction Summary
=================================================================================
Install    1 Package(s)
Update     0 Package(s)
Remove     0 Package(s)

Total download size: 946 k
Is this ok [y/N]: y
```

Note

Using an asterisk on the command line, as shown in the preceding example, may include more packages than you intend. It is best to check the list of packages `yum` intends to install first, and install only the packages you want to install. ■

A good reason for using `yum localinstall` instead of the `rpm` command to install RPM packages is that `yum` will check whether the package you are installing is dependent on any other packages being installed. If `yum` finds that it needs other packages, it will search any `yum` repositories you have configured (at least the main Fedora repository) to download and install what you need.

In this example, `yum` found that joe didn't require installing any additional packages. Therefore, typing **y** at the prompt caused only the one package to be installed.

Using yum for listing packages

Besides downloading and installing new RPM packages, `yum` can also be used to list available packages, as well as those that are already installed. The following examples illustrate some uses of `yum`.

If you want to see a list of all packages that are installed or available for download from the repositories you have configured, type the following:

```
# yum list | less
```

Adding the `less` command to the end enables you to scroll through the list of software (it could be long, depending on which repositories you point to). If you try to install a package and it fails with a message like `package xyzpackage needs xyzfile (not provided)`, you can check for packages that include the missing file using the `provides` option as follows:

```
# yum provides missingfile
```

With the `provides` option, `yum` will search your repositories for whatever file you enter (instead of *missingfile*) and return the name of any packages it finds that include that file. Be sure to include the full path to the missing file.

To search software descriptions in repositories for a particular string, use the `search` option. For example, the following command searches for `arcade` in any package description (this search will find some games):

```
# yum search arcade
```

Because `yum` packages are not automatically deleted after being installed, you might want to go through them occasionally and clean them out. To clear out packages from subdirectories of the `/var/cache/yum` directory, type the following:

```
# yum clean packages
```

Removing packages with yum

If you no longer want to use a package (or you just want to recover some disk space), use the `erase` option to remove that package and all of its dependencies:

```
# yum erase package
```

Using the yum-utils package

There are several utilities in the yum-utils package for working with yum repositories and managing software packages. To get these utilities, type the following yum command:

```
# yum install yum-utils
```

These utilities provide different ways of cleaning up repositories, getting packages without installing them, and doing different types of queries against repositories. Here are some examples:

- **package-cleanup** — Checks your local RPM database for dependency problems and packages that are not needed. Options include --problems (to check dependency problems in the RPM database), --orphans (to list packages not currently available in any of your repositories), and --oldkernels (to remove old kernel and kernel-devel packages). You can add --keepdevel when running --oldkernels, to keep the associated kernel-devel packages.

- **repoclosure** — Checks remote yum repositories for dependency problems. By default, this checks repositories configured for your machine. To check a specific repository, use the -r repoid option (get the repoid from the first line of the /etc/yum.repos.d file for the repository). Other options include -c file (to use a different configuration file containing repositories) or -a arch (to indicate which base architecture to check for the repository). Note that this command consumes a lot of memory and can take a long time to run.

- **yumdownloader** — Downloads a package from a repository to a selected directory. This tool also downloads all dependent packages along with the requested package by adding the --resolve option. You can specify a download directory (--destdir directory) or just list the URL from which the package would be downloaded (--urls) without actually downloading. Use --source to download source packages as well.

- **repoquery** — Queries yum repositories for information about packages and groups. This command is similar to using rpmquery to query your local RPM database. You can list descriptions of a package (-i), list package dependencies (--requires), and show name, version, and release information (-nvr). Type **repoquery --help** for other options.

Getting Fedora software updates

With new exploits being discovered daily, any computer connected to the Internet should get regular software updates to patch any potential holes and fix broken code.

Yum offers several ways of getting updates for Fedora. For Fedora, the GUI utility for getting updates is called PackageKit.

Being alerted to available updates

The first time you log in to Fedora and display the desktop, you will probably see an orange star icon in the upper-right corner, alerting you that updates are available. That icon represents the PackageKit Update Applet. Anytime updates are available, that icon will appear.

Click the orange star icon. The PackageKit Update System window will open, listing the number of available updates. You can select Review Updates to view and optionally select only particular packages to update. Click the Install Updates button and all selected updates will be downloaded to your computer and installed. Figure 5-1 shows an example of the PackageKit Update System window.

FIGURE 5-1

Check for software updates with the PackageKit Update System window.

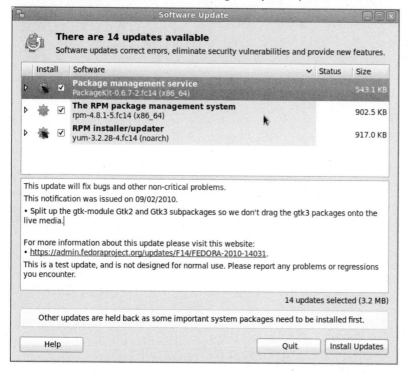

Getting manual updates with yum

At any time you can check whether updates are available for RPM packages installed on your Fedora system. Before doing updates with yum, however, you should always update yum itself first:

```
# yum update yum
```

Next, you can check for updates. Then you can choose to update either selected packages or all available packages. Here is how:

```
# yum check-update
```

The `check-update` option causes `yum` to check the software repositories for available updated versions of RPM packages you have installed. If you see a package you want to update, you can use the `update` option. For example, to update the nmap-frontend package, type the following:

```
# yum update nmap-frontend
```

To update all packages that have updates available, type the following:

```
# yum update
```

This command can take a while to complete, depending on how long it has been since the last time you installed updates and how many total packages are installed on your computer. If, instead of trying to remember to do updates, you want them to happen automatically, the following section describes how to do that.

Managing RPM Packages

Both graphical and command-line tools are available for managing your Fedora system. The PackageKit Add/Remove Software window lets you display categories of software packages installed on and available for your system. The `rpm` command offers an extensive range of features for installing, uninstalling, listing, and verifying your RPM packages.

Note

In recent Fedora releases, PackageKit has grown beyond a simple application you can call to install packages. PackageKit is now more of an integrated facility to update packages, automatically find a package that you need to play certain types of content, and grab those packages for you. When Fedora 12 was released, PackageKit added a feature that let nonroot users install any signed package without providing a password. After some concern about the security of this approach as the default behavior, the Fedora project decided to reverse it. Your Fedora system now requires the root password to install packages as soon as you select to get the most recent round of Fedora updates. ∎

Using the PackageKit Add/Remove window

Unless you installed every package that comes with Fedora, as you go through this book you will probably find that you want to add some Fedora software packages after the initial installation. To do that, you can use the `yum` command (as already described). You can also use `rpm`, a general-purpose command for installing any software packages in RPM format, described in the following section. However, the application with the most user-friendly interface is the PackageKit Add/Remove Software window, which provides a graphical interface for installing packages.

To open the Add/Remove Software window in Fedora, select System ➪ Administration ➪ Add/Remove Software from the menu on the top panel.

With the Add/Remove Software window displayed, you can find both available and installed packages as follows:

- Select a category from the left column to see all packages from that category in the right column.

- Enter all or part of a package name into the search box and select Find to have all packages that include that term appear in the right column.

Packages appear with open box icons if they are installed, or closed box icons if they are not. Select a package to see information about the contents of that package. With a package selected, you can choose to either install it or remove it (depending on its current state).

Note

Not all packages in a repository will necessarily appear in the groups shown on the left window pane. Therefore, if you believe a package you want is in an enabled repository but you can't browse for it, use the Find box to search for it by name. ∎

The Add/Remove Software window is shown in Figure 5-2. In this example, after searching for xfce and displaying all packages with that term in the right column, I selected one of the packages. In the bottom of the window, I can then see a description of the package. From the Selection menu, I can choose to see a complete list of files the package contains and any packages it depends on or that depend on it. From the Selection menu, I can also go to the project's home page or select to install the package.

FIGURE 5-2

Get additional software packages using the PackageKit Add/Remove Software window.

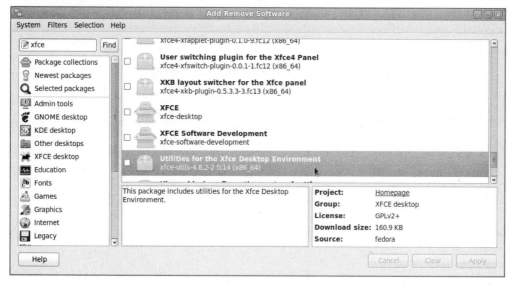

Using the rpm command

The original command used to work with RPM package files is rpm. Unlike yum, the rpm command is not designed to work with repositories. Instead, rpm is best used to install individual packages, verify the contents of packages (before or after you install them), and query information about packages you have installed or are about to install.

The rpm command has the following modes of operation:

- install (-i)
- upgrade (-U)
- freshen (-F)
- query (-q plus options such as -l, -i, -c, -d, -f, -p, and others)
- verify (-V)
- signature check (--checksig or -K)
- uninstall (-e)
- rebuild database (--rebuilddb)
- fix permissions (--setperms)
- set owners/groups (--setugids)
- show RC (--showrc)

With these options, you can install RPM packages and verify that their contents are properly installed, so you can correct any problems that occur. Using the -q option, you can query installed packages for various information from the list of locally installed packages or add -p to query that same information from packages before they are installed. You can also do special things, such as rebuild the RPM database and modify ownership. You must be logged in as the root user to add or remove packages. You may, however, list installed packages, query packages for information, or verify a package's contents without root permission.

The following sections describe how to use rpm to install and work with your RPM applications.

Note

Although the rpm command is good for installing a single RPM from a local directory (or from a URL), once your system is installed the yum command is often a better choice for installing software. Some advantages to using yum are that, for the package you request, it will search your configured repositories, grab the latest available version, and automatically find dependent packages.

Even if you have an RPM package in a local directory or on a DVD, if the package is dependent on other packages, installing with yum localinstall will try to grab extra needed packages from online repositories (while the rpm command would just fail). See the section "Using yum to install packages locally" earlier in this chapter. ■

Verifying rpm package integrity

When you add repositories to your yum facility, in the cases of RPMFusion.org, ATRPMs, and others that offer a release RPM (such as rpmfusion-free), yum is automatically configured to use a valid GPG/DSA key and point to a valid online repository. When you ask to install a package from one of those repositories using yum, the GPG/DSA key is typically used to validate each package before it is installed. Conversely, if you are simply installing a local RPM package, you need to do some manual work to verify its contents.

To check all digests and signatures included in an RPM (to ensure that it is original and not corrupted), you can use the --checksig option to RPM. For example, if I have a copy of the dvgrab RPM (which is part of Fedora) in my local directory and I want to check it, I could run the following command:

```
# rpm --checksig dvgrab-3.5-1.fc13. x86_64.rpm
dvgrab-3.5-1.fc13.x86_64.rpm: rsa sha1 (md5) pgp md5 OK
```

The preceding output shows that the GPG/DSA key was found and used to check that the package's digital signatures (rsa, sha1, and md5) were correct. If, however, you got a package for which you didn't have the GPG/DSA key installed, you would need to get and import that key before you could verify the package.

If you trust the Internet site from which you are getting the RPM you want to install, look for an indication that the site has signed its packages. Then download the GPG public key and import it. That will enable you to check the validity of the packages from that site. For example, I decided I wanted to use the KDE-redhat project (http://apt.kde-redhat.org/linux/kde-redhat) to replace all my KDE packages from Fedora. I downloaded the digikam package and tried to verify it as follows:

```
# rpm --checksig digikam-1.4.0-0.1.fc13.i686.rpm
digikam-1.4.0-0.1.fc13.i686.rpm: (SHA1) DSA sha1 md5 (GPG) NOT OK
(MISSING KEYS: GPG#ff6382fa)
```

Because the GPG public key was not installed, the contents couldn't be verified as correct. Therefore, I went to the KDE-redhat project site and downloaded the GPG public key to the current directory. Then I imported the key as follows:

```
# rpm --import gpg-pubkey-ff6382fa-3e1ab2ca
```

With the GPG public key imported, the second check of the RPM showed that it was clean:

```
# rpm --checksig digikam1.4.0-0.1.fc13.i686. rpm
digikam-1.4.0-0.1.fc13.i686.rpm: (sha1) dsa sha1 md5 gpg OK
```

Most of the GPG public keys you need for the basic repositories used with Fedora are included in the fedora-release package. GPG public keys from other repositories should also be stored with those keys in the /etc/pki/rpm-gpg directory.

Remember, however, that it is best to get packages automatically from known repositories with yum (or related tools). Besides checking the signatures of packages, yum will also ensure that all dependencies are cleared up.

Installing with rpm

To install an RPM archive file that is not yet installed on your system with the rpm command, most people generally use the same options they would if they were upgrading (the -U option). Here's an example of a command line you could use to install a new RPM package or upgrade an existing one:

```
# rpm -U [options] package
```

Package is the name of the RPM archive file. This package may be in the current directory, on a DVD or CD (e.g., /media/disk/Packages/*whatever*.i386.rpm), or on an accessible FTP site (e.g., ftp://ftp.example.com/pub/*whatever*.i386.rpm).

Caution

Interrupting rpm during a package installation can leave stale lock files and possibly corrupt the database. As a result, subsequent rpm commands may hang. If this happens, you can probably correct the problem by removing old database locks. If that doesn't work, you can also try checking whether the database is corrupt; if so, rebuild the RPM database. However, rebuilding the database can take a long time, so only do it if the other options don't resolve the problem. Here's how to remove lock files, check the database, and rebuild the database (as root user):

```
# rm -f /var/lib/rpm/__db*
# rpm --rebuilddb            ■
```

Along with the -U option, you can use the following options to get feedback during a new installation:

- -v — Prints verbose information during installation. This is a good way to see everything that happens during the install process. (This output can be long, so you may want to pipe it to the less command.) You can get additional debug information by adding multiple -v options (for example, -vv).

- -h — Prints 50 hash marks (#) as the package unpacks. The intent is to see the progress of the unpacking process (so you can tell if the program is still working or stalled).

- --percent — Prints the percentage of the total package that has been installed throughout the install process.

Before installing a package, rpm checks to ensure that it is not overwriting newer files or installing a package that has dependencies on other packages that are not installed. The following install options can be used to override conditions that may otherwise cause the installation to fail:

- --force — Forces the contents of the current package to be installed, even if the current package is older than the one already installed, the current package contains files placed there by other packages, or the current package is already installed. (This is the same as using the `oldpackage`, `replacefiles`, and `replacepkgs` options.) Although it is dangerous to do so, people often use this option to override any issue that might cause the package install to fail (such as an older RPM).

- `--oldpackage` — Forces the package to be installed, even if the current package is older than the one already installed.

- `--replacefiles` — Forces files in the package to be installed, even if the files were placed there by other packages.

- `--replacepkgs` — Forces packages in this archive to be installed, even if they are already installed on the system. (This can be used to restore package components that were deleted by mistake.)

- `--nodeps` — Skips package dependency checks and installs the package, even if packages it depends on are not installed. Use this option with extreme caution! By not resolving dependencies properly, you can end up with broken software.

- `--ignorearch` — Forces the package to be installed, even if the binaries in the package don't match the architecture of your host computer.

- `--excludedocs` — Excludes any man pages, texinfo documents, or other files marked as documentation.

- `--ignoreos` — Forces the package to be installed, even if the binaries in the package don't match the architecture of your operating system.

The following is a simple `rpm` command line used to install an RPM package:

```
# rpm -U dvgrab-3.5-1.fc13.x86_64.rpm
```

I like to see some feedback when I install something (by default, `rpm` is suspiciously quiet when it succeeds). Here is what the command looks like after adding the `-vv` option to get more verbose feedback, along with some of the output:

```
# rpm -Uvv dvgrab-3.5-1.fc13.x86_64.rpm
D: =============== dvgrab-3.5-1.fc13.x86_64.rpm
D: loading keyring from pubkeys in /var/lib/rpm/pubkeys/*.key
D: couldn't find any keys in /var/lib/rpm/pubkeys/*.key
D: loading keyring from rpmdb
D: opening  db environment /var/lib/rpm cdb:mpool:joinenv
D: opening  db index       /var/lib/rpm/Packages rdonly mode=0x0
D: locked   db index       /var/lib/rpm/Packages
D: opening  db index       /var/lib/rpm/Name rdonly mode=0x0
D:  read h#    1406 Header sanity check: OK
D: added key gpg-pubkey-97a1071f-4c49d6fe to keyring .
     .
     .
     .
```

From this output, you can see that rpm finds one binary package in this archive, verifies the checksum, opens the RPM database, installs the packages, and closes the database when done. Another way to verify that the install is actually working is to add the -h option, as follows:

```
# rpm -Uvh ~/dvgrab-3.5-1.fc13.x86_64.rpm
Preparing...    ########################################### [100%]
   1:dvgrab      ########################################### [100%]
```

With the -h option, rpm chugs out 50 hash marks (#) until the package is done installing. As you can see, when everything goes well, installing with rpm is quite simple. Some problems can occur, however. Here are a couple of them:

- **Package dependencies errors** — If the package you are installing requires an additional package for it to work properly, you will see an error noting the missing components. You should get and install the packages containing those components before trying your package again. (You can override the failure with install options described previously, but I don't recommend that because your package may not work without the dependent package.)

- **Nonroot user errors** — If rpm -U is run by someone who is not the root user, the command will fail. The output will likely indicate that the /var/lib/rpm database could not be opened. Log in as root user and try again. (You may also get an error about missing dependencies.)

Upgrading packages with rpm

The upgrade option (-U) with rpm can, as you might expect, be used to upgrade existing packages. The format is the same as described previously:

```
# rpm -U [options] package
```

Tip

Although there is a separate install option (-i), I recommend using the -U option whether you are doing a new install or an upgrade. With -U, the package installs in either case, so rpm -U always works (with one exception), whereas rpm -i fails if the package is already installed.

The exception is when you are installing kernel packages. Use -i when installing a new kernel; otherwise, your old (and presumably, working) kernel will be removed and you could be stuck with an unbootable system! ■

One issue when upgrading is installing an older version of a package. For example, if you install a new version of some software and it doesn't work as well, you will want to go back to the old version. To do this, you can use the --oldpackage option as follows:

```
# rpm -U --oldpackage AnotherLevel-0.7.4-1.noarch.rpm
```

If a later package of this name already exists, it is removed and the older version is installed.

Freshening packages with rpm

An option that is similar to the upgrade (-U) option is the freshen (-F) option. The main difference between the two is what happens when the RPM you are updating or freshening is not already installed on your Fedora system. The -U can do either a new install or an upgrade. The -F will do only an upgrade (so if the package is not already installed, rpm -F will do nothing).

One great use for freshen presents itself when you have a directory full of updated RPM files that you want to install on your system, but you want to update only those packages that are already installed. In other words, you may have a lot of RPMs in the directory you don't want. Freshen lets you update just the packages you already have.

Let's say that you downloaded a directory of RPMs and you want to selectively freshen the ones you have installed. With the directory of RPMs as your current directory, you could type

```
# rpm -Fhv *.rpm
```

Packages already installed are updated with the new RPMs. All other RPMs are skipped.

Caution

Do not use freshen or upgrades on kernel packages because it might cause your only working kernel to be removed when you add the new one. ■

Removing packages with rpm

If you no longer want to use a package (or you just want to recover some disk space), use the -e option to remove the package. In its simplest form, you use rpm with the -e option as follows:

```
# rpm -e package
```

If there are no dependencies on this package, it is silently removed. Before you remove a package, however, you may want to do a quick check for dependencies. The -q option is used for a variety of query options. (Checking for dependencies isn't necessary because rpm checks for dependencies before it removes a package. You may want to do this for your own information, however.) To check for dependencies, do the following:

```
# rpm -q --whatrequires package
```

If you decide to remove the package, I recommend using the -vv option with rpm -e. This lets you see the actual files that are being removed. I also suggest that you either direct the output to a file or pipe it to the less command because the output often runs off the screen. For example:

```
# rpm -evv dvgrab | less
```

This example removes the dvgrab package and shows you the files that are being removed one page at a time. (Press the Spacebar to page through the output.)

Other options that you can run with `rpm -e` can be used to override conditions that would prevent the package from being removed or to prevent some processing (such as not running preuninstall and postuninstall scripts). Three of those options are as follows:

- `--nodeps` — Uninstalls the package without checking for dependencies
- `--noscripts` — Uninstalls the package without running any pre-uninstall or post-uninstall scripts
- `--notriggers` — Uninstalls the package without executing scripts that are triggered by removing the package

If you feel nervous about boldly removing a package, you can always run the uninstall in test mode (`--test`) before you do the real uninstall. Test mode shows you everything that would happen in the uninstall without actually uninstalling. (Add the `-vv` option to see the details.) Here's an example:

```
# rpm -evv --test dvgrab
D: loading keyring from pubkeys in /var/lib/rpm/pubkeys/*.key
D: couldn't find any keys in /var/lib/rpm/pubkeys/*.key
D: loading keyring from rpmdb
D: opening  db environment /var/lib/rpm cdb:mpool:joinenv
D: opening  db index       /var/lib/rpm/Packages rdonly mode=0x0
D: locked   db index       /var/lib/rpm/Packages
   .
   .
   .
D:      erase: dvgrab-3.5-1.fc13 has 7 files, test = 1
D: closed   db index       /var/lib/rpm/Requirename
D: closed   db index       /var/lib/rpm/Basenames
D: closed   db index       /var/lib/rpm/Name
D: closed   db index       /var/lib/rpm/Packages
D: closed   db environment /var/lib/rpm
```

If the results look fine, you can run the command again without the `--test` option to remove the package.

Querying packages with rpm

You can use the query options (`-q`) of `rpm` to get information about RPM packages. This can be simply listing the packages that are installed or printing detailed information about a package. Here is the basic format of an `rpm` query command (at least one option is required):

```
# rpm -q [options]
```

The following list shows some useful options you can use with an `rpm` query:

- `-qa` — Lists all installed packages
- `-qf file` — Lists the package that owns `file`. (The file must include the full path name or `rpm` assumes the current directory.)

- -qi *packagename* — Lists detailed information about a *package*
- -qR *packagename* — Lists components (such as libraries and commands) that *package* depends on
- -ql *packagename* — Lists all the files contained in *package*
- -qd *packagename* — Lists all documentation files that come in *package*
- -qc *packagename* — Lists all configuration files that come in *package*
- -qp *[option] packagefile* — Queries package files that are not yet installed. Using this option along with other query options enables you to query packages you have that are not yet installed. Without -p, the rpm command queries only locally installed packages.

To list all the packages installed on your computer, use the -a query option. Because this is a long list, you should either pipe the output to less or, possibly, use grep to find the package you want. The following command line displays a list of all installed RPM packages, and then shows only those names that include the string of characters xorg. (The -i option to grep says to ignore case.)

```
# rpm -qa | grep -i xorg
```

If you are interested in details about a particular package, you can use the rpm -i query option. In the following example, information about the dosfstools package (for working with DOS file systems in Linux) is displayed:

```
# rpm -qi dosfstools
Name        : dosfstools               Relocations: (not relocatable)
Version     : 3.0.9                     Vendor: Fedora Project
Release     : 3.fc14                    Build Date: Mon 31 May 2010 03:30:28 AM CDT
Install Date: Mon 13 Sep 2010 07:06:29 PM CDT
Build Host: x86-04.phx2.fedoraproject.org
Group       : Applications/System       Source RPM: dosfstools-3.0.9-3.fc14.src.rpm
Size        : 200161                    License: GPLv3+
Signature   : RSA/SHA256, Sat 24 Jul 2010 03:07:34 AM CDT, Key ID
421caddb97a1071f
Packager    : Fedora Project
URL         : http://www.daniel-baumann.ch/software/dosfstools/
Summary     : Utilities for making and checking MS-DOS FAT filesystems on Linux
Description:
The dosfstools package includes the mkdosfs and dosfsck utilities,
which respectively make and check MS-DOS FAT filesystems on hard
drives or on floppies.
```

To find out about a package's contents, you can use the -l (list) option with your query. The following example shows the complete path names of files contained in the dosfstools package:

```
# rpm -ql dosfstools | less
/sbin/dosfsck
/sbin/fsck.msdos
/sbin/fsck.vfat
```

```
/sbin/mkdosfs
/sbin/mkfs.msdos
/sbin/mkfs.vfat
/usr/share/man/man8/dosfsck.8.gz
     .
     .
     .
```

Would you like to know how to use the components in a package? Using the -d option with a query will display the documentation (man pages, README files, HOWTOs, and so on) that is included with the package. If you are having trouble getting your X Window System running properly, you can use the following command line to find documents that may help:

```
# rpm -qd xorg-x11-server-Xorg | less
/usr/share/man/man1/Xorg.1.gz
/usr/share/man/man1/cvt.1.gz
/usr/share/man/man1/gtf.1.gz
/usr/share/man/man4/exa.4.gz
/usr/share/man/man4/fbdevhw.4.gz
/usr/share/man/man5/xorg.conf.5.gz
```

Many packages have configuration files associated with them. To see what configuration files are associated with a particular package, use the -c option with a query. For example, type the following to find configuration files that are used with the ppp package:

```
# rpm -qc ppp
/etc/logrotate.d/ppp
/etc/pam.d/ppp
/etc/ppp/chap-secrets
/etc/ppp/options
/etc/ppp/pap-secrets
```

If you ever want to know which package a particular command or configuration file came from, you can use the -qf option. In the following example, the -qf option displays the fact that the chgrp command comes from the fileutils package:

```
# rpm -qf /bin/chgrp
coreutils-8.5-4.fc14.i386
```

Before you install a package, you can do the same queries on it that you would do on an installed package. This can be a great tool for finding information from a package while it is in your current directory, or even in a software repository. Here is an example of using the -qp option with -i to see the description of a package in a software repository:

```
# rpm -qp -i \
http://apt.kde-redhat.org/linux/kde-redhat/fedora/14/x86_64/RPMS.stable/↵
kdeutils-4.5.1-2.fc14.x86_64.rpm
Name        : kdeutils        Relocations: (not relocatable)
Version     : 4.5.1           Vendor: Fedora Project
```

```
Release      : 2.fc14              Build Date: Tue 07 Sep 2010 10:57:45 AM CDT
Install Date: (not installed)      Build Host: x86-16.phx2.fedoraproject.org
Group        : Applications/System Source RPM: kdeutils-4.5.1-2.fc14.src.rpm
Size         : 2366637             License: GPLv2
Signature    : DSA/SHA1, Tue 07 Sep 2010 11:51:20 AM CDT, Key ID efe4780cff6382fa
Packager     : Fedora Project
URL          : http://www.kde.org
Summary      : KDE Utilities
Description :
Utilities for KDE 4.
Includes:
   * kcharselect: character selector
   * kfloppy: floppy formatting tool
   * okteta: binary/hex editor
   * superkaramba
   * sweeper: clean unwanted traces the user leaves on the system
```

In the previous example, the long command line shown on two lines should actually be typed on one line. If you are concerned about the content or legality of downloading a package, this example demonstrates a way to read the description of a package before you even download it.

In the following example, the command lists the files contained in a package that is in the current directory:

```
# rpm -qp -l dvgrab-3.5-1.fc13.x86_64.rpm
```

Again, this is an excellent way to find out what is in a package before you install it.

Verifying installed packages with rpm

If something in a software package isn't working properly, or if you suspect that your system has been tampered with, the verify (-V) option of rpm can help you verify installed software against its original software package. Information about each installed package is stored on your computer in the RPM database. By using the verify option, you can check whether any changes were made to the components in the package.

Note

The verify option uses the uppercase letter (-V); the verbose option uses the lowercase (-v). ∎

Various file size and permissions tests are done during a verify operation. If everything is fine, there is no output. Any components that have changed since they were installed will be output, along with information indicating how they were changed. Here's an example:

```
# rpm -V ppp
S.5....T. c /etc/ppp/chap-secrets
S.5....T. c /etc/ppp/options
S.5....T. c /etc/ppp/pap-secrets
```

This output shows that the ppp package (used to dial up a TCP/IP network such as the Internet using PPP, the Point-to-Point Protocol) contains three files that have changed since it was installed. The notation at the beginning shows that the file size (S), the MD5 sum (5), and the modification time (T) have all changed. The letter c shows that these are all configuration files. By reviewing these files to confirm that the changes were only those that I made to get PPP working, I can verify that the software is okay.

You may see the following indicators when you verify the contents of a configuration file:

- 5 (MD5 Sum) — An MD5 checksum indicates a change to the file contents.
- S (File size) — The number of characters in the file has changed.
- L (Symlink) — The file has become a symbolic link to another file.
- T (Mtime) — The modification time of the file has changed.
- D (Device) — The file has become a device special file.
- U (User) — The user name that owns the file has changed.
- G (Group) — The group assigned to the file has changed.
- M (Mode) — The ownership or permission of the file has changed.

Using RPM in rescue mode

Because yum is a front end to RPM, sometimes you may find it handy to be able to use RPM as a low-level tool to fix broken packages. If you boot into rescue mode via a bootable CD/DVD, RPM will mount your root file system by default to /mnt/sysimage. If you are trying to install RPMs from /media/dvd/Packages, for example, you can run the following:

```
# rpm --root /mnt/sysimage -Uvh \
    --replacepkgs /media/dvd/Packages/coreutils-*.rpm
```

This will reinstall the files from coreutils onto your Fedora system and update the RPM database found in /mnt/sysimage, rather than in the installer's image (/). If the coreutils package were broken somehow on your system, this would reinstall the package and, hopefully, fix the problem.

Using Software in Different Formats

There may not be RPMs available for every piece of software you want to install on your Fedora system. Likewise, you may find that an RPM isn't configured exactly the way you would want it, so that you would be better served by building your own RPM from an RPM source code package. The following sections describe various forms in which you may encounter open-source software and different ways of building and installing that software for you to use.

Understanding software package names and formats

Whenever possible, install the applications you use with Fedora from software packages in RPM format (files with a .rpm extension). However, if an RPM isn't available, the software that you want may be available in other package formats.

Say you just downloaded a file from the Internet that contains a lot of names, numbers, dots, gzs, and tars. What does all that stuff mean? Well, when you break it down, it's really not that complicated.

Most of the names of archive files containing Linux applications follow the GNU-style package-naming conventions. The following example illustrates the package-naming format:

```
mycoolapp-4.2.3-1.i386.rpm
mycoolapp-4.2.3.tar.gz
mycoolapp-4.2.3.src.tar.gz
mycoolapp-4.2.3.bin.SPARC.tar.gz
mycoolapp-4.2.3.bin.ELF.static.tar.gz
```

These examples represent several different packages of the same software application. The name of this package is mycoolapp. Following the package name is a set of numbers that represent the version of the package. In this case, it is version 4.2.3 (the major version number is 4, followed by minor version number and patch level 2.3). After the version number is a dot, followed by some optional parts, which are followed by indications of how the file is archived and compressed.

The first line shows a package that is in the RPM Package Management (.rpm) format. The .i386 before the .rpm indicates that the package contains binaries that are built to run Intel i386 architecture computers (in other words, PCs). The -1 indicates the build level (the same package may have been rebuilt multiple times to make minor changes). See the sidebar "Using Binary RPMs versus Building from Source" for the pros and cons of using prebuilt RPM binary packages as opposed to compiling the program yourself.

Using Binary RPMs versus Building from Source

Binaries created in RPM format are easily installed, managed, and uninstalled using tools such as rpm and yum. This is the recommended installation method for Fedora Linux. Sometimes, however, building an application from source code may be preferable. Here are some arguments on both sides:

- **RPM** — Installing applications from a binary RPM archive is easy. After the application is installed, there are both shell commands and GUIs for managing, verifying, updating, and removing the RPM package. You don't need to know anything about Makefiles or compilers. When you install a binary RPM package, RPM tools even check to ensure that other packages that the package depends on are installed. Because Red Hat has released RPM under the GPL, other Linux distributions also use it to distribute their software. Thus, most Linux applications are, or will be, available in RPM format.

continued

continued

- **Source code** — Not all source-code packages are made into RPM binaries. If you use RPM, you may find yourself with software that is several versions old, when you could simply download the latest source code and run a few `tar` and `make` commands. Also, by modifying source code, you can tailor the package to better suit your needs.

Refer to Appendix A for information on getting source code for Fedora RPM binary packages that are included on the DVD that comes with this book. You can modify that source code yourself and rebuild the RPM binaries. The rebuilt binaries can be tuned to your hardware and include the features you want with the package. For more information on RPMs, refer to the *Red Hat RPM Guide* by Eric Foster-Johnson (Red Hat Press/Wiley, 2003).

In the next two lines of the previous example, each file contains the source code for the package. The files that make up the package were archived using the `tar` command (`.tar`) and compressed using the `gzip` command (`.gz`). You use these two commands (or just the `tar` command with the `-z` option) to expand and uncompress the packages when you are ready to install the applications.

Between the version number and the `.tar.gz` extension there can be optional tags, separated by dots, which provide specific information about the contents of the package. In particular, if the package is a binary version, this information provides details about where the binaries will run. In the third line, the optional `.src` tag was added because the developer wanted to differentiate between the source and binary versions of this package. In the fourth line, the `.bin.SPARC` detail indicates that it is a binary package, ready to run on a SPARC workstation. The final line indicates that it is a binary package, consisting of statically linked ELF format executables.

Instead of using `gzip`, many software packagers today use the `bzip2` utility to compress their software archives. In that case, filenames shown in the preceding examples might instead end with `.bz2` or `.tar.bz2` extensions.

Here is a breakdown of the parts of a package name:

- **name** — This is generally an all-lowercase string of characters that identifies the application.
- **dash** (-)
- **version** — This is shown as major to minor version number from left to right.
- **dot** (.)
- **src** or **bin** — This is optional, with `src` usually implied if no indication is given.
- **dot** (.)
- **type of binary** — This is optional and can include several different tags to describe the content of the binary archive. For example, i386 indicates binaries intended for Intel architectures (Pentium CPU), and SPARC indicates binaries for a Sparc CPU.

- dot (.)
- **archive type** — Often tar is used (.tar).
- **compression type** — Often gzip is used (.gz).

Using different archive and document formats

Many of the software packages that are not associated with a specific distribution (such as Fedora or Debian) use the tar/gzip method for archiving and compressing files. However, you may notice files with different suffixes at software project sites.

Table 5-1 describes the different file formats that you will encounter as you look for software at a Linux FTP site. Table 5-2 lists some of the common document formats that are used in distributing information in Linux.

TABLE 5-1

Linux Archive File Formats

Format	Extension	Description
gzip file	.gz or .z	File was compressed using the GNU gzip utility. It can be uncompressed using the gzip or gunzip utilities (they are both the same).
tar file	.tar	File was archived using the tar command. tar is used to gather multiple files into a single archive file. You can expand the archive into separate files using tar with different options.
tar and gzip file	.tgz	A common practice for naming files that are tar archives that were compressed with gzip is to use the .tgz extension.
bzip2	.bz2	File was compressed with the bzip2 program.
tar and bzip2	.tbz2	Files that are tar archives that were compressed with bzip2.
Tar/compressed	.taz or .tz	File was archived with tar and compressed with the Unix compress command.
Linux Software Map	.lsm	File contains text that describes the content of an archive.
Debian Binary Package	.deb	File is a binary package used with the Debian Linux distribution. (See descriptions of how to convert Debian to Red Hat formats later in this chapter.)
RPM Package Management	.rpm	File is a binary package used with Fedora. Format also available to other Linux distributions.

TABLE 5-2

Linux Document Formats

Format	Extension	Description
Hypertext Markup Language	`.html` or `.htm`	File is in hypertext format for reading by a Web browser program (such as Mozilla).
PostScript	`.ps`	File is in PostScript format for outputting on a PostScript printer.
SGML	`.sgml`	File is in SGML, a standard document format. SGML is often used to produce documents that can later be output to a variety of formats.
PDF	`.pdf`	File is in Portable Document Format, which is gradually replacing PostScript for use in documentation.
DVI	`.dvi`	File is in DVI, the output format of the LaTeX text-processing tools. Convert these files to PostScript or Hewlett-Packard's PCL using the `dvips` and `dvilj` commands.
Plain text		Files in Fedora without a suffix are sometimes plain-text files (in ASCII format). (A note of caution: A lot of the commands in Linux, such as those in `/usr/bin` and `/usr/sbin`, have no extension either. If you have a file with no extension, it's best to use the `file` command on it before proceeding with any operation. In fact, using `file` on a previously untested file can prevent problems. A `.txt` file full of binary code could be used to exploit a text editor and do malicious things to the system.)

If you are not sure of a file's format, use the `file` command as follows:

```
$ file filename
```

This command tells you if it is a GNU `tar` file, RPM, `gzip`, or other file format. (This is a good technique if a file was renamed and lost its extension.)

If you would like to convert a software package from one of the formats described, you can try the alien utility (`http://freshmeat.net/projects/alien`). Although alien is not considered stable enough to use with important system packages, it can be a good tool for trying out some simple software packages on your Fedora system.

Building and installing from source code

If no binary version of the package that you want is available, or if you just want to tailor a package to your needs, you can always install the package from source code. To begin, you can get the source code (SRPM) version of any binary packages in Fedora from the Fedora software repository (see Appendix A for details). You can modify the source code and rebuild it to suit your needs.

Software packages that are not available in RPM format are typically available in the form of a *tarball* (a bunch of files grouped together into a single file formatted by the tar utility) that has been compressed (typically by the gzip utility). Although the exact instructions for installing an application from a source code archive vary, many packages that are in the .bz2, .tar.bz2, .tgz, .gz and .tar formats follow the same basic procedure.

Tip

Before you install from source code, you need to install a variety of software development packages. If you have the disk space, I recommend that you install all software development packages that are recommended during Fedora installation. ■

The following is a minimal list of C-programming software development tools:

- **gcc** — Contains the gcc (GNU C compiler) compiler
- **make** — Contains the make command for making the binaries from Makefiles
- **glibc** — Contains important shared libraries, the C library, and the standard math library
- **glibc-devel** — Contains standard header files needed to create executables
- **binutils** — Contains utilities needed to compile programs (such as the assembler and linker)
- **kernel-devel** — Contains the Linux kernel source code and is needed to rebuild the kernel
- **rpm-build** — Contains the rpmbuild utility for building the RPM binary package from source code
- **libc** — Contains libraries needed for programs that were based on libc 5, so older applications can run on glibc (libc 6) systems. If you use C++, there are a number of packages to get, especially libstdc++ and libstdc++-devel.

Installing software in SRPM format

To install a source package from the Fedora source directory, do the following:

1. Refer to Appendix A for information on obtaining Fedora source code.
2. Download the package you want to the current directory.

3. Install the source code package using the following command:

```
# rpm -iv packagename*.src.rpm
```

4. (Replace *packagename* with the name of the package you are installing.) Starting with Fedora 10, the source is installed by default in a directory called (`rpmbuild/SOURCES`) in your home directory. Spec files are copied to `rpmbuild/SPECS`. Prior to Fedora 10, the default was `/usr/src/redhat/SOURCES` and `/usr/src/redhat/SPECS`.

5. Change to the `SPECS` directory as follows:

```
# cd ~/rpmbuild/SPECS
```

6. Unpack the source code as follows (note that you may need to install the `rpm-build` package):

```
# rpmbuild -bp packagename*.spec
```

7. The package's source code is installed to the `rpmbuild/BUILD/package` directory, where package is the name of the software package.

8. You can now make changes to the files in the package's `BUILD` directory. Read the README, Makefile, and other documentation files for details on how to build the individual package.

The `--rebuild` option to `rpmbuild` can be used to rebuild the RPM without installing it first. The resulting binary will be in `rpmbuild/RPMS/arch`, where *arch* is replaced by i386 or another architecture for which you are building the RPM.

Installing software in tar.gz or tar.bz2 formats

Here are some generic instructions that you can use to install many Linux software packages that are in the `gzip` or `tar` format:

1. Get the source-code package from the Internet or from a CD distribution and copy it into an empty directory (preferably using a name that identifies the package).

2. To check the contents of your tar archive before extracting it to your hard drive, you could use the following command:

```
# tar ztvf package.tar.gz
```

Note
Use the command `tar tvjf` if the file is compressed using bzip2. ∎

3. Assuming the file is compressed using `gzip`, uncompress the file using the following command:

```
# gunzip package.tar.gz
```

The package will be uncompressed and the `.gz` removed from the package name (for example, *package*.tar). (If your package ends in bz2, use the bzip2 command instead of gunzip.)

4. From the resulting tar archive, run the tar command as follows:

`tar xvf` *package*`.tar`

This command extracts the files from the archive and copies them to a subdirectory of the current directory. (Using `tar xvfz` *package*`.tar.gz` you can do Steps 2 and 3 in one step. For a compressed bzip2 file, run `tar xvfj` *package*`.tar.bz2` instead.)

5. Change directories to the new subdirectory created in Step 3, as follows:

`cd` *package*

6. Look for a file called INSTALL or README. One of these files should give you instructions on how to proceed with the installation. In general, the make command is used to install the package. Here are a few things to look for in the current directory:

If there is a Make.in file, try running the following:

```
# ./configure -prefix=/usr/local
# make all
```

7. If there is an Imake file, try running this:

```
# xmkmf -a
# make all
```

8. If there is a Makefile, try running this:

```
# make all
```

After the program is built and installed, you might have to do additional configuration. You should consult the man pages or the HOWTOs that come with the software for information on how to proceed.

Tip

With some `tar.gz` files that include an RPM spec file, you could run the command `rpm-build -ta file.tar.gz` to build an RPM from that tarball. ■

Using Fedora to Run Applications

Although operating systems are nice (and necessary), people use desktop computers to run application programs. There has been a common belief that although Fedora can work well as a server, it is not ready to challenge Microsoft's dominance of the desktop arena. There are several reasons why, I believe, Fedora can replace Microsoft Windows on the desktop, if you are committed to doing it:

- Every category of desktop application now has an open-source offering that will run in Linux. For example, although Adobe Photoshop doesn't run natively in Linux, you can use The GIMP or other applications to work with digital images in Linux.

- The Windows applications that you absolutely must have can usually be run without problems using Windows emulators or compatibility programs, such as QEMU and WINE. Particular efforts have been made to get Windows games (Transgaming.com) and office productivity applications (Codeweavers.com) running in Linux.

- With viruses and worms running rampant in Microsoft systems, many people believe that Linux systems offer a more secure alternative, particularly if the desktop system is being used primarily for Web browsing and e-mail. With Linux, corporations that deploy hundreds or even thousands of desktop systems can exercise a great deal of control over the security and features in their employees' systems. In addition, most Linux administration can be done remotely using ssh, which offers encryption and authentication along with all the advantages of a Linux shell.

- In the long run, as Linux systems become more profitable targets for viruses and malware, learning good practices in choosing software, using file ownership/permissions, and monitoring system resources will become more important. However, such tools (including virus scanners like klamav and clamscan) are already available for any Linux system that chooses to include them. (For more information, refer to www.clamav.net and http://klamav.sourceforge.net.)

- A huge development community is working on open-source applications to meet the needs of the Linux community. If you feel more secure having a company back up your mission-critical applications, some strong commercial software offerings are available for Red Hat systems (www.redhat.com/apps/isv_catalog).

- Hundreds of popular desktop software packages such as Firefox, OpenOffice.org, and Thunderbird, and workstation software, such as compilers and IDEs (Eclipse), are available prepackaged for you. Installing and updating your favorite applications does not require exploring dozens of different software download sites.

The bottom line is that it will take some effort for most people to discard their Microsoft Windows operating systems completely. However, if you are committed to making Fedora your sole application platform, there are several ways to ease that transition. Emulation programs enable you to run many programs that were created for other operating systems. Conversion programs can help you convert graphics and word-processing data files from other formats to those supported by Linux applications.

Cross-Reference
See Chapter 6 for information on importing and exporting word processing and graphics files. ■

If you are running Linux on a PC, chances are good that you already paid for a Microsoft Windows operating system. You can either run Linux on a different PC than you use for Windows or have Windows and Linux on separate partitions of your hard disk on the same PC.

The latter requires you to reboot each time you want to switch operating systems. (See Chapter 2 for information on setting up a Linux/Windows dual-boot system.) Recently, a third option has been added, whereby you can run a virtual Windows system on your Linux system (see the descriptions of Xen and KVM in Chapter 23).

The following section describes applications that run in Fedora that you can use to replace the Windows applications you are used to.

Finding common desktop applications in Linux

If you are going to use Linux as a desktop computer system, you have to be able to write documents, work with graphics, and crunch numbers. You probably also have other favorite applications, such as a music player, Web browser, and e-mail reader.

Note

Using WINE technology, the people at CodeWeavers, Inc., offer a CrossOver Office product that enables you to install and run Microsoft Office in Linux. See the section "Running Windows Applications with WINE" later in this chapter. ■

To give you a snapshot of what desktop applications are available, Table 5-3 contains a list of popular Windows applications, equivalent Linux applications, and where you can find the Linux applications. Although many of these applications have not reached the level of sophistication of their Windows counterparts, they can be cost-effective alternatives.

TABLE 5-3

Windows-Equivalent Linux Applications

Windows Applications	Linux Applications	Where to Get Linux Applications	Cost
Microsoft Office (office productivity suite)	OpenOffice.org (`openoffice.org`)	Included on Fedora DVD	Free
	KOffice	Included on Fedora DVD	Free
Microsoft Word (word processor)	OpenOffice.org Writer	Included on Fedora DVD	Free
	AbiWord	Included on Fedora DVD	Free
	KWord	Included on Fedora DVD	Free

continued

TABLE 5-3 *(continued)*

Windows Applications	Linux Applications	Where to Get Linux Applications	Cost
Microsoft Excel (spreadsheet)	OpenOffice.org Calc	Included on Fedora DVD	Free
	gnumeric	Included on Fedora DVD	Free
	KSpread	Included on Fedora DVD	Free
Microsoft PowerPoint (presentation)	OpenOffice.org Impress	Included on Fedora DVD	Free
	KPresenter	Included on Fedora DVD	Free
Microsoft Internet Explorer (Web browser)	Firefox	Included on Fedora DVD	Free
	SeaMonkey	Included on Fedora DVD	Free
	epiphany	Included on Fedora DVD	Free
	konqueror	Included on Fedora DVD	Free
	Opera	`www.opera.com`	Free
Microsoft Outlook (e-mail reader)	evolution	Included on Fedora DVD	Free
	kmail	Included on Fedora DVD	Free
	Thunderbird	Included on Fedora DVD	Free
	Mozilla Lightning	`www.mozilla.org/ projects/calendar/ lightning/`	Free
Adobe Photoshop (image editor)	The Gimp (gimp)	Included on Fedora DVD	Free
Microsoft Expression or Front Page (HTML editor)	quanta	Included on Fedora DVD	Free
Quicken or Microsoft Money (personal finance)	gnucash	Included on Fedora DVD	Free
AutoCAD (computer-aided design)	LinuxCad	`www.linuxcad.com`	$99
	NX	`www.plm.automation. siemens.com/`	See vendor
	ProEngineer	`www.ptc.com/ products/ proengineer/`	See vendor

The following sections describe how to find and work with application programs that are included with or available specifically for Linux.

Investigating your desktop

More and more high-quality desktop applications are being packaged with or made available for Fedora, many as part of the GNOME or KDE desktop environments. In other words, to start finding some excellent office applications, games, multimedia players, and communications tools, you don't have to look any further than the Applications menu button on your desktop panel.

Therefore, before you start hunting around the Internet for the software you need, see if you can use something already installed with Fedora. The chapters that follow this one describe how to use publishing tools, work with multimedia, and communicate over the Internet — all with programs that either are on the DVD that comes with this book or are easily attainable.

Using your Fedora desktop to run applications is relatively easy. If you have used Microsoft Windows operating systems, you already know the most basic ways to run an application from a graphical desktop. X, however, provides a much more flexible environment for running native Linux applications.

Cross-Reference
See Chapter 3 for information on setting up an X desktop. ∎

Starting applications from a menu

From the GNOME or KDE desktops in Fedora, open the Applications menu, select the category, such as Office, and then select the application to run. You can install both GNOME and KDE applications on your Linux system, where they will appear together on the Applications submenus.

Starting applications from a Run Application window

Not all installed applications appear on the menus provided with your window manager. For running other applications, some window managers provide a window, similar to the Run Application window, that lets you type in the name of the program you want to run.

To access the Run Application window:

1. Right-click the panel and select Add to Panel.
2. Select Run Application and click Add. The Run Application icon should appear on the panel.
3. Click the Run Application button. The Run Application window appears.
4. Click Show List of Known Applications, click the program you want, and then click Run.
5. If the application you want isn't on the list, you can either type the command you want to run (along with any options) and click Run, or you can click Run with File to browse through directories to select a program to run. If you are running a program that needs to run in a terminal window, such as the vi command, click the Run in Terminal button before running the command. Figure 5-3 shows an example of the Run Application window.

FIGURE 5-3

Select a program to run from the list in the Run Application window.

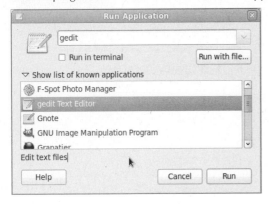

Starting applications from GNOME Do

GNOME Do provides an application launcher similar to that of QuickLaunch on the Macintosh. When you run GNOME Do from the Applications ⇨ Accessories menu or from an icon on the panel, you'll see a spare two-paned window. Start typing the name of a command and you'll see an icon for the application in the pane on the left, as shown in Figure 5-4.

FIGURE 5-4

Quickly launch applications with GNOME Do.

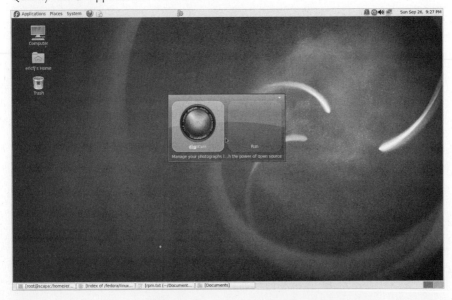

Click Enter to run the application.

GNOME Do does more than just launch applications, though. It provides shortcuts to many common tasks such as playing music, sending e-mail, or launching Firefox to view a particular site. See http://do.davebsd.com for more on GNOME Do.

Starting applications from a Terminal window

I often prefer to run an X application, at least for the first time, from a terminal window. There are several reasons why I prefer a terminal window to selecting an application from a menu or Run Application window:

- If there is a problem with the application, you see the error messages. Applications started from a menu or Run Application usually just fail silently.

- Applications from menus run with set options. If you want to change those options, you have to change the configuration file that set up the menu and make the changes there.

- If you want to try out a few different options with an application, a terminal window is an easy way to start it, stop it, and change its options.

When you have found an application and figured out the options that you like, you can add it to a menu or a panel (if your window manager supports those features). That way, you can run a program exactly as you want, rather than how it is given to you on a menu.

Here is a procedure to run X applications from a terminal window:

1. Open a Terminal window from your desktop via Applications ⇨ System Tools ⇨ Terminal.

2. Enter the following:

```
$ echo $DISPLAY
```

The result should be something similar to this:

```
:0.0
```

3. This indicates that the terminal window will, by default, direct any X application you run from this window to display 0.0 on your local system. (If you don't see a value when you type that command, type **export DISPLAY=:0.0** to set the display value.)

4. With the xmms package installed, type the following command:

```
$ xmms &
```

5. The xmms program should appear on your desktop, ready to work with. If you do not have the xmms command, use the command yum install xmms to install the program. Note the following:

   - The xmms command runs in the background of the terminal window (&). This means that you can continue to use the terminal window while xmms is running.

   - I encountered no errors running xmms on this occasion. With other applications, however, text sometimes appeared in the terminal window after the command was run. The text may say that the command can't find certain information or that certain fonts or colors cannot be displayed. That information would have been lost if the command were run from a menu.

6. To know what options are available, type

   ```
   $ xmms --help
   ```

7. Try it with a few options. For example, if you wanted to begin by playing a file and you have an Ogg Vorbis audio file named file.ogg, you could type

   ```
   $ xmms file.ogg
   ```

8. When you are ready to close the xmms window, you can either do so from the xmms box window (right-click on the xmms window and select Exit) or you can kill the process in the terminal window. Type **jobs** to see the job number of the process. If it were job number 2, for example, you would type **kill %2** to kill the xmms program. If instead you want to continue running xmms in the background, press Ctrl+Z (to put it in the background) and bg (to continue running it in the background).

Try running a few other X commands, such as xev, xclock, or xdpyinfo.

Running remote X applications

Applications written for the X Window System are the most flexible of Linux applications because X lets you start an application from anywhere on the network and have it show up on your X display. Instead of being limited by the size of your hard disk and the power of your CPU and RAM, you can draw on resources from any computer that gives you access to those resources.

Given the proper permissions, you can work with files, printers, backup devices, removable drives, other users, and any other resources on the remote computer as though you were on that computer. With this power, however, comes responsibility. You need to protect the access to your display, especially in networks where the other machines and users are not known or trusted. For example, you wouldn't want to allow anyone to display a login screen on your display, encouraging you to inadvertently give some cracker your login and password.

Traditionally, to run remote X applications, you basically only need to know how to identify remote X displays and how to use whatever security measures are put in place to protect your network resources. Using ssh to launch X applications is even simpler and more secure than the traditional method. Those issues are described in the following sections.

Traditional method to run remote X applications

If an X application is installed on another computer on your network and you want to use it from your desktop, follow these steps:

1. Open permissions to your X server so that the remote application can use your display.

2. Identify your X server display to the application when it starts up.

When you run an X client on your local system, your local display is often identified as :0, which represents the first display on the local system. To identify that display to a remote system, however, you must add your computer's host name. For example, if your computer were named *whatever*, your display name would be

```
whatever:0
```

Tip

In most cases, the host name is the TCP/IP name. For the computers on your local network, the name may be in your /etc/hosts file, or it may be determined using the Domain Name System (DNS) service. You could also use a full domain name, such as hatbox.handsonhistory.com. X does support other types of transport, although transports other than TCP/IP aren't used much anymore. ■

You will probably use the display name in this form most of the time you run a remote X application. In certain cases, however, the information may be different. If your computer has multiple X displays (keyboard, mouse, and monitor), you may have numbers other than :0 (:1, :2, and so on). It is also possible for one keyboard and mouse to be controlling more than one monitor, in which case you could add a screen number to the address, like this:

```
whatever:0.1
```

This address identifies the second screen (.1) on the first display (:0). The first screen is identified as .0 (which is the default because most displays have only one screen). Unless you have multiple physical screens, however, you can skip the screen identifier.

There are two ways to identify your display name to a remote X application:

- **DISPLAY shell variable** — The DISPLAY shell variable can be set to the system name and number identifying your display. After this is done, the output from any X application run from that shell will appear on the display indicated. For example, to set the DISPLAY variable to the first display on whatever, type one of the following:

  ```
  export DISPLAY=whatever:0
  ```

  or

  ```
  setenv DISPLAY whatever:0
  ```

  The first example shows how you would set the DISPLAY variable on a bash or ksh shell. The second example works for a csh shell.

- **-display** option — Another way to identify a remote display is to add the `-display` option to the command line when you run the X application. This overrides the DISPLAY variable. For example, to open an `xterm` window on a remote system so that it appears on the first display on `whatever`, type the following:

```
xterm -display whatever:0
```

You may need to install the xterm package with `yum` first. With this information, you should be able to run an X application from any computer that you can access from your local computer. The following sections describe how you may use this information to start a remote X application.

Launching a remote X application

Suppose you want to run an application from a computer named `remote1` on your local area network (in your same domain). Your local computer is `local1`, and the remote computer is `remote1`. The following steps show how to run an X application from `remote1` from your X display on `local1`.

You may need to enable your X server to support networked connections. To determine whether you need to enable networked connections, run the following command:

```
$ ps uax | grep Xorg
root      1941  0.0  2.1  54276 44972 tty1     Ss+ 11:14  0:04 ↵
/usr/bin/Xorg :0 -nr -verbose -auth↵
/var/run/gdm/auth-for-gdm-D9SKms/database vt1 -nolisten tcp ↵
ericfj    6034  0.0  0.0   4212   724 pts/0↵
    R+  12:21   0:00 grep Xorg
```

If you see `-nolisten tcp` in the Xorg command, you need to enable networked connections. To do so, edit the file `/etc/gdm/gdm.schemas` if you are using the GNOME display manager, the Fedora default. Look for the following block in this XML file:

```
<schema>
  <key>security/DisallowTCP</key>
  <signature>b</signature>
  <default>true</default>
</schema>
```

Change this setting to the following:

```
<schema>
  <key>security/DisallowTCP</key>
  <signature>b</signature>
  <default>false</default>
</schema>
```

After this, restart your system. Log in and make sure the `-nolisten tcp` argument is no longer present:

```
$ ps uax | grep Xorg
root    2141  0.0  2.1  54276 44972 tty1    Ss+  12:04   0:04 /usr↵
/bin/Xorg :0 -nr -verbose -auth /var/run/gdm/auth-for-gdm-sZV27d/database vt1
```

Once completed, follow these steps to enable remote applications to connect to your desktop:

1. Open a terminal window on the local computer.

2. Allow access for the remote computer (e.g., remote1) to the local X display by typing the following from the terminal window:

   ```
   $ xhost +remote1
   ```

   ```
   remote1 being added to access control list
   ```

Caution

Using the xhost command in this way is inherently insecure and requires that you trust all users on computers to which you allow access. If you require a more secure method, refer to the section "Using SSH to run remote X applications" later in this chapter. ■

3. Log in to the remote computer using any remote login command. For example, if you want to log in as user joe on the remote computer, you could use the following:

   ```
   $ ssh joe@remote1
   ```
   You will be prompted for a password.

   ```
   joe@remote1's password:
   ```

4. Type the password for the remote user login. (You are now logged in as the remote user in the terminal window.)

5. Set the DISPLAY variable on the remote computer to your local computer. For example, if your computer were named pine in the local domain, the command could appear as follows:

   ```
   $ export DISPLAY=pine:0
   ```

   If you are using a csh shell on the remote system, you may need to type **setenv DISPLAY pine:0**.

6. At this point, any X application you run from the remote system from this shell will appear on the local display. For example, to run a remote terminal window so that it appears locally, type the following:

   ```
   $ xterm
   ```

   The terminal window appears on the local display.

Note the following about the remote application that appears on your display:

- If you only use the login to run remote applications, you can add the line exporting the DISPLAY variable to a user configuration file on the remote system (such as .bashrc, if you use the bash shell). After that, any application that you run will be directed to your local display.

- Even though the application looks as though it is running locally, all the work is being done on the remote system. For example, if you ran a word processing program remotely, it would use the remote CPU; and when you save a file, it is saved to the remote file system.

Caution

Don't forget when a remote shell or file editor is open on your desktop. Sometimes people forget that a window is remote and then edit an important configuration file on the remote system accidentally (such as the /etc/fstab file). You could damage the remote system with this type of mistake. ■

Using user-based security

As you've just seen, xhost enables all users from a remote host to connect to your display. This can be dangerous, as any user on that system would be able to do screen captures, key logging, or even control your desktop. Therefore, it may not be a good idea to use xhost. You can disable xhost with the command xhost -remote1:

```
$ xhost -remote1
```

After you have enabled the X server to listen on TCP, you can use the xauth command, which uses shared keys to enable only specific users that have your shared key to connect to your display. To see your shared key, on your X server run the following:

```
$ xauth list
pine/unix:0  MIT-MAGIC-COOKIE-1  2e64617669646475666665792e636f6d
```

This shared key is what allows your locally running X applications to communicate over the unix socket for your display. You need to add an additional line to allow connections over TCP. You can do this by copying and pasting the relevant parts, but leave out /unix and run xauth add with the name of the system you want to grant access, a system called pine in this case:

```
$ xauth add pine:0  MIT-MAGIC-COOKIE-1 \
2e64617669646475666665792e636f6d
```

Now you need to enable your remote1 client to be able to communicate with your X server running on pine. Do this by adding pine to the DISPLAY variable and then running xauth to add the shared key on remote1:

```
$ export DISPLAY=pine:0
$ xauth add pine:0  MIT-MAGIC-COOKIE-1 \
2e64617669646475666665792e636f6d
```

Now any commands you run as that user from remote1 will display on pine:0. Because you did not use xhost, no other users on remote1 will be able to connect to pine's display unless they have access to that user's ~/.Xauthority file.

Caution

While xauth **provides authentication, neither** xhost **nor** xauth **provides encryption, and anyone sniffing the network may be able to capture your X activity and keystrokes.** ■

Using SSH to run remote X applications

Not only does the ssh command provide a secure mechanism for logging in to a remote system, it also provides a way to securely run remote X applications. With X11 forwarding enabled, any X application you run from the remote location during your ssh session will appear on your local desktop.

After you log in to the remote computer using ssh, you can use that secure channel to forward X applications back to your local display. Here is an example:

1. Type the following ssh command to log in to a remote computer (the -X option enables X11 forwarding):

   ```
   $ ssh -X jake@remote1
   jake@remote1's password: *******
   ```

2. Check that the display variable is set to forward any X applications you run through this ssh session to your local display (this value is controlled by the X11DisplayOffset setting in /etc/ssh/sshd_config):

   ```
   $ echo $DISPLAY
   localhost:10.0
   ```

3. After you are logged in, type any X command and the window associated with that command appears on your local display. For example, to start the gedit command, type

   ```
   $ gedit &
   ```

For this to work, you don't need to open your local display (using xhost). That's because the SSH daemon (sshd) on the remote system sets up a secure channel to your computer for X applications. In order to not interfere with any real display numbers, the SSH daemon (by default) uses the display name of localhost:10.0. The ssh command also creates an xauth shared key on both sides of the connection so that no other users from localhost can connect to localhost:10.0. Note that xauth must be installed and working (which is the default).

This X forwarding feature is on by default in the latest version of Fedora (see the X11Forwarding yes value set in the /etc/ssh/sshd_config file). It is off in other systems, however, so you may need to change the X11Forwarding value on those systems.

Running Microsoft Windows and DOS Applications

Linux is ready to run most applications that were created specifically for Linux, the X Window System, and many Unix systems. Many other applications that were originally created for other operating systems have also been ported to Linux. However, there are still many applications created for other operating systems for which there are no Linux versions.

Linux can run some applications that are intended for other operating systems using *emulator* programs. An emulator, as the name implies, tries to act like something it is not. In the case of an operating system, an emulator presents an environment that looks to the application like the intended operating system.

Note

The most popular of these emulators, called WINE, is not really an emulator at all. WINE is a mechanism that implements Windows application-programming interfaces; rather than emulate Microsoft Windows, it provides the interfaces that a Windows application would expect. In fact, some people claim that WINE stands for "WINE Is Not an Emulator." ■

The following sections describe emulators that enable you to run applications that are intended for DOS or Windows systems.

As for Mac OS X applications, because that operating system is based on a Unix-like operating system called Darwin, many open-source applications written for Mac OS X also have versions available that run in Linux. If you find an application that you like in Mac OS X and want to run in Linux, check the Sourceforge.net site to see if the project that created the Mac OS X application offers a Linux version of it as well (or at least the source code for building the application yourself).

Note

In theory, any application that is Win32-compatible should be able to run using software such as WINE (described later). Whether or not a Microsoft Windows application will run in an emulator in Linux must be checked on a case-by-case basis. ■

Available emulation programs include the following:

- DOSBox (www.dosbox.com), for running many classic DOS applications that won't run on new computers. (Install it from Fedora by typing **yum install dosbox** as root.)

- DOSEMU, also for running classic DOS applications. (Refer to the DOSEMU site at http://dosemu.sourceforge.net for information. Select the Stable Releases link to find RPM binaries of DOSEMU that run in Fedora.)

- WINE, which enables you to run Windows 3.1, Windows 95, Windows 98, Windows 2000, Windows NT, Windows XP, Windows Vista, and Windows 7 binaries. (It is not yet known how well supported Windows 7-specific applications will be.) However, because many Windows applications are written to work in earlier Windows systems, they will run just fine in WINE as well. Check the documentation for the Windows application.

In general, the older and less complex the program, the better chance it has to run in an emulator. Character-based applications generally run better than graphics-based applications. Programs tend to run slower in emulation, due sometimes to additional debugging code put into the emulators. However, because WINE "is not an emulator," any application that doesn't make system calls should run as fast in WINE as it does natively in Windows.

Yet another approach to running applications from other operating systems on Linux is to use virtualization products. One popular virtual machine product is VMware player (`www.vmware.com/products/player`). However, included in Fedora itself is Xen virtualization software. Another approach to virtualization, called KVM, was added to Fedora starting in Fedora 7. (Both Xen and KVM are described in Chapter 23.)

Running DOS applications

Because Linux was originally developed on PCs, a variety of tools were created to help developers and users bridge the gap between Linux and DOS systems. A set of Linux utilities called `mtools` enables you to work with DOS files and directories within Linux. A DOS emulator called `DOSbox` enables you to run DOS applications within a DOS environment that is actually running in Linux (much the way a DOS window runs within a Microsoft Windows OS). DOSEMU is another DOS emulator that is available outside of the Fedora repository.

Using mtools

The `mtools` package contains a set of utility programs, mostly DOS commands that have the letter *m* in front of them and that run in Linux (although there are a few exceptions that are named differently). Using these commands, you can easily work with DOS files and file systems. Table 5-4 lists `mtools` that are available with Linux (if you have the `mtools` package installed).

TABLE 5-4

mtools Available with Linux

Command	Description
mattrib	The DOS `attrib` command, which is used to change an MS-DOS file attribute flag
mcd	The DOS `cd` command, which is used to change the working directory to another DOS directory. (The default directory is A:\.)
mcheck	The DOS `check` command, which is used to verify a file
mcopy	The DOS `copy` command, which is used to copy files from one location to another
mdel	The DOS `del` command, which is used to delete files
mdeltree	The DOS `deltree` command, which deletes an MS-DOS directory along with the files and subdirectories it contains

continued

TABLE 5-4	(continued)
Command	**Description**
mdir	The DOS dir command, which lists a directory's contents
mdu	The Linux du command, which is used to show the amount of disk space used by a DOS directory
minfo	Prints information about a DOS device, such as a hard disk
mkmanifest	Creates a shell script that restores Linux filenames that were truncated by DOS commands
mlabel	The DOS label command, which is used to make a DOS volume label
mmd	The DOS md command, which is used to create a DOS directory
mmount	Mounts a DOS disk in Linux
mmove	The DOS move command, which is used to move a file to another directory and/or rename it
mrd	The DOS rd command, which is used to remove a DOS directory
mren	The DOS ren command, which is used to rename a DOS file
mshowfat	Shows the FAT entry for a file in a DOS file system
mtoolstest	Tests the mtools configuration files
mtype	The DOS type command, which is used to display the contents of a DOS text file
mzip	Performs operations with Zip disks, including eject, write protect, and query

You can use mtools utilities to copy files between your Linux system and a Windows system that is not on your network. Using mcopy, you can copy files using drive letters instead of device names. For example, to copy vi.exe from drive C: to the current directory in Linux, you would type the following:

```
# mcopy c:\vi.exe .
```

Using DOSBox

To run your classic DOS applications, Fedora includes the dosbox package. To install dosbox, type the following as root user:

```
# yum install dosbox
```

With dosbox installed, just type **dosbox** to open a DOSBox window on your desktop. From that window, you have an environment where you can run many classic DOS applications. Assuming you already have some DOS applications you want to run stored on your Fedora system, you can make those applications available by mounting the directory containing them. For example, to mount the /home/chris directory to drive C in DOSBox, type the following:

```
Z:\> mount c /home/chris
```

At this point, you can use standard DOS commands to access and run applications from the directory you just mounted. For example, type **dir c:** to see the contents of the directory you just mounted. Type **c:** to go to that directory. Then just run the DOS applications stored in that directory by typing its name.

To mount a CD-ROM, you need to indicate the file system type when you mount it. For example:

```
Z:\> mount d /media/disk -t cdrom
```

For information on using special keys and features in dosbox, refer to the dosbox README file (/usr/share/doc/dosbox-*/README).

Running Microsoft Windows applications in Linux

There are several promising approaches you can take to get your Windows applications to work during a running Linux session. Here are a two of them:

- **WINE** — The WINE project (www.winehq.org) has been making great strides in getting applications that were created for Microsoft Windows to run in Linux and other operating systems. WINE is not truly an emulator because it doesn't emulate the entire Windows operating system. Instead, because it implements Win32 application programming interfaces (APIs) and Windows 3.x interfaces, the WINE project is more of a "Windows compatibility layer." WINE doesn't require that Windows be installed. It can, however, take advantage of Windows .dll files if you have some to add.

- **QEMU** — QEMU (http://wiki.qemu.org/ is an open-source project that acts as a processor emulator. It can either emulate a full system or work in user mode emulation (where it can be used to test processes compiled for different CPUs). In full system emulation, QEMU can run a variety of operating systems, including Windows.

  To try applications intended for other operating systems, QEMU can also run several Linux (e.g., Fedora, KNOPPIX, Mandrake, Morphix, Debian) and other Unix-like systems (e.g., NetBSD, Solaris). QEMU can take advantage of virtualization features, using KVM, that have recently been added to the Linux kernel.

  With the open-source QEMU project, you can simultaneously run Microsoft Windows and Linux operating systems on the same PC. (Go to http://wiki.qemu.org/Manual and click QEMU Official OS Support List for a complete list of supported operating systems.)

Cross-Reference

In general, Windows applications are less likely to break in QEMU than they are in WINE (because you actually run the whole Windows operating system), but performance may not be as good (because you run an operating system within another operating system). See Chapter 23 for more on QEMU and its virtualization utility. ∎

The rest of this section describes how to get and use WINE to run Windows applications in Linux. To get WINE for your Fedora system, you can go to the following places:

- **WINE in Fedora** — As of Fedora 7, WINE became part of the main Fedora software repository. The wine and wine-core packages are needed to use WINE. Additional WINE support comes in the following packages: `wine-alsa` (ALSA support), `wine-capi` (ISDN support), `wine-cms` (color management), `wine-esd` (ESD sound support), wine-jack (JACK sound support), `wine-ldap` (LDAP support), `wine-nas` (NAS sound support), `wine-pulseaudio` (PulseAudio support), and `wine-twain` (scanner support). Add `wine-docs` for further documentation, or `wine-devel` for WINE development components.

- **Cedega** — A commercial version of WINE called Cedega (formerly called WineX) is available from TransGaming, Inc. (`www.transgaming.com`). TransGaming focuses on running Windows games in Linux, using WINE as its base.

- **CodeWeavers** — If you need Microsoft Office or Web browser plugins, CodeWeavers (`www.codeweavers.com`) offers CrossOver Linux. Although CrossOver Linux isn't free, it offers friendly interfaces for installing and managing the Windows software. A 30-day free trial is available.

While it's true that you can run several Windows applications using WINE, some fiddling is still required to get many Windows applications to work. If you are considering moving your desktop systems from Windows to Linux, you should test how well WINE runs your remaining Windows-only applications.

In addition to developing software, the WINE project maintains a database of applications that run under WINE (`http://appdb.winehq.org`). More than 8,000 applications are listed, although many of them are only partially operational. The point is that the list of applications is growing, and special attention is being paid to getting important Windows applications running.

Tip

If you want to migrate your desktop systems from Windows to Linux, you can start by moving to cross-platform systems that run on both Windows and Linux. For example, move from Microsoft Office to OpenOffice.org. Move from Internet Explorer to Firefox and from Outlook to Thunderbird. Doing this will substantially ease the final migration to Linux. ∎

Running Windows Applications with WINE

In order for WINE to let you run Microsoft Windows applications, it needs an environment set up that looks like a Microsoft Windows system. You can install WINE from the Fedora yum repository by typing the following:

```
# yum install wine wine-core wine-docs
```

Although you only need the `wine` and `wine-core` packages, `wine-docs` offers some useful documents in the `/usr/share/doc/wine-docs*` directory for developing software and using

WINE. The `yum` command line just shown will also pull in other WINE packages from the Fedora repository (such as those that include additional support for sound, scanners, and other features mentioned earlier).

The location of the basic Microsoft Windows operating-system directories for WINE is the `$HOME/.wine/drive_c` directory for each user, which looks like the C: drive to WINE. The `$HOME/.wine` directory is created automatically in your home directory the first time you run Wine Configuration (select Applications ➪ Wine ➪ Wine Configuration) or type the `winecfg` command:

```
$ winecfg
```

This opens the Wine configuration window, where you can do most of your activities to add applications, configure the operating system, and integrate with the desktop. Figure 5-5 shows an example of the Wine configuration window.

FIGURE 5-5

Set up your Windows applications in Linux from the Wine configuration window.

Assigning drive letters

Before you begin installing Windows applications in WINE, you should become familiar with your WINE environment. Drive letters are assigned in the `$HOME/.wine/dosdevices` directory. Select the Drives tab in the Wine configuration window to see which drive letters are assigned. At least drive C: and drive Z: should be set.

To configure additional drive letters, you can select Add (to add an individual drive) or Autodetect (to have WINE assign all your partitions to drive letters) in the Windows configuration window.

Within the `$HOME/.wine/drive_c` directory (that is, your C: drive), you should see some familiar things if you are coming from an older Windows environment: `Program Files` and `windows` directories.

Note

For details on configuring WINE, see the Wine User Guide. That guide (`wineusr-guide.pdf`) is stored in the `/usr/share/doc/wine-docs*` directory when you install the wine-docs RPM. ∎

Installing applications in WINE

For Windows applications that are included on CD or DVD, you can try installing them by simply running the setup program on that medium with the `wine` command. Therefore, with a CD containing the application you want to install inserted and mounted, you would run a command like the following:

```
# wine d:\Setup.exe
```

Launching applications

Depending on how the application's installer set up the application, there are a couple of ways you might launch your Windows application in WINE:

- **Control panel** — If the application set up an applet for the Windows control panel, you can open a Windows control panel and then select the applet to launch the application from there. To start a Windows control panel, type the following:

  ```
  $ wine control
  ```

- **WINE file system browser** — If you installed the wine-core package, you can launch the `winefile` command to see the Wine File window. This window displays a tree structure of the file system, as it relates to the drives you have configured for WINE. Select the drive letter containing the application you want to launch, browse to the application, and double-click it to start.

Just as you launched the application's installer, as described earlier, you can also launch a Windows application installed on your file system from the command line. Again, you can use drive letters to indicate the location of the application you want to launch. However, to have the path to the application interpreted properly, you should typically surround it with quotes:

```
$ wine "C:\program files\appdir\app.exe"
```

For a Windows file path you use backslashes (\) instead of slashes (/) to separate subdirectories. Instead of using double quotes, you can add an extra backslash before each space or backslash.

Once you have a working `wine` command line to run your Windows application, you can add that command to a launcher on your Fedora desktop.

Cross-Reference

See Chapter 3 for information on adding application launchers to your panel, menus, or desktop area. ∎

Tuning and configuring WINE

Because the Windows applications you run with WINE expect to find Windows resources on a Linux system, those resources either have to be provided by WINE or need to be mapped into the existing Linux system. For example, an application may require a specific DLL file that WINE doesn't include; or you may need to map your COM or LPT ports to where WINE expects to find them.

Here are some tips to help you tune your WINE configuration:

- **Windows version** — Different versions of Windows provide different environments for applications to run in. WINE emulates Windows XP by default, but enables you to have WINE run nearly a dozen different Windows versions for each application. From the Wine configuration window, select the Applications tab and choose the Add application button. Choose the Windows application you want from your file system and then choose the Windows version you want it to run under.

- **Changing registry entries** — When you need to change Windows registry entries, WINE provides three files you can work with: `system.reg`, `user.reg`, and `userdef.reg`. All of these files are in the user's `$HOME/.wine` directory. You can use the `wineprefixcreate` utility to update your registry, but normally you should no longer need to, as this should happen automatically.

- **Configuring ports** — As with Windows drive letters, you can add links to serial and parallel ports to your `$HOME/.wine/dosdevices` directory. For example, to add entries for your first parallel port (LPT1) and serial port (COM1), you could run the following commands from your `$HOME/.wine/dosdevices` directory:

```
$ ln -s /dev/lp0 lpt1
$ ln -s /dev/ttyS0 com1
```

- **Adding DLLs** — WINE provides many of the basic libraries (DLL files) needed for a functioning Windows system. However, some DLLs that may be required for your application may not be included, or some that are included may not work properly for your application. Using the Windows configuration window (Libraries tab), you can replace DLLs provided by WINE or add other DLLs you have from applications you install.

- **Graphics settings** — You can change settings associated with your graphics display from the Graphics tab on the Windows configuration window. In particular, you can change how closely your Windows applications will be managed on your Linux desktop.

- **Adding fonts** — To add fonts to your WINE installation, copy TrueType fonts (`.ttf` files) to the `C:\windows\fonts` directory on your WINE virtual drive.

For further information on configuring WINE to run your Windows applications in Linux, refer to the Wine User Guide (www.winehq.org/docs/en/wineusr-guide.html).

Finding more Windows applications for WINE

For information on Windows applications that have been tested to run in WINE, refer to the Wine Application Database (http://appdb.winehq.org). CodeWeavers also keeps its own database of applications that have been tested to run under WINE. Refer to the CodeWeavers Compatibility Center (www.codeweavers.com/compatibility) for information on running Windows applications. From there, you can view CodeWeavers' own application database of more than 3,300 Windows applications.

Another website for information about WINE applications is Frank's Corner (www.frankscorner.org). This site is loaded with good tips for getting graphics, Internet, multimedia, office, games, and other applications running in WINE.

Cross-Reference

Chapter 23 covers virtualization in Linux. Using virtualization, you can run Windows, Linux, Unix, or other operating systems hosted on your Linux system. ■

Summary

Between applications written directly for Linux and other Unix systems, those that have been ported to Linux, and those that can run in emulation, thousands of applications are available for use with Fedora systems. With the Fedora repository, the number of high-quality software packages available to run on Fedora continues to grow rapidly.

To simplify the process of installing and managing your Linux applications, Red Hat developed the RPM Package Management (RPM) format. Using tools developed for RPM, such as the rpm command, you can easily install, remove, and perform queries on Linux RPM packages. Tools for finding, downloading, and installing RPM packages include the yum utility and the PackageKit window.

Of the types of applications that can run in Linux, those created for the X Window System provide the greatest level of compatibility and flexibility when used in Linux. However, using emulation software, it is possible to run applications intended for DOS and Microsoft Windows 95/98/2000/NT/XP/Vista/7 operating systems. Also, as covered in Chapter 23, virtualization software such as Xen and KVM enable multiple operating systems to run as guests on Fedora. That, in turn, provides a means for running a variety of applications within those systems on Fedora.

Working in a Linux Office

To survive as a desktop system, an operating system must be able to perform at least one task well: produce documents. It's no accident that, after Windows, Microsoft Word (which is bundled into Microsoft Office) is the foundation of Microsoft's success on the desktop. Fedora includes tools for producing documents, manipulating images, scanning, and printing. Almost everything you would expect a publishing system to do, you can do with Fedora.

This chapter describes popular Linux office suites (such as OpenOffice.org and KOffice) for creating documents, presentations, and spreadsheets. For page layouts, Scribus is an excellent application that can be used to create brochures and pamphlets. For working with images, we cover the GNU Image Manipulation Program (GIMP). For working with vector graphics, we describe the Inkscape vector graphics editor. To display the content you create, several different viewers are available for viewing output in PDF and PostScript formats.

IN THIS CHAPTER

Running the OpenOffice.org suite

Displaying PDF files

Creating documents with Groff and LaTeX

Creating DocBook documents

Doing page layout with Scribus

Working with graphics

Capturing screen images

Making Inkscape vector graphics

Using scanners driven by SANE

Running the OpenOffice.org Suite

OpenOffice.org, available from www.openoffice.org, is a powerful open-source office suite available as part of the Fedora distributions. Based on the Sun Microsystems StarOffice productivity suite (now called Oracle Office), OpenOffice.org includes a word processor, spreadsheet, presentation manager, and other personal productivity tools. In many cases, OpenOffice.org can act as a drop-in replacement for Microsoft Office, in both its features and its ability to read and save files in Word, Excel, PowerPoint, and other

Microsoft formats. You can work in a mixed environment, whereby some users run Microsoft Office applications and others OpenOffice.org applications. As long as you export the OpenOffice.org files to the Microsoft formats, most users won't ever notice the difference.

Note

The OpenOffice.org suite runs on Windows, Linux, Mac OS X, and Solaris. This means you can migrate your organization to a free office suite, saving a lot of money compared to the costs of Microsoft Office. In addition, if you want to migrate a Windows-based organization to Linux, you can start with migrating from Microsoft Office to OpenOffice.org, while remaining on Windows. Such a migration may actually be easier on your users than migrating from, say, Office 2003 to Office 2007, because the 2007 version introduced a lot of user interface changes. I'd also suggest moving to the Firefox Web browser and Thunderbird e-mail clients — Internet applications that run on Windows and Linux. Then, when your users are successful with free software, start the eventual migration to Linux.

See Chapter 8 for more on Firefox and Thunderbird. ∎

Fedora includes the entire OpenOffice.org suite of desktop applications. The latest OpenOffice.org version (3.3.0) is included with Fedora 14. OpenOffice.org consists of the following office-productivity applications:

- **OpenOffice.org Writer** — A word processing application that can work with documents in file formats from Microsoft Word and several others. Writer also has a full set of features for using templates, working with fonts, navigating your documents, including images and effects, and generating tables of contents.

- **OpenOffice.org Calc** — A spreadsheet application that enables you to incorporate data from Microsoft Excel, Oracle Office, Dbase, and several other spreadsheet formats. Some nice features in Calc enable you to create charts, set up database ranges (to easily sort data in an area of a spreadsheet), and use the data pilot tool to arrange data from different points of view.

- **OpenOffice.org Draw** — A drawing application that enables you to create, edit, and align objects; incorporate textures; include textures and colors; and work with layers of objects. You can also incorporate images, vector graphics, AutoCAD, and a variety of other file formats into your drawings. Then, you can save your drawing in the OpenOffice.org Drawing or Oracle Office Draw formats.

- **OpenOffice.org Math** — A calculation program that enables you to create mathematical formulas.

- **OpenOffice.org Impress** — A presentation application that includes a variety of slide effects. Using Impress, you can create and save presentations in the Microsoft PowerPoint, Draw, and Impress formats.

- **OpenOffice.org Base** — A low-end database, similar to Microsoft's Access database. Base can also act as a front end to other databases.

Unlike other applications that were created to work with Microsoft document and data formats, OpenOffice.org (although not perfect) does a very good job of opening and saving files from many different versions of Microsoft Word (.doc and .docx) and Excel (.xls and .xlsx) formats with fewer problems. Very basic styles and formatting that open in OpenOffice.org often don't look noticeably different from the way they appear in Microsoft Office. In fact, OpenOffice.org Writer supports older versions of Word and older Word documents better than the latest Microsoft Office suites.

Note

The Open Office XML (OOXML) format, a 6,000-page tome and no relation to the OpenOffice.org suite, represents Microsoft's recent efforts in its claim to support standard document formats. This format is the default document type in Word 2007. Some people in the open-source community, however, claim that OOXML is so specific in requiring support for Microsoft product features, without providing any guidance about how those Microsoft proprietary features can be implemented, that it is unusable as a standard. In other words, don't assume that because Microsoft claims to support certain standards that you will ever be able to fully use Microsoft document formats on other platforms.

Furthermore, the OOXML format is, in part, patented by Microsoft. This has serious future implications: While the technology may exist to read and write this XML format, you may not be legally allowed to do so, at least in countries such as the United States that allow software patents. This is another reason to avoid the OOXML file format. ■

By default, the OpenOffice.org suite saves files in ODF, or Open Document Format. Other Linux-based office applications, such as AbiWord and KOffice, support this file format.

Tip

If you are willing to pay $40 to $70, CrossOver Linux from Codeweavers.com enables you to install and run different versions of Microsoft Office (97, 2000, XP, 2003, and 2007) from your Linux desktop. See www.codeweavers.com/products/cxlinux for more on CrossOver Linux. ■

Whether you are writing a letter, a memo, or a book, you usually begin with a word processor, in most cases Openoffice.org Writer. Other word processing applications available with Linux systems include several open-source offerings, such as AbiWord and KOffice. AbiWord is especially good for systems with low memory or slower CPUs. Commercial office suites include Oracle Office, which contains not only a word processor, but also applications for creating and working with spreadsheets, presentations, and other office-oriented content. (Oracle Office is the commercial version of the OpenOffice.org suite.)

To open OpenOffice.org Writer, Impress, Calc, and other office application, click Office from the Applications menu. Then select the OpenOffice.org application you want to open. Figure 6-1 shows an example of OpenOffice.org Writer with a document file that was originally created in Microsoft Word.

FIGURE 6-1

Using Writer from OpenOffice.org to edit a document created in Microsoft Word.

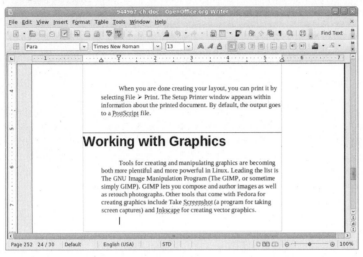

The Linux file browsers, such as GNOME's Nautilus and KDE's Dolphin, will launch the appropriate OpenOffice.org application when you double-click on document files, as shown in Figure 6-2.

FIGURE 6-2

Double-click on a Word document in the GNOME Nautilus file browser to launch the OpenOffice.org Writer application.

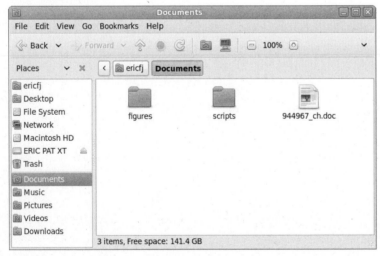

Using Writer

The controls in OpenOffice.org Writer are similar to the ones you would find in Word prior to Word 2007, so if you were comfortable with those controls you should find it easy to transition to OpenOffice.org Writer. In fact, you might find it easier than using the latest versions of Microsoft Word because many people found the transition to Word 2007 or 2010 difficult.

Toolbars in OpenOffice.org Writer include boxes for identifying filenames, and changing styles, font types, and font sizes. Buttons enable you to save and print the file, change the text alignment, and cut, copy, and paste text. In other words, Writer includes almost everything you expect in an advanced word processor. In addition, Writer includes a handy PDF button to output a file directly to the PDF format. This is very useful for exchanging documents or placing data on the Internet.

If you are just starting out with OpenOffice.org Writer, here are a few features you can try:

- **Wizards** — Use a wizard to start a letter, fax, agenda, presentation, Web page, Document Converter, or Euro Converter. Select File ➪ Wizards and then choose one of the document types just mentioned. The Document Converter Wizard enables you to convert a directory of Microsoft documents to OpenDocument format. Use the Euro Converter to convert files containing different European currencies to euros.

- **Document styles and formatting** — Create the format of your documents using character, paragraph, frame, page, and numbering styles (select Format ➪ Styles and Formatting). From the Styles and Formatting window, choose the type of style you want to change, right-click in the Styles box, and choose New to create your own style.

- **Outputting PDF or other formats** — Writer provides a toolbar button that will output your current document to PDF format. PDF is a good format for sharing documents that you want others to be able to read or print, but don't necessarily want to give them the ability to modify the document. You can also save Writer documents to other useful formats, including HTML (to publish your document to the Web) or Rich Text Format (to be able to share the document with different word processors).

Other Office Applications

The OpenOffice.org suite includes a reasonable replacement for MS Excel and PowerPoint in addition to Writer described here. Furthermore, the OpenOffice.org suite isn't the only game in town. Linux offers quite a few options, including the following.

AbiWord

The AbiWord word processor (`abiword` command) is a very nice, free word processor from the AbiSource project (`www.abisource.com`). If you are creating documents from scratch, AbiWord includes many of the basic functions you need to create good-quality documents. In addition to working with files in its own AbiWord format (`.abw` and `.zabw`), AbiWord can import files in Microsoft Word and several other formats.

If you have slow hardware, AbiWord offers better performance than OpenOffice.org Writer. If you are working in a cross-platform environment, you can get versions of AbiWord that run in Windows, Mac OS X, QNX, and most Unix derivatives (Linux, BSD, Solaris, and so on).

KOffice

The KOffice package contains a set of office productivity applications designed for the KDE desktop. Installing the koffice-suite package will pull in most of the software you need to use. KOffice includes a word processor (KWord), a spreadsheet (KSpread), a presentation creator (KPresenter), and a diagram drawing program (KChart). These applications can be run separately or within a KOffice Workspace. The koffice package is on the DVD that comes with this book. You can learn more about it from the KOffice website at `www.koffice.org`.

Use the command `yum install koffice-suite` to install the KOffice suite.

Note
In general, the OpenOffice.org suite provides closer compatibility with documents created in Microsoft Office than the KOffice suite. ∎

TextMaker

TextMaker is another popular commercial word-processing package for Linux (`www.softmaker .com/english/tml_en.htm`). This word processor requires much less memory than OpenOffice. org Writer but still contains many powerful features. TextMaker is part of the SoftMaker Office 2010 suite.

Cross-Reference
If you only need to edit a plain-text document, you can begin with a simple text editor. See Chapter 4 for more on Linux text editors. ∎

GNUmeric

GNUmeric is the official spreadsheet of the GNOME desktop project. It aims to provide a very close match to Microsoft's Excel.

Displaying PDF Files

The Portable Document Format (PDF) provides a way to store documents as they would appear in print. With Adobe Acrobat Reader, you can view PDF files in a very friendly way. Adobe Acrobat makes it easy to move around within a PDF file. A PDF file may include hyperlinks, a table of contents, graphics, and a variety of type fonts.

PDF files are used extensively on the Internet as a means to exchange documents. Traditionally, the PDF file has been considered more secure than other formats such as Microsoft Word, although there have been PDF security issues as well. In addition, as a read-only document format, PDF files serve better than Word documents when an organization wants to distribute documents.

Fedora Linux comes with Evince, the GNOME PDF-viewing application, as well as Okular, the KDE desktop's program. The best way to launch Evince is to right-click on a PDF file in a Nautilus file-browser window and choose Open With ⇨ Document Viewer.

You can download the official Adobe Acrobat Reader application from `get.adobe.com/ reader/`. As of this writing, the most recent version is 9.3.4. See `www.adobe.com/products/ reader/dlm/firefox_steps.html` for instructions on how to install the Adobe PDF Reader plug-in for Firefox.

Acrobat Reader is distributed by default as a `.bin` file, a binary executable. A better option is to use the RPM version. Click on the Different language or operating system? link to select a Linux RPM version.

Using Traditional Linux Publishing Tools

The first document and graphics tools for Linux were mostly built on older, text-based tools. Despite their age, many of the older publishing tools such as Groff and LaTeX are still used by people in the technical community. With these old-school text processors you can ignore document appearance while writing. Plain-text macros instruct post-processors how to lay out a document for printing after writing is done. With word processors (such as OpenOffice.org Writer), you mark up text and see the basic layout of the document as you write.

Some attributes of the traditional Linux publishing tools make them particularly well suited for certain types of document publishing. Groff and LaTeX (which is based on TeX) are included with Fedora and have been popular for several reasons, including the following:

- You can manipulate files in plain text. Using tools such as `sed` and `grep`, you can scan and change one document or hundreds with a single command or script.

- Scientific notation is supported. With `geqn`, you can create complex equations. LaTeX and TeX are suited for technical notation. Some math publications require LaTeX.

- Editing can be faster because traditional Linux documents are created with a text editor. You usually get better performance out of a text editor than a word processor.

Simple page layouts work well with Linux documentation tools. For example, a technical book with a few flowcharts and images can be easily produced and maintained using Groff or TeX documentation tools. Letters and memos are also easy to do with these tools; and, of course, Linux man pages are created with text-based tools.

The drawback to the traditional Linux document tools is that they are not intuitive. Rarely will a beginner try to use these tools, unless they have a need to support legacy Unix or Linux documents (such as manual pages or old Unix guides). Although there are some easier front ends to LaTeX (see the description of LyX later), if you are creating documents in a text editor, you need to learn what macros to type into your documents and which formatting and print commands to use.

Creating Documents in Groff or LaTeX

You can create documents for either of Linux's Groff (troff/nroff) or LaTeX (TeX) styles of publishing using any text editor. Fedora comes with several text editors, or you can download others from the Internet.

Cross-Reference
See the section "Using Text Editors," in Chapter 4, for more information. ∎

The process of creating documents in Groff or LaTeX consists of the following general steps:

1. Create a document with any text editor. The document will contain text and markup.

2. Format the document using a formatting command that matches the style of the document you created (e.g., `groff` or `latex`). During this step, you may need to indicate that the document contains special content, such as equations (`eqn` command), tables (`tbl` command), or line drawings (`pic` command).

3. Send the document to an output device. The device may be a printer or display program.

If you are used to a word processor with a GUI, you may find these publishing tools difficult. In general, Groff is useful to create man pages for Linux. LaTeX is useful if you need to produce mathematical documents, perhaps for publication in a technical journal.

Text processing with Groff

The `nroff` and `troff` text formatting commands were the first interfaces available for producing typeset-quality documents with the Unix system. They aren't editors; rather, they are commands that you send your text through, with the result being formatted pages.

The `groff` command is the front end for producing `nroff/troff` documentation. Because Linux man pages are formatted and output in Groff, most of the examples here help you create and print man pages with Groff. Groff includes a number of macro packages, including the following:

- man — The `man` macros are used to create Linux man pages. You can format a man page using the `-man` option to the `groff` command.

- mm — The `mm` macros (memorandum macros) were created to produce memos, letters, and technical white papers. This macro package includes macros for creating a table of contents, lists of figures, references, and other features that are helpful for producing technical documents. You can format an `mm` document using the `-mm groff` option.

Groff macro packages are stored in `/usr/share/groff/*/tmac`. The `man` macros are called from the `an.tmac` file and `mm` macros are from `m.tmac`. The naming convention for each macro package is *xxx*.`tmac`, where *xxx* is replaced by one or more letters representing the macro package.

Tip

Instead of noting a specific macro package, you can use `-mandoc` **to choose a macro package.** ■

When you run the `groff` formatting command, you can indicate on the command line which macro packages you are using. You can also indicate that the document should be run through any of the following commands that preprocess text for special formats:

- `eqn` — Formats macros that produce equations in `groff`
- `pic` — Formats macros that create simple line drawings in `groff`
- `tbl` — Formats macros that produce tables within `groff`

The formatted Groff document is output for a particular device type. The device can be a printer, a window, or (for plain text) your shell, with `ps` (for PostScript printers) or `dvi` (a device-independent format for output to a variety of other devices) being the most popular formats.

Formatting and printing documents with Groff

You can try formatting and printing an existing Groff document using any man pages on your Fedora system, such as those in `/usr/share/man/*`. (Those man pages are compressed, so you can copy them to a temporary directory and unzip them to try out Groff.)

In the following example, the `chown` man page (`chown.1.gz`) is copied to the `/tmp` directory, unzipped (using `gunzip`), and output in plain text (`-Tascii`) using the man macros (`-man`). The output is piped to `less`, for paging through it on your screen. Instead of piping to `less` (`| less`), you can direct the output to a file (`> /tmp/chown.txt`).

```
$ cp /usr/share/man/man1/chown.1.gz /tmp
$ gunzip /tmp/chown.1.gz
$ groff -Tascii -man /tmp/chown.1 | less
```

To format a man page for typesetting, you can specify PostScript or HP LaserJet output. You should direct the output either to a file or to a printer. Here are a couple of examples:

```
$ groff -Tps -man /tmp/chown.1 > /tmp/chown.ps
$ groff -Tlj4 -man -l /tmp/chown.1
```

The first example creates PostScript output (`-Tps`) and directs it to a file called `/tmp/chown.ps`. That file can be read by a PostScript previewer (such as Ghostscript) or sent to a printer (`lpr /tmp/chown.ps`). The second example creates HP LaserJet output (`-Tlj4`) and directs it to the default printer (`-l` option).

Text processing with TeX/LaTeX

TeX (pronounced *tech*) is a collection of commands used primarily to produce scientific and mathematical typeset documents. The most common way to use TeX is by calling a macro package, which enhances your ability to create documents, building on top of the basic TeX capabilities. The most popular macro package for TeX is LaTeX, which takes a higher-level approach to formatting TeX documents. TeX and LaTeX tools are contained in the `tetex-latex` package.

Popular macro files that you can use with TeX include the following:

- `amstex` — Mathematical publications, including the American Mathematical Society, use this as their official typesetting system.
- `eplain` — Includes macros for indexing and tables of contents.
- `texinfo` — Macros used by the Free Software Foundation to produce software manuals. Text output from these macros can be used with the Linux `info` command.

You can create a TeX/LaTeX file using any text editor. After the text and macros are created, you can run the `tex` command (or one of several other related utilities) to format the file. The input file is in the form `filename.tex`. The output is generally three different files: `filename.dvi`, `filename.log`, and `filename.aux`.

The `.dvi` file produced can be formatted for a particular device. For example, you could use the `dvips` command to output the resulting `.dvi` file to your PostScript printer (`dvips filename .dvi`). Alternately, you could use the `xdvi` command to preview the `.dvi` file in X.

Creating and formatting a LaTeX document

The best way to get started with LaTeX is to use the LyX editor. LyX provides a GUI for creating LaTeX documents. It also contains a variety of templates you can use, rather than create a document from scratch.

Note

The LyX editor is available from the Fedora repository; you can install it by typing yum install lyx. ∎

If you want to edit LaTeX in a regular text editor, you need to be familiar with the LaTeX commands. For a complete listing of the LaTeX commands, type the command `info latex` and then go to the section "Commands within a LaTeX document."

Creating DocBook documents

Documentation projects often need to produce documents that are output in a variety of formats. For example, the same text describing how to use a software program may need to be output as a printed manual, an HTML page, and a PostScript file. The standards that have been embraced most recently by the Linux community for creating what are referred to as *structured documents* are SGML, XML, and DocBook.

DocBook's focus is on marking content, rather than indicating a particular look (that is, font type, size, position, and so on). It includes markup that enables you to automate the process of creating indices, figure lists, and tables of contents, to name a few. Tools in Fedora enable you to output DocBook documents into HTML, PDF, DVI, PostScript, RTF, and other formats.

DocBook is important to the Linux community because many open-source projects are using DocBook to produce documentation. For example, the following organizations use DocBook to create the documents that describe their software:

- Linux Documentation Project (`www.tldp.org/LDP/LDP-Author-Guide`)
- GNOME Documentation (`http://library.gnome.org/devel/gdp-handbook/`)
- KDE Documentation Project (`www.kde.org/documentation`)
- FreeBSD Documentation Project (`www.freebsd.org/docproj`)

If you want to contribute to any of the preceding documentation projects, refer to the websites for each organization. In all cases, they publish writers' guides or style guides that describe the DocBook tags that they support for their writing efforts.

Cross-Reference
You can find official documentation for DocBook at `www.docbook.org`. ■

Fedora includes a number of utilities for converting DocBook files in the `docbook-utils` and `docbook-utils-pdf` packages.

Doing Page Layout with Scribus

For brochures, magazines, newsletters, catalogs, and other materials that require more sophisticated layouts than you can achieve with a word processor, you need a page layout application. The most popular open-source page layout application is Scribus (`www.scribus.net`).

Although Scribus is intended primarily to produce print publications, you can also use Scribus to produce what are referred to as *intelligent PDFs*. With PDFs that you create with Scribus, you can include JavaScript and other features that enable others to interact with your text (such as by filling in forms). Scribus is similar to the Publisher application available with Windows.

To use Scribus in Fedora, install the `scribus` package, which includes templates and samples you can use to start your own projects (usually in `/usr/share/scribus/`).

With the `scribus` package installed, you can start Scribus from the GNOME desktop by selecting Applications ➪ Graphics ➪ Scribus. After Scribus is running on your desktop, begin by selecting a template (select File ➪ New from Template). Choose a brochure, newsletter, presentation, or text-based layout.

When you are done creating your layout, you can print it by selecting File ⇨ Print. The Setup Printer window appears with information about the printed document. By default, the output goes to a PostScript file.

Working with Graphics

Tools for creating and manipulating graphics are becoming both more plentiful and more powerful in Linux. Leading the list is The GNU Image Manipulation Program (The GIMP, or sometimes simply GIMP). GIMP enables you to compose and author images, as well as retouch photographs. Other tools included with Fedora for creating graphics include Take Screenshot (a program for taking screen captures) and Inkscape, for creating vector graphics.

Cross-Reference
See Chapter 7 for descriptions of other multimedia applications, such as gPhoto2, for working with images from digital cameras. ■

Manipulating images with GIMP

To create images with GIMP, you can either import a drawing, photograph, or 3D image, or you can create one from scratch. To start GIMP, from the Applications menu click Graphics ⇨ GNU Image Manipulation Program or type `gimp&` from a terminal window.

In many ways, GIMP 2.6.11 is similar to Adobe Photoshop. Some people feel that GIMP's scripting features are comparable to, or even better than, Actions in Adobe Photoshop. One capability in which GIMP has been behind Photoshop has been in the area of color management. With the latest features of GIMP, however, you can calibrate screens and work with color profiles from your cameras and scanners (`http://docs.gimp.org/en/gimp-imaging-color-management.html`).

Tip
If you make a mistake while editing an image, select Edit ⇨ Undo from the GIMP menu or press Ctrl+Z. To redo undone changes, press Ctrl+Y. ■

Taking screen captures

If you want to show examples of the work you do on Fedora, you can use the Take Screenshot program to capture screen images. The GNOME desktop comes with the Take Screenshot program.

Note
If you don't have GNOME installed, you can also use GIMP to capture screenshots of your desktop. ■

To open Take Screenshot, from the Applications menu click Accessories ⇨ Take Screenshot (or type `gnome-screenshot`).

When Take Screenshot first opens, it provides options for capturing the contents of a window or the entire desktop. You can also delay the screenshot for a set number of seconds. Once you take a screenshot, you are prompted to save it. You can also copy the image to the clipboard. Take Screenshot saves images in the PNG format. You can use GIMP to convert to another format.

Creating vector graphic images with Inkscape

When you need maximum flexibility while working with graphics and text, a vector graphic editor enables you to deal with geometric elements (such as lines, curves, and boxes) instead of dots (as you do with image editors). As a result, you usually get cleaner edges on your fonts and graphics, and the capability to bend and shape those elements as you like. Inkscape (`http://inkscape.org`) is a popular vector graphics editor that is available with Fedora.

With Inkscape, you have an application with features similar to those you find in commercial products such as Adobe Illustrator and CorelDraw. Inkscape creates images in Scalable Vector Graphics (SVG) format — an open standard from the W3C (`www.w3.org/Graphics/SVG`). Thousands of SVG graphics and clipart elements are available in the public domain or under Creative Commons licenses.

In Fedora, install the `inkscape` package to get Inkscape. I recommend you also install the `openclipart` package, which provides hundreds of clipart items for use in your Inkscape creations. With the inkscape and openclipart packages installed, select Applications ➪ Graphics ➪ Inkscape Vector Graphics Editor to open an Inkscape window. Figure 6-3 shows an example of the Inkscape window.

You can start by opening one of the dozens of templates available with Inkscape (select File ➪ New and choose from web banner, business card, DVD cover, or other templates).

FIGURE 6-3

Inkscape lets you manipulate vector graphics and text.

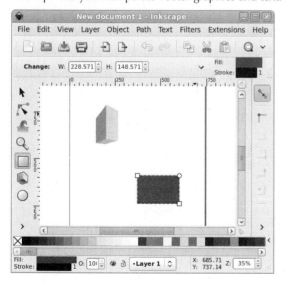

When you are done creating your vector graphic, you can print it by selecting File ⇨ Print. From the Print window's Rendering tab, you can select to have the image in vector or bitmap form.

Using Scanners Driven by SANE

Software for using a scanner with Linux is being driven by an effort called *Scanner Access Now Easy* (*SANE*). This effort standardized how device drivers for equipment such as scanners, digital still cameras, and digital video cameras are created, and helped simplify the interfaces for applications that use those devices.

SANE is now included with the Fedora distributions. The `sane-backends`, `sane-frontends`, `simple-scan`, `xsane`, and `xsane-gimp` packages are all on the DVD included with this book. You can get the latest SANE driver packages from `www.sane-project.org`.

Someone who wants to use Linux as a publishing platform is generally interested in two scanner issues: which scanners are supported and which applications are available to use the scanners. In the past, more SCSI scanners were supported than parallel scanners, which have since given way to the more convenient USB scanners.

Because of ongoing development effort, new scanners are being supported all the time. You can find a current list of supported scanners at `www.sane-project.org/sane-supported-devices.html`. As for applications, the following are currently available with Fedora:

- `simple-scan` — This is an X-based graphical front end for SANE scanners; `simple-scan` can work as a GIMP plugin or as a separate application. (From the Applications menu, select Graphics ⇨ Simple Scan.) Beginning with Fedora 13, `simple-scan` replaces the older program `xsane`.

- `scanimage` — This is a command-line interface for obtaining scanned images. The command acquires the scanned image and then directs the data to standard output (so you can send it to a file or pipe it to another program). This program is included in the `sane-backends` package.

In addition to these applications, the OpenOffice.org suite supports SANE.

The architecture of SANE scanner drivers makes it possible to separate scanner drivers from scanner applications, which makes it possible to share scanners across a network.

Summary

Tools available in Linux for publishing words and images on paper and the Web can compete with similar software available commercially. For producing hardcopy documents, you have word processors such as OpenOffice.org Writer, AbiWord, and KOffice. To lay out pages, there is Scribus. To work with photos, you have GIMP, or for vector graphics you can use Inkscape.

Music, Video, and Images in Linux

Nearly every kind of audio and video format available today can be played, displayed, encoded, decoded, and managed in Linux. With the development of the Theora video codec, there are now patent-free, royalty-free formats available for every major type of multimedia content available today. If you are starting from scratch, you can legally create, manipulate, and share your own multimedia content from Linux using all free applications and codecs.

This chapter covers many different tools that are included with Fedora for playing or displaying digital music, video, and images. It also takes a swipe at explaining some of the legal issues surrounding software for playing commercial movie DVDs, MP3 music, and various audio/video formats in Linux.

Video content that is readily available on the Internet for playing movie clips, commercial films, and other content can be viewed using several different players in, or available for, Fedora. Also, you can view live television and video using TV Tuner cards (or TV cards for short) and webcams.

Because CD-ROM is the physical medium of choice for recorded music, this chapter describes how to set up and use CD burners to create your own music CDs. After your CD burner is set up to record music, you can use the same CD burner to back up your data or create software CDs. (The same tools can be used to burn DVDs as well.)

Understanding Multimedia and Legal Issues in Linux

You can't play commercial (encrypted) DVD movies or MP3 music with software delivered with Fedora because there are patent claims associated with the formats used to store, encode, and decode that content that would prevent open-source software that worked with that content from being freely distributed. Commercial Linux vendors, including Red Hat, have decided not to add software codecs (which encode and decode multimedia formats), even if they were written from scratch and covered under the GPL, that are encumbered by contentious software patents. After Thomson and Fraunhofer Gesellschaft (which control the MP3 patent) began requesting licensing fees in 2002 of $.075 for MP3 decoders (per system), Red Hat Linux dropped MP3 support. (See www.mp3licensing.com/royalty for details.)

Just to clarify, I am not talking about copyright here. Nobody can rightly claim that it is okay to copy someone else's commercial code and release it as free software. It would clearly violate copyright laws. What we are talking about are patents.

The effect of a patent is to allow someone to control the rights regarding who can make, sell, offer to sell, use, or import an invention that the patent applicant dreamed up. As it relates to multimedia software in particular, the encoding and decoding of audio and video content for many commercially released music and video formats are covered by patents. Therefore, even if open-source developers write every piece of code from scratch to encode and decode content, it may not be legal to distribute it without paying a royalty to the patent owner.

Major efforts are underway (especially in Europe) to oppose software patents. (Refer to the Foundation for a Free Information Infrastructure website at http://ffii.org for further information.) The contention is that so many ideas related to software are being patented that it could severely cripple the ability to innovate (especially for open-source developers or small software companies without huge legal teams).

Patents have been granted in Europe for common items that might appear on a Web page, such as selling things over a network, using an electronic shopping cart, and using rebate codes (see http://webshop.ffii.org). Although there are now laws in Europe that are aimed at preventing any further software patents, some software patents are still being granted, and existing patents are still being used to discourage innovation.

Despite efforts against software patents, however, the fact remains that Fedora does not include some of the software that you would want to use to play your digital media. That doesn't mean, however, that there is nothing you can do to legally play the commercial audio and video content you want to play in Linux. This chapter includes discussions about how to find the codecs you want and use them legally, when possible.

Extending Freedom to Codecs

Fedora may not be able to give you the audio decoders you need to play every kind of media you want, but it gives you the freedom (and the tools) to go out and get those decoders yourself. For example, you can purchase codecs for non-free audio and video formats, such as MPEG4 video, Windows Media, and others. Or, if you are in a country where software patents are not recognized, Fedora finds and automatically downloads open-source software that can play many different types of patent-encumbered codecs.

A company called Fluendo (www.fluendo.com), which is responsible for the GStreamer multimedia framework used in Fedora, purchased an unlimited MP3 license that allows you to download the Fluendo MP3 Audio Decoder for free, to play your MP3 audio files. You can pay a small fee to get audio/video codecs such as Dolby AC3 Audio Decoder, Windows Media MMS Network Stream Reader, MPEG2 Video Decoder, or MPEG4 Part 2 Video Decoder. Read the licensing agreement that appears before you accept the download. Unlike software that comes with Fedora, you cannot freely redistribute the codecs you get from Fluendo.

Listening to Music in Linux

Good-quality sound hardware is considered a necessity for today's desktop and laptop computer systems. Whether playing songs downloaded from the Internet, sound tracks to digital movies, or audio from a TV card, any user-friendly operating system has to support a healthy list of sound hardware and audio applications.

Most popular sound devices for the PC, whether on separate cards or built into your computer's motherboard, are automatically detected when a Fedora system boots up. Appropriate modules will be loaded, so you can immediately begin using your sound card.

Beginning with Fedora 8, PulseAudio (www.pulseaudio.org) became the default sound system used with Fedora, taking over that spot from Advanced Linux Sound Architecture (ALSA). PulseAudio basically provides the interfaces between audio applications and your sound card. A major improvement over other audio systems is that it enables you to control volume levels separately for different applications. Also, by incorporating plugins, PulseAudio enables you to use audio applications that were designed for ALSA. (Fedora 13 and beyond add improved integration between PulseAudio and the KDE desktop.)

To control playback volume and audio input and output devices, the pulseaudio package includes the PulseAudio Sound Preferences window. The alsa-utils RPM package contains the commands and configuration files you can use to tune your sound card and adjust audio levels. Other friendly graphical tools have been added by the GNOME and KDE projects for managing sound.

After your sound card is working and audio levels are adjusted, you can use any of the dozens of audio applications that come with Linux with your sound card. Those applications include music players, video players, video conferencing applications, games, and audio recorders, to name a few.

As for audio content, the following list describes the types of audio content you might want to play, which players can be used for each type of content, and whether or not the software comes with Fedora. (If it doesn't come with Fedora, I describe where you can get software to play that content and the issues associated with getting and using the software.)

- **Music CDs (CDDA)** — Nearly all commercial music CDs are stored in the Compact Disc Digital Audio system (CDDA). Rhythmbox can play music CDs, as well as import songs to your hard disk (using Sound Juicer) so you can manage your music from one location. Other applications in Fedora that can play audio files from CDs include xmms and grip. Fedora's default CD player for GNOME is Rhythmbox.

- **Ogg Vorbis Audio** — If you are compressing and storing music from scratch, Ogg Vorbis is probably the best choice if you want to avoid any royalty issues completely. The libvorbis codec, included with Fedora, makes it possible to play audio encoded in Ogg Vorbis format in a variety of Linux music players, including xmms, Rhythmbox, ogg123, and many others. The vorbis-tools package also includes utilities for encoding (oggenc) and decoding (oggdec) Ogg Vorbis content to or from WAV and raw music formats. The Xiph.org Foundation develops both Ogg Vorbis audio formats and Theora video formats.

- **MP3 Audio** — MPEG Audio Layer 3 (MP3) has become the standard format for storing audio files that are transmitted over computer networks (such as the Internet). Because of licensing issues associated with distributing MP3 players, the Fedora Project does not include codecs needed to encode or decode MP3 audio files in any of its distributions. However, Fedora does give you the opportunity to download free, legal MP3 decoders from Fluendo.

    Another way to get MP3 support, which may not be legal where you are, is to install the xmms-mp3 package, which contains software needed by Linux audio players to play MP3 audio files with the xmms music player. You need the package named lame to create compressed audio files from WAV, AIFF, or raw audio files that play on MP3 players. Many use the mpg321 command-line MP3 player, which is available in the mpg321 package. (All of these packages are available from the rpmfusion.org RPM repository. See Chapter 5 for more info on installing software from the rrpmfusion.org repository.)

- **FLAC Audio** — FLAC is an open-source lossless audio format. *Lossless* means that it compresses the audio as much as possible without losing sound quality. Comparing the same song compressed in Ogg Vorbis and FLAC (using default settings), FLAC files are on average about six times the size of the Ogg Vorbis files.

    Many of the same applications that can play Ogg Vorbis files can play FLAC files as well. Rhythmbox, ogg123, and xmms can all play FLAC files. You can encode FLAC audio using Sound Juicer or the flac command, among others.

- **Other Audio Formats** — While the audio formats mentioned previously are the most common ones used for music files today, there are other audio formats you may want to play from Linux. Refer to the description of the sox utility for several audio formats that are supported by that utility. Use the play command (which comes with the sox package) or aplay (which is in the alsa-utils package) to play content stored in any of those supported formats.

Audio formats that are sometimes included with video files are described in the section "Playing Video," later in this chapter. For an official description of which contentious multimedia encoding software (and other software) Fedora doesn't include, refer to the Fedora Project Forbidden Items page (http://fedoraproject.org/wiki/ForbiddenItems).

Configuring a sound card

Configuring a sound card in Linux consists primarily of having the right modules loaded (which usually happens automatically at boot time) and then using the sound utilities you choose (such as the PulseAudio Sound Preferences, alsamixer, or aumix) to adjust the settings for the sound card. Today's sound cards often have more than the old Mic-In, Line-In, Speaker-out, and Joystick ports, so when you want to adjust your audio levels there are more items you need to learn about.

Sound card features

Sound cards can hold an amazing number of features these days. Most current PCs come with built-in sound support. Here are some of the features you should look for if you want to purchase a sound card separately:

- **Sound recording and playback quality** — When you record and play back audio, quality and file size are determined, in part, by word length (the number of bits that are used to hold a numerical value) and sample rates. Typical word lengths include 8-bit (less popular), 16-bit, or 24-bit digital sizes. To convert the sound, the board samples the sound in waves from 8 kHz to 96 kHz, or 8,000 to 96,000 times per second. (Of course, the higher the sampling, the better the sound and larger the output.)

- **Full-duplex support** — This allows for recording and playback to occur at the same time. This is particularly useful for bidirectional Internet communication or simultaneous recording and playback.

- **PCI or USB interface** — Most people purchase a PCI sound card to put in the case of their desktop system when sound ports on the computer's motherboard are not sufficient. However, if you are using a PC with limited slots (such as a Shuttle) or a laptop, there are USB sound cards that are supported in Linux.

Several different ports on the board enable you to connect input/output devices. These ports can include some or all of the following:

- **Line-In (blue)** — Connects an external CD player, cassette deck, synthesizer, MiniDisc, or other device for recording or playback. If you have a TV card, you might also patch that card's line-out to your sound card's line-in.

- **Microphone (red)** — Connects a microphone for audio recording or communications.

- **Headphone/Line-Out/Speaker Out (green)** — Connects speakers, headphones, or a stereo amplifier. (On sound cards I've tested, this is marked as Headphone in mixer utilities.)

- **Joystick/MIDI (15-pin connector)** — Connects a joystick for gaming or MIDI devices. (Some sound cards no longer have these ports because they are now available with most motherboards.)

- **Digital out (orange)** — A digital out connector can be used to connect a digital audio tape (DAT) device or CD recordable (CD-R) device.

- **Rear out (black)** — Can be used to deliver audio output to powered speakers or an external amplifier.
- **Internal CD Audio** — This internal port connects the sound card to your computer's internal CD-ROM drive (typically, this port isn't exposed when the board is installed, which makes it more difficult to directly connect these devices).

For some sound applications, you need to identify the device files used to communicate with the sound card and other sound hardware. While your system may not have all these available, the devices that the audio programs use to access audio hardware in Fedora include the following:

- **/dev/cdrom** — Device representing your first CD-ROM drive. (Additional CD-ROM drives are located at `/dev/cdrom1`, `/dev/cdrom2`, and so on.)
- **/dev/dsp, /dev/dsp1, and /dev/adsp** — Digital sampling devices, which many audio applications identify to access your sound card. This requires the snd-pcm-oss kernel module.
- **/dev/mixer, /dev/mixer1** — Sound-mixing devices.
- **/dev/sequencer** — Device that provides a low-level interface to MIDI, FM, and GUS.
- **/dev/midi00 and /dev/midi** — Devices that provide raw access to midi ports.
- **/dev/snd/*** — ALSA native sound device interfaces.

Note

Nodes in the `/dev` directory, such as `/dev/cdrom`, aren't just regular files. They represent access points to the physical devices (hard disks, COM ports, and so on) that are connected to your system, or to pseudo-devices (such as terminal windows). For example, to find out the device of your current terminal window, type tty. Then send some data to that device. For example, if your device name is `/dev/pts/0`, type the following:

```
$ echo "Hello There" > /dev/pts/0
```

The words "Hello There" appear in that terminal window. You can try sending messages among several terminal windows. If a user who is logged on to the computer has terminal permissions open, you can send messages to him or her in this way, too. (I've known people who would send a dictionary file to an unsuspecting user's terminal. Although it wasn't destructive, it was annoying if you were trying to get work done.) ■

To get information about your sound cards from the ALSA service, list the contents of the following files (for example, `cat /proc/asound/devices`):

- **/proc/asound/devices** — Contains available capture, playback, and other devices associated with your sound system
- **/proc/asound/cards** — Contains the names, model numbers, and IRQs of your sound cards

For general information about sound in Linux, see the Sound-HOWTO (for tips about sound cards and general sound issues) and the Sound-Playing-HOWTO (for tips on software for playing different types of audio files). You can also refer to the Linux Audio Users Guide (`http://lau.linuxaudio.org`).

Note

You can find Linux HOWTOs at www.tldp.org. ■

Detecting your sound card driver

Unlike earlier releases, sound card detection should "just work" in current releases. You can adjust sound settings and see what sound cards were detected from the Sound Preferences window. From the System menu, select Preferences ⇨ Sound. Then choose the Hardware tab. Figure 7-1 shows an example of the Sound Preferences window.

FIGURE 7-1

The Sound Preferences window lets you check and adjust audio settings.

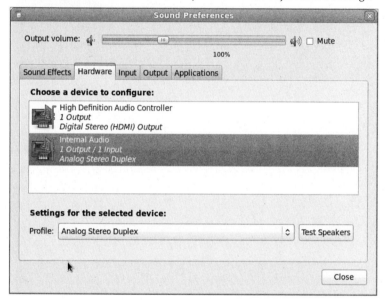

Note

Audio may be muted when you first install Fedora. If you are not able to hear the test of your sound card, use Sound Preferences or alsamixer (described later in this chapter) to unmute and adjust the volume on your audio input. ■

At this point, you can check the audio hardware that was detected, adjust input and output volume, and see sliders (on the Applications tab) for audio applications that are running.

Try playing an audio file. Insert a CD and Fedora should ask you whether you want to open Rhythmbox or one of the audio players described in the following sections. When you play the CD, if you don't hear any sound but the utility seems to have detected your sound card, refer to the next section and try adjusting your audio levels. If that doesn't work, try some of the debugging procedures suggested in the ALSA Wiki (http://alsa.opensrc.org/).

Tip

If there is a data CD in your CD drive, you may not be able to simply eject it to play your music CD. To eject a data CD, close any windows that may have an open file from the CD, and then unmount the CD in your drive (if one is mounted) by typing `umount /media/cdrecorder` **as root user from a terminal window (the mount point name may be something other than** `cdrecorder`**). Then you can eject the old CD and place an audio CD in the drive. If the CD appears as an icon on the desktop, you can right-click the CD icon and select Eject to eject the disc.** ■

Adjusting sound levels

Every audio output (playback) and input (capture) device associated with your sound cards can be adjusted or muted using one of several different tools that come with Fedora. From the Sound Preferences window described earlier, select the Applications tab to adjust sound levels for individual applications.

A separate menu option available with the applet on the top bar of the desktop allows you to quickly mute the sound. In addition, if you simply click the applet, GNOME presents a volume slider to make it easy to adjust the current volume — the most likely operation when it comes to sound.

The alsamixer utility is an ncurses application, which means that it is viewed graphically from a shell. It can be used to manage sound levels for more than one sound card on a computer, each with multiple devices representing it. Type **alsamixer** from a terminal window to start it in playback mode (to adjust audio output) or **alsamixer -V capture** (to select an audio capture device and adjust audio capture level).

Here are some ways to adjust your audio with alsamixer:

- Use the right and left arrow keys to move among the different sound tracks.
- Use the up and down arrow keys to adjust the levels of the current tracks.
- Press M to mute or unmute the current track (playback mode only).
- Press the spacebar to make the current track the capture device, for devices such as microphone or line-in that are appropriate for capturing audio. Then adjust the Capture bar to set the level at which audio is captured. (Note that this feature works in capture mode only: `alsamixer -V capture` or by pressing F4 in alsamixer.)

Tracks that are muted appear with an MM at the bottom of the slider. When unmuted and at the lowest volume level, 00 appears instead. If more tracks are available than can appear on the screen, the right arrow key enables you to scroll to the right to display additional track bars.

If two channels are available on a track, you can adjust them individually. With the track selected, use the q, w, and e keys to adjust the left, both, and right channels up, respectively. Use z, x, and c to adjust those same channels down, respectively. When you are done using alsamixer, press the Esc key to exit.

Here are a few general rules for adjusting your audio channels:

- To avoid unwanted noise on playback or record, mute any tracks you are not using.

- An icon representing your Sound Preferences utility should appear on your desktop panel. The single slider associated with that icon may be set to adjust your master volume or headphone port output. Right-click that icon and select Preferences to change to a different port.

- To test that your audio channels are working, use the `speaker-test` command. For example, `speaker-test -c4` will send a tone to each of four speakers in turn (front left, front right, rear left, and rear right) to confirm that each is working. Note that the tone output may surprise you with its loudness.

Tip

By default, alsamixer will try to use an emulated device provided by PulseAudio and will likely have only one or two mixers to control. If you want to control the underlying real ALSA device and all of its associated controls, press F6 in alsamixer to choose your sound card. If you have more than one sound card, each sound card is identified by a number, with zero identifying the first sound card. For example, to start alsamixer for your second sound card, type `alsamixer -c 1`. ■

Setting your sound card to record

I added this section on setting your sound card to record because people often miss this step. You may run a communications application (such as Ekiga) and wonder why nothing records. The reason is that you need to identify the capture device to use before you record and make sure its level is set high enough to work.

The easiest way to set the channel to use for audio capture is to use the Sound Preferences window described earlier. Click the Input tab and choose the device that controls your computer microphone (or other input device). Then make sure that all audio devices are muted except the one you want to record from. Available devices might include microphone, line-in, and CD. A red X through a microphone icon beneath each capture device indicates that it is muted.

Move the slider for your capture device up to an appropriate level. Then connect your microphone or input device (to line-in) and start the application you want to record from.

Tip

Audacity is a nice application for recording and working with recorded sound in Fedora. You can install the audacity package from the Fedora repository (type `yum install audacity`). ■

Choosing audio players

There are audio players in Fedora for playing music and sound files in a variety of formats. Without adding any software, you can play commercial music CDs and Ogg Vorbis audio (which you can rip and encode yourself). MP3 support can be added to some of these players, while MP3 players outside of the Fedora distribution are also available.

- **KsCD player (kscd)** — The KsCD player comes with the KDE desktop. To use KsCD, the kdemultimedia package must be installed. From the Applications menu (KDE desktop), select Sound & Video ➪ KsCD (or type **kscd** from a terminal window). This player enables you to get title, track, and artist information from the CD database, and submit information you type in yourself to a CD database (if your CD isn't found there).

- **Rhythmbox (rhythmbox)** — Import and manage your music collection with Rhythmbox music management and playback software for GNOME. Rhythmbox uses GStreamer and Sound Juicer to extract music from a CD, and then compresses that music using Ogg Vorbis, FLAC, or a low-quality WAV (for speech) audio format. Besides enabling you to create playlists of your music library, Rhythmbox also has features for playing Internet radio stations. Open Rhythmbox from the Applications menu by selecting Sound & Video ➪ Music Player.

- **XMMS (xmms)** — The X Multimedia System (XMMS) audio player provides a simple, graphical player for playing Ogg Vorbis, WAV, FLAC, and other audio formats. XMMS has a fairly simple Windows winamp-like look and feel, which you can adjust using a few dozen skins. (The xmms package is available in the Fedora repository. To add CD playing support to xmms, install the xmms-cdread package as well.)

- **ogg123, mpg321, aplay, or play** — If you don't have access to the desktop, you can use the text-based ogg123, mpg321, or play commands. The ogg123 command comes with the vorbis-tools package, aplay is part of the alsa-utils package, and play comes with the sox package in Fedora. The mpg321 command comes in the mpg321 package, which is available from the rpmfusion.org RPMs site. (The mpg321 command is covered under the GPL. There is an mpg123 project, which is no longer maintained and is not fully covered under the GPL.)

The default CD audio player is Rhythmbox for the current release. One advantage of Rhythmbox and other GStreamer audio applications is that they will work with the free and legal MP3 codecs you can download.

Note
If you try some of these CD players and your CD-ROM drive is not working, see the sidebar "Troubleshooting Your CD-ROM" for further information. ∎

Automatically playing CDs

When you put an audio CD into your CD-ROM drive, a dialog box automatically pops up on your desktop and asks if you want to open Rhythmbox or use some other CD player or audio extraction tool. If you are using the GNOME desktop, you can use the application launcher to handle music CDs (as well as other removable media) from a Nautilus folder window.

If you want to have CDs automatically start playing or if you want to use a different CD player by default, you can change that behavior from the File Management Preferences window in Nautilus. Open any folder in Nautilus and select Edit ➪ Preferences and choose the Media tab. From the Media tab, select the box next to CD Audio and select your preferred option when an audio CD is encountered.

Troubleshooting Your CD-ROM

If you are unable to play CDs on your CD-ROM drive, here are a few things you can check to correct the problem:

- Verify that your sound card is installed and working properly (see "Configuring a sound card" earlier in this chapter).

- Most CD-ROM drives have a special audio cable that runs from the drive to your sound card. If you don't have one installed, you will have to rip the audio from the CD, rather than play it directly.

- Verify that the CD-ROM drive was detected when you booted Linux. If your CD-ROM drive is an IDE drive, type **dmesg | grep -i cd**. You should see messages about your CD-ROM that look like this: `ata2.00: ATAPI: HL-DT-STCD-RW/DVD DRIVE GCC-4242N, 0201, max UDMA/33`.

- If you see no indication of a CD-ROM drive, verify that the power supply and cables to the CD-ROM are connected. To ensure that the hardware is working, you can also boot to DOS and try to access the CD.

- Try inserting a software CD-ROM. If you are running the GNOME or KDE desktop, a desktop icon should appear indicating that the CD is mounted by itself. If no such icon appears, go to a terminal window and try to mount the device, represented by the device file `/dev/cdrecorder`. For example, type **mkdir /mnt/cdrecorder** to create a directory for mounting the device, then type **mount /dev/cdrecorder /mnt/cdrecorder**. Then list the contents using the `ls /mnt/cdrecorder` command. This tells you if the CD-ROM is accessible.

- Check that your CD-ROM drive is not blacklisted because of buggy firmware or other issues. See `www.tldp.org/HOWTO/Hardware-HOWTO/cdrom.html`.

Playing and managing music with Rhythmbox

Rhythmbox is a tool for gathering, managing, and playing your music collection from one application. You can import music (from a CD, URL, or folder), and then select and sort your music by album, artist, title, or other variables from the Rhythmbox window. Rhythmbox also lets you play Internet radio stations.

The first time you run Rhythmbox, consider setting some Rhythmbox Preferences by selecting Edit ⇨ Preferences. On the Music tab, you can tell Rhythmbox the folder in which to store your music files, as shown in Figure 7-2. (Remember this folder name. You will need it later when you configure Sound Juicer to rip CDs.)

Tip

The location you choose for your music collection could require a lot of disk space. Some people add a hard disk or at least have a large, dedicated disk partition for storing their music and other multimedia content. Having this separate disk area can be useful later for doing backups; and if you later want to reinstall your operating system, you can do so without harming your music collection. ■

FIGURE 7-2

Define where you store your music with Rhythmbox.

After you set your Music folder and other preferences, close the Preferences menu and begin using the main music player (see Figure 7-3).

Note

To get MP3 support for Rhythmbox, you can use the Fluendo codecs or codecs available from `rpmfusion.org`. ∎

Here are a few ways to use Rhythmbox:

- **Scan removable media** — Extract tracks from an audio CD by selecting Music ➪ Scan Removable Media. If an audio CD is found, Sound Juicer launches to rip and compress the music from your CD (see the section "Extracting music CDs with Sound Juicer" for more on ripping audio CDs).

- **Create playlist** — To create a playlist, select Music ➪ Playlist. If you have a very large music collection, select New Automatic Playlist. A pop-up window lets you choose search criteria to find songs, artists, titles, or other criteria to load into your playlist. You can also create a new, empty playlist (New Playlist) or load a stored playlist from a file. Once a playlist is created, you can add songs to the list by importing (from a CD, URL, or folder) or dragging and dropping from a Nautilus window. Right-click on a song to copy, cut, or delete it.

FIGURE 7-3

View your music library and play selected songs or albums with Rhythmbox.

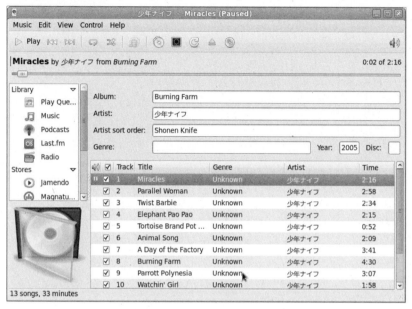

- **Check statistics** — Rhythmbox stores the number of times a song has been played, when it was last played, and how you rate it (one to five stars). Select Edit ⇨ Preferences to select to have columns of that information appear on your Rhythmbox window.

- **Play music tracks** — With your music available, you can play it by double-clicking an album (to play the whole album), an artist (to play the artist's first album you have), or a track (to start with that track). Use the buttons at the top of Rhythmbox to play/pause or go forward or backward a track. Select Shuffle or Repeat boxes on the bottom of Rhythmbox to randomly play the songs in an album or play the same album repeatedly. Use the slider to move ahead or back in a song, and select the speaker icon to adjust volume.

- **Play Internet radio** — Rhythmbox can also play Internet radio stations. The easiest way to do this is to find a streaming radio station (you want to look for Shoutcast PLS files, usually with a .pls extension). Save the PLS file, right-click the file in the Nautilus file browser, and then select Open with Music Player. Nautilus is configured to launch Rhythmbox for playing audio. The sites www.di.fm and www.shoutcast.com list a number of free Internet radio channels. You can also click Radio or Last.Fm in the Rhythmbox Library window.

If you are looking for new music, selections under Stores on the Rhythmbox window let you connect to Magnatune and Jamendo online music services. Select either of those services to see lists of music you can try out free. You can also search those services for music that interests you.

Magnatune makes money by licensing the music of the artists it represents for use in movies, websites, commercials, or other media. You can also purchase a whole album or physical music CD through those services. Jamendo provides the music of its artists free, to help promote the music to a worldwide audience. In either case, these services provide a way for you to explore different kinds of music. If you install MP3 codecs, then you can use any store that supports the MP3 format, such as Amazon.

Playing music with XMMS Audio Player

The XMMS (X Multimedia System) Audio Player provides a graphical interface for playing music files in MP3, Ogg Vorbis, WAV, and other audio formats. XMMS has some nice extras, too, including an equalizer, a Playlist Editor, and the capability to add more audio plugins. If the player looks familiar to you, that's because it is styled after the Windows winamp program.

Note

Because XMMS is not a GStreamer application, the MP3 support you can get from Fluendo doesn't work with XMMS. You can get MP3 support by installing the lame package from the rpmfusion.org repository. ■

The xmms package is available from the Fedora repository (type **yum install xmms** to install the xmms package). Start the XMMS Audio Player from the Applications menu by selecting Sound & Video ➪ Audio Player or by typing the xmms command from a terminal window. You can also install nyxmms2, a newer-generation music player based on some of the original ideas in xmms. Figure 7-4 consists of the XMMS Audio Player with the associated equalizer (below on the left) and the Playlist Editor (to the right). Note how small the user interface and controls are.

Note

Although the default theme is one that matches the Fedora blue color scheme, you can download different themes from www.xmms.org/skins.php. **Copy the skin's ZIP file to the** /usr/share/doc/xmms/Skins **directory. Then change the look of the player by right-clicking on XMMS and selecting Options ➪ Skin Browser.** ■

FIGURE 7-4

Play Ogg Vorbis and other audio files from the XMMS playlist.

As noted earlier, you can play several audio file formats. Supported audio file formats include the following:

- MP3 (with added xmms-mp3 package)
- Ogg Vorbis
- FLAC (with added xmms-flac package)
- WAV
- AU
- CD Audio
- CIN Movies

You can get many more audio plugins from the Fedora repository or directly from `www.xmms.org`. The XMMS Audio Player can be used in the following way to play music files:

1. Obtain music files in one of the following ways:
   - Rip songs from a CD or copy them from the Web so that they are in an accessible directory.
   - Insert a music CD in your CD-ROM drive (xmms expects the CD to be accessible from `/dev/cdrom`).

2. From the Applications menu, select Sound & Video ➪ XMMS. The X Multimedia System player appears.

3. Click the Eject button. The Load files window appears.

4. If you have inserted a CD, the content of that CD appears in the Files pane. (If it doesn't, change to `/dev/cdrom`, `/media/cdrom`, or `/media/cdrecorder`, as appropriate.) Select the files you want to add to your Playlist and click the Add Selected Files or the Add All Files in Directory button to add all songs from the current directory. To add audio files from your file system, browse your files and directories and click the same buttons to add the audio files you want. Select Close.

5. Click the Play List button (the tiny button marked PL) on the console. A Playlist Editor window appears.

6. Double-click the music file. It will start to play.

7. With a file selected and playing, here are a few actions you can take:
   - **Control play** — Buttons for controlling play are what you would expect to see on a physical CD player. From left to right, you can go to a previous track, play, pause, stop, go to the next track, or eject the CD. The Eject button opens a window from which you can load the next file.
   - **Adjust sound** — In the main player window, use the left slider bar to adjust the volume. Use the right slider bar to change the right-to-left balance.

- **Display time** — Click in the elapsed time area to toggle between elapsed time and time remaining.

- **View file information** — Click the small infinity-like button in the upper-left corner of the main player window to see the XMMS menu. Then select View File Info. You can often find out a lot of information about the file: title, artist, album, comments, and genre. For an Ogg file, you can see specific information about the file itself, such as format, bit rate, sample rate, frames, file size, and more. You can change or add to the tag information and click Save to keep it.

8. When you are done playing music, click the Stop button to stop the current song. Then click the X in the upper-right corner of the display to close the window.

Special features of the XMMS Audio Player enable you to adjust high and low frequencies using a graphic equalizer and gather and play songs using a Playlist Editor. In the main player window, click the button marked EQ next to the balance bar on the main player window to open the Equalizer. Click the button marked PL next to that to open the Playlist Editor.

Using the Equalizer

The Equalizer provides slider bars to set different levels to different frequencies played. Bars on the left adjust lower frequencies; those on the right adjust higher frequencies. In the main player window, click the EQ button to open the Equalizer (shown open in Figure 7-4). Here are tasks you can perform with the Equalizer:

- If you like the settings you have for a particular song, you can save them as a preset. Set each frequency as you like it and click the Preset button. Then choose Save ⇨ Preset. Type a name for the preset and click OK.

- To reload a preset you created earlier, click the Preset button and select Load ⇨ Preset. Select the preset you want and click OK to change the settings.

The small display in the center/top of the Equalizer window shows the sound wave formed by your settings. You can adjust the Preamp bar on the left to boost different levels in the set range.

Using the Playlist Editor

The Playlist Editor lets you put together a list of audio files that you want to play. You can add and delete files from this list, save them to a file, and use them again later. In the main player window, click the PL button in the XMMS window to open or close the Playlist Editor (shown open in Figure 7-4).

The Playlist Editor allows you to:

- **Add files to the playlist** — Click the Add button. The Load Files window appears. Select the directory containing your audio files (it's useful to keep them all in one place) from the left column. Then either select a file from the right column and click Add selected files or click Add all files in the directory. Click OK. The selected file or files appear in the playlist. You can also drag music files from the Nautilus file manager onto the playlist window to add the files to the playlist.

- **Select files to play** — To select from the files in the playlist, use the previous track and next track buttons in the main XMMS window. The selected file is highlighted. Click the Play button to play that file. Alternatively, you can double-click on any file in the playlist to start playing it.

- **Delete files from the playlist** — To remove files from the playlist, select the file or files you want to remove (next/previous track buttons), right-click the playlist window, and click Remove ⇨ Selected. The selected files are removed. You can also click on the – File (minus File) button to remove a file.

- **Sort files on the playlist** — To sort the playlist in different ways, click and hold the Misc Opt. button and move the mouse to select Sort List. Then you can select Sort List to sort by Title, Filename, Path and Filename, or Date. You can also randomize or reverse the list.

- **Save the playlist** — To save the current playlist, hold the mouse button down on the Load List button and then select Save. Browse to the directory you want, and then type the name you want to assign to the playlist and click OK.

- **Load the playlist** — To reload a saved playlist, click the Load List button. Select a previously saved playlist from the directory in which you saved it and click OK.

There is also a tiny set of buttons on the bottom of the Playlist Editor screen. These are the same buttons as those on the main screen used for selecting different tracks or playing, pausing, stopping, or ejecting the current track.

Using ogg123, mpg321, and play command-line players

Command-line music players are convenient if you happen to be working from a shell (no GUI) or if you want to play audio files from a shell script. Here are a few command-line players that might interest you:

- **ogg123** — The `ogg123` command is a good way to play Ogg Vorbis or FLAC audio files from the command line (you may need to install the vorbis-tools package). From the command line, you can play a file (pass the file name on the command line, such as `abc.ogg`), a playlist containing multiple music files (`--list=/tmp/myownlist`), or a file stored on the network and available from an HTTP or FTP server (`http://example.com/song.ogg`). The following is an example of the `ogg123` command playing an Ogg Vorbis file from the current directory:

```
$ ogg123 01-Rhapsody_in_Blue.ogg
Audio Device:   PulseAudio output

Playing: 01-Rhapsody_in_Blue.ogg
Ogg Vorbis stream: 2 channel, 44100 Hz
Title: Rhapsody in Blue
```

```
Artist: George Gershwin
Track number: 1
Tracktotal: 8
Album: Rhapsody in Blue
Genre: Instrumental
Time: 00:20.36 [15:29.65] of 15:50.01 (181.6 kbps) Output Buffer  96.9%
```

To stop ogg123 from playing a single song, press Ctrl+C. Do two Ctrl+C keystrokes to quit ogg123 when multiple tracks are queued up. This command is part of the vorbis-tools package, which you can install with yum.

- **play** — The play command can be used to play any of the wide range of audio formats supported by SoX. The syntax is simply play *file.xx*. To see what file formats can be played by the play command, type **sox -h** to see a list. The play command is useful if you are looking in directories of sound effects, voice content, or other audio files that aren't your typical mainstream multimedia audio types. (You need the sox package installed, which comes with Fedora, to be able to use play.)

- **mpg321** — This is similar to the ogg123 command, but it's used (as you might guess) to play MP3 audio files. Like ogg123, you can play a file (pass the file name on the command line, such as abc.mp3), a playlist containing multiple music files (--list /tmp/myownlist), or an HTTP or FTP location (http://example.com/song.mp3). Unlike ogg123, mpg321 doesn't come with Fedora. You can get the mpg321 package from the rpmfusion.org site.

Using MIDI audio players

MIDI stands for Musical Instrument Digital Interface. MIDI files are created from synthesizers and other electronic music devices. MIDI files tend to be smaller than other kinds of audio files because, rather than store the complete sounds, they contain the notes played. The MIDI player reproduces the notes to sound like a huge variety of MIDI instruments.

You can download MIDI files from many sites on the Internet. Try the Ifni MIDI Music site (www.ifnimidi.com), which contains pop hits, classic rock, dance, punk, and more organized by group. Most of the MIDI music is pretty simple, but you can have some fun playing with it.

Fedora comes with the kmid MIDI player. Kmid is not installed by default (find it in the kmid2 package on the DVD). It provides a GUI for MIDI music, including the capability to display karaoke lyrics in real time. The timidity MIDI player (from the timidity++ package on the DVD) enables you to run MIDI audio from a terminal window.

Note

Use the timidity MIDI player if your sound card doesn't include MIDI support (install the timidity++ package). It can convert MIDI input into WAV files that can play on any sound card. To start timidity, type timidity *file.mid* at the command-line prompt. ■

To start kmid, type **kmid &** from a terminal window.

Converting audio files with SoX

If you have a sound file in one format, but you want it to be in another format, Linux offers some conversion tools you can use to convert the file. The sox command can translate to and from a huge number of audio formats, including FLAC, Ogg Vorbis, WAV, AIFF, AU, and a host of old formats.

Tip

Type sox -h **to see the supported audio types, including options and effects.** ■

With optional packages, you can convert additional file formats such as AMR-WB/AMR-NB and MP3 files. You need to install additional libraries. See http://sox.sourceforge.net for more on SoX.

If you are unsure about the format of an audio file, you can add the .auto extension to the filename. This triggers the sox command to guess what kind of audio format is contained in the file. The .auto extension can be used only for the input file. If sox can determine the content of the input file, it translates the content to the sound type for the output file you request.

In its most basic form, you can convert one file format (such as a WAV file) to another format (such as an AU file) as follows:

```
$ sox file1.wav file1.au
```

To see what sox is doing, use the -V option. For example:

```
$ sox -V file1.wav file1.au
sox: SoX v14.3.1
sox INFO formats: detected file format type `wav

Input File      : file1.wav
Channels        : 2
Sample Rate     : 44100
Precision       : 16-bit
Duration        : 00:05:02.57 = 13343346 samples = 22692.8 CDDA sectors
File Size       : 4.36M
Bit Rate        : 115k
Sample Encoding: 16-bit Signed Integer PCM
Endian Type     : little
Reverse Nibbles: no
Reverse Bits    : no

Output File     : file1.au
Channels        : 2
Sample Rate     : 44100
Precision       : 16-bit
Duration        : 00:05:02.57 = 13343346 samples = 22692.8 CDDA sectors
Sample Encoding: 16-bit Signed Integer PCM
Endian Type     : big
Reverse Nibbles: no
Reverse Bits    : no
```

```
sox INFO sox: effects chain: input     44100Hz 2 channels
sox INFO sox: effects chain: output     44100Hz 2 channels
```

You can apply sound effects during the sox conversion process. The following example shows how to change the sample rate (using the -r option) from 10,000 kHz to 5,000 kHz:

```
$ sox -r 10000 file1.wav -r 5000 file1.voc
```

To reduce the noise, you can send the file through a low-pass filter. Here's an example:

```
$ sox file1.voc file2.voc lowp 2200
```

For more information on SoX and to get the latest download, go to the SoX (Sound eXchange) home page (http://sox.sourceforge.net).

Extracting and encoding music

Storing your music collection on your computer's hard disk makes it easy to manage and play your music. Using ripping software, you can copy music tracks from a music CD to your hard disk. As part of the same process (or as a separate step), you can encode each track into another form. That encoding is usually done to reduce the size of the audio files.

Tools provided with Fedora for extracting audio tracks from CDs and copying them to your hard disk include the Sound Juicer window and the cdparanoia command. Encoders that come with Fedora that are typically used for encoding music include oggenc and flac. Although encoding is often done as part of the extraction process (for example, in Sound Juicer), I provide an example showing how to use oggenc to encode WAV files to Ogg Vorbis format on the command line.

Extracting music CDs with Sound Juicer

Sound Juicer is an intuitive graphical tool for extracting music tracks from commercial music CDs. It can read the tracks of a music CD; get CD album, artist, and track information about the CD (provided you have an Internet connection); and save the tracks to your hard disk. During that process, you can also have Sound Juicer encode the tracks in Ogg Vorbis, FLAC, or voice-quality WAV format.

Note
You can use the Fluendo codecs, described earlier in this chapter, to get support for MP3 playback. There is a fee for the MP3 decoding software. ■

To start Sound Juicer, select Applications ⇨ Sound & Video ⇨ Audio CD Extractor (or type **sound-juicer** or select Music ⇨ Import Audio CD from Rhythmbox). Figure 7-5 shows an example of the Sound Juicer window.

FIGURE 7-5

Extract songs from music CDs and encode them using Sound Juicer.

Here's how to use Sound Juicer to extract songs from an audio CD and encode them to any supported encoding type:

1. After starting Sound Juicer, insert an audio CD into your computer's CD drive and select Re-Read Disc from the Disc menu. (If another audio player starts, you can close it.)

2. Select Edit ➪ Preferences. The Preferences window appears, as shown in Figure 7-5.

3. Set the following Preferences:

   - **CD Drive** — If you have multiple CD drives, choose the one you want to extract from.

   - **Music Folder** — Choose the folder to which the music tracks will be written. Ensure that the disk partition containing the folder has enough space to store your music collection. As noted earlier, a separate partition is a good idea for a large collection.

   - **Track Names** — Here's where you identify the names that will be used to store your music. The Folder hierarchy is set to the artist's name, followed by the Album title. Therefore, multiple albums by the same artist are in the same folder. The tracks themselves, indicated by the File name box, are stored by track number and song title, separated by a dash. You can choose different ways of indicating the files and folder names used to store your music.

- **Output Format** — This sets the type of encoding that is done to each track. Your options are FLAC, Ogg Vorbis, and WAV. With a gstreamer-plugins-mp3 package installed, you should have the option of MP3 as well. I normally use Ogg Vorbis because the quality is good and it takes less disk space. When I want higher-quality output (with some compression), I tend to use FLAC. Choose WAV to store the file without compression (highest quality, largest size).

Close the Preferences window and click the Extract button in Sound Juicer. The tracks are extracted, encoded, and stored on your hard disk to the folder you selected.

Extracting and encoding music CDs from commands

Instead of using a graphical tool (such as Sound Juicer) to extract and encode your music CDs, you can use commands. Using these commands, you also have more flexibility in setting options to use for your encoding.

This procedure takes you through the process of extracting tracks from CD (`cdparanoia`) and encoding them to Ogg Vorbis (`oggenc`):

1. Create a directory to hold the audio files, and change to that directory. Make sure the directory can hold up to 660MB of data (less if you are burning fewer songs). For example:

```
# mkdir /tmp/cd
# cd /tmp/cd
```

2. Insert the music CD into your CD-ROM drive. (If a CD player opens on the desktop, close it.)

3. Extract the music tracks you want by using the `cdparanoia` command. By default, Fedora sets up users to allow access to the CD-ROM device. Run the following command:

```
$ cdparanoia -B
```

This example reads all of the music tracks from the CD-ROM drive (the location of your CD drive may be different). The `-B` option says to output each track to a separate file. By default, the `cdparanoia` command outputs the files to the WAV audio format.

Instead of extracting all songs, you can choose a single track or a range of tracks to extract. For example, to extract tracks 3 through 5, add the "3+5" option. To extract just track 9, add "9".

Watch the "output smiles" on the progress bar as the tracks are extracted. Normal operation (low/no jitter) is represented by a smiley face :-), whereas errors cause faces that are progressively more worried: `:-|`, `:-/`, `:-P`, and so on.

4. To encode your WAV files to Ogg Vorbis, you can use the `oggenc` command. In its most basic form, you can use `oggenc` with one or more WAV or AIFF files following it. For example:

```
$ oggenc *.wav
```

This command would result in Ogg Vorbis files created from all files ending with `.wav` in the current directory. An Ogg file is produced for each WAV file, with `oggenc` substituting `.ogg` for `.wav` as the file suffix for the compressed file.

Instead of using oggenc to convert the WAV files to Ogg Vorbis, you can use the `flac` command to convert the WAV files to FLAC format (`*.flac`). To give you an idea of the space consumed by each format, I started with a WAV file of 27MB. When I encoded it with FLAC, it went to 11MB, whereas encoding the WAV file to Ogg Vorbis ended in 1.5MB.

Tip

Another tool for ripping and compressing a music CD is grip. Grip enables you to select `oggenc` **or other tools to do the file compression. You can get grip from the Fedora repository (type** `yum install grip`**).** ■

Creating your own music CDs

Fedora contains tools for burning CDs and DVDs from either the command line or the graphical window. CD and DVD burners are great for backing up your data and system files. The following sections describe how to use CD/DVD burning software specifically to create audio CDs.

Creating audio CDs with cdrecord

You can use the `cdrecord` command to create either data or music CDs. You can create a data CD by setting up a separate file system and copying the whole image of that file system to CD. Creating an audio CD consists of selecting the audio tracks you want to copy and copying them all at once to the CD.

Note

Instead of the cdrecord package, Fedora now uses the wodim package (`www.cdrkit.org`**) to implement the** `cdrecord` **command. Fedora and other Linux distributions switched to the CDR Kit project because cdrecord licensing was changed to the Sun CDDL license, which is believed to be incompatible with the GPL. Now,** `cdrecord` **is a link to the** `wodim` **command, although it supports the same options that** `cdrecord` **supported before the switch to** `wodim`**.** ■

This section focuses on using `cdrecord` to create audio CDs. The `cdrecord` command can use audio files in `.au`, `.wav`, or `.cdr` format, automatically translating them when necessary. If you have audio files in other formats, you can convert them to one of the supported formats by using the `sox` command (described previously in this chapter).

Cross-Reference

See Chapter 12 for information on how to use cdrecord **to create adata CDs.** ∎

Start by extracting music tracks from your audio CD (using a tool such as cdparanoia, described earlier in this chapter). After you have created a directory of tracks (in WAV format) from your CD, you can copy those files to your CD writer as follows:

```
# cdrecord -v dev=/dev/cdrom -audio *.wav
```

The options to cdrecord tell the command to create an audio CD (-audio) on the writable CD device located at /dev/cdrom. The cdrecord command writes all files from the current directory that end in .wav. The -v option causes verbose output.

To change the order of the tracks, you can type the track names in the order you want them written (rather than use *.wav). If you don't indicate a recording speed, cdrecord will try to choose an appropriate one. If you get errors while you are recording, sometimes reducing the recording speed helps. For example, try speed=2 or speed=4 on the cdrecord command line.

After you have created the music CD, indicate the contents of the CD on the label side of the CD. The CD should then be ready to play on any standard music CD player.

Creating audio and data CDs with K3b

For anyone who has struggled to get the options just right with cdrecord, the K3b CD/DVD Burning Facility is a wonderful tool (install the k3b package). Modeled after popular CD recording tools you can find in Windows environments, K3b provides a very intuitive way to master and burn your own CDs and DVDs.

Among the best uses of K3b are copying audio CDs and burning ISO images (perhaps containing a Linux distribution you want to try out) that you download from the Internet. To start K3b, select Sound & Video ➪ K3b from the Applications menu. Figure 7-6 shows an example of the K3b interface.

Creating a new audio CD

If you have a bunch of audio tracks you want to put together for your own CD, here's how to do that from the K3b window:

1. Select the New Audio CD project icon from the main K3b window.

2. Open a folder window and go to the folder that contains the music track files you want to burn to CD.

3. Drag-and-drop the music tracks you want to the Current Projects pane on the bottom of the K3b screen.

4. Right-click on any track to see properties of that track. You can change or add to the information there. To change the order, you can drag tracks to different locations within the pane.

5. Select the Burn button in the upper-left corner of the K3b Current Projects screen.

6. From the Audio Project window that appears, select options for doing the burn and click the Burn button to burn the CD. Alternatively, you can select Only Create Image, to create an ISO image of all the files that you can burn to CD later.

FIGURE 7-6

Master and burn CDs and DVDs using the K3b window.

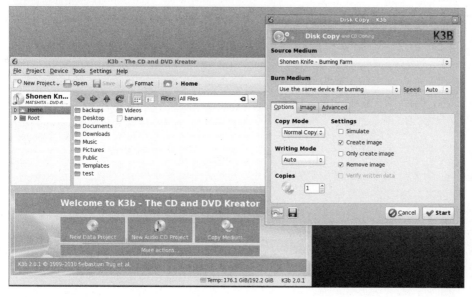

Copying a CD

If you want to copy an audio or data CD, you can do so from the K3b window as follows:

1. Insert the CD you want to copy into your CD drive.

2. Select Tools ➪ Copy Medium from the K3b window. The Disk Copy window appears.

3. Choose options for the CD copy, such as the CD reader and burner devices (they can be the same if you have only one). You can also choose to do a normal copy or a clone copy. Assuming you have only one CD drive (and it's a burner), you need to set a temporary directory that can hold the entire contents of the CD.

4. When you are happy with the options, click Start. K3b begins copying the source disk to the temporary directory you indicated.

5. When prompted, remove the original CD and insert a blank CD into the CD drive.

6. Click Start to continue. K3b will tell you when the copy is complete.

7. Eject the CD and mark it appropriately.

Burning an ISO image to CD

Before your songs are copied to CD, they are gathered together into a single archive, referred to as an ISO image. You can download ISO images of software (such as the DVD or CD images used to install Fedora). Although an ISO image only looks like one big file before you burn it, after it is burned to a CD it appears as a file system containing multiple files.

Note

Copying an ISO file is a lot different than burning an ISO image. You can treat the ISO images as plain old files, and copy or move these files. Burning an ISO image treats the ISO file as a binary blob containing the entire contents of a CD or DVD, including the file system on the disc. ■

To burn any of the images just described to a CD using K3b, do the following:

1. Download or otherwise copy an ISO image to a directory on your hard disk. A CD image can be up to about 700MB, while a DVD image can be over 4GB.

2. From the K3b window, select Tools ⇨ Burn Image. A Burn CD Image window appears.

3. Next to the Image to Burn box, select the folder icon to browse your file system to find the ISO image. After you select the image, it is loaded into the Burn CD Image window, which displays information about the image, including its MD5sum.

4. Check the MD5sum and compare it with the MD5sum provided with the ISO image when you downloaded it. (There is likely a file ending with md5 in the directory from which you downloaded the image.)

5. If the MD5sums match, continue by checking the settings on the Burn CD Image window. I've had generally good luck using the default settings. However, if you get a bad burn, changing the speed from Auto to a slower speed that is auto-detected will often result in a good burn.

6. Click Start to begin burning the image to CD. When the writing is done, K3b tells you whether it considered the burn process successful.

The descriptions for burning CDs apply to DVDs as well (provided you have a DVD burner). Remember that you are going to need a lot more temporary space on your hard disk to work with DVDs than you would to work with CDs.

Creating audio and data CDs with Brasero

The Brasero Disc Burner, shown in Figure 7-7, provides the default GNOME application for creating CDs.

Brasero can burn CDs as well as DVDs and offers a number of advanced features. You can preview the audio tracks, normalize the volume, and check the integrity of the disks. In addition, Brasero offers a CD cover editor that enables you to create the tray cards and front cards to fit into CD jewel cases.

See http://projects.gnome.org/brasero/ for more on Brasero.

FIGURE 7-7

Brasero provides the default GNOME CD creation tool.

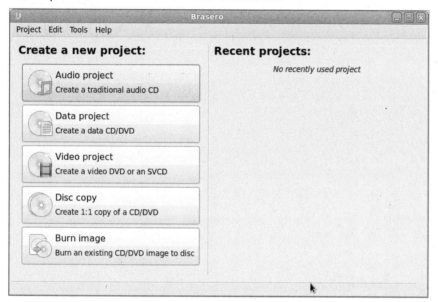

Viewing TV, Video Conferencing, and Using Webcams

Getting TV cards, webcams, and other video devices to play in Linux can still be a bit of an adventure. Most manufacturers of TV cards and webcams are not losing sleep to produce Linux drivers. As a result, most drivers that bring video to your Linux desktop have been reverse-engineered (that is, they were created by software engineers who watched what the video device sent and received, rather than seeing the actual code that runs the device).

The first, and probably biggest, trick is to get a TV card or webcam that is supported in Linux. Once you are getting video output from that device (typically available from /dev/video0), you can try out a couple of applications to begin using it. This section describes the tvtime application for watching television and the Ekiga program for video conferencing.

Watching TV with tvtime

The tvtime program (tvtime command) enables you to display video output — in particular, television channels — on your desktop. You can change the channels, adjust volume, and fine-tune your picture. In addition, tvtime sports a slick onscreen display and support for a wide-screen display.

tvtime will display, by default, any device producing video on the /dev/video0 device. (Use the -d option to specify a different device.)

Therefore, you can use tvtime to view webcams as well as receive television channels. The following sections describe how to choose a TV capture card and use tvtime to watch television on your desktop.

Note

tvtime will not display output from some low-quality webcams. To use your webcam, consider obtaining the xawtv package, which is available by typing yum install xawtv. ∎

Getting a supported TV card

Video4Linux is the video interface included with Fedora. It supports a variety of TV capture cards and cameras. To see a list of supported TV cards that you can use with tvtime, refer to the list of supported cards in the tvtime documentation, which you'll find in the following location on your Linux system: /usr/share/doc/tvtime*/html/index.html

Look for the help, FAQ (frequently asked questions), and the list of supported cards.

Video4Linux is designed to autodetect your TV capture card and load the proper modules to activate it. Therefore, physically install the TV-card hardware (with the appropriate connection to your TV reception), boot Fedora, and run the tvtime command as described in the next section. You should be able to see video displayed on your tvtime window.

If your card doesn't seem to be working, here are a few things you can try:

- To determine if your TV card was properly seated in its slot and detected by Linux, type the following:

```
$ /sbin/lspci | less
```

  This will return a list of all valid PCI cards on your computer. If nothing shows up for the card that says something like "Multimedia video controller," you probably have a hardware problem. My Hauppauge WinTV Go card (with Brooktree chipset support) appears as follows:

```
Multimedia video controller: Brooktree Corporation Bt878 ↵
Video Capture
```

- It is possible that the card is there but the right card type is not being detected. Improper detection is most likely the issue when you have a card for which there are several revisions, with each requiring a different driver. If you think your card is not being properly detected, find your card in the CARDLIST files. Then add the appropriate line to the /etc/modprobe.conf file. For example, to add a Prolink PV-BT878P, revision 9B card, add the following line to /etc/modprobe.conf:

```
options    bttv    card=72
```

You can also add other options listed in the Insmod-options file for the bttv driver. If you are still having problems getting your card to work, use the following mailing list to ask questions about Video4Linux issues: http://listman.redhat.com/mailman/listinfo/video4linux-list

One reason you might not see any video when you try to run tvtime or other video applications is that another person or video application already has the video driver open. Only one application can use the video driver at a time in Fedora. Another quirk of Video4Linux is that the first person to open the device on your system becomes the owner, so you might need to open the permissions of the device file (such as /dev/video0) to allow people other than the first person to use it to access the video4linux driver (for example, chmod 666 /dev/video0).

Starting tvtime

To start up the tvtime viewer, simply select the tvtime Television Viewer option from the Sound & Video menu. Alternately, type the following from a terminal window on your desktop:

```
$ tvtime &
```

A video screen should appear in a window on the desktop. Click the left mouse button on the window to see the current channel number, current time, and current video source (Television, Composite1, and so on). Click the right mouse button to see the onscreen Setup menu.

If your card seems to have been detected and the needed modules were properly loaded, but you don't see any video, try using the keyboard arrow keys to step forward until you find a valid channel. If that doesn't work, try going through the following adjustments (most important, the video source and television standard), to get tvtime working properly:

- **Configure input** — This option allows you to change the video source, choose the television standard (which defaults to NTSC for the USA), and change the resolution of the input. To change the video source to Composite1, S-Video, Television, or other input source, right-click the tvtime window, select Input configuration ➪ Change video Source. To change Television standard, select Television standard and choose NTSC (U.S.), PAL (Europe), or other available settings.

- **Set up the picture** — Adjust the brightness, contrast, color, and hue. Right-click the tvtime window, select Picture settings, and then choose Brightness, Contrast, Saturation, or Hue to adjust those attributes.

- **Adjust the video processing** — You can control the attempted frame rate, configure the deinterlacer, or add an input filter. Right-click the tvtime window, select Video processing, and then choose Attempted framerate (to slow the frame rate) or a Deinterlacer option (to change other processing features). You can also try Input filters to do some fun things like invert color, flip the video as though in a mirror image, or put the video in black and white (using Chroma killer).

If you view television often from your computer, consider adding an icon to your panel (right-click the panel and select Add to Panel ➪ Application Launcher ➪ Sound & Video ➪ TVtime). With tvtime running, you can put it on top by right-clicking the title bar and selecting On Top.

Selecting channels in tvtime

With video input working and the picture adjusted to your liking, you should set up your channels. Right-click the tvtime window, select Channel management ➪ Scan channels for signal. tvtime will scan for all available channels and note which ones have active signals. Once channels have been scanned, you can use your mouse wheel to switch among the active channels. If tvtime missed an active channel, use your keyboard arrow keys to go to the missed channel and select Channel management ➪ Current channel active in list.

Tip
The XMLTV Project provides a means to identify and download TV listings for your area. tvtime includes support for xmltv listing files, enabling you to display current television shows and station names while you go through tvtime channels. It can be tricky getting xmltv going. If you are interested, I suggest you start at the XMLTV Project site (http://wiki.xmltv.org/index.php/Main_Page). ■

Video conferencing and VOIP with Ekiga

The Ekiga application (formerly called GnomeMeeting) enables you to communicate with other people over a network through video, audio, and typed messages. Because Ekiga supports the H323 protocol, you can use it to communicate with people using other video-conferencing clients, such as Microsoft NetMeeting, Cu-SeeMe, and Intel VideoPhone. Besides video conferencing, Ekiga also supports VOIP and IP telephony, to make telephone calls over the Internet.

To be able to send video, you need a webcam that is supported in Linux. Although not all webcams are supported in Linux, you have a few dozen models from which to choose. The following sections show you how to set up your webcam and use Ekiga for video conferencing.

Getting a supported webcam

As with support for TV capture cards, webcam support is provided through the Video4Linux interface. Some of the supported cameras have a parallel-port interface, although most webcams currently supported in Linux require a USB port.

- Finding a webcam to work in Linux used to be a bit of an adventure. Few (if any) webcams come with Linux drivers or the specs needed to enable open-source developers to create those drivers. Webcam drivers that have been created often have limited features and sometimes break with new kernel releases. Also, webcam vendors sometimes switch the chip sets they are using without changing the webcam's name; and sometimes the same webcam is marketed under different names. Even so, with Fedora 14, you'll find quite a few webcams supported out of the box.

Check out the following websites for a complete list of webcams that are (and are not) supported in Linux. Keep in mind, however, that not all of the drivers for these webcams will work in the latest kernels in Fedora.

- Linux USB Device Drivers (`www.linux-usb.org/devices.html`)
- Linux Webcams (`http://302found.com/linux_webcams/`)

The Logitech QuickCam Pro 300 webcam that I used for examples in this chapter works well with the pwc driver that comes with Fedora. To confirm that it was working, I ran the lsmod command to verify that the pwc driver was loaded and associated with the videodev module:

```
# lsmod
pwc                  43392     0
compat_ioctl32        5569     1 pwc
videodev              5120     1 pwc
```

To see information about the pwc module (which is specific to this webcam), I typed the following modinfo command:

```
# modinfo -p pwc
dev_hint:Device node hints
leds:LED on,off time in milliseconds
compression:Preferred compression quality. Range 0 (uncompressed) ↵
to 3 (high compression)
power_save:Turn power save feature in camera on or off
trace:For debugging purposes
mbufs:Number of external (mmap()ed) image buffers
fbufs:Number of internal frame buffers to reserve

fps:Initial frames per second. Varies with model, useful range 5-30
size:Initial image size. One of sqcif, qsif, qcif, sif, cif, vga
```

Running Ekiga

To start Ekiga, select Applications ⇨ Internet ⇨ Ekiga Softphone. To start Ekiga from a terminal window, type **ekiga &**. If it is not installed, you can install the ekiga package from the DVD that comes with this book. The first time you run Ekiga, the Ekiga Configuration Assistant starts. Using the assistant, you can enter the following information:

- **Personal Data** — Your first name, last name, e-mail address, comment, and location. You can also specify whether you want to be listed in the Ekiga ILS directory.
- **Ekiga.net accounts** — To go forward without such an account, check the box at the bottom that you don't want to set up an account on these screens.

- **Connection Type** — Indicate the speed of your Internet connection (56K modem, ISDN, DSL/Cable, or LAN).
- **Audio Devices** — Typically, you would choose the defaults.
- **Video Devices** — Typically, you would choose the default as detected by Ekiga.

Note

If you want to reconfigure Ekiga later, run the following command to clean out the old settings:

```
ekiga-config-tool --clean
```

Make sure all instances of Ekiga are stopped before running that configuration tool. In addition, be sure to shut down the panel application, which may still be running even after stopping Ekiga. Run `ekiga` again to re-enter your settings. You can also choose Configuration Assistant from the Edit menu. Ekiga supports SIP accounts and devices. See `www.ekiga.net` for more information on this. ∎

In the Ekiga window that opens, you can click Address Book from the Chat menu icon to open an address book. From the address book, select Ekiga.net Directory. By typing a name into the search filter, you can search for people who might be connected to the Ekiga server — by first name, last name, e-mail address, or location. Select a person from the list that appears and, if he or she accepts your call, you can begin video conferencing. The Call History tab shows a log of your activities.

Taking webcam videos and snapshots with Cheese

With a supported webcam (described earlier), you can use the Cheese application (`www.gnome.org/projects/cheese`) to capture images from your webcam with a few simple mouse clicks.

To install Cheese, type the following from a terminal window as root user:

```
# yum install cheese
```

Then, with your webcam connected, either select Applications ➪ Sound & Video ➪ Cheese Webcam Booth from the GNOME menu or type `cheese` from a terminal window to launch Cheese. Figure 7-8 shows an example of the Cheese window.

As your webcam output is displayed live in the top of the Cheese window, you can use the Photo or Video buttons to select what you want to capture. Toggle the middle button to either Take a Photo or Start Recording. For photos, you have a three-second pause to get ready for the shot. For videos, recording starts and you need to click Stop Recording when you have captured all you want.

Before grabbing an image or video, you can select Effects to change the images to produce effects such as Black-and-White, Hulk (everything turns green), or some weird Warp or Vertigo effects. Select No Effect to turn off the special effects.

Each photo or video you grab is represented by a thumbnail on the bottom of the window. Right-click on the image you want and you can select to open it, save it, or move it to the trash.

FIGURE 7-8

Take pictures or videos from your webcam and apply effects with Cheese.

Playing Video

Video recording (encoding) and playback (decoding) remain among the most contentious areas of potential litigation in open-source software. On the one hand, you have patent holders of complex video formats that might ask for royalties for open-source codecs (even when the software was written from scratch). On the other, you have the movie industry that has taken aim at those publishing what they had hoped were secret encryption techniques (DeCSS), to prevent the open-source decoding of commercial movies. The problem is that the same technique that enables you to play movies in Linux also can be used to copy and share them.

Note
Codec stands for COder/DECoder or COmpressor/DECompressor, depending on whom you ask. Either way, codecs are what make it possible to process and encode audio and video on computers. ■

As with audio recording, if you are starting from scratch, at the time of this writing there is an open-source codec called Theora (www.theora.org) that you can use without paying any royalties. Provided you own the content you are recording, you can freely distribute that content as well and allow others to play it back. (See the sidebar "Converting Video to Theora" for details.)

Converting Video to Theora

There are not a lot of tools yet for creating Theora video. To get a video to try out, I shot a video with my Sony Handycam, which stores video in 30-minute, 1.4GB mini DVDs. I downloaded a tool, recommended from the Theora.org site, called ffmpeg2theora (www.v2v.cc/~j/ffmpeg2theora). My video camera stored my home movie as a VOB file, which I copied to my hard disk and converted to Theora/Ogg Vorbis as follows:

```
$ ffmpeg2theora VTS_01_1.VOB
Input #0, mpeg, from 'VTS_01_1.VOB':
  Duration: 00:00:00.6, start: 0.197311, bitrate: -2147483 kb/s
  Stream #0.0: Video: mpeg2video, 704x480, 29.97 fps, 9300 kb/s
  Stream #0.1: Audio: ac3, 48000 Hz, stereo, 256 kb/s
  Resize: 704x480 => 320x240
  Resample: 48000Hz => 44100Hz        .
      .
      .
```

The original file was stored in mpeg-2 video (720 x 480 pixels) and ac3 audio (48,000 Hz). The ffmpeg2theora command resized the video to 704 x 480 pixels and resampled the audio to 44,100 Hz. The result was a second file (same filename with a .ogg extension added) that was 82MB, compared to the original 1.1GB.

When it comes to including video codecs (other than the free Theora), the Fedora Project has taken the cautious approach. While Fedora now includes the Totem video player (described later in this chapter) as part of the GNOME desktop, and has added other media players such as Xine, those players do not include contentious codecs. If you want to play commercial movies, popular video clips, or other video content in a Fedora system, you have to get those codecs elsewhere.

This section describes some of the issues surrounding playing and creating video in Linux. It also describes video players that come with Fedora, as well as those you can obtain to play a wide variety of video content.

Examining laws affecting video and Linux

I need to start out by reminding everyone that I am not a lawyer, so you need to take responsibility yourself regarding any software you put on your computers. However, several themes have arisen in regard to playing video content with open-source software in Linux:

- **Licensing fees for patented codecs may be required.** While many video codecs are covered by patents, some patent holders don't charge for personal use. However, you should check current policies of companies who own patents on codecs you plan to use, as the terms of use are constantly changing. For example, the following statement that previously appeared on the DivX website is no longer there: "Personal use of DivX video software is free. Commercial use is not and requires that you obtain a commercial use license from DivXNetworks." (Refer to www.divx.com for information on DivX licensing.)

Because MPEG-2 and MPEG-4 video formats are covered by a variety of patents, groups of patent holders have joined together to charge licensing fees for related encoders and decoders. These efforts are not sponsored by standards organizations that spearheaded the creation of those formats and may not cover every patent holder related to the software you are paying for. See the MPEG Industry Forum for details on MPEG patent issues (www.m4if.org/patents).

Keep in mind that there are now ways to purchase codecs for many popular audio/video formats for use with Linux. See the section "Extending Freedom to Codecs" for information on purchasing codecs from Fluendo.

- **Unauthorized copying of copyright-protected material is never legal.** Even legal video codecs do not make it legal to copy commercial movies and other protected content and distribute them to others. There are questions as to whether or not, for example, it is legal to make a personal backup copy of a DVD movie (a commonly accepted legal practice with computer software); but any redistribution of movie, music, or other media content is not legal without the owner's permission.

Because patenting eliminates trade secret protection for the subject matter disclosed in the patent (or published patent application), many people have raised the question of why someone can't freely distribute libdvdcss (based on DeCSS decryption) to play DVD movies. Without copyright or patent coverage on CSS, it should not be illegal to distribute libdvdcss and there's nobody to pay a license fee to for using it. In regards to libdvdcss, another issue arose in the United States: the Digital Millennium Copyright Act (DMCA). DMCA might make DeCSS illegal because the technology is used to break an encryption scheme to circumvent copyrighted material.

As for the software patent issues, those are being fought on several fronts besides those relating to multimedia content. As noted earlier, the contention held by many open-source proponents is that software should be copyrighted and not patented. (See the section "Understanding Multimedia and Legal Issues in Linux" earlier in this chapter.)

With all that said, the next parts of this chapter describe which players are available to play a wide range of video content in Linux. It is up to you to work out the maze of which codecs are free for you to use and in what ways.

Understanding video content types

Before launching into the video players themselves, I want to try to clear up a bit of confusion relating to video file formats and codecs:

- **Video file formats** — A video file format essentially describes the structure of a video file for combining audio and video content. That structure can also define such things as subtitles and how audio and video are synchronized. However, a variety of video and audio codecs may have been used to encode that content. Therefore, just because you can play a video file that is marked as MPEG (.mpg), Audio Video Interleaved (.avi), QuickTime (.mov), RealMedia (.rm), Windows media (.wvm), Advanced Streaming Format (.asf), Ogg (.ogg), or another file format, it doesn't mean that you can play all video files marked as such.

● **Video and audio codecs** — Codecs are used to encode and decode video and audio content. A video encoded entirely with free software might use Theora to encode the video and Vorbis to encode the audio. Popular video codecs include MPEG-4, DivX, Xvid, RealVideo, and MJPEG.

Not all video codecs and file formats are suitable for streaming video. For example, AVI and MPEG-2 are not streamable. However, RealMedia, MPEG-4, and ASF format can be streamed, which reduces the load on a server and means you don't have to download an entire video to start watching. Check the descriptions of video players in the following sections for information on which players can support which codecs.

If you have a video file on your hard disk and you'd like to know what type of content it contains, you can use the file command. Here's an example of the file command for checking the contents of a movie trailer:

```
$ file movie.avi
movie.avi: RIFF (little-endian) data, AVI, 640 x 272, 23.98 fps,
video: DivX 3, audio: MPEG-1 Layer 3 (stereo, 44100 Hz)
```

This example shows that the file contains DivX 3 video and MPEG-1 Layer 3 audio. The size of the video is 640 × 272 pixels. Video was captured at 23.98 frames per second. This can lead you to the type of video player you need to play the content. Assuming that the right codecs are installed, Totem, Dragon, MPlayer, Xine, VLC, or several other players would be able to play this content.

Watching video with Xine

At the base of the Xine video player (www.xine-project.org) is the xine-lib core engine. While Xine has its own xlib-based user interface, you can choose different video player front ends to use with the core engine instead (including Totem, Kaffeine, Dragon, and aaxine). You can also use Xine as a Mozilla plugin, to have videos play in a browser window.

The Xine player is an excellent application for playing a variety of video and audio formats. You can get Xine from www.xine-project.org/releases. The basic Xine player is available in Fedora (xine-ui package). However, to get most of the codecs you need to make Xine useful, you must download RPMs from http://rpmfusion.org. (See Chapter 5 for information on using rpmfusion.org and other software repositories for getting Fedora software. If yum is configured to point to one of those repositories, you should be able to install Xine by typing **yum install xine***.)

Note

The Xine project offers the following disclaimer before you download or use its software:

Some parts of Xine (especially audio/video codecs) may be subject to patent royalties in some countries.

If you provide pre-compiled binaries or intend to build derivative works based on the Xine source please consider this issue. The Xine project is not warranting or indemnifying you in any way for patent royalties. You are solely responsible for your own actions. ■

You can start the Xine player by typing **xine&** from a terminal window. The Xine Setup window lets you choose various settings for the video player, such as a different user interface, if one is available. Below the Xine window is the Xine controller, which has buttons that work like many physical DVD players. Right-click the main window to see a menu of options. Select Settings ⇨ Video to display another controller for adjusting hue, saturation, brightness, and contrast.

Xine supports a bunch of video and audio file formats and codecs. However, not all of these codecs are distributed with Xine:

- MPEG (1, 2, and 4)
- QuickTime (see the section "Xine tips" later in this chapter if this content won't play)
- RealMedia (see the section "Xine tips" later in this chapter if this content won't play)
- WMV (see the section "Xine tips" later in this chapter if this content won't play)
- Motion JPEG
- MPEG audio (MP3)
- AC3 and Dolby Digital audio
- DTS audio
- Ogg Vorbis audio

Using the Xine controller, you can select to play content directly from a DVD, DVB, VCD, VCDO, or CD disk. If you are playing an audio CD (or any audio file), you can choose different visualizations (right-click, and then choose Audio ⇨ Visualization and select goom, oscope, fftscope, or fftgraph) to appear in the Xine windows as music plays.

Xine can understand different file formats that represent streaming audio and video. These include .mpg (MPEG program streams), .ts (MPEG transport streams), .mpv (raw MPEG audio/video streams), .avi (MS AVI format), and .asf (Advanced Streaming format). While Xine can play video CDs and DVDs containing other content, it can't play encrypted DVDs or video-on-CD hybrid format without adding other software (because of the legal issues mentioned earlier related to decrypting DVDs).

Using Xine

With Xine started, right-click in the Xine window to see the controls. The quickest way to play video is to click one of the following buttons, and then press the Play button (right arrow or Play, depending on the skin you are using):

- VCD (looks for a video CD)
- DVD (looks for a DVD in /dev/dvd)
- CDA (looks for a music CD in /dev/cdaudio)
- DVB (looks for a DVB device supported by linuxtv drivers)

Next, you can use the Pause/Resume, Stop, Play, Fast motion, Slow motion, or Eject buttons to work with video. You can also use the Previous and Next buttons to step to different tracks. The controls are very similar to what you would expect on a physical CD or DVD player.

To select individual files, or to put together your own list of content to play, you can use the Playlist feature.

Creating playlists with Xine

Click the Playlist button on the left side of the Xine control window. A Playlist Editor appears, showing the files on your current playlist. You can add and delete content from this list, and then save the list to call on later. The Xine content is identified as media resource locators (MRLs). Each MRL is identified as a file, DVD, or VCD. Files are in the regular file path (/path/file) or preceded by file:/, fifo:/, or stdin:/. DVDs and VCD are preceded by dvd and vcd, respectively (for example, vcd://01).

The following options are available in the Xine Playlist Editor:

- **CDA, DVD, or VCD** — Click any of the buttons that represent a particular CD or DVD. All content from that CD or DVD is added to the playlist.
- **Add** — Click the Add button to see the MRL Browser window. From that window, click File to choose a file from your Linux file system to add to the list. Click Select to add that file to the Playlist Editor.
- **Move up/Move down** — Use the Move up selected MRL and Move down selected MRL buttons to move up and down the playlist.
- **Delete** — Click the Delete Selected MRL button to remove the current selection.
- **Delete all** — Click the Delete All Entries button to clear the whole playlist.
- **Save** — Click the Save button to save the playlist to your home directory ($HOME/ .xine/playlist.tox or give it another name).
- **Load** — To read in the playlist you saved, click the Load button.

To play your playlist, click the Play button (arrow key) on the Playlist Editor.

Xine tips

Getting video and audio to work properly can sometimes be a tricky business. Here are a few quick tips to using Xine:

- **Xine won't start.** To work best, Xine needs an X driver that supports xvid. If there is no xvid support for your video card in X, Xine will shut down immediately when it tries to open the default Xv driver. If this happens to you, try starting the `xine` command with the X11 video driver (which is slower, but should work) as follows:

```
$ xine -V XShm
```

- **Don't run as root.** Run `xine` as a regular user, instead of as root. Once Xine is installed, you should be able to run it from the Applications menu on your panel by selecting Sound & Video ⇨ Xine Media Player. Although recently vulnerabilities have been identified in some open-source media players related to streaming media, that problem was fixed; but it highlights the fact that running applications as a regular user, whenever possible, is a good idea.

- **Run `xine-check`.** To get an idea of how happy Xine is running on your system, run the `xine-check` command (as the user who will be using Xine). It will tell you if there are problems running Xine on your current operating system, kernel, and processor, among other things.

- **Xine playback is choppy.** If playback of files from your hard disk is choppy, you can check a couple of settings: 32-bit IO and DMA. (If these two features are supported by your hard disk, they will generally improve hard disk performance.)

Caution

Improper disk settings can result in destroyed data on your hard disk. Run the `hdparm` **command at your own risk. The** `hdparm` **command is only for IDE hard drives (not SCSI)! Also, be sure to have a current backup and no activity on your hard disk if you change DMA or I/O settings as described here.** ∎

- First, test the speed of hard disk reads. To test the first IDE drive (in Fedora 7 and prior versions, it may appear as /dev/hda instead of /dev/sda), type the following:

```
# hdparm -t /dev/sda
Timing buffered disk reads: 64 MB in 19.31 seconds = 3.31 MB/sec
```

- To see your current DMA and IO settings, as root user type the following:

```
# hdparm -c -d /dev/sda
/dev/sda:
 I/O support = 0 (default 16-bit)
 using_dma   = 0 (off)
```

- This shows that both 32-bit IO and DMA are off. To turn them on, type the following:

```
# hdparm -c 1 -d 1 /dev/sda
```

```
/dev/sda:
 I/O support = 1 (32-bit)
 using_dma   = 1 (on)
```

- If you have problems with the DMA setting, run the command without the -d 1 option. Now, test the disk again:

```
# hdparm -t /dev/sda
```

```
Timing buffered disk reads: 64 MB in 2.2 seconds = 28.83 MB/sec
```

As you can see from this example, buffered disk reads of 64MB went from 19.31 seconds to 2.2 seconds after changing the parameters described. Playback should be much better now.

- **Xine won't play particular media.** Messages such as no input plug-in mean that either the file format you are trying to play is not supported or it requires an additional plugin (as is the case with playing DVDs). If the message is maybe xyx is a broken file, the file may be a proprietary version of an otherwise supported format. For example, I had a QuickTime video fail that required an SVQ3 codec (which is currently not supported under Linux), although other QuickTime files will play fine.

  If a particular multimedia format is not supported, but you have Windows Dynamic Link Libraries (DLLs) available that support it, you can add those DLL files to the /usr/lib/win32 directory. Some of these codec DLLs are available from www.mplayerhq.hu/design7/dload.html#binary_codecs in a package called essential. Choose a mirror site from the table under the Binary Codec Packages heading.

Note

The CrossOver Plugin (described in Chapter 8) can be used to play a variety of content, including the version of QuickTime just mentioned. ■

Using Totem movie player

The Totem movie player (www.gnome.org/projects/totem) comes with the GNOME desktop environment. In Fedora, Totem can play video in Theora format with Vorbis audio. Totem is based on GStreamer (http://gstreamer.freedesktop.org), so it can be used with other video software from that project. In particular, free and fee-based codecs that you can purchase from www.fluendo.com for playing a variety of commercial audio/video formats will work with Totem.

Totem also supports a Xine back end that enables it to play a wide range of video content (in other words, anything Xine supports). To play commercial DVD movies, you need to install the gstreamer-plugins-ugly package from the rpmfusion.org repository and the libdvdcss package from the livna.org repository.

Launch Totem from the Applications menu on your panel by selecting Sound & Video ⇨ Movie Player.

Besides common controls you would expect with a movie player (play, pause, skip forward, skip backwards, and so on), with Totem you can create playlists, take a snapshot of the current frame, and adjust the volume. You can also change preferences, which enable you to add proprietary plugins, select your DVD device, and balance color. Figure 7-9 shows an example of the Totem window.

FIGURE 7-9

Totem plays Theora video, plus any codecs supported by Xine and GStreamer.

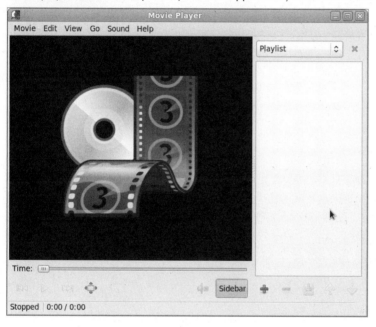

Using a Digital Camera

With the GNOME Volume Manager features in Fedora, getting images from a digital camera can be as easy in Linux as it is in any desktop operating system. With most digital cameras that can be connected to a USB port on your computer, simply plugging the camera into a USB port (with the camera set to send and receive) causes the GNOME Volume Manager to do the following:

- Immediately prompt you to ask whether you want to download images from your camera

- Run the digiKam image viewer on the KDE desktop or the Shotwell application on the GNOME desktop to look at, manipulate, and download the contents of your digital camera

Although the GNOME Volume Manager will open your camera's contents in an image viewer, you can treat the storage area in your camera much as you would the storage area on a hard disk or a pen drive.

When it first starts, digiKam will ask you a few configuration questions and then it will load in your pictures. Shotwell does the same thing.

Displaying images in Fedora

The GNOME Volume Manager mounts the contents of your USB camera, treating the memory of your camera as it would any file storage device. When I tried it with an Olympus digital camera, my images were available from the `/media/usbdisk/dcim/100olymp` directory. Figure 7-10 shows an example of the Shotwell photo manager window displaying the images from a digital camera.

FIGURE 7-10

Download images from digital cameras with the Shotwell photo manager.

Shotwell provides a user interface very similar to that of iPhoto on the Mac. It was designed to help you manage collections of images from a camera or other devices. Shotwell will automatically organize your photos into events based on the dates from the photos as shown in Figure 7-10.

With your camera connected and the Shotwell window open, here are some things you can do with the images on your camera:

- **Download images** — You can import photos from a variety of sources, including the F-Spot Photo Library as well as any camera supported by gPhoto, Linux software that works with digital cameras.

- **View slide show** — Select View ⇨ Slide Show. A full-screen slide show appears on your display, with the images changing every few seconds. The toolbar that appears at the top lets you display information about the photo name, date, and size (click Image Info), go forward and back through the images, and zoom in or out.

- **Manipulate images** — Double-click an image to open it, and select the Photo menu, which offers a set of tools for enhancing, resizing, cropping, or otherwise transforming the image. You can also adjust the color balance, hue/saturation, and brightness contrast.

- **Assign categories** — With an image selected, right-click and select Add Tags. The Add Tags pop-up window lets you assign the image to a tag or category to help you organize your photos.

- **Organize** — One of Shotwell's main purposes is to enable you to organize your photos into different events. While Shotwell automatically organizes photos by the date the pictures were taken, you can create additional events and organize them as desired — by family gathering, subject matter, or anything else that strikes your fancy.

After images are downloaded to your computer's hard disk, you can continue to work with them using Shotwell or any of a number of tools available for manipulating digital images (e.g., GIMP, KView, digiKam, and Kuickshow, to name a few).

Note

If your camera saves images to SD or CF cards, you can purchase a USB card reader and view these files from Linux. ∎

Check the gPhoto2 website (`www.gphoto.org/proj/libgphoto2/support.php`) for information on supported cameras as well as other topics related to gPhoto.

Using your camera as a storage device

As I noted with my example of an Olympus camera with a USB connector, the GNOME Volume Manager can detect that camera once it is connected, and mount its contents as a storage device.

With the contents of a digital camera mounted, you can use your camera as a USB mass storage device as follows:

- Open the mounted directory in a folder window and use any file manager features to work with the images.
- Change to the mounted directory from the shell and use commands to copy, move, rename, or delete digital images.

Of course, with your camera mounted as a file system, you are not limited to using it only for digital images. You can use it to store any kind of files you like, essentially using the camera as a storage device. The following list is a partial summary of digital cameras that can be used as a USB storage device:

- **Casio** — Supported models: QV-2400UX, QV-2x00, QV-3x00, QV-4000, and QV-8000
- **Fuji** — FinePix 1300, 1400Zoom, 2300Zoom, 2400Zoom, 2800Zoom, 4200Z, 4500, 4700 Zoom, 4900 Zoom, 6800 Zoom, A101, A201, and S1 Pro
- **HP** — PhotoSmart 315, 318xi, 618, and C912
- **Konica** — KD200Z, KD400Z, and Revio KD300Z
- **Kyocera** — Finecam s3
- **Leica** — Digilux 4.3
- **Minolta** — Dimage 5, Dimage 7, and Dimage X
- **Nikon** — CoolPix 2500, 885, 5000, 775, and 995
- **Olympus** — Brio Zoom D-15, C-100, C-200Z, C-2040, C-220Z, C-2Z, C-3020Z, C-3040Z, C-4040Zoom, C-700, C-700UZ, C-860L, D-510, D-520Z, E-10, and E-20
- **Pentax** — EI2000, Optio 330, and Optio 430
- **Sony** — DSC-F505, DSC-F505V, DSC-F707, DSC-P1, DSC-P20, DSC-P5, DSC-P71, DSC-S30, DSC-S70, DSC-S75, DSC-S85, MVC-CD300, and MVC-FD92
- **Vivitar** — Vivicam 3550
- **Yashica** — Finecam s3

Playing Games on Linux

Every type of PC gaming is available now with Linux. Whether you are looking for a solitaire game to fill time or a full-blown online 3D gaming experience, you have dozens (or hundreds) of options on the Linux desktop. A strong gaming special-interest group within the Fedora Project has ensured that many open-source games not only run but run well in Fedora.

Although some companies, such as ID Software (Quake) and Epic Games (Unreal Tournament) have worked to port their games to Linux, others have used third-party developers (such as RuneSoft) to port commercial games to Linux. Independent games developers, such as Frictional Games (http://frictionalgames.com) and Introversion Software (www.introversion.co.uk) are now producing high-quality gaming experiences in Linux.

Some experts predict that gaming will be the software category that brings Linux into homes. The unfortunate truth is that many of the current "hot" titles still need to be coaxed onto Linux with some kind of Win32 emulation (such as Cedega, at www.cedega.com or CrossOver Games at www.codeweavers.com/products/cxgames); but even this is getting easier and more dependable. While the number of popular game applications is currently fairly limited, like everything else in Linux, more games are becoming available each day.

One area where gaming-related software has grown in Linux is in tools for producing high-quality 3D animations. For example, Blender (www.blender.org) is an open-source project for doing animations, 3D models, post-production, and rendering that is being used today to produce commercial games and movie animations. Blender's features are beginning to rival those of commercial 3D animation software such as Maya (www.autodesk.com/maya).

Note
You can participate in a community of Blender artists and game developers at the BlenderArtists.org site, which offers many useful forums on blender, including several active forums on the Blender Game Engine. ∎

Jumping into Linux gaming

If you have a Linux system running and want to get started playing a game right now, here are some suggestions:

- **Check the Games menu** — Default installations of Fedora come with a bunch of games already installed. If you are running a GNOME desktop in Linux, select Applications ➪ Games from the panel. You should be able to select a variety of arcade, card, board, tactical, and other games to keep you busy for a while.

- **Games packaged for your Linux distribution** — Many of the most popular open-source games are packaged to run on your Linux distribution. In Fedora, open the Add/Remove Software (PackageKit) window and select Games to see a list of more than 200 games you can download and play.

- **Other open-source games** — If the open-source game you want is not packaged for your distribution, try going to the game's project site to get it. There are Internet sites that contain lists of games, and links to each game's site. The Wikipedia Linux Gaming page (http://en.wikipedia.org/wiki/Linux_gaming), the Wikipedia list of open-source games (http://en.wikipedia.org/wiki/List_of_open_source_games), and the Linux Game Tome (http://happypenguin.org) are good places to start.

- **Commercial Windows games** — The latest commercial computer games are not all ported to run in Linux. Boxed commercial games for Linux include versions of Unreal Tournament, as well as some 50 first-rate commercial games that have been ported to run in Linux. Using Cedega from cedega.com, you can get hundreds of popular

Windows games to run. To see if the game you want is verified to run in Cedega, visit the Transgaming Games Database (www.cedega.com/gamesdb/) to see its status. Also see the CrossOver Games site (www.codeweavers.com/products/cxgames/) for more on the CrossOver Games product.

- **Other gaming sites** — The Linux Gamer's FAQ (http://icculus.org/lgfaq) contains a wealth of information about free and commercial Linux games. For a list of Linux games without additional information, see http://icculus.org/lgfaq/gamelist.php. You can also purchase Linux games from Linux Game Publishing (www.linuxgame-publishing.com), and Tux Games (www.tuxgames.com).

Cross-Reference

Chapter 5 covers more on WINE, the basic technology behind Cedega and CrossOver Games. See Chapter 23 for more on running Windows operating systems through virtualization.

Chapter 3 provides more information on graphics cards on Linux. ∎

Before you can play some of the more demanding 3D games, you need to confirm that your hardware can handle them. Some games requiring support for 3D hardware acceleration need more RAM, faster processors, and particular video cards to run in Linux.

Here is a quick list of games that are available on Fedora, and many other Linux distributions that you can try out. I've listed them in the order of "simple and addicting" to "more complex and addicting":

- **Frozen Bubble** (www.frozen-bubble.org) — The Frozen Bubble game is often mentioned as the most addictive Linux Game. Shoot up frozen bubbles and colored groups of bubbles as they slowly descend on you. Clear the bubbles in sets of three or more until they are all gone (or come down and freeze you). The game can be played with multiple players. (Install the frozen-bubble package and select it from the Games menu.)

- **Gweled** (http://sebdelestaing.free.fr/gweled) — In this clone of the popular Bejeweled game, exchange two jewels on the board to match three or more jewels (vertically or horizontally). (Install the gweled package and select Gweled from the Games menu.)

- **WarZone 2100** (http://wz2100.net/) — This 1999 real-time strategy game was released in open source in 2004. Build a base from which you design and build vehicles and weapons, set up structures, and research new technologies to fight a global war. (Install the warzone2100 package and select Warzone 2100 from the Games menu.)

- **Quake 3 Arena** (ftp.idsoftware.com) — Several first-person shooter games in the Quake series are available for download from id Software. (Install the quake3 package and select Quake 3 Arena from the games menu.) The application that starts lets you download a demo version of the Quake3 data files, which can be freely downloaded. Read and accept the licensing terms to download the data files and begin playing the Quake 3 Arena demo. Note that id Software's FTP site, `ftp.idsoftware.com`, includes Linux downloads for Quake 4 and other games.

- **Vega Strike** (`http://vegastrike.sourceforge.net`) — Explore the universe in this 3D action, space simulation game. Accept missions to transport cargo, become a bounty hunter, or patrol space. In this 3D environment you can chat with bartenders or watch news broadcasts to keep up with events in the universe. (To play this game in Fedora, install the vegastrike package and select Vega Strike from the Games menu.)

Note
Despite gains in gaming support in Linux, a lot of popular Windows games still don't run in Linux. For that reason, some PC gamers maintain a separate Windows partition on their computers so they can boot to Windows to play particular games. See Chapter 2 for more on dual booting Linux and Windows. ∎

Basic Linux gaming information

There are more than 200 software packages in the Games group in the Fedora software repository, so if you are just looking for a few diverting games or old commercial games that are now publicly available, you can start by looking there. However, if you want to learn more about new commercial games that run in Linux, or find out about the general state of Linux gaming, there are several sites on the Web you should check out, as mentioned previously.

The GNOME games consist of some old card games and a bunch of games that look suspiciously like the games you would find on Windows systems. If you are afraid of losing your favorite desktop diversion (such as Solitaire, FreeCell, or Minesweeper) when you leave Windows, have no fear. You can find clones of many of them under GNOME games.

If you install KDE, there are a lot of games in the kdegames package. If you didn't install the KDE desktop, you can install the kdegames package separately from the DVD that accompanies this book or using `yum` over the Internet (`yum install kdegames`). To see the KDE games (along with some GNOME games) on the Applications menu, select Games and then choose the game you want. I find Shisen-Sho, a Mahjongg variant, especially addicting.

Summary

This chapter walked you through the steps of setting up and using audio, video, and digital cameras in Fedora. It covered topics such as troubleshooting your sound card and explained how to find software to play music through that card. Many popular music players included with Fedora, such as KsCD and Rhythmbox, are described.

With nearly every type of audio and video format available today in Linux, the biggest trick is figuring out which software is legal to use freely. Because the Fedora Project tends to be conservative when it comes to patent claims to multimedia, you might need to dig up the audio and video codecs you need on your own. I outlined some of the legal issues surrounding multimedia software patents, so you can make informed decisions.

Linux provides a number of video players, along with webcam support. With a TV card, you can display live video and engage in video conferencing.

If your computer has a CD burner, you can also burn complete CD or DVD ISO images using the K3b window.

While Linux doesn't have the same commercial support for gaming that Windows does, you can still play a wide variety of games on your Linux system. Using packages that can run Windows applications such as Cedega or CrossOver Games, you can play many of your favorite games on Linux.

Using the Internet and the Web

## 8

With your Fedora system connected to the Internet, you can take advantage of dozens of tools for browsing the Web, downloading files, getting e-mail, and communicating live with your friends. In most cases, you have several options of GUI and command-line applications for using Internet services from your Linux desktop or shell.

This chapter describes some of the most popular tools available with Fedora for working with the Internet. These descriptions cover Web browsers, e-mail readers, instant messaging clients, and commands for login and remote execution. Many specialty applications (such as BitTorrent file sharing) are available to Fedora users from the Fedora repository.

Overview of Internet Applications and Commands

When it comes to features and ease-of-use issues, applications that come with Fedora for accessing the Internet rival those of any operating system. For every major type of Internet client application, there are at least three or four graphical and command-line tools to choose from.

While Linux has offered high-quality servers for Web, mail, FTP, and other Internet services for years, current versions of these desktop Internet applications have become both solid and rich in content. If Web browsing and e-mail are your primary needs in a desktop system, Fedora is fully capable of handling those tasks, enabling you to leave your Windows desktop systems behind.

IN THIS CHAPTER

Understanding Internet tools

Browsing the Web

Communicating via e-mail

Participating in newsgroups

Using Pidgin Instant Messaging

Using BitTorrent cooperative software distribution

Using remote login, copy, and execution commands

If you are using Fedora as a desktop system, the browsers and e-mail clients make requests to servers available on your LAN or the Internet. Software for configuring a computer as a Web, mail, FTP, or other server type is also included with Fedora systems. Someone starting out with Linux, however, can use applications for using the Internet as they would from any Windows or other desktop system.

The following Internet applications available in Fedora are covered in this chapter:

- **Web browsers** — Most Web browsers available for Linux today follow from the legacy of Netscape Navigator. The open-source Mozilla project, which was originally spawned from Netscape source code, is responsible for the award-winning Firefox Web browser. Another browser included with Fedora is the Konqueror browser. (The Mozilla suite was renamed SeaMonkey and is available with Fedora in the seamonkey package.)

  Relatively new ways for gathering content from the Web include RSS news feed readers, such as the liferea and Akregator RSS/RDF feed readers. Several browsers, such as lynx and w3m, can also run from the command line (with no graphical interface required).

- **E-mail clients** — The Evolution e-mail client has evolved into a full-fledged groupware suite, combining an e-mail reader with features for managing contacts, calendars, and tasks, as well as connecting to Microsoft Exchange servers. Thunderbird provides an e-mail client from the Mozilla project (SeaMonkey mail is also available from the same organization). For those who prefer old-school e-mail readers, the mutt and mail commands enable you to read mail from the command line, often with limited capabilities to handle attachments, HTML, or other modern e-mail features.

- **FTP clients** — If you use the FTP protocol to download files from FTP servers, or to upload Web pages to your server, graphical tools for doing those tasks include the gFTP and kGet applications. There are also many shell commands available for accessing FTP servers to look for files, download files, or upload files. Those commands include lftp, ncftp, and tftp.

- **BitTorrent clients/servers** — BitTorrent is the popular open-source software project for sharing files among many computers at the same time. With BitTorrent, as you download a file you can simultaneously safely upload that same file to others. BitTorrent is particularly useful for publishing CD or DVD images containing large software distributions (such as Fedora) the minute they become available, without overstressing the original servers releasing the software.

- **Instant messaging and chats** — Typing real-time messages to friends, family, and associates has become a vital activity for some of us. Empathy provides the official GNOME IM client. Pidgin is an instant messaging (IM) client that enables you to connect to a host of servers, including AIM, IRC, MSN, Google, ICQ, and others. XChat is a popular Internet Relay Chat (IRC) client, a popular protocol among Linux enthusiasts for online chats. Kopete is an instant messaging client that integrates with a KDE desktop.

- **Remote commands (login, file copy, etc.)** — As you spend more time working with Linux, you will find that it is often quicker and more convenient to run commands than it is to run graphical applications. Some very powerful command-line tools exist in Linux for doing such things as remote login and remote execution (ssh) and remote file copy (wget, scp, and rsync).

Note

Besides the applications mentioned here, many more Internet-enabled applications are described in other parts of the book. For example, music players and video players described in Chapter 7 can get audio and video files or streaming media from the Internet. Likewise, software installation tools such as `yum` get software packages from software repositories on the Internet. ∎

Because the Internet client applications featured in Fedora are designed to be intuitive, if you are accustomed to using the Internet from Windows or Mac the transition to Linux shouldn't be that difficult. While I describe many of the basic features included in these Internet applications, learning a few tricks will help you get the most out of them:

- **Tuning your browser** — While Firefox has made great strides in supporting different kinds of Web content, getting some multimedia, image, and document formats to play in Firefox can require some extra steps. In most cases, this is because software for playing many popular multimedia formats cannot be freely distributed, so you have to add them later. I'll describe some plugins and other software that you will want to add to Firefox (or another Web browser) to get it to play many popular types of content that it can't handle by default.

- **Managing e-mail** — As e-mail volume continues to increase, tools for managing it are becoming more important. In the discussion of e-mail, I explain how to use filter rules to sort your e-mail and how to identify junk mail. You'll also learn ways to manage and use mailing lists effectively.

- **Useful command options** — In addition to learning some useful commands for remote login, file copying, and command execution, you'll learn some options that are particularly helpful to use with them.

To get started with Internet applications in Linux, you need to set up a connection to the Internet from your Linux system (as described in Chapters 14 and 15). Most graphical Internet applications in Fedora are available from menus on the GNOME or KDE desktops. Click Applications ⇨ Internet to see a list of Internet applications you can choose from. Icons to launch the Firefox browser and Evolution e-mail client are directly on the panel on the top of the display.

Browsing the Web

The most important client Internet program these days is the Web browser. In Fedora, you have several Web browser options, including the following:

- **Firefox** — The Firefox browser is touted as the flagship Web browser from the Mozilla project and is aimed squarely at the dominance of Microsoft Internet Explorer in the browser space. Firefox offers easy-to-use features for dealing cleverly with issues that have wreaked havoc with other Internet browsers, such as viruses, spyware, and pop-ups. Firefox, the featured Web browser in Fedora, also runs on Windows and Mac OS X.

- **Chrome** — Google's Chrome browser, called Chromium on Linux, provides some innovative advances in managing browser tabs, Web pages that use up system resources, and all-around speed.

- **Epiphany** — The Epiphany browser is the official Web browser of the GNOME project. It is powered by the Mozilla Layout Engine (sometimes referred to as Gecko). While Epiphany doesn't have all the features you find in Firefox, it is designed to be fast and efficient.

- **Konqueror** — Although Konqueror was once the file manager for the KDE desktop, it is now used primarily to display Web content. Using Konqueror, you can easily go back and forth between websites and local files and folders. A testament to Konqueror's quality is the fact that the Mac OS X Safari and iPhone browsers use the WebKit rendering engine, which is based on the Konqueror KHTML and kjs engines.

If you are working from a shell, several command-line utilities enable you to browse the Web without a graphical interface, including the links, w3m, and lynx commands.

Browsing the Web with Firefox

The Firefox Web browser offers real competition to Microsoft Internet Explorer. Firefox is lightweight (so it performs fast), includes many ease-of-use features, and was built with security as a high priority. If you haven't switched to Fedora yet, you can get Firefox for Windows, Mac OS X, and other Linux systems. With the Fedora CD and DVD that come with this book, you can try Firefox out right now.

Because Firefox is the default browser for the current Fedora, if you have done an install that includes the desktop, Firefox should already be installed. (If it's not, you need to install the firefox package from the Fedora DVD.) To start Firefox from your Fedora desktop, either select the globe icon from your panel or select Internet ➪ Firefox Web Browser from the Applications menu. Firefox makes some of its best features available right in its main window (as shown in Figure 8-1). Here are some examples:

- **Tabbed browsing** — Instead of opening multiple windows to have several Web pages available at a time, Firefox includes a very efficient tabbed browsing feature. Select File ➪ New Tab (or press Ctrl+T). Then type the URL for the new Web page you want. Figure 8-1 shows the Firefox window with two open browsing tabs. Tab options set from the Preferences window (Edit ➪ Preferences ➪ Tabs) can be set to automatically force new links to be opened in a new tab or open links from other applications in a new tab. This can help preserve screen real estate by containing multiple Web pages in one window.

  To close a tab, open a new tab, bookmark one or a group of tabs, or reload one or all tabs, right-click one of the tabs at the top of the pane. A drop-down menu enables you to choose the function you want. One of the easiest ways to open a link in a tab is to right-click over it on an HTML page. Select the Open Link in New Tab option. Clicking the middle button on a three-button mouse will open a link in a new tab.

FIGURE 8-1

Firefox makes it easy to search, do tabbed browsing, and get plugins in a secure way.

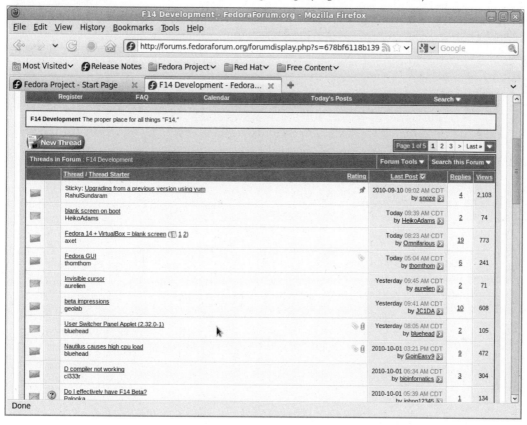

- **Live Bookmarks** — For websites that have RSS news and blog headlines available, a small RSS logo icon appears in the location box of the Firefox screen (see Figure 8-1). Using that icon, you can bookmark the advertised RSS feed so that live headlines from that site can be displayed from your Bookmarks menu.

  Try a site such as `http://fedoraforum.org`. Click the RSS button. When prompted, choose to Subscribe Now to Live Bookmarks for the site. Select Bookmarks, and then select the new bookmark. To the right of the bookmark, a list of current articles available from the site appears. You can click to go straight to an article that looks interesting; or, you can choose Open All in Tabs to open all the articles in separate tabs.

  Many sites include RSS support. Try `packers.com`, `cnn.com`, `slashdot.org`, `abcnews.com`, or `cbssportsline.com` for other examples of sites that offer RSS news feeds.

Note

If you visit a website that you know is an RSS site but the headlines you want appear in XML code, it means the page is not identifying itself to Firefox as an RSS site. You can add a Live Bookmark for the site anyway by selecting Bookmarks ➪ Subscribe to This Page. If Firefox recognizes the site as an RSS feed, it will display a Subscribe Now button at the top of the page. If this does not work, add the site as a normal bookmark. From the Library screen (choose Organize Bookmarks to get there), select Organize ➪ New Bookmark. When prompted, enter a name for the live bookmark, and then type (or paste) the location of the RSS page into the Feed Location box and click OK. That new live bookmark, and today's articles from that site, will appear in your Bookmarks list. ■

- **Using the sidebar** — Select View ➪ Sidebar to choose to have Bookmarks or History appear as a sidebar in the Firefox window. Add your own bookmarks, return to pages from your history list, or use the Search box to search for content from those lists. Type Ctrl+B and Ctrl+H to toggle on and off Bookmarks and History sidebars, respectively.

- **Web searches** — A box for doing keyword searches from Google is built right into the Firefox navigation toolbar. A drop-down menu enables you to search Yahoo!, Answers. com, Creative Commons, Amazon.com, Wikipedia, or eBay.

- **Finding text** — Click Edit ➪ Find to open a toolbar at the bottom of the window for searching the current page for a text string. This enables you to search the page for text without a little pop-up window getting in your way. After typing the text string, click Next or Previous to search for the string. You can also click Highlight to highlight all instances of the string on the page. As a shorthand, type a forward slash character, /, to display a Quick Find toolbar.

- **Resizing text on Web page** — A nice keyboard shortcut enables you to quickly resize the text on most Web pages in Firefox. Hold the Ctrl key and press the plus (+) or minus (-) keys. The text on the Web page (in most cases) gets larger or smaller, respectively. That page with the insanely small type font is suddenly readable. (Remember to hold the Shift key to type a + character.)

- **Checking history** — Select History ➪ Show All History to have the History appear on the Library screen. From that window, you can do keyword searches for sites you have visited, display the site names you have visited in various ways (by date, site name, most visited, and last visited), and browse through and select to revisit a site.

Some of the best features in Firefox are not as near the surface. In particular, Firefox was designed for safe computing, so it is very careful about what it will allow by default. Here are some important features of Firefox that can contribute to safe and fun Web browsing:

- **Blocking pop-ups** — In Firefox, pop-up windows are blocked by default. To see or change how pop-ups are handled from Firefox, select Edit ➪ Preferences and select Content. The Block pop-up windows option is either selected (to block pop-ups) or unselected (to allow them). If pop-ups are blocked, you can select Exceptions to add selected sites from which you will allow pop-ups. You can add additional restrictions to JavaScript code in Web pages by clicking the Advanced button associated with the Enable JavaScript check box.

- **Advanced Security Features** — With Firefox, you have a lot of control over what content can be played and what software can be downloaded to your computer. You can view or change many security features from the Preferences window (select Edit ➪ Preferences). Use the Content tab to enable Java or JavaScript, load images, or block pop-up windows. The Privacy tab enables you to manage cookies, passwords, history, and cache information.

To help with security, you can use the location box, shown in Figure 8-2, to verify sites you visit and that HTTPS URLs are actually encrypted.

FIGURE 8-2

Verify sites from the location box.

The example shown in Figure 8-2 shows what happens when you click the icon on the left side of the location box when visiting a secured site. In this case, Akamai verifies the authenticity of the site and that communications are encrypted. By selecting the star on the right side, you can work with bookmark information for a page and modify that information. Other icons that might appear in the location box include a variety of security warnings, such as alerts about possible forged or dangerous content.

See the Mozilla Firefox site (www.mozilla.org/products/firefox) for more information on Firefox. For help transitioning from Internet Explorer to Firefox, see the Firefox site at www.mozilla.org/products/firefox/switch.html.

Setting up Firefox

You can do many things to configure Firefox to run like a champ. The following sections describe some ways to customize your browsing experience in Firefox.

Setting preferences

You can set your Firefox preferences in the Preferences window. To open Firefox Preferences, click Edit ⇨ Preferences. The Firefox Preferences window appears, as shown in Figure 8-3.

FIGURE 8-3

Change settings for navigating the Web from the Firefox Preferences window.

The following list describes some preferences you might want to change from the Firefox Preferences window:

- **Choosing a home page** — To choose a home page from the Main tab, you can simply type a URL in the location box. It can be a local file (file://) or a Web page (http://). You can also have multiple home pages, with each appearing on a separate tab when Firefox starts, by separating URLs with a pipe (e.g., http://linuxtoys.net|http://redhat.com).

To fill in your home page locations, you can also select buttons. Use Current Pages adds the current pages on all tabs of your browser as your home pages. The Use Bookmarks button lets you choose home pages from your bookmarks list. Selecting Show a blank page sets your home page to about:blank.

- **Saving browsing information** — Select the Privacy tab to specify how information about your Web browsing is saved. On the Privacy tab, you can specify whether Firefox should save data that may be of special concern due to privacy, such as your browsing history, data you enter into forms, passwords, downloaded files, and cookies. You can select to clear your history, forms data, passwords, download history, cookies, and cached Web pages. Clearing this information is a good idea if you are using Firefox on someone else's machine and want to keep your browsing private.

- **Blocking or enabling content** — Some content you encounter can be annoying or even dangerous to play or display from your browser. From the Content tab, select what to allow and block in regard to pop-up windows, sites trying to install extensions or themes, image display, Java content, and JavaScript content. You can also set exceptions to the general rules you set for handling the content just mentioned. There are numerous Firefox extensions you can use to aid in blocking content as well.

Note

Firefox helps you block forged websites by displaying a Suspected Web Forgery pop-up message when it encounters a page that has been reported as forged. You can choose to not display the page or ignore the warning. If you suspect a forged page that doesn't display that message, select Help ⇨ Report Web Forgery to suggest that the page be added to the Google Web Forgery list. ■

- **Defining tabbed browsing** — Use selections on the Tabs tab to determine how tabs are used when opening new content or closing the browser.

- **Download manager and folder** — Choose whether or not a download manager is displayed when file downloads are being done. You can also either select to be asked where to place each file chosen for download or select a default folder.

The Advanced Preferences tab can be used to fine-tune your Web browsing experience. Here are some Advanced Preferences that might interest you:

- **General settings** — Some settings on the General tab in the Advanced section let you change accessibility settings, browsing features (such as scrolling), and system defaults.

- **Choosing connection settings** — If you have direct access to the Internet, you don't need to change any proxy settings; but if you need to access the Internet via a proxy server, you can identify the location of that server (or servers) by selecting Network ⇨ Connection Settings from the Advanced tab. To access the Web via proxy servers, you must explicitly identify the proxy server to use for each type of content you request (HTTP, SSL, FTP, Gopher, and SOCKS).

- **Get browser updates** — From the Update tab, Firefox can be set to automatically check for updates available for the search engine or installed extensions and themes. Select Show Update History to see a history of updates you have installed for Firefox.

- **Choose security settings** — From the Encryption tab of the Advanced section, choose which protocols (SSL and TLS) are acceptable for Firefox to use for secure browsing. The Certificates section enables you to manage certificates to verify the authenticity of secure sites or authenticate yourself to remote sites. (See the section "Securing Firefox" for further information on securing Web browsing with Firefox.)

Extending Firefox

Firefox can handle most standard Web content (HTML, JPEG, text files) without any trouble. As with any browser, however, some content requires additional plugins or helper applications in order to play or display that content. Firefox also enables you to add extensions that enhance its features.

Using plugins

From Firefox, you can see what plugins are installed to Firefox by typing **about:plugins** in the location box. As Firefox is delivered in Fedora systems, you will have at least a NPAPI plugins wrapper installed by default. The NPAPI plugin enables you to use some plugins that were not built for Linux.

To find plugins that will work for Firefox in Linux systems, try the Mozilla Plugins page (http://plugindoc.mozdev.org/linux.html). Here are a few plugins that you might want to add to Firefox:

- **Adobe Reader Plugin** (www.adobe.com/downloads) — Displays files in the Adobe Systems PDF (Portable Document Format) format. (Without this plugin installed, Firefox will use the evince command to display PDF files in a separate window.)

- **Adobe Flash Player** (www.adobe.com/downloads) — With the explosion of YouTube and other sites carrying Flash video content, the Adobe Flash Player has become indispensible on desktop systems. Follow the links from the Adobe Flash Player site to find the Linux plugin you need. I recommend the yum version, which will install the plugin, get updates, and install related software.

- **MPlayer Plugin** (http://mplayerplug-in.sourceforge.net) — This plugin implements the popular mplayer video player to play embedded video content in the browser window. An RPM package of this plugin (mplayerplug-in) is available from http://rpmfusion.org. See Chapter 5 for more on using rpmfusion.org.

- **Java Runtime Environment** (java-1.6.0-openjdk-plugin) — To be able to play Java content from your Web browser, you need a plugin that provides the functionality you get with the Java Runtime Environment (JRE) Web plugin from Oracle (http://java.com/en/download). Instead of using proprietary code from Oracle, however, Fedora Project has added a completely free equivalent version by combining software from the OpenJDK project and IcedTea project (`http://fedoraproject.org/wiki/Features/IcedTea`).

To ensure that the plugin is working, restart Firefox and type **about:plugins** in the location box. You'll see a list of Java content handled by the GCJ Web Browser Plugin. You can also try different websites that contain Java content to try out your Java plugin. For example, you can visit the Java.com test page: `http://java.com/en/download/help/testvm.xml`

If you are unable to see the Java content, open the PackageKit Update Applet and look for an updated nspluginwrapper package. Installing that updated package and restarting your Firefox browser should enable you to see the Java content.

- **CrossOver Plugin** (`www.codeweavers.com`) — Linux plugins are not yet available for some of the more interesting and popular plugins. QuickTime 5 movies, Shockwave Director multimedia content, and various Microsoft movie, file, and data formats simply will not play natively in Firefox. Using software built on WINE for Linux on x86-based processors, CodeWeavers created the CrossOver Plugin. Although no longer offered as a separate product (you must buy the entire CrossOver Linux product for $39.95), the CrossOver Plugin enables you to play some content that you could not otherwise use in Linux. (Download a demo from `www.codeweavers.com/site/products/download_trial`.)

  After you install the CrossOver Plugin, you see a nice Plugin Setup window that enables you to selectively install plugins for QuickTime, Windows Media Player, Shockwave, Flash, iTunes, and Lotus Notes, as well as Microsoft Word, Excel, and PowerPoint viewers. (Support for later versions of these content formats may be available by the time you read this.) You can also install other multimedia plugins, as well as a variety of fonts to use with those plugins.

For some plugins, you are prompted for a location for the plugin. You can install them so they are available either to all users on the system or to only the current user. To add a plugin for the current user only, place it in the `~/.mozilla/plugins` directory. To have the plugin available for all users who run Firefox on the system, put the plugin in the `/usr/lib/firefox-*/plugins` directory. (On 64-bit Linux systems, this will be in the `/usr/lib64/firefox-*/plugins` directory.)

Note

When Firefox doesn't have a plugin assigned to handle a particular data type, a pop-up window asks if you want to use the default application from your desktop environment to handle the data. For GNOME, the `/usr/share/applications/defaults.list` file defines system-wide default applications. For your own desktop, you can change the defaults used to open a particular file type as follows: Open the Nautilus file manager; right-click on any file of the type you want to change; select Properties; select the Open With tab; and choose the application you want to use for that file type from the list. If the application you want to add isn't on the list, click Add to add it. ∎

While plugins are available for playing select types of content, add-ons can be used to add features to the browser itself.

Getting add-ons

To extend Firefox to handle content beyond what is delivered with Fedora, start from the Mozilla. org Firefox product page (`www.mozilla.com/en-US/firefox/`). From there, follow links to Firefox add-ons. Here are some of the most popular add-ons to Firefox that are available from Mozilla.org:

Note

Some Firefox add-ons have been known to cause performance problems with Firefox, primarily from using excessive amounts of memory. If you notice poor performance after installing an add-on, close all Firefox windows, and then restart Firefox in safe mode from a terminal window by typing the following:

```
firefox -safe-mode
```

Refer to `http://kb.mozillazine.org/Safe_Mode` **for more information on using safe mode to debug Firefox problems.** ■

Changing Firefox themes

Several themes are available for Firefox for changing the look and feel of your Firefox window. From the Mozilla update site (`https://addons.mozilla.org`), select Themes. When you download a theme for Firefox, it knows that it is a Firefox theme and, in the download window, gives you the option to install the theme by clicking the Use Theme button.

To change a theme later or get more Themes, select Tools ➪ Add-ons ➪ Get Add-ons and then Click on the Browse All Add-ons link. Select Themes as the category and look for themes that appeal to you. After you have installed a new theme and selected it as your current theme, restart Firefox for the new theme to take effect.

Securing Firefox

Security is one of the strongest reasons why people switch to Firefox. By prohibiting the most unsafe types of content from playing in Firefox, and by warning you of potentially dangerous or annoying content before displaying it, Firefox has become the Web browser of choice for many security-conscious users. Here are some ways that Firefox helps make your Web browsing more secure:

- **ActiveX** — Because of major security flaws found in ActiveX, Firefox will simply not play ActiveX content.

- **Pop-ups** — Pop-up windows are disabled by default in Firefox. You can set preferences to enable all pop-ups or to enable only pop-ups from selected sites.

- **Privacy preferences** — From the Privacy window in Firefox (select Edit ➪ Preferences, and then click the Privacy button), you can clear different categories of stored private information from your browser in a single click. This is a particularly good feature if you have just used a computer other than your own to browse the Web.

- **Certificates** — In Firefox, you can install and manage certificates that can be used for validating a website and safely performing encryption of communications to that site. Using the Preferences window (select Edit ⇨ Preferences, and then click the Advanced button), you can manage certificates under the Encryption tab. Select View Certificates to display a window where you can import new certificates or view certificates that are already installed. Firefox will verify that certificates you encounter are valid (and warn you if they are not). See Chapter 13 for more information on using certificates.

Along with all the excellent security features built into Firefox, it's important that you incorporate good security practices in your Web browsing. Download and install software only from sites that are secure and known to you to be safe. For any online transactions, make sure you are communicating with a secure site (look for the `https` protocol in the location box and the closed lock icon in the lower-right corner of the screen). Be careful about being redirected to another website when doing a financial transaction. An IP address in the site's address or misspellings on a screen where you enter credit card information are warning signs that you may have been directed to an untrustworthy site.

Because new exploits are being discovered all the time, it's important that you keep your Web browser up to date. That means that, at least, you need to get updates of Firefox from the Fedora project as they become available (see Chapter 5 for information on using `yum` and PackageKit to get the latest software). To keep up on the latest security news and information about Firefox and other Mozilla products, refer to the Mozilla Security Center (`www.mozilla.org/security`).

Tips for using Firefox

There are so many nice features in Firefox, it's hard to cover all of them. Just to point you toward a few more fun and useful features, here are some extra tips about Firefox you might enjoy:

- **Add smart keywords** — Many websites include their own search boxes to enable you to look for information on their site. With Firefox, you can assign a smart keyword to any search box on the Web, and then use that keyword from the location box in the Firefox browser to search that site.

  For example, go to the Linux Documentation Project site (`http://tldp.org`). Right-click in the Search/Resources search box. Select Add a Keyword for this Search from the menu that appears. Add a name (Linux Documentation) and a keyword (tldp) and select Add to add the keyword to your Bookmarks.

  After you have added the keyword, you can use it by simply entering the keyword and one or more search terms to the Firefox location box (on the navigation toolbar). For example, I entered **tldp Lego Mindstorms** and came up with a list of HOW-TOs for using Lego Mindstorms in Linux. This list is returned just as if you had visited the site and typed the text **Lego Mindstorms** into the search box on that site.

- **Check config** — Firefox has hundreds of configuration preferences available to set as you please. You can see those options by typing **about:config** in the location box. For true/false options, you can simply click the preference name to toggle it between the two values. For other preferences, click the preference to enter a value into a pop-up box. While many of these values can be changed through the Preferences menu (Edit ⇨ Preferences), some technical people prefer to look at settings in a list like the one shown on the about:config page. The about:buildconfig page lists the options used to build Firefox.

- **Multiple home pages** — Instead of just having one home page, you can have a whole set of home pages. When you start Firefox, a separate tab will open in the Firefox window for each address you identify in your home page list. To do this, create multiple tabs (File ⇨ New Tab) and enter the address for each page you want in your list of home pages. Then select Edit ⇨ Preferences ⇨ Main and click the Use Current Pages button. The next time you open Firefox, it will start with the selected tabs open to the home pages you chose. (Clicking the Home icon will open new tabs for all the home pages.)

There are many more things you can do with Firefox than I have covered in this chapter. If you have questions about Firefox features or you just want to dig up some more cool stuff about it, I recommend checking out the MozillaZine forum for Firefox support (http://forums .mozillazine.org/viewforum.php?f=38).

Browsing the Web with Chrome

Google's Chrome Web browser focuses on simplicity in the user interface, speed, and better separation between various Web pages you view. For example, in Chrome, each browser tab is sandboxed for security purposes, so that problems in one tab should not affect your system or other tabs, and hence other Web pages you view.

Many advanced Internet users choose Chrome, with its rich set of developer tools, overall speed, and slimmed-down user interface.

Note
On Fedora, Chrome is called Chromium. ■

By default, Chrome does not come with Fedora. In fact, if you query for packages starting with *chrom*, you'll see an entry for chromium-bsu, a space shooter game. To get Chrome, you have two main options:

- Download from Google — Go to http://google.com/chrome and download the RPM for Linux. Be sure to download the RPM version for Fedora/openSUSE and choose the proper version of Linux, 32-bit or 64-bit.

- Download the RPMs, as well as sources, from the Chromium repository at http:// repos.fedorapeople.org/repos/spot/chromium/.

Installing Chromium

To install Chromium from the RPM repository, run the following commands as the root user:

```
# cd /etc/yum.repos.d/
# wget http://repos.fedorapeople.org/repos/spot/chromium/fedora-chromium.repo
# yum install chromium
```

The first two commands set up a new repository in /etc/yum/repos.d. (See Chapter 5 for more on yum repositories.) The third command installs the application, using the new repository you just set up.

Running Chromium

Once installed, you can run Chromium by selecting Applications ⇨ Internet ⇨ Chromium Web Browser from the desktop. When you first launch chromium (as built from the RPMs at http://repos.fedorapeople.org/repos/spot/chromium), you need to select which search engine to use — Google, Yahoo, or Bing. Next, you'll see the main Chromium browser window, as shown in Figure 8-4.

FIGURE 8-4

The main Chromium window enables you to search and browse the Web.

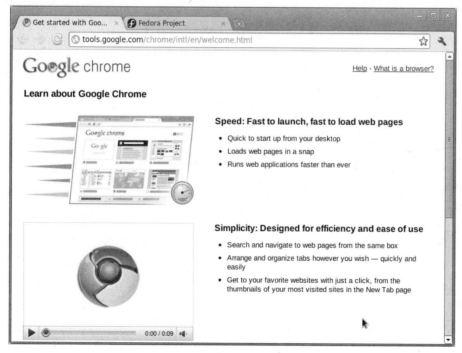

With its simple interface, you won't see a menu bar. Instead, right-click over a tab to see the tab menu, or click the wrench icon to the far right.

See `www.google.com/chrome` for more on Chrome.

Using text-based Web browsers

If you become a Linux administrator or power user, over time you will inevitably find yourself working on a computer from a remote login or location where no desktop GUI is available; and at some point while you are in that state, you will probably want to check an HTML file or a Web page. To solve the problem, Fedora includes several text-based Web browsers.

With text-based Web browsers, any HTML file available from the Web, your local file system, or a computer where you're remotely logged in can be accessed from your shell. There's no need to fire up your GUI or read pages of HTML markup if you just want to take a peek at the contents of a Web page. Besides letting you call up Web pages, move around within those pages, and follow links to other pages, some of these text-based browsers even display graphics right in a terminal window!

Which text-based browser you use is a matter of which one you are more comfortable with. Available browsers include the following:

- **links** — With links (elinks package), you can open a file or a URL, and then traverse links from the pages you open. Use search forward (`/string`) and back (`?string`) features to find text strings in pages. Use up and down arrows to go forward and back among links. Then press Enter to go to the current link. Use the right and left arrow keys to go forward and back among pages you have visited. Press Esc to see a menu bar of features.

  While links doesn't allow you to display images inline, if you select an image it will be displayed on your desktop in gThumb image viewer (by default). You also have the option to save the image to your local hard disk.

- **lynx** — The lynx browser includes a good set of help files (press the ? key). Step through pages using the spacebar. Although lynx can display pages containing frames, it cannot display them in the intended positioning. Use the arrow keys to display the selected link (right arrow), go back to the previous document (left arrow), select the previous link (up arrow), and select the next link (down arrow). One nice feature of lynx is that it prompts you when remote sites want to set cookies.

  As with links, lynx lets you display a selected image. However, lynx uses ImageMagick instead of gThumb to display the image you choose.

- **w3m** — The w3m text-based Web browser can display HTML pages containing text, links, frames, and tables. There are both English and Japanese help files available (press H with w3m running). You can also use w3m to page through an HTML document in plain text (for example, `cat index.html | w3m -T text/html`). Use the Page Up and Page Down keys to page through a document. Press Enter on a link to go to that link. Press the B key to go back to the previous link. Search forward and back for text using the / and ? keys, respectively. Type **q** to quit.

Note

You must install the elinks package to get links; the lynx package to get lynx; and the w3m package to get w3m. All of them are in the Fedora repository. ■

The w3m command seems the most sophisticated of these browsers. It features a nice default font selection, handles frames neatly, and its use of colors makes it easy to use. The links browser lets you use the mouse to cut and paste text.

You can start any of these text-based Web browsers by giving it a filename, or, if you have an active connection to the network, a Web address. For example, to read the w3m documentation (which is in HTML format) with a w3m browser, you can type the following from a terminal window or other shell interface:

```
$ w3m /usr/share/doc/w3m-0*/doc/MANUAL.html
```

An HTML version of the *w3m Manual* is displayed, or you can give w3m a URL to a Web page, such as the following:

```
$ w3m www.handsonhistory.com
```

After a page is open, you can begin viewing it and moving around to links included in the page. Start by using the arrow keys to move around and select links. Use the Page Up and Page Down keys to page through text.

Communicating with E-mail

Running a close second to Web browsers is the e-mail reader (referred to in network standards terms as a Mail User Agent, or MUA). Evolution is the recommended e-mail client for Fedora.

Other e-mail options include Mozilla Thunderbird, the Sylpheed mail client, and the KDE KMail program. Mail programs that have been around in Linux and other Unix systems since the time when most mail was plain text include mutt and mail. In other words, there is no shortage of options for e-mail clients in Linux.

Here are some pros and cons for different e-mail clients that are available for Fedora:

- **Evolution** — This is a full-featured e-mail client that also includes ways to manage your contacts, calendars, and tasks. Because it is so easy to use and rich in features, it provides one of the best ways to transition from Windows e-mail clients (such as Outlook). There are also features in Evolution for connecting to Microsoft Exchange and Novell GroupWise servers. The complaint I hear most often about Evolution is that it demands a lot of resources, so with slow-processor and low-RAM systems, you would probably find other e-mail clients less frustrating to use over time.

- **Thunderbird** — As with Firefox in the browser arena, Thunderbird is the flagship mail client from the Mozilla project. It was designed from the ground up to be secure, fast, and loaded with important features. It has versions available on Windows and Mac OS X, so you can use the same mail client on different platforms. Not much on the downside here: Thunderbird doesn't include a lot of the groupware features you get in Evolution. You can use the Sunbird calendar or the Lightning plugin to Thunderbird to add the capability to manage your calendar. See `www.mozilla.org/projects /calendar/`.

- **KMail** — People who are frustrated with Evolution's performance often seem to switch to KMail. Because KMail is a KDE desktop project, it integrates particularly well with the KDE desktop environment. However, many people insist that KMail runs well in GNOME, too. The look and feel is similar to Evolution (folders in the left column and message headers and messages on the right). As with Evolution, KMail can easily integrate with clamav (anti-virus software) and spamassassin (e-mail spam-checker software).

- **Sylpheed** — The Sylpheed mail client is good for low-end computers on which you still want to use a graphical mail client. Sylpheed is used on bootable business-card Linux systems, such as Damn Small Linux. You can install Sylpheed simply by typing `yum` **install sylpheed**.

- **Text-based mail** — Many technical people who often work from the command line prefer to use a text-based mail reader as well. That way, they can do remote shell login or not even fire up a GUI to read their mail. The mutt e-mail client will run in a shell, handle some modern features well (such as attachments), and beat out any graphical e-mail client for performance by a wide margin. The downside is a longer learning curve than you will have with point-and-click interfaces.

Cross-Reference

If you don't have an e-mail account, you can set up your own e-mail server using Fedora. For information on setting up a mail server, see Chapter 18. You can also get free e-mail accounts from Yahoo!, Google (gmail), and others. ∎

Using Evolution e-mail

Evolution is the preferred application for sending and managing e-mail on default GNOME desktops for Fedora. Fedora developers gave it a prime spot on the desktop, just to the right of the System menu and Web browser icon. After you launch Evolution for the first time and run the Setup Assistant, the Evolution window appears, showing the different types of operations you can perform.

If you want to change your default e-mail application in GNOME from Evolution, select System ⇨ Preferences ⇨ Preferred Applications. When the Preferred Applications window appears, select the Internet tab and choose the mail reader you want from the Select drop-down box. (You can also change your default Web browser and terminal window from the Preferred Applications window.) In KDE, from the main KDE menu, select System Setting ⇨ Default Applications ⇨ Email Client. Then either use the default KMail client or select the "Use a different email client" button to choose from a list of known applications you can use as your e-mail client.

Figure 8-5 shows an example of the Evolution window.

Evolution is a groupware application, combining several types of applications that help groups of people communicate and work together. Features include the following:

- **Mail** — A complete set of features for getting, reading, managing, composing, and sending e-mail on one or more e-mail accounts.

- **Calendars** — Create and manage appointments on your personal calendar. You can e-mail appointment information to others and do keyword searches of your calendar.

- **Contacts** — Create contact information for friends and associates, such as names, addresses, and telephone numbers. A Categories feature helps you remember who gets birthday and anniversary gifts.

- **Tasks** — Organize ongoing tasks into folders.

- **Exchange** — Connect to an Exchange server. If your organization gets its mail from an Exchange server, the Evolution Connector software (included with this version of Evolution) enables you to configure this e-mail client to access that server.

FIGURE 8-5

Evolution can be used to manage your e-mail, appointments, and tasks.

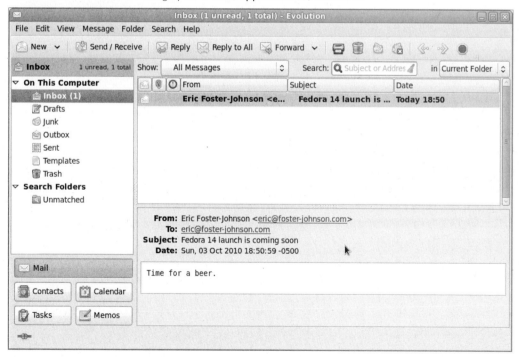

Setting Evolution preferences

To really make Evolution your own, you can set preferences that are particular to you, such as how your e-mail is gathered and sorted. You can change Mail Accounts settings by performing the following steps:

1. From the Evolution main window, select Edit ➪ Preferences.

2. Click Mail Accounts in the left column.

3. Select the mail account to change and click Edit. The Evolution Account Editor appears.

4. Here are a few items you may want to change for your e-mail account:

   - **Signature** — Have a signature appear on every e-mail message you send. Either click the signature box and select Autogenerated (to use name and e-mail address as a signature) or click Add New Signature to create a signature in a text editor.

   - **Receiving options** — By default, Evolution doesn't check your mail server for your messages unless specified. You can change that by clicking the "Automatically check for new mail every . . ." box on the Receiving Options tab. The default, which you can change, checks your mail server for your mail every 10 minutes. Once downloaded, each message is erased from the server. Select Leave messages on server to change that behavior.

   - **Automatic copy** — You can have every message you send copied to one or more other users. This is a nice feature if you write important e-mail that you want to archive to a different e-mail account. Select the Defaults tab, and then click the check box next to Always carbon-copy (cc) or Always blind carbon-copy (bcc). Then type the correct e-mail address.

   - **Security** — To help validate that you are who you say you are and keep your e-mail private, Evolution lets you use PGP/GPG (Pretty Good Privacy/GNU Privacy Guard) encryption keys. Click the Security tab, and then enter your PGP/GPG Key ID. Choose settings for signing and encryption as appropriate.

5. Click OK to apply the changes.

Receiving, composing, and sending e-mail

Evolution offers a full set of features for sending, receiving, and managing your e-mail. The folder bar in the left part of the Evolution window makes it easy to create and use multiple mail folders.

Here are some tips for sending, reading, and receiving mail:

- **Read e-mail** — Click Inbox in the Folder column. Your messages appear to the right.

- **Delete e-mail** — After you have read a message, select it and press the Delete key. Click View ➪ Show Deleted Messages to toggle whether or not you see deleted messages. Right-click on the Trash folder and select Empty Trash to permanently remove the deleted messages.

- **Send and receive** — Click the Send/Receive button to send any e-mail queued to be sent and receive any e-mail waiting for you on your mail server.

- **Compose e-mail** — Click New ➪ Mail Message (or click the New button in the tool-bar). A Compose Message window appears. Type the e-mail address, a message for the subject line, and the body of the message. Click Send when you are finished. Use buttons on the Compose window to add attachments, cut and paste text, choose a format (HTML or plain text), and sign the message (if you have set up appropriate keys).

- **Create folders** — If you like to keep a lot of old messages, you may want to save them outside your Inbox (so it won't get too crowded). Right-click on the Inbox, and then select New Folder. Type a folder name and click Create (to store it as a subfolder to your Inbox).

- **Organize messages** — With new folders created, you can easily organize messages from your Inbox to another folder. The easiest way is to simply drag and drop each message (or a set of selected messages) from the message pane to the new folder.

- **Search messages** — With your Inbox or other mail folder selected, type a keyword in the search box over your e-mail message pane and select whether to search by message subject line, sender, recipient, or message body. Click Find Now to search for the keyword. After viewing the messages, click Clear to have the other messages reappear.

- **Filter messages** — You can take action on an e-mail message before it even lands in your Inbox. Click Message ➪ Create Rule. From the menu that appears, you can add filters to deal with incoming or outgoing messages. Select the type of filter you want. For example, you could have all messages from a particular sender, subject, date, status, or size sorted to a selected folder; or you could have messages matching your criteria deleted, assigned a color, or respond by playing a sound clip.

Cross-Reference

Refer to Chapter 18 for information on using SpamAssassin, along with Evolution filters, to sort out spam from your real e-mail messages. Evolution also includes built-in junk e-mail filtering, using Bayesian statistical analysis. ■

Besides the features mentioned in the previous sections, Evolution supports many common features, such as printing, saving, and viewing e-mail messages in various ways. The help system that comes with Evolution (click the Help button) includes a good manual, FAQ, and service for reporting bugs.

Using Evolution to manage your schedule and contacts

You can also use Evolution to manage your calendar, tasks, contacts, and memos. In this regard, Evolution is a lot like Outlook on Windows, providing a heavyweight client for managing your work.

Click any of the buttons in the lower-left corner of the Evolution window to select Tasks, Memos, Contacts, or Calendar.

Connecting to Microsoft Exchange servers

You can also configure Evolution to work with Microsoft's Exchange servers. To do this, install the evolution-exchange package while Evolution is not running. Then, restart Evolution and go to Edit ➪ Preferences. Click Mail Accounts in the left column. Click Add to create a new e-mail account. Enter your name and the e-mail address for your exchange account and then click Forward. On the next screen, select Microsoft Exchange as the server type. Enter all the information necessary to talk to your exchange server. While the integration isn't perfect, you'll find this goes a long way towards making your Linux system fit into a Windows-centric environment.

Thunderbird mail client

As a companion to its Firefox Web browser, the Mozilla project created the Thunderbird e-mail client. If you installed Thunderbird (thunderbird package) from the Fedora media that comes with this book, you can launch it from your Applications menu by selecting Internet ➪ Thunderbird.

The first time you run Thunderbird, an account-creation wizard opens, which provides a handy way to set up a new e-mail account. For example, you can just enter your name, your e-mail address, and your password. Thunderbird figures out the rest by trying IMAP and POP3 servers, as well as following standard conventions for mail server names. Have information about your e-mail account (user name, incoming and outgoing servers, and so on) ready so you can enter it just in case Thunderbird cannot autodetect your configuration. Figure 8-6 shows an example of the Thunderbird window.

In many ways, the layout and selections in the Thunderbird client are similar to those in Evolution. In general, however, Thunderbird seems to offer better performance and a simpler user interface than Evolution. Here are some features of Thunderbird that may interest you:

- **Display threads** — Click a small callout icon (such as a small outline) in the header of the Thunderbird message pane. Then, instead of simply sorting your messages by date, subject, or sender, messages are sorted by threads (so all messages created in response to a message are sorted together).

- **Junk mail controls** — Select Edit ➪ Preferences and click the Security tab to configure how Thunderbird deals with messages that appear to be junk mail. From the preferences window, select to Delete or Move to the Junk folder any messages you mark as junk mail. To manage your junk mail, click in the junk mail column (next to the date column, by default) next to any messages you deem junk mail that arrive in your inbox. By marking messages as junk mail, you can train Thunderbird's adaptive junk mail filter to learn when a message is junk mail and mark new messages that arrive as such. Select Tools ➪ Run Junk Mail Controls on Folder to apply junk mail filtering to the current folder.

- **HTML messages** — You have the option to create HTML markup in the mail messages you compose. When you write a mail message, from the Compose window you can choose what type of text to use, change font sizes, add bullets or numbers, set text justification, and add emoticons, to name a few features. (Note that in many news groups and mailing lists you should not use HTML markup because some people like to use text-only mail clients to access those groups.)

FIGURE 8-6

Thunderbird is an efficient e-mail client that includes advanced junk mail and message filtering.

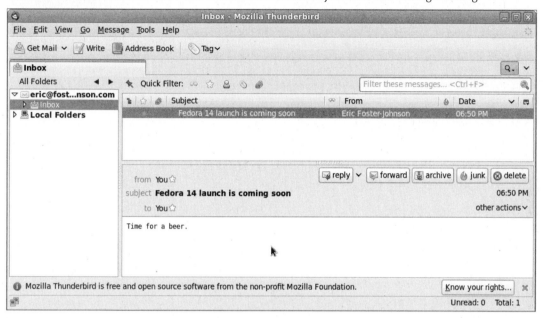

After using the Thunderbird e-mail client, the biggest improvement over other graphical e-mail clients I have used is performance. Sorting and searching messages is much faster than I've experienced on other clients. Switching to different mail folders and opening messages also seems to work much faster.

Text-based mail programs

If you don't mind text-based interfaces, or if you are a Unix person who likes to `sort`, `grep`, `troff`, `col`, and `cat` your e-mail, there are still plenty of Unix-like mail tools around. The `mail` command itself provides an easy-to-use interface for plain-text messages sent to other users on your Unix system or your LAN. Text-based mail applications, such as the `mutt` command, enable you to handle mail attachments and connect to remote mail servers.

Many text-based mail programs have been around for a long time, so they are full of features and have been well debugged. Because they are not used much anymore, however, don't expect them to have the latest spiffy features. As a group, text-based mail clients are not very intuitive. The following sections describe some text-based mail clients.

Tip

Most of these programs use the value of your $MAIL environment variable as your local mailbox. Usually, that location is /var/spool/mail/*user*, where *user* is your user name. To set your $MAIL so that it points to your Mozilla mailbox (so you can use a text-based mail program or graphical mail client), add the following line to one of your startup files:

```
export MAIL=$HOME/.thunderbird/*.default/Mail/accountname/Inbox
```

If you usually use Thunderbird for mail, set this variable temporarily to try out some of these mail programs. If the account isn't stored in the Mail directory, look in the ImapMail directory instead:

```
$HOME/.thunderbird/*.default/ImapMail/accountname/INBOX
```

If your mailbox is not on your local system, use a mail reader such as mutt to get mail directly from the server. For example:

```
mutt -f imap://chris@linuxtoys.net ■
```

Mail readers and managers

The mail readers described in the following sections are text-based and use the entire screen. Although some features are different, menu bars show available options right on the screen.

Mutt mail reader

The mutt command is a text-based, full-screen Mail User Agent for reading and sending e-mail. The interface is quick and efficient. After installing the mutt package, type **mutt** to start the mail program. Click the up and down arrow keys to select from your listed messages. Press Enter to see a mail message, and type **i** to return to the Main menu.

The menu bar indicates how to mark messages to delete or undelete them, save messages to a directory, or reply to a message. Type **m** to compose a new message and it opens your default editor (for me, vi) to create the message. Type **y** to send the message. If you want to read mail without having your fingers leave your keyboard, mutt is a nice choice. (It even handles attachments!)

Mail reader

The mail command was the first mail reader for Unix. It is text-based, but not screen-oriented. Type **mail** and you will see the messages in your local mailbox. Because mail is not screen-oriented, you just get a prompt after message headings are displayed — you are expected to know what to do next. (You can use the Enter key to step through messages.) Type **?** to see which commands are available.

While in mail, type **h** to see mail headings again. Simply type a message number to see the message. Type **d#** (replacing # with a message number) to delete a message. To create a new message, type **m**. To respond to a message, type **r#** (replacing # with the message number). Type **man mail** to learn more about the mail command.

Participating in Newsgroups

Usenet news is another feature that has been around almost as long as the Internet. Using a newsreader, and even many regular mail readers, you can select from literally thousands of topics and participate in discussions on those topics. To participate, you simply read the messages people have posted to the group, respond to those that you have something to say about, and send your own messages to start a discussion yourself.

To get started, you basically need a newsreader and access to a news server computer. The Thunderbird e-mail client includes support for accessing Usenet accounts. A popular newsreader that works with Fedora is called Pan.

Tip
If you have never used a newsgroup before, check out the `news.announce.newusers` **newsgroup. This newsgroup exists to answer questions from new users.** ■

The Pan newsreader is a graphical application for reading, managing, and interacting with newsgroups. It is particularly adept at displaying attached pictures and downloading binaries. The interface is very intuitive and easy to use.

Note
You can get the pan package by typing `yum install pan.` ■

To open the Pan newsreader, type **pan** from the shell. The first time you start Pan, the Pan wizard runs to enable you to set up the newsreader. Have your e-mail address and your news server's name ready. When the wizard is done, you can download the list of newsgroups available from your news server.

Instant Messaging

Fedora offers several instant messaging clients, including the popular Pidgin, and Empathy, the default client for the GNOME desktop.

Instant messaging with Pidgin

Pidgin is the predominant instant messaging client in Linux, and it supports Windows and Unix as well. Originally based on the America Online (AOL) Open IM architecture (www.aim .com) and called GAIM, the project was forced to change its name due to legal issues and became Pidgin. Pidgin supports a wide variety of instant messaging protocols, including the following:

- **Oscar** — Because Oscar is the official AIM protocol created by AOL, it is the most popular one used for Pidgin. To work in Pidgin, Oscar had to be reverse engineered because it is a proprietary protocol of AOL. Therefore, not all features that you might find in AOL's own instant messenger are supported. Messaging is done over TCP-based networks (typically, the Internet), with all messages going through AOL servers, except in the case of direct connections (which are difficult to get working properly).

- **MSN Messenger** — This protocol was based originally on the MSN Messenger Service 1.0 protocol (www.hypothetic.org/docs/msn/ietf_draft.txt). That protocol has been "enhanced" so significantly by Microsoft since it was first published that the version included with Pidgin had to be reverse engineered. To find out more about MSN Messenger (from Pidgin or otherwise), see the MSN Messenger Protocol Resources/Links page (www.hypothetic.org/docs/msn/resources/links.php).

- **Google Talk** — Pidgin supports the Google Talk service as well as general XMPP communications (called the Jabber protocol, and available from www.jabber.org). Another XMPP server is OpenFire, available from www.igniterealtime.org/.

- **ICQ** — Pidgin uses the open-source icqlib library to implement the ICQ protocol. Because of recent changes to the ICQ protocol, it is usually recommended that you use Oscar to connect to the ICQ network, rather than icqlib.

- **IRC** — The Internet Relay Chat protocol is based on the Internet standard RFC 1459. Although there are differences in implementation of that standard on different IRC servers, this TCP-based protocol should work fine on most IRC servers.

- **Yahoo! Messenger** — This enables you to communicate with others using Yahoo! Messenger servers.

There are other messaging protocols supported by Pidgin as well. These include Napster (instant messaging and buddy lists, but not music downloads), Groupwise Messenger (Novell's instant messaging), Sametime (Lotus messaging from http://meanwhile.sourceforge.net), TOC (a rarely used AOL AIM service for unofficial clients), and Zephyr (an IM system from MIT). Pidgin not only supports multiple protocols, but also allows you to communicate over multiple protocols at the same time. In addition, there are available Jabber servers you can get to run your own Jabber instant messaging server, such as Ejabberd (www.ejabberd.im). (Type yum **install ejabberd** to install that package.)

To use Pidgin, you need to install the pidgin package.

To start Pidgin from the Applications menu, choose Internet ⇨ Pidgin Instant Messenger.

If you have never used instant messaging before, you can sign up for free accounts from AOL (https://my.screenname.aol.com/) or MSN (http://messenger.msn.com). Click Accounts from the initial Pidgin window and add your account. Select your account from the Account list, enter the password, and select Sign on.

Once you are signed on — for example, to AOL — from the Buddy List that appears, select the IM button to connect to another IM user who is online. Alternately, select Chat to enter the name of a chat room you want to enter. You can add buddies to your list as appropriate.

A small icon shaped like a word balloon appears in the system tray on your desktop when Pidgin is running. Click that icon to have your buddy list appear or disappear. Right-click that icon for a menu from which you can send a new message, join a chat, or work with Pidgin account and preference settings.

Using other instant message clients

Empathy provides the official GNOME messaging client. It supports essentially the same protocols as Pidgin. Empathy will also import your account settings from Pidgin, making it easy to switch from Pidgin, if you so desire.

To start Empathy from the Applications menu, choose Internet ⇨ Empathy IM Client. Empathy is installed by default with the GNOME desktop.

Kopete is the KDE messaging client. Like Pidgin and Empathy, Kopete supports multiple IM protocols including AIM, Windows Live Messenger, Yahoo, and Jabber. Kopete comes standard with the KDE desktop as part of the `kdenetwork` package.

Finch provides a command-line messaging client. Finch uses the ncurses library to create text-based windows inside a Terminal client or other shell window. If you don't have a graphics display, Finch is a good choice.

Sharing Files with BitTorrent

BitTorrent is a tool for distributing software content to a large number of clients over a network. What makes BitTorrent unique is that as you download a file to your computer, someone else can be downloading the same file from your computer. That way, the server originally offering the file isn't hammered and a potentially unlimited number of people can get the file quickly.

BitTorrent is an excellent tool for the free and open-source software community. For example, when a new release of Fedora is released (now including more than 13GB of software), using BitTorrent means you don't have to wait for days for traffic on the Fedora mirror servers to cool down. Likewise, someone who wants to share home videos with the world can do so without having industrial-size server and bandwidth. Of course, there are also those who are concerned that BitTorrent makes it easy to share files people shouldn't share, such as commercial movies, music, and software.

Both a text-based and graphical (bittorrent-gui) BitTorrent client are available from the Fedora repository. You can get both clients by typing the following as root user from a terminal window:

```
# yum install bittorrent-gui
```

To use BitTorrent, visit a website that offers software downloads and look for a link to a torrent file representing the software, video, or other type of file you want to download. Download the torrent file to your computer. Next, open the BitTorrent window (select Applications ⇨ Internet ⇨ BitTorrent File Transfer), and then open the torrent file (look for a file with a .torrent extension) you downloaded by selecting File ⇨ Open torrent file.

Use the slider on the BitTorrent window to control how much bandwidth you will allow for others to upload the files from you that you are downloading. The more you supply, the faster you will be allowed to download the file. You can continue to make the file available to others after you are finished downloading.

To create your own torrent file for a file or directory of files you want to share, select File ⇨ Make new torrent. While you can always publish your own torrent on a public server, your firewall may limit your ability to publish your own torrent to the Internet.

Another friendly BitTorrent client is Transmission, from www.transmissionbt.com. Transmission provides Gtk (GNOME), Qa (KDE), and Mac clients.

For more information on BitTorrent, refer to the BitTorrent Introduction at www.bittorrent .org/introduction.html.

Using Remote Login, Copy, and Execution

This section describes some features for allowing users to use resources across a network. They are the telnet, ssh, lftp, and wget commands.

Cross-Reference
Only the ssh service is turned on by default in Fedora because the other remote login, execution, and copy commands described here do not provide encrypted communications by default, and therefore can represent significant security risks. For information on how to enable the services described in this chapter on a Fedora server, refer to Chapter 13. ∎

This section includes descriptions of the text-based lftp and ncftp FTP clients, as well as the graphical gFTP. The ssh command is typically used as a secure remote login command, although it can be used for remote execution as well.

Two newer commands for copying files over the network are wget and rsync. Both of these tools can be used to efficiently download files that you can identify on the network. Note that wget requires a Web server.

Getting files with FTP

FTP is a protocol that is available on many different operating systems. Archives of files on the Internet are stored on what are called FTP servers. To connect to those servers from Fedora, you can either type the URL of that server into a Web browser or use the lftp command or graphical FTP windows such as gFTP. Of the other FTP client programs available for Fedora, my favorite is the ncftp command.

Using the lftp command

The `lftp` command is available on Fedora for copying files to and from FTP servers. The `lftp` command has a command mode or you can use it to connect directly to a remote computer. For example:

```
$ lftp maple
lftp maple:~>
```

In this example, `lftp` connects to a computer called maple (`ftp maple`). Unless you use the `-u username` option, you are automatically logged in using the anonymous user account. See Chapter 19 for details about how to set up your own FTP server.

Unlike ssh, instead of being in a regular Linux shell after you log in with an FTP client, you are placed in FTP command mode. Command mode with FTP includes a whole lot of commands for moving around the remote file system and copying files (which is the main job of an FTP client).

Note

If you are behind a firewall and having trouble connecting to FTP servers, learn about active and passive FTP. Refer to the following: `http://slacksite.com/other/ftp.html`. ∎

FTP directory commands

To get your bearings and move around the remote file system, you could use some of the following commands from the `lftp host:~>` prompt. The commands work with both the remote and local directories associated with the FTP connection.

- `pwd` — Shows the name of the current directory on the remote system
- `ls` — Lists the contents of the current remote directory using the Linux `ls` command. You can use any valid `ls` options with this command, provided they are supported by the particular FTP server you are connected to.
- `dir` — Same as `ls`
- `cd` — Use the `cd` command to move to the named directory on the remote system
- `lpwd` — Shows the name of your current directory on your local system
- `lcd` — Use the `lcd` command to move to the named directory on the local system

If you want to make changes to any of the remote files or directories, use the following commands:

- `mkdir` — Creates a directory on the remote system
- `mv` — Moves file or directory to a new location on the remote system
- `rmdir` — Removes a remote directory
- `rm` — Removes a remote file

Depending on how the FTP server is configured, you may or may not be able to execute some of the file and directory commands shown. In general, if you log in as the anonymous user, you will not be able to modify any files or directories; you will only be able to download files. If you have a real login account, you will typically have the same read and write permission you have when you enter the computer using a standard login prompt.

FTP file copying commands

Before you copy files between the remote and local systems, consider the type of transfer you want to do. The two types of transfer modes are as follows:

- **binary** — For transferring binary files (such as data files and executable commands). This is also referred to as an *image transfer*.

- **ascii** — For transferring plain-text files.

The Linux lftp command sets the default to binary when you start it. Binary seems to work well for either binary or text files. However, binary transfers may not work when transferring ASCII files from non-Unix systems. If you transfer an executable file in ASCII mode, the file may not work when you try to run it on your local system.

Most file copying is done with the get and put commands. Likewise, you can use the mget and mput commands to transfer multiple files at once. Some FTP servers will even allow you to use matching characters (e.g., mget abc* to get all files beginning with the letters abc). Here are descriptions of those commands:

- **get file** — Copies a file from the current directory on the remote file system and copies it to the current directory on the local file system. You can use a full path along with the filename. Here are some examples:

```
ftp> get route
ftp> get /tmp/sting
```

The first example takes the file route from the current remote directory and copies it to the current local directory. The second example copies the file /tmp/sting from the remote system to the file tmp/sting relative to the current directory on the local system. If your current directory were /home/jake, ftp would try to copy the file to /home/jake/tmp/sting.

- **put file** — Copies a file from the current local directory to the current remote directory. The usage of this command is essentially the same as the get command, except that files are copied from the local to the remote system.

Note

Anonymous FTP sites (described later) usually let you copy files *from* them, but not *to* them. If they do allow you to put files on their servers, it will usually be in a restricted area. ∎

- **mget file . . .** — Use this command to download multiple files at once. You can specify multiple files either individually or by using metacharacters (such as the asterisk). If you run the `prompt` command (see below), FTP prompts you for each file to ensure that you want to copy it.

- **mput file . . .** — Use this command to put multiple files on the remote computer. Like `mget`, `mput` can prompt you before transferring each file.

Another useful FTP command is the `prompt` command. After `prompt` is run, `mget` and `mput` commands will display a prompt asking if you want to download each file in the list you requested as it is ready to download.

FTP exiting commands

While a connection is open to a remote computer from an FTP client in Fedora, you can use several commands to either temporarily or permanently exit from that connection. Here are some useful commands:

- **!** — Temporarily exits you to the local shell. After you have done what you need to do, type **exit** to return to your FTP session. You can also use this command to run other local commands. For example, you can type **!pwd** to see what the current directory is on the local system, **!uname -a** to remind yourself of your local system name, or **!ls -l** to see the contents of your current directory.

- **bye** — Closes the connection and exits the `ftp` command. You can also use **quit** in place of **bye**.

Using the ncftp command

By virtue of being an FTP client program, the `ncftp` command supports all the standard commands you would expect to find in an FTP client (`get`, `put`, `ls`, `cd`, and so on). However, `ncftp` has added features that make it more efficient and friendlier than some other FTP clients.

Note

You can install the ncftp package by typing `yum install ncftp`. ∎

With `ncftp`, you can connect to an FTP server in the same way you did with `ftp`. One convenient difference is that if you don't enter a user name, `ncftp` assumes you want to use the anonymous user name and just logs you in. Here is an example:

```
$ ncftp ftp.mozilla.org
NcFTP 3.2.4 (Apr 07, 2010) by Mike Gleason
(http://www.NcFTP.com/contact/).
Connecting to ftp.mozilla.org...
...Logging in...
...
Login successful.
Logged in to ftp.mozilla.org.
ncftp / >
```

To log in as a user name other than anonymous, add a -u *user* option, where *user* is replaced by the name you want to log in as. Enter the password as prompted to continue.

Using ncftp

After you are logged in with the ncftp session running, you can use a few nice features that aren't available with other FTP clients. Here are some examples:

- bookmark — If you are visiting a site you want to return to, type the bookmark command and enter a name to identify that site. The next time you start an ncftp session, type the bookmark name as an option. Not only are you logged into the FTP site you bookmarked, you are taken to the directory where you set the bookmark.

- lls, lcd, lmkdir, lpwd — This set of commands enables you to move around the local file system. Just place the letter l in front of standard shell commands such as ls, cd, mkdir, pwd, rm, and rmdir and you can move around and work with your local file system while you are in ncftp.

- rhelp — Use rhelp to see commands that are recognized by the remote FTP server. To see commands that are specific to the FTP server, type **help** while you are in an ncftp session.

- **Auto-resume** — If you are disconnected in the middle of a large download, you will appreciate this feature. After a connection is broken during a download, reconnect to the FTP site and begin downloading the file again in the same local directory. The ncftp command resumes downloading where it left off.

- **Tab completion** — Press the Tab key to have ncftp complete filenames and paths.

Using ncftp for background transfers

If you are moving around to different parts of the FTP site, or jumping between different sites, you might not want to wait for a file transfer to complete before you can go somewhere else. The ncftp command has an excellent feature for placing transfer commands in a spool file and then running them in the background immediately or later.

To select a file for background transfer, use the bgget command. Here is an example:

```
ncftp /pub > bgget wireless.doc
+    Spooled: get wireless.doc
ncftp /pub > jobs
---Scheduled-For-----Host-----------Command-------------------
2010-11-01  18:38 maple            GET wireless.doc
ncftp /pub > bgstart
Background process started.
Watch the "/home/ericfj/.ncftp/spool/log" file to see how it
is progressing
```

In this example, the bgget command (short for *background get*) spools the wireless.doc file from the remote current directory (/pub) and sets it to be copied to the local current directory.

Typing the `jobs` command shows that the job (`GET wireless.doc`), from the host named `maple`, is scheduled to run immediately (6:38 p.m., November 1, 2010). By running the `bgstart` command, this process and any other spooled jobs are run immediately.

Instead of starting the background transfers immediately, you can do them later. For background jobs spooled for transfer, the transfer begins when you either quit `ncftp`, leave your current FTP site, or go to another FTP site. This way, the program that does the transfer (`ncftpbatch`) can take over your current login session to do the transfer.

If you wanted to wait even longer to do the transfers, you can pass an option to the `bgget` command to have it start the transfer at a particular time. Here is an example:

```
ncftp /pub > bgget -@ 20110104010000 wireless.doc
```

With this command, the transfer is set to run at 1 a.m. on January 4, 2011 to transfer the file called `wireless.doc`. Again, you can check the `.ncftp/spool/log` file in your home directory to see if the transfer has completed. The file transfer is completed by an `ncftp` daemon process.

Using the gFTP window

If you prefer a more graphical interface for accessing FTP servers, you can use the gFTP window. (Install gFTP by typing `yum` **install gftp**.) You can open a gFTP window by typing **gftp**. Figure 8-7 shows an example of the gFTP window.

Unlike the `ftp` command, the gFTP window enables you to simultaneously see the contents of the current remote and local directories. To transfer a file from one side to the other, simply double-click it or drag and drop it to the other pane. (Normally, you will just be copying files from FTP sites, unless a site provides you with permission to write to it.)

Follow this procedure to connect to an FTP site:

1. Type the name of the FTP server to which you want to connect (e.g., `ftp.mozilla.org`) into the Host box.

2. Type the port number on the FTP server (you can leave this blank to use the default port number 21).

3. Type the user name used to log in to the FTP server. Use the default `anonymous` if you don't have a specific user name and the server is publicly accessible. You can also leave this blank for many public FTP sites. For private sites, you will need a user name and password for the site.

4. Type the password for the user name you entered. The convention with anonymous FTP servers is to use your e-mail address as the password, although for many sites you do not need to enter any password.

5. Click the icon displaying two little monitors to connect to the FTP site.

FIGURE 8-7

View local and remote files simultaneously from the gFTP window.

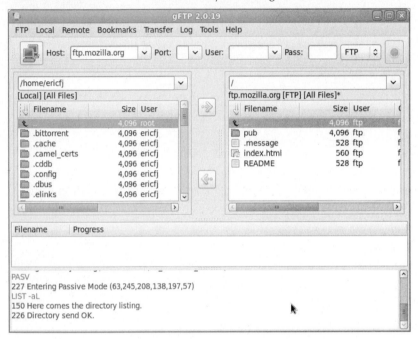

6. If you entered the information correctly, the bottom pane on the window shows that the transfer was complete and the right pane shows the contents of the current directory of the FTP site. Here are some actions you can take once you are connected:

- **Move around** — Double-click a directory to move to that directory or double-click on the two dots (. .) to move up a level. You can do this on both the remote and local directories.

- **Drag and drop files** — Drag and drop files from the FTP site on to the left pane (representing your current local directory).

- **Save this site** — To return to the site later, choose Bookmarks ➪ Add Bookmark. A pop-up window lets you name the site for the Bookmarks list. After you do, you can select that entry from the list later to connect to that site. The gFTP window stores not only the host name, but also the port, user name, and password. Therefore, you are just one click away from connecting. This is one of the best features of graphical FTP programs such as gFTP.

A nice feature of gFTP is that it stores log information. Choose Log ➪ View. A window appears showing you the conversations that have taken place between your computer and each FTP site. You can look at these messages to see what is wrong if you are unable to connect to a site or to remember where you have been and what you have done on an FTP site.

Note

The Bookmarks list includes several entries under the Fedora Sites and Red Hat Sites menus that enable you to connect directly to FTP sites that have software packaged as RPMs. While those sites were useful at one time, it's usually better these days to use yum or PackageKit to get software packages. Many of the sites in this Bookmarks list contain out-of-date RPMs and won't automatically take care of dependency issues. ■

Getting files with wget

If you already know where a file is on the network, there are more efficient ways to download that file than opening an FTP session, moving around the FTP server, and running the get command. The wget command is a simple, efficient tool for doing non-interactive downloads of files over the Internet.

Note

Another great command for copying files over the network is the rsync command. I often use rsync to do backups over the network. See Chapter 12 for information about using rsync to do backups. ■

If you want to download a file from an FTP site or Web server (HTTP), and you know exactly where the file is, wget is a good way to download. This command is very useful if you want to copy a whole site, recursively, from one computer to another (for example, containing user home directories). When downloading from FTP sites, wget enables you to just download as the anonymous user or add your own user name and password to the command line.

Downloading a single file

Here is an example of using wget to get a file from a Web server:

```
$ wget http://download1.rpmfusion.org/nonfree/fedora/development/↵
x86_64/os/xmms2-nonfree-0.7-1.fc14.x86_64.rpm
--2009-11-01 20:07:03--  http://download1.rpmfusion.org/nonfree/↵
fedora/development/x86_64/os/xmms2-nonfree-0.7-1.fc12. x86_64.rpm
Resolving download1.rpmfusion.org... 193.28.235.60
Connecting to download1.rpmfusion.org|193.28.235.60|:80... connected.
HTTP request sent, awaiting response... 200 OK
Length: 16436 (16K) [application/x-rpm]
Saving to: ` xmms2-nonfree-0.7-1.fc12. x86_64.rpm

100%[======================================>] 16,436 52.5K/s  in 0.3s

2011-01-04 20:07:03 (52.5 KB/s) -
` xmms2-nonfree-0.7-1.fc12. x86_64.rpm
saved [16436/16436]
```

The first part of the URL (http://), enables wget to determine that you are copying a file from an HTTP server to the current directory (.) on the local host. After resolving the address (download1.rpmfusion.org), wget connects to the site and transfers the file. As the file downloads, wget shows the progress of the download and then exits.

Downloading a file with user name and password

If you are doing an FTP file copy and need to log in as a user other than anonymous, you can add that information to the command line or to a `.netrc` file in your home directory (type **man netrc** to see the format of that file). Here is an example of adding the password to the command line:

```
$ wget ftp://joe:my67chevy@ftp.handsonhistory.com/memo1.doc
```

Caution

Adding a password to a command line leaves the password exposed to onlookers, so this practice is generally discouraged except in cases where no one can see your monitor or your history files or view your command line by running the `ps` **command. You can add passwords to your** `~/.wgetrc` **file to keep your password from being seen. If you do so, ensure that no one else can read this file by running the** `chmod 400 .wgetrc` **command.** ■

In the previous example, the user logs in as `joe` with the password `my67chevy`. The `wget` command then copies the file `memo1.doc` from the current directory on the host computer named `ftp.handsonhistory.com`. That current directory is most likely `/home/joe`.

Downloading a whole website

Using `wget`, you can download a large number of files from Web servers as well. The `wget` command downloads files using the HTTP protocol if file addresses begin with `http://`. Downloading a single file, you would use the same form as you would for an FTP file (e.g., `wget http://host/file.`). The best `wget` option for HTTP downloads is `-r` (recursive).

A recursive download enables you to choose a point at a website and download all content below that point. Here is an example of a recursive download used to download the contents of the `www.example.com` website.

```
$ wget -r http://www.example.com
```

In this example, the HTML pages, images, and other content on the `www.example.com` website are copied below the current directory in a new directory named `www.example.com`. This is useful if you want to gather the contents of a website but don't have login access to that site. Because content is taken by following links, if there is content in a directory at the website that isn't in a link, it won't be downloaded.

Downloading an entire website can result in a massive amount of data being downloaded. If you want only part of a website, start from a point lower in the site's structure. Or, as an alternative, you can limit the number of levels that `wget` will access in the site structure. Using the `-l` option (l as in level), the following example gets two levels of HTML content:

```
$ wget -r -l 2 http://www.example.com
```

To mirror a site, you can use the `-m` option instead of `-r`. Using `wget -m http://site` is comparable to asking to download an infinite number of levels recursively (`-r -l inf`), keep current time stamps (`-N`), and keep FTP directory listings (`-nr`). Note that `wget` will honor a website's `robots.txt` file, which might restrict the ability of `wget` to recursively access multiple levels of links from a website.

Continuing a download

In the old days, when you were downloading a particularly large file (such as an ISO image of a CD or DVD), if the download stopped for some reason (a disconnected network or errant reboot), you needed to start all over. With wget, you can choose to restart a download and have it continue right where it left off. This has been a lifesaver for me on many occasions.

Let's say you were downloading a 4GB DVD ISO image named mydvd.iso from the site ftp://ftp.example.com and you killed the wget process by mistake after about 3GB of download. Ensure that your current directory is the one that contains the partially downloaded ISO. Then run the same wget command you did originally, adding the -c (continue) option as follows:

```
$ wget -c ftp://ftp.example.com/mydvd.iso
```

If you had not used the -c option, in this case a new download would have started using the filename mydvd.iso.1 to download to.

Note

Another command that you might be interested in, similar to wget, is the curl command. Like wget, curl can download files using FTP or HTTP. Curl can also do multiple file transfers on the same connection. ∎

Using ssh for remote login/remote execution

Although the telnet and rlogin login commands and rsh remote execution command have been around much longer, the ssh command is the preferred tool for remote logins and executions. That's because ssh provides encrypted communication, so you can use it securely over insecure, public networks between hosts that don't know each other.

In the following example, ssh is used to log in to a computer named maple. Because no user is specified, ssh tries to log in as the current user (which is the root user in this case).

```
# ssh maple
root@maple's password:
```

If you wanted to log in as a different user, you could use the -l option. For example, to log in to the computer named maple as the user named jake, you could type the following:

```
# ssh -l jake maple
jake@maple's password:
```

The ssh command can also be used to execute a command on the remote computer. For example, if you wanted to monitor the messages file on a remote computer for a minute, you could type the following command:

```
# ssh root@maple "tail -f /var/log/messages"
root@maple's password:
```

After you typed the password in the preceding case, the last several lines of the /var/log/messages file on the remote computer would be displayed. As messages were received, they would continue to be displayed until you decided to exit (press Ctrl+C to exit the tail command).

Cross-Reference
To learn how to use public keys for passwordless login to ssh, refer to Chapter 13. Find out more about the ssh **command from the SSH website** (www.openssh.org). ■

Using scp for remote file copy

The scp command is a simple yet secure way of copying files among Linux systems. It uses the underlying ssh facility, so if ssh is enabled, so is scp. Here is an example of using scp to copy a file from one computer to another:

```
# scp myfile toys.linuxtoys.net:/home/chris
root@toys.linuxtoys.net's password: ******
```

In this example, the file myfile is copied to the computer named toys.linuxtoys.net in the /home/chris directory. If you don't provide a user name, scp assumes you are using the current user name. Unlike some tools that provide remote login, scp and ssh do allow you to log in as root user over the network, by default. (Many people turn off this feature for security reasons.)

To use scp with a different user name, you can append the user name with an @ character. For example, chris@toys.linuxtoys.net:/home/chris would attempt to log in as the user named chris to do the file copy.

The first time you connect to a remote computer using scp or ssh, those commands try to establish the authenticity of the remote host. If it cannot establish the host's authenticity, it will display the RSA key fingerprint and ask you if you want to continue. If you type yes, scp will not question the authenticity of that computer again for subsequent scp commands.

However, if the RSA key fingerprint should change in the future for the remote computer (which will happen if, for example, the operating system is reinstalled on that computer), scp will refuse to let you connect to that remote computer. To override that refusal, you need to edit your $HOME/.ssh/known_hosts file and delete the entry for the remote computer. You can then verify the authenticity of the remote computer and continue to use scp.

The sftp command, which also communicates using secure ssh protocols, is a command for copying files from an FTP server. It is considered a more secure way to get files from an FTP server that has an sshd server running. You can disable the sftp command on the server by commenting out the sftp line in the sshd_config directory.

Using the "r" commands: rlogin, rcp, and rsh

The rlogin, rcp, and rsh commands all use the same underlying security mechanism to enable remote login, remote file copy, and remote execution, respectively, among computers.

These commands are included with Fedora to be compatible with legacy Unix systems. Because "r" commands are inherently insecure, however, most people use ssh and scp commands to provide the same functionality in a more secure way.

Summary

Most use of the World Wide Web centers on the Web browser. Firefox is the most popular Web browser to use with Fedora and most other Linux systems, and it is accessible from a button on your desktop. Epiphany, Konqueror, and various text-based Web browsers are also available with Fedora. The original Mozilla Application Suite is now packaged with Fedora under the name SeaMonkey.

Evolution, which can also be used to manage your e-mail, is now the preferred mail reader for Fedora. Thunderbird is the latest e-mail application from the Mozilla Project. There are also many text-based mail readers, such as mutt, pine, and mail.

Command-line tools for downloading files include wget, ftp, and many others. A popular download tool that offers both command-line and graphical interfaces is BitTorrent. With BitTorrent, you can not only download files, but also simultaneously upload the files you get to others.

Legacy remote login and file copy commands (rlogin, rcp, and rsh) are still available in Fedora. However, improved programs for remote login and file copy, such as ssh, scp, and sftp, are more often used now.

Part III

Administering Fedora

Understanding System Administration

## 9

Fedora, like other Linux and Unix systems, was intended for use by more than one person at a time. Multiuser features enable many people to have accounts in Linux, with their data kept secure from others. Multitasking enables many people to use the computer at the same time. Sophisticated networking protocols and applications make it possible for a Linux system to extend its capabilities to network users and computers around the world. The person assigned to manage all of this is referred to as the *system administrator*.

Even if you are the only person using a Linux system, system administration is still set up to be separate from other computer use. To do most administrative tasks, you need to be logged in as the root user (also referred to as the super user) or gain temporary root privileges. Other users cannot change, or in some cases, even see some of the configuration information for a Linux system. In particular, security features such as secure passwords are protected from general view.

This chapter describes the general principles of Fedora system administration. In particular, this chapter covers some of the basic tools you need to administer your Linux system. It also helps you learn how to work with file systems and monitor the setup and performance of your Linux system.

Security Enhanced Linux (SELinux) adds another dimension to administering a Fedora system. Instead of giving the root user full control of the entire Linux system, you can assign access to data, programs, devices, and processes to different roles. Because Fedora is delivered with only a limited set of SELinux features enabled (targeted policy), the root user maintains most of its traditional role (whether SELinux is off or on). SELinux is described at the end of this chapter.

IN THIS CHAPTER

Using the root user account

Learning about administrative commands, configuration files, and log files

Graphical administration tools

Working with the file system

Configuring hardware devices

Monitoring system performance

Managing battery power on laptops

Using Security Enhanced Linux (SELinux)

Using the root user Account

The traditional role of the root user in Linux systems is to have complete control over the operation of your Fedora system. That user can open any file or run any program. The root user also installs software packages and adds accounts for other people who use the system.

During the Fedora installation process, you are required to add a password for the root user. You need to remember and protect this password. You will need it to log in as root or to obtain root permission while you are logged in as some other user.

The home directory for the root user is /root. The home directory and other information associated with the root user account is assigned in the /etc/passwd file. Here is what the root entry looks like in the /etc/passwd file:

```
root:x:0:0:root:/root:/bin/bash
```

This shows that for the user named root, the x indicates that the password is stored in /etc/shadow, the user ID is set to 0 (root user), and the group ID is set to 0 (root group). The home directory is /root and the shell for that user is /bin/bash.

Cross-Reference
It's best to make changes to /etc/passwd with the User Manager window or the usermod command. See the section on modifying accounts in Chapter 10 for more information about the /etc/passwd file. ■

Among the defaults that are set for the root user are aliases for certain commands that could have dangerous consequences. Aliases for the rm, cp, and mv commands allow those commands to be run with the -i option. The -i option causes each deletion, copy, or move to prompt you before removing or overwriting any files from those commands. This prevents massive numbers of files from being removed, copied, or moved by mistake.

Becoming the Super User: The su Command

Although one way to become the super user is to log in as root, sometimes that isn't convenient. For example, you may be logged into a regular user account and just want to make a quick administrative change to your system without having to log out and log back in. Or you may need to log in over the network to make a change to a Linux system but find that the system doesn't allow root users in from over the network (a common practice).

The solution is to use the su command.

Caution
In general, it is safer to use the sudo command to run a single Linux command as the super user, rather than run the su command. See the description of the sudo command later in this chapter. ■

From any terminal window or shell, you can simply type the following:

```
$ su
Password: ******
#
```

When you are prompted, type in the root user's password. The prompt for the regular user ($) will be changed to the super user prompt (#). At this point, you have full permission to run any command and use any file on the system. However, one thing that the su command doesn't do when used this way is read in the root user's environment. As a result, you may type a command that you know is available and get the message "command not found." To fix this problem, you can use the su command with the dash (-) option instead, as follows:

```
$ su -
Password: ******
#
```

You still need to type the password, but after you do that, everything that normally happens at login for the root user will happen after the su command is completed. Your current directory will be root's home directory (probably /root), and things like the root user's PATH variable will be used. If you became the root user by just typing su, rather than su -, you would not have changed directories or the environment of the current login session.

Tip

When you become the root user during someone else's session, a common mistake is leaving files or directories in the user's directories that are owned by root. If you do this, be sure to use the chown or chmod command to make the files and directories you modify open to the user that you want to own them. Otherwise, you will probably soon get a phone call, asking you to fix it. ■

You can also use the su command to become another user other than root. For example, to have the permissions of a user named chum, you could type the following:

```
$ su - chum
```

Even if you were the root user before you typed this command, you would have only the permission to open files and run programs that are available to chum. As the root user, however, after you type the su command to become another user, you don't need a password to continue. If you type that command as a regular user, you must type the new user's password.

When you are finished using super user permissions, return to the previous shell by exiting the current shell. To do so, press Ctrl+D or type **exit**.

Caution

If you are the administrator for a computer that is accessible to multiple users, don't leave a root shell open on someone else's screen (unless you want to let that person do anything they like to the computer)! ■

Besides opening a shell session using su (to run a bunch of commands as root), you can instead just apply root permission to a single command or window. This approach is considered more secure than leaving a shell open with root permission if you are just doing one administrative task. For example:

- **GUI admin tools** — When you run GUI administration tools as a regular user, you are usually prompted for the root password (as described in "Using graphical administration tools" later in this chapter).

- **sudo command** — You can run the visudo command to configure a user in /etc/sudoers to be allowed to run administrative commands. After that is done, that user can run the sudo command, followed by a single administrative command, to run that command as root would. When that single command completes, the root permission to run that command ends as well. (See the description of the sudo command later in this chapter.)

Learning About Administrative GUI Tools, Commands, Configuration Files, and Log Files

Fedora systems have advanced enough in recent releases that you can now do most system administration from your desktop GUI, bypassing the shell altogether. Whether you administer Linux from the GUI or a shell, however, underlying your activities are many administrative commands, configuration files, and log files.

Understanding where GUI administrative tools, commands, and files are located and how they are used will help you effectively maintain your Linux system. Although most administrative features are intended for the root user, other administrative users (described later in this section) have limited administrative capabilities.

Using graphical administration tools

The trend over the past few versions of Fedora has been to steer clear of the massive administrative interfaces (such as linuxconf and Webmin) and instead offer graphical windows that perform individual administrative tasks. Instead of sharing one monolithic interface, they share common menus. Individual graphical windows for configuring a network, adding users, or setting up printers can be launched from those menus.

To administer your Fedora system through the GNOME or KDE desktops, the Fedora Project has provided a common set of administrative tools that are accessible from menus on the panel. Selections for starting most graphical administration windows are available from the following menus:

- **Administration** — Select System ⇨ Administration from the GNOME desktop panel (or Administration from the KDE menu) to select tools for updating software, configuring your system. These include tools for adding users, setting date and time, configuring your network, and setting up printers.

- **System Tools** — Select Applications ⇨ System Tools from the GNOME desktop panel (or System from the KDE menu) to select tools to monitor and work with your system. These include tools for analyzing disk usage, monitoring the system, and checking network activity.

Because these administrative tasks require root permission, if you are logged in as a regular user you must enter the root password before the GUI application's window opens, or if you try to perform a protected action within the program. For example, if you launch the Date & Time settings window (System ⇨ Administration ⇨ Date & Time) from the desktop panel as a regular user, you see the pop-up window shown in Figure 9-1.

FIGURE 9-1

Enter the root password to open system administration windows from a regular user's GUI.

After you have entered the root password, most of the system configuration tools will open without requiring you to retype the password during this login session. Authorization expires after five minutes by default.

Note

As you configure different features on your Fedora system, you are asked to launch different individual graphical windows. In general, if you have a choice of tools for configuring a server or adding a feature, I recommend using the tool provided with your distribution. That's because the Fedora GUI tools are integrated closely with the way Fedora systems store and manage their configuration information. ■

The following list describes administrative tools you can start from the Administration menu (System ⇨ Administration). The name of the package that must be installed to get the feature is shown in parentheses:

- **Add/Remove Software (gnome-packagekit)** — Add and remove software packages.
- **Authentication (authconfig-gtk)** — Change how users are authenticated on your system. Usually, Shadow Passwords and MD5 Passwords are selected. However, if your

network supports LDAP, Kerberos, SMB, NIS, or Hesiod authentication, you can select to use any of those authentication types.

- **Boot Loader (system-config-boot)** — Configure the default boot entry and timeout value (in seconds) for your GRUB boot loader.

- **Date & Time (system-config-date)** — Set the date and time or choose to have an NTP server keep system time in sync. Figure 9-2 shows the Date/Time Properties window.

FIGURE 9-2

Choose an NTP server by clicking Synchronize date and time over the network.

- **Firewall (system-config-firewall)** — Configure your firewall to allow or deny services to computers from the network.

- **Language (system-config-language)** — Select the default language used for the system.

- **Logical Volume Management (system-config-lvm)** — Display and manage logical volumes and related disk partitions.

- **Network (system-config-network)** — Manage your current network interfaces, as well as add interfaces.

- **Network Device Control (system-config-network)** — Activate and deactivate network interfaces.

- **Printing (system-config-printer)** — Configure local and network printers.

- **Root Password (system-config-rootpassword)** — Change the root password.

- **Samba (system-config-samba)** — Configure Windows (SMB) file sharing. (To configure other Samba features, you can use the SWAT window. SWAT is described in Chapter 17.)

- **SELinux Management (policycoreutils-gui)** — Configure SELinux security policies.

- **Services (system-config-services)** — Display and change which services are running on your Fedora system at different run levels.

- **Software Sources (gnome-packagekit)** — Choose which repositories to use for yum and other package management tools.

- **Software Update (gnome-packagekit)** — Display updates available for the packages you have already installed. You can update individual packages or all selected.

- **Users (accountsdialog)** — Control your own user account, and create and modify other user accounts. See Chapter 10.

- **Users & Groups (system-config-users)** — Add, display, and change user and group accounts for your Fedora system.

The following tools associated with system administration can be started from the System Tools menu (Applications ⇨ System Tools):

- **Configuration Editor (gconf-editor)** — Change settings associated with your GNOME desktop system.

- **Disk Usage Analyzer (gnome-utils)** — Display and analyze data on the use of your computer's hard disks.

- **Disk Utility (gnome-disk-utility)** — Manage hard disks, partitions, mount points, and RAID. (The command is palimpsest.)

- **Kickstart (system-config-kickstart)** — Create a Kickstart configuration file that can be used to install multiple Fedora systems without user intervention.

- **Log File Viewer (gnome-system-log)** — Display messages (by date) for log files stored in the /var/log directory.

- **System Monitor (gnome-system-monitor)** — Shows information about running processes and resource usage.

The Applications ⇨ System Tools menu also includes programs for working with SELinux, described later in this chapter. Procedures for using the various system graphical administrative tools are discussed throughout the book.

Administrative commands

Many commands are intended only for root. When you log in as root, your $PATH variable is set to include some directories that contain commands for the root user. These include the following directories:

- **/sbin** — Contains commands for modifying your disk partitions (such as fdisk), changing boot procedures (grub), and changing system states (init).

- **/usr/sbin** — Contains commands for managing user accounts (such as useradd) and checking network traffic (wireshark). Commands that run as daemon processes are also contained in this directory. (Look for commands that end in "d" such as sshd, pppd, and crond.)

Some administrative commands are contained in regular user directories (such as /bin and /usr/bin). This is especially true of commands that have some options available to everyone. An example is the /bin/mount command, which anyone can use to list mounted file systems, but only the root user can mount file systems. In addition, starting with Fedora 10, /sbin and /usr/sbin were added to the default paths for all users.

Commands that are needed very early in the boot process are found in /bin and /sbin instead of /usr. This is because the kernel mounts only the root file system, so commands like init (the first process to execute), mount, and lvm are needed to mount the other file systems, like /usr.

To find commands that are intended primarily for the system administrator, check out the section 8 manual pages (usually in /usr/share/man/man8). They contain descriptions and options for most Linux administrative commands. For example, type the following to see the man page for the fdisk command (/usr/share/man/man8/fdisk.8.gz):

```
$ man fdisk
```

Some third-party applications add administrative commands to directories that are not in your PATH. For example, an application may put commands in /usr/local/bin (this is the most common location), /opt/bin, or /usr/local/sbin. Although /usr/local/bin and /usr/local/sbin are already in each user's path, you may need to add /opt/bin or other directories to your PATH.

Administrative configuration files

Configuration files are another mainstay of Linux administration. Almost everything you set up for your particular computer — user accounts, network addresses, or GUI preferences — is stored in plain-text files. This has some advantages and some disadvantages.

The advantage of plain-text files is that it is easy to read and change them. Any text editor will do. On the downside, however, as you edit configuration files, no error checking is occurring. You have to run the program that reads these files (such as a network daemon or the X desktop) to find out if you set up the files correctly. A comma or a quote in the wrong place can sometimes cause an entire interface to fail.

Throughout this book, I describe the configuration files you need to set up the different features that make up Fedora systems. In terms of a general perspective on configuration files, however, there are several locations in a Fedora file system where configuration files are stored. Here are some of the major locations:

- **$HOME** — All users store information in their home directories that directs how their login accounts behave. Most configuration files in $HOME begin with a dot (.), so they don't appear as a user's directory when you use a standard ls command (you need to type ls -a to see them). There are dot files that define how each user's shell behaves, the desktop look and feel, and options used with your text editor. There are even files (such as .ssh/* and .rhosts) that can configure network permissions for each user.

- **/etc** — This directory contains most of the basic Linux system-configuration files. The following /etc configuration files are of interest:

  - **adjtime** — Holds the data to adjust the hardware clock (see the hwclock man page).

  - **aliases** — Can contain distribution lists used by the Linux mail service.

  - **bashrc** — Sets system-wide defaults for bash shell users. (By default, it sets the shell prompt to include current user name, hostname, current directory, and other values.)

  - **crontab** — Sets cron environment and times for running automated tasks.

  - **csh.cshrc (and csh.login)** — Sets system-wide defaults for csh (C shell) users.

  - **dovecot** — Contains information needed to support the dovecot IMAPv4/POP3 mail service.

  - **exports** — Contains a list of local directories that are available to be shared by remote computers using the Network File System (NFS).

  - **fedora-release** — Contains a string identifying the current Fedora release. For Red Hat Enterprise Linux (RHEL) releases, the file is named redhat-release.

  - **fstab** — Identifies the devices for common storage media (hard disk, floppy, CD-ROM, and so on) and locations where they are mounted in the Linux system. This is used by the mount command to choose which file systems to mount.

  - **group** — Identifies group names and group IDs (GIDs) that are defined on the systems. Group permissions in Linux are defined by the second of three sets of rwx (read, write, execute) bits associated with each file and directory.

  - **gshadow** — Contains shadow passwords for groups.

  - **host.conf** — Sets the locations in which domain names (e.g., redhat.com) are searched for on TCP/IP networks (such as the Internet) used by applications that use the old-style resolver. By default, the local hosts file is searched, and then any nameserver entries in resolv.conf.

  - **hosts** — Contains IP addresses and hostnames that you can reach from your computer. (Usually this file is used just to store names of computers on your LAN or small private network.)

  - **hosts.allow** — Lists host computers that are allowed to use certain TCP/IP services compiled with tcpwrapper support from the local computer.

- `hosts.deny` — Lists host computers that are *not* allowed to use certain tcpwrapper enabled TCP/IP services from the local computer).

- `inittab` — Contains information that defines which programs start and stop when Linux boots, shuts down, or goes into different states (runlevels) in between. This is the most basic configuration file for starting Linux. (See Chapter 11 for more on this file.)

- `issue` — Contains the lines that are displayed when a terminal is ready to let you log in to your Fedora system from a local terminal, or the console in text mode.

- `issue.net` — Contains login lines that are displayed to users who try to log in to the Linux system from a computer on the network using the telnet service.

- `mail.rc` — Sets system-wide parameters associated with using mail.

- `modprobe.conf` — Optional file containing aliases and options related to loadable kernel modules used by your computer. Also look at files stored in `modprobe.d`.

- `mtab` — Contains a list of file systems currently mounted.

- `mtools.conf` — Contains settings used by DOS tools in Linux.

- `named.conf` — Contains DNS settings if you are running your own DNS server.

- `nsswitch.conf` — Sets the locations in which domain names (e.g., redhat.com) are searched for on TCP/IP networks (such as the Internet). By default, the local hosts file is searched, and then any nameserver entries in `resolv.conf`.

- `ntp.conf` — Includes information needed to run the Network Time Protocol (NTP).

- `passwd` — Stores account information for all valid users for the system. Also includes other information, such as the home directory and default shell.

- `printcap` — Contains definitions for the printers configured for your computer, automatically populated by the CUPS daemon.

- `profile` — Sets system-wide environment and startup programs for all users. This file is read when the user logs in.

- `protocols` — Sets protocol numbers and names for a variety of Internet services.

- `redhat-release` — Contains a string identifying the current Red Hat release. This file exists on Red Hat Linux and Red Hat Enterprise Linux systems. On Fedora systems, this file exists as a link to the `fedora-release` file, so that applications that look for release information in the `redhat-release` file won't fail.

- `resolv.conf` — Identifies the locations of DNS name server computers that are used by TCP/IP to translate Internet host.domain names into IP addresses and which domains to search by default.

- `rpc` — Defines remote procedure call names and numbers.

- `services` — Defines TCP/IP services and their port assignments.

- `shadow` — Contains encrypted passwords for users defined in the `passwd` file. (This is considered a more secure way to store passwords than the original encrypted password in the `passwd` file. The `passwd` file needs to be publicly readable, whereas the `shadow` file can be unreadable by all but the root user.)

- `shells` — Lists the shell command-line interpreters (`bash`, `sh`, `csh`, and so on) that are available on the system, as well as their locations.

- `sudoers` — Sets commands that can be run by users, who may not otherwise have permission to run the command, using the `sudo` command. In particular, this file is used to provide selected users with root permission.

- `rsyslog.conf` — Defines what logging messages are gathered by the `syslogd` daemon and what files they are stored in. (Typically, log messages are stored in files contained in the `/var/log` directory.)

- `/etc/X11` — Contains subdirectories that each contain system-wide configuration files used by X and different X window managers available for Linux. The optional `xorg.conf` file (which makes your computer and monitor usable with X) and configuration directories containing files used by `xdm` and `xinit` to start X are in here.

Directories relating to window managers contain files that include the default values that a user will get if that user starts one of these window managers on your system. The `fontpath.d` directory contains a file for configuring font server settings.

Note

Some files and directories in `/etc/X11` are linked to other locations. ∎

- `/etc/alternatives` — Contains links that the alternatives facility uses to enable a system administrator to exchange one service with another in a way that is invisible to users.

- `/etc/amanda` — Contains files and directories that allow the amanda facility to do network backups of other Linux and Unix systems.

- `/etc/cron*` — Directories in this set contain additional crond crontab files (crond.d) or executables that run on a daily (`cron.daily`), hourly (`cron.hourly`), monthly (`cron.monthly`), or weekly (`cron.weekly`) schedule.

- `/etc/cups` — Contains files that are used to configure the CUPS printing service.

- `/etc/default` — Contains files that set default values for various utilities. For example, the file for the `useradd` command defines the default group number, home directory, password expiration date, shell, and skeleton directory (`/etc/skel`) that are used when creating a new user account.

- `/etc/httpd` — Contains a variety of files used to configure the behavior of your Apache Web server (specifically, the httpd daemon process).

- `/etc/init.d` — Contains links to the run-level scripts.

- `/etc/mail` — Contains files used to configure your sendmail mail service.

- `/etc/pcmcia` — Contains configuration files that enable you to configure a variety of PCMCIA cards for your computer. (PCMCIA slots are the openings on your laptop that enable you to have credit card-size cards attached to your computer. You can attach such devices as modems and external CD-ROMs.)

- `/etc/postfix` — Contains configuration files for the postfix Mail Transport Agent.

- /etc/ppp — Contains several configuration files used to set up Point-to-Point protocol (so that you can have your computer dial out to the Internet).

- /etc/rc?.d — There is a separate rc?.d directory for each valid system state: rc0.d (shutdown state), rc1.d (single-user state), rc2.d (multiuser state), rc3.d (multiuser plus networking state), rc4.d (user-defined state), rc5.d (multiuser, networking, plus GUI login state), and rc6.d (reboot state).

- /etc/security — Contains files that set a variety of default security conditions for your computer. These files are part of the pam (pluggable authentication modules) package.

- /etc/skel — Any files contained in this directory are automatically copied to a user's home directory when that user is added to the system. By default, most of these files are dot (.) files, such as .gnome2 (a directory for setting GNOME desktop defaults) and .bashrc (for setting default values used with the bash shell).

- /etc/squid — Contains configuration files for the Squid proxy caching server.

- /etc/sysconfig — Contains important system configuration files that are created and maintained by various system services (including iptables, samba, and most networking services).

- /etc/vsftpd — Contains configuration files used to set up the vsftpd FTP server.

- /etc/xinetd.d — Contains a set of files, each of which defines a network service that the xinetd daemon listens for on a particular port. When the xinetd daemon process receives a request for a service, it uses the information in these files to determine which daemon processes to start to handle the request.

Administrative log files

One of the things that Linux does well is keep track of itself. This is important when you consider how much can go wrong with a complex operating system. Sometimes you are trying to get a new facility to work and it fails without giving you the foggiest reason why. Other times you want to monitor your system to see if people are trying to access your computer illegally. In either of those cases, you can use log files to help track down the problem.

The main utilities for logging error and debugging messages for Linux are the rsyslogd and klogd daemons. General system logging is done by rsyslogd. Logging that is specific to kernel activity is done by klogd, from the optional sysklogd package. Logging is done according to information in the /etc/rsyslog.conf file. Messages are typically directed to log files that are usually in the /var/log directory.

As root user, you can view log files with the less command or watch messages as they are logged using the tail command (tail -f /var/log/messages).

Using other administrative logins

You don't hear much about other administrative logins (besides root) being used with Linux. It was a fairly common practice in Unix systems to have several different administrative logins that allowed administrative tasks to be split among several users.

In any case, these administrative logins are available with Linux, so you may want to look into using them. At the very least, because individual software packages such as bind, squid, and amanda set up permissions for their log files and configuration files based on their administrative logins, maintaining those permissions can impede someone who hacks into one of those services from gaining control of the whole computer.

Tip

Because most Fedora administrative features are expected to be administered by the root user, e-mail for other administrative accounts is routed to the root user. If you want other administrative users to receive their own e-mail, delete the aliases for those users from the /etc/aliases **file. ∎**

Understanding administrative logins

Here are some of the administrative logins, also called system accounts, that are configured automatically for Linux systems. Usually these logins are assigned UID numbers under 100. Here are examples:

- **lp** — This user can control some printing features. Having a separate lp administrator allows someone other than the super user to do such things as move or remove lp logs and print spool files. The home directory for lp is /var/spool/lpd.

- **mail** — This user can work with administrative e-mail features. The mail group has group permissions to use mail files in /var/spool/mail (which is also the mail user's home directory).

- **uucp** — This user owns various uucp commands (once used as the primary method for dial-up serial communications). It is the owner of log files in /var/log/uucp, spool files in /var/spool, administrative commands (such as uuchk, uucico, uuconv, and uuxqt) in /usr/sbin, and user commands (uucp, cu, uuname, uustat, and uux) in /usr/bin. The home directory for uucp is /var/spool/uucp.

- **bin** — This user owns many commands in /bin in traditional Unix systems. This is not the case in Fedora because root tends to own most executable files. The home directory of bin is /bin.

Tip

Most administrative logins have no passwords by default. They also typically have /sbin/nologin **assigned as their shell, so if you try to log in as one of these users, you see a** This account is currently not available **message. That's why you can't use an administrative login separately until you assign it a password and shell (such as** /bin/bash**). ∎**

Using sudo to assign administrative privilege

One way to give full or limited root privileges to any nonroot user is to set up the sudo facility. That simply entails adding the user to /etc/sudoers and defining what privileges you want that user to have. Then the user can run any command he or she is privileged to use by preceding that command with the sudo command.

The following example shows how to use the sudo facility to cause any users who are added to the wheel group to have full root privileges:

1. As the root user, edit the /etc/sudoers file by running the visudo command:

```
# /usr/sbin/visudo
```

2. By default, the file is opened in vi, unless your EDITOR variable happens to be set to some other editor acceptable to visudo (e.g., export EDITOR=gedit). The reason for using visudo is that the command will lock the /etc/sudoers file and do some basic sanity-checking of the file to ensure it was edited correctly.

Cross-Reference
If you are stuck here, refer to the vi tutorial ("Using the vi text editor") in Chapter 4 for information. ■

3. Uncomment the following line to allow users in the group named wheel to have full root privileges on the computer:

```
%wheel      ALL=(ALL)      ALL
```

4. The previous line causes the user to be prompted for a password to be allowed to use administrative commands. To allow users in the wheel group to have that privilege without using a password, uncomment the following line instead:

```
%wheel      ALL=(ALL)      NOPASSWD: ALL
```

5. Save the changes to the /etc/sudoers file.

6. Still as root user, open the /etc/group file using the vigr -s command and add the users you want to have root privilege to the wheel line. For example, if you were to add the users mary and jake to the wheel group, the line would appear as follows:

```
wheel:x:10:root,mary,jake
```

The -s option on the vigr command ensures that /etc/gshadow is updated properly as well.

At this point, the users mary and jake can run the sudo command to run commands, or parts of commands, that are normally restricted to the root user. The following is an example of a session by the user jake after he has been assigned sudo privileges:

```
[jake]$ sudo umount /mnt/win
[sudo] Password: *********
[jake]$ mount /mnt/win
mount: only root can mount /dev/sda1 on /mnt/win
[jake]$ sudo mount /mnt/win
[jake]$
```

In the preceding session, the user `jake` runs the `sudo` command so he can unmount the `/mnt/win` file system (using the `umount` command). He is asked to provide his password.

Tip

This is the user jake's password, *not* the root password. ∎

Notice that even after `jake` has given the password, he must still use the `sudo` command to run the command as root (the first mount fails, but the second succeeds). In addition, he was not prompted for a password for the second `sudo` because after entering his password successfully he can enter as many `sudo` commands as he wants for the next five minutes without having to enter it again. (You can change the timeout value from five minutes to however long you want by setting the `passwd_timeout` value in the `/etc/sudoers` file.)

The preceding example grants a simple all-or-nothing administrative privilege to everyone you put in the `wheel` group. However, the `/etc/sudoers` file gives you an incredible amount of flexibility in permitting individual users and groups to use individual applications or groups of applications. See the `sudoers` and `sudo` man pages for information about how to tune your `sudo` facility.

Using PolicyKit for assigning administrative privilege

PolicyKit provides a system for graphical applications to run privileged operations without granting full root access to the applications. Since its inception with Fedora 8, PolicyKit has grown to manage more applications so that only certain operations run as root. This is in contrast to the normal applications on the System ⇨ Administration menu, where you enter the root password and the entire application runs with root privileges.

For example, the Clock applet on the GNOME desktop shows the current time and date. If you place this applet on your desktop, right-click on it and choose Preferences ⇨ Time Settings ⇨ Set System Time, you will see a PolicyKit Authenticate dialog like the one shown in Figure 9-3.

FIGURE 9-3

The Authenticate dialog protects operations in programs that normally run with only user privileges.

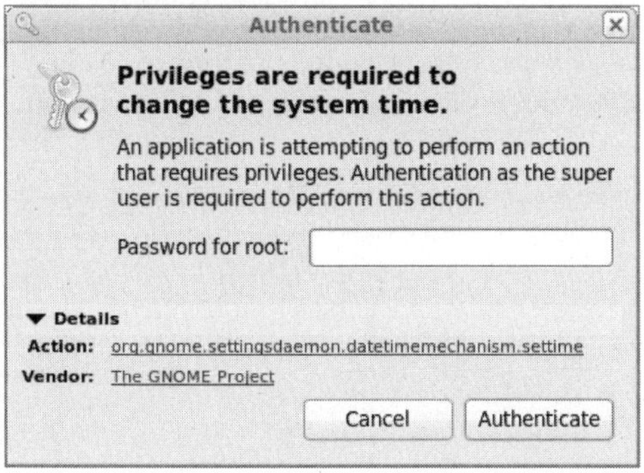

If you think about this, it makes perfect sense. There is no real security issue with letting users know the date and time, so the Clock applet should run with plain old user privileges. Changing the system time, however, should be protected, as this could cause quite a bit of disruption to a Linux system that runs various tasks at specified times.

Fedora 12 shipped with the 1.0 release of PolicyKit, called PolicyKitOne. This required a rewrite of PolicyKit to allow for integration with FreeIPA and other directory services. Fedora 13 included PolicyKitOneQt to fully integrate the new PolicyKit with QT and the KDE desktop, using KAuth to authenticate the higher privileges. With time, more and more applications will take the approach of running with user privileges except for a small set of protected operations. This helps security by reducing the amount of privileges granted to applications. See `http://hal.freedesktop .org/docs/polkit/` for more on PolicyKit.

Administering Your Linux System

Your Linux system administrator duties don't end after you have installed Fedora. Your ongoing job as a Linux system administrator includes the following tasks, which are covered in this chapter:

- **Configuring hardware** — Often when you add hardware to your Fedora computer, that hardware is automatically detected and configured by tools such as HAL. In cases where the hardware was not properly set up, you can use commands such as `lsmod`, `modprobe`, `insmod`, and `rmmod` to configure the right modules to get the hardware working.

- **Managing file systems and disk space** — You must keep track of the disk space being consumed, especially if your Fedora system is shared by multiple users. At some point, you may need to add a hard disk or track down what is eating up your disk space. (You can use commands such as `find`, `du`, and `df` to do this.)

- **Monitoring system performance** — You may have a runaway process on your system or you may just be experiencing slow performance. Tools that come with Fedora can help you determine how much of your CPU and memory are being consumed.

Cross-Reference

Other chapters cover other administrative topics, such as managing user accounts (Chapter 10), automating system tasks (Chapter 11), performing system backups and restores (Chapter 12), and securing your system (Chapter 13). Tasks related to network and server administration are covered in Chapters 14 through 23. Ways of getting updates to your Linux software (using the Add/Remove Software window and `yum` command) are described in Chapter 5. ∎

Configuring Hardware

For many hardware items that you attach to your computer, Linux will simply detect them and configure them. During system boot time, the kernel will probe and identify your IDE drives,

SCSI drives, PCI cards, and other hardware. After the Linux desktop is running, USB devices that you plug in (such as pen drives or digital cameras) will be detected, and any file systems they contain will be automatically mounted.

The following sections describe how to add and reconfigure hardware in Linux. This includes sections on checking your hardware, using HAL (for detecting and configuring hardware) and commands for working with loadable modules when hardware isn't being detected and configured properly.

Checking your hardware

Sometimes the fact that Fedora can't properly detect and configure your hardware may make it impossible for you to install Linux. In those cases, try to determine what hardware you have before you install. See Chapter 2 for information on checking your hardware before install-ing Fedora (you can try the bootable Fedora live CD that comes with this book to test your hardware).

Managing hardware with the DeviceKit

In prior releases of Fedora, a program called kudzu ran at boot time and checked your hardware against a saved configuration. Kudzu enabled you to reconfigure your hardware when it detected new devices.

Starting with Fedora 9, kudzu was replaced by another system called HAL, short for Hardware Abstraction Layer. HAL maintains a list of devices on your system and provides a programming API for applications to access. A background process, hald, looks for changes to your installed hardware.

Then, starting with Fedora 11, HAL was deprecated in favor of a newer replacement called DeviceKit. (Note the pattern here.) In Fedora 12, two main systems were migrated to the DeviceKit framework: power management and disks. Going forward, DeviceKit is working closer and closer with udev, the dynamic device manager used by Fedora. As part of this, the old pack-age devkit-disks has been renamed *udisks,* and the package devkit-power has been renamed *upower.* In Fedora 14, the old commands such as devkit-disks and devkit-power remain, but they are links to the newer commands udisks and upower.

To see a list of disks managed by the DeviceKit, run a command like the following:

```
# udisks --enumerate
```

You can then get information on a single device by running a command like this:

```
# udisks --show-info /dev/sda1
```

Note that you enter the Linux device file, not the name of the device as known by DeviceKit, /org/freedesktop/UDisks/devices/sda1 in this case.

Note

Removable devices, such as digital cameras, USB flash drives, and webcams, are detected and configured on-the-fly using the hald daemon. The hald daemon relies on the Udev device management facility to dynamically create devices and mount points (if needed) when those types of devices are connected. See Chapter 7 for descriptions of how CDs and digital cameras are detected. ■

Configuring modules

In a perfect world, after installing and booting Linux, all your hardware should be detected and available for access. While Fedora systems are rapidly moving closer to that ideal, sometimes you must take special steps to get your computer hardware working.

Fedora systems come with tools for configuring the drivers that stand between the programs you run (such as CD players and Web browsers) and the hardware they use (such as CD-ROM drives and network cards). The intention is to have only the most critical drivers your system needs built into the kernel; these are called *resident drivers*. Other drivers that are added dynamically as needed are referred to as *loadable modules*. The idea is to keep the basic kernel as lean as possible, so that each running system has only a few resident drivers and can dynamically add what it needs.

Listing loaded modules

To see which modules are currently loaded into the running kernel on your computer, you can use the lsmod command. Here's an example:

```
# lsmod
Module                  Size   Used by
vfat                    8579   1
fat                    45956   1 vfat
fuse                   61363   3
rfcomm                 67220   4
sco                    17180   2
bnep                   15390   2
l2cap                  51240   16 rfcomm,bnep
sunrpc                201180   1
.
.
.
nf_conntrack_ipv6      18078   7
ip6table_filter         1687   1
ip6_tables             17481   1 ip6table_filter
ipv6                  286249   50 ip6t_REJECT,nf_conntrack_ipv6
.
.
.
firewire_core          45817   1 firewire_ohci
crc_itu_t               1563   1 firewire_core
usb_storage            45875   0
nouveau               410336   2
ttm                    55006   1 nouveau
```

This output shows a variety of modules that have been loaded on a Linux system. The modules loaded on this system include several to support various types of file storage, including fuse, a module that provides a file system in user space.

To find information about any of the loaded modules, you can use the `modinfo` command:

```
# modinfo fuse
filename:       /lib/modules/2.6.35.6-46.fc14.x86_64/kernel/fs/fuse/fuse.ko
alias:          devname:fuse
alias:          char-major-10-229
license:        GPL
description:    Filesystem in Userspace
author:         Miklos Szeredi <miklos@ZZZZZZZZ>
srcversion:     5655074B2781008EDB812DA
depends:
vermagic:       2.6.35.6-46.fc14.x86_64 SMP mod_unload
parm:           max_user_bgreq:Global limit for the maximum number of
backgrounded requests an unprivileged user can set (uint)
parm:           max_user_congthresh:Global limit for the maximum congestion
threshold an unprivileged user can set (uint)
```

This output provides the location of the module (filename), the author, and a description, among other information. You can use the `-d` option to list just the description, the `-a` option to see the author of the module, or `-n` to see the object file representing the module. The author information often includes the e-mail address of the driver's creator (obscured here so as not to show someone's real e-mail address) so you can contact the author if you have problems or questions about it.

Loading modules

You can load any module that has been compiled and installed (to the `/lib/modules` directory) into your running kernel using the `modprobe` command. The most common reasons to load a module are that you want to use a feature temporarily (such as loading a module to support a special file system on a floppy you want to access) or to identify a module that will be used by a particular piece of hardware that could not be autodetected.

Here is an example of the `modprobe` command being used to load the parport module, which provides the core functions to share parallel ports with multiple devices:

```
# modprobe parport
```

After parport is loaded you can load the parport_pc module to define the PC-style ports available through the interface. The parport_pc module lets you optionally define the addresses and IRQ numbers associated with each device sharing the parallel port. For example:

```
# modprobe parport_pc io=0x3bc irq=auto
```

In this example, a device is identified as having an address of 0x3bc. The IRQ for the device is autodetected.

The modprobe command loads modules temporarily. At the next system reboot, the modules you enter disappear. To permanently add the module to your system, add the modprobe command line to one of the startup scripts that are run at boot time. A shell script that ends with the extension of .modules in /etc/sysconfig/modules will be executed automatically at boot time by the rc.sysinit script.

Note

An alternative to using modprobe **is the** insmod **command. The advantage of using** modprobe**, however, is that** insmod **will load only the module you request, whereas** modprobe **will try to load other modules that the one you requested is dependent on.** ■

Removing modules

You can remove a module from a running kernel using the rmmod command. For example, to remove the module parport_pc from the current kernel, type the following:

```
# rmmod parport_pc
```

If the module is not currently busy, the parport_pc module is removed from the running kernel. (Instead of rmmod, you can use modprobe -r to remove the module, plus related modules.)

Note

Sometimes a piece of hardware is improperly detected, and a module is loaded that is either the wrong module or simply a broken module. In any of these cases, consider adding the name of the offending driver to the /etc/modprobe.d/blacklist.conf **file, to prevent that module from being loaded. After that, consider loading the proper module manually or by adding a** modprobe **command to load the module you want from a system startup file.** ■

Managing File Systems and Disk Space

File systems in Linux are organized in a hierarchy, beginning from root (/) and continuing downward in a structure of directories and subdirectories. As an administrator of a Fedora system, it is your duty to ensure that all the disk drives that represent your file system are available to users of the computer. It is also your job to ensure that there is enough disk space in the right places in the file system for users to store what they need.

File systems are organized differently in Linux than they are in Microsoft Windows operating systems. Instead of drive letters (e.g., A:, B:, C:) for each local disk, network file system, CD-ROM, or other type of storage medium, everything fits neatly into the directory structure. For hard drive partitions, it is up to administrators to create a mount point in the file system and then connect the disk to that point. For removable media (such as CD, DVD, USB flash drives, or digital cameras), mount points are automatically created and connected (in the /media directory) when those items are connected or loaded.

Cross-Reference

Chapter 2 provides instructions for using Disk Setup (formerly Disk Druid) to configure disk partitions. Chapter 4 describes how the Linux file system is organized. ■

The organization of your file system begins when you install Linux. Part of the installation process is to divide your hard disk (or disks) into partitions. Those partitions can then be assigned to:

- A part of the Linux file system
- Swap space for Linux
- Other file system types (perhaps containing other bootable operating systems)

For our purposes, we'll focus on partitions that are used for the Linux file system. To see what partitions are currently set up on your hard disk, use the fdisk command as follows:

```
# fdisk -1
Disk /dev/sda: 500.1 GB, 500107862016 bytes
255 heads, 63 sectors/track, 60801 cylinders
Units = cylinders of 16065 * 512 = 8225280 bytes
Disk identifier: 0xa44f8c47

   Device Boot      Start         End      Blocks   Id  System
/dev/sda1               1           5       40131   de  Dell Utility
/dev/sda2               6        1918    15360000    7  HPFS/NTFS
/dev/sda3   *        1918        2020      819200   83  Linux
/dev/sda4            2021       60801   472158382+   5  Extended
/dev/sda5            2021        4060    16384000   82  Linux swap / Solaris
/dev/sda6            4060       60801   455774207+  83  Linux
```

This output shows the disk partitioning for a computer able to run both Linux and Microsoft Windows. You can see that the Linux partition on /dev/sda6 has most of the space available for data. There is a Windows partition (/dev/sda2) and a Linux swap partition (/dev/sda5), and a small /boot partition (788MB) on /dev/sda3. In this case, a special recovery partition exists on /dev/sda1.

Next, to see what partitions are actually being used for your Linux system, you can use the mount command (with no options). The mount command can show you which of the available disk partitions are actually mounted and where:

```
# mount
/dev/sda6 on / type ext4 (rw)
proc on /proc type proc (rw)
sysfs on /sys type sysfs (rw)
devpts on /dev/pts type devpts (rw,gid=5,mode=620)
/dev/sda3 on /boot type ext3 (rw)
tmpfs on /dev/shm type tmpfs ↵
(rw,rootcontext="system_u:object_r:tmpfs_t:s0")
none on /proc/sys/fs/binfmt_misc type binfmt_misc (rw)
```

```
sunrpc on /var/lib/nfs/rpc_pipefs type rpc_pipefs (rw)
nfsd on /proc/fs/nfsd type nfsd (rw)
gvfs-fuse-daemon on /home/ericfj/.gvfs type fuse.gvfs-fuse-daemon ↵
(rw,nosuid,nodev,user=ericfj)
/dev/sda2 on /mnt/windows type fuseblk (rw,allow_other,blksize=4096)
/dev/sr0 on /media/Fedora 14 i386 DVD type iso9660 ↵
(ro,nosuid,nodev,uhelper=udisks,
uid=500,gid=500,iocharset=utf8,mode=0400,dmode=0500)
```

Note

You may notice that /proc, /sys, /dev/pts, /proc/sys/fs/binfmt_misc, /dev/shm, **and other entries not relating to a partition are shown as file systems. That's because they represent different file system types (** proc **and** devpts, **and so on).** ∎

The mounted Linux partitions in this case are /dev/sda3, which provides space for the /boot directory (which contains data for booting Linux) using the older ext3 file system type, and /dev/sda6, which provides space for the rest of the Linux file system beginning from the root directory (/). This system has a Windows NT file system partition mounted on /mnt/windows.

Beginning with Fedora Core 3, mount points for removable media (CDs, DVDs, USB pen drives, and so on) moved from /mnt to the /media directory. In this example, an IDE combination CDRW/DVD-ROM drive was mounted on /media/Fedora 14 i386 DVD. With most GUIs, the CD or DVD is typically mounted automatically when you insert it. In this example, the uhelper (unprivileged unmount request helper) is assigned to the DeviceKit daemon user udisks so that the DeviceKit facility can unmount the CD as an otherwise nonprivileged user.

After the word type, you can see the type of file system contained on the device. (See the description of different file system types in the next section.) Particularly on larger Linux systems, you may have multiple partitions for several reasons:

- **Multiple hard disks** — You may have several hard disks available to your users. In that case you would have to mount each disk (and possibly several partitions from each disk) in different locations in your file system.

- **Protecting different parts of the file system** — If you have many users on a system and they consume all the file system space, the entire system can fail. For example, there may be no place for temporary files to be copied (so the programs writing to temporary files may fail), and incoming mail may fail to be written to mail boxes. With multiple mounted partitions, if one partition runs out, others can continue to work.

- **Backups** — There are some fast ways to back up data from your computer that involve copying the entire image of a disk or partition. If you want to restore that partition later, you can simply copy it back (bit by bit) to a hard disk. With smaller partitions, this approach can be done fairly efficiently.

- **Protecting from disk failure** — If one disk (or part of one disk) fails, by having multiple partitions mounted on your file system you may be able to continue working and just fix the one disk that failed.

When a disk partition is mounted on the file system, all directories and subdirectories below that mount point are then stored on that partition. For example, if you were to mount one partition on / and one on /usr, everything below the /usr mount point would be stored on the second partition, while everything else would be stored on the first partition. If you then mounted another partition on /usr/local, everything below that mount point would be on the third partition, while everything else below /usr would be on the second partition.

Tip

What if a remote file system is unmounted from your computer and you try to save a file in that mount point directory? You write the file to that directory and it is stored on your local hard disk. When the remote file system is remounted, however, the file you saved will seem to disappear. To get the file back, you have to unmount the remote file system (causing the file to reappear), move the file to another location, remount the file system, and copy the file back there. ■

Mount points that are often mentioned as being candidates for separate partitions include /, /boot, /home, /usr, and /var. The root file system (/) is the catchall for directories that aren't in other mount points. The root file system's mount point (/) is the only one that is required. The /boot directory holds the images needed to boot the operating system. The /home file systems is where all the user accounts are typically stored. Applications and documentation are stored in /usr. Below the /var mount point is where log files, temporary files, server files (Web, FTP, and so on), and lock files are stored (that is, items that need disk space for your computer's applications to keep running).

Cross-Reference

See Chapter 2 for further information on partitioning techniques. ■

The fact that multiple partitions are mounted on your file system is invisible to people using your Linux system. The only times they will care is when a partition runs out of space or they need to save or use information from a particular device (such as a floppy disk or remote file system). Of course, any user can check this by typing the mount command.

Mounting file systems

Most of your hard disk partitions are mounted automatically for you. When you installed Fedora, you were asked to create partitions and indicate the mount points for those partitions. When you boot Fedora, all Linux partitions residing on hard disk should typically be mounted. For that reason, this section focuses mostly on how to mount other types of devices so that they become part of your Linux file system.

Besides being able to mount other types of devices, you can also use mount to mount other kinds of file systems on your Linux system. This means that you can store files from other operating systems or use file systems that are appropriate for certain kinds of activities (such as writing large block sizes). The most common use of this feature for the average Linux user, however, is to allow that user to obtain and work with files from USB drives or CD-ROMs.

Supported file systems

To see file system types that are currently available for use on your system, type **cat /proc/ filesystems**. The following file system types are supported in Linux, although they may not be in use at the moment or they may not be built into your current kernel (so they may need to be loaded as modules):

- `adfs` — This is the acorn disc file system, which is the standard file system used on RiscOS operating systems.

- `affs` — This file system is used with Amiga computers.

- `befs` — This is the file system used by the BeOS operating system.

- `brtfs` – Currently, this new file system remains experimental. Similar to ext4, Brtfs provides a copy-on-write file system focusing on fault tolerance and ease of administration. See `http://btrfs.wiki.kernel.org` for more on Brtfs.

- `cifs` — The Common Internet File System (CIFS) is the virtual file system used to access servers that comply with the SNIA CIFS specification. CIFS is an attempt to refine and standardize the SMB protocol used by Samba and Windows file sharing.

- `ext3` — The ext file systems are the most common file systems used with Linux. The ext3 file system is the default file system type in many older Linux systems. It is also referred to as the *third extended file system*. The ext3 file system includes journaling features that improve a file system's ability to recover from crashes, relative to ext2 file systems.

- `ext4` — An enhancement to ext3, this type of file system performs and scales better to larger numbers of files. Fedora 9 introduced the ext4 file system type as a preview release. With Fedora 11, ext4 became the default file system for Fedora. The root file system (/) is typically ext4 (although you can use other file systems too). Some older versions of Linux cannot handle a `/boot` file system of type ext4 (you need to use ext2 or ext3), but Fedora 12 and higher fully support a `/boot` in the ext4 file system type.

- `ext2` — The default file system type for versions of Red Hat Linux previous to 7.2. Features are the same as ext3, except that ext2 doesn't include journaling features.

- `ext` — This is the first version of the ext file system. It is not used very often anymore and I recommend you don't use it.

- `fuse` — Fuse behaves like a user-space remote file system. A local user can use ssh tools to mount a remote file system locally, without the remote file system being made available, purely on the basis of the permissions of the user you log in as. It provides a very cool way to mount a remote file system without administrative intervention on the remote side.

- `hpfs` — This file system is used to do read-only mounts of an OS/2 HPFS file system.

- `iso9660` — This file system evolved from the High Sierra file system (the original standard used on CD-ROM). Extensions to the High Sierra standard (called Rock Ridge extensions), allow iso9660 file systems to support long filenames and Unix-style information (such as file permissions, ownership, and links). This file system type is used when you mount a CD-ROM.

- **jfs** — This file system is based on the JFS file system IBM used for OS/2 Warp. It became an open-source project in 2000. JFS is best suited for enterprise systems. Like XFS, JFS is tuned for large file systems and high-performance environments.

- **kafs** — This is the AFS client file system. It is used in distributed computing environments to share files with Linux, Windows, and Macintosh clients.

- **minix** — This is the Minix file system type, used originally with the Minix version of Unix. It supports filenames of up to 30 characters only.

- **msdos** — This is an MS-DOS file system. You can use this type to mount floppy disks that come from Microsoft operating systems.

- **ncpfs** — This relates to Novell NetWare file systems. NetWare file systems can be mounted over a network.

- **nfs** — This is the Network File System (NFS) type of file system. File systems mounted from another computer on your network use this type of file system.

- **ntfs** — NTFS support was added to the Fedora repository with Fedora 7. Many people who set up dual-boot computers want to be able to access the Windows (ntfs) drives.

- **proc** — This is not an on-disk system, but rather a file-system interface to the Linux kernel. You probably won't do anything special to set up a proc file system. However, the /proc mount point should be a proc file system. Many utilities rely on /proc to gain access to Linux kernel information.

- **reiserfs** — This is a journaling file system that used to be the default file system for some other Linux distributions (including SUSE, Slackware, and Linspire). Reiserfs is not considered to be well-supported in Fedora systems. (You must add reiser to the boot prompt when you install Fedora to enable reiserfs partitions. Also, SELinux doesn't support reiserfs file systems.)

- **squashfs** — This is a compressed file system, whereby files are uncompressed on-the-fly as they are requested. It is often used with live CDs, including all official Fedora live CDs.

- **swap** — This is used for swap partitions. Swap areas are used to hold data temporarily when RAM is currently used up. Data is swapped to the swap area, and then returned to RAM when it is needed again.

- **ufs** — This file system is popular on Solaris and SunOS.

- **vfat** — This is the Microsoft extended FAT (VFAT) file system.

- **xenix** — This was added to be compatible with Xenix file systems (one of the first PC versions of Unix). It is obsolete and will probably be removed eventually.

- **xfs** — This journaling file system is useful in high-performance environments. It includes full 64-bit addressing. An xfs file system can scale up to systems that include multiple terabytes of data that transfer data at multiple gigabytes per second.

- **xiafs** — This file system supports long filenames and larger inodes than file systems such as minux.

The ext4 file system is the latest version of the ext file system (with ext3 being the prior standard). An ext4 file system can be mounted as an ext3 file system. Starting with Fedora 11, ext4 became the default file system for Linux. See the Ext4 FAQ for information on creating and working with ext4 file systems:

```
http://ext4.wiki.kernel.org/index.php/Frequently_Asked_Questions
```

A how-to document helps you get started with ext4 file systems:

```
http://ext4.wiki.kernel.org/index.php/Ext4_Howto
```

You can convert an ext3 file system to ext4 by using a command like the following:

```
# tune2fs -O extents -E test_fs /dev/DEV
```

With a command like the following, you can also adjust the inode setting — for example, from 128 to 256 — to improve efficiency:

```
# tune2fs -I 256 /dev/DEV
```

Encrypted file systems can be used to protect your data if your computer should become lost or stolen. In particular, this feature was created with laptops in mind. Someone stealing your laptop would not be able to mount or access data on an encrypted file system without your password. The `cryptsetup` command from the `cryptsetup-luks` package is used to create cryptographic volumes. Any file system, other than root (/), can be encrypted in Fedora. To learn more, refer to the Encrypted Filesystems Feature page:

```
http://fedoraproject.org/wiki/Releases/FeatureEncryptedFilesystems
```

You can use dm-crypt, short for *device mapper encryption*, to provide transparent encryption to block devices, such as disks. Here, transparent means that programs don't need to worry whether the contents of your disk are encrypted, as the mapping layer adds this feature. This enables you to work with word processors, text editors, drawing programs, and so on, without messing with encryption, but your files are stored safely protected. (Well, as safe as current encryption technology can be.)

To use dm-crypt, you must have a 2.6 or higher Linux kernel with dm-crypt support. For more on dm-crypt, see `www.saout.de/misc/dm-crypt/`.

Using the fstab file to define mountable file systems

The hard disks on your local computer and the remote file systems you use every day are probably set up to mount automatically when you boot Linux. The definitions for which of these file systems are mounted are contained in the `/etc/fstab` file. Here's an example of an `/etc/fstab` file:

```
#
# /etc/fstab
# Created by anaconda on Mon Sep 13 18:58L:29 2010
```

```
#
# Accessible filesystems, by reference, are maintained under '/dev/disk'
# See man pages fstab(5), findfs(8), mount(8) and/or blkid(8) for more info
#
/dev/VolGroup00/LogVol00 /                        ext4    defaults      1 1
LABEL=/boot /boot                     ext3    defaults      1 2
swap                      swap      defaults      0 0
tmpfs                     /dev/shm              tmpfs   defaults      0 0
devpts                    /dev/pts              devpts  gid=5,mode=620 0 0
sysfs                     /sys                  sysfs   defaults      0 0
proc                      /proc                 proc    defaults      0 0
/dev/sda2                 /mnt/windows          ntfs    noauto        0 0
```

Note

You will likely see UUID (universal identifiers) such as UUID=866237bb-d845-4118-a1b3-ba0cdcf253e48f **before the names of the file systems. I pulled those out to make the** fstab **file's contents clearer.** ■

All file systems listed in this file are mounted at boot time, except for those set to noauto in the fourth field. In this example, the root (/) and swap hard disk partitions are configured as logical volume management (LVM) volumes. This means that they may consist of multiple hard disk partitions. You can use the pvdisplay command to see what physical volumes make up each logical volume. An advantage of LVM volumes is that if you run out of space in a logical volume, you can simply attach a new physical volume (such as a disk partition) to extend its size. You don't have to resize or create a new partition.

The /proc, /sys, /dev/shm, and /dev/pts file systems are not associated with particular devices. The floppy disk and CD-ROM drive entries are no longer included in the /etc/fstab file by default. That's because those media types are now handled by the udisks-disks daemon and mounted automatically when they are inserted. The actual mount points vary according to the CD's or DVD's volume name (implanted on that medium itself).

I also added one additional line for /dev/sda1, which enables me to mount the Windows (vfat in this case, but ntfs support could be used as well) partition on my computer so I don't need to always boot Windows to get at the files on my Windows partition.

Note

To access the Windows partition described previously, I must first create the mount point (by typing mkdir /mnt/win**). I can then mount it when I choose by typing (as root)** mount /mnt/win**.** ■

You find the following in each field of the fstab file:

- **Field 1** — The name of the device representing the file system. The word none is often placed in this field for file systems (such as /proc and /dev/pts) that are not associated with special devices. Notice that this field can now include the LABEL or UUID options. Using UUID, you can indicate a universally unique identifier (UUID). LABEL indicates a volume label instead of a device name. The advantage to the LABEL approach is that, because the partition is identified by volume name, you can move a volume to a different device name without having to change the fstab file.

- **Field 2** — The mount point in the file system. The file system contains all data from the mount point down the directory tree structure, unless another file system is mounted at some point beneath it.

- **Field 3** — The file system type. Valid file system types are described in the "Supported file systems" section earlier in this chapter.

- **Field 4** — Options to the mount command. In the preceding example, the noauto option prevents the indicated file system from being mounted at boot time. Also, ro says to mount the file system read-only (which is reasonable for a CD-ROM drive). Commas must separate options. See the mount command manual page (under the -o option) for information on other supported options.

Tip

Normally, only the root user is allowed to mount a file system using the mount command. However, to allow any user to mount a file system (such as a file system on a floppy disk), you could add the user or owner option to Field 4 of /etc/fstab. ∎

- **Field 5** — The number in this field indicates whether or not the indicated file system must be backed up by a backup system called dump. A number 1 assumes that the file system needs to be backed up, or *dumped*. A number 0 assumes that the file system doesn't need to be dumped. Most Linux users do not use the dump program for backups.

- **Field 6** — The number in this field indicates whether or not the indicated file system needs to be checked with fsck. A zero indicates that the file system should not be checked. A number 1 assumes that the file system needs to be checked first (this is used for the root file system). A number 2 assumes that the file system can be checked at any point after the root file system is checked.

If you want to add an additional local disk or an additional partition, you can create an entry for the disk or partition in the /etc/fstab file.

Using the mount command to mount file systems

Your Fedora system automatically runs mount -a (mount all file systems) each time you boot. For that reason, you would typically use only the mount command for special situations. In particular, the average user or administrator uses mount in two ways:

- To display the disks, partitions, and remote file systems that are currently mounted

- To temporarily mount a file system

Any user can type the mount command (with no options) to see what file systems are currently mounted on the local Linux system. The following is an example of the mount command. It shows a single hard disk partition (/dev/sda6) containing the root (/) file system, and proc and devpts file system types mounted on /proc and /dev/pts, respectively:

```
$ mount
/dev/sda6 on / type ext4 (rw)
```

```
proc on /proc type proc (rw)
sysfs on /sys type sysfs (rw)
devpts on /dev/pts type devpts (rw,gid=5,mode=620)
/dev/sda3 on /boot type ext3 (rw)
tmpfs on /dev/shm type tmpfs
(rw,rootcontext="system_u:object_r:tmpfs_t:s0")
none on /proc/sys/fs/binfmt_misc type binfmt_misc (rw)
sunrpc on /var/lib/nfs/rpc_pipefs type rpc_pipefs (rw)
nfsd on /proc/fs/nfsd type nfsd (rw)
gvfs-fuse-daemon on /home/ericfj/.gvfs type fuse.gvfs-fuse-daemon ↵
(rw,nosuid,nodev,user=ericfj)
```

The most common devices to mount by hand are USB drives and your CD-ROM. However, by default now in Fedora and other Linux systems, CD-ROMs, floppy disks (for older systems), and USB drives are mounted automatically when you insert them. (In some cases, the autorun program may also run automatically. For example, autorun may start a CD music player or software package installer to handle the data on the medium.)

Mounting removable media

If you want to mount a file system manually, the /etc/fstab file helps make it simple to mount a file system from any disk partition, floppy disk, or a CD-ROM. Although Fedora no longer automatically adds entries for CDs and floppy disks (for those with older hardware) to the /etc/fstab file, you could add entries manually if you wanted to mount those media in different locations. Here are examples of entries you could add to your /etc/fstab file:

```
/dev/cdrom  /mnt/cdrom  auto noauto,user,exec,ro 0 0
/dev/fd0  /mnt/floppy auto noauto,owner        0 0
```

The /mnt directory is the location traditionally used to mount removable or temporary file systems in Linux. If you are adding mount points manually, it's best to use a location such as /mnt, instead of the newer /media directory, so you don't cause a conflict with any file systems Fedora mounts automatically in the /media directory.

With entries added such as those just shown, you can use the mount command with a single option to indicate what you want to mount, and information is taken from the /etc/fstab file to fill in the other options. The following are cases when you could mount a CD or floppy disk file system using a single option (based on the /etc/fstab file shown previously):

- **CD-ROM** — If you are mounting a CD-ROM that is in the standard ISO 9960 format (as most software CD-ROMs are), you can mount that CD-ROM by placing it in your CD-ROM drive and typing the following:

  ```
  # mount /mnt/cdrom
  ```

  By default, your CD-ROM is mounted on a point in the /media directory. The command just shown, however, mounts the /dev/cdrom device on the /mnt/cdrom directory. Run this command only if Fedora does not automatically mount your CDs.

- **Floppy disk** — If you are mounting a floppy disk that is in the standard Linux file system format (ext4), based on the /etc/fstab file entry shown previously, you can mount that floppy disk by inserting it in your floppy drive and typing the following:

```
# mount /mnt/floppy
```

The file system type (ext4), device (/dev/fd0), and mount options are filled in from the /etc/fstab file. You should be able to change to the floppy disk directory (cd /mnt/floppy) and list the contents of the floppy's top directory (ls).

Note

In both of the two previous cases, you could give the device name (/dev/cdrom or /dev/fd0, respectively) instead of the mount point directory to get the same results. ∎

Of course, you might get floppy disks you want to use that are in many formats. Someone may give you a floppy containing files from a Microsoft operating system (in MS-DOS format); or you may get a file from another Unix system. In those cases, you can fill in your own options, rather than rely on options from the /etc/fstab file. In some cases, Linux autodetects that the floppy disk contains an MS-DOS (or Windows vfat) file system and mounts it properly without additional arguments. However, if it doesn't, the following example shows how to mount a floppy containing MS-DOS files:

```
# mount -t msdos /dev/fd0 /mnt/floppy
```

This shows the basic format of the mount command you would use to mount a floppy disk. You could change msdos to any other supported file system type (described earlier in this chapter) to mount a floppy of that type. Instead of using floppy drive A: (/dev/fd0), you could use drive B: (/dev/fd1) or any other accessible drive. Instead of mounting on /mnt/floppy, you could create any other directory and mount the floppy there.

Here are some other useful options you could add along with the mount command:

- **-t auto** — If you aren't sure exactly what type of file system is contained on the floppy disk (or other medium you are mounting), use the -t auto option to indicate the file system type. The mount command will query the disk to try to determine what type of data it contains.
- **-r** — If you don't want to make changes to the mounted file system (or can't because it is a read-only medium), use this option when you mount it. This will mount it read-only.
- **-w** — This mounts the file system with read/write permission.

Mounting CD or DVD images

Another valuable way to use the mount command has to do with ISO disk images. If you download a CD, DVD, or floppy disk image from the Internet and you want to see what it contains, you can do so without burning it to CD or floppy. With the image on your hard disk, create a mount point and use the `-o loop` option to mount it locally. Here's an example of what to type (as root user):

```
# mkdir /mnt/mycdimage
# mount -o loop whatever-i386-disc1.iso /mnt/mycdimage
```

In this example, the disk image file (`whatever-i386-disc1.iso`) residing in the current directory is mounted on the `/mnt/mycdimage` directory I just created. I can now change to that directory using the `cd` command, view its contents, and copy or use any of its contents. This is useful for downloaded CD images that you want to install software from without having to burn the image to CD. When you are done, just type **umount/mnt/mycdimage** to unmount it.

Mounting Windows file systems

If your system has Windows partitions, you can mount those partitions using the `mount` command. For example, to mount a Windows Vista partition from Linux, you can use commands like the following:

```
# mkdir /mnt/windows
# mount -t ntfs /dev/sda2 /mnt/windows
```

In this example, the partition associated with `/dev/sda2` is an NTFS file system created by Windows Vista. The first command creates the mount point, the directory where the NTFS partition will be mounted. The second command mounts the file system.

Other options to mount are available only for a specific file system type. See the `mount` manual page for those and other useful options.

Using the umount command to unmount a file system

When you are done using a temporary file system, or you want to unmount a permanent file system temporarily, you can use the `umount` command. This command detaches the file system from its mount point in your Linux file system. To use `umount`, you can give it either a directory name or a device name. For example, the following unmounts the device (probably `/dev/sda2` in the preceding examples) from the mount point `/mnt/windows`:

```
# umount /mnt/windows
```

You also could have done this using the form:

```
# umount /dev/sda2
```

In general, it's better to use the directory name because the `umount` command will fail if the device is mounted in more than one location.

If you get a message that the "device is busy," the `umount` request has failed. The reason is because either a process has a file open on the device or you have a shell open with a directory on the device as a current directory. Stop the processes or change to a directory outside of the device you are trying to unmount for the `umount` request to succeed.

An alternative for unmounting a busy device is the -l option. With umount -l (a lazy unmount), the unmount happens as soon as the device is no longer busy. To unmount a remote NFS file system that is no longer available (e.g., the server is down), use the umount -f option to forcibly unmount the NFS file system.

With the fuser command, you can list all the processes that are accessing a given file or file system. This can help you track down why a device is busy. For example, to list all the processes accessing the /home file system, run the following command:

```
# fuser -m /mnt/windows
```

Replace /mnt/windows with the file system you are trying to unmount.

You'll see a number of process IDs listed in the output. After each process ID, fuser places one or more characters to indicate the type of access, such as *e* to indicate an executable being run, *c* for the current directory, and *r* for the root directory.

Run the man fuser command to see more on how to use fuser.

Using the mkfs command to create a file system

It is possible to create a file system, for any supported file system type, on a disk or partition that you choose. This is done with the mkfs command. While this is most useful for creating file systems on hard disk partitions, you can create file systems on floppy disks or rewritable CDs as well.

Here is an example of using mkfs to create a file system on a floppy disk:

```
# mkfs -t ext3 /dev/fd0
mke2fs 1.41.12 (17-May-2010)
Filesystem label=
OS type: Linux
Block size=1024 (log=0)
Fragment size=1024 (log=0)
184 inodes, 1440 blocks
72 blocks (5.00%) reserved for the super user
First data block=1
1 block group
8192 blocks per group, 8192 fragments per group
184 inodes per group

Writing inode tables: done

Filesystem too small for a journal
Writing superblocks and filesystem accounting information: done

The filesystem will be automatically checked every 23 mounts or
180 days, whichever comes first. Use tune2fs -c or -i to override.
```

You can see the statistics that are output with the formatting done by the `mkfs` command. The number of inodes and blocks created are output. Likewise, the number of blocks per group and fragments per group are also output. You could now mount this file system (`mount /mnt/floppy`), change to it as your current directory (`cd /mnt/floppy`), and create files on it as you please.

Adding a hard disk

Adding a new hard disk to your computer so that the disk can be used by Linux requires a combination of steps described in previous sections. The general steps are as follows:

1. Install the hard disk hardware.
2. Identify the partitions on the new hard disk.
3. Create the file systems on the new hard disk.
4. Mount the file systems.

The easiest way to add a hard disk to Linux is to have the entire hard disk devoted to a single Linux partition. You can have multiple partitions of different sizes, however, and assign them each to different types of file systems and different mount points, if you like. The following procedure describes how to add a hard disk containing a single Linux partition. Along the way, it also notes which steps you need to repeat to have multiple file systems with multiple mount points.

Note

This procedure assumes that Fedora is already installed and working on the computer. If this is not the case, follow the instructions for adding a hard disk on your current operating system. Later, when you install Fedora, you can identify this disk when asked to partition your hard disk(s). ■

1. Install the hard disk into your computer. Follow the manufacturer's instructions for physically installing and connecting the new hard disk. If, presumably, this is a second hard disk, you may need to change jumpers on the hard disk unit itself to have it operate as a slave hard disk. You may also need to change the BIOS settings.

2. Boot your computer to Linux.

3. Determine the device name for the hard disk. As root user from a shell, type the following:

```
# dmesg | less
```

4. From the output, look for an indication that the new hard disk was found. For example, if it is a second hard disk, you should see `sdb:` in the output. Be sure to identify the right disk or you will erase all the data from disks you probably want to keep!

Note

Prior to Fedora 7, IDE hard drives began with `/dev/hd` and SCSI drives began with `/dev/sd`. Now, both IDE and SCSI drives begin with `/dev/sd`, as in `/dev/sda` and `/dev/sdb`. ■

5. Use the `fdisk` command to create partitions on the new disk. For example, if you are formatting the second hard disk (sdb), you could type the following:

```
# fdisk /dev/sdb
```

If the disk had existing partitions on it, you can change or delete those partitions now. Or, you can simply reformat the whole disk to remove everything. Use p to view all partitions and d to delete a partition.

6. To create a new partition, type the following:

```
n
```

7. You are asked to choose an extended or primary partition. To choose a primary partition, type the following:

```
p
```

8. You are asked the partition number. If you are creating the first partition (or for only one partition), type the number 1:

```
1
```

9. You are asked to enter the first cylinder number (with 1 being the default).

10. To begin at the second cylinder, type the number 2 as follows:

```
2
```

11. You are asked to enter the last cylinder. If you are using the entire hard disk, use the last cylinder number shown. Otherwise, choose the ending cylinder number or indicate how many megabytes the partition should have.

12. To create more partitions on the hard disk, repeat Steps 6 through 10 for each partition. You need to change the partition number, cylinder numbers, and so on as appropriate.

13. Type **w** to write changes to the hard disk. At this point, you should be back at the shell.

14. To make a file system on the new disk partition, use the `mkfs` command. By default, this command creates an ext2 file system, which is useable by Linux. To create an ext4 file system on the first partition of the second hard disk, type the following:

```
# mkfs -t ext4 /dev/sdb1
```

15. If you created multiple partitions, repeat this step for each partition (e.g., `/dev/sdb2`, `/dev/sdb3`, and so on).

Tip

If you don't use `-t ext4` as shown above, an ext2 file system is created by default. Use other commands, or options to this command, to create other file system types. For example, use `mkfs.vfat` to create a VFAT file system, `mkfs.msdos` for DOS, or `mkfs.reiserfs` for Reiser file system type. The `tune2fs` command, described later in this section, can be used to change an ext2 file system to an ext3 file system. ■

16. Once the file system is created, you can have the partition permanently mounted by editing the /etc/fstab file to add the new partition. Here is an example of a line you might add to that file:

```
/dev/sdb1              /abc            ext4          defaults        1 1
```

17. In this example, the partition (/dev/sdb1) is mounted on the /abc directory as an ext4 file system. The defaults keyword causes the partition to be mounted at boot time. The numbers 1 1 cause the disk to be checked for errors. Add one line like the one shown above for each partition you created.

18. Create the mount point. For example, to mount the partition on /abc (as shown in the previous step), type the following:

```
# mkdir /abc
```

19. Create your other mount points if you created multiple partitions. The next time you boot Linux, the partition will be automatically mounted on the /abc directory, as will any other partitions you added.

After you have created the file systems on your partitions, a nice tool for adjusting those file systems is the tune2fs command. Using tune2fs, you can change volume labels, the frequency at which the file system is checked, and error behavior. You can also use tune2fs to change an ext2 file system to an ext3 file system so the file system can use journaling. For example:

```
# tune2fs -j /dev/sdb1
tune2fs 1.41.12 (17-May-2010)
Creating journal inode: done
This filesystem will be automatically checked every 38 mounts or
180 days, whichever comes first. Use tune2fs -c or -i to override.
```

By adding the -j option to tune2fs, you can either change the journal size or attach the file system to an external journal block device. After you have used tune2fs to change your file system type, you need to correct your /etc/fstab file to change the file system type from ext2 to ext3.

Using RAID

RAID (Redundant Arrays of Independent Disks) spreads the data used on a computer across multiple disks, while appearing to the operating system as if it is dealing with a single disk partition. Using the different RAID specifications, you can achieve the following advantages:

- **Improved disk performance** — RAID0 uses a feature called *striping*, whereby data is striped (or placed) across multiple RAID partitions. Striping can improve disk performance by spreading the hits on a computer's file system across multiple partitions, which are presumably on multiple hard disks. Striping does not provide redundancy.

- **Mirroring** — RAID1 uses partitions from multiple hard disks as mirrors. That way, if one of the partitions becomes corrupted or the hard disk fails, the data exists on a partition from another disk because it has continuously maintained an exact mirror image of the original partition. If the primary partition becomes corrupt, though, the mirrored drive can also get corrupted.

- **Parity** — Although striping can improve performance, it can increase the chance of data loss because any hard-disk crash in the array can potentially cause the entire RAID device to fail. Using a feature called *parity*, information about the layout of the striped data is kept so that data can be reconstructed if one of the disks in the array crashes. RAID3, 4, and 5 implement different levels of parity.

During installation of Fedora, you can use the Disk Setup window to create RAID0, RAID1, and RAID5 disk arrays. The following procedures describe how to set up RAID disks during installation.

Before you begin creating RAID partitions when you install Fedora, you will probably want to start with a computer that has two or more hard disks. Otherwise, without multiple hard disks, you won't get the performance gains that result from spreading the hits on your computer among multiple disks. Likewise, mirroring will be ineffective if all RAID partitions are on the same disk because the failure of a single hard disk would still potentially cause the mirrored partitions to fail as well.

For example, you might begin with 30GB of free disk space on your first hard disk (/dev/sda) and 30GB of free disk space on your second hard disk (/dev/sdb). During Fedora installation, select to create a custom layout. Then follow this procedure:

1. From the Disk Setup window, click the RAID button. A RAID Options window appears.

2. Select Create a Software RAID Partition, and click OK. The Add Partition window appears.

3. With Software RAID selected as the File System Type, choose the drive you want to create the partition on and choose the size (in megabytes). Then click OK.

4. Repeat Steps 2 and 3 (presumably creating software RAID partitions on different hard disks until you have created all the RAID partitions you want).

5. Click the RAID button again. Select Create a RAID Device [default=/dev/md0] and click OK. The Make RAID Device window appears.

6. You need to specify the following information about your RAID device and click OK:

   - **Mount Point** — The point in the file system associated with the RAID device. You might be creating the RAID device for a part of the file system for which you expect a lot of hits on the hard disk (such as the /var partition).

   - **File System Type** — For a regular Linux partition, choose ext4. You can also select LVM, swap, or VFAT as the file system type.

   - **RAID Device** — The first RAID device is typically md0 (for /dev/md0).

   - **RAID Level** — Allowable RAID levels are RAID0, RAID1, and RAID5. RAID0 is for striping (essentially dividing the RAID device into stripes across RAID partitions you have selected). RAID1 is for mirroring, which duplicates the data across all RAID partitions. RAID5 is for parity, so there is always one backup disk if a disk goes bad. You need at least three RAID partitions to use RAID5.

- **RAID Members** — From the RAID partitions you created, select which ones are going to be members of the RAID device you are creating.

- **Number of spares** — Select how many spares are available to the RAID device.

The new RAID device should appear on the Disk Setup window. Click Next to continue with installation.

Once installation is complete, you can check your RAID devices by using a variety of tools included with Fedora. Commands for working with software RAID partitions are in the mdadm package. Using mdadm commands, you can list and reconfigure your RAID partitions. If your computer has a low-cost ATA RAID controller, often referred to as "fake" hardware RAID due to its heavy reliance on the operating system, you can manage it with the dmraid command.

Checking system space

Running out of disk space on your computer is not a happy situation. Using tools that come with Fedora, you can keep track of how much disk space has been used on your computer, and keep an eye on users who consume a lot of disk space.

Checking disk space with Disk Usage Analyzer

The Disk Usage Analyzer, which is part of the gnome-utils package, provides an easy way to see how much and where space is being consumed on your hard disk. To start Disk Usage Analyzer from the GNOME desktop, select Applications ➪ System Tools ➪ Disk Usage Analyzer.

At first, Disk Usage Analyzer displays only the size of the hard disk and the amount of space that has been consumed on that disk. However, you can see how much disk space is consumed by files in a particular folder (and its subfolders) by selecting the Folder icon and browsing for the folder that interests you. Figure 9-4 shows a music folder containing several music subfolders. You can sort each subfolder alphabetically or by disk space consumed.

Displaying system space with df

You can display the space available in your file systems using the df command. To see how much space is available on all the mounted file systems on your Linux computer, type **df** with no options:

```
$ df
Filesystem          1K-blocks      Used  Available Use% Mounted on
/dev/sda6          448621348   5550340  420282300   2% /
/dev/sda3             806288     34260     731068   5% /boot
tmpfs                2018084       728    2017356   1% /dev/shm
/dev/sda2           15359996   7477104    7882892  49% /mnt/windows
/dev/sdc1           15652928   3419200   12233728  22% /media/BACKUP
```

FIGURE 9-4

Determine where disk space is being used with Disk Usage Analyzer.

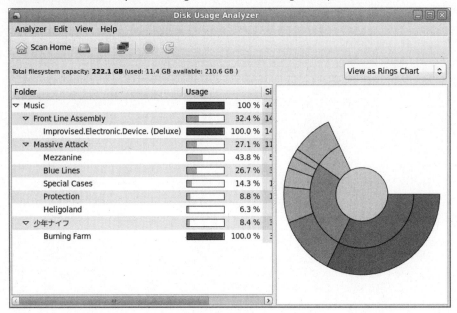

The output here shows the space available on the hard disk partition mounted on the root partition (/dev/sda6), /boot partition (/dev/sda3), a Windows disk partition (/dev/sda2), and the USB drive mounted on the /media/BACKUP directory (/dev/sdc1). Disk space is shown in 1K blocks. To produce output in a more human-readable form, use the -h option:

```
$ df -h
Filesystem      Size  Used Avail Use% Mounted on
/dev/sda6       428G  5.3G  401G   2% /
/dev/sda3       788M   34M  714M   5% /boot
tmpfs           2.0G  728K  2.0G   1% /dev/shm
/dev/sda2        15G  7.2G  7.6G  49% /mnt/windows
/dev/sdf1        15G  3.3G   12G  22% /media/BACKUP
```

With the df -h option, output appears in a friendlier megabyte or gigabyte listing. Other options with df enable you to do the following:

- Print only file systems of a particular type (-t type)
- Exclude file systems of a particular type (-x type)
- Include file systems that have no space, such as /proc and /dev/pts (-a)
- List only available and used inodes (-i)
- Display disk space in certain block sizes (--block-size=#)

Checking disk usage with du

To find out how much space is being consumed by a particular directory (and its subdirectories), you can use the du command. With no options, du lists all directories below the current directory, along with the space consumed by each directory. It returns total disk space used within that directory structure.

The du command is a good way to check how much space is being used by a particular user (du /home/user1) or in a particular file system partition (du /var). By default, disk space is displayed in 1K block sizes. To make the output more friendly (in kilobytes, megabytes, and gigabytes), use the -h option as follows:

```
$ du -h /home/ericfj
1.8M    /home/ericfj/cover_images
4.0K    /home/ericfj/Desktop
4.0K    /home/ericfj/Documents
4.0K    /home/ericfj/Downloads
2.2M    /home/ericfj/Music/reggae/dub
4.3M    /home/ericfj/Music/reggae
4.0K    /home/ericfj/Music/polka
2.2M    /home/ericfj/Music/alternative
2.2M    /home/ericfj/Music/punk/80s
4.3M    /home/ericfj/Music/punk
11M     /home/ericfj/Music
2.2M    /home/ericfj/Pictures/chap09_images
2.2M    /home/ericfj/Pictures
4.0K    /home/ericfj/Public
4.0K    /home/ericfj/Templates
4.0K    /home/ericfj/Videos
22M     /home/ericfj
```

The preceding output shows the disk space used in each directory under the home directory of the user named ericfj (/home/ericfj). Disk space consumed is shown in kilobytes (k) and megabytes (M). Total space consumed by /home/ericfj appears on the last line. To avoid listing all the subdirectories and to see a total for all files and directories below a certain directory, add the -s option as follows:

```
$ du -sh /home/ericfj
22M    /home/ericfj/
```

Finding disk consumption with find

The find command is a great way to find file consumption of your hard disk using a variety of criteria. You can get a good idea of where disk space can be recovered by finding files that exceed a certain size or were created by a particular person.

Note
You must be root user to run this command effectively, unless you are just checking your personal files. ∎

In the following example, the find command searches the root file system (/) for any files owned by the user named jake (-user jake) and prints the filenames. The output of the find command is then listed with a long listing in size order (ls -ldS). Finally, that output is sent to the file /tmp/jake. When you read the file /tmp/jake, you will find all the files owned by the user jake, listed in size order. Here is the command line:

```
# find / -xdev -user jake -print0 | xargs -0 ls -ldS > /tmp/jake
```

Tip

The -xdev option prevents file systems other than the selected file system from being searched. This is a good way to eliminate a lot of junk that may be output from the /proc file system. It can also keep large remotely mounted file systems from being searched. ∎

The next example is similar to the previous one, except that instead of looking for a user's files, this command line looks for files that are larger than 1,000 kilobytes (-size +1000k):

```
# find / -xdev -size +1000k -print0 | xargs -0 ls -ldS > /tmp/size
```

You can save yourself a lot of disk space by just removing some of the largest files that are no longer needed. If you open the /tmp/size file in this example, files are sorted by size.

Monitoring System Performance

If your Linux system is being used as a multiuser computer, sharing the processing power of that computer can be a major issue. Likewise, anytime you can stop a runaway process or reduce the overhead of an unnecessary program running, your Linux server can do a better job serving files, Web pages, or e-mail to the people who rely on it.

Utilities are included with Linux that can help you monitor the performance of your Linux system. The kinds of features you want to monitor in Linux include CPU usage, memory usage (RAM and swap space), and overall load on the system. The following sections describe tools for monitoring Linux.

Watching computer usage with System Monitor

If you like visual representations of your system use, System Monitor provides a great way to see your system usage. To open System Monitor from the Applications menu on the GNOME panel, select System Tools ➪ System Monitor. Figure 9-5 shows the System Monitor window with the Resources tab selected.

In the Resources tab, lines scroll from right to left, indicating the percentage of your CPU usage as it rises and falls. You can also see how much of your total memory (RAM) is being used at the moment (and over time), and the amount of swap space being used. The bar at the bottom of the window shows the amount of data being sent and received over your computer's network interfaces.

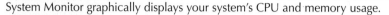

FIGURE 9-5

System Monitor graphically displays your system's CPU and memory usage.

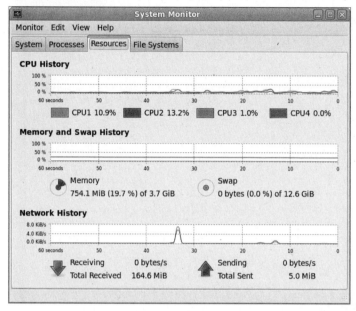

Click the Processes tab to see a listing of processes running for the current user. Click the columns in that tab to sort processes by name, memory use, percentage of CPU being consumed by the process, or process ID.

Click the File Systems tab to see the storage devices (hard disk partitions, CD, USB flash drive, or other) currently mounted on your computer. Click columns to sort the devices by device name, directory name, file system type, total disk space, free disk space, or used disk space.

The example in Figure 9-5 shows a computer that is running with 3.7GB of RAM. Although a fair amount of activity is on the System Monitor in this example, plenty of user memory is available. However, if user memory on your system is running near the maximum, it would indicate the likely occurrence of performance problems as RAM fills up and data has to be moved to swap space. The CPU used shows a fairly low percentage, spread over four processors, which indicates that the CPU is currently keeping up with the demand.

Monitoring CPU usage with top

If you start the top utility in a terminal window, it displays the top CPU-consuming processes on your computer. Every five seconds, top will determine which processes are consuming the most CPU time and display them in descending order onscreen.

By adding the -S option to top, the display will show you the cumulative CPU time that the process, as well as any child processes that may already have exited, has spent. To change how often the screen is updated, add the -d *secs* option, where *secs* is replaced by the number of seconds between updates.

By default, processes are sorted by CPU usage. You can sort processes numerically by PID (press N), by resident memory usage (press M), by time (press T), or back to CPU usage (press P). The following output shows an example of top running, with information sorted by memory use. The system shown is running a GNOME desktop, with OpenOffice.org Writer, Firefox Web browser, and several other applications active. Notice that the amount of memory free is very low. To get good performance out of a Fedora desktop system, 256MB (as shown here) may not be enough once you start running a lot of big applications.

```
top - 16:11:41 up 10:27,  2 users,  load average: 1.60, 0.51, 0.18
Tasks: 107 total,   2 running, 103 sleeping,   0 stopped,   2 zombie
Cpu(s): 16.6%us,  6.5%sy,  0.0%ni,  0.0%id, 76.9%wa,  0.0%hi,  0.0%si,  0.0%st
Mem:    252424k total,   249224k used,     3200k free,     2360k buffers
Swap:  1020088k total,    14240k used,  1005848k free,    86820k cached

  PID USER      PR  NI  VIRT  RES  SHR S %CPU %MEM   TIME+  COMMAND
 4242 chris     18   0  183m  37m  25m R 19.9 15.0  0:05.86 swriter.bin
 4217 chris     15   0  137m  31m  17m S  0.0 12.9  0:07.27 firefox-bin
 4244 chris     15   0 39148  18m 7684 S  0.0  7.6  0:04.94 beagled-helper
 4138 chris     15   0  101m  14m 9.8m S  0.0  5.9  0:06.87 baobab
```

Monitoring power usage on laptop computers

To effectively use a laptop computer, you need to be able to monitor and manage the laptop's power usage. Using tools provided in Fedora, you can configure your laptop to do all of the following:

- Monitor the battery level

- Notify you when the battery is low

- Notify you when the battery is fully charged

- Show you when the laptop is plugged in

- Suspend the current session

Fedora offers two facilities that do power management: APM and ACPI.

- **Advanced Power Management (APM)** — APM can be used to monitor the battery of your notebook and notify user-level programs to tell you when your battery is low. It can also be used to put your laptop into suspend mode.

- **Advanced Configuration and Power Interface (ACPI)** — Besides monitoring power features on your laptop, ACPI can also do thermal control and motherboard configuration, and change power states.

Many older laptops do not include support for ACPI in the BIOS, so you must use APM to monitor and manage your batteries. For some newer laptops, ACPI may be required. In general, ACPI offers a more complete feature set for power management, but APM has more user-level support today.

To check whether ACPI or APM are supported on your Linux system, you can use the `dmesg` command after a reboot. For example, type:

```
# dmesg | less
```

Page through the output looking for lines beginning with text strings `ACPI` or `apm`. On a computer where APM wasn't working, I saw the message "apm: overridden by ACPI." When ACPI wasn't working, I saw the message "ACPI: System description tables not found."

The procedure in the following section was performed on a laptop that uses ACPI to manage power events. It describes how to use the GNOME Power Manager applet on the desktop to monitor your battery.

Note

If it seems that either ACPI or APM are interfering with the proper operation of your laptop, you can turn off either service when you boot your computer. Add either `acpi=off` **or** `apm=off` **to the end of the kernel line (from the GRUB boot screen or the** `/boot/grub/grub.conf` **file) to turn off ACPI or APM, respectively.** ■

Using the GNOME Power Manager applet

If you are using the GNOME desktop, the GNOME Power Manager applet should automatically appear on your panel to keep track of your battery's power levels (if a battery is present). The following procedure outlines the steps to add the monitor to your panel (if it isn't already there) and configure the applet to behave as you like:

1. Move the mouse pointer over the battery icon in the top panel. A tooltip should indicate your battery's current charge level.

2. Right-click the battery icon and select Preferences. The Power Management Preferences window appears.

3. Change any of the following values related to your battery monitor:

    - **On AC Power** — From the On AC Power tab, you can select how many minutes of idle time should elapse before putting the computer or display to sleep. You can also set what happens when the laptop lid is closed (Blank Screen Suspend, Hibernate, or Shutdown). For the display, you can set how long to wait before putting the display to sleep (40 minutes is the default) or whether you want to dim the display when it is idle.

    - **On Battery Power** — The same options described for running on AC power are available when your laptop is running on battery power. You can set what happens to the CPU and display after specified amounts of idle time.

    - **General** — From this tab, you can set the type of notification that occurs when the laptop's power button is pressed or when the suspend button is pressed. You can also set when the battery icon is displayed (when a battery is present, when it is low, or when it is charging or discharging).

The power applet can also show you information about the usage of your battery, such as graphs of charging profiles.

Using apm to enter suspend mode

If the apm service is running, the apm command enables you to view information about your computer's power management, and put the computer in suspend mode (if that's supported on your laptop). Following are some examples using the apm command. With the -m option, the apm command displays the number of minutes of battery life remaining (if that information is available):

```
# apm -m
```

It may also indicate the status showing how the battery is charging and whether or not the laptop is currently plugged in.

The -s option of apm causes the laptop to enter suspend mode:

```
# apm -s
```

You can start up the laptop again, in most cases, by pressing a key on the keyboard.

Using acpi_listen to monitor ACPI events

If ACPI is running on your system, you can monitor ACPI events using the acpi_listen command. As root user, type the following from a terminal window:

```
# acpi_listen
ac_adapter AC 00000080 00000000
processor CPU 00000080 00000000
processor CPU 00000081 00000000
battery BAT0 00000080 00000001
ac_adapter AC 00000080 00000001
processor CPU 00000080 00000000
processor CPU 00000081 00000000
battery BAT0 00000080 00000001
button/lid LID 00000080 00000001
button/lid LID 00000080 00000002
```

The preceding message appeared when the AC power was disconnected, the power was reconnected, the laptop's lid was closed, and the lid was again opened.

You can install the acpi package (yum install acpi) if you would like a command-line tool similar to apm to provide battery information. Once installed, you can run a command such as the following to get information on the AC power adapter:

```
# acpi -a
Adapter 0: on-line
```

If you disconnect the power cord, you'll see output like the following:

```
# acpi -a
Adapter 0: off-line
```

Fixing Your System with the FirstAidKit

Starting with Fedora 10, an included package called FirstAidKit helps you fix many issues that may strike your system. Built on top of a pluggable architecture, FirstAidKit is an automated recovery tool that applies common techniques to try to rescue your system.

To use FirstAidKit, you first need to install the package:

```
# yum install firstaidkit
```

The most common way to run the program is to let it do what it thinks ought to be done — this is the automated part of the recovery tool. To do so, run the following command:

```
# firstaidkit -a
```

The program reports what it finds and the actions it takes.

FirstAidKit works with special plugins designed to help with a particular task. You can install the package `firstaidkit-plugin-all` to get all available plugins. I also recommend installing the `firstaidkit-gui` package to get a GUI for the tool, as shown in Figure 9-6.

FIGURE 9-6

Control FirstAidKit from a graphical window.

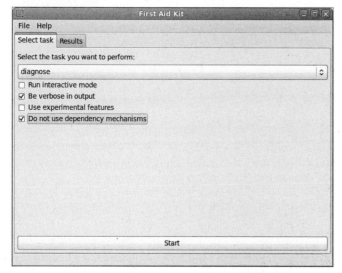

To see a list of the available plugins, use the following command:

```
# firstaidkit --list
```

See `https://fedorahosted.org/firstaidkit/` for more information about FirstAidKit.

Choosing Software Alternatives

Because several software packages are available for every major service available in Linux (such as mail, printing, Java environments, and so on), there will be times when people using the system prefer one service over another. Software packages that have been designed to work with the `alternatives` system can be configured in Fedora to let an administrator choose which of the alternatives to a particular service he or she wants to use by default.

Selecting Java alternatives

If you are developing Java applications, an addition to the alternatives feature lets you switch between using a proprietary Java virtual machine (JVM) or the Open JDK (openjdk), to using the GNU compiler for Java (gcj). Type the following to see which implementation of Java is currently in use on your system:

```
# alternatives --display java
```

Selecting mail alternatives

The main use of the alternatives feature enables you to choose the mail transport services. If the Sendmail, Postfix, and Exim Mail Transport Agents are installed, as an administrator you can choose which of those services is the default for sending and receiving e-mail.

As an administrator, you still need to configure each alternative service to work. Descriptions for configuring Sendmail and Postfix mail-transport agents are contained in Chapter 18.

In terms of defining which alternative you want for mail services, much of the work of creating links so that the services can be chosen is already done. Links relating to the default services are set up in the `/etc/alternatives` directory. Definitions that identify the alternative components of Sendmail, Postfix, and Exim mail servers are contained in the `/var/lib/alternatives` directory.

Because much of the configuration has been done in advance, the first step in switching between the different mail services installed on your computer is only a couple of clicks away. Follow these steps to switch the default mail services on your computer:

1. To switch mail service, type **system-switch-mail**. The switcher window appears. Install the system-switch-mail package if this command is not installed.

2. Click the service you want to switch to — Sendmail, Postfix, or Exim for mail, depending on which are installed. (If the one you want is already selected, you can just cancel.)

3. If the switch is successful, a pop-up window tells you to restart the new service.

4. Click OK to complete the switch and close the pop-up window.

The next time your computer boots, your new mail service takes over that service. All the links are in place and the startup scripts are changed. However, your system is still running the old service. The following startup scripts for those services are in the /etc/init.d directory:

- sendmail — For the Sendmail mail service
- postfix — For the Postfix mail service
- exim — For the Exim mail service

To stop the old service so that the new one can take over, type the following (replacing *servicename* with the name of the service you want to stop):

```
# service servicename stop
```

To start the new service, type the following (replacing *servicename* with the name of the service you want to start):

```
# service servicename start
```

Assuming the new service was configured properly, it should now be available to users.

Using mail alternatives

The mail-transport services that the alternatives facility allows you to change rely on many of the same command names. For example, both Postfix and Sendmail have a newalias command and mailq commands for updating aliases and checking the mail queue, respectively.

Therefore, to the user, a change in the local mail service should (in theory) be nearly invisible. Users can send mail as they always did and the fact that a different mail transport is being used should make no difference.

Using Security Enhanced Linux

Security Enhanced Linux (SELinux) is a security model that offers the potential to compartmentalize and secure every component of a Linux system (processes, files, directories, users, devices, and so on). Instead of the all-or-nothing, either-you-have-root-privilege-or-you-don't approach to security in traditional Linux and Unix systems, SELinux offers much finer granularity in how permissions to run and alter components on the computer are handed out. With SELinux, you can drastically limit the damage caused by a person who cracks one part of a Linux system.

When you first install Fedora, SELinux is installed and enabled, using a default targeted policy. Targeted policies focus on services with vulnerable daemon processes, as well as the resources the services can access.

Targeted policies limit the impact that an attack on the following services can have on your server as a whole: Apache (Web server), Samba (Windows file and print sharing), FTP (file transfer protocol), NFS (network file system), and others. The targeted set of policies is practical and provides additional boundaries around what are already quite secure features. In most cases, you can use this policy set without modification.

The following sections provide an overview of SELinux. They describe how to turn on SELinux in Fedora, how Fedora's targeted policy is set up for you, and how you can modify the targeted SELinux policies to personalize your SELinux policy settings.

With traditional Unix and Linux systems, when a user got root access to your computer, he or she owned the machine. The root user (or whoever took over as root user) could override ownership, read/write/execute permissions, and processor scheduling priorities. Likewise, an attack on a Web server (httpd daemon) could allow an attacker full privileges of the apache user account, rather than limit the attack to a single set of virtual host resources.

Organizations such as the United States National Security Agency (NSA) recognized the need for operating systems in secure environments to be able to separate information in terms of confidentiality and data integrity. The standard security model made Linux and Unix systems unacceptable for highly secure environments, where the risk of one exploit taking down the whole operating system was unacceptable. The mechanism that the NSA recommended to implement highly secure systems is referred to as *Mandatory Access Control (MAC)*.

Traditional Unix and Linux permissions are *Discretionary Access Controls (DAC)*, because determining who has permission to access a resource is left to the discretion of the resource owner. For example, users can make their files group- or world-readable or writable. With SELinux, however, a mandatory policy declares that even if users set files in their home directory to world-readable or writable, other daemons, even running as root, would not be allowed to read or write to those files.

The SELinux project aims to provide MAC functionality in the Linux kernel. By implementing rules governing what all operating system components can and can't do, an application that has security flaws or that has been taken over for malicious intent can be contained. In other words, gaining control of one component of a system doesn't allow a cracker to take over the entire computer.

Types and roles in SELinux

The mechanisms for implementing security rules in SELinux are referred to as *policies*. Any system that implements SELinux selects a particular policy (strict, targeted, and so on) that results in a consistent set of rules that meet the level of security required on the system. Fedora defaults to a targeted policy.

Using policy configuration files, SELinux implements two different security models: *Type Enforcement (TE)* and *Role-Based Access Control (RBAC)*.

- **Type Enforcement** — Under the TE model, every object in the operating system is bound to a security attribute called a *type*. Every process is bound to a security attribute called a *domain*. This approach allows for very tight control of every object in the operating system. Every user is allowed to access objects in the operating system based on the domain in which he or she is allowed to operate.

- **Role-Based Access Control** — Using the RBAC model, SELinux lets each user operate in a specific role. The roles are arranged in a hierarchy, with specific permissions associated with each role provided by type enforcement.

In traditional Linux, a user is assigned a specific user ID (UID) and group ID (GID), which affords that user certain access to system resources. For instance, it gives the user certain rights to read, write, or execute files and directories based on whether that user owns the file or directory or is part of a group assigned to that file or directory.

In SELinux, a data file, directory, or application can have many more attributes associated with it. SELinux helps ensure that having access to the component wouldn't necessarily give that user control of that component in a way that could be exploited beyond what the security policies allow the user to do.

Users in SELinux

The model that SELinux uses to define the rights that users have on an SELinux-enabled system can coexist with the existing Linux user model, rather than replace it. With SELinux enabled, Linux users still have their accounts defined through definitions in the /etc/passwd file. A user who is also assigned a role in SELinux is referred to as a *defined user*.

Special user identities in SELinux include the system_u (the user identity assigned to system processes) and user_u (the assignment used to indicate if general users, in particular those without specific user identities, are allowed to use the feature in question). There is also a root identity, which is retained to allow compatibility with existing file contexts. This allows existing files to remain valid if they have root as their user identity.

Policies in SELinux

As noted earlier, with Fedora you have the choice of either turning off SELinux or turning it on. The values set in the /etc/selinux/config file determine which type of policy is on (only the targeted policy is available by default, but a strict policy is also available) and whether or not SELinux is the following:

- **Enforcing** — The current SELinux policy is turned on and its policies are enforced.
- **Permissive** — The current SELinux policy is on but not enforced (so you only see warning messages describing how the policy would be enforced).
- **Disabled** — SELinux is off, so only standard Linux permissions are enforced (as they always were on systems not including SELinux).

Fedora contains a compiled policy file for the targeted policy it delivers. For example, in the current version of Fedora, /etc/selinux/targeted/policy/policy.24 is the compiled policy set used when that policy is active.

Tools in SELinux

Tools available with SELinux enable you to work with and change policy settings in SELinux. Many of these tools come in the selinux-policy, policycoreutils, setroubleshoot, and setroubleshoot-server packages in the current release of Fedora. Tools include the following:

- **SELinux Troubleshooter** — The SELinux Troubleshooter will start an icon in the desktop panel when SELinux detects something that violates SELinux policy. Click that icon to display the `setroubleshoot` browser window to see descriptions and potential fixes for the problem. You can also start the `setroubleshoot` browser directly by selecting Applications ➪ System Tools ➪ SELinux Troubleshooter.

- **SELinux Policy Generation tool** — Graphical tool for generating your own SELinux policy framework. Application developers or systems administrators can use this tool to confine users or applications to access only those resources they need.

- **SELinux Administration window** — Open the SELinux Administration window (select System ➪ Administration ➪ SELinux Management) to change the status of SELinux (Permissive, Disabled, or Enforcing) or change the default policy type (targeted by default). You can also modify SELinux settings for users, files and directories, policy modules, and network ports.

- **SELinux commands** — A set of command-line tools can be used to modify SELinux policies. These commands include `chcon` (to label files and directories) and `setsebool` (to turn on and off SELinux attributes). To get information on how specific daemon processes are being handled in SELinux, refer to various SELinux policy man pages such as ftpd_selinux, httpd_selinux, kerberos_selinux, named_selinux, nfs_selinux, nis_selinux, rsync_selinux, and ypbind_selinux.

Using SELinux in Fedora

If you use the targeted SELinux policy (which is delivered and on by default), you can still administer Linux as you always have. The following procedure describes the software packages you need to use SELinux and starts you off working with the default targeted policy. If you need additional information, refer to the following:

- **Red Hat Enterprise Linux 4 SELinux Guide** — Describes how to use, administer, and troubleshoot SELinux in Red Hat Enterprise Linux 4. While some of the specific policy settings are different for the most recent Fedora and RHEL versions, this is an excellent guide for understanding how SELinux works in RHEL and Fedora systems. You can find this document at `www.redhat.com/docs/manuals/enterprise/RHEL-4-Manual/ selinux-guide/`.

- **SELinux Documentation** — Most of the documents that come in the selinux-doc package are standards-type documents from the U.S. National Security Agency (NSA). A Fedora 13 SELinux user guide is available online at `http://docs.fedoraproject. org/en-US/Fedora/13/html/Security-Enhanced_Linux/`. Look in the `/usr/`

`share/doc/selinux-doc*` directory of your Fedora system for these files, using your Web browser or PDF file viewer. (You may need to install the `selinux-doc` package.)

Getting SELinux

Support for SELinux is built into the Linux kernel. In fact, SELinux is on by default in the latest releases of Fedora. If you prefer to have SELinux off, after you boot the desktop you can open the SELinux Administration window (select System ➪ Administration ➪ SELinux Management) and set the Enforcing Current selection to Permissive. Permissive causes SELinux to check and note where SELinux would fail, but doesn't actually fail.

With SELinux enabled, you might also want the following software packages installed:

- **checkpolicy** — Contains the SELinux policy compiler named `checkpolicy`. Use this package to build or check policies for SELinux. Using `checkpolicy`, you create binary policy files from policy configurations and parameters in a `policy.conf` file. (Type **man checkpolicy** to read about `checkpolicy`.)

- **libselinux** — Contains the application programming interface for SELinux applications. It includes components used by application programs to check SELinux status.

- **policycoreutils** — Contains basic utilities needed to operate an SELinux system. Commands include `fixfiles` (to check and possibly correct security attributes on file systems), `restorecon` (to set security attributes for selected files), `audit2allow` (to translate messages from `/var/log/messages` to rules that SELinux can use), `newrole` (to open a shell in a new role), `load_policy` (to load a policy file), `run_init` (to run an init script using the correct context), `sestatus` (to check whether SELinux is currently enabled), and `setfiles` (to set the security contexts of files).

- **selinux-doc** — Contains a lot of SELinux documentation that is stored in the `/usr/share/selinux-doc` directory.

- **selinux-policy-mls** — Contains the multilevel security translation table for SELinux.

- **selinux-policy-targeted** — Contains the sample policy file used to incorporate the targeted SELinux policy into a running Linux system, as well as contexts files and the `booleans` file needed to make run-time changes to SELinux.

- **setools** — Contains tools for managing parts of a running policy that define what access users have to different components of the Linux system.

Checking whether SELinux is on

After Fedora is installed, you can check the `/etc/selinux/config` file to see if SELinux is enabled and, if so, which policies are in effect. That file sets two critical variables for a Fedora system configured to use SELinux:

- **SELinux State** — The `SELINUX` variable sets the state of SELinux. If you enable SELinux during Fedora installation this starts out as `SELINUX=enforcing` (which causes security policies for SELinux to be enforced). If SELinux is disabled, `SELINUX=disabled` is set instead. A third option is to set `SELINUX=permissive`, which prints warnings based on the policies you have set, instead of enforcing them.

- **SELinux Policy Type** — The `SELINUXTYPE` variable indicates the type of policy to use. `SELINUX=targeted` protects only selected network daemons (as set in files located in the `/etc/selinux/targeted` directory).

For most practical purposes, if you use SELinux you will want to enable the SELinux targeted policy (which is the default). While not locking down all Fedora components under SELinux, the targeted policy does lock down those daemon processes that are most critical to protect from attacks. Standard Linux security protects everything else in the operating system.

You can override your default settings to place SELinux into permissive mode from the Linux boot prompt by adding the following to the end of the kernel line from the GRUB screen when you boot Fedora:

```
setenforce 0
```

With SELinux in permissive mode (`setenforce 0`), you can still log in and use the system, with any potentially devastating permission failures simply resulting in error messages. If SELinux is in permissive mode, you can likewise return SELinux to enforcing mode from the boot prompt by typing `setenforce 1`. You can change the SELinux state permanently, using the SELinux Administration window.

Checking SELinux status

There are many tools for checking the status of SELinux on your Fedora system. To check whether or not SELinux is enabled, type the following:

```
# sestatus -v | less
SELinux status:         disabled
```

The preceding output shows that SELinux is not enforced on the current system. If SELinux were set to enforcing, the output would look more like the following:

```
SELinux status:                 enabled
SELinuxfs mount:                /selinux
Current mode:                   enforcing
Mode from config file:          enforcing
Policy version:                 24
Policy from config file:        targeted

Process contexts:
Current context:        unconfined_u:unconfined_r:unconfined_t:s0-s0:c0.c1023
Init context:           system_u:system_r:init_t:s0
/sbin/mingetty          system_u:system_r:getty_t:s0
/usr/sbin/sshd          system_u:system_r:sshd_t:s0-s0:c0.c1023
```

```
File contexts:
Controlling term: unconfined_u:object_r:user_devpts_t:s0
/etc/passwd       system_u:object_r:etc_t:s0
/etc/shadow       system_u:object_r:shadow_t:s0
/bin/bash         system_u:object_r:shell_exec_t:s0
/bin/login        system_u:object_r:login_exec_t:s0
/bin/sh           system_u:object_r:bin_t:s0 -> system_u:object_r:shell_exec_t:s0
/sbin/agetty      system_u:object_r:getty_exec_t:s0
/sbin/init        system_u:object_r:bin_t:s0 -> system_u:object_r:init_exec_t:s0
/sbin/mingetty    system_u:object_r:getty_exec_t:s0
/usr/sbin/sshd    system_u:object_r:sshd_exec_t:s0
/lib/libc.so.6    system_u:object_r:lib_t:s0 -> system_u:object_r:lib_t:s0
/lib/ld-linux.so.2  system_u:object_r:lib_t:s0 -> system_u:object_r:ld_so_t:s0
```

Press the spacebar to page through the output. Besides showing that SELinux is enabled and running in enforcing mode, this output shows the process contexts and file contexts that are set.

To see and change basic SELinux settings from a graphical interface, you can open the SELinux Administration window. From the GNOME Desktop, select System ➪ Administration ➪ SELinux Management. From that window, you can set whether SELinux is Disabled, Enforcing, or Permissive. You can also set the SELinux policy to use (targeted is the default).

Changing the policy type or turning the SELinux service from off to on requires that you also relabel the entire file system. Changing policy should never be done lightly. If you do decide to change policy through the SELinux Administration window, that change also requires that the file system be relabeled. By changing the policy through this window, the file system will be relabeled automatically the next time you reboot your computer (or you can select the check box to prevent relabeling the file system on the next reboot).

Note
Relabeling the file system can be a long and time-consuming activity. Again, remember that changing policies is a major change to your operating system. The more nodes there are in your file system, the longer it will take to relabel your file system the next time you boot your computer. ■

You can check the security context in which you are operating using the id command with the -Z option. The following example shows that the current context is the root user, the role is the system_r role, and the type is unconfined_t:

```
# id -Z
unconfined_u:unconfined_r:unconfined_t:s0-s0:c0.c1023
```

SELinux is capable of turning out a lot of error messages. By default, they are directed to the /var/log/messages file.

Working with SELinux on a server

While SELinux supports many advanced features such as categorization (classifying resources usable by only certain departments) and multilevel security (MLS) to implement restricted information flow (secret, top secret), system administrators are usually concerned with only domain and context type compartmentalization. Fedora has made great strides in making SELinux usable for the typical Fedora server and desktop. If you have setroubleshoot installed, you are notified via the GUI and in /var/log/messages when an SELinux enforcement occurs, with possible hints on how to enable the particular access that was denied.

Most of the GNU utilities have been modified to accept the -Z option to see process domains (ps -eZ), files (ls -Z), and so on. If you think SELinux is denying one of your applications access to a particular resource (e.g., a PHP script running via Apache), running the SELinux Management GUI will enable you to set a boolean value to turn off SELinux for that particular daemon or specific features of that daemon.

Here are some brief examples of using SELinux on a typical server:

```
setsebool -P httpd_enable_homedirs on ↵
# allow Apache to read user home directories
restorecon -r /var/www/html
# reset file context by consulting the context database
chcon -t public_content_rw_t /var /ftp/incoming
# manually set a file context
```

You can explore the currently loaded SELinux policy with the sesearch command as follows:

```
# sesearch --allow -s ftpd_t -p write -c dir -t public_content_rw_t -C
Found 2 semantic av rules:
DT allow ftpd_t public_content_rw_t : dir { ioctl read write create getattr ↵
setattr lock unlink link rename add_name remove_name reparent search rmdir ↵
open } ; [ allow_ftpd_anon_write ]
DT allow ftpd_t public_content_rw_t : dir { ioctl read write create getattr ↵
setattr lock unlink link rename add_name remove_name reparent search rmdir ↵
open } ; [ allow_ftpd_full_access ]
```

The preceding example is searching the policy for any allow rules (--allow) that allow the domain ftpd_t (-s) to write (-p write) a directory (-c dir) that has the context type public_content_rw_t (-t), and display any booleans that need to be set to enable the rule (-C). As shown in the output, this rule would be active if allow_ftpd_anon_write is enabled.

Given the helpful nature of setroubleshoot, the ease of use of the SELinux Management GUI, and the fine-grained control to enable or disable specific rules in SELinux, there should be very few cases for which you need to turn SELinux completely off.

Learning more about SELinux

To dig deeper into SELinux, a variety of technical reports, FAQs, and component documents are available. Here are a few places you can try:

- **SELinux FAQs** (`http://docs.fedoraproject.org/en-US/Fedora/13/html/ SELinux_FAQ/`) — This site provides information specific to the SELinux implementation in Fedora.

- **SELinux Wiki** (`http://fedoraproject.org/wiki/SELinux`) — Provides more up-to-date information than the SELinux FAQs

- **SELinux Documentation** (`www.nsa.gov/research/selinux/docs.shtml`) — This site provides links to published papers, technical reports, and presentations related to SELinux.

- **SELinux project** (`http://selinuxproject.org/`) — This site contains a Wiki and FAQ about SELinux.

Summary

Although you may be using Fedora as a single-user system, many of the tasks you must perform to keep your computer running are defined as administrator tasks. A special user account called the root user is needed to do many of the things necessary to keep a Linux system performing as required. If you are administering a Linux system that is used by a lot of people, the task of administration becomes even larger. You must be able to add and support users, maintain the file systems, and ensure that system performance serves your users well.

To help the administrator, Fedora comes with a variety of command-line utilities and graphical windows for configuring and maintaining your system. The FirstAidKit program can be used to diagnose, fix, and recover from system problems. Commands such as mkfs and mount enable you to create and mount file systems, respectively. Tools such as System Monitor and top enable you to monitor system performance.

SELinux adds a new layer of security on top of existing Linux security methods. As a systems administrator, you can choose whether or not to turn on SELinux. You can also choose which of your system services are protected by SELinux.

Setting Up and Supporting Users

## 10

One of the more fundamental and important tasks of administering a Linux system is setting up and supporting user accounts. Computers, after all, are tools to be used by people. Apocalyptic science fiction plots aside, computers have no purpose without users.

Note

When you install Fedora, you automatically create an account, called the *root* user account, to administer the system. The first time you boot Fedora, you are asked to create a regular user account, using any name you choose. Several other administrative user accounts that you will probably never use directly are set up automatically as well (such as apache, ftp, and lp). For a description of the root user account and how to use it, see Chapter 9. ■

This chapter discusses the basics of setting up user accounts and offers tips on easing the burden of supporting a large number of Linux users.

IN THIS CHAPTER

Creating user accounts

Setting user defaults

Extending user authentication

Creating portable desktops

Providing support to users

Deleting user accounts

Checking disk quotas

Sending mail to all users

Creating User Accounts

Every person who uses your Fedora system should have a separate user account. Having a user account provides each person with a dedicated area in which to securely store files. A user account also defines which files and directories a user is permitted to create, modify, or delete throughout the computer's file system.

Some user accounts are automatically created when you install your Linux system. Administrative user accounts (originally UID 0-99, although now UIDs up to 499 are used) are created to maintain separate control of system files and services from regular user accounts. Of the administrative user accounts, you will probably use only root (when some system administration is required).

Regular user accounts are created using any names you choose, starting (by default) with a user ID (UID) of 500. Regular users you add to your Fedora system typically fall into one of two categories:

- **Desktop users** — A desktop user is one whom you expect to use your computer via a graphical interface (typically GNOME or KDE). Create this kind of user account for yourself and anyone else you want to be able to log in directly to your computer (or from a thin client over the network). Most of this section describes how to add this type of user.

- **Server users** — If you are configuring Fedora as a server (Web, mail, FTP, and so on), you may want to add accounts for users who should have only limited access to your system. You may want those users to be able to add content to a Web server or access a mail server but have only a shell login account (or possibly no login account). See the section "Adding user accounts to servers" later in this chapter for information on adding these types of accounts.

Cross-Reference

If you have multiple users, you'll also need to be concerned about backup and recovery issues for those users. See Chapter 12 for more information. ■

You can add user accounts to your Fedora system in several ways. This chapter describes how to use the `useradd` command to add user accounts to Fedora from the command line, and how to use the User Manager window to add users from the desktop.

Adding users with useradd

The most straightforward method for creating a new user from the shell is with the `useradd` command. After opening a terminal window with root permission, simply invoke the `useradd` command at the command prompt, with details of the new account as parameters.

The only required parameter to `useradd` is the login name of the user, but you will probably want to include some additional information. Each item of account information is preceded by a single-letter option code with a dash in front of it. Table 10-1 lists the options that are available with the `useradd` command.

TABLE 10-1

useradd Command Options

Option	Description
`-b base_dir`	Defines a base directory and is needed if you do not specify the `-d` option for the home directory. Appends the user name onto the end of the base directory to define the user's home directory. The directory must exist unless you also use the `-m` option.

Option	Description
-c "comment"	Provides a description of the new user account. Usually this is just the person's full name. Replace comment with the name of the user account. If the comment contains multiple words, use quotation marks.
-d home_dir	Sets the home directory to use for the account. The default is to name it the same as the login name and to place it beneath /home. Replace home_dir with the directory name to use.
-D	Rather than create a new account, saves the supplied information as the new default settings for any new accounts that are created. Stores defaults in the file /etc/default/useradd.
-e expire_date	Assigns the expiration date for the account in MM/DD/YYYY or MM-DD-YYYY format. Replace expire_date with the expiration date to use. This is best used with temporary employees who need the account for only a limited time.
-f inactivity	Sets the number of days after a password expires until the account is permanently disabled. Setting this to 0 disables the account immediately after the password has expired. Setting it to -1 turns off the option, causing the password never to expire, which is the default behavior. Replace inactivity with the number to use.
-g group	Sets the primary group (as listed in the /etc/group file) that the new user will be in. Replace group with the group name to use. The default is to assign the user name as the group name.
-G grouplist	Adds the new user to the supplied comma-separated list of groups.
-k skel_dir	Sets the skeleton directory containing initial configuration files and login scripts that should be copied to a new user's home directory. This parameter can be used only in conjunction with the -m option. Replace skel_dir with the directory name to use.
-K name=value	Allows you to override environmental settings in /etc/login.defs. Pass the name of the environment variable to override, as well as its value.
-m	Automatically creates the user's home directory and copies the files in the skeleton directory (/etc/skel) to it.
-M	Does not create the new user's home directory, even if the default behavior is set to create it.
-N	Turns off the default behavior of creating a new group that matches the name and user ID of the new user.
-o	Uses -u uid to create a user account that has the same user ID as another user name. (This effectively lets you have two different users with authority over the same set of files and directories.)

continued

TABLE 10-1	(continued)
Option	**Description**
`-p passwd`	Enters a password for the account you are adding. This must be an encrypted password. Instead of adding an encrypted password here, you can simply use the `passwd user` command later to add a password for `user`. The user should be asked to immediately change the password you set.
`-r`	Allows you to create a new account with a user ID in the range reserved for system accounts.
`-s shell`	Specifies the command shell to use for this account. Replace `shell` with the command shell.
`-u user_id`	Specifies the user ID number for the account. The default behavior assigns the next available number automatically. Replace `user_id` with the ID number.
`-U`	Creates a group with the same name as the user and adds the user to that group. Normally, this is the default action.
`-Z SELinuxUser`	Defines the SELinux user for the new user's login. If a user is not specified, the system picks the default SELinux user.

As an example, create an account for a new user named John Smith with a login name of `jsmith`. First, log in as root, and then type the following command:

```
# useradd -c  "John Smith" -m jsmith
```

Tip

When you choose a user name, don't begin with a number (e.g., 06jsmith). Also, it is best to use all lowercase letters; no control characters, tabs, special characters, or spaces; and a maximum of eight characters. The `useradd` command allows up to 32 characters, but some applications can't deal with user names that long. Tools such as `ps` display UIDs instead of names if names are too long. Having users named Jsmith and jsmith can cause confusion with programs (such as sendmail) that don't distinguish case. Also, some very old applications may not be able to handle user names with more than eight characters. ∎

Next, set John's initial password using the `passwd` command. The `password` command prompts you to type the password twice. (Asterisks are shown here to represent the password you type. Nothing is actually displayed when you type the password.)

```
# passwd jsmith
Changing password for user jsmith.
New password: *******
Retype new password: *******
```

The `passwd` command will let you know if it thinks you selected a bad password, one that could be easily guessed by using a dictionary or one that is too short or too simple.

The `chage` command, covered in the section on resetting a user's password, allows you to change the password aging and expiration options.

Cross-Reference

See Chapter 13 for tips on creating good passwords. ∎

In creating the account for John, the useradd command performs several actions:

- Reads the /etc/login.defs and /etc/default/usradd files to get default values to use when creating accounts.

- Checks command-line parameters to determine which default values to override.

- Creates a new user entry in the /etc/passwd and /etc/shadow files based on the default values and command-line parameters.

- Creates any new group entries in the /etc/group file.

- Creates a home directory based on the user's name and places it in the /home directory.

- Copies any files located within the /etc/skel directory to the new home directory. This usually includes login and application startup scripts.

The preceding example uses only two of the available useradd options. Most account settings are assigned using default values. Here's an example that uses a few more options:

```
# useradd -m -g users -G wheel,sales -s /bin/tcsh -c "Mary Smith" mary
```

In this case, the useradd command is told to create a home directory for the user mary (-m), make users the primary group she belongs to (-g), add her to the groups wheel and sales (-G), and assign tcsh as her primary command shell (-s). Note that the wheel and sales groups must already exist for this example to work. This results in a line similar to the following being added to the /etc/passwd file:

```
mary:x:502:100:Mary Smith:/home/mary:/bin/tcsh
```

In the /etc/passwd file, each line represents a single user account record. Each field is separated from the next by a colon (:) character. The field's position in the sequence, from left to right, determines what it is. As you can see, the login name is first. The password field contains an x because Fedora is using a shadow password file in which to store encrypted password data. The user ID (UID) selected by the useradd command is 502. The primary group ID (GID) is 100, which corresponds to the users group in the /etc/group file. The comment field was correctly set to Mary Smith, the home directory was automatically assigned as /home/mary, and the command shell was assigned as /bin/tcsh, exactly as specified with the useradd options.

If you omit many of the options (as in the first useradd example), defaults are assigned in most cases. For example, if you didn't use -g users or -G wheel,sales, a group named mary would have been created and assigned to the new user. Likewise, omitting -s /bin/tcsh causes /bin/bash to be assigned as the default shell.

The /etc/group file holds information about the different groups on your Fedora system and the users who belong to them. Groups are useful for allowing multiple people to share access to

the same files while denying access to others. If you peek at the /etc/group file, you should find
something similar to this:

```
root:x:0:root
bin:x:1:root,bin,daemon
daemon:x:2:root,bin,daemon
sys:x:3:root,bin,adm
adm:x:4:root,adm,daemon
tty:x:5:
disk:x:6:root
lp:x:7:daemon,lp
mem:x:8:
kmem:x:9:
wheel:x:10:root,joe,mary
          .
          .

          .
nobody:x:99:
users:x:100:mary
chris:x:500
sheree:x:501
sales:x:601:bob,jane,joe,mary
```

Each line in the group file contains the name of a group, the group ID number associated with
it, and a list of users in that group. By default, each user is added to his or her own group, beginning with GID 500. Note that mary was added to the wheel and sales groups instead of having
her own group.

Adding mary to the wheel group is actually rather significant. By doing this, you can easily grant
her the capability to use the sudo command to run commands as the root user, provided that
the wheel line is uncommented from the /etc/sudoers file (as described in Chapter 9), which
it is not by default. (The wheel group is used by convention as a sudoers group. You can define
other such groups as well.)

This example used the -g option to assign mary to the users group. If you omit the -g parameter, the default behavior is for useradd to create a new group with the same name and ID number as the user; this group is assigned as the new user's primary group. For example, consider the
following useradd command:

```
# useradd -m -G wheel,sales -s /bin/tcsh -c "Mary Smith" mary
```

That would result in an /etc/passwd entry like this:

```
mary:x:502:502:Mary Smith:/home/mary:/bin/tcsh
```

It would also result in a new group entry like this:

```
mary:x:502:
```

Note that the UID and GID fields now have the same number. If you set up all of your users this way, you will have a unique group for every user on the system, thus allowing for increased flexibility in the sharing of files among your users.

Adding users with the Account Information dialog

Starting with Fedora 13, you can use the Account Information dialog to add users. Part of the `accountsdialog` package, this program is intended to replace applications such as `system-config-users` and `gnome-about-me`. As of Fedora 14, though, the `accountsdialog` program does not yet support editing groups, and so is not installed by default. To install this program, run the `yum install accountsdialog` command.

Installing the `accountsdialog` package will also install the `accountsservice` and `apg` (automatic password generator) packages. To launch the application from the GNOME desktop, select System ➪ Administration ➪ Users. You'll see a window like that in Figure 10-1.

Add user accounts from the Account Information dialog.

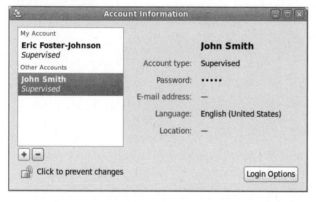

As shown in Figure 10-1, the Account Information dialog sports a minimalist interface similar to that of Mac OS X. You can add new users or perform minimal account editing. To add a new user, first click the lock icon to make changes. You'll be prompted for the root user password. Next, click the plus icon to add a new user. Then, start typing the user's real name. The application will create a user name for you. You can also specify whether the account is Standard, for an Administrator, or Supervised. Accounts created by the `useradd` command, and the account you create for yourself on the first boot of Fedora, appear as Supervised. (Don't worry about the differences, the accounts are created the same way for Supervised and Standard.)

One nice feature is that you can create a new user account with a password set now, or allow the user to choose a password on the next login. Furthermore, the program will handily help you choose a good password. To do this, click the password entry for a user (you'll see a series of dots that represent the user's password). As you mouse over the entry, you'll see an effect like a button. Click this to invoke a window like that shown in Figure 10-2.

FIGURE 10-2

You can test the strength of passwords from the useraccounts program.

Choose an Action, such as Disable account, Choose password at next login, or Set a password now. Click the gear icon (this is not an easy program to understand) to see a list of reasonably complex passwords. A handy meter indicates the password strength.

In addition, if you add a picture for yourself (any picture) from the GNOME About Me dialog (System ➪ Preferences ➪ About Me), then you can click the picture to change it or take a picture if your system has a built-in webcam.

Tip

As of Fedora 14, this application is not yet complete and may well induce all sorts of frustration. Neither the no-password nor the set password at next login options work. However, the application does help choose reasonably good passwords, and you can use the webcam to take a snapshot. ∎

Adding users with User Manager

If you prefer the older graphical window for adding, changing, and deleting user accounts, try the User Manager window instead. To open the window from the GNOME desktop, select System ➪ Administration ➪ Users and Groups (or type **system-config-users** from a terminal window as root user). Figure 10-3 shows an example of the User Manager window.

FIGURE 10-3

Manage users from the User Manager window.

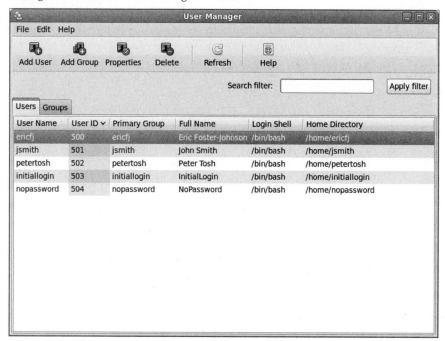

Opening the User Manager window displays a list of all regular users currently added to your computer. Administrative users (UID 1 through 499) are not displayed (but can be by changing preferences). For each user, you can see the user name, UID, primary group, full name, login shell, and home directory. Click any of those headings to sort the users by that information.

To add a new user from the User Manager window, do the following:

1. Click the Add User button to open the Add New User dialog (see Figure 10-4).

2. Enter the requested information in the following fields:

   ● **User Name** — A single word to describe the user. Typically, the user name is eight characters, all lowercase, containing the user's real first name, last name, or (more often) a combination of the two (such as jwjones).

   ● **Full Name** — The user's full name (usually first name, middle initial, and last name). This name is typically used only for display, so using uppercase and lowercase is fine.

   ● **Password** — The user's initial password. (Ask users to change this password the first time they log in to the new account, which they can do by running the `passwd` command.)

- **Confirm Password** — Type the password again, to ensure it was entered correctly.
- **Login Shell** — This is the default shell (for entering typed commands) that the user sees when first logging in to Fedora from a character display.
- **Create home directory** — By default, this check box is selected and the user's home directory (as indicated by the Home Directory field) is created automatically.
- **Home Directory** — By default, the user is given a home directory of the user's name in the /home directory. (For example, the user sheree would be assigned /home/sheree as her home directory.) Change this field if you want to assign the user to a different home directory.
- **Create a private group for the user** — Check this box if you want a group with the same name as the user created for this user. The name is added to the /etc/group file. This feature is referred to as a user private group (UPG).
- **Specify user ID manually** — Typically, you would not check this box, so that the UID for the new user would be assigned automatically. New UIDs for regular users start at 500. However, if you want to assign a particular UID for a user (e.g., if you want to match the UID with the UID from another computer on your network), select this box and type the number you want to use in the UID box.
- **Specify group ID manually** — Like the user ID, you would typically just have the group ID automatically assigned; but you can assign a different GID to have the user assigned to a particular group.

3. Click OK when you are done. The new user is added to the /etc/passwd and /etc/group files. The user account is now available for that user to log in.

FIGURE 10-4

The Add New User dialog.

Tip

Fedora uses a user private group (UPG) scheme, which makes Unix groups easier to use. The UPG scheme does not add or change anything in the standard Unix way of handling groups; it simply offers a new convention. Whenever you create a new user, by default that user has a unique group. You can extend this scheme for sharing files among several users. Here's an example:

```
# useradd -m projectx
# mkdir /usr/local/x
# chown root.projectx /usr/local/x
# chmod 2775 /usr/local/x
# ls -ld /usr/local/x
drwxrwsr-x 2 root projectx 4096 Aug 18 01:54 /usr/local/x
# gpasswd -a nextuser projectx
```

This example creates a user named projectx (with a group named projectx); creates a /usr/local/x directory and has it owned by root user and the projectx group; sets the setgid bit to be on for the group (2); opens full read/write/execute permissions for user and group (77); and opens read and execute permissions for everyone else (5). Add each user to the group that you want to be able to write to the projectx directory (replace nextuser with the user you want to add). After that, regardless of a user's primary group, any file created in the /usr/local/x directory by a user can be read or modified by anyone in the projectx group. ∎

Setting User Defaults

The useradd command and User Manager window both determine the default values for new accounts by reading the /etc/login.defs and /etc/default/useradd files. You can modify those defaults either by editing those files manually with a standard text editor or by running the useradd command with the -D option. If you choose to edit the files manually, here is what you face:

```
# *REQUIRED*
# Directory where mailboxes reside, _or_ name of file, relative to the
# home directory. If you _do_ define both, MAIL_DIR takes precedence.
# QMAIL_DIR is for Qmail
#
#QMAIL_DIR Maildir
MAIL_DIR     /var/spool/mail
#MAIL_FILE .mail

# Password aging controls:
#
# PASS_MAX_DAYS Maximum number of days a password may be used.
# PASS_MIN_DAYS Minimum number of days allowed between password changes.
# PASS_MIN_LEN  Minimum acceptable password length.
# PASS_WARN_AGE Number of days warning given before a password
# expires.
#
```

```
PASS_MAX_DAYS      99999
PASS_MIN_DAYS      0
PASS_MIN_LEN       5
PASS_WARN_AGE      7


#
# Min/max values for automatic uid selection in useradd
#
UID_MIN                  500
UID_MAX                  60000


#
# Min/max values for automatic gid selection in groupadd
#
GID_MIN                  500
GID_MAX                  60000


#
# If defined, this command is run when removing a user.
# It should remove any at/cron/print jobs etc. owned by
# the user to be removed (passed as the first argument).
#
#USERDEL_CMD /usr/sbin/userdel_local


#
# If useradd should create home directories for users by default.
# On RH systems, we do. This option is overridden with the -m flag on
# useradd command line.
#
CREATE_HOME yes
# The permission mask is initialized to this value. If not
# specified, the permission mask will be initialized to 022.
UMASK             077

# This enables userdel to remove groups if no members exist.
#
USERGROUPS_ENAB yes

# Use SHA512 encrypt password.

ENCRYPT_METHOD SHA512
```

Lines beginning with a hash mark (#) are ignored. All other lines contain keyword/value pairs. For example, the keyword MAIL_DIR is followed by some white space and the value /var/spool/mail. This tells useradd that the initial user e-mail mailbox is created in that directory. Following that are lines which enable you to customize the valid range of automatically assigned user ID numbers or group ID numbers. A comment section explaining that keyword's purpose precedes each keyword. Altering a default value is as simple as editing the value associated with that keyword and then saving the login.defs file.

Default settings that can be modified with the useradd command are stored in the /etc/default/useradd file. Here is an example of that file:

```
GROUP=100
HOME=/home
INACTIVE=-1
EXPIRE=
SHELL=/bin/bash
SKEL=/etc/skel
CREATE_MAIL_SPOOL=yes
```

You can view and modify that file directly. Alternatively, you could view the defaults by typing the useradd command with the -D option as follows:

```
# useradd -D
```

You can also use the -D option to change defaults. When run with this flag, useradd refrains from actually creating a new user account; instead, it saves any additionally supplied options as the new default values in /etc/default/useradd. Not all useradd options can be used in conjunction with the -D option. You can use only the five options listed in Table 10-2.

TABLE 10-2

useradd Options for Changing User Defaults

Options	Description
-b *default_home*	Sets the default directory in which user home directories will be created. Replace *default_home* with the directory name to use. Usually this is /home.
-e *default_expire_date*	Sets the default expiration date on which the user account is disabled. The *default_expire_date* value should be replaced with a date in the form MM/DD/YYYY — for example, 10/15/2010.
-f *default_inactive*	Sets the number of days after a password has expired before the account is disabled. Replace *default_inactive* with a number representing the number of days.
-g *default_group*	Sets the default group in which new users will be placed. In Fedora, useradd creates a new group with the same name and ID number as the user, so this value is ignored. To set a different primary group for a user, you must set it explicitly with the -g option on the command line.
-s *default_shell*	Sets the default shell for new users. Typically this is /bin/bash. Replace *default_shell* with the full path to the shell that you want as the default for new users.

To set any of the defaults, use the -D option first, then add any of the defaults you want to set. For example, to set the default home directory location to /home/everyone and the default shell to /bin/tcsh, type the following:

```
# useradd -D -b /home/everyone -s /bin/tcsh
```

Besides setting up user defaults, administrators can create default files that are copied to each user's home directory for use. These files can include login scripts and shell configuration files (such as .bashrc). The following sections describe some of these files.

Supplying initial login scripts

Many Linux applications, including the command shell itself, read a configuration file at startup. Typically, these configuration files are stored in the users' home directories. This enables each user to customize the behavior of the command shell and other applications without affecting that behavior for other users. Global defaults can be assigned from /etc/profile, and then those settings can be customized by a user's personal files.

The bash command shell, for example, looks for a file called .bashrc in the current user's home directory whenever it starts up. Similarly, the tcsh command shell looks for a file called .tcshrc in the user's home directory. You may see a repeating theme here. Startup scripts and configuration files for various applications usually begin with a dot (.) character and end in the letters rc (which stands for *run commands*). You can supply initial default versions of these and other configuration files by placing them in the /etc/skel directory. When you run the useradd command, these scripts and configuration files are copied to the new user's home directory.

Supplying initial .bashrc and .bash_profile files

By supplying your users with initial .bashrc and .bash_profile files, you give them a starting point from which they can further customize their shell environments. This also ensures that files are created with the appropriate access permissions, in order not to compromise system security without the user's knowledge.

The .bash_profile script is run each time the user starts a new bash shell and, in turn, runs the .bashrc script. Therefore, security is a concern. The .bash_profile file sets the original PATH used by the user, so it is a good place to add directories containing binaries you want the user to be able to run at your location. You can also add other startup programs you want to run automatically for every user. Here's an example of the .bash_profile file:

```
# .bash_profile

# Get the aliases and functions
if [ -f ~/.bashrc ]; then
        . ~/.bashrc
fi

# User specific environment and startup programs
```

```
PATH=$PATH:$HOME/bin
export PATH
```

The `.bashrc` file is a good place to supply useful command aliases and additions to the command search path. Here's an example of a `.bashrc` file:

```
# .bashrc


# Source global definitions
if [ -f /etc/bashrc ]; then
        . /etc/bashrc
fi
# User specific aliases and functions
alias rm='rm -i'
alias cp='cp -i'
alias mv='mv -i'
```

This sample `.bashrc` file executes `/etc/bashrc` (if it exists) to read any additional global bash values. Next, the file creates aliases for the `rm`, `cp`, and `mv` commands, which results in an `-i` option always being used (unless overridden with the `-f` option). This protects against the accidental deletion of files.

Supplying an initial .tcshrc file

The following example `.tcshrc` file does basically the same thing as the preceding `.bashrc` example. However, this file (which is for the root user) has the additional task of setting the appearance of the command prompt:

```
# .tcshrc

# User specific aliases and functions

alias rm 'rm -i'
alias cp 'cp -i'
alias mv 'mv -i'

setenv PATH "$PATH:/usr/bin:/usr/local/bin"

set prompt='[%n@%m %c]# '
```

Instead of using the `export` command to set environment variables, the `tcsh` shell uses the `setenv` command. In the example, `setenv` is used to set the `PATH` variable. The shell prompt is set to include your user name (%n), your computer name (%m), and the name of the current directory (%c). So, if you were to use the `tcsh` shell as the root user on a computer named `maple` with `/tmp` as your current directory, your prompt would appear as follows:

```
[root@maple /tmp]#
```

The .tcshrc file can also be named .cshrc. The tcsh shell is really an extended version of the csh shell (in fact, you can invoke it with the csh name). When a tcsh shell is started, it first looks for a .tcshrc file in the current user's home directory. If it can't find a file by that name, it looks for the other name, .cshrc. Thus, either name is appropriate.

Configuring system-wide shell options

Allowing individually customizable shell startup files for each user is a very flexible and useful practice; but sometimes you need more centralized control than that. You may have an environment variable or other shell setting that you want set for every user, without exception. If you add that setting to each individual shell, the user can edit that file and remove it. Furthermore, if that setting needs to be changed in the future, you must change it in every single user's shell startup file.

Configuring system-wide bash options

Fortunately, there is a better way. There are default startup files that apply to all users of the computer that each command shell reads before reading the user-specific files. In the case of the bash command shell, it reads the /etc/bashrc file before doing anything else.

Note
While you can put system-wide options in the /etc/bashrc file, users can override these settings. ∎

Configuring system-wide tcsh options

Similarly, the tcsh shell reads the /etc/csh.cshrc file before processing the .cshrc or .tcshrc file found in the user's home directory.

The /etc/cshrc and /etc/bashrc files set a variety of shell environment options. If you want to modify or add to the shell environment supplied to every single user on the system, the /etc/bashrc or /etc/cshrc file is the place to do it.

Setting system profiles

Some of the most basic information assigned to each user is added from the /etc/profile file. Therefore, if you want to change any of the following information, you can start from /etc/profile. The contents of the /etc/profile file is sourced into each user's shell only to the initial login shell. Here are some values contained in /etc/profile:

- **PATH** — Assigns the default PATH for the root user and for all other users. You might change this value to add PATHs to local directories containing applications that all users need.

- **Environment variables** — Shell environment variables that are needed for standard operation are assigned in this file. These include USER (set by the id -un command), LOGNAME (same as USER), MAIL (set to /var/spool/mail/$USER), HOSTNAME (set to the output of the command /bin/hostname), and HISTSIZE (which sets shell command history to 1,000 items).

The last thing the /etc/profile file does is look at the contents of the /etc/profile.d directory and source in the files that it finds. Each file contains settings that define environment variables or aliases that affect how users can use the shell. For example, the lang.sh and lang.csh files identify the locations of foreign-language files. The vim files create aliases that cause vim to be used when vi is typed. The which2.sh file defines a set of options used by the which command.

You can modify the profile.d files or add your own to have environment variables and aliases set for all of your users. In fact, if you do want to modify the shell startup settings across the entire system, it is best to put your changes into a new file in /etc/profile.d instead of editing /etc/profile directly.

Adding user accounts to servers

When you set up a server, you often want to allow users to either upload files to it or download files or messages from it. However, you may not want to allow those people access to the entire server. You can begin limiting access to those users when you first create their user accounts.

To prevent a remote user from logging in and accessing a shell (via ssh, telnet, or another login service), you can set the default shell for a user to nologin. For example:

```
# useradd -s /sbin/nologin jerryb
```

With the shell set to nologin, this user would not be able to log in to the server to open a shell. However, the user could still use this account to log in to an FTP service on the server (if the service is available and the user has a password). By default, the user's home directory in this example when he logged in via FTP would be /home/jerryb.

Cross-Reference
See Chapter 19 for ways in which you can restrict this user to access only his home directory in a chroot environment. ■

Another approach to FTP-only access to a server is to use /usr/libexec/openssh/sftp-server as a user's login shell. While this allows users access to the entire file system that is available to the user account, it restricts them to accessing the server via secured FTP only.

A common practice with Web hosting is to allow a user to place content on the server, often in that user's /home/username/public_html directory, using FTP (but no shell login). However, the administrator could choose to assign the location for the Web content to be any directory, including the system-wide Web server directory. The following command assigns the user named webuser to use /var/www/html as his home directory (you should also change ownership of the files to belong to webuser for this to work):

```
# useradd -s /sbin/nologin -d /var/www/html webuser
```

If you were adding a user for mail service access only, you might choose to prevent any access to FTP as well. One way to do that is to point the user's home directory to /dev/null:

```
# useradd -s /sbin/nologin -d /dev/null jerryb
```

Once you have set up a limited user account, you can further define what your server's users can and cannot access, using features associated with the particular service.

Creating Portable Desktops

Linux is an operating system that was born on the Internet, so it is not surprising that it has strong networking capabilities. This makes Linux an excellent server, and it also enables Linux to be an excellent desktop workstation, especially in a highly networked environment. Fedora enables you to easily set up your users with a portable desktop that follows them from computer to computer, something you can't do as easily with other leading desktop operating systems.

Typically, a Linux user's home directory is located within the /home directory. As an alternative, within the home directory you can create a directory named after the system's host name. Within that directory, create the users' home directories. Thus, on a Linux system named dexter, the user mary would have a home directory of /home/dexter/mary instead of /home/mary. There is a very good reason for doing this.

If you are logged in to the Linux system ratbert and would like to access your home directory on dexter as if it were stored locally, the best approach is to use Network File System (NFS) to mount dexter's /home directory on the /home on ratbert. As a result, you have the same contents of your home directory available to you no matter which machine you log in to.

To mount dexter's /home directory as described, add a line similar to the following in ratbert's /etc/fstab file:

```
dexter:/home /home nfs defaults 0 0
```

Also add an entry such as the following in dexter's /etc/exports directory:

```
/home ratbert(sync)
```

Now, when ratbert boots up, dexter's home partition is automatically mounted over the network. This enables you to treat the remote files and directories on dexter's /home as if they were locally stored on ratbert. Unfortunately, this has the side effect of "covering up" ratbert's actual /home directory.

This is where the extra directory level based on the system name comes to the rescue. With all of dexter's home directories located in /home/dexter and all of ratbert's home directories located in /home/ratbert, you can remove the danger of one system covering up the home directories of another. In fact, let's take this example one step further: Imagine a scenario in which the systems dexter, ratbert, and daffy all have portable desktops that are shared with the other systems. The /etc/fstab and /etc/exports files for each system should have the following lines added to them as indicated:

/etc/exports file

```
/home/dexter ratbert,daffy
```

/etc/fstab file

```
ratbert:/home/ratbert /home/ratbert nfs defaults 0 0
daffy:/home/daffy     /home/daffy   nfs defaults 0 0
```

The /etc/exports and /etc/fstab files for ratbert are as follows:

/etc/exports file

```
/home/ratbert dexter,daffy
```

/etc/fstab file

```
dexter:/home/dexter /home/dexter nfs defaults 0 0
daffy:/home/daffy   /home/daffy   nfs defaults 0 0
```

The /etc/exports and /etc/fstab files for daffy are as follows:

/etc/exports file

```
/home/daffy ratbert,dexter
```

/etc/fstab file

```
ratbert:/home/ratbert /home/ratbert  nfs defaults 0 0
dexter:/home/dexter   /home/dexter   nfs defaults 0 0
```

As you can see, each system uses NFS to mount the home directories from the other two systems. A user can travel from server to server and see exactly the same desktop on each system.

Providing Support to Users

Creating new user accounts is just one small administrative task among many. No single chapter can adequately discuss all the tasks that are involved in the ongoing support of users; but I'll share with you a few hints and procedures to ease that burden.

Creating a technical support mailbox

E-mail is a wonderful communication tool, especially for the overworked system administrator. People usually put more thought and effort into their e-mail messages than into their voicemail messages. A text message can be edited for clarity before being sent, and important details can be copied and pasted from other sources. This makes e-mail an excellent method for Linux users to communicate with their system administrators.

In an office with only a few users, you can probably get away with using your personal mailbox to send and receive support e-mails. In a larger office, however, you should create a separate mailbox reserved for technical support issues. This has several advantages over using your personal mailbox:

- Support messages will not be confused with personal, nonsupport-related messages.
- Multiple people can check the mailbox and share administrative responsibility without needing to read each other's personal e-mail.
- Support e-mail is easily redirected to another person's mailbox when you go on vacation. Your personal e-mail continues to go to your personal mailbox.

One easy solution is to simply create a support e-mail alias that redirects messages to an actual mailbox or list of mailboxes. For example, suppose you want to create a support alias that redistributes e-mail to the user accounts for support staff members Joe, Mary, and Bob. Log in as root, edit the /etc/aliases file, and add lines similar to the following:

```
# Technical support mailing list
support: joe, mary, bob
```

After saving the file, you need to run the newaliases command to recompile the /etc/aliases file into a database format. Now your users can send e-mail to the support e-mail address, and the message will be automatically routed to everyone on the list. When a member of the list responds to that message, he or she should use the Reply To All option so that the other support staff members also see the message. Otherwise, multiple people may attempt to solve the same problem, resulting in duplication of effort.

You may also choose to create a support user account. The technical support staff would log in to this account to check messages and send replies. This way, all replies are stamped with the support login name, not the personal e-mail address of a staff member.

Resetting a user's password

One common (if not *the* most common) problem that your users may encounter is the inability to log in for one of the following reasons:

- They have the Caps Lock key on.

- They have forgotten the password.
- The password has expired.

If the Caps Lock key is not on, you probably need to reset the user's password. You can't look up the password because Linux stores hashed forms of passwords. Instead, use the passwd command to assign a new password to the user's account. Give the user the new password (preferably in person), but then set the password to expire soon so that he or she must choose one (let's hope one that is more easily remembered).

If you must reset a user's password, do so with the passwd command. While logged in as root, type **passwd** followed by the login name you are resetting. You are prompted to enter the password twice. For example, to change the password for mary, type:

```
# passwd mary
```

After resetting the password, set it to expire so the user has to change it the next time she logs in. You can use the chage command to set an expiration period for the password and to trick the system into thinking that the password is long overdue to be changed:

```
# chage -M 30 -d 0 mary
```

The -M 30 option tells the system to expire Mary's password every 30 days. The -d 0 option tricks the system into thinking that her password has not been changed since January 1, 1970. (Keep in mind that using chage activates password aging for any account on which it is used. Adding a -1 to the chage command line disables password aging.)

Modifying Accounts

Occasionally a user needs more done to an account than just a resetting of the password. You may need to change the groups that a user is in, the drive on which a home directory resides, or a person's name may change because of a change in marital status. The following sections explain how to modify user accounts using one of two methods: usermod or the User Manager application.

Modifying user accounts with usermod

The usermod command is similar to the useradd command and even has some of the same options. However, instead of adding new accounts, it enables you to change various details of existing accounts. When invoking the usermod command, you must provide account details to change followed by the login name of the account. Table 10-3 lists the available options for the usermod command.

TABLE 10-3

usermod Options for Changing Existing Accounts

Options	Description
-a	Adds the user to the supplemental groups when used with the -G option.
-c "comment"	Changes the description field of the account. Nonroot users can use the chfn command to change this field for themselves. Replace comment with a name or other description of the user account. Because the comment can contain multiple words, the quotation marks are necessary.
d home_dir	Changes the home directory of the account to the specified new location. If the -m option is included, copies the contents of the home directory as well. Replace home_dir with the full path to the new directory.
-e expire_date	Assigns a new expiration date for the account, replacing expire_date with a date in the MM/DD/YYYY format.
-f inactivity	Sets the number of days after a password expires until the account is permanently disabled. Setting inactivity to 0 disables the account immediately after the password has expired. Setting it to -1 turns off the option, which is the default behavior.
-g group	Changes the primary group (as listed in the /etc/group file) that the user is in. Replace group with the name of the new group.
-G grouplist	Sets the list of groups, besides the user's private group, to which the user belongs. Replace grouplist with a comma-separated list of groups. (If you don't use -G with the -a option, the user is removed from existing supplemental groups when the new ones are added.)
-1 login_name	Changes the login name of the account to the name supplied after the -1 option. Replace login_name with the new name. This does not automatically change the name of the home directory; use the -d and -m options for that.
-L	Locks a password and places a ! in the password field. To lock an account, also set the expiration date to 1.
-m	This option is used only in conjunction with the -d option. It causes the contents of the user's home directory to be copied to the new directory.
-o	This option is used only in conjunction with the -u option. It removes the restriction that user IDs must be unique.
-p passwd	Enters a password for the account you are modifying. This must be an encrypted password. Rather than set an encrypted password here, you can simply use the passwd user command later to add a password for user. The user should be asked to immediately change the password you set.

Options	Description
`-s` *shell*	Specifies a new command shell to use with this account. Replace *shell* with the full path to the new shell.
`-u` *user_id*	Changes the user ID number for the account. Replace *user_id* with the new user ID number. Unless the `-o` option is used, the ID number must not be in use by another account.
`-U`	Unlocks a user password.
`-Z` *SELinuxUser*	Defines the SELinux user for the user's login. If no user is specified, the system picks the default SELinux user.

Assume that a new employee named Jenny Barnes will be taking over Mary's job. We want to convert the mary account to a new name (`-l jenny`), new comment (`-c "Jenny Barnes"`), and home directory (`-d /home/jenny`). You can do that with the following command:

```
# usermod -l jenny -c "Jenny Barnes" -m -d /home/jenny mary
```

Furthermore, if after converting the account you learn that Jenny prefers the `tcsh` shell, you can make that change with the `-s` option (`-s /bin/tcsh`):

```
# usermod -s /bin/tcsh jenny
```

Instead, you can use the `chsh` command to change the shell. The following is an example:

```
$ chsh -s /bin/tcsh jenny
```

The `chsh` command is handy because it enables regular users to change their own shell setting to any shell listed in the `/etc/shells` file. (The root user can change his or her own shell to any command desired.) Simply omit the user name parameter when invoking the command, and `chsh` assumes the currently logged-in user as the account to change.

Users can also change their own user information using the `chfn` command. This information is stored in the `/etc/passwd` file and displayed when you type the `finger` command (e.g., `finger jenny`, to get information on a given user). In this example, the full name, office name, office phone, home phone, and work phone are set by the user jenny:

```
$ chfn -f "J Smith" -o "A-111" -p 555-1212 -h 555-2323 jenny
```

Users can also add information about themselves in the `.plan`, `.project`, `.forward`, and `.pgpkey` files in their home directory. That information will then be picked up by the `finger` command. The `finger` command "fingers" users, or more politely, tells you who a user is (from information in `/etc/passwd`, `.forward`, and `.pgpkey` files) and what the user is working on (from information in the `.plan` and `.project` files). The `finger` command is part of the `finger` package, and is not installed by default.

Note

The `finger` command opens potential security issues. Finger gives out personal information that can be useful to those who want to crack your system. In addition, malicious users can flood your servers with `finger` requests. So, be careful about what information you provide to the system in these files. You may also want to block ports 79 and 2003 (the `finger` ports) with your firewall. See Chapter 13 for more on firewalls. ∎

Modifying user accounts with User Manager

To use the desktop to change an existing account, use the User Manager. Here's how to modify a user account from the User Manager application:

1. Select System ➪ Administration ➪ Users and Groups (or type `system-config-users` from a terminal window as root user). The main User Manager application window appears.

2. Select the user name of the account you want to modify, and then click the Properties button to open the User Properties dialog (see Figure 10-5).

FIGURE 10-5

The User Properties dialog allows you to modify a user account.

3. There are four tabs of information you can modify for the user you selected:

    *   **User Data** — This tab contains the user information you created when you first added the user account.

    *   **Account Info** — Select the Enable Account Expiration check box, and then type a date if you want the account to become inaccessible after a particular date. Select the Local Password Is Locked check box if you want to prevent access to the account but not delete it. (This is a good technique when an employee is leaving the com-

pany or you want to lock out a customer whose account is temporarily disabled. The information isn't removed; it just isn't accessible.)

- **Password Info** — Select Enable Password Expiration if you want to control expiration of the user's password. By default, passwords don't expire. Here are your options: "Days before change allowed" (forces the user to keep the password for at least a set number of days before it can be changed); "Days before change required" (allows the user to keep the same password for at least the set number of days); "Days warning before change" (sets how many days before the password expiration day that the user is warned to change the password); "Days before account inactive" (sets the number of days after which the account is deactivated).

- **Groups** — Select from the list of available groups to add the user to one or more of those groups.

4. Click OK to apply the changes to the user account.

Deleting User Accounts

Occasionally, it is necessary to remove a user account from your Linux system. This can be done with either the userdel command or the User Manager window.

Deleting user accounts with userdel

The userdel command takes a single argument: the login name of the account to delete. If you supply the -r option, it also deletes the user's home directory and all the files in it. With the -f option, you force the removal of the account even if the user is logged in, which is useful if you suspect malicious activity. To delete the user account with login name mary, type the following:

```
# userdel mary
```

To wipe out her home directory along with her account, type this:

```
# userdel -r mary
```

Before wiping these files out, you should verify that the files are no longer needed (or ensure you have a good backup of the files).

Files owned by the deleted user but not located in the user's home directory will not be deleted. The system administrator must search for and delete those files manually. The find command comes in very handy for this type of task. I won't describe all the capabilities of the find command (that would take a very fat chapter of its own). I do, however, provide a few simple examples of how to use find to locate files belonging to a particular user, even when those files are scattered across a file system. You can even use the find command to delete or change the ownership of files as they are located. Table 10-4 has a few examples of the find command in action.

TABLE 10-4

Using find to Locate and Change User Files

Find Command	Description
find / -user mary	Searches the entire file hierarchy (start at /) for all files and directories owned by mary and prints the filenames to the screen.
find /home -user mary -exec rm -i {} \;	Searches for all files and subdirectories under /home owned by mary. Run the rm command interactively to delete each file.
find / -user mary -exec chown jenny {} \;	Searches for all files and subdirectories under /home that are owned by user mary and runs the chown command to change each file so that it is owned by jenny instead.
find / -uid 500 -exec chown jenny {} \;	Basically the same as the previous example but uses the user ID number instead of the user name to identify the matching files. This is useful if you have deleted a user before converting the user's files.

There are a few common things about each invocation of the find command. The first parameter is always the directory to start the recursive search in. After that are the file attributes to match. You can use the -exec parameter to run a command against each matching file or directory. The {} characters designate where the matching filename should be filled in when find runs the -exec option. The \; at the end simply tells Linux where the command ends. These are only a few of find's capabilities. I encourage you to read the online man page to learn more about find. (Type **man find** to view the page.)

Deleting user accounts with User Manager

To delete a user from the User Manager window, simply click the line representing the user account, and then click the Delete button.

- Information about the user is removed from the /etc/passwd file; thus, the user can no longer log in.
- The home directory and all files owned by the user will still exist. However, a listing of files previously owned by that user (ls -l) will show only the former user's UID, but no name, as the owner.

See the description in the previous section for information about how to find and remove files previously owned by the user.

Checking Disk Quotas

Limited disk space can be another source of user support calls. Fedora offers the quotas software package for limiting and displaying the amount of disk space that a user can consume. You can also use the du command to see how much disk space has been used in a particular directory (and related subdirectories). To automate the process of checking for disk space, you can create your own script. The following sections describe these ways of dealing with potential disk space problems.

Using quota to check disk usage

A careless or greedy user can gobble up all the space on your hard disk, and possibly bring your computer to a halt. By using disk quotas, you can limit the amount of disk resources a user or group can use.

The quota package contains a set of tools that enables you to limit the amount of disk space (based on disk blocks) and files (based on inodes) that a user can consume. Using quotas, you can limit the amount of usage (on a per-user and per-group basis) for each file system on your computer. The general steps for setting disk quotas are as follows:

1. Edit the /etc/fstab file.
2. Create quota files.
3. Create and start a quota startup script.
4. Create quota rules.
5. Check quotas.

You set quotas on file systems listed in your /etc/fstab file. For computers that are shared by many users, there might be a separate /home or /var partition where users are expected to put all their data. That kind of partition boundary can prevent an entire disk from being consumed by one user. Quotas on the /home or /var partition can ensure that the space within those partitions is shared fairly among your computer's users.

Tip
When you begin setting user disk quotas, keep track of the total amount of disk space that can be consumed by the users you assign. Although quotas can limit how much each user can consume, they don't prevent your system from running out of disk space when the total amount of disk space allocated exceeds the total amount available. ∎

The procedure that spans the next few sections assumes that you have a separate /home partition on your computer for which you want to create quotas. You could use any partition, not just the /home partition shown in the procedure. For example, if you have only one partition mounted at the root of the file system (/), you could set quotas for your entire file system by replacing /home with / in the following example.

Editing the /etc/fstab file

To add quota support to the file system, edit the /etc/fstab file and add the usrquota option to field number four of the partition for which you want to set quotas. The fourth field represents the options to the mount command, options that will apply when the system mounts the disk. Here is an example of a line from /etc/fstab:

```
/dev/sda2  /home  ext4   defaults,usrquota,grpquota     1 2
```

You may see a Universal Unique Identifier (UUID) value in place of the device name shown here as /dev/sda2. In this example, the /home file system is used to allow disk quotas for all users' home directories under the /home directory.

Before the usrquota option can take effect, the file system must be remounted. This happens automatically when you reboot, which you have to do if you are setting quotas for the root (/) file system. Otherwise, you might be able to use the umount and mount commands to cause the usrquota option to take effect, or run mount with the remount option.

Creating quota files

You need to have aquota.user and/or aquota.group files in the root directory of the partition on which you want to establish disk quotas. To add quotas based on individual users, you need an aquota.user file, while aquota.group is needed to set quotas based on groups. One way to create these files is with the quotacheck command. Here's an example of the quotacheck command to create an initial aquota.user file:

```
# quotacheck -c /home
```

A /home/aquota.user file is created from the previous command. (To create an initial aquota.group file, type **touch /home/aquota.group**.) Next, you must create the disk usage table for the partition. Here's an example of how to do that:

```
# quotacheck -vug /home
```

The quotacheck command in this example looks at the file system partition mounted on /home and builds a table of disk usage. The -v option produces verbose output from the command, the -u option causes user quotas to be examined, and the -g option causes group quotas to be examined.

Creating a quota startup script

If the quota package doesn't include a startup script (and it doesn't with the current Fedora distribution), you can create your own. You want this script to check quotas (quotacheck command), start the quota service (quotaon command), and turn off the service (quotaoff command).

Open a new file called /etc/rc.d/init.d/quota as root user, using any text editor. Listing 10-1 shows an example of the content you can add to that file.

LISTING 10-1

A Quota Startup Script

```
#!/bin/bash

# init file for quota
#
# description: Checks disk quotas
```

```
#
# processname: quota
# chkconfig: - 90 90
# source function library
. /etc/rc.d/init.d/functions

case "$1" in
  start)
    echo -n "Checking quotas: "
        daemon /sbin/quotacheck -avug
    echo
    echo -n "Starting quotas: "
        daemon /sbin/quotaon -avug
    echo
    ;;
  stop)
    echo -n "Shutting down quotas: "
    daemon /sbin/quotaoff -a
    echo
    ;;
  restart)
        $0 stop
        $0 start
        ;;
  *)
    echo "Usage: quota {start|stop|restart}"
    exit 1
esac

exit 0
```

The quota script, when started, first runs the `quotacheck` command to check all file systems for which quota checking is on. Then it turns on quota checking with the `quotaon` command. The line `#  chkconfig: - 90  90` identifies the names assigned to the startup script (S90quota or K90quota) when it is added to the individual run-level directories. When you run `chkconfig --add quota` in the next step, those scripts are automatically put in the correct run-level directories.

Turning on the quota startup script

If you created a quota file, as described in the previous step, you need to make it executable and set it to start automatically when you start Fedora. To do those things, type the following as root user:

```
# chmod 755 /etc/rc.d/init.d/quota
# chkconfig --add quota
# chkconfig quota on
```

At this point, links are created so that your quota script starts when Fedora boots.

Creating quota rules

You can use the edquota command to create quota rules for a particular user or group. (Valid users and groups are listed in the /etc/passwd and /etc/group files, respectively). Here is an example of an edquota command to set quotas for a user named jake.

Note

The edquota **command uses the** vi **text editor to edit your quota files. To use a different editor, change the value of the** EDITOR **or** VISUAL **environment variable before running** edquota. **For example, to use the** emacs **editor, type the following before running** edquota:

```
#  export EDITOR=emacs
#  edquota -u jake
Disk quotas for user jake (uid 501)
  Filesystem            blocks    soft    hard    inodes    soft    hard
  /dev/sda2                596       0       0         1       0       0
~
~
~
"/tmp//EdP.aBY1zYC" 3L, 215C ■
```

This example shows that user quotas can be set for the user jake on the /dev/sda2 partition (which is /home in this example). Currently, jake has used 596 blocks (one block equals 1K on this ext3 file system). One file was created by jake (represented by 1 inode). To change the disk usage limits, you can edit the zeros (unlimited use) under the soft and hard heading for blocks and inodes.

Soft limits set limits that you don't want a user or group to exceed. Hard limits set the boundaries that you will not let a user or group exceed. After a set grace period when a soft limit has been exceeded (which is seven days, by default), the soft limit becomes a hard limit. (Type **edquota -t** to check and change the grace periods that you have set.)

Here is an example of how the line in the previous edquota example could be changed:

```
  /dev/sda2                596  512000  716800         1     800    1000
```

In this example, the soft limit on the number of blocks that the user jake could consume on the /dev/sda2 device (/home) is 512000 blocks (or 500MB); the hard limit is 716800 blocks (or 700MB). Soft and hard limits on inodes are 800 and 1,000, respectively. If either of the soft limits is exceeded by the user jake, he has seven days to get back under the limit, or he will be blocked from using any more disk space or inodes.

Further attempts to write to a partition after the hard limit has been exceeded result in a failure to write to the disk. When this happens, users who try to create the file that exceeds their limit will see a message like the following:

```
    ide0(3,2): write failed, user block limit reached.
    cp: writing 'abc.odt: Disk quota exceeded
```

Exceeding disk quota can also prevent such users from logging in again because logging in from some graphical user interfaces requires being able to write to the user's home directory.

Instead of assigning quotas to users, you can assign quotas to any group listed in the /etc/group file. Instead of the -u option to edquota, use the -g option followed by a group name.

Updating quota settings

After you have changed quota settings for a user, rerun the quotacheck command. You should also run the quotacheck command periodically, to keep the quota records up to date. One way to do that is to run the quotacheck command weekly using a cron entry. (See Chapter 12 for more information on the cron facility.)

Checking quotas

To get information about how much disk space and how many inodes each user on your computer (for whom you have set quotas) has consumed, use the repquota command. Here's an example of the repquota command for reading quota data relating to all partitions that are using quotas:

```
# repquota -a
*** Report for user quotas on device /dev/sda2
Block grace time: 7days: Inode grace time: 7days
                        Block limits               File limits
User         used    soft    hard  grace    used  soft  hard grace
root    --  1973984     0       0           2506    0     0
jake    --     1296   700    1700  6days       3    0     0
```

In this example, jake has exceeded his soft limit of 700 blocks. He currently has six days left in his grace period to remove enough files so that the soft limit does not become the hard limit.

Using du to check disk use

You can discover the most voracious consumers of disk space by using the du command. Invoke du with the -s option and give it a list of directories; it reports the total disk space used by all the files in each directory. Add an -h option to display disk space used in numbers, followed by kilobytes (K), megabytes (M), or gigabytes (G). The -c option adds a total of all requested directories at the end. The following checks disk usage for several home directories:

```
# du -hcs /home/tom /home/bill /home/tina /home/sally
```

This should result in a list of all of your users' home directories preceded by the number of kilobytes (K), megabytes (M), or gigabytes (G) that each directory structure uses. It looks something like this:

```
339M    /home/tom
81M     /home/bill
31M     /home/tina
44K     /home/sally
1.45G   total
```

Removing temp files automatically

Some potential disk-consumption problems are set up to take care of themselves. For example, directories for storing temporary files used by applications (such as /tmp and /var/tmp) can consume a lot of disk space over time. To deal with the problem, Fedora includes the tmpwatch facility. The tmpwatch command runs from the cron file /etc/cron.daily/tmpwatch to delete unused temporary files. Here's what that file contains:

```
#! /bin/sh
flags=-umc
/usr/sbin/tmpwatch "$flags" -x /tmp/.X11-unix -x /tmp/.XIM-unix \
    -x /tmp/.font-unix -x /tmp/.ICE-unix \
    -x /tmp/.Test-unix -x '/tmp/hsperfdata_*' 10d /tmp
/usr/sbin/tmpwatch "$flags" 30d /var/tmp

for d in /var/{cache/man,catman}/{cat?,X11R6/cat?,local/cat?}; do
    if [ -d "$d" ]; then
    /usr/sbin/tmpwatch "$flags" -f 30d $d
    fi
done
```

Each day, this tmpwatch script runs to delete temporary files that haven't been used for some time. The flags (-umc) indicate that time access is based on the file's access time (u), modification time (m), and inode change time (c). It starts by identifying files that are not to be deleted (tmpwatch -x). Files such as those in the /tmp/.X11-unix directory represent sockets for active X servers, and would make an active GUI inaccessible if deleted. All other files from the /tmp and /var/tmp directories are removed after 10 and 30 days of not being accessed, respectively. Temporary man page files stored in /var/cache subdirectories are also checked and deleted after 30 days of disuse.

Sending Mail to All Users

Occasionally, you need to send messages to all users on your system. Warning users of planned downtime for hardware upgrades is a good example. Sending e-mail to each user individually is extremely time-consuming and inefficient; this is precisely the kind of task for which e-mail aliases and mailing lists were invented. Keeping a mailing list of all the users on your system can be problematic, however. If you are not diligent about keeping the mailing list current, it becomes increasingly inaccurate as you add and delete users. Also, if your system has many users, the mere size of the alias list can become unwieldy.

Listing 10-2 shows a script, called mailfile, which provides a simple method for working around these problems. It grabs the login names from the /etc/passwd file and sends e-mail to all users.

Note

Because regular user accounts begin with UID 500 in Fedora, the script excludes all UIDs under 500 (which are typically administrative accounts). It also skips UID 65534, which is the anonymous NFS user account. ■

LISTING 10-2

The mailfile Script for Sending a File to All Users

```
#!/bin/bash
# mailfile: This script mails the named file to all regular
#           users of the system.  It skips all administrative
#           accounts (accounts under UID 500) as well as the
#           anonymous NFS user (UID 65534).
#
# USAGE: mailfile "Subject goes here" filename.txt

# Check for a subject and file name
#
test -z "$1" && echo "Subject argument is missing" && exit
test -z "$2" && echo "Filename argument is missing" && exit
# Get the subject of the message
    subject=$1

# Check for a filename
    filename=$2

# Loop through all login names, skipping accounts under 500
# as well as the anonymous NFS account (65534)

for x in $(cut -d ":" -f 1,3 /etc/passwd)
do
    USER=$(echo $x | cut -d ":" -f1)
    ID=$(echo $x | cut -d ":" -f2)

    if [[ $ID -gt 499 && $ID -lt 65534 ]]; then

    # Mail the file
    echo Mailing to $USER
    mail -s "$subject" $USER < $filename

    # Sleep for a few seconds so we don't overload the mailer
    # On fast systems or systems with few accounts, you can
    # probably take this delay out.
    sleep 2
fi
done
```

The script accepts two parameters. The first is the subject of the e-mail message, which is enclosed in quotation marks. The second is the name of the file containing the text message to send. Thus, an e-mail message to all users warning them about an upcoming server hardware upgrade may look similar to the following:

```
mailfile "System upgrade at 5:00pm" upgrade.txt
```

The file upgrade.txt contains the text of the message to be sent to each user. The really useful thing about this approach is that you can save this text file and easily modify and resend it the next time you upgrade the system.

Tip

If your users log in to your system using text-based logins instead of graphical logins, you can add messages to the /etc/motd file to have them reach your users. Any text in that file will be displayed on each user's screen after the user logs in and before the first shell prompt appears. ■

Summary

It is not uncommon for a Linux system to be used as a single-task server with no actual users logging in. It sits quietly in a server room, serving Web pages or handling the domain name system service, never crashing, and rarely needing attention. This is not always the case, however. You may have to support users on your Linux system, and that can be the most challenging part of your system administration duties.

Fedora provides a variety of tools to help you with your administrative chores. The useradd, usermod, and userdel commands enable easy command-line manipulation of user account data. Furthermore, you can lighten your load even more by creating a support mailbox and building shell scripts to automate repetitive tasks. Fedora builds on top of the rich history of Unix and provides an ideal platform to support the diverse needs of your users.

## 11

Automating System Tasks

You'd never get any work done if you typed every command that needs to be run on your Fedora system when it starts. Likewise, you could work more efficiently if you grouped together sets of commands that you run all the time. Shell scripts can handle these tasks.

A *shell script* is a group of commands, functions, variables, or just about anything else you can use from a shell. These items are typed into a plain-text file. That file can then be run as a command. Fedora uses system initialization shell scripts during system startup to run commands needed to get things going. You can create your own shell scripts to automate the tasks you need to do regularly.

This chapter provides a rudimentary overview of the inner workings of shell scripts and how they can be used. You learn how simple scripts can be harnessed to a scheduling facility (such as cron or at) to simplify administrative tasks.

You also learn to fine-tune your machine to start at the most appropriate run level and to run only services you need. With that understanding, you'll be able to personalize your computer and reduce the amount of time you spend repetitively typing the same commands.

Understanding Shell Scripts

Have you ever had to repeatedly do a task that took a lot of typing on the command line? Do you ever think to yourself, "I wish there were just one command I could type to do all this of this"? Maybe a shell script is what you're after.

Shell scripts are the equivalent of batch files in MS-DOS, and they can contain long lists of commands, complex flow control, arithmetic evaluations, user-defined variables, user-defined functions, and sophisticated condition testing. Shell scripts are capable of handling everything from simple one-line commands to something as complex as starting up your Fedora system.

In fact, as you will learn in this chapter, Fedora does just that. It uses shell scripts (/etc/rc.d/rc.sysinit and /etc/rc) to check and mount all your file systems, set up your consoles, configure your network, launch all your system services, and eventually provide you with your login screen. There are nearly a dozen different shells available in Fedora, but the default shell is called bash, the Bourne-Again Shell.

Executing and debugging shell scripts

One of the primary advantages of shell scripts is that you can open them in any text editor to see what they do. A big disadvantage is that large or complex shell scripts often execute more slowly than compiled programs. There are two basic ways to execute a shell script:

- The filename is used as an argument to the shell (as in bash myscript). With this method, the file does not need to be executable; it just contains a list of shell commands. The shell specified on the command line is used to interpret the commands in the script file. This is most common for quick, simple tasks.

- The shell script may include the name of the interpreter placed in the first line of the script, preceded by #! (as in #!/bin/bash), and have its execute bit set (using chmod +x). You can then run your script just like any other program in your path simply by typing the name of the script on the command line.

Cross-Reference

See Chapter 4 for more details on chmod and read/write/execute permissions. ∎

When scripts are executed in either manner, options for the program may be specified on the command line. Anything following the name of the script is referred to as a *command-line argument*.

As with writing any software, there is no substitute for clear and thoughtful design and a lot of comments. The pound sign (#) prefaces comments and can take up an entire line or exist on the same line after script code. It's best to implement more complex shell scripts in stages, making sure the logic is sound at each step before continuing. Here are a few good, concise tips to ensure that things work as expected during testing:

- Place an echo statement at the beginning of lines within the body of a loop. That way, rather than execute the code, you can see what will be executed without making any permanent changes.

- To achieve the same goal, you could place dummy echo statements throughout the code. If these lines are printed, you know the correct logic branch is being taken.

- You could use `set -x` near the beginning of the script to display each command that is executed or launch your scripts using `bash -x myscript`.

- Because useful scripts have a tendency to grow over time, keeping your code readable as you go along is extremely important. Do what you can to keep the logic of your code clean and easy to follow.

Understanding shell variables

Often within a shell script, you want to reuse certain items of information. During the course of processing the shell script, the name or number representing this information may change. To store information used by a shell script in such a way that it can be easily reused, you can set variables. Variable names within shell scripts are case-sensitive and can be defined in the following manner:

```
NAME=value
```

The first part of a variable is the variable name, and the second part is the value set for that name. Be sure that the `NAME` and `value` touch the equal sign, without any spaces. Variables can be assigned from constants, such as text or numbers. This is useful for initializing values or avoiding a lot of typing for long constants. In the following examples, variables are set to a string of characters (`CITY`) and a numeric value (`PI`):

```
CITY="Springfield"
PI=3.14159265
```

In addition to constants holding things not likely to change (such as the mathematical definition of pi), you can also use variables as placeholders for the given items of interest, such as the filename to process, the directory you want to back up, and so on.

Variables can contain the output of a command or command sequence. You can accomplish this by preceding the command with a dollar sign and an open parenthesis, and following it with a closing parenthesis. For example, `MYDATE=$(date)` assigns the output from the `date` command to the `MYDATE` variable. Enclosing the command in backticks (`` ` ``) has the same effect.

Note

Keep in mind that characters such as the dollar sign ($), backtick (`` ` ``), asterisk (*), exclamation point (!), and others have special meaning to the shell, as you will see as you proceed through this chapter. To use those characters in an option to a command, rather than have the shell use its special meaning, you need to precede the character with a backslash (\) or surround it in quotes. One place you will encounter this is in files created by Windows users that might include spaces, exclamation points, or other characters. In Linux, to properly interpret a file named `my big! file!`, you need to either surround it in double quotes or type: `my\ big\! file\!` ■

These are great ways to get information that can change from computer to computer or from day to day. The following example sets the output of the `uname -n` command to the `MACHINE` variable. You can use parentheses to set NUM_FILES to the number of files in the current directory by piping (|) the output of the ls command to the word count command (wc -1):

```
MACHINE=`uname -n`
NUM_FILES=$(/bin/ls | wc -1)
```

Variables can also contain the value of other variables. This is useful when you have to preserve a value that will change so you can use it later in the script. Here, BALANCE is set to the value of the CurBalance variable:

```
BALANCE="$CurBalance"
```

The double quotes (") tell bash to substitute the value of the variable CurBalance. If you used single quotes ('), the shell would merely display the text $CurBalance as shown here:

```
$ CurBalance=5.00
$ echo "$CurBalance"
5.00

$ echo '$CurBalance'
$CurBalance
```

Note

When assigning variables, use only the variable name (for example, BALANCE). When referenced, meaning you want the *value* of the variable, precede it with a dollar sign (as in $CurBalance). The result of the latter is the value of the variable, not the variable name itself. ■

Special shell variables

There are special variables that the shell assigns for you. The most commonly used variables are called the *positional parameters* or *command-line arguments* and are referenced as $0, $1, $2, $3...$n. $0 is special and is assigned the name used to invoke your script; the others are assigned the values of the parameters passed on the command line. For instance, if the shell script named myscript were called

```
myscript foo bar
```

the positional parameter $0 would be myscript, $1 would be foo, and $2 would be bar. The following script, myscript, shows this:

```
#!/bin/sh

echo "0: $0"
echo "1: $1"
echo "2: $2"

echo "You passed $# arguments to $0"
```

Running the preceding script with the command-line parameters of foo and bar would result in output like the following:

```
$ sh myscript foo bar
0: myscript
1: foo
2: bar
You passed 2 arguments to myscript
```

The variable $# in the last line of the script tells you how many parameters your script was given. In the preceding example, $# would be 2. Another particularly useful special shell variable is $?, which receives the exit status of the last command executed. Typically, a value of zero means everything is OK, and anything other than zero indicates an error of some kind. For a complete list of special shell variables, refer to the bash man page.

Parameter expansion in bash

As mentioned earlier, if you want the value of a variable, you precede it with a $ (for example, $CITY). This is really just shorthand for the notation ${CITY}; curly braces are used when the value of the parameter needs to be placed next to other text without a space. Bash has special rules that allow you to expand the value of a variable in different ways. Going into all the rules is probably overkill for a quick introduction to shell scripts, but Table 11-1 presents some common constructs that you're likely to see in bash scripts you find on your Fedora box.

TABLE 11-1

Examples of bash Parameter Expansion

Construction	Description
${var:-value}	If the variable is unset or empty, expand this to value.
${var#pattern}	Chop the shortest match for pattern from the front of var's value.
${var##pattern}	Chop the longest match for pattern from the front of var's value.
${var%pattern}	Chop the shortest match for pattern from the end of var's value.
${var%%pattern}	Chop the longest match for pattern from the end of var's value.

For more on parameter expansion, see the bash man page or http://tldp.org/LDP/abs/html/parameter-substitution.html.

Try typing the following commands from a shell to test how parameter expansion works:

```
$ FOOD="Pizza"
$ FOOD=${FOOD:-"Not Set"}
$ SNACK=${SNACK:-"Not Set"}
```

```
$ echo $FOOD
Pizza
$ echo $SNACK
Not Set
```

In these examples, the FOOD variable is set to Pizza in the first line. The second line gives FOOD a default value, Not Set, if necessary. In this case, the value of FOOD is still Pizza because it has a value. The third line sets a default value for the variable SNACK. Because we never gave SNACK a value, it gets the default, Not Set in this case.

Note
The rest of this section shows how variables and commands may appear in a shell script. To try out any of the examples, you can simply type them into a shell as shown in the previous example. ■

In the following example, MYFILENAME is set to /home/digby/myfile.txt. Next, the FILE variable is set to myfile.txt and DIR is set to /home/digby. In the NAME variable, the filename is shortened to simply myfile; then, in the EXTENSION variable the file extension is set to txt. (To try these out, you can type them at a shell prompt as in the previous example, and then echo the value of each variable to see how it is set.)

```
MYFILENAME="/home/digby/myfile.txt"
FILE=${MYFILENAME##*/}     #FILE becomes "myfile.txt"
DIR=${MYFILENAME%/*}       #DIR becomes "/home/digby"
NAME=${FILE%.*}            #NAME becomes "myfile"
EXTENSION=${FILE#*.}       #EXTENSION becomes "txt"
```

Performing arithmetic in shell scripts

Bash uses *untyped* variables, meaning it normally treats variables as strings or text, but it can change them on-the-fly if you want it to. Unless you tell it otherwise with declare, your variables are just a bunch of letters to bash; but when you start trying to do arithmetic with them, bash converts them to numbers if it can. This makes it possible to do some fairly complex arithmetic in bash.

Integer arithmetic can be performed using the built-in let command or through the external expr or bc commands. After setting the variable BIGNUM value to 1024, the three commands that follow would all store the value 64 in the RESULT variable. (The command using bc will set the RESULT variable to 64.00000000000000000000.)

The last command gets a random number between 0 and 10 and echoes the results back to you.

```
BIGNUM=1024
let RESULT=$BIGNUM/16
RESULT=`expr $BIGNUM / 16`
RESULT=`echo "$BIGNUM / 16" | bc -l`
let foo=$RANDOM%10; echo $foo
```

You can also use arithmetic in line with the following double-parenthesis syntax:

```
$ RESULT=$((10*20))
$ echo $RESULT
200
```

Note

While most elements of shell scripts are relatively free-form (where whitespace, such as spaces or tabs, is insignificant), both let and expr are particular about spacing. The let command insists on no spaces between each operand and the mathematical operator, whereas the syntax of the expr command requires whitespace between each operand and its operator. In contrast to those, bc isn't picky about spaces, but it can be trickier to use because it does floating-point arithmetic. ∎

To see a complete list of the kinds of arithmetic you can perform using the let command, type **help let** at the bash prompt.

Using programming constructs in shell scripts

One of the features that make shell scripts so powerful is that their implementation of looping and conditional execution constructs is similar to those found in more complex scripting and programming languages. You can use several different types of loops, depending on your needs.

The "if...then" statements

The most commonly used programming construct is conditional execution, or the if statement. It is used to perform actions only under certain conditions. There are several variations, depending on whether you're testing one thing, or want to do one thing if a condition is true, but another thing if that condition is false, or if you want to test several things one after the other.

The first if...then example that follows tests whether VARIABLE is set to the number 1. If it is, then the echo command is used to say that it is set to 1. The fi (if backwards) then indicates that the if statement is complete and processing can continue.

```
VARIABLE=1
if [ $VARIABLE -eq 1 ] ; then
    echo "The variable is 1"
fi
```

Instead of using -eq, you can use the equals sign (=), as shown in the following example. The = works best for comparing string values, while -eq is often better for comparing numbers.

```
STRING="Friday"
if [ $STRING = "Friday" ] ; then
    echo "WhooHoo.  Friday."
else
    echo "Will Friday ever get here?"
fi
```

Using the else statement in this example, different words can be echoed if the criterion of the if statement isn't met ($STRING = "Friday"). Keep in mind that it's good practice to put strings in double quotes.

You can also reverse tests with an exclamation mark (!). In the following example, if STRING is not Monday, then "At least it's not Monday" is echoed:

```
STRING="FRIDAY"
if [ "$STRING" != "Monday" ] ; then
    echo "At least it's not Monday"
fi
```

Tip

Leave a space before and after the square brackets, as [is actually a Linux command in /usr/bin **(and built into the bash shell).** ■

In the following example, elif (which stands for "else if") is used to test for an additional condition (is filename a file or a directory):

```
filename="$HOME"

if [ -f "$filename" ] ; then
    echo "$filename is a regular file"
elif [ -d "$filename" ] ; then
    echo "$filename is a directory"
else
    echo "I have no idea what $filename is"
fi
```

As you can see from the preceding examples, the condition you are testing is placed between square brackets, [ ]. When a test expression is evaluated, it returns either a value of 0, meaning it is true, or a 1, meaning it is false. Note that the echo lines are indented. This is optional but makes the script more readable.

Table 11-2 lists the conditions that are testable and is quite a handy reference. (If you're in a hurry, you can type **help test** on the command line to get the same information.)

TABLE 11-2

Operators for Test Expressions

Operator	What Is Being Tested?
-a *file*	Does the file exist? (same as -e)
-b *file*	Is the file a special block device?
-c *file*	Is the file character special (e.g., a character device)? Used to identify serial lines and terminal devices.

Operator	What Is Being Tested?
-d *file*	Is the file a directory?
-e *file*	Does the file exist? (same as -a)
-f *file*	Does the file exist, and is it a regular file (e.g., not a directory, socket, pipe, link, or device file)?
-g *file*	Does the file have the set-group-id bit set?
-G *file*	Does your group own the file?
-h *file*	Is the file a symbolic link? (same as -L)
-k *file*	Does the file have the sticky bit set?
-L *file*	Is the file a symbolic link? (same as -h)
-n *string*	Is the length of the string greater than 0 bytes?
-N *file*	Has the file been modified since it was last read?
-O *file*	Do you own the file?
-p *file*	Is the file a named pipe?
-r *file*	Is the file readable by you?
-s *file*	Does the file exist, and is it larger than 0 bytes?
-S *file*	Does the file exist, and is it a socket?
-t *fd*	Is the file descriptor connected to a terminal?
-u *file*	Does the file have the set-user-id bit set?
-w *file*	Is the file writable by you?
-x *file*	Is the file executable by you?
-z *string*	Is the length of the string 0 (zero) bytes?
expr1 -a *expr2*	Are both the first expression and the second expression true?
expr1 -o *expr2*	Is either of the two expressions true?
file1 -nt *file2*	Is the first file newer than the second file (using the modification timestamp)?
file1 -ot *file2*	Is the first file older than the second file (using the modification timestamp)?
file1 -ef *file2*	Are the two files associated by a hard link?
var1 = *var2*	Is the first variable equal to the second variable?

continued

TABLE 11-2   *(continued)*

Operator	What Is Being Tested?
`var1 -eq var2`	Is the first variable equal to the second variable?
`var1 -ge var2`	Is the first variable greater than or equal to the second variable?
`var1 -gt var2`	Is the first variable greater than the second variable?
`var1 > var2`	Does the first variable sort after the second variable?
`var1 -le var2`	Is the first variable less than or equal to the second variable?
`var1 -lt var2`	Is the first variable less than the second variable?
`var1 < var2`	Does the first variable sort before the second variable?
`var1 != var2`	Is the first variable not equal to the second variable?
`var1 -ne var2`	Is the first variable not equal to the second variable?

There is also a special shorthand method of performing tests that can be useful for simple *one-command* actions. In the following example, the two pipes (||) indicate that if the directory being tested for doesn't exist (`-d dirname`), then make the directory (`mkdir $dirname`). The two pipe characters make for a logical OR test:

```
# [ test ] || {action}
# Perform simple single command {action} if test is false
dirname="/tmp/testdir"
[ -d "$dirname" ] || mkdir "$dirname"
```

Instead of pipes, you can use two ampersands (&&) to test if something is true. In the following example, a command is being tested to see if it includes at least three command-line arguments. The two ampersands make a logical AND test:

```
# [ test ] && {action}
# Perform simple single command {action} if test is true
[ $# -ge 3 ] && echo "There are at least 3 command line arguments."
```

The case command

The `case` command can take the place of several nested `if` statements. A general form of the `case` statement is as follows:

```
case "VAR" in
    Result1)
        { body };;
    Result2)
        { body };;
    *)
```

```
        { body } ;;
esac
```

Note that you need to replace "VAR" with the variable or command to test, and each { body } block with the actual commands to run, as shown in the example that follows. One use for the case command might be to help with your backups. The following case statement tests for the first three letters of the current day (case `date +%a` in). Then, depending on the day, a particular backup directory (BACKUP) and tape drive (TAPE) are set.

```
# Our VAR doesn't have to be a variable,
# it can be the output of a command as well
# Perform action based on day of week
case `date +%a` in
    "Mon")
            BACKUP=/home/myproject/data0
            TAPE=/dev/rft0
# Note the use of the double semi-colon to end each option
            ;;
# Note the use of the "|" to mean "or"
    "Tue" | "Thu")
            BACKUP=/home/myproject/data1
            TAPE=/dev/rft1
            ;;
    "Wed" | "Fri")
            BACKUP=/home/myproject/data2
            TAPE=/dev/rft2
            ;;
# Don't do backups on the weekend.
    *)
            BACKUP="none"

            TAPE=/dev/null
            ;;
esac
```

The asterisk (*) is used as a catchall, similar to the default keyword in the C programming language. In this example, if none of the other entries are matched on the way down the loop, the asterisk is matched, and the value of BACKUP becomes none. Note the use of esac, or case spelled backwards, to end the case statement.

The "for...do" loop

Loops perform actions repeatedly until either a condition is met or all data has been processed. One of the most commonly used loops is the for...do loop, which iterates through a list of values, executing the body of the loop for each element in the list. The syntax follows:

```
for VAR in LIST
do
    { body }
done
```

The `for` loop assigns the values in LIST to VAR one at a time. Then for each value, the body in braces between do and `done` is executed. VAR can be any variable name, and LIST can be composed of pretty much any list of values or anything that generates a list.

```
for NUMBER in 0 1 2 3 4 5 6 7 8 9
do
    echo The number is $NUMBER
done

for FILE in `/bin/ls`
do
    echo $FILE
done
```

You can also write it as follows, which is somewhat cleaner:

```
for NAME in John Paul Ringo George ; do
    echo $NAME is my favorite Beatle
done
```

Each element in the LIST is separated from the next by whitespace. This can cause trouble if you're not careful because some commands, such as `ls -l`, output multiple fields per line, each separated by whitespace. The string done ends the `for` statement.

If you're a die-hard C programmer, bash allows you to use C syntax to control your loops:

```
LIMIT=10
# Double parentheses, and no $ on LIMIT even though it's a variable!
for ((a=1; a <= LIMIT ; a++)) ; do
    echo "$a"
done
```

The "while...do" and "until...do" loops

Two other possible looping constructs are the `while...do` loop and the `until...do` loop. The structure of each is presented here:

```
while condition      until condition
do                   do
    { body }            { body }
done                 done
```

The `while` statement executes while the condition is true. The `until` statement executes until the condition is true — in other words, while the condition is false.

Here is an example of a `while` loop that outputs the number 0123456789:

```
N=0
while [ $N -lt 10 ] ; do
```

```
        echo -n $N
        let N=$N+1
    done
```

Another way to output the number 0123456789 is to use an `until` loop as follows:

```
    N=0
    until [ $N -eq 10 ] ; do
        echo -n $N
        let N=$N+1
    done
```

Some useful external programs

Bash is great and has a lot of built-in commands, but it usually needs some help to do anything really useful. Some of the most common useful programs you'll see used are `grep`, `cut`, `tr`, `awk`, and `sed`. As with all the best Unix tools, most of these programs are designed to work with standard input and standard output, so you can easily use them with pipes and shell scripts.

The general regular expression parser (grep)

The name *general regular expression parser* sounds intimidating, but `grep` is just a way to find patterns in files or text. Think of it as a useful search tool. Becoming proficient with regular expressions is quite a challenge, but many useful things can be accomplished with just the simplest forms.

For example, you can display a list of all regular user accounts by using `grep` to search for all lines that contain the text `/home` in the `/etc/passwd` file as follows:

```
    grep /home /etc/passwd
```

Or you could find all environment variables that begin with `HO` using the following command:

```
    env | grep ^HO
```

Note
The ^ above is the actual caret character, ^, not what you commonly see for a backspace, ^H. Type ^, H, and O (the uppercase letter) to see what items start with the uppercase characters *HO*. ■

To find a list of options to use with the `grep` command, type **man grep**.

Remove sections of lines of text (cut)

The `cut` command can extract specific fields from a line of text or from files. It is very useful for parsing system configuration files into easy-to-digest chunks. You can specify the field separator and the fields you want, or you can break up a line based on bytes.

The following example lists all home directories of users on your system. Using an earlier example of the `grep` command, this line pipes a list of regular users from the `/etc/passwd` file, then displays the sixth field (-f6) as delimited by a colon (-d':'). The hyphen at the end tells cut to read from standard input (from the pipe).

```
grep /home /etc/passwd | cut -f6 -d':' -
```

Translate or delete characters (tr)

The tr command is a character-based translator that can be used to replace one character or set of characters with another or to remove a character from a line of text.

The following example translates all uppercase letters to lowercase letters and displays the words "mixed upper and lower case" as a result:

```
FOO="Mixed UPpEr aNd LoWeR cAsE"
echo $FOO | tr [A-Z] [a-z]
```

In the next example, the tr command is used on a list of filenames to rename any files in that list so that any tabs or spaces (as indicated by the [:blank:] option) contained in a filename are translated into underscores. Try running the following code in a test directory:

```
for file in * ; do
    f=`echo $file | tr [:blank:] [_]`
    [ "$file" = "-d" ] || mv -i "$file" "$f"
done
```

The Stream Editor (sed)

The sed command is a simple scriptable editor, and as such can perform only simple edits, such as removing lines that have text matching a certain pattern, replacing one pattern of characters with another, and other simple edits. To get a better idea of how sed scripts work, there's no substitute for the online documentation, but here are some examples of common uses.

You can use the sed command to essentially do what I did earlier with the grep example: search the /etc/passwd file for the word home. In the following example, the sed command searches the entire /etc/passwd file for the word home, and prints any line containing the word home:

```
sed -n '/home/p' /etc/passwd
```

In the next example, sed searches the file somefile.txt and replaces every instance of the string Mac with Linux. Notice that the letter g is needed at the end of the substitution command to cause every occurrence of Mac on each line to be changed to Linux. (Otherwise, only the first instance of Mac on each line is changed.) The output is then sent to the fixed_file.txt file. The output from sed goes to stdout, so this command redirects the output to a file for safekeeping.

```
sed 's/Mac/Linux/g' somefile.txt > fixed_file.txt
```

You can get the same result using a pipe:

```
cat somefile.txt | sed 's/Mac/Linux/g' > fixed_file.txt
```

By searching for a pattern and replacing it with a null pattern, you delete the original pattern. This example searches the contents of the somefile.txt file and replaces extra blank spaces at the end of each line (s/ *$) with nothing (//). Results go to the fixed_file.txt file.

```
cat somefile.txt | sed 's/ *$//' > fixed_file.txt
```

Trying some simple shell scripts

Sometimes the simplest scripts can be the most useful. If you type the same sequence of commands repetitively, it makes sense to store those commands (once!) in a file. Here are a couple of simple, but useful, shell scripts.

A simple telephone list

This idea has been handed down from generation to generation of old Unix hacks. It's really quite simple, but it employs several of the concepts just introduced:

```
#!/bin/bash
# (@)/ph
# A very simple telephone list
# Type "ph new name number" to add to the list, or
# just type "ph name" to get a phone number

PHONELIST=~/.phonelist.txt

# If no command line parameters ($#), there
# is a problem, so ask what they're talking about.
if [ $# -lt 1 ] ; then
    echo "Whose phone number did you want? "
    exit 1
fi

# Did you want to add a new phone number?
if [ $1 = "new" ] ; then
    shift
    echo $* >> $PHONELIST
    echo $* added to database
    exit 0
fi

# Nope. But does the file have anything in it yet?
# This might be our first time using it, after all.
if [ ! -s $PHONELIST ] ; then
    echo "No names in the phone list yet! "
    exit 1
else
    grep -i -q "$*" $PHONELIST    # Quietly search the file
    if [ $? -ne 0 ] ; then        # Did we find anything?
        echo "Sorry, that name was not found in the phone list"
```

```
        exit 1
    else
        grep -i "$*" $PHONELIST
    fi
fi
exit 0
```

Therefore, if you created the file ph in your current directory, you could type the following from the shell to try out your ph script:

```
$ chmod 755 ph
$ ./ph new "Mary Jones" 608-555-1212
Mary Jones 608-555-1212 added to database
$ ./ph Mary
Mary Jones 608-555-1212
```

The chmod command makes the ph script executable. The ./ph command runs the ph command from the current directory with the new option. This adds Mary Jones as the name and 608-555-1212 as the phone number to the database ($HOME/.phonelist.txt). The next ph command searches the database for the name Mary and displays the phone entry for Mary. If the script works, add it to a directory in your PATH (such as $HOME/bin).

A simple backup script

Because nothing works forever and mistakes happen, backups are just a fact of life when dealing with computer data. This simple script backs up all the data in the home directories of all the users on your Fedora system:

```
#!/bin/bash
# (@)/my_backup
# A very simple backup script
#

# Change the TAPE device to match your system.
# Check /var/log/messages to determine your tape device.
# You may also need to add scsi-tape support to your kernel.
TAPE=/dev/rft0

# Rewind the tape device $TAPE
mt -f $TAPE rew
# Get a list of home directories
HOMES=`grep /home /etc/passwd | cut -f6 -d': '`
# Backup the data in those directories
tar cvf $TAPE $HOMES
# Rewind and eject the tape.
mt -f $TAPE rewoffl
```

Cross-Reference

See Chapter 12 for details on backing up and restoring files and getting the mt command (part of the ftape-tools packages that must be installed separately). ■

Initializing the System

When you turn on your computer, a lot happens even before Fedora starts up. Here are the basic steps that occur each time you boot up your computer to run Fedora:

1. **Boot hardware** — Based on information in the computer's read-only memory (referred to as the BIOS), your computer checks and starts the hardware. Some of that information tells the computer which devices (floppy disk, CD, hard disk, and so on) to check to find the bootable operating system.

2. **Start boot loader** — After checking that no bootable operating system is ready to boot in your floppy, CD, or DVD drive, typically, the BIOS checks the master boot record on the primary hard disk to see what to load next. With Fedora installed, the GRUB boot loader is started, enabling you to choose to boot Fedora or another installed operating system.

3. **Boot the kernel** — Assuming that you selected to boot Fedora, the Linux kernel is loaded. That kernel mounts the basic file systems and transfers control to the init process. The rest of this section describes what happens after the kernel hands off control of system startup to the init process.

Starting init

In the boot process, the transfer from the kernel phase (the loading of the kernel, probing for devices, and loading drivers) to init is indicated by the following lines:

```
Welcome to Fedora
Press "I" to enter interactive startup.
```

The init program, part of the upstart RPM package, is now in control. The output from ps always lists init (known as "the father of all processes") as PID (process identifier) 1.

Prior to Fedora 9, a special script, /etc/inittab, directed the actions of the init program. Starting in Fedora 9, a new initialization system called upstart replaced the older SysV Unix-style init program.

With upstart, the /etc/inittab file controls only the default run level. Everything else is run from a special script for each run level; for example, /etc/init/rc5.conf for run level 5. Upstart is based on the concept of launching programs based on *events,* rather than run levels. Upstart can restart services that terminate, and it isn't as fragile as the older SysV init system.

Note

Upstart has been changing in recent versions of Fedora. Up through Fedora 12, the system initialization files were in /etc/event.d/rcN, **such as** /etc/event.d/rc5. **Starting in Fedora 13, these files are in** /etc/ init **and have a** .conf **filename extension. Fedora 14 offers an updated version of the upstart launch. Expect a lot of changes in this area.** ■

Starting with Fedora 14, a new system called systemd replaces upstart. Systemd is compatible with older SysV init scripts, and at this time not all startup scripts have been migrated to the new system. Systemd has been designed to start fewer services at boot time by starting many services on demand later, and to start them faster by running commands in parallel.

With systemd, configuration files are located in /etc/systemd/system and the services are defined in /lib/systemd/system. Systemd uses the concepts of services, devices, and mounts as units defined in /lib/systemd/system that systemd can work with. Systemd also uses target files that define multiple units grouped together. For example, the multi-user.target file defines a target for multiuser mode (init level 3) and the graphical.target file defines init level 5 running the X Window System.

Systemd associates each target, such as multi-user.target, with a set of things the target wants, that is, things the target depends on, stored in the multi-user.target.wants directory. This directory holds the list of things to start when running a given target, mostly services such as the dbus.service. If you have used Samba, the configuration files used by systemd should appear familiar. The following file, for example, shows the configuration for the display manager:

```
#  This file is part of systemd.
#
#  systemd is free software; you can redistribute it and/or modify it
#  under the terms of the GNU General Public License as published by
#  the Free Software Foundation; either version 2 of the License, or
#  (at your option) any later version.

[Unit]
Description=Display Manager
After=syslog.target livesys-late.service rc-local.service

# On Fedora gdm/X11 is on tty1. We explicitly cancel the getty here to
# avoid any races around that.
Conflicts=getty@tty1.service plymouth-quit.service

[Service]
ExecStart=/etc/X11/prefdm -nodaemon
Restart=restart-always
RestartSec=0

[Install]
Alias=display-manager.service
```

ExecStart defines the command to run and Restart tells systemd whether it should restart the command if it ever stops. See the systemd.service man page for more information on what configuration options you can set. Most of these options relate to the before and after settings. With systemd, you can define a service to start before or after another systemd unit. That enables you to define the dependencies between services.

Even with systemd, you'll see that most services are still defined in /etc/rc.d/init.d. You can continue to use those files if you desire.

Note

See www.freedesktop.org/wiki/Software/systemd and http://0pointer.de/blog/projects/ systemd.html **for more information on** systemd. **Most older commands, such as** service start **and** chkconfig, **still work under** systemd. **See** http://docs.fedoraproject.org/en-US/Fedora/14/ html/Installation_Guide/s2-boot-init-shutdown-init.html **for more information on upstart.** ∎

Because so many Linux programs make assumptions about the init system, however, upstart, starting with Fedora 10, and systemd, starting with Fedora 14, uses the old /etc/inittab file to determine the default system run level. In that file, you'll see a line like the following, indicating run level 5 (run the X Window System and graphics) is the default run level:

```
id:5:initdefault
```

The other common initdefault level is run level 3 (often used for servers that boot up in text mode and often have no GUI). Table 11-3 describes each of the run levels and should help you choose the level that is most suitable as the default in your environment.

TABLE 11-3

Possible Run Levels

Run Level	Description
0	All processes are terminated and the machine comes to an orderly halt. As the inittab comments point out, this is not a good choice for initdefault because as soon as the kernel, modules, and drivers are loaded, the machine halts.
1, s, S	This is single-user mode, frequently used for system maintenance and instances where it may be preferable to have few processes running and no services activated. In single-user mode, the network is nonexistent, the X server is not running, and it is possible that some file systems are not mounted.
2	Multiuser mode. Multiple user logins are allowed, all configured file systems are mounted, and all processes except X, the at daemon, the xinetd daemon, and NIS/NFS are started. If your machine doesn't have (or perhaps doesn't need) a permanent network connection, this is a good choice for initdefault.
3	Multiuser mode with network services. Run level 3 is the typical value for initdefault on a Fedora server.
4	Run level 4 is available as a user-defined run level. It is nearly identical to run level 3 in a default Fedora configuration.
5	Multiuser mode with network services and X. This run level starts the X server and presents a graphical login window, visually resembling any of the more expensive Unix-based workstations. This is a common initdefault value for a Fedora workstation or desktop system.
6	All processes are terminated and the machine is gracefully rebooted. Again, the comments in the inittab file mention that this is not a good choice for initdefault, perhaps even worse than run level 0. The effect is a possibly infinite cycle of booting, followed by rebooting.

Starting Up and Shutting Down the System

During system startup, a series of scripts are run to start the services that you need. These include scripts to start network interfaces, mount directories, and monitor your system. Most of these scripts are run from subdirectories of /etc/rc.d. The program that starts most of these services when you boot and stops them when you shut down is the /etc/rc.d/rc script. The following sections describe run-level scripts and what you can do with them.

Starting run-level scripts

Any change of run level causes the /etc/rc.d/rc script to be executed, with the new run level as an argument. Here's a quick rundown of what the /etc/rc.d/rc script does:

- **Checks that run-level scripts are correct** — The rc script verifies that each run-level script exists and excludes those that represent backup scripts left by rpm updates.

- **Determines current and previous run levels** — Checks current and previous run levels to determine which run-level scripts to stop (previous level) and start (current level).

- **Decides whether to enter interactive startup** — If the confirm option is passed to the boot loader at boot time, all server processes must be confirmed at the system console before starting.

- **Kills and starts run-level scripts** — Stops run-level scripts from the previous level, and then starts run-level scripts from the current level.

In Fedora, most of the services that are provided to users and computers on the network are started from run-level scripts.

Understanding run-level scripts

A software package that has a service to start at boot time (or when the system changes run levels) can add a script to the /etc/init.d directory. That script can then be linked to an appropriate run-level directory and run with either the start or stop option (to start or stop the service, respectively).

Note

Note that the /etc/init.d directory is really a link to /etc/rc.d/init.d, but most documentation refers to /etc/init.d. If you want to modify files, work in /etc/rc.d/init.d; otherwise, you can use /etc/init.d. ∎

Table 11-4 lists many of the typical run-level scripts that are found in /etc/init.d and explains their function. Depending on the Fedora software packages you installed on your system, you may have dozens more run-level scripts than those shown here. (Later, I describe how these files are linked into particular run-level directories.)

TABLE 11-4

Run-Level Scripts Contained in /etc/init.d

Run-Level Scripts	Description
acpid	Controls the Advanced Configuration and Power Interface daemon, which monitors events in the kernel and reports them to user level.
atd	Starts or stops the at daemon to receive, queue, and run jobs submitted via the at or batch commands.
autofs	Starts and stops the automount daemon, for automatically mounting file systems (so, for example, a CD can be automatically mounted when it is inserted).
bluetooth	Starts services such as authentication, discovery, and human interface devices for communicating with Bluetooth devices.
crond	Starts or stops the cron daemon to periodically run routine commands.
dhcpd	Starts or stops the dhcpd daemon, which automatically assigns IP addresses to computers on a LAN.
firstboot	Checks to see if firstboot needs to be run and, if so, runs it. This is typically done after Fedora is first installed.
haldaemon	Starts the hald daemon to discover and set up hardware. Used to mount removable media, manage power, or auto-play multimedia.
halt	Terminates all processes, writes out accounting records, removes swap space, unmounts all file systems, and either shuts down or reboots the machine (depending on how the command was called).
httpd	Starts the httpd daemon, which enables your computer to act as an HTTP server (that is, to serve Web pages).
ip6tables	Starts the ip6tables firewall daemon, which manages any iptables-style firewall rules set up for your computer for Ipv6 networking.
iptables	Starts the iptables firewall daemon, which manages any iptables-style firewall rules set up for your computer.
killall	Shuts down any subsystems that may still be running prior to a shutdown or reboot.
messagebus	Runs the dbus-daemon for broadcasting system messages to interested applications.
netfs	Mounts or unmounts network (NFS, SMB, and NCP) file systems.
network	Starts or stops all configured network interfaces and initializes the TCP/IP and IPX protocols.
NetworkManager	Switches automatically to the best-available network connections.

continued

TABLE 11-4 *(continued)*	
Run-Level Scripts	**Description**
nfs	Starts or stops the NFS-related daemons (`rpc.nfsd`, `rpc.mountd`, `rpc.statd`, and `rcp.rquotad`) and exports shared file systems.
ntpd	Runs the Network Time Protocol daemon (`ntpd`), which synchronizes system time with Internet standard time servers.
openvpn	Runs the OpenVPN virtual private network service.
rsyslog	Starts or stops the `klogd` and `rsyslogd` daemons that handle logging events from the kernel and other processes, respectively.
sendmail	Controls the `sendmail` daemon, which handles incoming and outgoing SMTP (Simple Mail Transport Protocol) mail messages.
smb	Starts or stops the `smbd` and `nmbd` daemons for allowing access to Samba file and print services.
snmpd	Starts or stops the `snmpd` (Simple Network Management Protocol) daemon, which enables others to view machine-configuration information.
sshd	Runs the secure shell daemon (`sshd`), which listens for requests from ssh clients for remote login or remote execution requests.
vsftpd	Runs the Very Secure FTP server (`vsftpd`) to provide FTP sessions to remote clients for downloading and uploading files.
winbind	Runs the winbind service for Samba file and print services.

Each script representing a service that you want to start or stop is linked to a file in each of the run-level directories. For each run level, a script beginning with K stops the service, whereas a script beginning with S starts the service.

The two digits following the K or S in the filename provide a mechanism to select the priority at which the programs are run. For example, S12syslog is run before S90crond. However, the file S110my_daemon is run before S85gpm even though you can readily see that 85 is less than 110. This is because the ASCII collating sequence orders the files, which simply means that one positional character is compared to another. Therefore, a script beginning with the characters S110 is executed between S10network and S15netfs in run level 3.

All of the programs within the /etc/rcX.d directories (where X is replaced by a run-level number) are symbolic links, usually to a file in /etc/init.d. The /etc/rcX.d directories include the following:

- /etc/rc0.d: Run level 0 directory
- /etc/rc1.d: Run level 1 directory

- /etc/rc2.d: Run level 2 directory
- /etc/rc3.d: Run level 3 directory
- /etc/rc4.d: Run level 4 directory
- /etc/rc5.d: Run level 5 directory
- /etc/rc6.d: Run level 6 directory

In this manner, /etc/rc0.d/K05atd, /etc/rc1.d/K05atd, /etc/rc2.d/K05atd, /etc/rc3.d/S95atd, /etc/rc4.d/S95atd, /etc/rc5.d/S95atd, and /etc/rc6.d/K05atd are all symbolic links to /etc/init.d/atd. Using this simple, consistent mechanism, you can customize which programs are started at boot time.

Understanding what startup scripts do

Despite all the complicated rc*X*s, Ss, and Ks, the form of each startup script is really quite simple. Because they are in plain text, you can just open one with a text editor to see what it does. For the most part, a run-level script can be run with a start option, a stop option, and possibly a restart option. For example, the following lines are part of the contents of the smb script, defining what happens when the script is run with different options to start or stop the Samba file and print service:

```
#!/bin/sh
#
# chkconfig: - 91 35
# description: Starts and stops the Samba smbd daemon \
#              used to provide SMB network services.
        .
        .
        .
start() {
        KIND="SMB"
        echo -n $"Starting $KIND services: "
        daemon smbd $SMBDOPTIONS
        RETVAL=$?
        echo

        [ $RETVAL -eq 0 ] && touch /var/lock/subsys/smb || \
            RETVAL=1
        return $RETVAL
}

stop() {
        KIND="SMB"
        echo -n $"Shutting down $KIND services: "
        killproc smbd
        RETVAL=$?
        echo
```

```
                      [ -$RETVAL -eq 0 ] && rm -f /var/lock/subsys/smb
                      return $RETVAL
        }

    restart() {
            stop
            start
    }
            .
            .
            .
```

To illustrate the essence of what this script does, I skipped some of the beginning and the end of the script (where it checks if the network is up and running and sets some values). Here are the actions smb takes when it is run with start or stop:

- **start** — This part of the script starts the smbd server when the script is run with the start option.

- **stop** — When run with the stop option, the /etc/init.d/smb script stops the smbd server.

The restart option runs the script with a stop option followed by a start option. If you want to start the smb service yourself, type the following command (as root user):

```
# service smb start
Starting SMB services:                     [ OK ]
```

To stop the service, type the following command:

```
# service smb stop
Shutting down SMB services:                [ OK ]
```

The smb run-level script is different from other run-level scripts in that it supports several options other than start and stop. For example, this script has options (not shown in the example) that enable you to reload the smb.conf configuration file (reload) and check the status of the service (status).

Changing run-level script behavior

Modifying the startup behavior of any such script merely involves opening the file in a text editor.

For example, the atd daemon queues jobs submitted from the at and batch commands. Jobs submitted via batch are executed only if the system load is not above a particular value, which can be set with a command-line option to the atd command.

The default *limiting load factor* value of 0.8 is based on the assumption that a single-processor machine with less than 80 percent CPU utilization could handle the additional load of the batch job. However, if you were to add another CPU to your machine, 0.8 would only represent 40 percent of the computer's processing power, so you could safely raise that limit without affecting overall system performance.

This load limit is set in a file of options for the atd daemon. You can determine which file by looking into the /etc/init.d/atd script. After the initial comments near the top, you'll see lines like the following:

```
prog="atd"
[ -e /etc/sysconfig/$prog ] && . /etc/sysconfig/$prog
```

These lines check for the existence of the file /etc/sysconfig/atd, and if the file exists, sources in the commands (and settings) in that file.

In the /etc/sysconfig/atd file, you'll see a commented-out set of options:

```
#example
#OPTS="-1 4 -b 120"
```

Notice how the example shows a load level of 4.

You can change the limiting load factor to 1.6 to accommodate the increased processing capacity. To do this, simply modify the OPTS line:

```
#OPTS="-1 4 -b 120"
```

Remove the comment marker, #, and then set the value you want after the -1 option, to specify the new minimum system load value:

```
OPTS="-1 1.6 -b 120"
```

After saving the file and exiting the editor, you can reboot the machine or just run any of the following three commands to begin using the new batch threshold value:

```
# service atd reload
# service atd restart
# service atd stop ; service atd start
```

Note

Always make a copy of a run-level script before you change it. In addition, keep track of changes you make to run-level scripts before you upgrade the packages they come from. You need to make those changes again after the upgrade. ■

Many of the startup scripts use a file in the /etc/sysconfig directory to set their options, similar to the atd script. Check the /etc/sysconfig directory to see if there is a file by the same name as the script you want to modify. If there is, that file probably provides values that you can set to pass options to the startup script. Sysconfig files exist for atd, crond, dhcpd, ntpd, samba, squid, and others.

Reorganizing or removing run-level scripts

There are several ways to deal with removing programs from the system startup directories, adding them to particular run levels, or changing when they are executed. From a terminal window, you can use the chkconfig command. From a GUI, use the Service Configuration window.

Caution

You should never remove the run-level file from the /etc/init.d **directory. Because no scripts are run from the** /etc/init.d **directory automatically, it is okay to keep them there. Scripts in** /etc/init.d **are only accessed as links from the** /etc/rcX.d **directories. Keep scripts in the** init.d **directory so you can add them later by relinking them to the appropriate run-level directory.** ■

To reorganize or remove run-level scripts from the GUI, use the Service Configuration window. Either select System ➪ Administration ➪ Services or log in as root user and type the following command in a terminal window:

```
# system-config-services &
```

Figure 11-1 shows an example of the Service Configuration window, where you can reconfigure services for run levels 2, 3, 4, and 5. Icons next to each service indicate whether the service is currently enabled (green) or disabled (red) for the current run level and whether the service is currently running. (In this figure, only the NetworkManager, acpid, and auditd services are running.) Select a service to see a description of it. Here is what you can do from this window:

- **Enable** — With a service selected, click the Enable button to enable the service to start when you start your computer (run levels 2, 3, 4, and 5).

- **Disable** — With a service selected, click Disable to have the service not start when you boot your computer (or otherwise enter run levels 2, 3, 4, or 5).

- **Customize** — With a service selected, click Customize and select the run levels at which you want the service to start.

- **Start** — Click a service on the list. Select Start to request the service to immediately start.

Some administrators prefer text-based commands to manage run-level scripts and other system services that start automatically. The chkconfig command can be used to list whether services are configured to be on or off. To see a list of all system services, and whether they are on or off, type the following:

```
# chkconfig --list | less
```

You can then page through the list to see those services. If you want to view the status of an individual service, you can add the service at the end of the list option. For example, to see whether the Common Unix Printing Service (CUPS) starts in each run level, type the following:

```
# chkconfig --list cups
cups        0:off   1:off   2:on    3:on    4:on    5:on    6:off
```

FIGURE 11-1

Reorganize, add, and remove run-level scripts from the Service Configuration window.

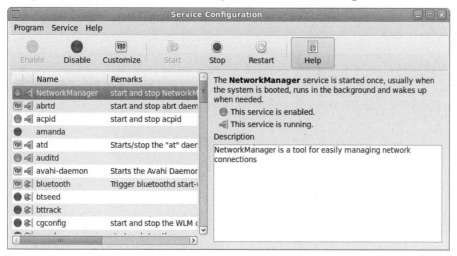

This example shows that the Common Unix Printing Service (CUPS) is set to be on for run levels 2, 3, 4, and 5, but off for run levels 0, 1, and 6.

Another tool you can run from the shell to change which services start and do not start at various levels is the ntsysv command. Type the following as root user from the shell:

```
# ntsysv
```

A screen appears with a list of available services. Use the up and down arrow keys to locate the service you want. With the cursor on a service, press the spacebar to toggle the service on or off. Press the Tab key to highlight the OK button, and press the spacebar to save the change and exit. The ntsysv tool changes services for the current run level only. You can run ntsysv with the --level # option, where # is replaced by the run level for which you want to change services.

Adding run-level scripts

Suppose you want to create and configure your own run-level script. For example, after installing the binaries for the fictitious my_daemon program, it needs to be configured to start up in run levels 3, 4, and 5, and terminated in any other run level. You can add the script to the /etc/init.d directory, and then use the chkconfig command to configure it.

To use chkconfig, ensure that the following lines are included in the /etc/init.d/my_daemon script:

```
# !/bin/sh
#
```

```
# Service my_daemon starts and stops the my_daemon daemon
#
# chkconfig: 345 82 28
# description: Starts the my_daemon daemon,  \
#              nicely.

### BEGIN INIT INFO
# Provides: my_daemon
# Required-Start: $local_fs
# Required-Stop: $local_fs
# Default-Start: 3 4 5
# Default-Stop: 0 1 2 6
# Short-Description: Starts/stop the "my_daemon" daemon
# Description:     Runs commands scheduled by the "my_daemon"
#        and provides a chkconfig example.
### END INIT INFO
```

Note

The line `chkconfig: 345 82 28` sets the script to start in run levels 3, 4, and 5. It sets start scripts to be set to 82 for those run levels. It sets stop scripts to be set to 28 in all other levels. You'll see these numbers in the file names for the scripts in the `/etc/rcN.d` directories as shown in the script names example following. These numbers help ensure the scripts are run in a certain order based on how Linux sorts the file names in the directories. ∎

You need both the old-style `chkconfig` lines at the top and the newer-style LSB (Linux Standard Base) init information blocks as comments in your script. The init information block takes precedence over the information at the top of the file as well.

In this case, the default start levels are 3, 4, and 5.

Note

You will see quite a variation in the information in the default set of `/etc/init.d` scripts. If `chkconfig` detects problems but still has enough information to set up your service, you will likely end up with a service that is off for each run level. ∎

With those lines in place, simply run the following command:

```
# chkconfig --add my_daemon
```

Appropriate links are created automatically. This can be verified with the following command:

```
# chkconfig --list my_daemon
```

The resulting output should look like this:

```
my_daemon 0:off 1:off 2:off 3:on 4:on 5:on 6:off
```

The script names that are created by `chkconfig` to make this all work are as follows:

```
/etc/rc0.d/K28my_daemon
/etc/rc1.d/K28my_daemon
/etc/rc2.d/K28my_daemon
/etc/rc3.d/S82my_daemon
/etc/rc4.d/S82my_daemon
/etc/rc5.d/S82my_daemon
/etc/rc6.d/K28my_daemon
```

Managing xinetd services

Several services, particularly network services, are not handled by separate run-level scripts. Instead, a single run-level script called `xinetd` (formerly `inetd`) is run to handle incoming requests for these services. For that reason, `xinetd` is sometimes referred to as the *super-server*. The `xinetd` run-level script (along with the `xinetd` daemon that it runs) offers the following advantages:

- **Fewer daemon processes** — Instead of one (or more) daemon processes running on your computer to monitor incoming requests for each service, the `xinetd` daemon can listen for requests for many different services. As a result, when you type `ps -ax` to see what processes are running, dozens of fewer daemon processes will be running than there would be if each service had its own daemon.

- **Access control and logging** — By using `xinetd` to oversee the management of services, consistent methods of access control (such as PAM) and consistent logging methods (such as the `/var/log/messages` file) can be used across all the services.

When a request comes into your computer for a service that `xinetd` is monitoring, `xinetd` uses the `/etc/xinetd.conf` file, if present, to read configuration files contained in the `/etc/xinetd.d` directory. Then, based on the contents of the `xinetd.d` file for the requested service, a server program is launched to handle the service request (provided that the service is not disabled).

Each server process is one of two types: single-thread or multithread. A single-thread server handles only the current request, whereas a multithread server handles all incoming requests for the service as long as a client holding the process is still open. Then the multithread server closes and `xinetd` begins monitoring that service again.

You will see entries in the `/etc/xinetd.d` directory for the network services you installed that are managed by `xinetd`, such as rsync.

Other services that can be launched by requests to `xinetd` include services for remote telnet requests, Samba configuration requests (swat), and Amanda network backups. A short description of each service is included in its `/etc/xinetd.d` file. Many of the services handled by `xinetd` are legacy services, including `rlogin`, `rsh`, and `finger`, that are considered insecure by today's security standards because they use clear-text passwords.

Manipulating run levels

Aside from the run level chosen at boot time (usually 3 or 5) and the shutdown or reboot levels (0 and 6, respectively), you can change the run level at any time while you're logged in (as root user). The telinit command (really just a symbolic link to init) enables you to specify a desired run level, causing the termination of all system processes that shouldn't exist in that run level, and starting all processes that should be running.

For example, if you encounter a problem with your hard disk on startup, you may be placed in single-user mode (run level 1) to perform system maintenance. After the machine is stable, you can execute the command as follows:

```
# telinit 5
```

The init command handles terminating and starting all processes necessary to present you with a graphical login window.

Determining the current run level

You can determine the machine's current run level with the aptly named runlevel command. Using the previous example of booting into single-user mode and then manually changing the run level, the output of the runlevel command would be as follows:

```
# runlevel
S 5
```

This means that the previous run level was S (for single-user mode) and the current run level is 5. If the machine had booted properly, the previous run level would be listed as N to indicate that there wasn't a previous run level.

Changing to a shutdown run level

Shutting down the machine is simply a change in run level. With that in mind, other ways to change the run level include the reboot, halt, poweroff, and shutdown commands. The reboot command runs the halt command and executes a shutdown -r now, terminating all processes and rebooting the machine. The halt command executes shutdown -h now, terminating all processes and leaving the machine in an idle state (but still powered on).

Similarly, the poweroff command executes a change to run level 0, but if the machine's BIOS supports Advanced Power Management (APM), it will switch off the power to the machine.

Note

A time must be given to the shutdown command, specified either as +m (representing the number of minutes to delay before beginning shutdown) or as hh:mm (an absolute time value, where hh is the hour and mm is the minute that you would like the shutdown to begin). Alternatively, now is commonly used to initiate the shutdown immediately. ∎

Scheduling System Tasks

Frequently, you need to run a process unattended or at off-hours. The `at` facility is designed to run such jobs at specific times. Jobs you submit are spooled in the directory `/var/spool/at`, awaiting execution by the `at` daemon `atd`. The jobs are executed using the current directory and environment that was active when the job was submitted. Any output or error messages that haven't been redirected elsewhere are e-mailed to the user who submitted the job.

The following sections describe how to use the `at`, `batch`, and `cron` facilities to schedule tasks to run at specific times. These descriptions also include ways to view which tasks are scheduled and delete scheduled tasks that you don't want to run anymore.

Using at.allow and at.deny

There are two access control files designed to limit which users can use the `at` facility. The file `/etc/at.allow` contains a list of users who are granted access, and the file `/etc/at.deny` contains a similar list of those who may not submit `at` jobs. If neither file exists, then only the super user is granted access to `at`. If a blank `/etc/at.deny` file exists (as in the default configuration), then all users are allowed to utilize the `at` facility to run their own `at` jobs. If you use either `at.allow` or `at.deny`, you aren't required to use both.

Specifying when jobs are run

There are many different ways to specify the time at which an `at` job should run (most of which look like spoken commands). Table 11-5 has a few examples. These are not complete commands — they provide only an example of how to specify the time that a job should run.

TABLE 11-5

Samples for Specifying Times in an at Job

Command Line	Description
at now	The job is run immediately.
at now + 2 minutes	The job will start two minutes from the current time.
at now + 1 hour	The job will start one hour from the current time.
at now + 5 days	The job will start five days from the current time.
at now + 4 weeks	The job will start four weeks from the current time.
at now next minute	The job will start in exactly 60 seconds.
at now next hour	The job will start in exactly 60 minutes.

continued

TABLE 11-5 *(continued)*

Command Line	Description
at now next day	The job will start at the same time tomorrow.
at now next month	The job will start on the same day and at the same time next month.
at now next year	The job will start on the same date and at the same time next year.
at now next fri	The job will start at the same time next Friday.
at teatime	The job will run at 4 p.m. They keywords noon and midnight can also be used.
at 16:00 today	The job will run at 4 p.m. today.
at 16:00 tomorrow	The job will run at 4 p.m. tomorrow.
at 2:45pm	The job will run at 2:45 p.m. on the current day.
at 14:45	The job will run at 2:45 p.m. on the current day.
at 5:00 Apr 14 2011	The job will begin at 5 a.m. on April 14, 2011.
at 5:00 4/14/11	The job will begin at 5 a.m. on April 14, 2011.

Submitting scheduled jobs

The at facility offers a lot of flexibility regarding how you can submit scheduled jobs. There are three ways to submit a job to the at facility:

- **Piped in from standard input** — For example, the following command will attempt to build the Perl distribution from the source in the early morning hours while the machine is likely to be less busy, assuming the Perl sources are stored in /tmp/perl:

```
echo "cd /tmp/perl; make ; ls -al" | at 2am tomorrow
```

An ancillary benefit to this procedure is that a full log of the compilation process will be e-mailed to the user who submitted the job.

- **Read as standard input** — If no command is specified, at will prompt you to enter commands at the special at> prompt, as shown in the following example. You must indicate the end of the commands by pressing Ctrl+D, which signals an End of Transmission (<EOT>) to at.

```
$ at 23:40
at> cd /tmp/perl
at> make
at> ls -al
at> <Ctrl-d>
```

- **Read from a file** — When the -f command-line option is followed by a valid filename, the contents of that file are used as the commands to be executed, as in the following example:

```
$ at -f /root/bin/runme now + 5 hours
```

This runs the commands stored in /root/bin/runme in five hours. The file can be either a simple list of commands or a shell script to be run in its own subshell (that is, the file begins with #!/bin/bash or the name of another shell).

Viewing scheduled jobs

You can use the atq command (effectively the same as at -l) to view a list of your pending jobs in the at queue, showing each job's sequence number, the date, and time the job is scheduled to run, and the queue in which the job is being run.

The two most common queue names are a (which represents the at queue) and b (which represents the batch queue). All other letters (uppercase and lowercase) can be used to specify queues with lower priority levels. If the atq command lists a queue name as =, it indicates that the job is currently running. Here is an example of output from the atq command:

```
# atq
2    Sun Jan 9 00:51 a  ericfj
3 Sun Jan 9 00:52 a  ericfj
4 Sun Jan 9 23:52 a  ericfj
```

Here you can see that three at jobs are pending (job numbers 2, 3, and 4, all indicated as a). After the job number, the output shows the date and hour each job is scheduled to run.

Deleting scheduled jobs

If you decide that you'd like to cancel a particular job, you can use the atrm command (equivalent to at -d) with the job number (or more than one) as reported by the atq command. For example, using the following output from atq:

```
# atq
18      Sat Jan 1 03:00 a  ericfj
19      Sat Jan 29 05:27 a  ericfj
20      Sun Jan 30 05:27 a  ericfj
21      Fri Jan 14-14 00:01 a  ericfj
22      Sat Jan 1 03:00 a  ericfj
```

you can remove the jobs scheduled to run at 5:27 a.m. on January 29 and January 30 from the queue with the following command:

```
# atrm 19 20
```

Using the batch command

If system resources are at a premium on your machine, or if the job you submit can run at a priority lower than normal, the `batch` command (equivalent to `at -q b`) may be useful. It is controlled by the same `atd` daemon, and it allows job submissions in the same format as `at` submissions (although the time specification is optional).

However, to prevent your job from usurping already scarce processing time, the job will run only if the system load average is below a particular value. The default value is 0.8, but specifying a command-line option to `atd` can modify this. This was used as an example earlier in the description of startup and shutdown. Here is an example of the `batch` command:

```
$ batch
at> du -h /home > /tmp/duhome
at> <Ctrl+d>
```

In this example, after I type the `batch` command, the `at` facility is invoked to enable me to enter the command(s) I want to run. Typing the `du -h /home > /tmp/duhome` command line has the disk usages for everything in the `/home` directory structure output to the `/tmp/duhome` file. On the next line, pressing Ctrl+D ends the batch job. As soon as the load average is low enough, the command is run. (Run the `top` command to view the current load average.)

Using the cron facility

Another way to run commands unattended is via the `cron` facility. Part of the cronie rpm package, `cron` addresses the need to run commands periodically or routinely (at least, more often than you'd care to manually enter them) and allows a lot of flexibility in automating the execution of the command. (The cronie package contains an extended version of the `cron` utility for scheduling tasks to run at a particular time, as well as adding security enhancements.)

As with the `at` facility, any output or error messages that haven't been redirected elsewhere are e-mailed to the user who submitted the job. Unlike using `at`, however, `cron` jobs are intended to run more than once and at a regular interval (even if that interval is only once per month or once per year).

Also like the `at` facility, `cron` includes two access control files designed to limit which users can use it. The file `/etc/cron.allow` contains a list of users who are granted access, and the file `/etc/cron.deny` contains a similar list of those who may not submit `cron` jobs. If neither file exists (or if `cron.deny` is empty), all users are granted access to `cron`.

There are four places where a job can be submitted for execution by the `cron` daemon `crond`:

- The `/var/spool/cron/`*username* file — This method, whereby each individual user (indicated by *username*) controls his or her own separate file, is the method used on Unix System V systems.

- The `/etc/crontab` file — This is referred to as the *system crontab file*, and was the original crontab file from BSD Unix and its derivatives. Only root has permission to modify this file.

- **The /etc/cron.d directory** — Files placed in this directory have the same format as the /etc/crontab file. Only root is permitted to create or modify files in this directory.
- **The /etc/cron.hourly, /etc/cron.daily, /etc/cron.weekly, and /etc/cron. monthly directories** — Each file in these directories is a shell script that runs at the times specified in the /etc/crontab file (by default, at one minute after the hour every hour; at 4:02 a.m. every day; Sunday at 4:22 a.m.; and 4:42 a.m. on the first day of the month, respectively). Only root is allowed to create or modify files in these directories.

The standard format of an entry in the /var/spool/cron/*username* file consists of five fields specifying when the command should run: minute, hour, day of the month, month, and day of the week. The sixth field is the actual command to be run.

The files in the /etc/cron.d directory and the /etc/crontab file use the same first five fields to determine when the command should run. However, the sixth field represents the name of the user submitting the job (because it cannot be inferred by the name of the file as in a /var/spool/cron/*username* directory), and the seventh field is the command to be run. Table 11-6 lists the valid values for each field common to both types of files.

TABLE 11-6

Valid /etc/crontab Field Values

Field Number	Field	Acceptable Values
1	minute	Any integer between 0 and 59
2	hour	Any integer between 0 and 23, using a 24-hour clock
3	day of the month	Any integer between 0 and 31
4	month	Any integer between 1 and 12, or an abbreviation for the name of the month (Jan, Feb, Mar, Apr, May, Jun, Jul, Aug, Sep, Oct, Nov, Dec)
5	day of the week	Any integer between 0 and 7 (as a convenience, both 0 and 7 can represent Sunday, 1 is Monday, 2 is Tuesday, and so on), or abbreviation for the day (Sun, Mon, Tue, Wed, Thu, Fri, Sat)

The latest version of cron (cronie and crontabs packages) includes the capability to indicate that a cron job be run at boot time.

Refer to the crontab man page (type **man 5 crontab**) for information on using the reboot option to have a command run once at startup time.

An asterisk (*) in any field indicates all possible values for that field. For example, an asterisk in the second column is equivalent to 0, 1, 2 . . . 22, 23, and an asterisk in the fourth column means

Jan, Feb, Mar . . . Nov, Dec. In addition, lists of values, ranges of values, and increments can be used. For example, to specify the days Monday, Wednesday, and Friday, the fifth field could be represented as the list Mon, Wed, Fri. To represent the normal working hours in a day, the range 9–17 could be specified in the second field. Another option is to use an increment, as in specifying 0–31/3 in the third field to represent every third day of the month, or */5 in the first field to denote every five minutes.

Lines beginning with a # character in any of the `crontab`-format files are comments, which can be very helpful in explaining what task each command is designed to perform. It is also possible to specify environment variables (in Bourne shell syntax, such as `NAME="value"`) within the `crontab` file. Any variable can be specified to fine-tune the environment in which the job runs, but one that may be particularly useful is `MAILTO`. The following line sends the results of the `cron` job to a user other than the one who submitted the job:

```
MAILTO=otheruser
```

If the following line appears in a `crontab` file, all output and error messages that haven't already been redirected will be discarded:

```
MAILTO=
```

Modifying scheduled tasks with crontab

The files in `/var/spool/cron` should not be edited directly. They should only be accessed via the `crontab` command. To list the current contents of your own personal `crontab` file, type the following command:

```
$ crontab -l
```

All `crontab` entries can be removed with the following command:

```
$ crontab -r
```

Even if your personal `crontab` file doesn't exist, you can use the following command to begin editing it:

```
$ crontab -e
```

The file automatically opens in the text editor that is defined in your `EDITOR` or `VISUAL` environment variables, with vi as the default. When you're done, simply exit the editor. Provided there were no syntax errors, your `crontab` file will be installed. For example, if your user name is jsmith, you have just created the file `/var/spool/cron/jsmith`. If you add a line (with a descriptive comment, of course) to remove any old core files from your source code directories, that file may look similar to this:

```
# Find and remove core files from /home/jsmith/src
5 1 * * Sun,Wed find /home/jsmith/src \↵
-name core.[0-9]* -exec rm {} \; > /dev/null 2>&1
```

In this example, the > /dev/null sends the normal output (stdout) of the command to /dev/null (essentially ignoring the output). The 2>&1 syntax sends the error output (stderr) to the same location as the normal output (ignoring errors as well).

Because core files in Fedora consist of the word core, followed by a dot (.) and process ID, this example will match all files beginning with core. and followed by a number. The root user can access any user's individual crontab file by using the -u *username* option to the crontab command.

Understanding cron files

Separate cron directories are set up to contain cron jobs that run hourly, daily, weekly, and monthly. These cron jobs are all set up to run from the /etc/crontab file. The default /etc/crontab file is empty. Under the hood, however, cron runs the hourly, daily, weekly, and monthly jobs as if the crontab file looks like this:

```
SHELL=/bin/bash
PATH=/sbin:/bin:/usr/sbin:/usr/bin
MAILTO=root
HOME=/

# run-parts
01 * * * * root run-parts /etc/cron.hourly
02 4 * * * root run-parts /etc/cron.daily
22 4 * * 0 root run-parts /etc/cron.weekly
42 4 1 * * root run-parts /etc/cron.monthly
```

The first four lines initialize the run-time environment for all subsequent jobs (the subshell in which jobs run, the executable program search path, the recipient of output and error messages, and that user's home directory). The next five lines execute (as the user root) the run-parts program that controls programs you may want to run periodically.

run-parts is a shell script that takes a directory as a command-line argument. It then sequentially runs every program within that directory (shell scripts are most common, but binary executables and links are also evaluated). The default configuration executes programs in /etc/cron.hourly at one minute after every hour of every day; /etc/cron.daily at 4:02 a.m. every day; /etc/cron.weekly at 4:22 a.m. on Sundays; and /etc/cron.monthly at 4:42 a.m. on the first day of each month.

Here are examples of files that are installed in cron directories for different software packages:

- /etc/cron.daily/logrotate — Automates rotating, compressing, and manipulating system log files
- /etc/cron.daily/makewhatis.cron — Updates the whatis database (contains descriptions of man pages), which is used by the man -k, apropos, and whatis commands to find man pages related to a particular word

- **/etc/cron.daily/mlocate.cron** — Updates the /var/lib/mlocate/mlocate.db database (using the updatedb command), which contains a searchable list of files on the machine

- **/etc/cron.daily/tmpwatch** — Removes files from /tmp, /var/tmp, and /var/catman that haven't been accessed in 10 days

The makewhatis.cron script installed in /etc/cron.weekly is similar to the one in /etc/cron.daily but it completely rebuilds the whatis database, rather than just updating the existing database.

Finally, the /etc/cron.d directory contains files that have the same format as /etc/crontab files.

Summary

Shell scripts are an integral part of a Fedora system for configuring, booting, administering, and customizing Fedora. They are used to eliminate typing repetitive commands; and they are frequently executed from the scheduling facilities within Fedora, providing a lot of flexibility in determining when and how often a process should run. They also control the startup of most daemons and server processes at boot time.

The init daemon and its configuration file, /etc/inittab, also factor heavily in the initial startup of your Fedora system. They implement the concept of run levels, which are carried out by the shell scripts in /etc/rc.d/init.d, and they provide a means by which the machine can be shut down or rebooted in an orderly manner.

To have shell scripts configured to run on an ongoing basis, you can use the cron facility. cron jobs can be added by editing cron files directly or by running commands such as at and batch to enter the commands to be run.

Backing Up and Restoring Files

I f you've ever suffered a hard drive crash, you know just how aggravating it can be. You can lose irreplaceable data. You will likely spend countless hours reinstalling your operating system and applications. It is not a fun experience. It need happen only once for you to learn the importance of making regular backups of your critical data.

Today, larger and faster backup media can simplify the process of backing up your data. Fedora supports many different types of media — such as writable CD (CD-R and CD-RW), DVD (DVD-R, DVD+R, DVD+RW, and DVD-RW), and magnetic tape — for creating backups. Using tools such as cron, you can configure backups to run unattended at scheduled times.

This chapter describes how to create a backup strategy and how to select media for backing up data on your Fedora system. It tells you how to do automated backups, and backups over a network. It also describes how to restore individual files, or entire file systems, using tools such as the `restore` command.

Making a Simple Backup Archive

Improvements in the GNOME desktop for handling removable media (CDs, DVDs, USB flash drives, and so on) can help you do a quick backup of your personal data. With the GNOME desktop running on your Fedora system, use the following procedure to back up all the data in your home directory:

1. Insert a blank CD or DVD into your computer's drive. You'll see either an icon on the desktop or a dialog asking you what to do when inserting CDs or DVDs. An icon appears on the desktop, indicating that a blank disc is ready to be used.

2. Double-click the Blank Disc icon to see the CD/DVD Creator window. Alternately, select CD/DVD Creator from the window that pops up.

3. Open the folder icon representing your home directory (such as Joe's Home) on the desktop and browse to the /home folder.

4. Drag-and-drop your home directory from the /home folder on to the CD/DVD Creator window.

5. Add other files and folders you want to back up to the CD/DVD Creator window in the same way.

6. When all the files and folders you want to back up are copied to the CD/DVD Creator window, click Write to Disc. The Disc Burning Setup pop-up window will appear.

7. Type a disc name for the backup medium and optionally choose the write speed. (The disc name will be used as the name of the mount point if you later open the CD/DVD on the GNOME desktop).

This procedure results in a standard ISO9660 image (with Rock Ridge extensions) being burned to the CD or DVD. That disc can be read from Linux, Windows, or other systems that support that ISO standard. While this procedure is a quick way to save your critical files, you should consider using other backup tools described in this chapter for more flexible and powerful backup methods.

Note

Your home directory will likely have configuration files in dot-directories (hidden directories whose names start with a period) that go levels deeper than the normal CD formats can support. ISO9660 can only support directories eight levels deep. Thus, CDs are not always good for backing up your home directory. You can create ZIP or gzipped files to compress your home directory structure and then write those files to the CD. In addition, the mkisofs tool, described later in this chapter in the section on writing to DVDs, helps create a CD image on your hard disk that will shorten the long directory depths, especially those created in ~/.openoffice.org. ∎

Doing a simple backup with déjà-dup

Inexpensive hard disk space, fast networks, and some really neat new tools have given Linux users some nice backup alternatives to the old reliable removable media (such as tapes and CDs). To back up your personal data or the data from a small office computer, the examples in this section provide fairly simple ways of creating usable backups of your data.

To do this procedure, you need to have hard disk space on a computer that is at least slightly larger than the hard disk you are backing up. That hard disk space could be on the following:

- **A different partition** — By backing up to a separate disk partition on the same disk drive, you are protected in case the partition you are backing up becomes corrupted. However, you are not protected if your hard disk goes bad.

- **A different hard disk** — Backing up to a separate hard disk can protect from a corrupted disk, but won't help you if your computer is hit by lightning, a flood, or other acts of God. It is also good to place the separate hard disk on a separate disk controller.

- **A different computer** — By backing up over the network, you can back up to another computer that is as far away from the source of your data as you are comfortable with. You can back up to the computer down the hall or one across the country.

Starting in Fedora 13, you can perform some of the simplest backups using the déjà-dup tool. Déjà-dup provides a very simple user interface on top of the command-line tool duplicity.

With déjà-dup, you can back up to local or remote systems, as well as upload backups to Amazon S3 servers in the cloud. On remote systems, you can use FTP, SSH, WebDAV or store to a Windows share. You can also back up to any disk mounted locally. If déjà-dup is not available on your system, you need to install the `deja-dup` and `duplicity` packages.

When you start déjà-dup from the System Tools menu under Applications, the tool presents a simple two-button user interface, as shown in Figure 12-1. From here, you can either back up or restore a previous backup.

FIGURE 12-1

Déjà–dup's startup window offers to back up or restore from a backup.

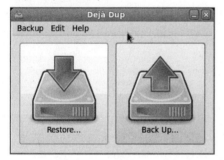

1. To get started, click Backup and then select the server or disk to use for backups. For example, you can create a directory on a local disk called `backups` to store your backups. (It is probably a good idea to back up to a different disk than what you use for your work.) Figure 12-2 shows the preferences for a simple home system backup.

   Notice how the backups directory itself is excluded from backups, to avoid a recursive attempt to save your data.

FIGURE 12-2

Configuring a backup location.

2. You then need to define an encryption password, as déjà-dup protects your backup data.

3. Next, back up your data. When you are done, you can specify when déjà-dup should perform the next backup.

Behind the scenes, déjà-dup uses duplicity, a command-line tool that creates encrypted backups. Duplicity in turn creates encrypted tar-formatted backups and uses the rsync code to send only changes to the backup server. You can also use rsync alone to perform backups.

Doing a simple backup with rsync

The rsync command is like a remote copy command (similar to rcp) on steroids. In essence, rsync lets you copy files from one location to another. However, it also has some nice extra features that enable you to do the following:

- **Transfer differences only** — If you transfer a file that was transferred during an earlier backup, rsync uses a checksum-search algorithm to determine the differences between the old file and the new one. Then it sends only the data needed to account for the differences between the two files. This results in less traffic being transferred over your network and less use of hardware I/O.

- **Transfer data securely** — rsync combines with ssh (or another remote shell) to encrypt the data, so it can travel securely across a network. Note that by default, rsync does not encrypt data. You need to set it up to use ssh as the transport mechanism, as described next in the section "Backing up files remotely."

- **Maintain ownership** — The transferred files can keep their same permissions, ownership, timestamps, and group designations. (Because ownership is based on numeric UID and GID, matching user and group accounts must be set up between machines in order for the files to appear to be owned by the same users and groups after the files are copied.)

The following sections show examples of the `rsync` command at work.

Backing up files locally

The first example shows a simple backup of a user's personal files. Here I'm copying the `/home/chris` directory (including all its files and subdirectories) to another directory on the local computer. That directory (`/mnt/backup/homes`) could be on a separate partition (see Chapter 2 for creating separate partitions), a hard disk (see Chapter 9 to add a hard disk), or a remote file system (see Chapter 17 to set up Samba to access Windows file shares or to create a system that serves up Windows file shares):

```
# rsync -av /home/chris /mnt/backup/homes/
```

Note

Notice that there's no trailing slash after `/home/chris` (it's not `/home/chris/`). Without that trailing slash, `rsync` will copy files from that directory to a target directory named `chris` (`/mnt/backup/homes/chris`). With a trailing slash, all files from `/home/chris/` are copied directly to the `homes` directory (`/mnt/backup/homes/`). ∎

In this example, the entire contents of the `/home/chris` directory structure are added to the `/mnt/backup/homes/chris` directory. All files, subdirectories, links, devices, and other file types are copied. By using the archive option (`-a`), all ownership, permissions, and creation times are maintained on the copied files. Using the `-a` option enables you to avoid entering the following options individually: `-r` (recursive), `-l` (copy symbolic links), `-p` (preserve permissions), `-t` (preserve times), `-g` (preserve group), `-o` (preserve owner), and `-D` (preserve devices and special files). The verbose option (`-v`) results in more messages being displayed as `rsync` progresses and can be helpful for diagnostic work.

If `/mnt/backup/homes` is on a separate disk, you now have your entire `/home/chris` directory copied in two places on the same machine. If the `/mnt/backup/homes` directory is an NFS shared directory (with write permission on), the files are now backed up to another machine.

Because the example is a backup of my personal files, which don't change too often, after a few days of changes to the files I might want to run the exact same command again:

```
# rsync -av /home/chris /mnt/backup/homes/
```

This time, any new files are copied to the target directory and the changes to any files I modified are applied to the original backup files. Any files I deleted from my home directory will still be in the target directory (`rsync` doesn't remove deleted files unless you specifically tell it to). The result is, again, a complete copy of the `/home/chris` directory at the moment the `rsync` command is run, plus any files that have been deleted from any `/home/chris` directories. You can also create backup scripts that can be used to back up, copy, and archive data to many different locations.

Note

If you want files that were deleted from the sending directory to be likewise deleted from the target directory, you can add the --delete **option to** rsync. ∎

Backing up files remotely

The previous example was a quick, informal backup method. With more critical data, you want to ensure that the data is being backed up to another computer and that the backup is done at regular intervals. This can be accomplished by using rsync in concert with ssh and cron.

Having ssh as the transport mechanism ensures that data will be encrypted when it is transferred; and because the SSH service (sshd) is enabled by default on many Fedora systems, you need only a user name and password to the remote system to do the backup. (As long as you can use ssh to connect to the remote machine and rsync is installed remotely, you can use the rsync command to transfer files there.) Here's an example:

```
# rsync -azv -e ssh /home/chris duck:/mnt/backup/homes/
root@duck's password: *******
sending incremental file list
```

In this example, I identify the remote computer (named *duck* in this case) by putting it before the remote directory name, separated with a colon. I use some different options as well. To the archive (-a) and verbose (-v) options, I add the -z option to compress the data (making it more efficient to transfer). I also use the -e ssh option to have rsync use an ssh remote shell to transfer data. The password prompt you see is the ssh login prompt. The -a option is important if you want to be able to restore files exactly as they were copied because it recursively copies a whole directory structure as it preserves ownership, date/time stamps, and permissions.

Note

If you want to use a different port, pass the -p **option with the port number after the** -e ssh **option in the command above. For example:**

```
# rsync -azv -e ssh -p 8989 /home/chris duck:/mnt/backup/homes ∎
```

When you connect for the first time to a remote system, ssh will tell you about the RSA fingerprint and ask you if you want to continue. (Answer yes unless you typed the command incorrectly.)

You can repeat this command each time you want to back up your files. However, the more efficient way to do this is to set up this command to run as a cron job so that the backups happen automatically at set intervals.

In order for rsync to run automatically, you can't have it prompt you for a password. To have the rsync command run without prompting for a password, follow this procedure:

1. Set up SSH to do no-password logins for the user who is going to perform the backup (see the section "Using ssh, scp, and sftp without passwords" in Chapter 13 for information on how to do this).

2. Decide how often you want the backup to run. For example, if you want to run the rsync command once each day, as root user you could create a file called /etc/cron.daily/mybackup. See Chapter 11 for more on cron.

3. Set permissions to be executable:

```
# chmod 755 /etc/cron.daily/mybackup
```

4. Add the command line to the mybackup file that you want to use:

```
rsync -azv -e ssh /home/chris chris@duck:/mnt/backup/homes/
```

5. Notice that I added the user name Chris as the login user name on the remote computer (duck). For you, this will be the name of the person for whom you set up a no-password login in Step 1. Also note that with the verbose (-v) option, a lot of output is sent as an e-mail from cron. Once you have verified everything works, you can remove the -v option.

At this point, a backup will be done once each day to the machine specified.

Note

With the simple backup command just shown, you can build on more complex features. In particular, you might want to think about building in a snapshot feature. Snapshots enable you to go back to a particular date and time to restore a backed-up file. Mike Rubel has an excellent procedure for doing rsync snapshots at www.mikerubel.org/computers/rsync_snapshots/ entitled "Easy Automated Snapshot-Style Backups with Linux and Rsync."

Another useful feature is the --bwlimit= option, which prevents rsync commands from consuming too much of the available network bandwidth. For example, --bwlimit=100 would limit the maximum transfer rate to 100 kilobytes per second. ∎

Choosing Backup Tools

While the deja-dup and rsync commands are some of the best choices for doing backups, these are by no means the only tools available. Many Linux systems administrators use a variety of commands for doing backups, often writing scripts to combine commands to work together. They might group together files in a single archive using tar or cpio, compress files to backup using bzip2 or gzip, or write whole directory structures of files using mkisofs.

The tools described in this chapter focus on those that are particularly designed for backups. The dump and restore commands are traditional Unix commands for backing up and restoring files. The mkisofs and cdrecord commands can combine to gather a file system into an ISO image and copy that image to CD or DVD. As for networked backup features, the Amanda facility is described later in this chapter. The pax facility provides a means of creating cpio and tar archives.

If the tools for backing up files described in this chapter are not exactly what you are looking for, there are many open-source backup facilities that you can add to your Fedora system. Here are a few examples:

- **Bacula** (`www.bacula.org`) — Bacula is a tool for managing network backups. It includes features to make it easy to recover files that have been lost or damaged. Support for backup media includes tape, CD, and hard disk media.

- **Mondo Rescue** (`www.mondorescue.org`) — Mondo supports backups from LVM, RAID, ext2, ext3, JFS, XFS, ReiserFS, and VFAT file systems. Backups can be done to CD-R, CD-RW, NFS, or hard disk.

- **BackupPC** (`http://backuppc.sourceforge.net`) — BackupPC is useful for backing up both Linux and Windows systems over a network. Using BackupPC, you can extract backups using Samba, `tar` (over `ssh`, `rsh`, or `nfs`), or `rsync`.

Selecting a Backup Strategy

While it is tempting to do the quick-and-easy backup, backing up important data requires more planning and forethought. Several approaches can be taken to backing up your data. You need to ask yourself a few questions to decide which approach is best for you, such as the following:

- In the event of a crash, how much downtime can I tolerate?
- Will I need to recover older versions of my files or is the most recent revision sufficient?
- Do I need to back up files for just one computer or for many computers on a network?

Your answers to these questions will help you determine how often to do full backups and how often to do incremental backups. If the data is particularly critical, you may even decide that you need to have your data duplicated constantly, using a technique called *disk mirroring*. The following sections describe different backup methods.

Tip

For most Linux home users, the `deja-dup` **or the** `rsync` **methods discussed previously will work fine as a backup strategy.** ■

Full backup

A full backup is one that stores every file on a particular disk or partition. If that disk should ever crash, you can rebuild your system by restoring the entire backup to a new disk. Whatever backup strategy you decide on, some sort of full backup should be part of it. You may perform full backups every night or perhaps only once every week; it depends on how often you add or modify files on your system, and the capacity of your backup equipment.

Incremental backup

An incremental backup is one that contains only those files that have been added or modified since the last time a more complete backup was performed. You may choose to do incremental backups to conserve your backup media.

Incremental backups also take less time to complete because they only back up data that has changed since the most recent backup (full or incremental). Incremental and other partial backup types can be important when systems are in high use during the workweek and running a full backup would degrade system performance. Full backups can be reserved for the weekend when the system is not in use.

Disk mirroring

Full and incremental backups can take time to restore, and sometimes you just can't afford that downtime. By duplicating your operating system and data on an additional hard drive, you can greatly increase the speed with which you can recover from a server crash.

With disk mirroring, it is usually common for the system to continuously update the duplicate drive with the most current information. In fact, with a type of mirroring called RAID1 (described in Chapter 9), the duplicate drive is written to at the same time as the original, and if the main drive fails, the duplicate can immediately take over. This is called *fault-tolerant* behavior, which is a must if you are running a mission-critical server of some kind.

You can tailor different RAID levels to use features other than mirroring. Other RAID levels use *striping* (storing data in sections — called *stripes* — across multiple disks) and can be tuned for performance, data redundancy, and cost. Software RAID is supported in the Linux kernel, and several hardware vendors have RAID controller cards for SATA, IDE, and SCSI disk configurations that work well in Linux. See `http://tldp.org/HOWTO/Software-RAID-HOWTO.html` for further information on RAID in Linux.

Tip

While RAID may help protect your data, RAID is not a substitute for backups. You still want to back up your files. ∎

Network backup

All of the preceding backup strategies can be performed over a network. This is good because you can share a single backup device with many computers on a network. This is much cheaper and more convenient than installing a tape drive or other backup device in every system on your network. If you have many computers, however, your backup device will require a lot of capacity. In such a case, you might want to consider a mechanical tape loader, DVD-RW drive, or CD or DVD jukebox (which is capable of recording multiple CDs or DVDs without operator intervention).

It is even possible to do a form of disk mirroring over the network. For example, a Web server may store a duplicate copy of its data on another server. If the first server crashes, a simple TCP/IP hostname change can redirect the Web traffic to the second server. When the original server is rebuilt, it can recover all of its data from the backup server and be back in business.

Selecting a Backup Medium

Armed with a backup strategy in mind, it's time to select a backup medium. Several types of backup hardware and media are available for use with Fedora. Each type has its advantages and disadvantages.

The type of medium to choose depends largely on the amount of data you need to archive, how long you will store backups, how often you expect to recover data from your backups, and how much you can afford to spend. Table 12-1 compares the most common backup media.

TABLE 12-1

Comparison of Common Backup Media

Backup Medium	Advantages	Disadvantages
Magnetic tape	High capacity, low cost for archiving massive amounts of data.	Sequential access medium, so recovery of individual files can be slow.
Writable CDs	Random access medium, so recovery of individual files is easier. Backups can be restored from any CD-ROM drive.	Limited storage space (up to 700MB per CD). Shelf life for optical media (CDs, DVDs) may be as low as 5 years, although most manufacturers claim 20–30 years.
Writable DVDs	Large capacity (4.7GB, although the actual capacity you can achieve might be less) random access medium. DVDR-9 and DVD-9 DVDs can store up to 8.5GB of data.	Same shelf-life issues as other optical media.
Additional hard drive	Allows faster and more frequent backups. Fast recovery from crashes. No media to load. Data can be located and recovered more quickly. You can configure the second disk to be a virtual clone of the first disk, so that you can boot off of the second disk if the first disk crashes.	Data cannot be stored offsite; thus there is a risk of data loss if the entire server is destroyed. This method is not well suited to keeping historical archives of the many revisions of your files. The hard drive will eventually fill up. By using removable hard drives, you can overcome this limitation by removing the backup drive when it is full and moving it to a secure location.

The following sections describe how to use magnetic tape, writable DVDs, and writable CDs as backup media. Using additional hard drives as backup media is described later in this chapter.

Magnetic tape

Magnetic tape was for years the most common medium used for backing up large amounts of computer data. Tapes provide a low-cost, convenient way to archive your files. Today's high-capacity tape drives can back up many gigabytes of data on an amazingly small tape, allowing vast amounts of information to be safely stored. Tapes are also easy to transport offsite so that data will be secure in case of fires, hurricanes, or other disasters.

The primary disadvantage of magnetic tape is that it is a sequential access medium. This means that tapes are read or written from beginning to end, and searching for a particular file can be time-consuming. For this reason, tape is a good choice for backing up and restoring entire file systems, but not the ideal choice to recover individual files on a regular basis.

Fedora can use a wide variety of tape drives. Most SCSI tape drives will work without loading special modules. Even many IDE tape drives are now supported natively, without requiring the drive to operate in a "SCSI emulation" mode. Some drives, however, require installation of additional software.

Using ftape tools for magnetic tape

If your tape drive is attached to an IDE floppy controller cable, you will need to use the ftape driver to access it. Fortunately, the ftape loadable module is bundled with the Linux 2.6 kernel. When your Linux system boots, it should autodetect the tape drive and load the ftape driver. To verify that your system loaded the tape driver, type the following command shortly after you boot your computer:

```
dmesg | grep ftape
```

This searches the most recent kernel messages for lines containing the word ftape. If the ftape module was loaded, you should see output on the device.

If the module was not loaded, then you should check whether your kernel is compiled with support for the ftape module and your particular tape drive. It should be available and ready to include as a loadable module.

In most cases, an ftape device can be accessed just like a SCSI device. The primary difference is that an ftape device file contains the letters qft (for QIK Floppy Tape), whereas a SCSI tape contains st. For example, the device file for the first SCSI tape on your system will probably be /dev/st0; the device file for the first floppy tape will likely be /dev/qft0.

All of the standard tape- and archiving-related programs should work fine with both types of hardware. Nevertheless, there are a few extra programs that you might find useful when working with a floppy tape drive. These programs can be found in the mt-st package in Fedora. The mt command is used to control magnetic tape operation. The stinit command can initialize SCSI magnetic tape drives.

Testing the magnetic tape drive

With the mt-st package installed, you should now be ready to test your tape drive. Insert a blank tape into the tape drive and type the following commands:

```
$ mt -f /dev/qft0 status
$ mt -f /dev/qft0 rewind
```

The first command will present a status of the tape drive. After the second command, you should hear the tape spin as the system rewinds it. This will be a very short process if the tape is already rewound. The mt command provided with the mt-st package is used to scan, rewind, and eject magnetic tapes in a tape drive.

Writable DVD and CD drives

Another backup medium that is gaining popularity is the writable DVD or CD drive. Writable disc drives have several advantages over tape, the primary one being that CDs and DVDs are random access media. This means that the CD drive can quickly locate a particular file on the CD without sequentially scanning through the entire disc. This is useful when you need to keep a revision history of frequently changing data files (such as source code for a software project or drafts of legal documents).

Although people used to believe that CDs and DVDs had a very long life span, that belief has recently come into question. Even if your Robyn Hitchcock CD from 1984 still sounds good, CDs and DVDs are probably still a good choice if the backup will be needed for two years or less. For longer time periods, a tape backup will generally last longer than a writable disc. If your backups are intended for short-term storage, you should probably consider a rewritable or DVD-RW or CD-RW CD drive. A rewritable disc (unlike plain writable discs) can be reformatted and used to store new backups.

The biggest drawback is that a CD can store, at most, about 700MB of data. In contrast, DVDs can store 4.7GB of data (or about 8.5GB for dual-layer CDs) and many tape drives can store multiple gigabytes of data. For example, DAT DDS-3 tapes can hold up to 24GB of compressed data, while 8mm AIT-2 tapes can hold up to 100GB of compressed data.

Note

When manufacturers say 4.7GB, they are talking about 1,000MB per GB, not 1,024MB. Therefore, you can really only store up to about 4.3GB of data on a DVD (or, more precisely, 4,294,967,296 bytes). ∎

The commands to write CDs or DVDs are the same. In the following examples I use the term DVD, but you can use whatever media your drive supports.

Getting cdrecord for writable DVDs

To write CDs or DVDs with Fedora, you can use the wodim, cdparanoia, and genisoimage packages, which are installed by default. These packages contain components such as the cdrecord, devdump, isodump, isoinfo, isovfy, and readcd commands.

Note

If you want to create DVDs interactively, use the CD/DVD Creator covered previously or the Brasero Disc Burner application (covered in Chapter 7). This section discusses older command-line tools because that is what you need for running automated backups. ■

Writing to DVDs

DVD-R is a similar write-once DVD format with a capacity of about 4.7GB. Discs in the DVD-RW format can be written and rewritten many times. DVD+RW is a read-write format that provides for faster writing of data, and DVD+R is a similar write-once format. Typically, a DVD-burning drive will support the plus (DVD+RW, DVD+R) or the minus (DVD-RW, DVD-R) formats. Some drives support both. It is important you purchase discs compatible with your hardware. Using a writable DVD drive and the cdrecord command, you can back up your data to DVD-R, DVD-RW, DVD+R, and DVD+RW disks.

Because data written to write-once discs, such as DVD-R, DVD+R, CD-R or CD+R, becomes permanent once it is written, you need to format the disc and copy files to it all in one step. If you formatted it first, you would end up with an empty file system on a disc that can no longer be written to.

Note

Using a command called growisofs (described later in this chapter), you can write to a disc in such a way that the session is not closed. Later, you can add more data, in multiple sessions, before you finally close the DVD. The cdrecord command itself also now supports a -multi option, which can keep the session open for further writing. Not all DVD drives will support multisession writing (which requires that the hardware support CD-ROM XA mode 2 form 1). ■

The first step is to create an image of the DVD file system as a file on your computer. You do this with the mkisofs command. The second step is to burn the image to CD or DVD using a tool such as the cdrecord command.

Note

In recent releases of Fedora, the cdrecord command has been replaced by a command called wodim from the CDR Kit project (http://cdrkit.org). Fedora and other Linux distributions switched to the CDR Kit project because cdrecord licensing was changed to the Sun CDDL license, which is believed to be incompatible with the GPL. Because wodim is backward compatible with cdrecord and that command is linked to cdrecord, you can still use the cdrecord command. ■

As an example, imagine that you want to back up the home directory for user mary. You would invoke the mkisofs command and pass it the name of the file system image file to create, followed by the directory to base it on:

```
$ mkisofs -R -o /var/tmp/mary.iso /home/mary
```

This creates an ISO9660 file system image in a file named mary.iso located in the /var/tmp directory. The -R option causes Linux-specific file ownership and long filenames to be used. If your /var partition does not have enough room for the image, choose a different location.

Tip

By default, `mkisofs` preserves the ownership and access rights of files and directories when it creates the file system image. This is appropriate when you are making a backup, but not when you are creating a software distribution DVD. In such a case, add the `-r` option instead of `-R` as the first parameter to `mkisofs`. It will then store all files as publicly readable and, where appropriate, executable. ■

If you have a modern DVD or CD drive, you no longer need a SCSI ID for that drive to be able to record to it. You could enter the device name instead of the SCSI ID (such as `dev=/dev/cdrom`). However, if you have a SCSI DVD or CD drive, before you can write the image file to a disc, you must first discover the SCSI bus number, device ID number, and Logical Unit Number (LUN) of the drive. To find out which SCSI device ID the drive, in this instance a CD drive, is using, invoke the `cdrecord` command with the single parameter `-scanbus`:

```
# cdrecord -scanbus
```

You should see a response similar to the following:

```
scsibus0:
        0,0,0     0) 'IDE-CD ' 'R/RW 4x4x24  ' '1.04' Removable CD-ROM
        0,0,1     1) *
        0,0,2     2) *
        0,0,3     3) *
        0,0,4     4) *
        0,0,5     5) *
        0,0,6     6) *
        0,0,7     7) *
```

This tells you that the CD drive is using SCSI ID zero. The LUN in this case should always be zero, so you now have all three numbers. You supply them to `cdrecord` as part of the `dev` parameter. On a system with a writable DVD drive, you may see something more like the following:

```
scsibus0:
        0,0,0     0) *
        0,0,1     1) 'TSSTCorp' 'DVD+-RW TS-H653G' 'D200' Removable CD-ROM
        0,0,2     2) *
        0,0,3     3) *
        0,0,4     4) *
        0,0,5     5) *
        0,0,6     6) *
        0,0,7     7) *
```

The SCSI bus number is listed first; it is followed by the ID number, and then by the LUN. The entire command to write the DVD from the first example should look similar to this:

```
# cdrecord -v speed=2 dev=0,0,0 -data /var/tmp/mary.iso
```

Note

The `wodim` command (called `cdrecord` in this example for backward compatibility) will warn you that the `dev=0,0,0` pseudo-SCSI syntax may not be supported in future versions. ■

For modern DVD or CD drives, with the drive as /dev/cdrom, your command line might appear as follows instead:

```
# cdrecord -v speed=2 dev=/dev/cdrom -data /var/tmp/mary.iso
```

Several additional parameters are included in the command. The -v parameter tells cdrecord to supply verbose output to the screen. The speed parameter tells cdrecord what speed to record at (in this case X2). (You might choose to omit speed=2 and let cdrecord autodetect the record speed of your disc burner.) The -data parameter tells cdrecord to burn WAV or AU files as data, instead of audio tracks. (Without that option, those file types are burned as audio tracks while all other files are burned as data.)

In addition to /dev/cdrom, common device names include /dev/dvd and /dev/dvdrw.

Before running cdrecord live, you might consider adding the -dummy option, which runs through the disc burn process without actually turning on the laser. You can add the -eject parameter to eject the disc when it is done. As it works, cdrecord should display status messages that look similar to the following:

```
wodim: No write mode specified.
wodim: Asuming -tao mode.
wodim: Future versions of wodim may have drive dependent defaults.

Device type      : Removable CD-ROM
Version       : 5
Response Format: 5
Capabilities  :
Vendor_info      : MATSHITA '
Identifikation : 'DVD-R  UJ-898      '
Revision      : 'HC10'
Device seems to be: Generic mmc2 DVD-R/DVD-RW.
  .
  .
  .
Using generic SCSI-3/mmc   DVD-R(W) driver (mmc_mdvd).
...
Starting new track at sector: 0
Track 01:  322 of 322 MB written (fifo 100%) [buf  99%]   2.0x.
Track 01: Total bytes read/written: 338395136/338395136 (165232 sectors).
Writing  time:  1110.710s
Average write speed   2.0x.
Fixating...
Fixating time:  126.108s
BURN-Free was never needed.
wodim: fifo had 5331 puts and 5331 gets.
wodim: fifo was 0 times empty and 5262 times full, min fill was 96%.
```

Note

This output mentions `wodim` because that is the command actually run when you type in `cdrecord`. These commands are interchangeable. I used `cdrecord` on the command line for the examples because most users are more familiar with `cdrecord`. ∎

After `cdrecord` finishes writing the DVD and your shell prompt returns, you can delete the file system image file `/var/tmp/mary.iso`. Label the disc appropriately and store it in a safe place.

If you need any files that were copied to the DVD, just return the disc to the DVD drive. If it doesn't automatically open a window displaying the contents of the DVD, type **mount /media/cdrecorder**. Open `/media/cdrecorder` in a folder window and copy the files you want.

Note that the mount point name for the DVD drive may be something other than `/media/cdrecorder`. In the latest version of Fedora, the `udev` facility uses generic names such as `cdrecorder`, `disk`, or `cdrom` for CDs or DVDs that include no volume ID. However, if a volume ID was added to the DVD header when the disc was created, that name will be used as the mount point. For example, a game DVD with a volume ID of `GAMEDISK` would be mounted as `/media/GAMEDISK`.

Cross-Reference

See Chapter 7 for more information on `cdrecord`. You can also learn more about installing and troubleshooting writable disc drives from the CD-Writing-HOWTO. If you are using a desktop Fedora system, you might want to use a graphical DVD or CD writer instead. Chapter 7 also describes the Brasero graphical tool for copying and burning CDs and DVDs. ∎

You should also be aware of a few other issues related to using DVD media to record from Linux:

- While most new writable DVD drives today support both DVD-R and DVD+R formats, some older drives may not support DVD+R.

- DVD+RW media that has not been formatted must be formatted before you can write to it. However, you can use `cdrecord` on an unformatted DVD+RW because it will automatically detect and format an unformatted disk. To force a format, you can use the `-format` option to `cdrecord`. There is also a `dvd+rw-format` command that you can use to format a DVD drive (just run `dvd+rw-format` with your DVD device as the option).

- You don't need to reformat DVD-RW media more than once. Multiple reformats can make the DVD-RW media unusable.

Writing CD or DVDs with growisofs

Instead of doing separate `mkisofs` and `cdrecord` commands, as just shown, you can use the `growisofs` command to combine the function of those two commands. The `growisofs` command is particularly useful for the mastering of large ISO images (such as those for double-layer DVD recording). That's because instead of copying the ISO image you create to a file (as `mkisofs` does), `growisofs` sends the ISO image directly to the CD or DVD to be burned.

The growisofs command is also nice for backups because it has simple options for doing multi-session DVDs. For example, if you want to back up your /home/chris directory today, and then back up your /var/www directory later, you start the first backup as follows:

```
$ growisofs -Z /dev/cdrom -R -J /home/chris
```

The -Z indicates that this is an initial session being written to the CD or DVD. The device file for the CD/DVD drive is /dev/cdrom. The -R and -J options allow longer Linux filenames on ISO9660 images (so the disk can be read by other operating systems, yet still retain Linux extensions). The last option (in this case, /home/chris) is whatever directories or files you want to copy to DVD.

When you are ready to write more to the CD or DVD, use the -M options instead to indicate that you are adding on to an existing CD or DVD. Here is an example:

```
$ growisofs -M /dev/cdrom -R -J /var/www
```

Here, the -M indicates to add a new session to the existing session on the CD or DVD. The content of the /var/www directory (and its subdirectories) is written to the media. You can mount the media between sessions. Just be sure to unmount it before you try to write to it again (using the umount command).

Backing Up to a Hard Drive

As noted in the simple backup procedure in the beginning of this chapter, removable media such as tapes, DVDs, and CDs are not the only choice for backing up your data. You may find it useful to install a second hard drive in your system and use that drive for backups. This has several advantages over other backup media:

- Data can be backed up quickly and throughout the day; thus, backed-up data will be more current in the event of a crash.

- There's no medium to load. Data can be located and recovered more quickly.

- You can configure the second disk to be a virtual clone of the first one. If the first disk crashes, you simply boot off of the second disk, rather than install new hardware. With disk mirroring software, this process can even be automated. The downside to this approach is that a mirrored drive that is online all the time is more prone to error than would be the case when copying files to removable media and then removing the media to a safe location.

- With new, cost-effective removable hard drives (including those connected via USB and FireWire), you have the convenience of removable media with what was once usually thought of as non-removable media.

There are some disadvantages to backing up to a hard drive. For example, the hard drive backup method is not well suited to keeping historical archives of the many revisions of your files because the hard drive will eventually fill up. This problem can be reduced substantially, however, by using rsync snapshots, which store changes that are applied to modified files.

The simplest form of second-hard-drive backup is to simply copy important files to the other drive using the cp or tar command. The most sophisticated method is to provide fault-tolerant disk mirroring using RAID software.

A method in between RAID and a simple cp command is to add an rsync command to a cron file so that backups are done automatically as often as you please. For example, you can add a script that does your rsync backup to /etc/cron.hourly, /etc/cron.daily, /etc/cron.weekly, or /etc/cron.monthly, to have your backup run automatically each hour, day, week, or month, respectively. Keep in mind that you would have to catch any problems within the set time frame (an hour, a day, and so on) before the bad data overwrites the backup. (I describe how to use the cron facility to do backups with dump next.)

Backing Up Files with dump

The dump command was historically one of the most commonly used tools for performing backups on Unix systems. This command traces its history back to the early days of Unix and thus is a standard part of nearly every version of Unix. Likewise, the dump package is included in Fedora. If it was not installed by default when you first set up your Linux system, you can install it from the dump RPM file located on the Fedora installation DVD.

Note

The dump and restore commands, while widely used for many years, are not considered to be particularly reliable or robust backup and restore tools these days. Also, they can be used only on ext2 and ext3 file system types, and it is safest to use dump and restore on unmounted file systems. Descriptions of those tools are included here to support those with legacy backup media and automated scripts that still use those commands. ■

The dump package actually consists of several commands. You can read online man pages for more information about them. Table 12-2 provides a short description of the programs.

TABLE 12-2

Programs in the dump Package

Command	Description
dump	Creates backup archives of whole disk partitions or selected directories.
restore	Can be used to restore an entire archive or individual files from an archive to the hard drive.
rmt	A program used by the dump and restore commands to copy files across the network. You should never need to use this command directly.

When making a file system backup using the dump command, you must supply parameters specifying the dump level, the backup media, and the file system to back up. You can also supply optional parameters to specify the size of the backup media, the method for requesting the next tape, and the recording of file system dump times and status.

The first parameter to dump is always a list of single-letter option codes. This is followed by a space-separated list of any arguments needed by those options. The arguments appear in the same order as the options that require them. The final parameter is always the file system or directory being backed up:

```
# dump options arguments filesystem
```

Table 12-3 lists the various one-letter option codes for the dump command.

TABLE 12-3

Options to dump

Dump Options	Description
0-9	The dump level. Selecting a dump level of 0 backs up all files (a full dump). A higher number backs up only those files modified since the last dump of an equal or lower number (in essence, an incremental dump). The default dump level is 9.
-B records	The number of dump records per volume. Basically, the amount of data you can fit on a tape. This option takes a numeric argument.
-b kbperdump	The number of kilobytes per dump record. Useful in combination with the -B option. This option takes a numeric argument.
-h level	Files can be marked with a nodump attribute. This option specifies the dump level at or above which the nodump attribute is honored. This option takes a numeric argument of 1-9.
-f file	The name of the file or device to write the dump to. This can even be a file or device on a remote machine.
-d density	Sets the tape density. The default is 1,600 bits per inch. This option takes a numeric argument.
-n	When a dump needs attention (such as to change a tape), dump will send a message to all of the users in the operator group. This option takes no arguments.
-s feet	Specifies the length, in feet, of the dump tape. This calculation is dependent on tape density (option d) and the dump record (options B and b). This option takes a numeric argument.
-u	Records this backup in the /etc/dumpdates file. It is a good idea to use this option, especially if you create incremental backups.

continued

TABLE 12-3	*(continued)*
Dump Options	**Description**
-T *date*	Specifies a date and time on which to base incremental backups. Any files modified or added after that time will be backed up. This option causes dump to ignore the /etc/dumpdates file. It takes a single argument, a date in the format specified by the ctime man page.
-W	This option causes dump to list the file systems that need to be backed up. It does this by looking at the /etc/dumpdates file and the /etc/fstab file.
-w	This works like the W option but lists the individual files that should be backed up.

Thus, a typical dump command looks similar to the following:

```
# dump 0uBf 500000 /dev/qft0 /dev/sda6
```

This command results in dump performing a level zero (full) backup of the /dev/sda6 file system, storing the backup on the tape drive /dev/qft0, and recording the results in /etc/dumpdates. The B option is used to increase the expected tape block count to 500000; otherwise, dump would prompt for a new tape far earlier than required. The dump command prints status messages to the screen, letting you know how far along the backup has progressed and estimating how much time it will take to complete.

Automating Backups with cron

You can automate most of your backups with shell scripts and the cron daemon. Use the su command to become root, and then cd to the /usr/local/bin directory. Use any text editor to create a shell script called backups.sh that looks similar to the script in Listing 12-1.

LISTING 12-1

The backups.sh backup Script

```
#!/bin/sh
#
# backups.sh - A simple backup script, by Thad Phetteplace
#
# This script takes one parameter, the dump level.
# If the dump level is not provided, it is
# automatically set to zero. For level zero (full)
# dumps, rewind and eject the tape when done.
#

if [ $1 ]; then
        level=$1
```

```
else
        #
        # No dump level was provided, so set it
        # to zero
        #
        level="0"
fi

/sbin/dump $level'uf' /dev/nrft0 /
/sbin/dump $level'uf' /dev/nrft0 /home
/sbin/dump $level'uf' /dev/nrft0 /var
/sbin/dump $level'uf' /dev/nrft0 /usr

#
# If we are doing a full dump, rewind and eject
# the tape when done.
#
if [ $level = "0" ]; then
        /bin/mt -f /dev/nrft0 rewind
        /bin/mt -f /dev/nrft0 offline
fi
```

You might have to change the partitions being backed up to match your setup, but this script should otherwise work quite well for you. You could also modify this script to run the backup tool of your choice, using this file as an example to lead you through the task of setting up a cron-based backup. After saving and exiting the editor, change the permissions on the file so that it is executable and readable only by root:

```
# chmod 700 backups.sh
```

You can now back up your entire system by running the backups.sh script when logged in as root. The script accepts the dump level as its only parameter. If you omit the parameter, a level zero dump is automatically assumed. Thus, the following two commands are equivalent:

```
# backups.sh
# backups.sh 0
```

You may need to customize this script for your situation. For example, I am using the tape device /dev/nrft0. You might be using a different tape device. Whatever device you use, you should probably use the version of its device name that begins with the letter *n*. That tells the system that after it finishes copying data to the tape, it should *not* rewind the tape. For example, I used /dev/nrft0 instead of /dev/rst0 in the preceding script. If I had used /dev/rst0, each successive incremental backup would have overwritten the previous one.

Other things that you may change in this script include the partitions being backed up and the dump level at which the tape is ejected. It is common practice to eject the tape after the last incremental backup just before performing a full backup.

The most useful thing about this script is that you can easily configure your system to run it automatically. Simply add a few lines to the root `crontab` file, and the `cron` daemon will invoke the script on the days and times specified. While logged in as root, enter the `crontab` command with the `-e` option:

```
# crontab -e
```

This opens the root `crontab` file in an editor. Add the following lines at the end of the file:

```
0 22 * * 0 /usr/local/bin/backup.sh 0
0 22 * * 1 /usr/local/bin/backup.sh 9
0 22 * * 2 /usr/local/bin/backup.sh 8
0 22 * * 3 /usr/local/bin/backup.sh 7
0 22 * * 4 /usr/local/bin/backup.sh 6
0 22 * * 5 /usr/local/bin/backup.sh 5
0 22 * * 6 /usr/local/bin/backup.sh 4
```

Save and exit the file. The `cron` daemon will now run the backup script at 10:00 p.m. (22:00 in military time) every day of the week. This example implements the dump schedule outlined earlier. A full dump is performed on Sunday, and the tape is ejected when it is done. A new tape should be loaded on Monday, and then incremental backups will be written to that same tape for the rest of the week. The next full dump will be written to the end of that tape, unless someone is around on Sunday to eject and replace the tape before 10:00 p.m. Keep in mind that the person set to receive e-mail for the root user will be the one notified of the actions of this, or any, root-owned cron script.

Restoring Backed-Up Files

The `restore` command is used to retrieve files from a backup tape or other medium that was created by `dump`. You can use `restore` to recover an entire file system or to interactively select individual files. It recovers files from the specified media and copies them into the current directory (the one you ran the `restore` command in), recreating subdirectories as needed. Like the `dump` command, the first parameter passed to `restore` is a list of single-character option codes, as shown in Table 12-4.

TABLE 12-4

Restore Command Options

Restore Options	Description
-r	Restores the entire dump archive.
-C	Compares the contents of the dump file with the files on the disk. This is used to check the success of a restore.

Restore Options	Description
-R	Starts the restore from a particular tape of a multitape backup. This is useful for restarting an interrupted restore.
-X filelist	Extracts only specific files or directories from the archive. This option takes one argument, a list of files or directories to extract.
-T file	Lists the contents of the dump archive. If a file or directory is given as an argument, lists only the occurrence of that file, directory, or anything within the directory.
-i	Restores files in interactive mode.
-b blocksize	Specifies the block size of the dump, in kilobytes. This option takes a numeric argument.
-D filesystem	Specifies the name of the file system to be compared when using the -C option. The file system name is passed as an argument.
-F script	Specifies the name of the dump archive to restore from. This option takes an alphanumeric argument.
-h	If this option is specified, restore recreates directories marked for extraction but will not extract their contents.
-m	Files are extracted by inode number instead of name. This is generally not very useful.
-N	Instead of extracting files, prints their names.
-s file#	Specifies the dump file to start with on a multiple file tape. This takes a numeric argument.
-T directory	Tells restore where to write any temporary files. This is useful if you booted from a floppy disk (which has no space for temporary files).
-v	Runs in verbose mode. This causes restore to print information about each file as it restores it.
-y	The restore command will always continue when it encounters a bad block, rather than ask if you want to continue.

Restoring an entire file system

Let's say your system suffered a disk crash last Friday. You installed a shiny new hard drive and your backup tapes are in hand. It is time to restore the files. For the purposes of this example, I assume that the crashed drive contained only the /home partition and that the Linux operating system is still intact. If the crashed drive contained the Linux operating system, you would first have to reinstall Linux before restoring the backup.

With your new disk installed, run the fdisk command to partition the disk, as described in Chapter 2 in the section on partitioning your hard disks.

Before any files can be recovered to your new hard drive, an empty file system must be created on it. You use the mkfs command to do this. The mkfs command can accept a variety of parameters, but usually you need to supply only the name of the device to create the file system on. Thus, to prepare the new hard drive, type the following:

```
# mkfs -t ext4 /dev/sdb1
```

Alternatively, because your /home drive is listed in the /etc/fstab file, you can simply specify the /home mount point and mkfs will figure out the correct device. Thus, the preceding command could be replaced with this:

```
# mkfs /home
```

Caution

Exercise extreme caution when using the mkfs command. If you specify the wrong device name, you could unintentionally wipe out all data on an existing file system. ■

After creating a file system on your new disk, mount the partition to a temporary mount point:

```
# mkdir /mnt/test
# mount /dev/sdb1 /mnt/test
```

This connects the new file system to the /mnt/test directory. Now change into the directory (cd /mnt/test) and use the restore command to recover the entire file system off of your backup tape. Of course, it is assumed that you have loaded the tape into the tape drive.

```
# cd /mnt/test
# restore rf /dev/nrft0
```

When the restore is finished, you can unmount the partition and remount it to the appropriate mount point. If you have restored the file system to a physical partition other than the one it was originally on, be sure to modify the /etc/fstab file appropriately so that the correct partition is mounted next time the system is rebooted.

You can also restore individual files, as described in the restore man page.

Configuring Amanda for Network Backups

Using Amanda (the Advanced Maryland Automatic Network Disk Archiver), you can use a single large-capacity tape drive on a server to back up files from multiple computers over a network. The Amanda packages (amanda, amanda-client, and amanda-server) include a variety of commands, of which you will use the amdump command the most, since amdump is the program that performs the automatic Amanda backups.

Before you can get started, you need to configure a few things on both the backup server (the system with the tape drive) and the backup clients (the systems being backed up). On Amanda clients, you need to install the amanda and amanda-client packages. On the Amanda server, you need to install the amanda-server package as well.

Creating Amanda directories

You need to create some directories to hold the Amanda configuration files and to provide a location to write Amanda log files. The configuration files go in the /etc/amanda directory, and the log and database files go in /var/lib/amanda. In both cases, you should log in as the amandabackup user and create subdirectories within those directories, one subdirectory for each backup schedule that you intend to run and an index file, as shown in the following example.

```
# su - amandabackup
$ mkdir -p /var/lib/amanda/normal/index
$ mkdir -p /etc/amanda/normal
```

Note

For security reasons and to ensure that Amanda commands can access all the necessary files they need, you should do all Amanda administration as the amanda user, amandabackup. To do this, the root user can create a password for amandabackup by typing passwd amandabackup **and entering the new password. A better alternative, however, might be to lock the amanda user account and then simply type** su-amandabackup **(as in the following example) to do Amanda tasks as root user without an extra password. The rest of this procedure assumes that you are logged in as the amandabackup user.** ■

For the purpose of this example, I have created only a normal backup configuration that backs up the data drives on several machines. You may also decide to create an upgrade backup configuration that backs up the operating system partitions. You could then run that backup before you perform any operating system upgrades.

You also need to specify a holding disk that Amanda can use to spool backups temporarily before it writes them to disk. This directory should have a lot of free space. I have a large /home partition on my server, so I created an Amanda directory there to use as a holding disk:

```
# mkdir /home/amanda
# chmod 700 /home/amanda
# chown amandabackup /home/amanda
# chgrp disk /home/amanda
```

Creating the amanda.conf file

As the amandabackup user, you must create two configuration files for Amanda and store them in the /etc/amanda/normal directory: amanda.conf and disklist. You can start by copying samples of these files from the /etc/amanda/DailySet1 directory as follows:

```
$ cd /etc/amanda/DailySet1
$ cp amanda.conf disklist /etc/amanda/normal
```

The amanda.conf file sets a variety of general configuration values, and the disklist file defines which machines and partitions to back up. The amanda.conf file can be rather complicated but fortunately most of its values can be left at their defaults. Here is a simplified amanda.conf file with some comments embedded in it to help explain things:

```
# amanda.conf - sample Amanda configuration file. See amanda.conf(5)↵
```

```
# for   details

org        "GLACI"              # your organization name for reports
mailto     "amandabackup"       # space separated list of operators at
your ↵
site
dumpuser   "amandabackup"       # the user to run dumps under

# Specify tape device or tape changer.

runtapes 1      # number of tapes to be used in a single run of amdump
tapedev "tape:/dev/nrft0"        # tape changer or device to use

# Specify holding disks.  These are used as a temporary staging area
# for dumps before they are written to tape and are recommended for ↵
# most sites.

holdingdisk hd1 {
    comment "main holding disk"
    directory "/dumps/amanda"     # where the holding disk is
    use -100 Mb                   # how much space can we use on it
                                  # a non-positive value means:
                                  # use all space but that value
    chunksize 1Gb   # size of chunk if you want big dump to be
                    # dumped on multiple files on holding disks
                    #  N Kb/Mb/Gb split images in chunks of size N
                    #       The maximum value should be
                    #       (MAX_FILE_SIZE - 1Mb)
                    #        0 same as INT_MAX bytes
    }

# Note that, although the keyword below is infofile, it is only so
# for historic reasons, since now it is supposed to be a directory
# (unless you have selected some database format other than the
# `text' default)
infofile "/etc/amanda/DailySet1/curinfo"     # database DIRECTORY
logdir   "/etc/amanda/DailySet1"             # log directory
indexdir "/etc/amanda/DailySet1/index"       # index directory

# tapetypes

# Define the type of tape you use here, and use it in "tapetype"
# above.  Some typical types of tapes are included here.
# The tapetype tells amanda how many MB will fit on the tape,
# how big the filemars are, and how fast the tape devise is.

define tapetype HP-DAT {
```

```
        comment "DAT tape drives"
        # data provided by Rob Browning <rlb@cs.utexas.edu>
        length 1930 mbytes
        filemark 111 kbytes
        speed 468 kbytes
    }


# dumptypes
#
# These are referred to by the disklist file.

define dumptype global {
        comment "Global definitions"
        # This is quite useful for setting global parameters,
        # so you don't have to
    }

define dumptype always-full {
        global
        comment "Full dump of this filesystem always"
        compress none
        priority high
        dumpcycle 0


    }
```

This example amanda.conf file was trimmed down from a larger example I copied from the /etc/amanda/DailySet1 directory. The example amanda.conf file provides additional information on the available configuration options. Also, the online man page for Amanda should be helpful (type **man amanda** to read it). Generally, you have to do the following:

- Modify the org name for reports.
- Change the device names set for tapedev to match your tape device.
- Select a tape type entry that is appropriate for your tape drive.
- Change the name of the directory specified in the holding disk section to match the directory you created earlier.

Creating a disklist file

You also must create a disklist file in the /etc/amanda/normal directory. This simply contains a list of the systems and disk partitions to back up. The qualifier always-full is included on each entry to tell Amanda what type of backup to perform. It means to use full, rather than incremental, backups:

```
# sample Amanda2 disklist file, derived from CS.UMD.EDU's disklist
# File format is:
```

```
#
#     hostname diskdev dumptype
#
# where the dumptypes are defined by you in amanda.conf.

dexter.handsonhistory.com sda5 always-full
dexter.handsonhistory.com sda6 always-full
dexter.handsonhistory.com sda7 always-full
dexter.handsonhistory.com sda8 always-full

daffy.handsonhistory.com sda5 always-full
daffy.handsonhistory.com sda6 always-full
daffy.handsonhistory.com sda7 always-full
daffy.handsonhistory.com sdb1 always-full
daffy.handsonhistory.com sdb2 always-full
```

Tip

Use fully qualified host names for the systems you want backed up. ∎

This example file backs up two systems, `dexter.handsonhistory.com` and `daffy.handson-history.com`. The order of the systems and the partitions is selected so that the most important data is backed up first. This way, if a tape drive becomes full, you have still backed up the most important data.

Adding Amanda network services

Amanda is designed to perform backups over a network. The following amanda services are defined in the `/etc/services` file:

```
amanda          10080/udp
amanda          10080/tcp
kamanda         10081/tcp
kamanda         10081/udp
amandaidx       10082/tcp
amidxtape       10083/tcp
```

Of these, the ports 10081, 10082, and 10083 are not officially allocated by IANA, the Internet Assigned Numbers Authority. See `www.iana.org/assignments/port-numbers` for details.

On the Amanda server

To offer these services to the network in Fedora, you need to configure the `xinetd` daemon to listen for those services. This enables Amanda to accept requests from the client system and to start the backup process without any user intervention.

Next, enable the service for the `xinetd` daemon. To do this, edit the configuration file for Amanda in the `/etc/xinetd.d` directory and change the disable setting from yes to no. Then, on the `server_args` line, add `amindexd` and `amidxtaped` after `amdump` to the `-auth-bsd` option.

You need to tell the `xinetd` daemon to reload the `/etc/xinetd.d` files before this change takes effect. You can do this by typing the following as root user:

```
# /etc/init.d/xinetd reload
```

On each Amanda client

Now you need to configure the `.amandahosts` file in the `/var/lib/amanda` directory on each computer (client) that the Amanda server will back up from. This file should contain the fully qualified host and domain name of any backup servers that will connect to this client. When you begin, only your localhost is defined in this file as your backup server. To add another computer as a backup server, type the following (replacing *amandahost* with the name of the backup server, while you are logged in as the `amanda` user):

```
$ echo amandahost >> /var/lib/amanda/.amandahosts
```

Note that you may need to include the Amanda user name:

```
$ echo amandahost amandabackup >> /var/lib/amanda/.amandahosts
```

You also need to ensure that the Amanda client daemon is configured to run on the client. You do this by enabling the `amanda` service by typing the following (as root user):

```
# chkconfig amanda on
```

This enables the Amanda client to communicate with the Amanda server. You need to tell the `xinetd` daemon to reload the `/etc/xinetd.d` files before this change takes place. Do this by typing the following as root user:

```
# /etc/init.d/xinetd reload
```

Performing an Amanda backup

Now that everything is configured, you are ready to perform an Amanda backup. Before running the actual backup, run `amcheck` to check your drive and configuration. While logged in as root, change to the amandabackup user and then type the following commands:

```
$ /usr/sbin/amcheck normal
$ /usr/sbin/amdump normal
```

This runs the `amdump` command and tells it to read the configuration files it finds in the `/etc/amanda/normal` directory created earlier. It then works its way down the list of systems and partitions in the `disklist` file, backing up each partition in the order it occurs. The results of the `amdump` are written to the `/var/lib/amanda/normal` directory. Read the files you find there to check the results of the backup. (See the previous section on how to create a `disklist` file to understand the process that `amdump` goes through.)

You can, of course, automate this process with `cron`. To create an `amdump` schedule similar to the regular dump schedule discussed earlier, do the following. While logged in as root, enter the `crontab` command with the `-e` option:

```
# crontab -e
```

This opens the root `crontab` file in an editor. Add the following lines to the end of the file:

```
0 22 * * 0 /usr/sbin/amdump normal
0 22 * * 1 /usr/sbin/amdump incremental
0 22 * * 2 /usr/sbin/amdump incremental
0 22 * * 3 /usr/sbin/amdump incremental
0 22 * * 4 /usr/sbin/amdump incremental
0 22 * * 5 /usr/sbin/amdump incremental
0 22 * * 6 /usr/sbin/amdump incremental
```

Save and exit the file. The `cron` daemon will now run `amdump` at 10:00 p.m. (22:00 in military time) every day of the week. This example assumes that a second incremental configuration has been created. You can do this by creating a subdirectory named `incremental` under `/etc/amanda` and populating it with appropriately modified `amanda.conf` and `disklist` files. You must also create a subdirectory named `incremental` under `/var/lib/amanda` so that `amanda` has somewhere to write the log files for this configuration.

It may be a bit of work to get it all in place, but when you do, Amanda can make your network backups much easier to manage. It may be overkill for a small office, but in a large enterprise network, it enables Fedora to act as a powerful backup server.

Using the pax Archiving Tool

Over the years, a variety of Unix operating systems have arisen, resulting in a variety of similar but incompatible file archiving formats. Even tools that go by the same name may use slightly different storage formats on different systems. This can lead to big problems when trying to archive and retrieve data in a multi-platform environment. Fortunately, there is a solution.

The `pax` program is a POSIX standard utility that can read and write a wide variety of archive formats. An RPM package for pax is included with Fedora. If it is not already installed, install with the `yum install pax` command.

The `pax` command takes a variety of command-line options. The last parameter is usually the file or directory to archive. You may use wildcard characters such as * or ? to specify multiple files or directories. The options you will use most often include the `-r` and `-w` parameters for specifying when you are reading or writing an archive, respectively. These are usually used in conjunction with the `-f` parameter, which specifies the name of the archive file.

By using pax parameters in different combinations, it is possible to extract an archive, create an archive, list the contents of an archive, or even copy an entire directory hierarchy from one location to another. Table 12-5 shows a few examples of the pax command in action.

TABLE 12-5

Examples of pax Use

The pax Command	Description
pax -f myfiles	Lists the contents of the archive named myfiles
pax -r -f myfiles	Extracts the contents of the archive named myfiles
pax -w -f myfiles /etc	Creates an archive named myfiles containing everything within the /etc directory
pax -w -f myfiles *.txt	Archives all files in the current directory that have a .txt file extension
pax -r -w /olddir /newdir	Copies the entire contents of the directory /oldir into a new directory called /newdir
pax -w -x cpio -f myfiles *	Archives the contents of the current directory into an archive file named myfiles using the cpio format
pax -r -U mary -f backups	Extracts all files owned by user mary from the archive named backups

Note that by omitting both the -r and -w options, you cause pax to simply list the contents of the archive. If you specify both the -r and -w options, then you should omit the -f option and supply source and destination directories instead. This will cause the source directory to be completely cloned in the specified destination directory.

You can use additional parameters to further modify the pax command's behavior. See the online documentation for more on pax with the man pax command. As you can see, pax is a very flexible and powerful archiving tool. It can be particularly helpful in migrating data from older legacy systems to your new Linux system. When you are faced with the task of recovering archived data from an antiquated or even nonfunctioning Unix system, the multiple file format support of pax can be a literal lifesaver.

Summary

I hope that you never experience a major hard drive crash, but if you do, the effort of making backups will repay itself many times over. A variety of low-cost backup hardware is available for use with your Fedora system. The traditional tape drive is an excellent choice for backing up large amounts of data or data that you need to keep for years. However, simply copying your /home directories to another medium offers some level of protection for your data.

For convenience, a writable DVD or CD drive is a good choice. As for the tools you choose to do your backups, the dump and restore commands are old favorites, dating back to the early Unix days (although they are considered somewhat unreliable these days). The Amanda backup facility is excellent for network backups. If you are dealing with backups in several different formats, the pax command might be helpful.

Computer Security Issues

With the growth of the Internet, computer and network security have become more important than ever. Assaults on your Fedora system can come in many forms, such as denial-of-service (DoS) attacks, break-in attempts, or hijacking your machine as a spam relay, to name a few.

In many cases, good practices for setting and protecting passwords, monitoring log files, and creating good firewalls will keep out many would-be intruders. Keeping up with critical security software updates will help patch vulnerabilities as they become known. The addition of SELinux adds another layer of protection on your Linux system. Sometimes, more proactive approaches are needed to respond to break-ins. This chapter will familiarize you, as a Linux administrator, with the dangers that exist and the tools available to protect your system.

Linux Security Checklist

While Linux offers all the tools you need to secure your computer, if you are careless, someone can (and probably will) harm your system or try to steal your data. The following checklist covers a range of security measures to protect your Linux desktop or server:

- **Add users and passwords** — Creating separate user accounts for each user (each with a good password) is your first line of defense in keeping your data secure. Users are protected from each other, as well as from an outsider who takes over one user account. Setting up group accounts can extend the concept of ownership to multiple users. See Chapter 10 for more on setting up user accounts, and "Using Password Protection" later in this chapter.

IN THIS CHAPTER

Linux security checklist

Using password protection

Protecting Linux with the iptables firewall

Control system access with TCP wrappers

Checking log files

Using the Secure Shell (SSH) package

Understanding attack techniques

Securing servers with SELinux

Scanning for security problems with OpenSCAP

Protecting servers with encryption and certificates

Managing identities with FreeIPA

- **Read, write, and execute permissions** — Every item in a Linux file system (including files, directories, applications, and devices) can be restricted by read, write, and execute permissions for that item's owner and group, as well as by all others. In this way, you can, for example, let other users run a command or open a file, allowing them to change it. See Chapter 4 for information on setting file and directory permissions.

- **Protect root** — In standard Linux systems, the root users (as well as other administrative user accounts such as apache) have special permissions to use and change your Linux system. Protect the root account's password and don't use the root account unless it is necessary. An open shell or desktop owned by the root user can be a target for attack. Running `system-config-*` windows as a regular user (and then entering the root password as prompted) and running administrative commands using `sudo` can reduce exposure to attacks on your root account. See Chapter 9 for information on handling the root user account.

- **Use trusted software** — While there are no guarantees with any open-source software, you have a better chance of avoiding compromised software by using an established Linux distribution (such as Fedora). Software repositories from which you get add-on packages or updates should likewise be scrutinized. Using valid GPG public keys (which use signatures and encryption), you can ensure that the software you install comes from a valid vendor. Of course, always be sure of the source of data files you receive before opening them in a Linux application.

- **Get software updates** — As vulnerabilities and bugs are discovered in software packages, every major Linux distribution (including Fedora) offers tools for getting and installing those updates. Be sure to get those updates, especially if you are using Linux as a server. See Chapter 5 for information on using PackageKit and yum to get software updates.

- **Use secure applications** — Even with software that is valid and working, some applications offer better protection from attack or invasion than others. For example, if you want to log in to a computer over the Internet, the Secure Shell service (SSH) is considered more secure than `rlogin` or `telnet` services. Also, some services that are considered insecure if you expose them on the Internet (such as Samba and NFS) can be used more securely over the Internet through virtual private network (VPN) tunnels (such as IPsec or CIPE).

- **Use restrictive firewalls** — A primary job of a firewall is to accept requests for services from a network that you want to allow and to deny requests that you don't (primarily based on port numbers requested). A desktop system should refuse requests that come in on most ports. A server system should allow requests for a controlled set of ports. This chapter describes how to set up a firewall using iptables.

- **Enable only services you need** — To offer services in Linux (such as Web, file, or mail services), a daemon process listens on a particular port number. Don't enable services you don't need. In fact, don't install server software you don't need. See Chapter 11 for information on using system services. For even better security, don't install any software you don't use, be it server software or any other kind.

Note

A program that runs quietly in the background handling service requests (such as sendmail) is called a *daemon*. Usually, daemons are started automatically when your system boots up, and they keep running until your system is shut down. Daemons may also be started on an as-needed basis by `xinetd`, a special daemon that listens on a large number of port numbers, and then launches the requested process. ■

- **Limit access to services** — You can restrict access for a service you want to a particular host computer, domain, or network interface. For example, a computer with interfaces to both the Internet and a Local Area Network (LAN) might limit access to a service such as NFS to computers on the LAN, but not offer those same services to the Internet. Services may limit access in their own configuration files or by using TCP/IP wrappers (described later in this chapter).

- **Check your system** — Linux has numerous tools available for checking your system's security. After you install Linux, you can check access to its ports using nmap, or watch network traffic using Wireshark (formerly called Ethereal). You can also add popular security tools such as Nessus or sectool to get a more complete view of your system security.

- **Monitor your system** — You can log almost every type of activity on your Linux system. System log files, using the rsyslogd and klogd facilities, can be configured to track as much or as little of your system activity as you choose. The logwatch facility provides an easy way to have potential problem messages forwarded to your administrative e-mail account. Linux logging features are described later in this chapter. You can get add-on packages such as tripwire and portsentry to check your system for tampering and deal with someone scanning your ports, respectively.

- **Use SELinux** — SELinux is an extraordinarily rich (and complex) facility for managing the access of nearly every aspect of a Linux system. It addresses the if-I-get-root-access-I-own-your-box shortcomings of Linux and Unix systems for highly secure environments. Fedora offers a useful, limited set of SELinux policies that are turned on by default. Chapter 9 provides an overview of SELinux, along with explanations of how it is implemented in Fedora.

This checklist should give you a good starting point with many aspects of security in Linux. Each of these topics is covered in greater depth in this chapter and other chapters throughout this book as indicated. However, computer security is an ongoing battle, so I recommend you check out the following websites to get a deeper, continuing experience with Linux security:

- **CERT** (www.cert.org) — The CERT Coordination Center follows computer security issues. Check their home page for the latest vulnerabilities. The site has articles on security practices (http://www.cert.org/search_pubs/search.php); and recommendations about what to do if your computer has been compromised (www.cert.org/tech_tips/win-UNIX-system_compromise.html), although this is now considered somewhat dated.

- **Red Hat Security and Identity Management** (www.redhat.com/security) — For RHEL security issues (that typically relate to Fedora systems as well), you should check out the resources available from this site. From here you can look for and read about available updates. You can also get information on security training and consulting from Red Hat, Inc.

- **Red Hat Enterprise Linux 6 Security Guide** — This guide provides an in-depth look at Linux security, specifically as it relates to Red Hat Enterprise Linux and Fedora (`http://docs.redhat.com/docs/en-US/Red_Hat_Enterprise_Linux/6/html/Security_Guide/index.html`).

Using Password Protection

Passwords are the most fundamental security tool of any modern operating system, and therefore the most commonly attacked security feature. It is natural to want to choose a password that is easy to remember, but this often means choosing a password that is easy to guess. Crackers know that on any system with more than a few users, at least one person is likely to have an easily guessed password.

Note
The opposite approach, that of requiring all users to select really complicated passwords, may seem much better but you end up with passwords so complex that users write them down. That means any person who finds the note can get in. Ideally, passwords should be somewhere in between — easy to remember but hard to crack. ∎

By using the "brute force" method of attempting to log in to every account on the system and trying the most common passwords on each of these accounts, a persistent cracker has a good chance of finding a way in. Remember that crackers automate these attacks, so thousands of login attempts are not out of the question. Obviously, choosing good passwords is the first and most important step to having a secure system.

Here are some things to avoid when choosing a password:

- Do not use any variation of your login name or your full name. Even if you use varied case; append or prepend numbers or punctuation; or type it backwards; this will still be an easily guessed password.

- Do not use a dictionary word, even if you add numbers or punctuation to it.

- Do not use proper names of any kind.

- Do not use passwords based on a contiguous line of letters or numbers on the keyboard (such as qwerty, 1q2w3e4r, or asdfg).

Choosing good passwords

A good way to choose a strong password is to take the first letter from each word of an easily remembered sentence. The password can be made even better by adding numbers, punctuation, and varied case. The sentence you choose should have meaning only to you, and should not be publicly available (choosing a sentence on your personal Web page is a bad idea). Table 13-1 lists examples of strong passwords and the tricks used to remember them.

TABLE 13-1

Ideas for Good Passwords

Password	How to Remember It
Mrci7yo!	My rusty car is 7 years old!
2emBp1ib	2 elephants make BAD pets, 1 is better
ItMc?Gib	Is that MY coat? Give it back

The passwords look like gibberish, but are actually rather easy to remember. As shown, you can place emphasis on words that stand for capital letters in the password. You set your password using the passwd command. Type the passwd command within a command shell, and it will enable you to change your password. First, it prompts you to enter your old password. To protect against someone *shoulder surfing* (looking over your shoulder and watching you type) and learning your password, the password is not displayed as you type.

As long as you type your old password correctly, the passwd command will prompt you for the new password. When you type in your new password, the passwd command checks the password against cracklib to determine whether it is a *good* or a *bad* password. Nonroot users are required to try a different password if the one they have chosen is not a good password. The root user is the only user who is permitted to assign *bad* passwords. Once the password has been accepted by cracklib, the passwd command asks you to enter the new password a second time to ensure there are no typos, which are hard to detect when you can't see what you are typing! When running as root, it is possible to change a user's password by supplying that user's login name as a parameter to the passwd command. Typing

```
# passwd joe
```

results in the passwd command prompting you for joe's new password. It does not prompt you for his old password in this case. This allows root to reset a user's password when that user has forgotten it (an event that happens all too often).

The passwd command will complain but still let the root user change the password if the chosen password is too short, too simple, the same as the user name, or based on dictionary words.

Using a shadow password file

In early versions of Unix, all user account and password information was stored in a file that all users could read (although only root could write to it). This was generally not a problem because the password information was encrypted. The password was encrypted using a *trapdoor algorithm*, meaning the non-encoded password could be encoded into a scrambled string of characters, but the string could not be translated back to the non-encoded password.

How does the system check your password in this case? When you log in, the system encodes the password you entered, compares the resulting scrambled string with the scrambled string that is stored in the password file, and grants you access only if the two match. Have you ever asked a system administrator what the password on your account was only to be told that the system administrator doesn't know? If so, this is why: The administrator really doesn't have the password, only the encrypted version. The non-encoded password exists only at the moment you type it.

Breaking encrypted passwords

There is a problem with people being able to see encrypted passwords, however. Although it may be difficult (or even impossible) to reverse the encryption of a trapdoor algorithm, it is very easy to encode a large number of password guesses and compare them to the encoded passwords in the password file. This is, in order of magnitude, more efficient than trying actual login attempts for each user name and password. If crackers can get a copy of your password file, they have a much better chance of breaking into your system.

Fortunately, Linux and all modern Unix systems support a shadow password file by default. The shadow file is a special version of the passwd file that only root can read. It contains the encrypted password information, so passwords can be left out of the passwd file, which any user on the system can read. Linux supports the older, single-password file method as well as the newer shadow password file. You should always use the shadow password file (it is used by default).

Checking for the shadow password file

The password file is named passwd and can be found in the /etc directory. The shadow password file is named shadow and is also located in /etc. If your /etc/shadow file is missing, then it is likely that your Linux system is storing the password information in the /etc/passwd file instead. Verify this by displaying the file with the less command:

```
# less /etc/passwd
```

Something similar to the following should be displayed if your system is not using shadow passwords:

```
root:DkkS6Uke799fQ:0:0:root:/root:/bin/bash
bin:*:1:1:bin:/bin:/sbin/nologin
daemon:*:2:2:daemon:/sbin:/sbin/nologin
  .
  .
  .
mary:KpRUp2ozmY5TA:500:500:Mary Smith:/home/mary:/bin/bash
joe:OsXrzvKnQaksI:501:501:Joe Johnson:/home/joe:/bin/bash
jane:ptNoiueYEjwX.:502:502:Jane Anderson:/home/jane:/bin/bash
bob:Ju2vY7AOX6Kzw:503:503:Bob Renolds:/home/bob:/bin/bash
```

Each line in this listing corresponds to a single user account on the Linux system; and each line is made up of seven fields separated by colon (:) characters. From left to right the fields are the login name, the encrypted password, the user ID, the group ID, the description (usually a person's name), the home directory, and the default shell. The first line indicates that it is for the root account and has an encrypted password of DkkS6Uke799fQ. You can also see that root has a user ID of zero, a group ID of zero, and a home directory of /root, and root's default shell is /bin/bash.

All these values are quite normal for a root account, but seeing that encrypted password should set off alarm bells in your head. It confirms that your system is not using the shadow password file. At this point, you should immediately convert your password file so that it uses /etc/shadow to store the password information. You do this by using the pwconv command. Simply log in as root (or use the su command to become root) and enter the pwconv command at a prompt. It prints no messages, but when your shell prompt returns, you should have an /etc/shadow file and your /etc/passwd file should now look like this:

```
root:x:0:0:root:/root:/bin/bash
bin:x:1:1:bin:/bin:/sbin/nologin
daemon:x:2:2:daemon:/sbin:/sbin/nologin

       .
       .
       .

mary:x:500:500:Mary Smith:/home/mary:/bin/bash
joe:x:501:501:Joe Johnson:/home/joe:/bin/bash
jane:x:502:502:Jane Anderson:/home/jane:/bin/bash
bob:x:503:503:Bob Renolds:/home/bob:/bin/bash
```

Encrypted password data is replaced with an x. Password data has been moved to /etc/shadow.

To check the type of password authentication your system is using, open the Authentication window (System ⇨ Administration ⇨ Authentication from the GNOME desktop). This tool lets you choose to use MD5 passwords, LDAP authentication, FreeIPA, or other authentication methods. The default for Fedora 14 is to use shadow passwords on local accounts as well as the SHA512 hashing algorithm. SHA512 is stronger than previous algorithms such as MD5 and SHA256. (See the Advanced Options tab for these settings.)

To work with passwords for groups, you can use the grpconv command to convert passwords in /etc/groups to shadowed group passwords in /etc/gshadow. If you change passwd or group passwords and something breaks (you are unable to log in to the accounts), you can use the pwunconv and grpunconv commands, respectively, to reverse password conversion.

So, now you are using the shadow password file and picking good passwords. You have made a great start toward securing your system. You may also have noticed by now that security is not just a one-time job. It is an ongoing process, requiring constant vigilance. Keep reading to learn more.

Securing Linux with the iptables Firewall

In the noncomputer world, a firewall is a physical barrier that keeps a fire from spreading. *Computer firewalls* serve a similar purpose, but the "fires" that they attempt to block are attacks from crackers on the Internet. In this context, a firewall, also known as a *packet filter*, is a physical piece of computer hardware that sits between your network and the Internet, regulating and controlling the flow of information.

The most common types of firewalls used today are *filtering firewalls*. A filtering firewall filters the traffic flowing between your network and the Internet, blocking certain things that may put your network at risk. It can limit access to and from the Internet to specific computers on your network. It can also limit the type of communication as well as selectively permit or deny various Internet services.

For Fedora to act as a filtering firewall, you can use the iptables feature.

Note

The iptables feature replaced the older ipchains as the default Fedora Linux firewall several releases ago. ∎

This chapter describes the iptables facility and the Firewall Configuration window for starting out with a simple iptables firewall.

Using the Firewall Configuration window

When you first installed your Fedora system, you were given the opportunity to create a basic iptables firewall for your system. Using the Firewall Configuration window, you can see those settings and modify them further.

If you are not familiar with firewalls in general, or iptables in particular, it can be a bit daunting at first. To make iptables easier for new users, Fedora systems offer the Firewall Configuration window, shown in Figure 13-1. Look through the settings on this window, and then refer to other iptables descriptions that follow for more details on each feature.

To open the Firewall Configuration window, from the System menu select Administration ➪ Firewall (or type **system-config-firewall**).

Note

When you launch this program, you'll see a long, serious dialog pointing out the limitations of the Firewall Configuration window and warning you that if you need to customize your firewall, you really should edit the files by hand. ∎

FIGURE 13-1

Set up a basic firewall using the Firewall Configuration window.

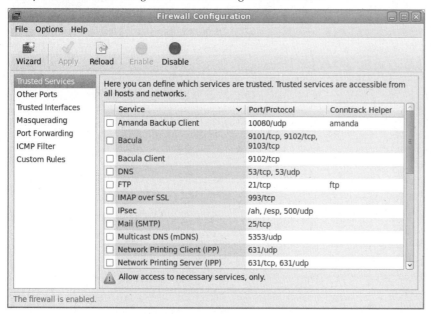

You can enable or disable the firewall using the checkboxes in this window. If you are connected to the Internet or other public network, I strongly suggest you enable your firewall. Even if you are on a trusted LAN, you should turn the firewall on but possibly open some services you might not expose to the Internet (such as NFS and Samba). If the firewall is enabled, select from the following topics in the left panel to configure your firewall.

- **Trusted Services** — You can open access to ports associated with your network interfaces to provide the services you want to make available from your system. Some services, such as Samba, require that multiple ports be open.

  The only service that is selected (open) by default is SSH (Secure Shell). Other services available from this screen include DNS, FTP, IMAP over SSL, IPsec, Mail (SMTP), Multicast DNS, Network Printing (IPP client and server), NFS4, OpenVPN, POP-3 over SSL, RADIUS, the Red Hat Cluster Suite, Samba, secure WWW (HTTPS), TFTP, and standard WWW (HTTP). Note that the firewall doesn't configure services; it just opens a way to get to the services.

Note

If you need more information about what a particular service is used for, hover your mouse over the service name that interests you in this window for a more detailed description. You need to start each service as well as open a hole in your firewall for that service. ∎

- **Other Ports** — You can allow access to any other port numbers by adding them to the Other Ports box. Select Add and then select the protocol type (TCP or UDP) and port number pair you want to allow. To enable ports not in the list, select the User Defined box, type the port number, and select the protocol you want to enable. Click OK when you are done.

- **Trusted Interfaces** — You can identify any of your network interfaces as being trusted. No incoming ports are blocked from requests from a trusted interface. You should never assign an external interface to a public network to be trusted. However, you might have a dedicated network connection or a connection to a small local LAN that you want to be trusted.

- **Masquerading** — By identifying an interface as a masquerading interface, you can allow other computers on your LAN with private IP addresses to use your computer as a router to the Internet (or other network). This presumes that your Fedora system has another network interface with a route to the Internet. By selecting at least one network interface as providing IP masquerading, packet-forwarding support is automatically turned on. (See descriptions of masquerading later in this chapter.)

- **Port Forwarding** — You indicate that traffic directed to a specific port on the local interface be redirected to either another local port or to a port on another computer. This is one way to allow a server behind the firewall to provide public Web, SSH, FTP, or other service.

- **ICMP Filter** — Allow or disallow Internet Control Message Protocol (ICMP) error messages to be sent between networked computers. For example, a `ping` request is often used to check if a computer on the network is up and running. `Ping` requests can also be used for denial-of-service attacks. By default, all ICMP packets are allowed.

- **Custom Rules** — Creating custom rules can be a bit trickier than simply opening access for a port. You can create an iptables rule in a separate file (in `iptables-save` format, as described later in this chapter) and assign that rule to a filter, NAT, or mangle iptables table. Click Add and indicate the address type (IPv4 or IPv6), type of table, and file containing the rule. Click OK to add the rule.

Before clicking Apply to save your settings, consider that doing so will overwrite your existing firewall rules. If you have done any hand editing of the configuration file (`/etc/sysconfig/iptables` or `/etc/sysconfig/ip6tables` for the IPv6 firewall), those changes will be overwritten. Make a backup copy of these files before continuing.

You can configure iptables to set up logging, port forwarding, network address translation, and other features manually, as described in the following sections.

Configuring an iptables firewall

The remaining sections on iptables in this chapter describe a more manual way of working with your iptables firewall in Linux. Also covered is how to implement special iptables features that are not available from the Firewall Configuration window (e.g., NAT).

Turning on iptables

The iptables firewall feature (also referred to as *netfilter*) is the default firewall software available when you install Fedora. This section describes how to enable iptables and set up firewall rules for several different types of situations. It also explains how to enable firewall-related features that allow your iptables firewall to do Network Address Translation (NAT), IP masquerading, port forwarding, and transparent proxies.

Note

The Fedora startup scripts will "punch a hole" through your firewall if you use certain services, and will therefore work even if they are not explicitly enabled in your `iptables` **configuration. For example, NTP (which sets your system time from a network time server) and DNS resolution (which lets you contact a DNS server to resolve addresses) both open the ports they need in your firewall.** ■

The following procedure describes how to get `iptables` going on your Fedora system:

1. Set the iptables script to start automatically at boot time:

```
# chkconfig iptables on
```

Note

Fedora includes two versions of the iptables system: iptables for IPv4 networking and ip6tables for IPv6 networking. The systems are configured similarly. Look for `/etc/sysconfig/ip6tables` **for configuring the IPv6 firewall. The IPv4 networking controls NAT, or Network Address Translation, services. Most of the examples show how to edit** `iptables`**. You can make similar changes to** `ip6tables`**.** ■

2. Before you can start iptables you must have a working set of rules that has been placed in your `/etc/sysconfig/iptables` file. To create those rules, refer to the examples in the following sections. (Without the configuration file in place, iptables fails silently.)

Tip

If you are new to iptables, you can start with a workable set of default values by configuring your firewall during Fedora installation. I recommend selecting to enable the firewall and enabling only those services you are ready to offer. The resulting `/etc/sysconfig/iptables` **file will let you study how Fedora creates its firewalls rules.** ■

3. If you are doing NAT or IP masquerading, turn on IP packet forwarding. With IP forwarding, your Linux system can forward network requests from multiple systems on your local network to the Internet. Outside your local network, all the packets appear to be coming from the same machine, your Linux system, hiding internal details of your network. One way to allow this is to change the value of `net.ipv4.ip_forward` to 1 in the `/etc/sysctl.conf` file. Open that file as root user with any text editor and change the line to appear as follows:

```
net.ipv4.ip_forward = 1
```

4. Restart your network interfaces to have IP packet forwarding take effect:

```
# /etc/init.d/network restart
```

Tip

You can also use `sysctl -p` to have the kernel pick up forwarding changes. I recommend restarting networking, though. ∎

5. Once the rules file is in place, start iptables:

    ```
    # /etc/init.d/iptables start
    ```

6. At this point, iptables is installed as your firewall. You can confirm that the modules used by iptables are loaded by using the `lsmod` command. Here are some examples:

    ```
    # lsmod |less
    Module                  Size   Used by
    Ip6t_REJECT             4716   2
    nf_conntrack_ipv6       18784  2
    ip6table_filter         3360   1
    ip6_tables              11684  1 ip6table_filter
    ```

7. If you want to allow passive FTP or IRC connections from computers on your LAN, you may need to load those modules by adding them to the `/etc/modprobe.conf` file. The basic connection tracking module, `ip_conntrack`, should be loaded by default already. (See the description of passive FTP and IRC after the firewall-example sections.)

If there is an error in your `/etc/sysconfig/iptables` file, you can make a copy of that file and then try to make a workable configuration by running `system-config-firewall` and setting up a basic firewall. You can then make changes to your firewall to add the features that you need. The following sections contain examples of iptables firewall rules.

Tip

As you add iptables rules, more modules will need to be loaded. Appropriate modules should be loaded automatically when a new rule is entered. Run `lsmod | less` again after you have added a few rules to see which modules were added. Note that these modules will not be unloaded if you decide to stop iptables. They stay loaded until the next reboot or until you remove them (`modprobe -r`). ∎

Creating iptables firewall rules

One way to configure iptables is to start by adding and deleting rules to your kernel from the command line. Then when you have a set of rules that you like, save the rules that are currently running on your system. The tools you use to create your firewall rules and then make them permanent are as follows:

*   `iptables` — Use this command to append (`-A`), delete (`-D`), replace (`-R`), or insert (`-I`) a rule. Use the `-L` option to list all current rules.
*   `service iptables save` — Use this command to save the rules from the kernel and install them in the configuration file.
*   `/etc/sysconfig/iptables` — This is the configuration file that contains the rules that were saved from the `service iptables save` command.

- `/etc/sysconfig/iptables-config` — You can add settings for managing your iptables rules to the `iptables-config` file. For example, any iptables modules, such as `ip_conntrack` and others described later in this chapter, can be added to the `IPTABLES_MODULES` line to be loaded automatically. You can also set whether the iptables table in your running kernel is saved to a file when iptables stops.

- `/etc/rc.d/init.d/iptables` — This is the iptables start-up script that must run automatically each time Fedora reboots. When it starts, it clears all iptables rules and counters, and installs the new rules from the `/etc/sysconfig/iptables` file. You can also use this script with different options from the command line to check the status of iptables (`status`) or to run `iptables-save` for you to save the current rules (`save`).

Note

For each of these commands and files, there is an IPv6 version too. ■

To get you started with iptables, I'm providing a sample set of iptables rules along with descriptions of how you might change those rules for different situations. Here's how you could load and save any of the sets of rules described in the following example:

1. Stop iptables and clear all existing rules:

   `# /etc/rc.d/init.d/iptables stop`

2. Add the rules shown in the following example to a file, using any text editor. Modify the rules to suit your situation and save the file.

3. As root user, run the file as a shell script. For example, if you named the file `fire-script`, you could run it as follows:

   `# sh firescript`

4. See how the rules were loaded into the kernel:

   `# iptabrc.d/les -L`

5. If everything looks OK, save the rules that are now in the kernel into the `/etc/sysconfig/iptables` file:

   `# cp /etc/sysconfig/iptables /etc/sysconfig/iptables-old`
   `# service iptables save`

6. Start iptables:

   `# /etc/init.d/iptables start`

From now on, the rules will be read each time you reboot or restart iptables. Save a copy of the script you used to create the rules, in case you ever need it again.

You can also use the commands `iptables-save` and `iptables-store` to help manage your rules. To save the current rules, run the `iptables-save` command:

```
# iptables-save > /root/iptables.bak
```

You can then restore these rules with the `iptables-restore` command:

```
# iptables-restore -c /root/iptables.bak
```

Firewall configurations can be vastly different depending on what you are trying to achieve, so the following examples illustrate how to configure firewalls based on several different example setups. These setups combine different levels of security requirements.

Example 1: Firewall for shared Internet connection (plus servers)

This example features a home or small-office LAN with a Fedora system acting as an iptables firewall between the LAN and the Internet. The firewall computer also acts as a Web server, FTP server, and DNS server. Figure 13-2 shows this configuration.

FIGURE 13-2

Using iptables as a firewall between the Internet and a LAN.

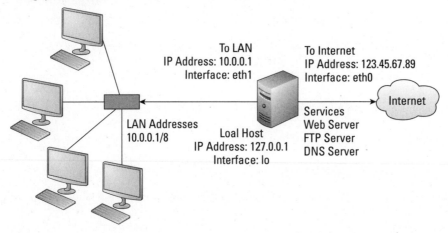

Note

To improve security, separate the network services for systems inside your network from the services to the outside world. ∎

If you want to use the sample firewall script that follows, you must change the following information to match your configuration.

The firewall computer is set up as follows:

- **Local host** — 127.0.0.1 (IP address) and lo (interface). You shouldn't need to change these.

- **Connection to the Internet** — 123.45.67.89 (IP address) and eth0 (interface). Replace them with the static IP address and interface name associated with your connection to the Internet, respectively.

- **Connection to the LAN** — 10.0.0.1 (IP address) and eth1 (interface). Replace 10.0.0.1 and eth1 with the static IP address and interface name associated with your connection to your LAN, respectively.

- **Computers on the LAN** — Each computer on the LAN in the example has an IP address from 10.0.0.2 to 10.0.0.254. Change all the 10.0.0.x values to a number that matches your LAN's range of addresses.

Listing 13-1 shows an example script to load firewall rules that could be used for the configuration shown in Figure 13-2:

LISTING 13-1

Iptables Rules

```
# (1) Policies (default)
iptables -P INPUT DROP
iptables -P OUTPUT DROP
iptables -P FORWARD DROP

# (2) User-defined chain for ACCEPTed TCP packets
iptables -N okay
iptables -A okay -p TCP --syn -j ACCEPT
iptables -A okay -p TCP -m state --state ESTABLISHED,RELATED \
-j ACCEPT
iptables -A okay -p TCP -j DROP

# (3) INPUT chain rules

# Rules for incoming packets from LAN
iptables -A INPUT -p ALL -i eth1 -s 10.0.0.0/24 -j ACCEPT
iptables -A INPUT -p ALL -i lo -s 127.0.0.1 -j ACCEPT
iptables -A INPUT -p ALL -i lo -s 10.0.0.1 -j ACCEPT
iptables -A INPUT -p ALL -i lo -s 123.45.67.89 -j ACCEPT
iptables -A INPUT -p ALL -i eth1 -d 10.0.0.255 -j ACCEPT

# Rules for incoming packets from the Internet

# Packets for established connections
iptables -A INPUT -p ALL -d 123.45.67.89 -m state --state \
ESTABLISHED,RELATED -j ACCEPT
```

```
# TCP rules
iptables -A INPUT -p TCP -i eth0 --destination-port 21 -j okay
iptables -A INPUT -p TCP -i eth0 --destination-port 22 -j okay
iptables -A INPUT -p TCP -i eth0 --destination-port 80 -j okay
iptables -A INPUT -p TCP -i eth0 --destination-port 113 -j okay

# UDP rules
iptables -A INPUT -p UDP -i eth0 --destination-port 53 -j ACCEPT
iptables -A INPUT -p UDP -i eth0 --destination-port 2074 -j ACCEPT
iptables -A INPUT -p UDP -i eth0 --destination-port 4000 -j ACCEPT

# ICMP rules
iptables -A INPUT -p ICMP -i eth0 --icmp type 8  j ACCEPT
iptables -A INPUT -p ICMP -i eth0 --icmp-type 11 -j ACCEPT

# (4) FORWARD chain rules
# Accept the packets we want to forward
iptables -A FORWARD -i eth1 -j ACCEPT
iptables -A FORWARD -m state --state ESTABLISHED,RELATED -j ACCEPT

# (5) OUTPUT chain rules
# Only output packets with local addresses (no spoofing)
iptables -A OUTPUT -p ALL -s 127.0.0.1 -j ACCEPT
iptables -A OUTPUT -p ALL -s 10.0.0.1 -j ACCEPT
iptables -A OUTPUT -p ALL -s 123.45.67.89 -j ACCEPT

# (6) POSTROUTING chain rules
iptables -t nat -A POSTROUTING -o eth0 -j SNAT \
--to-source 123.45.67.89
```

I divided the commands in Listing 13-1 into the following six sections:

(1) Policies — The iptables -P commands set the default policies for INPUT, OUTPUT, and FORWARD chains. By assigning each of those policies to DROP, any packet that isn't matched is discarded. In other words, for a packet to get through, it has to be specifically matched with an ACCEPT by one of the other rules in the script.

(2) User-defined chain — A user-defined chain I call okay is created to do a few more checks on packets requesting certain TCP services that I'm going to allow through (Web, FTP, and DNS services). The -N okay option creates the okay chain. The next line says that a SYN packet (--syn), which requests a new connection, is fine to let through. The next line allows packets associated with an ESTABLISHED connection (one that has already had traffic pass through the interface) or a RELATED connection (one that is starting a new connection related to an already established connection). The final line in this set tells iptables to DROP packets that don't meet one of those checks.

(3) INPUT chain rules — The bulk of the packet filtering is done in the INPUT chain. The first set of input rules indicates to iptables when to always accept packets from the Internet and from the LAN. The next three sets determine which requests for specific protocols (`TCP`, `UDP`, and `ICMP`) are accepted:

- **Packets from LAN** — Because you want the users on your LAN and the firewall computer itself to be able to use the Internet, this set of rules allows packets that are initiated from those computers. The first line tells iptables to accept packets for `ALL` protocols for which the source is an acceptable address on your LAN (`-s 10.0.0.0/24`, which represents IP numbers `10.0.0.1` through `10.0.0.254`). The next three lines allow packets that come from all valid IP addresses on the firewall computer itself (`-s 127.0.0.1`, `10.0.0.1`, and `123.45.67.89`). The last line accepts broadcast packets (`-d 10.0.0.255`) on the LAN.

- **Packets from Internet (already connected)** — This line is split in two (the backslash is used to join the lines because the page wasn't wide enough to show it as one line). It `ACCEPT`s packets that are both associated with connections already established (`--state ESTABLISHED,RELATED`) and requested directly to the firewall's IP address (`123.45.67.89`).

- **TCP rules (new connections)** — Here is where you open up the ports for the TCP services you want to provide to anyone from the Internet. These lines open ports for FTP service (`--destination-port 21`), Secure Shell service (`22`), Web service (`80`), and `IDENTD` authentication (`113`), the last of which might be necessary for protocols such as IRC. You might also need to open port 20 for FTP. Instead of accepting these requests immediately, you jump to the `okay` chain you defined to confirm that the packets were formed properly.

Caution

Ensure that the services on the ports to which you are allowing access are properly configured before you allow packets to be accepted to them. ∎

- **UDP rules (new connections)** — These lines define the ports where connection packets are accepted from the Internet for UDP services. In this example, I chose to accept requests for DNS service (`--destination-port 53`) because the computer is set up as a DNS server. The example also illustrates lines that accept requests for a couple of other optional ports. Port 2074 is needed by some multimedia applications that users on your LAN might want to use, and port 4000 is used by the ICQ protocol (for online chats).

- **ICMP rules** — ICMP messages are really more for reporting conditions of the server, routers, and network interfaces than for actually providing services. Packets from the Internet that are accepted for ICMP protocol requests in our example are those for ICMP types 8 and 11. Type 8 service, which allows your computer to accept echo request messages, enables people to ping your computer to see if it is available. Type 11 service relates to packets whose time to live (TTL) was exceeded in transit, and for which you are accepting a Time Exceeded message that is being returned to you. (You need to accept Type 11 messages to use the `traceroute` command to find broken routes to hosts you want to reach.)

(4) FORWARD chain rules — Because this firewall is also acting as a router, FORWARD rules are needed to limit what the firewall will and will not pass between the two networks (Internet and local LAN). The first line forwards everything from the local LAN (-A FORWARD -i eth1). The second line forwards anything from the Internet that is associated with an established connection (--state ESTABLISHED,RELATED).

(5) OUTPUT chain rules — These rules exist to prevent anyone from your local computer from *spoofing* IP addresses (i.e., from saying packets are coming from somewhere that they are not). According to these three rules, each packet output from your firewall must have as its source address one of the addresses from the firewall computer's interfaces (127.0.0.1, 10.0.0.0.1, or 123.45.67.89).

(6) POSTROUTING chain rules — The POSTROUTING chain defines rules for packets that have been accepted but need additional processing. This is where the actual network address translation (NAT) work takes place. For the NAT table (-t nat), in the POSTROUTING chain, all packets going out to the Internet have their addresses translated to that of the firewall's external interface (--to -source 123.45.67.89). In this case, I used the Source Network Address Translation (SNAT) chain because a static IP address (123.45.67.89) is associated with my Internet connection. If I were using a dynamic IP address (via DHCP), I would use MASQUERADE instead of SNAT. I would also have to change any references to -d 123.45.67.89 to -i eth0. (Of course, you would be using a different IP address and possibly a different Ethernet interface.)

You need to modify the IP addresses to match those on your network.

Example 2: Firewall for shared Internet connection (no servers)

In this scenario, the firewall is protecting a Linux system (firewall) and several systems on the LAN that are used only to connect to the Internet. No servers are behind this firewall, so you want to prevent people from the Internet from requesting services.

You could use the same script shown in Example 1 but not use lines that request TCP services. Therefore, you could drop the user-defined chain in section 2 and drop the TCP rules from section 3. You could also remove the ICMP rules if you don't want your firewall to be visible to ping requests (Type 8) and if you don't care about receiving messages when your packets exceed their time-to-live values (Type 11), such as when a packet runs into a broken router.

Example 3: Firewall for single Linux system with Internet connection

In this example, there is one network interface, which connects your Fedora system to the Internet. You are not sharing that connection with other computers and you are not offering any services from your computer.

In this case, you could cut sections 2, 4, and 6. From section 3, you could cut all rules relating to incoming requests from the LAN and all TCP services. As mentioned in Example 2, you could also remove the Type 8 ICMP rule to make your firewall invisible to ping requests from the Internet, and the Type 11 ICMP rule to not accept messages about failed time-to-live packets.

Understanding iptables

Now that you've learned something about iptables rules and how you can get them going, step back a bit to see how iptables works. Basically, IP packets (i.e., network data) that enter or leave the firewall computer traverse a set of rules that define what is done with the packet. Each rule that you add essentially does both of the following:

- Checks whether a particular criterion is met (such as that a packet requests a particular service or comes from a particular address)
- Takes an action (such as dropping, accepting, or further processing a packet)

Different sets of rules are implemented for different types of tables. For example, tables exist for filtering (filter), network address translation (nat), and changing packet headers (mangle). Depending on the packet's source and destination, it traverses different chains. Most of the rules you create will relate to the filter table (which is implied if no other table is given).

The chains associated with the filter table are INPUT, OUTPUT, and FORWARD. You can add user-defined chains as well. You will probably be most interested in adding or removing particular TCP and UDP services using the basic rules shown in the previous example. Assign ACCEPT to packets you want to allow through and DROP to those you want to discard. You can also assign REJECT to drop a packet but return an ICMP message to the sender, or LOG to neither drop nor accept the message, but to log information about the packet.

A lot of great features are built into iptables. The following sections describe some cool things you can do with iptables and provide some tips about using it.

Using iptables to do SNAT or IP masquerading

As noted in the iptables example, you can use Source Network Address Translation (SNAT) or IP masquerading (MASQUERADE) to allow computers on your LAN with private IP addresses to access the Internet through your iptables firewall. Choose SNAT if you have a static IP address for your Internet connection, or MASQUERADE if the IP address is assigned dynamically.

When you create the MASQUERADE or SNAT rule, it is added to the NAT table and the POSTROUTING chain. For MASQUERADE you must provide the name of the interface (such as eth0, ppp0, or slip0) to identify the route to the Internet or other outside network. For SNAT you must also identify the actual IP address of the interface. Here is an example of a MASQUERADE rule:

```
# iptables -t nat -A POSTROUTING -o eth0 -j MASQUERADE
```

Here is an example of a SNAT rule:

```
# iptables -t nat -A POSTROUTING -o eth0 -j SNAT \
--to-source 12.12.12.12
```

You can add several source addresses if you have multiple addresses that provide a route to the Internet (e.g., --to-source 12.12.12.1-12.12.12.254). Although MASQUERADE uses some additional overhead, you probably need to use it instead of SNAT if you have a dial-up or other Internet connection for which the IP address changes on each connection.

Remember that you need to ensure that IP forwarding is turned on in the kernel. (It is off by default.) To turn it on permanently, edit the `/etc/sysctl.conf` file as described earlier. To turn it on temporarily, you can do the following:

```
# echo 1 > /proc/sys/net/ipv4/ip_forward
```

If you require dynamic IP addressing (in common cases where you don't know the IP address when you first establish the connection to the Internet through a dial-up, DSL, or cable modem connection), turn on that service:

```
# echo 1 > /proc/sys/net/ipv4/ip_dynaddr
```

Using iptables as a transparent proxy

With the `REDIRECT` target you can cause traffic for a specific port on the firewall computer to be directed to a different one. Using this feature you can direct host computers on your local LAN to a proxy service on your firewall computer without those hosts knowing it.

The following is an example of a set of command-line options to the `iptables` command that causes a request for Web service (port 80) to be directed to a proxy service (port 3128):

```
-t nat -A PREROUTING -p tcp --dport 80 -j REDIRECT --to-ports 3128
```

You can use `REDIRECT` targets in `PREROUTING` and `OUTPUT` chains only within a `nat` table. You can also provide a range of port numbers to spread the redirection across multiple port numbers. See the online documentation (type **man iptables**) for more information.

Using iptables to do port forwarding

What if you have only one static IP address but you want to use a computer other than your firewall computer to provide Web, FTP, DNS, or some other service? You can use the Destination Network Address Translation (DNAT) feature to direct traffic for a particular port on your firewall to another computer.

For example, if you want all requests for Web service (port 80) that are directed to the firewall computer (`-d 15.15.15.15`) to be directed to another computer on your LAN (such as `10.0.0.25`), you can use the following `iptables` command:

```
# iptables -t nat -A PREROUTING -p tcp -d 15.15.15.15 --dport 80 \
          -j DNAT --to-destination 10.0.0.25
```

(Note that the preceding example should actually appear on one line. The backslash indicates continuation on the next line.)

You can also spread the load for the service you are forwarding by providing a range of IP addresses (e.g., `--to-destination 10.0.0.1-10.0.0.25`). Likewise, you can direct the request to a range of ports as well.

Using logging with iptables

Using the LOG target you can log information about packets that meet the criteria you choose. In particular, you might want to use this feature to log packets that seem like they might be improper in some way. In other words, if you don't want to drop a packet for some reason, you can just log its activity and decide later if something needs to be corrected.

The LOG target directs log information to the standard tools used to perform logging in Fedora: dmesg and rsyslogd. Here's an example of a rule using a LOG target:

```
-A FORWARD -p tcp -j LOG --log-level info
```

Instead of info, you could use any of the following log levels available with rsyslog: emerg, alert, crit, err, warning, notice, info, or debug. Using the --log-prefix option as follows, you could also add information to the front of all messages produced from this logging action:

```
-A FORWARD -p tcp -j LOG --log-level info --log-prefix "Forward INFO"
```

Enhancing your iptables firewall

You can modify or expand on the iptables examples given in this chapter in many ways, as iptables is tremendously flexible.

When you actually create your own iptables firewall, you should refer to the iptables man page (type **man iptables**) for detailed descriptions of options, ways to match, ways to enter addresses, and other details. I also recommend an excellent iptables tutorial by Oskar Andreasson (www.frozentux.net/documents/iptables-tutorial/).

Here are a few tips for using iptables features:

- **Reduce rules** — Try to improve performance by reducing the number of rules. Using subchains can prevent a packet from seeing rules that don't apply to it.
- **Deal with fragments** — Use the -f option to refer to the second and subsequent packets of a packet that was split into fragments. In general, it is safe to not drop second and third fragments for which you don't have a first packet fragment because they won't be reassembled. If you use NAT, the fragments are assembled before filtering, so you shouldn't have problems with unfiltered fragments being sent through.
- **Opposite** — To make a rule its opposite, use an exclamation mark (!).
- **All interfaces** — To match all interfaces of a type, use a plus sign (+), as in eth+.
- **Blocking connections** — Use the --syn option to block SYN packets (that is, packets requesting connections). This option applies only to TCP packets.
- **Limiting** — Use the --limit option to restrict the rate of matches that result in log messages. This option allows matches to produce messages a specified number of times per second (the default is three per hour, with bursts of five). See man iptables for more on limiting.

- **Denial-of-service (DOS) attacks** — You can use the `--limit` option to reduce the impact of DOS attacks, but it still won't stop them altogether. As long as the traffic is directed at your server, your network bandwidth is being leeched away, and the machine still utilizes resources to ignore the data.

- **Table types** — The default table type is `filter`. The other types of tables are `nat` (for IP masquerading) and `mangle` (for altering packets). To use a table other than `filter`, you must add a `-t table_type` option, where `table_type` is either `nat` or `mangle`.

See `http://docs.redhat.com/docs/en-US/Red_Hat_Enterprise_Linux/6/html/Security_Guide/sect-Security_Guide-IPTables.html` for more on iptables.

Controlling Access to Services with TCP Wrappers

Completely disabling an unused service is fine, but what about the services you really need? How can you selectively grant and deny access to these services? In older versions of Red Hat Linux, the TCP wrapper daemon (`tcpd`) was used to facilitate this sort of selective access. In the current version of Fedora, TCP wrapper support has been integrated into `xinetd`, which looks at the files `/etc/hosts.allow` and `/etc/hosts.deny` to determine when a particular connection should be granted or refused for services such as rlogin, rsh, telnet, finger, and talk. TCP wrappers are also enabled by default for other services, such as a vsftpd FTP server (with `tcp_wrappers=YES` in your `vsftpd.conf` file).

When a service is requested that relies on TCP wrappers, the `hosts.allow` and `hosts.deny` files are scanned and checked for an entry that matches the IP address of the connecting machine. These checks are made when connection attempts occur:

- If the address is listed in the `hosts.allow` file, the connection is allowed and `hosts.deny` is not checked.

- If the address is in `hosts.deny` (but not the `hosts.allow` file), the connection is denied.

- If the address is in neither file, the connection is allowed.

It is not necessary (or even possible) to list every single address that may connect to your computer. The `hosts.allow` and `hosts.deny` files enable you to specify entire subnets and groups of addresses. You can even use the keyword `ALL` to specify all possible addresses. You can also restrict specific entries in these files so they apply only to specific network services. Consider an example of a typical pair of `hosts.allow` and `hosts.deny` files. Here's the `/etc/hosts.allow` file:

```
#
# hosts.allow     This file contains access rules which are used to
#                 allow or deny connections to network services that
```

```
#               either use the tcp_wrappers library or that have been
#               started through a tcp_wrappers-enabled xinetd.
#

sshd: 199.170.177., .linuxtoys.net
vsftpd: ALL
```

Here's the /etc/hosts.deny file:

```
#
# hosts.deny     This file contains access rules which are used to
#                deny connections to network services that either use
#                the tcp_wrappers library or that have been
#                started through a tcp_wrappers-enabled xinetd.
#

ALL: ALL
```

The preceding example is a rather restrictive configuration. It allows connections to the sshd service from certain hosts, and allows connections to the FTP service (vsftp) to all hosts. The hosts.deny file denies all other connections. Let's examine the files in detail.

As usual, lines beginning with a # character are comments, which are ignored by xinetd when it parses the file. Each noncomment line consists of a comma-separated list of daemons followed by a colon (:) character and then a comma-separated list of client addresses to check. In this context, a client is any computer that attempts to access a network service on your system.

A client entry can be a numeric IP address (such as 199.170.177.25) or a hostname (such as jukebox.linuxtoys.net), but it's more often a wildcard variation that specifies an entire range of addresses. A client entry can take four different forms. The online manual page for the hosts.allow file describes them as follows:

- **"A string that begins with a dot (.) character** — A hostname is matched if the last components of its name match the specified pattern. For example, the pattern .tue.nl matches the hostname wzv.win.tue.nl.

- **A string that ends with a dot (.) character** — A host address is matched if its first numeric fields match the given string. For example, the pattern 131.155. matches the address of (almost) every host on the Eindhoven University network (131.155.x.x).

- **A string that begins with an at (@) sign is treated as an NIS netgroup name** — A hostname is matched if it is a host member of the specified netgroup. Netgroup matches are not supported for daemon process names or for client user names.

- **An expression of the form n.n.n.n/m.m.m.m is interpreted as a *net/mask* pair** — A host address is matched if *net* is equal to the bitwise *and* of the address and the mask. For example, the net/mask pattern 131.155.72.0/255.255.254.0 matches every address in the range 131.155.72.0 through 131.155.73.255."

The example `host.allow` contains the first two types of client specification. The entry `199.170.177.` will match any IP address that begins with that string, such as `199.170.177.25`. The client entry `.linuxtoys.net` will match hostnames such as `jukebox.linuxtoys.net` or `picframe.linuxtoys.net`.

Let's examine what happens when a host named `jukebox.linuxtoys.net` (with IP address `199.170.179.18`) connects to your Fedora system using the SSH protocol:

1. `xinetd` receives the connection request.

2. `xinetd` begins comparing the address and name of `jukebox.linuxtoys.net` to the rules listed in `/etc/hosts.allow`. It starts at the top of the file and works its way down until it finds a match. Both the daemon (the program handling the network service on your Fedora box) and the connecting client's IP address or name must match the information in the `hosts.allow` file. In this case, the first rule that is encountered matches the request:

   `cups-lpd: 199.170.177., .linuxtoys.net`

3. Jukebox is not in the `199.170.177` subnet, but it is in the `linuxtoys.net` domain. `xinetd` stops searching the file as soon as it finds this match.

If Jukebox connects to your box using another protocol, it matches none of the rules in `hosts.allow`. `xinetd` continues on to the `hosts.deny` file. The entry `ALL: ALL` matches anything, so `xinetd` denies the connection.

The `ALL` wildcard was also used in the `hosts.allow` file. In this case, it is telling `xinetd` to permit absolutely any host to connect to the FTP service on the Linux box. This is appropriate for running an anonymous FTP server that anyone on the Internet can access. If you are not running an anonymous FTP site, you probably should not use the `ALL` flag.

A good rule of thumb is to make your `hosts.allow` and `hosts.deny` files as restrictive as possible and then explicitly enable only those services that you really need. Also, grant access only to those systems that really need access. Using the `ALL` flag to grant universal access to a particular service may be easier than typing in a long list of subnets or domains, but better a few minutes spent on proper security measures than many hours recovering from a break-in.

Tip

You can further restrict access to services using various options within the `/etc/xinetd.conf` file, even to the point of limiting access to certain services to specific times of the day. Read the manual page for `xinetd` (by typing man xinetd at a command prompt) to learn more about these options. ∎

Checking Log Files

Preparing your system for a cracker attack is only part of the battle. You must also recognize a cracker attack when it is occurring. Understanding the various log files in which Fedora records important events is critical to this goal. The log files for your Fedora system can be found in the /var/log directory.

Because the system logs are plain-text files, you can view the contents of logs directly using any text editor or paging command (such as less or more). The logwatch facility (included with Fedora) sends daily highlights from your log files in an e-mail message to the root user.

Understanding the rsyslogd service

Most of the files in the /var/log directory are maintained by the rsyslogd service. The rsyslogd daemon is the System Logging Daemon and it acts as an extension of a previous logging system called syslogd. It accepts log messages from a variety of other programs and writes them to the appropriate log files. This is better than having every program write directly to its own log file because it enables you to centrally manage how log files are handled. It is possible to configure rsyslogd to record varying levels of detail in the log files. It can be told to ignore all but the most critical message or it can record every detail.

The rsyslogd daemon can even accept messages from other computers on your network. This is particularly handy because it enables you to centralize the management and reviewing of log files from many systems on your network. There is also a major security benefit to this practice. If a system on your network is broken into, the cracker cannot delete or modify the log files because those files are stored on a separate computer.

It is important to remember, however, that those log messages are not, by default, encrypted. Anyone tapping into your local network may be able to eavesdrop on those messages as they pass from one machine to another. In addition, although crackers may not be able to change old log messages, they will be able to affect the system such that any new log messages should not be trusted.

It is not uncommon to run a dedicated loghost, a computer that serves no other purpose than to record log messages from other computers on the network. Because this system runs no other services, it is less likely that it will be broken into. This makes it nearly impossible for crackers to erase their tracks. It does not, however, mean that all the log messages are accurate after a cracker has broken into a machine on your network.

Redirecting logs to a loghost with rsyslogd

To redirect your computer's log files to another computer's rsyslogd, you must make some changes to your local rsyslogd configuration file. The file that you need to work with is /etc/rsyslog.conf. If you are not already root, become root and then open the /etc/rsyslog.conf file in a text editor (such as vi). You should see something similar to this:

```
#rsyslog v3 config file

# if you experience problems, check
# http://www.rsyslog.com/troubleshoot for assistance

#### MODULES ####
```

```
$ModLoad imuxsock.so # provides support for local system logging ...
$ModLoad imklog.so # provides kernel logging support (previously done by rklogd)
#$ModLoad immark.so # provides --MARK-- message capability
```

```
       .
       .
       .
```

```
#### RULES ####

# Log all kernel messages to the console.
# Logging much else clutters up the screen.
#kern.*                                   /dev/console

# Log anything (except mail) of level info or higher.
# Don't log private authentication messages!
*.info;mail.none;authpriv.none;cron.none    /var/log/messages

# The authpriv file has restricted access.
authpriv.*                                /var/log/secure

# Log all the mail messages in one place.
mail.*                                    -/var/log/maillog


# Log cron stuff
cron.*                                    /var/log/cron

# Everybody gets emergency messages
*.emerg                                        *

# Save news errors of level crit and higher in a special file.
uucp,news.crit                            /var/log/spooler

# Save boot messages also to boot.log
local7.*                                  /var/log/boot.log
```

```
       .
       .
       .
```

The lines beginning with a # character are comments. Other lines contain two columns of information, separated by spaces or tabs. The left field is a semicolon-separated list of message types and message priorities. The right field is the log file to which those messages should be written.

The most interesting part begins with the section named RULES.

Note

Notice the dash (-) before the `/var/log/maillog` file. Normally, each log file is synced after every logging. A dash preceding the full path to the log file indicates that the file is not synced after each logging. While this might result in lost information if your machine crashes before the log is written, it can result in better performance on your system if you run verbose logging. ∎

To send the messages to another computer (the loghost) instead of a file, simply replace the log filename with the @ character followed by the name of the loghost. For example, to redirect the output normally sent to the `messages`, `secure`, and `maillog` log files, make these changes to the previous file:

```
# Log anything (except mail) of level info or higher.
# Don't log private authentication messages!
*.info;mail.none;news.none;authpriv.none;cron.none   @loghost

# The authpriv file has restricted access.
authpriv.*                                 @loghost

# Log all the mail messages in one place.
mail.*                                     @loghost
```

The messages will now be sent to the `rsyslogd` running on the computer named loghost. The name loghost was not an arbitrary choice. It is customary to create such a hostname and make it an alias to the actual system acting as the loghost. That way, if you ever need to switch the loghost duties to a different machine, you need to change only the loghost alias; you do not need to re-edit the `rsyslog.conf` file on every computer.

Note

You will likely need to edit the iptables rules on the loghost to allow incoming packets on port 514, the default `rsyslogd` port number. ∎

Understanding the messages log file

Because of the many programs and services that record information to the messages log file, it is important that you understand the format of this file. Examining this file often gives you a good early warning of problems developing on your system. Each line in the file is a single message recorded by some program or service. Here is a snippet of an actual messages log file:

```
Feb 25 11:04:32 toys network: Bringing up loopback interface:  succeeded
Feb 25 11:04:35 toys network: Bringing up interface eth0:  succeeded
Feb 25 13:01:14 toys vsftpd(pam_unix)[10565]: authentication failure;
     logname= uid=0 euid=0 tty= ruser= rhost=10.0.0.5  user=chris
Feb 25 14:44:24 toys su: pam_unix(su-l:session): session opened for
     user root by chris(uid=500)
```

This is really very simple when you know what to look for. Each message is divided into five main parts. From left to right they are as follows:

- The date and time when the message was logged

- The name of the computer from which the message was sent
- The program or service name to which the message pertains
- The process number (enclosed in square brackets) of the program sending the message
- The actual text message

Let's examine the previous file snippet. The first two lines show that I restarted the network. The next line shows that I tried to log in as the user named chris to get to the FTP server on this system from a computer at address 10.0.0.5 (I typed the wrong password, so authentication failed). The last line shows that I used the su command to become root user.

By occasionally reviewing the messages file and the secure file, it is possible to catch a cracking attempt before it is successful. If you see an excessive number of connection attempts for a particular service, especially if they are coming from systems on the Internet, you may be under attack.

Tracking log messages with logwatch

Another way to keep up with the contents of your log files is with the logwatch facility. Logwatch flags messages that might reflect a problem with your system and forwards them each day in an e-mail message to your system's root user. If logwatch is not installed, run the yum install logwatch command. Based on the logwatch cron file (/etc/cron.daily/0logwatch), the logwatch facility will do the following:

- Run each morning at 4:00 a.m.
- Choose which log files to scan and where to send the e-mail message, based on the configuration file /etc/logwatch/conf/logwatch.conf. (The defaults are listed in /usr/share/logwatch/default.conf/.)
- Send to the local computer's root user an e-mail message that reports potentially suspicious activity on your system, based on the contents of your log files.
- Report on administrative activities that could reflect a problem with the system.

The kind of information logwatch reports on includes users and groups that have been deleted, packages installed or uninstalled, and disk space consumed. The daily messages also show login activity through SSH over the network and file transfer activities. Failure messages are flagged and reported for each log file scanned.

Review the /usr/share/logwatch/default.conf/logwatch.conf file to see the options you have for configuring your logwatch service. To change any options, you can add them to the /etc/logwatch/conf/logwatch.conf file. Here are examples of some logwatch settings:

```
LogDir = /var/log
TmpDir = /var/cache/logwatch
MailTo = root
MailFrom = Logwatch
Print =
```

```
Service = "-zz-network"       # Prevents execution of zz-network service, which
                              # prints useful network configuration info.
Service = "-zz-sys"           # Prevents execution of zz-sys service, which
                              # prints useful system configuration info.
Service = "-eximstats"        # Prevents execution of eximstats service, which
                              # is a wrapper for the eximstats program.
Range = yesterday
Detail = Low
Service = All
mailer = "sendmail -t"
```

LogDir sets the log file directory as /var/log (so any log files listed are shown as relative to that directory). The /var/cache/logwatch directory is used to hold temporary files. The daily e-mail report is sent to the root user on the local system (you can change MailTo to any valid e-mail address), with the sender (MailFrom) listed as Logwatch. You can change the Print value to Yes to have the report sent to standard output, instead of being mailed to the MailTo recipient. The Range is set to yesterday, which causes logwatch to search log files for the past day only. You can change the Range to All to search all past files available for a particular log file, as in messages, messages.1, messages.2, and so on. To increase the amount of detail (which is set to Low by default), you can identify Detail as Medium or High (or a number from 0 to 10).

Most of the action that takes place by logwatch is based on the value of the Service entry. With Service set to All, all files in the /usr/share/logwatch/conf/services directory are used to produce the logwatch report. Files in this directory are each related to a service that is checked by logwatch and defines the type of information gathered for that service. Precede any service name that you want to disable with a dash (-). (By default, zz-network, zz-sys, and eximstats are disabled.)

Using the Secure Shell Package

The Secure Shell package (SSH) provides shell services similar to other remote execution, remote copy, and remote login commands (such as the old Unix rsh, rcp, and rlogin commands) but encrypts the network traffic. It uses private-key cryptography, so it is ideal for use with Internet-connected computers. The Fedora distributions contain the following client and server software packages for SSH: openssh, openssh-clients, and openssh-server packages.

Starting the SSH service

If you have installed the openssh-server software package, the SSH server is automatically configured to start. The SSH daemon is started from the /etc/rc.d/init.d/sshd start-up script. To ensure that the service is set up to start automatically, type the following (as root user):

```
# chkconfig --list sshd
sshd       0:off   1:off   2:on    3:on    4:on    5:on    6:off
```

This shows that the sshd service is set to run in system states 2, 3, 4, and 5 (normal boot-up states) and set to be off in all other states. You can turn on the SSH service, if it is off, for your default run state, by typing the following as root user:

```
# chkconfig sshd on
```

This line turns on the SSH service when you enter run levels 2, 3, 4, or 5. To start the service immediately, type the following:

```
# /etc/rc.d/init.d/sshd start
```

Tip

If you aren't able to connect to the sshd service from another computer, confirm that the firewall is open on your server to allow access to tcp port 22. That's the default port on which sshd listens for requests. It will be more secure if you change the sshd service to listen on a nonstandard port and then open that port in your firewall, since attackers will go after the default port. ■

Using the ssh, sftp, and scp commands

Three commands you can use with the SSH service are ssh, sftp, and scp. Remote users use the ssh command to log in to your system securely. The scp command lets remote users copy files to and from a system. The sftp command provides a safe way to access FTP sites.

Like the normal remote shell services, SSH looks in the /etc/hosts.equiv file and in a user's .rhost file to determine whether it should allow a connection. It also looks in the ssh-specific files /etc/ssh/shosts.equiv and .shosts. Using the shosts.equiv and the .shosts files is preferable because it avoids granting access to the non-encrypted remote shell services. The /etc/ssh/shosts.equiv and .shosts files are functionally equivalent to the traditional hosts.equiv and .rhosts files, so the same instructions and rules apply. You can improve security by turning off the use of the .rhosts and .shosts files. Do this by uncommenting the following line in the /etc/ssh/sshd_config file (type **man hosts.equiv** and **man ssh** for further information):

```
#IgnoreRhosts yes
```

Now you are ready to test the SSH service. From another computer on which SSH has been installed (or even from the same computer if another is not available), type the ssh command followed by a space and the name of the system you are connecting to. For example, to connect to the system ratbert.glaci.com, type the following:

```
$ ssh ratbert.glaci.com
```

If this is the first time you have logged in to that system using the ssh command, you will be asked to confirm that you really want to connect. Type **yes** and press Enter when it asks this:

```
The authenticity of host 'ratbert.glaci.com (199.170.177.18)' ↵
can't be established.
RSA key fingerprint is xx:xx:xx:xx:xx:xx:xx:xx:xx:xx:xx:xx:xx:xx:xx:xx.
Are you sure you want to continue connecting (yes/no)? yes
```

Caution

If you see an auth request a second time, it could possibly be a man-in-the-middle attack. ∎

If you don't specify a user name when you start the ssh connection, the SSH daemon assumes you want to use the user name you are logged in as from the client. If you want to log in as a different user name (e.g., chris), you could type the following:

```
$ ssh chris@ratbert.glaci.com
```

or

```
$ ssh -l chris ratbert.glaci.com
```

Once you are logged in, a shell prompt appears and you can begin using the remote system as you would from a local shell.

The `scp` command is similar to the `rcp` command for copying files to and from Linux systems. Here is an example of using the `scp` command to copy a file called memo from the home directory of the user named jake to the `/tmp` directory on a computer called maple:

```
$ scp /home/jake/memo maple:/tmp
jake@maple's password: ********
memo          100%  177KB 101.3KB/s 00:02
```

Enter the password for your user name (if a password is requested). If the password is accepted, the remote system indicates that the file has been copied successfully.

Similarly, the `sftp` command starts an interactive FTP session with an FTP server that supports SSH connections. Many security-conscious people prefer `sftp` to other `ftp` clients because it provides a secure connection between you and the remote host. Here's an example:

```
$ sftp ftp.handsonhistory.com
Connecting to ftp.handsonhistory.com
jake@ftp.handsonhistory.com's password: ********
sftp>
```

At this point you can begin an interactive FTP session. Use `get` and `put` commands on files as you would using any FTP client, but with the comfort of knowing that you are working on a secure connection.

Tip

The `sftp` command, as with `ssh` and `scp`, requires that the SSH service be running on the server. If you can't connect to an FTP server using `sftp`, the SSH service may not be available. It might also be disabled in the `/etc/ssh/sshd_config` file on the server. ∎

Using ssh, scp, and sftp without passwords

For machines that you use a great deal, it is often helpful to set them up so that you don't need to use a password to log in. The following procedure shows you how to do that. These steps take you through setting up password-less authentication from one machine to another. In this example, the local user is named chester on a computer named host1. The remote user is also chester on a computer named host2.

1. Log in to the local computer (in this example, I log in as `chester` to `host1`).

Note
Run Step 2 only once as local user on your local workstation. Do not run it again unless you lose your ssh keys. When configuring subsequent remote servers, skip right to Step 4. ■

2. Type the following to generate the ssh key:

```
$ ssh-keygen -t dsa
Generating public/private dsa key pair.
Enter file in which to save the key
(/home/chester/.ssh/id_dsa): <Enter>
Enter passphrase (empty for no passphrase): <Enter>
Enter same passphrase again: <Enter>
Your identification has been saved in /home/chester/.ssh/id_dsa.
Your public key has been saved in /home/chester/.ssh/id_dsa.pub.
The key fingerprint is:
3b:c0:2f:63:a5:65:70:b7:4b:f0:2a:c4:18:24:47:69 chester@host1
The key's randomart image is:
+--[ DSA 1024]----+
|                 |
|       . .       |
|      o + .      |
|       + o o     |
|      o * S o    |
|     o + 0 = .   |
|      . * + E    |
|       = .       |
|       ..o       |
+-----------------+
```

3. Accept the default key file location by pressing Enter. Then press Enter again (twice) to assign a blank passphrase. (If you enter a passphrase, you will be prompted for that passphrase and won't be able to log in without it.)

4. You must secure the permissions of your authentication keys by closing permissions to your home directory, .ssh directory, and authentication files as follows:

```
$ chmod go-w $HOME
$ chmod 700 $HOME/.ssh
$ chmod go-rwx $HOME/.ssh/*
```

5. Type the following to copy the key to the remote server (replace `chester` with the remote user name and `host2` with the remote hostname):

```
$ cd ~/.ssh
$ scp id_dsa.pub chester@host2:/tmp
chester@host2's password: *******
```

6. Type the following to add the ssh key to the remote user's authorization keys (the code should be on one line, not wrapped):

```
$ ssh chester@host2 'cat /tmp/id_dsa.pub >>
/home/chester/.ssh/authorized_keys2'
```

Note

The previous two steps ask for passwords. This is OK. Also, you may want to use the `chmod` command to restrict access to the `authorized_keys2` file to just the user. See Chapter 4 for more on `chmod`. ∎

7. In order for the sshd daemon to accept the `authorized_keys2` file you created, your home directories and authentication files must have secure permissions. To secure those files and directories, type the following (note that the double quotes are needed to prevent the * from being interpreted by the local shell):

```
$ ssh chester@host2 chmod go-w $HOME
$ ssh chester@host2 chmod 700 $HOME/.ssh
$ ssh chester@host2 "chmod go-rwx $HOME/.ssh/*"
```

8. Type the following to remove the key from the temporary directory:

```
$ ssh chester@host2 rm /tmp/id_dsa.pub
```

Note that once you have this working, it will work regardless of how many times the IP address changes on your local computer. The IP address has nothing to do with this form of authentication.

Securing Linux Servers

Opening up your Fedora system as a server on a public network creates a whole new set of challenges when it comes to security. Instead of just turning away nearly all incoming requests, your computer will be expected to respond to requests for supported services (such as Web, FTP, or mail service) by supplying information or possibly running scripts that accept data.

Entire books have been filled with information about how to secure your servers. Many businesses that rely on Internet servers assign full-time administrators to watch over the security of their servers. This section provides an overview of some of the kinds of attacks to look out for and some tools available to secure your Fedora server.

Understanding attack techniques

Attacks on computing systems take different forms, depending on the goal and resources of the attacker. Some attackers want to be disruptive, while others want to infiltrate your machines and utilize the resources for their own nefarious purposes. Still others are targeting your data for financial gain or blackmail. Here are three major categories of attacks:

- **Denial-of-service (DoS)** — The easiest attacks to perpetrate are denial-of-service attacks. The primary purpose of these attacks is to disrupt the activities of a remote site by overloading it with irrelevant data. DoS attacks can be as simple as sending thousands of page requests per second to a website. Once you have a handle on where the attack is coming from, a simple phone call to the perpetrator's ISP will solve the problem. If a DoS attack spoofs the return address, you may need to do more work to track down the source.

- **Distributed denial-of-service (DDoS)** — More advanced DoS attacks are called *distributed denial-of-service attacks*. DDoS attacks are much harder to perpetrate and nearly impossible to stop. In this form of attack, an attacker takes control of hundreds or even thousands of weakly secured Internet-connected computers. The attacker then directs them in unison to send a stream of irrelevant data to a single Internet host. As a result, the power of one attacker is magnified thousands of times. Instead of an attack coming from one direction, as with a normal DoS, it comes from thousands of directions at once. The best defense against a DDoS attack is to contact your ISP to see if it can filter traffic at its border routers.

  To avoid having to consider security, many people use the excuse that they have nothing on their machine anyone would want. The problem with this argument is that attackers have a lot of reasons to *use* your machine. An attacker can turn your machine into an agent for later use in a DDoS attack.

Note
If your system or Web page is mentioned on a popular Internet site such as slashdot.org, you may experience what seems like a DDoS attack but in reality is just a very lot of people trying to view your site. ∎

- **Intrusion attacks** — To remotely use the resources of a target machine, attackers must first look for an opening to exploit. In the absence of inside information such as passwords or encryption keys, they must scan the target machine to see what services are offered. Perhaps one of the services is weakly secured and the attacker can use some known exploit to finagle his or her way in.

  A tool called *nmap* is generally considered the best way to scan a host for services (note that nmap is a tool that can be used for good and bad). Once the attacker has a list of the available services running on his target, he needs to find a way to trick one of those services into letting him have privileged access to the system. Usually, this is done with a program called an exploit.

While DoS attacks are disruptive, intrusion-type attacks are the most damaging. The reasons vary, but the result is always the same: An uninvited guest is now taking up residence on your machine and is using it in a way you have no control over.

Protecting against denial-of-service attacks

As explained earlier, a denial-of-service attack attempts to crash your computer or at least degrade its performance to an unusable level. There are a variety of denial-of-service exploits. Most try to overload some system resource, such as your available disk space or your Internet connection. Some common attacks and defenses are discussed in the following sections.

Mailbombing

Mailbombing is the practice of sending so much e-mail to a particular user or system that the computer's hard drive becomes full. There are several ways to protect your systems from mailbombing. You can use the Procmail e-mail-filtering tool or configure your sendmail daemon.

Cross-Reference

See Chapter 18 for a more complete description of sendmail. ∎

Blocking mail with Procmail

The Procmail e-mail-filtering tool is installed by default with Fedora and is tightly integrated with the sendmail e-mail daemon; thus, it can be used to selectively block or filter out specific types of e-mail. You can learn more about Procmail at the Procmail website: www.procmail.org.

To enable Procmail for your user account, create a .procmailrc file in your home directory. The file should be mode 0600 (readable by you but nobody else). Type the following, replacing *evilmailer* with the actual e-mail address that is mailbombing you:

```
# Delete mail from evilmailer
:0
* ^From.*evilmailer
/dev/null
```

The Procmail recipe looks for the From line at the start of each e-mail to see if it includes the string evilmailer. If it does, the message is sent to /dev/null (effectively throwing it away).

Blocking mail with sendmail

The Procmail e-mail tool works quite well when only one user is being mailbombed. If, however, the mailbombing affects many users, you should probably configure your sendmail daemon to block all e-mail from the mailbomber. Do this by adding the mailbomber's e-mail address or system name to the access file located in the /etc/mail directory.

Each line of the access file contains an e-mail address, hostname, domain, or IP address followed by a tab and then a keyword specifying what action to take when that entity sends a message. Valid keywords are OK, RELAY, REJECT, DISCARD, and ERROR. Using the REJECT keyword causes a sender's e-mail to be bounced back with an error message. The keyword DISCARD causes the message to be silently dropped without sending an error back. You can even return a custom error message by using the ERROR keyword.

Thus, an example /etc/mail/access file may look similar to this:

```
# Check the /usr/share/doc/sendmail/README.cf file for a description
# of the format of this file. (search for access_db in that file)
# The /usr/share/doc/sendmail/README.cf is part of the sendmail-doc
# package.

...

# by default we allow relaying from localhost...
Connect:localhost.localdomain          RELAY
Connect:localhost                      RELAY
Connect:127.0.0.1                      RELAY
#
# Senders we want to Block
#
From:evilmailer@yahoo.com    REJECT
From:stimpy.glaci.com        REJECT
From:cyberpromo.com          DISCARD
From:199.170.176.99          ERROR:"550 Die Spammer Scum!"
From:199.170.177             ERROR:"550 Email Refused"
```

As with most Linux configuration files, lines that begin with a pound (#) sign are comments. Our list of blocked spammers is at the end of this example file. Note that the address to block can be a complete e-mail address, a full hostname, a domain only, an IP address, or a subnet.

To block a particular e-mail address or host from mailbombing you, log in to your system as root, edit the /etc/mail/access file, and add a line to DISCARD mail from the offending sender.

After saving the file and exiting the editor, you must convert the access file into a hash-indexed database called access.db. The database is updated automatically the next time sendmail starts; or you can convert the database immediately, as follows:

```
# cd /etc/mail
# make
```

Sendmail should now discard e-mail from the addresses you added.

Spam relaying

Another way in which your e-mail services can be abused is by having your system used as a spam relay. *Spam,* of course, refers to the unsolicited junk e-mail that is a common occurrence on the Internet. Spammers often deliver their annoying messages from a normal dial-up Internet account. They need some kind of high-capacity e-mail server to accept and buffer the payload of messages. They deliver the spam to the server all in one huge batch and then log off, letting the server do the work of delivering the messages to the many victims.

Naturally, no self-respecting Internet service provider (ISP) will cooperate with this action, so spammers resort to hijacking servers at another ISP to do the dirty work. Having your mail server hijacked to act as a spam relay can have a devastating effect on your system and your reputation. Fortunately, *open mail relaying*, where your system is configured to send e-mail from any system on the Internet, is deactivated by default on Fedora installations. Open mail relaying is one security issue that you do not have to worry about.

You can allow specific hosts or domains to relay mail through your system by adding those senders to your `/etc/mail/access` file with keyword `RELAY`. By default, relaying is allowed only from the local host. Refer to Chapter 18, as well as the sendmail documentation, for more information.

Tip

One package you might consider using to filter out spam on your mail server is spamassassin. SpamAssassin examines the text of incoming mail messages and attempts to filter out messages that are determined to be spam. It is described in Chapter 18. You should also check out The Spamhaus Project (`www.spamhaus.org`), which maintains the Spamhaus Block List to help you block verified spam sources and spam operations. ∎

Smurf amplification attack

Smurfing refers to a particular type of denial-of-service attack aimed at flooding your Internet connection. It can be a difficult attack to defend against because it is not easy to trace the attack to the attacker.

The smurf attack makes use of the ICMP protocol, a service intended for checking the speed and availability of network connections. Using the `ping` command, you can send a network packet from your computer to another computer on the Internet. The remote computer will recognize the packet as an ICMP request and echo a reply packet to your computer. Your computer can then print a message revealing that the remote system is up and telling you how long it took to reply to the ping.

A smurfing attack uses a malformed ICMP request to bury your computer in network traffic. The attacker does this by bouncing a ping request off an unwitting third party in such a way that the reply is duplicated dozens or even hundreds of times. An organization with a fast Internet connection and a large number of computers is used as the relay. The destination address of the ping is set to an entire subnet, rather than a single host. The return address is forged to be your machine's address instead of the actual sender. When the ICMP packet arrives at the unwitting relay's network, every host on that subnet replies to the ping! Furthermore, they reply to your computer instead of the actual sender. If the relay's network has hundreds of computers, your Internet connection can be quickly flooded.

The best fix is to contact the organization being used as a relay and inform them of the abuse. Usually, they need only to reconfigure their Internet router to stop any future attacks. If the

organization is uncooperative, you can minimize the attack's effect by blocking the ICMP protocol on your router. This at least keeps the traffic off your internal network. Convincing your ISP
to block ICMP packets aimed at your network will help even more. ICMP is needed for network
traffic control, so you'll just want to block this temporarily. You can block Type 8 packets (echo
requests) permanently.

Protecting against distributed DOS attacks

As mentioned earlier, DDoS attacks are much harder to initiate and nearly impossible to stop.
A DDoS attack begins with the penetration of hundreds or even thousands of weakly secured
machines. These machines can then be directed to attack a single host based on the whims of
the attacker.

With the advent of DSL and cable modem, millions of people are enjoying Internet access with
virtually no speed restrictions. Because the vast majority of these people run Microsoft operating systems, they tend to be hit with worms and viruses rather quickly. After a machine has
been infiltrated, quite often the worm or virus installs a program on the victim's machine that
instructs it to quietly *call home* and announce that it is now ready to do *the master's bidding*.

At the whim of the master, the infected machines can then be used to focus a concentrated
stream of garbage data at a selected host. In concert with thousands of other infected machines,
a *scriptkiddie* (someone, often a youngster, who doesn't have the knowledge to create worms or
viruses but has the inclination and small bit of skill needed to find and launch them) now has the
power to take down nearly any site on the Internet.

Detecting a DDoS attack is similar to detecting a DoS attack. One or more of the following signs
are likely to be present:

- Sustained saturated data link
- No reduction in link saturation during off-peak hours
- Hundreds or even thousands of simultaneous network connections
- Extremely slow system performance

To determine if your data link is saturated, the act of pinging an outside host can tell much of the
story. Much higher than usual latency is a dead giveaway. Normal ping latency (that is, the time it
takes for a ping response to come back from a remote host) looks like the following:

```
# ping www.example.com
PING www.example.com (192.0.32.10) from 10.0.0.11: 56(84) bytes of data
64 bytes from 192.0.32.10: icmp_seq=1 ttl=49 time=40.1 ms
64 bytes from 192.0.32.10: icmp_seq=2 ttl=49 time=42.5 ms
64 bytes from 192.0.32.10: icmp_seq=3 ttl=49 time=39.5 ms
64 bytes from 192.0.32.10: icmp_seq=4 ttl=49 time=38.4 ms
64 bytes from 192.0.32.10: icmp_seq=5 ttl=49 time=39.0 ms
```

```
--- www.example.com ping statistics ---
5 packets transmitted, 5 received, 0% loss, time 4035ms
rtt min/avg/max/mdev = 38.472/39.971/42.584/1.432 ms
```

In the preceding example, the average time for a ping packet to make the round-trip was about 39 thousandths of a second.

A ping to a nearly saturated link will look like the following:

```
# ping www.example.com
PING www.example.com (192.0.32.10): from 10.0.0.11: 56(84)bytes of data
64 bytes from 192.0.32.10: icmp_seq=1 ttl=62 time=1252 ms
64 bytes from 192.0.32.10: icmp_seq=2 ttl=62 time=1218 ms
64 bytes from 192.0.32.10: icmp_seq=3 ttl=62 time=1290 ms
64 bytes from 192.0.32.10: icmp_seq=4 ttl=62 time=1288 ms
64 bytes from 192.0.32.10: icmp_seq=5 ttl=62 time=1241 ms

--- www.example.com ping statistics ---
5 packets transmitted, 5 received, 0% loss, time 5032ms
rtt min/avg/max/mdev = 1218.059/1258.384/1290.861/28.000 ms
```

In this example, a ping packet took, on average, 1.3 seconds to make the round-trip. From the first example to the second example, latency increased by a factor of 31! A data link that changes from working normally to slowing down by a factor of 31 is a clear sign that link utilization should be investigated.

For a more accurate measure of data throughput, a tool such as ttcp can be used. To test your connection with ttcp you must have installed the ttcp RPM package on machines inside *and* outside of your network. Install the ttcp package if needed using the yum command. If you are not sure whether the package is installed, simply type ttcp at a command prompt. You should see a message of help on the ttcp command-line parameters if the command is installed.

The first step is to start up a receiver process on the server machine:

```
# ttcp -rs
ttcp-r: buflen=8192, nbuf=2048, align=16384/0, port=5001  tcp
ttcp-r: socket
```

The -r flag denotes that the server machine will be the receiver. The -s flag, in conjunction with the -r flag, tells ttcp that you want to ignore any received data.

The next step is to have someone outside of your data link, with a network link close to the same speed as yours, set up a ttcp sending process. You may need to open port 5001 in your firewall.

```
# ttcp -ts server.example.com
ttcp-t: buflen=8192, nbuf=2048, align=16384/0, port=5001  tcp
-> server.example.com
ttcp-t: socket
ttcp-t: connect
```

Let the process run for a few minutes and then press Ctrl+C on the transmitting side to stop the testing. The receiving side will then take a moment to calculate and present the results:

```
# ttcp -rs
ttcp-r: buflen=8192, nbuf=2048, align=16384/0, port=5001  tcp
ttcp-r: socket
ttcp-r: accept from 64.223.17.21
ttcp-r: 2102496 bytes in 70.02 real seconds = 29.32 KB/sec +++
ttcp-r: 1226 I/O calls, msec/call = 58.49, calls/sec = 17.51
ttcp-r: 0.0user 0.0sys 1:10real 0% 0i+0d 0maxrss 0+2pf 0+0csw
```

In this example, the average bandwidth between the two hosts was 29.32 kilobytes per second. On a link suffering from a DDoS, this number would be a mere fraction of the actual bandwidth the data link is rated for.

If the data link is indeed saturated, the next step is to determine where the connections are coming from. A very effective way of doing this is with the netstat command, which is included as part of the base Fedora installation. Type the following to see connection information:

```
# netstat -tupn
```

Table 13-2 describes each of the netstat parameters used here.

TABLE 13-2

netstat Parameters

Parameter	Description
-t, --tcp	Shows TCP socket connections
-u, --udp	Shows UDP socket connections
-p, --program	Shows the PID and name of the program to which each socket belongs
-n, --numeric	Shows numerical address instead of trying to determine symbolic host, port, or user names

The following is an example of what the output might look like:

```
Active Internet connections (w/o servers)
Proto Recv-Q Send-Q Local Address     Foreign Address      State      PID/↵
Program name
tcp        0      0 65.213.7.96:22    13.29.132.19:12545   ESTABLISHED 32376/↵
sshd
tcp        0    224 65.213.7.96:22    13.29.210.13:29250   ESTABLISHED 13858/↵
sshd
tcp        0      0 65.213.7.96:6667  13.29.194.190:33452  ESTABLISHED 1870/↵
ircd
```

```
tcp      0      0 65.213.7.96:6667   216.39.144.152:42709 ESTABLISHED 1870/↵
ircd
tcp      0      0 65.213.7.96:42352 67.113.1.99:53        TIME_WAIT   -
tcp      0      0 65.213.7.96:42354 83.152.6.9:113        TIME_WAIT   -
tcp      0      0 65.213.7.96:42351 83.152.6.9:113        TIME_WAIT   -
tcp      0      0 127.0.0.1:42355    127.0.0.1:783        TIME_WAIT   -
tcp      0      0 127.0.0.1:783      127.0.0.1:42353      TIME_WAIT   -
tcp      0      0 65.213.7.96:9449678 19.15.11.1:25       TIME_WAIT   -
```

The output is organized into columns defined as follows:

- **Proto** — Protocol used by the socket.
- **Recv-Q** — Number of bytes not yet copied by the user program attached to this socket.
- **Send-Q** — Number of bytes not acknowledged by the host.
- **Local Address** — Address and port number of the local end of the socket.
- **Foreign Address** — Address and port number of the remote end of the socket.
- **State** — Current state of the socket. Table 13-3 provides a list of socket states.
- **PID/Program name** — Process ID and program name of the process that owns the socket.

TABLE 13-3

Socket States

State	Description
ESTABLISHED	Socket has an established connection
SYN_SENT	Socket actively trying to establish a connection
SYN_RECV	Connection request received from the network
FIN_WAIT1	Socket closed and connection shutting down
FIN_WAIT2	Connection closed, socket is waiting for remote end to shut down
TIME_WAIT	Socket is waiting after closing to handle packets still in the network
CLOSED	Socket is not being used
CLOSE_WAIT	The remote end has shut down, waiting for the socket to close
LAST_ACK	The remote end has shut down, and the socket is closed, waiting for acknowledgment
LISTEN	Socket is waiting for an incoming connection
CLOSING	Both sides of the connection are shut down, but not all of your data has been sent
UNKNOWN	The state of the socket is unknown

During a DoS attack, the foreign address is usually the same for each connection. In this case, it is a simple matter of typing the whois command, followed by the foreign IP address, to determine who owns the IP address of the machine causing the attack. If the source address has been spoofed (which is common), you may need to trace the attacks back to where they enter your ISP's network and then block the packets there. Your ISP should be able to help with this.

During a DDoS attack, the foreign address is often different for each connection. In this case, it is impossible to track down all of the offenders because there will likely be thousands of them. The best way to defend yourself is to contact your ISP to see if it can filter the traffic at its border routers.

Protecting against intrusion attacks

Intrusion attacks focus on exploiting weaknesses in your security, so the crackers can take more control of your system (and potentially do more damage) than they could from the outside.

Fortunately, there are many tools and techniques for combating intrusion attacks. This section discusses the most common break-in methods and the tools available to protect your system. Although the examples shown are specific to Fedora systems, the tools and techniques are generally applicable to any other Linux or Unix-like operating system.

Note

The tripwire **package, which is included in the Fedora repository, is a good tool for detecting whether intrusion attacks have taken place. Another useful tool is called** sectool. **You can install both tools with the** yum **command.** ∎

Evaluating access to network services

Fedora, Red Hat Enterprise Linux, and its Unix kin provide many network services, and with them many avenues for cracker attacks. You should know these services and how to limit access to them.

By network service, I am referring to a resource or facility that a remote user can request of the server machine, such as a login, file sharing, instant messaging, or other service. Routing e-mail is a network service. So is serving Web pages. Your Linux box has the potential to provide thousands of services. Many of them are listed in the /etc/services file. Here's a snippet of that file:

```
# /etc/services:
# service-name   port/protocol   [aliases ...]    [# comment]
chargen          19/tcp          ttytst source
chargen          19/udp          ttytst source
ftp-data         20/tcp
ftp-data         20/udp
# 21 is registered to ftp, but also used by fsp
ftp              21/tcp
ftp              21/udp          fsp fspd
ssh              22/tcp                           # SSH Remote Login Protocol
ssh              22/udp                           # SSH Remote Login Protocol
telnet           23/tcp
```

```
telnet              23/udp
# 24 - private mail system
smtp                25/tcp            mail
```

After comment lines, you will notice three columns of information. The left column contains the name of each service. The middle column defines the port number and protocol type used for that service. The rightmost field contains an optional alias or list of aliases for the service.

For example, examine the last entry in the file snippet. It describes the SMTP (Simple Mail Transfer Protocol) service, which is the service used for delivering e-mail over the Internet. The middle column contains the text 25/tcp, which indicates that the SMTP protocol uses port 25 and the Transmission Control Protocol (TCP) as its protocol type.

A *port number* is a unique number that has been set aside for a particular network service. It allows network connections to be properly routed to the software that handles that service. For example, when an e-mail message is delivered from some other computer to your Linux box, the remote system must first establish a network connection with your system. Your computer receives the connection request, examines it, sees it labeled for port 25, and thus knows that the connection should be handed to the program that handles e-mail (which usually happens to be sendmail).

I mentioned that SMTP uses the TCP protocol. Some services use UDP, the User Datagram Protocol. All you really need to know about TCP and UDP (for the purpose of this security discussion) is that they provide different ways to package the information sent over a network connection. A TCP connection provides error detection and retransmission of lost data. UDP doesn't check to ensure that the data arrived complete and intact; it is meant as a fast way to send non-critical information.

Disabling network services

Although there are hundreds of services (listed in /etc/services) that potentially could be available and subject to attack on your Fedora system, in reality only a few dozen services are installed, and only a handful of those are on by default. Most network services are started by either the xinetd process or by a start-up script in the /etc/rc.d/init.d directory.

xinetd is a daemon that listens on a great number of network port numbers. When a connection is made to a particular port number, xinetd automatically starts the appropriate program for that service and hands the connection to it. The xinetd daemon improves on its predecessor, inetd, by offering features that include more flexible access control, more logging settings, and denial-of-service prevention.

The configuration file /etc/xinetd.conf is used to provide default settings for the xinetd server. The directory /etc/xinetd.d contains files telling xinetd what ports to listen on and what programs to start. Each file contains configuration information for a single service, and the file is usually named after the service it configures. For example, to enable the rsync service, edit the rsync file in the /etc/xinetd.d directory and look for a section similar to the following:

```
service rsync
{
```

```
            disable = yes
            flags            = IPv6
            socket_type      = stream
            wait             = no
            user             = root
            server           = /usr/bin/rsync
            server_args      = --daemon
            log_on_failure   += USERID
        }
```

Note that the first line of this example identifies the service as rsync. This exactly matches the service name listed in the /etc/services file, causing the service to listen on port 873 for TCP and UDP protocols. You can see that the service is off by default (disable = yes). To enable the rsync services, change the line to read as follows:

```
        disable = no
```

Tip

The rsync **service is a nice one to enable if your machine is an FTP server. It allows people to use an** rsync **client (which includes a checksum-search algorithm) to download files from your server. With that feature, users can restart a disrupted download without having to start from the beginning.** ■

Because most services are disabled by default, your computer is only as insecure as you make it. You can double-check that insecure services, such as rlogin and rsh (which are included in the rsh-server package), are also disabled by ensuring that disabled = yes is set in the /etc/xinetd.d/rlogin and rsh files.

Tip

You can make the remote login service active but disable the use of the /etc/host.equiv **and** .rhosts **files, requiring** rlogin **to always prompt for a password. Rather than disable the service, locate the server line in the** rsh **file (**server = /usr/sbin/in.rshd**) and add a space followed by** -L **at the end. Of course, that doesn't change the fact that your password and data will still be sent unencrypted over the network.** ■

You now need to send a signal to the xinetd process to tell it to reload its configuration file. The quickest way to do that is to reload the xinetd service. As the root user, type the following from a shell:

```
# service xinetd reload
Reloading configuration:          [ OK ]
```

That's it — you have enabled the rsync service. Provided that you have properly configured your FTP server (see Chapter 19), clients should now be able to download files from your computer via the rsync protocol and be able to restart interrupted downloads.

Securing servers with SELinux

Red Hat, Inc., did a clever thing when it took its first swipe at implementing SELinux in Red Hat systems, and by extension, Fedora. Instead of creating policies to control every aspect of your

Linux system, it created a "targeted" policy type that focused on securing those services that are most vulnerable to attacks. Red Hat then set about securing those services in such a way that if they were compromised, a cracker couldn't compromise the rest of the system as well.

After you have opened a port in your firewall so others can request a service, and then started that service to handle requests, SELinux can be used to set up walls around the service. As a result, its daemon process, configuration files, and data can't access resources they are not specifically allowed to access. The rest of your computer, then, is safer.

Cross-Reference
See Chapter 9 for a more in-depth description of SELinux in Fedora. ■

Scanning for security problems with OpenSCAP

Starting in Fedora 14, OpenSCAP, or Open Security Content Automation Protocol, allows you to scan your system for security vulnerabilities. Combined with a handy plugin for FirstAidKit, you can use the OpenSCAP library to scan your system. You can also run the scanner separately with the `oscap` command.

To use OpenSCAP, you should install the following packages: `firstaidkit-plugin-open-scap`, `openscap-utils`, and `secstate`. See `www.open-scap.org/page/Main_Page` for more on OpenSCAP.

Protecting Web servers with certificates and encryption

Previous sections described how to lock the doors to your Fedora system to deny access to crackers. The best dead-bolt lock, however, is useless if you are mugged in your own driveway and have your keys stolen. Likewise, the best computer security can be for naught if you are sending passwords and other critical data unprotected across the Internet.

A savvy cracker can use a tool called a *protocol analyzer* or a *network sniffer* to peek at the data flowing across a network and pick out passwords, credit card data, and other juicy bits of information. The cracker does this by breaking into a poorly protected system on the same network and running software, or by gaining physical access to the same network and plugging in his or her own equipment.

You can combat this sort of theft by using encryption. The two main types of encryption in use today are *symmetric cryptography* and *public-key cryptography*.

Symmetric cryptography

Symmetric cryptography, also called *private-key* cryptography, uses a single key to both encrypt and decrypt a message. This method is generally inappropriate for securing data that will be used by a third party, because of the complexity of secure key exchange. Symmetric cryptography is generally useful for encrypting data for one's own purposes.

A classic use of symmetric cryptography is for a personal password vault. Anyone who has been using the Internet for any amount of time has accumulated a quantity of user names and passwords for accessing various sites and resources. A personal password vault enables you to store this access information in an encrypted form. As a result, you only have to remember one password to unlock all of your access information.

Until recently, the United States government was standardized on a symmetric encryption algorithm called DES (Data Encryption Standard) to secure important information.

As personal computing power has increased nearly exponentially, the DES algorithm has had to be retired. In its place, after a very long and interesting search, the U.S. government has accepted the Rijndael algorithm as what it calls the AES (Advanced Encryption Standard). Although the AES algorithm is also subject to *brute-force attacks*, in which malicious users apply lots of computing power to repeatedly try to guess passwords, it requires significantly more computing power to crack than the DES algorithm.

For more information on AES, including a command-line implementation of the algorithm, you can visit `http://aescrypt.sourceforge.net/`.

Public-key cryptography

Public-key cryptography does not suffer from key distribution problems, which is why it is the preferred encryption method for secure Internet communication. This method uses two keys, one to encrypt the message and another to decrypt the message. The key used to encrypt the message is called the public key because it is available for all to see. The key used to decrypt the message is the private key and is kept hidden. The entire process works as follows. Imagine that you want to send me a secure message using public-key encryption. Here is what we need:

1. I must have a public and private key pair. Depending on the circumstances, I may generate the keys myself (using special software) or obtain the keys from a key authority.

2. You want to send me a message, so you first look up my public key (or more accurately, the software you are using looks it up).

3. You encrypt the message with my public key. At this point, the message can be decrypted with the private key only (the public key cannot be used to decrypt the message).

4. I receive the message and use my private key to decrypt it.

Secure Sockets Layer

A classic implementation of public-key cryptography is with Secure Sockets Layer (SSL) communication. This is the technology that enables you to securely submit your credit card information to an online merchant. The elements of an SSL-encrypted session are as follows:

- SSL-enabled Web browser (Firefox, Chrome, Internet Explorer, Opera, Konquerer, and so on)

- SSL-enabled Web server (Apache)
- SSL certificate

To initiate an SSL session, a Web browser first makes contact with a Web server on port 443, also known as the HTTPS port (Hypertext Transport Protocol Secure). After a socket connection has been established between the two machines, the following occurs:

1. The server sends its SSL certificate to the browser.
2. The browser verifies the identity of the server through the SSL certificate by using the third-party certificate authority.
3. The browser generates a symmetric encryption key.
4. The browser uses the SSL certificate to encrypt the symmetric encryption key.
5. The browser sends the encrypted key to the server.
6. The server decrypts the symmetric key with its private key counterpart of the public SSL certificate.
7. The browser and server can now encrypt and decrypt traffic based on a common knowledge of the symmetric key.

Secure data interchange can now occur.

Creating SSL certificates

In order to be able to use SSL certificates for secure HTTP data interchange, you must have an SSL-capable Web server. The Apache Web server (httpd package), which comes with Fedora, is SSL-capable. Here are some of the files you need to create your own SSL certificates for the Apache Web server:

- /etc/httpd/conf/httpd.conf — Web server configuration file
- /etc/pki/tls/certs/Makefile — Certificate building script
- /etc/httpd/conf.d/ssl.conf — Primary Web server SSL configuration file (from the mod_ssl package)

Now that you're familiar with the basic components, take a look at the tools used to create SSL certificates:

```
# cd /etc/pki/tls/certs
# make
This makefile allows you to create:
  o public/private key pairs
  o SSL certificate signing requests (CSRs)
  o self-signed SSL test certificates

  ...2
```

The make command utilizes the Makefile to create SSL certificates. (The make command is used for a variety of software tasks with C and C++ programming.) Without any arguments the make command simply prints helpful information. The following defines each argument you can give to make:

- make server.key — Creates generic public/private key pairs
- make server.csr — Generates a generic SSL certificate service request
- make server.crt — Generates a generic SSL test certificate
- make stunnel.pem — Generates a generic SSL test certificate, but puts the private key in the same file as the SSL test certificate
- make genkey — Same as make server.key except it places the key in the ssl.key directory
- make certreq — Same as make server.csr except it places the certificate service request in the certs directory
- make testcert — Same as make server.crt except it places the test certificate in the private directory
- make server.crt SERIAL=1 — Generates the keys mentioned above using key serial numbers other than zero

Using third-party certificate signers

In the real world, I know who you are because I recognize your face, your voice, and your mannerisms. On the Internet, I cannot see these things and must rely on a trusted third party to vouch for your identity. To ensure that a certificate is immutable, it has to be signed by a trusted third party when the certificate is issued and validated every time an end user taking advantage of your secure site loads it. The following is a list of trusted third-party certificate signers:

- **GlobalSign** — www.globalsign.com
- **GeoTrust** — www.geotrust.com
- **VeriSign** — www.verisign.com
- **RapidSSL.com** — www.rapidssl.com
- **Thawte** — www.thawte.com
- **Entrust** — www.entrust.com
- **ipsCA** — www.ipsca.com
- **COMODO Group** — www.comodogroup.com

Note

Because of the fluid nature of the certificate business, some of these companies may not be in business when you read this, and others may have come into existence. To get a more current list of certificate authorities, from your Firefox browser select Edit ⇨ Preferences. From the Preferences window that appears, select Advanced ⇨ Encryption ⇨ View Certificates. From the Certificate Manager window that appears, refer to the Authorities tab to see certificate authorities from which you have received certificates. Consider using well-known certificate authorities for your publicly accessible resources. ∎

Each of these certificate authorities (CAs) has gotten a chunk of cryptographic code embedded into nearly every Web browser in the world. This chunk of cryptographic code allows a Web browser to determine whether or not an SSL certificate is authentic. Without this validation, it would be trivial for crackers to generate their own certificates and dupe people into thinking they are giving sensitive information to a reputable source.

Certificates that are not validated are called *self-signed certificates*. If you come across a site that has not had its identity authenticated by a trusted third party, your Web browser will display a warning message.

This does not necessarily mean that you are encountering anything illegal, immoral, or fattening. Many sites opt to go with *self-signed* certificates, not because they are trying to pull a fast one on you but because there may not be any reason to validate the true owner of the certificate and they do not want to pay the cost of getting a certificate validated. Some reasons for using a *self-signed* certificate include the following:

- **The website accepts no input** — In this case, you, as the end user, have nothing to worry about. No one is trying to steal your information because you aren't giving out any information. Most of the time this is done simply to secure the Web transmission from the server to you.

- **The website caters to a small clientele** — If you run a website that has a very limited set of customers, such as an Application Service Provider, you can simply inform your users that you have no certificate signer and that they can browse the certificate information and validate it with you over the phone or in person.

- **Testing** — It makes no sense to pay for an SSL certificate if you are just testing a new website or Web-based application. Use a self-signed certificate until you are ready to go live.

Using the Dogtag certificate system

Starting in Fedora 13, you can also use the Dogtag certificate system to manage your certificates and keys yourself. Dogtag can act as a certificate authority, data-recovery manager, registration authority, as well as manage smartcards.

The main focus is on large enterprises and managing a number of keys and certificates. See `http://pki.fedoraproject.org/wiki/PKI_Main_Page` for details.

Creating a Certificate Service Request

To create a third-party validated SSL certificate, you must first start with a Certificate Service Request (CSR). To create a CSR, enter the following on your Web server:

```
# cd /etc/pki/tls/certs
# make certreq
...

You are about to be asked to enter information that will be
```

```
incorporated  into your certificate request.
What you are about to enter is what is called
a Distinguished Name or a DN.
There are quite a few fields but you can leave some blank
For some fields there will be a default value,
If you enter '.', the field will be left blank.
-----
Country Name (2 letter code) [XX]: US
State or Province Name (full name) []: Connecticut
Locality Name (eg, city) [Default City]: Mystic
Organization Name (eg, company) [Default Company Ltd]: Acme Marina, Inc.
Organizational Unit Name (eg, section) []: InfoTech
Common Name (eg, your name or your server's hostname) []: www.acmemarina.com
Email Address []: webmaster@acmemarina.com
```

Note

Ensure that the hostname you provide, www.acmemarina.com in this case, matches the actual hostname for your website. If the names don't match, users will see what looks like a certificate error. Also, if you enter a password for the key, you will need to enter the password each time you restart httpd. ∎

To complete the process, you will be asked if you want to add any extra attributes to your certificate. Unless you have a reason to provide more information, you should simply press Enter at each of the following prompts to leave them blank:

```
Please enter the following 'extra' attributes
to be sent with your certificate request
A challenge password []:
An optional company name []:
```

Getting the CSR signed

Once your CSR has been created, you need to send it to a signing authority for validation. The first step in this process is to select a signing authority. Each signing authority has different deals, prices, and products. Check out each of the signing authorities listed in the "Using third-party certificate signers" section earlier in this chapter to determine which works best for you.

After you have selected your certificate signer, you have to go through some validation steps. Each signer has a different method of validating identity and certificate information. Some require that you fax articles of incorporation, while others require a company officer be made available to talk to a validation operator. At some point in the process you will be asked to copy and paste the contents of the CSR you created into the signer's Web form. Use commands like the following to access your CSR.

```
# cd /etc/pki/tls/certs
# cat localhost.csr
-----BEGIN CERTIFICATE REQUEST-----
MIIB6jCCAVMCAQAwgakxCzAJBgNVBAYTAlVTMRQwEgYDVQQIEwtDb25uZWN0aWN1
dDEPMA0GA1UEBxMGTXlzdGljMRowGAYDVQQKExFBY211IE1hcmluYSwgSW5jLjER
MA8GA1UECxMISW5mb1RlY2gxGzAZBgNVBAMTEnd3dy5hY211bWFyaW5hLmNvbTEn
```

```
MCUGCSqGSIb3DQEJARYYd2VibWFzdGVyQGFjbWVtYXJpbmEuY29tMIGfMA0GCSqG
SIb3DQEBAQUAA4GNADCBiQKBgQDcYH4pjMxKMldyXRmcoz8uBVOvwlNZHyRWw8ZG
u2eCbvgi6w4wXuHwaDuxbuDBmw//Y9DMI2MXg4wDq4xmPi35EsO1Ofw4ytZJn1yW
aU6cJVQro46OnXyaqXZOPiRCxUSnGRU+OnsqKGjf7LPpXv29S3QvMIBTYWzCkNnc
gWBwwwIDAQABoAAwDQYJKoZIhvcNAQEEBQADgYEANv6eJOaJZGzopNR5h2YkR9Wg
18oBl3mgoPH60Sccw3pWsoW4qbOWq7on8dS/++QOCZWZIlgefgaSQMInKZ1II7Fs
YIwYBgpoPTMC4bpOZZtURCyQWrKIDXQBXw7BlU/3A25nvkRY7vgNL9Nq+7681EJ8
W9AJ3PX4vb2+ynttcBI=
-----END CERTIFICATE REQUEST-----
```

You can use your mouse to copy and paste the CSR into the signer's Web form.

After you have completed the information validation, paid for the signing, and answered all of the questions, you have completed most of the process. In 48 to 72 hours you should receive an e-mail with your shiny new SSL certificate in it. The certificate will look similar to the following:

```
-----BEGIN CERTIFICATE-----
MIIEFjCCA3+gAwIBAgIQMI262Zd6njZgN97tJAVFODANBgkqhkiG9w0BAQQFADCB
ujEfMB0GA1UEChMWVmVyaVNpZ24gVHJ1c3QgTmV0d29yazEXMBUGA1UECxMOVmVy
aVNpZ24sIEluXy4xMzAxBgNVBAsTKlZlcmlTaWduIEludGVybmF0aW9uYWwgU2Vy
dmVyIENBICOgZ2xhc3MgMzFJMEcG10rY2gODd3d3LnZlcmlzaWduLmNvbS9DUFMg
SW5jb3JwLmJ51FJ1Zi4gTElBQklMSVRZIExURC4oYyk5NyBWZXJppU2lnbjAeFw0w
MzAxMTUwMDAwMDBaFwOwNDAxMTUyMzU5NTlaMIGuMQswCQYDVQQGEwJVUzETMBEG
A1UECBMKV2FzaG1uZ3RvHiThErE371UEBxQLRmVkZXJhbCBXYYXkxGzAZBgNVBAoU
EklETSBTZXJ2aWMlcywgSW5jLjEMMAoGA1UECxQDd3d3MTMwMQYDVQQLFCpUZXJt
cyBvZiB1c2UgYXQgd3d3LnZlcmlzawduLmNvbS9ycGGgKGMpMDAxFDASBgNVBAMU
C21kbXN1cnYuY29tMIGfMA0GCSqGSIb3DQEBAQUAA4GNADCBiQKBgQDaHSk+uzOf
7jjDFEnqT8UBalL3yFILXFjhj3XpMXLGWzLmkDmdJjXsa4x7AhEpr1ubuVNhJVIO
FnLDopsx4pyr4n+P8FyS4M5grbcQzy2YnkM2jyqVF/7yOW2pD13Ot4eacYYaz4Qg
q9pTxhUzjEG4twvKCAFWfuhEoGulCMV2qQ1DAQABo4IBJTCCASEwCQYDVR0TBAIw
ADBEBgNVHSAEPTA7MDkGC2CGSAGG+EUBBxcDMCOwKAYIKwYBBQUHAgEWHGh0dHBz
0i8vd3d3LnZlcmlzawduLmNvbS9ycGEwCwYDVRRPBAQDAgWgMCgGA1UdJQQhMB8G
CWCGSAGG+EIEMOOcOwIYBQUHAwEGCCsGAQUFBwmCMDQGCCsGAQUFBwEBBCgwJjAk
BggrBgEFBQcwAYYYaHROcDovL29jc2AudmVyaXNpZ24uY29tMEYGA1UdHwQ/MDOw
O6A5oDeGNWhOdHA6Ly9jcmwudmVyaXNpZ24uY29tLONsYXNzMOludGVybmF0aW9u
81LZXnaR+acHeStRO1b3rQPjgv2y1mwjkPmC1WjoeYfdxH7+Mbg/6fomnK9auWAT
WFOiFW/+a8OWRYQJLMA2VQOVhX4znjpGcVNY9AQSHm1UiESJy7vtdliX
-----END CERTIFICATE-----
```

Copy and paste this certificate into an empty file called `server.crt`, which must reside in the `/etc/pki/tls/certs` directory, and restart your Web server by typing:

```
# service httpd restart
```

Assuming your website was previously working fine, you can now view it in a secure fashion by placing an "s" after the http in the Web address. For example, if you previously viewed your website at `http://www.acmemarina.com`, you can now view it in a secure fashion by going to `https://www.acmemarina.com`.

Creating self-signed certificates

Generating and running a self-signed SSL certificate is much easier than having a signed certificate. To generate a self-signed SSL certificate, do the following:

1. Remove the key and certificate that currently exist:

   ```
   # rm /etc/pki/tls/certs/localhost.crt
   # rm /etc/pki/tls/private/localhost.key
   ```

2. Create your own server key:

   ```
   # make genkey
   ```

3. Create the self-signed certificate by typing the following:

   ```
   # make testcert
   umask 77 ; \
   /usr/bin/openssl req -utf8 -new -key ↵
   /etc/pki/tls/private/localhost.key
        -x509 -days 365 -out /etc/pki/↵
   tls/private/localhost.crt -set_serial 0
       .
       .
       .
   ```

At this point, it is time to start adding some identifying information to the certificate. Before you can do this, you must unlock the private key you just created. Do so by typing the password you typed earlier. Then follow this sample procedure:

```
You are about to be asked to enter information that will be
  incorporated into your certificate request.
What you are about to enter is what is called
a Distinguished Name or a DN.
There are quite a few fields but you can leave some blank
For some fields there will be a default value,
If you enter '.', the field will be left blank.
-----
Country Name (2 letter code) [GB]: US
State or Province Name (full name) [Berkshire]: Ohio
Locality Name (eg, city) [Newbury]: Cincinnati
Organization Name (eg, company) [My Company Ltd]: Industrial Press, Inc.
Organizational Unit Name (eg, section) []: IT
Common Name (eg, your name or your server's hostname) []: ↵
www.industrialpressinc.com
Email Address []: webmaster@industrialpressinc.com
```

The preceding generation process places all files in the proper place. All you need to do is restart your Web server and add `https` instead of `http` in front of your URL. Don't forget: you'll get a certificate validation message from your Web browser, which you can safely ignore.

Restarting your Web server

By now you've probably noticed that your Web server requires you to enter your certificate password every time it is started. This is to prevent someone from breaking into your server and stealing your private key. Should this happen, you are safe in the knowledge that the private key is a jumbled mess. The cracker will not be able to make use of it. Without such protection, a cracker could get your private key and easily masquerade as you, appearing to be legitimate in all cases.

If you just cannot stand having to enter a password every time your Web server starts, and are willing to accept the increased risk, you can remove the password encryption on your private key. Simply do the following:

```
# cd /etc/pki/tls/private
# /usr/bin/openssl rsa -in localhost.key -out localhost.key
```

Troubleshooting your certificates

The following tips should help if you are having problems with your SSL certificate:

- It's usual to use one SSL certificate per IP address. If you want to add more than one SSL-enabled website to your server, you usually bind another IP address to the network interface. Now, however, you can do SSL-enabled name-based virtual hosting, whereby multiple hosts share the same IP address and port, using the Apache mod_gnutls module. If that interests you, refer to www.g-loaded.eu/2007/08/10/ssl-enabled-name-based-apache-virtual-hosts-with-mod_gnutls/

- Make sure you aren't blocking port 443 on your Web server. All https requests come in on port 443. If you are blocking it, you won't be able to get secure pages.

- The certificate normally lasts for only one year. (Some sites sell five-year certificates.) When that year is up, you have to renew your certificate with your certificate authority. Each certificate authority has a different procedure for doing this; check the authority's website for details.

- Make sure you have the mod_ssl package installed. If it is not installed, you won't be able to serve any SSL-enabled traffic.

Managing Identities with FreeIPA

The FreeIPA project (www.freeipa.org) aims to provide software to manage security information across an entire enterprise or other computing environment. The "IPA" part of FreeIPA stands for identity (identifying and authenticating users and machines), policy (settings for access control of applications and machines), and audit (methods for collecting and auditing security events, logs, and user activities).

FreeIPA is still under development, so not all planned features are currently implemented. The "identity" area of FreeIPA represents the first set of FreeIPA features to be implemented. If you want to centralize management of security information, you can try these features in Fedora. You can use the current release of FreeIPA to configure IPA servers for user identity management and centralized authentication. Then use FreeIPA clients to work with that information.

The software features that FreeIPA works with in this initial release include the following:

- Fedora Linux
- Network Time Protocol (NTP) Daemon
- Domain Name System (DNS) Daemon
- Fedora Directory Server
- Kerberos Key Distribution

Caution

FreeIPA modifies the services just mentioned, so it is best to try FreeIPA only on test systems. In other words, don't use FreeIPA on your production servers. ■

Setting up the FreeIPA server

Both server and client FreeIPA features are available in Fedora 14. However, you need to start with a server system that can essentially be taken over in many respects by FreeIPA. To use a server that has not been updated to Fedora 14, you need to add the latest patches and upgrades. The server you use should have the following attributes:

- **Fedora 7 or later version** — If possible, start with a clean Fedora 14 system. You need the latest patches and upgrades to use FreeIPA on any earlier Fedora systems.

- **Installed FreeIPA Software** — To configure a FreeIPA server, you need to install the ipa-server and ipa-admintools packages. Support for SELinux and Radius are provided by the ipa-server-selinux, ipa-radius-server, and ipa-radius-admintools packages. You can get all FreeIPA packages by simply typing yum install ipa-* as root user.

- **Clean Fedora Directory Server** — Another reason for a clean install is that you cannot currently use FreeIPA on any system that has existing Directory Server instances. There is no upgrade feature included yet.

- **Fully Qualified Domain Name** — Your FreeIPA server must have a fully functional DNS hostname (not localhost) that can resolve forward and reverse addresses.

- **Available ports** — Port numbers for HTTP/HTTPS (80, 443, and 8080), LDAP/LDAPS (389 and 636), and Kerberos (88 and 464) associated with the TCP protocol must be available to FreeIPA and not assigned to other services. Likewise, port numbers for Kerberos (88 and 464) and NTP (123) must be available to FreeIPA for UDP protocol.

The amount of RAM and disk space you need on the server depends on the number of entries the server will hold. For details on configuring a FreeIPA server, first refer to the FreeIPA concepts page (www.freeipa.com/page/IpaConcepts). Next, follow the instructions on the FreeIPA

Install and Deploy page (www.freeipa.com/page/InstallAndDeploy). Because FreeIPA is under active development, check back to those pages for the latest information.

Setting up FreeIPA clients

Clients for FreeIPA services are available for a wide range of systems. Supported systems include Red Hat Enterprise Linux, Fedora, Solaris, AIX, HP-UX, Mac OS X, and Windows.

To use FreeIPA client services from a Fedora system, install the ipa-client and ipa-admintools packages. For more on setting up FreeIPA clients, see the FreeIPA Client Configuration Guide (www.freeipa.com/page/ClientConfigurationGuide).

Summary

If you connect your systems to the Internet, security becomes a critical issue. Properly using passwords, securely configuring network services, and monitoring log files are critical ways of keeping your computer secure. Using encryption keys, you can help verify the authenticity of those you communicate with, as well as make the data you transmit more secure. By following the recommendations in this chapter, you can begin to learn the techniques and tools that are available for keeping your Fedora systems secure.

Part IV

Fedora Network and Server Setup

Setting Up Network Connections

With computers becoming more mobile and wireless networks more common, setting up network connections varies more than it did in the days when most computers were at fixed locations and addresses; but whether you are connecting to your own Local Area Network (LAN) or a public wireless network, Fedora includes tools to set up the kind of network connections you want.

To enable you to interactively manage your network connections, Fedora includes NetworkManager. NetworkManager is described here for choosing and connecting to a wireless LAN (WLAN) because it includes an easy-to-use desktop applet that detects available wireless LANs and lets you choose the one you want to connect to.

In the home or in a small business, Fedora can help you connect to other Linux, Windows, and Macintosh computers so that you can share your computing equipment (files, printers, and devices). Add a connection to the Internet (described in Chapter 15), and Fedora can serve as a focal point for network computing in a larger enterprise. For times when you need more manual configuration for your LAN connections, this chapter describes how to use the Network Configuration window.

IN THIS CHAPTER

Using NetworkManager for network connections

Understanding Local Area Networks (LANs)

Connecting to a LAN with NetworkManager

Setting up a wired Ethernet LAN

Setting up a wireless LAN (WLAN)

Troubleshooting your LAN

Connecting to the Network with NetworkManager

NetworkManager is designed to make your network connections "just work." It finds your network interface cards, then connects to the network (when possible) or provides you with easy options for choosing your network connection. If you change network connections, NetworkManager will likewise try to change attributes of your connection, such as IP addresses, DNS servers, and routes.

In most cases with NetworkManager, connecting to an existing network is simple:

- **Wired network** — If a wired network interface is available and a Dynamic Host Configuration Protocol (DHCP) server is found, Fedora will automatically connect you to that interface and use it as your default route.

- **Wireless network** — If a wireless network interface is available, the NetworkManager applet menu shows all wireless networks that your wireless card can find. You simply choose the network you want and authenticate as needed.

Note
The NetworkManager also allows you to share connections. For example, if you have a wireless broadband card, you can share the connection with other computers on your network, regardless of whether they are wired or wireless. ■

If the NetworkManager service is enabled on your Fedora system, you should see a two-computer-screen icon on the desktop top panel, as shown in Figure 14-1.

FIGURE 14-1

The NetworkManager applet icon (second from the right) shows NetworkManager is running.

If you see the NetworkManager applet icon, you can immediately start using NetworkManager. If it is not displayed, confirm that NetworkManager is installed and start the service, as follows:

1. **Check for NetworkManager** — Type the following from a terminal window to see if NetworkManager packages are installed:

```
# rpm -qa NetworkManager*
NetworkManager-openconnect-0.8.1-1.fc14.x86_64
```

```
NetworkManager-glib-0.8.1-9.git20100831.fc14.x86_64
NetworkManager-vpnc-0.8.1-1.fc14.x86_64
NetworkManager-openvpn-0.8.1-1.fc14.x86_64
NetworkManager-pptp-0.8.1-1.fc14.x86_64
NetworkManager-0.8.1-9.git20100831.fc14.x86_64
NetworkManager-gnome-0.8.1-9.git20100831.fc14.x86_64
```

2. **Install NetworkManager** — If NetworkManager packages are not installed, type the following as root user from a terminal window:

   ```
   # yum install "NetworkManager*"
   ```

3. **Start NetworkManager** — Type the following commands (as root) to start the NetworkManager service immediately (service) and set it to start on every reboot:

   ```
   # service NetworkManager start
   # chkconfig NetworkManager on
   ```

With NetworkManager installed and running, you can begin using the NetworkManager applet on your GNOME desktop to manage your network interfaces. If you are using a KDE desktop, you need to run the `knetworkmanager` command to have the NetworkManager applet appear in your desktop panel.

With the NetworkManager service started, you can manage your network connections from the NetworkManager applet icon. Using NetworkManager, you can work with wireless and wired Ethernet connections, as well as select to set up a Virtual Private Network (VPN) from those connections.

If you see a red square with an X on the applet icon, this means your network is disconnected. Click the icon and select a network interface such as system `eth0` (the first physical Ethernet connection). This should activate your network.

Connecting to a wireless network

To see wireless networks detected by your computer, click the NetworkManager applet icon in the top panel. Provided that Fedora has a working driver for your wireless card, you will see a list of wireless networks that have been detected.

Note
Although Fedora has dramatically improved support for wireless LAN cards in recent releases, many wireless cards are still not supported out of the box. If your wireless card is not properly detected, refer to the section "Getting wireless drivers" later in this chapter for information about how to get and load appropriate wireless drivers. ■

Figure 14-2 shows an example of a NetworkManager applet menu that has found two wireless networks, and is connected to one of them.

FIGURE 14-2

The NetworkManager applet icon displays available wireless networks.

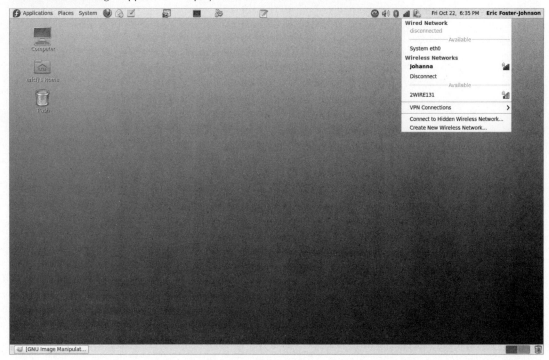

Assuming the network you want to connect to is displayed under the Wireless Networks heading, you can click on that network. Type a password or encryption key and click Connect when you see the Wireless Network Authentication Required window, shown in Figure 14-3.

FIGURE 14-3

Enter the password to connect to the selected wireless network.

If the password is correct, NetworkManager uses your new wireless connection as the default network route from your computer (disconnecting any wired Ethernet connection you may have).

Here are some other ways to work with wireless networks from the NetworkManager applet:

- **Existing Wireless Network** — If your wireless card is working but the network you want doesn't appear, click the NetworkManager icon and select Connect to Hidden Wireless Network to select a different wireless network by name.

- **New Wireless Network** — To create your own wireless network, click the NetworkManager icon and select Create New Wireless Network. When prompted, enter the network name and select the type of Wireless Security you want. You can then enter the passphrase that others would use to connect to your new wireless network.

- **Disable Wireless Network** — Right-click the NetworkManager applet icon and uncheck the Enable Wireless box (so the check box disappears).

After you have established a connection, you can check information about that connection by right-clicking the NetworkManager icon and selecting Connection information. You will see the interface name, connection speed, driver name, IP address, and locations of DNS servers (among other information).

Connecting to a wired network

As noted earlier, with your wired network plugged in and a DHCP server on the line, you probably don't have to do anything to start your wired Ethernet network interface. However, if you want instead to configure static IP addressing, I recommend that you use the Network Configuration window, described later in this chapter.

Once a wired network connection is working, however, you can use the NetworkManager applet to enable and disable the interface. To do that, right-click the NetworkManager applet icon and select Enable Networking. That will toggle the network interface on and off.

Using the NetworkManager command line

Starting with Fedora 13, you can interact with the NetworkManager from the command line. This provides help for administering headless servers or remote systems.

The nmcli command provides a command-line interface to the Fedora NetworkManager using a syntax whereby you specify the network-related object you're interested in along with a network command. For example, the dev object refers to the devices managed by the NetworkManager. To see the status of the network devices on your system, try a command like the following:

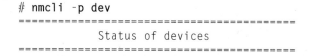

```
# nmcli -p dev
========================================
            Status of devices
========================================
```

```
DEVICE     TYPE                STATE
--------------------------------------------
eth0       802-3-ethernet      connected
```

The `-p` option tells `nmcli` to provide pretty (formatted) output. In addition to `dev`, you can use `nmcli` objects of `con`, short for connections, and `nm`, short for the NetworkManager service itself.

To get the status of your system's WiFi wireless network interface, use the following command:

```
# nmcli nm wifi
WIFI
enabled
```

You can then disable WiFi with the following command:

```
# nmcli nm wifi off
```

Use `on` to bring WiFi back up.

To list the detailed status of the hardwired Ethernet, you can use a command like the following:

```
# nmcli con list id "System eth0"
connection.id:                        System eth0
connection.uuid:                      5fb06bd0-0bb0-7ffb-45f1-d6edd65f3e03
connection.type:                      802-3-ethernet
connection.autoconnect:               no
connection.timestamp:                 0
connection.read-only:                 no
802-3-ethernet.port:                  not set
802-3-ethernet.speed:                 0
802-3-ethernet.duplex:                not set
802-3-ethernet.auto-negotiate:        yes
802-3-ethernet.mac-address:           C4:2C:03:37:13:85
802-3-ethernet.cloned-mac-address:not set
802-3-ethernet.mtu:                   auto
ipv4.method:                          auto
ipv4.dns:
ipv4.dns-search:
ipv4.addresses:
ipv4.routes:
ipv4.ignore-auto-routes:              no
ipv4.ignore-auto-dns:                 no
ipv4.dhcp-client-id:                  not set
ipv4.dhcp-send-hostname:              no
ipv4.dhcp-hostname:                   not set
ipv4.never-default:                   no
ipv6.method:                          ignore
ipv6.dns:
ipv6.dns-search:
```

```
ipv6.addresses:
ipv6.routes:
ipv6.ignore-auto-routes:        no
ipv6.ignore-auto-dns:           no
ipv6.never-default:             no
```

Note that in this case, System eth0 is the name, or ID, of the given connection. Use the nmcli list command to see the names of all available connections.

See the online manual page for nmcli for more on the commands you can use (with the man nmcli command).

Setting up a virtual private network connection

The NetworkManager applet offers some simple graphical tools for configuring your Fedora system to connect to a VPN. The following procedure describes how to configure NetworkManager to communicate with a remote OpenVPN server.

Sometimes the people and offices that have to work closely together are not physically close together. For example, you may have:

- Two branch offices that need to constantly share sales databases, or
- An employee who needs to access office computers, printers, and files from home.

Rather than purchase expensive leased lines from a phone company, you want to use an inexpensive network medium, like the Internet, to let the two sides communicate. The problem is that you don't want to open access to file sharing, print sharing, and other private services to the Internet. You also don't want communication between these sites to be exposed to anyone who is watching Internet traffic. One solution is to set up a VPN.

A VPN provides a way to create secure communications over an otherwise insecure network. With a VPN connection in place, the two sides of a connection can communicate as safely as they do on the same corporate LAN. To do this, a VPN usually offers the following features:

- **Authentication** — Using passwords or other techniques, two ends of a communication can prove that they are who they say they are before accepting a connection. After the connection is in place, communications can flow in both directions across it.
- **Encryption** — By encrypting all data being sent between the two points on the public network, you can be assured that even if someone could see the packets you send, they couldn't read them. Creating a connection between two public network addresses to use for exchanging encrypted data is known as *tunneling*.

Before you can set up a VPN connection with NetworkManager, the basic service needs to be installed and running. Also, ensure that the NetworkManager-openvpn and openvpn packages are installed. The following procedure assumes that NetworkManager is running and you can reach a computer on your network that has an active openvpn service. (See Chapter 15 for information on setting up a VPN server with OpenVPN.)

1. Click the NetworkManager applet icon, and then select VPN Connections ⇨ Configure VPN. A VPN Connections window appears.

2. Select Add to see the Create VPN Connection window. Select Forward to continue.

3. For this example, select OpenVPN (Cisco AnyConnect Compatible VPN, Cisco Compatible VPN, and Point-to-Point Tunneling Protocol clients are also available), and click Create. You are asked to enter VPN connection information.

4. Fill in the following information for your OpenVPN client connection:

   - **Connection name** — Name the connection anything you like.

   - **Gateway** — This is the name or IP address of the openvpn server that is acting as the gateway for your VPN connection.

   - **Type** — Select the default, Certificates (TLS), if you are using the example server from Chapter 15. You can also select Password, Password with Certificates (TLS), or Static Key. The following fields appear with Certificates (TLS):

     User Certificate — Identify the location of the client certificate you copied from the key server (possibly to /etc/openvpn/keys/client01.crt).

     CA Certificate — Identify the location of the root CA certificate you copied from the key server (possibly to /etc/openvpn/keys/ca.crt).

     Private Key — Identify the location of the client private key you copied from the key server (possibly to /etc/openvpn/keys/client01.key).

     Private Key Password — Identify the password associated with the private key.

5. If everything looks correct, select Apply to apply your new VPN connection.

6. If the openvpn server is up and running, you can try your new VPN connection. Select the NetworkManager applet. Then choose VPN Connects and select the name of the new VPN connection you just configured.

NetworkManager is still a work in progress, so the automated features may not extend as far as you would like. For example, when you change between wired and wireless interfaces, besides just bringing VPN interfaces up or down, you may also want to unmount and mount shared file systems. Work is underway in this area but has not yet been included in any formal release.

Understanding Local Area Networks

Connecting the computers in your organization via a LAN can save you a lot of time and money. Putting a small amount of money into networking hardware, even in a small configuration (fewer than five or six users), can save you from buying multiple printers, backup media, and other hardware.

With a LAN, you take advantage of the greatest potential of Linux — its ability to act as a server on a network. Because Fedora is a robust and feature-rich computing system, adding it to your LAN can provide a focal point to workstations that could use Linux as a file server, a mail server, a print server, or a boot server. (Those features are described later in this book.)

Creating and configuring a LAN consists of these steps:

1. **Planning, getting, and setting up LAN hardware** — This entails choosing a network topology, purchasing the equipment you need, and installing it (adding cards and connecting wires or using wireless antennas).

2. **Configuring TCP/IP** — To use most of the networking applications and tools that come with Linux, you must have TCP/IP configured. TCP/IP enables you to communicate not only with computers on your LAN, but also with any computers you can reach on your LAN, modem, or other network connection (particularly via the Internet).

Planning, getting, and setting up LAN hardware

Even with a simple LAN, you must make some decisions about network topology — that is, how computers are connected. You must also make some decisions about network equipment (network interface cards, wires, switches, and so on).

This section describes different types of network topologies you may be using:

- **Wired Ethernet LAN** — Most computers today on wired Ethernet networks use a *star topology*. In this arrangement, each computer contains a network interface card (NIC) that connects with a cable to a central network switch or hub. The cabling is typically Category 5e or 6 (unshielded twisted pair) wiring with RJ-45 connectors. Other equipment, such as printers and fax machines, can also be connected to the switch in a star topology, where the switch is the center and all the devices connect to it.

- **Wireless peer-to-peer** — In this topology, frames of data are broadcast to all nodes within range but are consumed only by the computers for which they are intended. This arrangement is useful if you are sharing file and print services among a group of client computers.

- **Wireless access point** — A wireless interface can act as an access point for one or more wireless clients. Clients can be configured to communicate directly with the access point, instead of with every client within range. This arrangement is useful for point-to-point connections between two buildings, where the access point acts as a gateway to the Internet or, for example, a campus intranet. It is also the most popular topology for home wireless LANs, where you typically have one wireless access point connected to the Internet and a number of wireless devices such as phones, laptops, or tablets.

- **Multiple wireless access points and roaming** — Each wireless network can be configured as a separate cell. Multiple cells can be joined together in what is called a *Managed Wireless LAN*. In this arrangement, each cell's access point acts as a bridge (in fact, its actions are referred to as *bridging*) by passing all data from the cell to other cells without changing any node's MAC address. In other words, the managed wireless LAN masks the fact that there are multiple wireless cells invisible to the clients on those cells. This arrangement enables users to roam among cells as they come in and out of range without losing continuity of communication.

For our purposes, we focus on star (wired) and peer-to-peer (wireless) topologies. Common to both of these topologies is the protocol used to send data over those wired and wireless media — the Ethernet protocol.

LAN equipment

The equipment that you need to connect your LAN can include some or all of the following:

Cross-Reference

For a complete description of wireless hardware, see the section "Choosing wireless hardware" later in this chapter. ■

- **Network Interface Card (NIC)** — Typically, one of these cards either is located on the computer's motherboard, goes into a slot, or plugs into a USB port. Common wired Ethernet cards transmit data at 10 Mbps, 100 Mbps, or 1,000 Mbps (Gigabit). An 802.11b wireless NIC can operate at speeds of up to 11 Mbps, while 802.11g cards operate at 54 Mbps and 802.11n cards can operate at up to 160 Mbps.

- **Cables** — For star topologies, cables are referred to as *twisted-pair*. Category 5e and Category 6 wiring, which contain four twisted-pair sets per wire, are common types of wiring used for LANs today. A connector at each end of the cable is an RJ-45 plug, similar to those used on telephone cables. Ethernet interfaces are 10Base-T (10 Mbps), 100Base-T (100 Mbps), and/or 1000Base-T (1,000 Mbps). These cables plug into the computer's NIC at one end and the switch at the other.

- **Hubs** — With the star topology, hubs were once the most popular ways to connect computers. With low-cost network switches now dominating the marketplace, however, hubs are less often used. Sometimes hubs are also referred to as *repeaters* because they receive signals from the nodes connected to them and send the signals on to other nodes.

- **Switches** — Switches are now more commonly used than hubs. Switches enable you to divide a LAN that is getting too large into manageable segments. A switch can reduce network traffic by directing messages intended for a specific computer directly to that computer. This is unlike a hub, which broadcasts all data to all nodes. Because switches are more affordable than they used to be, in most cases you should pay a few extra dollars to get a switch instead of a hub. Besides the common 10/100 Mbps switches, Gigabit switches (1,000 Mbps) are now available for economical prices.

One piece of equipment that I won't go into yet is a *router*, which is used to direct information from the LAN to other LANs or the Internet.

Cross-Reference
Machines that carry out routing functions are described in Chapter 15. ∎

LAN equipment setup

With an Ethernet NIC, appropriate cables, and a hub or switch, you are ready to set up your wired Ethernet LAN. Most new computers include built-in Ethernet ports. If your computer doesn't have one, most PCI Ethernet cards you can purchase for only a few dollars can be used with Linux. The steps for setting up an Ethernet LAN are as follows:

1. Power down each computer and physically install the NIC (following the vendor's instructions). Note that most system boards already include a NIC. You may not need to install any card in your computer.

2. Using cables appropriate for your NICs and switch, connect each NIC to the network switch.

3. Power up each computer.

4. If Fedora is not installed yet, install the software and reboot (as instructed). Chapter 2 explains how to configure your Ethernet card while installing Linux.

5. If Fedora is already installed, refer to the section "Configuring TCP/IP for your LAN" for information on configuring your Ethernet cards.

6. When the system comes up, your Ethernet card and interface (eth0) should be ready to use.

For most wired Ethernet cards, Linux will properly detect the card and load the module needed for that card to start communicating. Wireless cards, however, often require special firmware to be installed on your Fedora system. If your card is not immediately detected and configured, information later in this chapter will help you get the firmware and drivers you need.

If your card is working, you can continue to configure TCP/IP for that card. If not, refer to the section "Troubleshooting Your LAN" later in this chapter to learn how to check your Ethernet connection.

Configuring TCP/IP for your LAN

When you install Fedora, you can add your TCP/IP host name and IP address, as well as other information, to your computer, or choose to have that information automatically provided using DHCP. You also can set up a way to reach other computers on your LAN by name. With very small LANs, this can be done by adding computer names and IP addresses to your /etc/hosts file (as described here) or (with more than a few machines) using a DNS server.

Cross-Reference
DHCP is discussed in Chapter 21. ∎

If you did not configure your LAN connection during Linux installation, you can use either NetworkManager (described earlier) to connect to your wired or wireless networks or the Network Configuration window (run the `system-config-network` command to start it). Using the Network Configuration window, the IP address and hostnames can be assigned statically to an Ethernet interface or retrieved dynamically at boot time from a DHCP server.

Note

A computer can have more than one IP address and multiple network interfaces. Each network interface connected to the network should have an IP address (even if the address is assigned temporarily). Therefore, if you have two Ethernet cards (`eth0` and `eth1`), each should have its own IP address; the address `127.0.0.1` represents the local host, so users on the local computer can access services via the loopback interface. ∎

To use the Network Configuration window to define your IP address for your Ethernet interface, follow this procedure:

1. Start the Network Configuration. From the top panel, click System ➪ Administration ➪ Network. Alternately, as root user from a terminal window, type **system-config-network**. (If prompted, type the root password.) The Network Configuration window appears, as shown in Figure 14-4.

2. Click the Devices tab to see a list of your existing network interfaces.

FIGURE 14-4

Configure your LAN interface using the Network Configuration window.

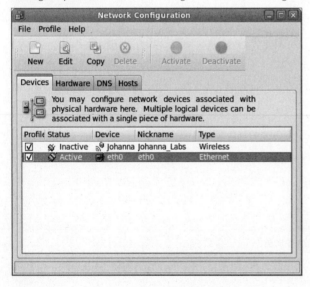

3. Double-click the eth0 interface (representing your first Ethernet card). A pop-up window appears, enabling you to configure your eth0 interface. Figure 14-5 shows the pop-up Ethernet Device window configuring eth0.

FIGURE 14-5

Configure your eth0 interface using the Ethernet Device window.

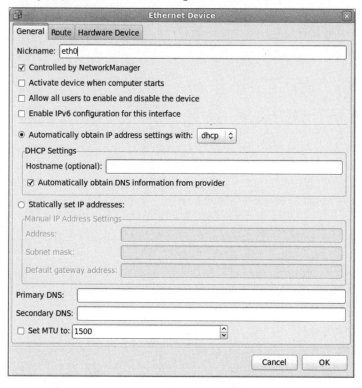

4. On the Ethernet Device window that appears, you can enter the following information:

   - **Controlled by NetworkManager** — Clear this check box to use this window to configure your network interface instead of having NetworkManager control this interface. You must do this to change the network interface from this window.

   - **Activate device when computer starts** — Check here to have eth0 start at boot time. If your network does not start up when you boot Fedora, look at this box first.

   - **Allow all users to enable and disable the device** — Check this to let nonroot users enable and disable the network interface.

   - **Enable IPv6 configuration for this interface** — Check here if you are connected to an IPv6 network. (Most networks are still IPv4.)

5. In the same window, you must choose whether to get your IP addresses from another computer at boot time or enter the addresses yourself:

- **Automatically obtain IP address settings with** — Select this check box if you have a DHCP or BOOTP server on the network from which you can obtain your computer's IP address, netmask, and gateway. DHCP is the most common way to connect to your ISP. Consider setting up your own DHCP server if you have more than just a few computers on your LAN. (See Chapter 21 for how to set up a DHCP server.) You can, optionally, set your own hostname, which can be just a name (such as jukebox) or a fully qualified domain name (such as jukebox.linuxtoys.net). BOOTP is a network protocol designed for configuring Internet terminals and other "dumb" devices. By nature, BOOTP is a very simple protocol and is designed to support limited-capability devices.

- **Statically set IP addresses** — If there is no DHCP or other boot server on your LAN, you can add necessary IP address information statically by selecting this option and adding the following information:

  - **Address** — Type the IP address of the computer into this box. The number must be unique on your network. For your private LAN, you can use private IP addresses (see "Understanding Internet Protocol Addresses" later in this chapter).

  - **Subnet mask** — Enter the netmask to indicate what part of the IP address represents the network. (Netmask is described later in this chapter.)

  - **Default gateway address** — If a computer or router connected to your LAN is providing routing functions to the Internet or another network, enter the IP address of the computer here. (Chapter 15 describes how to use NAT or IP Masquerading, using Fedora as a router.)

  - **Primary and Secondary DNS** — If you want to manually set which DNS servers to use when this interface is up, enter your DNS information here. If you want to automatically use the DNS server information from a DHCP server, leave these boxes blank. If you always want to try to use static DNS server(s), leave this section blank and globally set values as discussed in the next section.

  - **Set MTU to** — The maximum transfer unit (MTU) sets the number of 8-bit bytes that are available to the Internet Protocol in a link-layer frame. Click the check box and enter a number to change from the default 1500 MTU used by default for Ethernet interfaces in Linux. Lower rates can result in fewer packets being dropped on unreliable networks (some gamers like to lower the rate slightly, so fewer small actions are dropped). Higher rates can improve performance of large data transfers on reliable networks. In most cases, you don't need to modify this.

6. Click OK in the Ethernet Device window to save the configuration and close the window.

7. Click File ➪ Save to save the information you entered.

8. Click Activate in the Network Configuration window to start your connection to the LAN.

Identifying other computers (hosts and DNS)

Each time you use a name to identify a computer, such as when browsing the Web or using an e-mail address, the computer name must be translated into an IP address. To resolve names to IP addresses, Fedora goes through a search order (based on the contents of three files in the /etc directory: `resolv.conf`, `nsswitch.conf`, and `host.conf`). By default, it checks the following:

- Hostnames you add yourself (which end up in the /etc/hosts file)
- Hosts available via NIS (if an NIS server is running)
- Hostnames available via DNS

You can use the Network Configuration window to add the following:

- **Hostnames and IP addresses** — You might do this to identify hosts on your LAN that are not configured on a DNS server.
- **DNS search path** — By adding domain names to a search path (such as `linuxtoys.net`), you can browse to a site by its hostname (such as `jukebox`) and have Linux search the domains you added to the search path to find the host you are looking for (such as `jukebox.linuxtoys.net`).
- **DNS name servers** — A DNS server can resolve addresses for the domains it serves and contact other DNS servers to get addresses for all other DNS domains.

Note

If you are configuring a DNS server, you can use that server to centrally store names and IP addresses for your LAN. This saves you the trouble of updating every computer's /etc/hosts file every time you add or change a computer on your LAN. ■

To add hostnames, IP addresses, search paths, and DNS servers, do the following:

1. Start the Network Configuration. As root user from a terminal window, type **system-config-network**, or from the Desktop menu, click System Settings ⇨ Network. The Network Configuration window appears.
2. Click the Hosts tab to see a list of IP addresses, hostnames, and aliases.
3. Click New. A pop-up window appears asking you to add the IP address, hostname, and aliases for a host that you can reach on your network. Figure 14-6 shows the Network Configuration window and the pop-up window for adding a host.
4. Type in the IP address number, hostname, and, optionally, the host alias.
5. Click OK.
6. Repeat this process until you have added every computer on your LAN.
7. Click the DNS tab.
8. Type the IP address of the computers that serve as your DNS servers. You get these IP addresses from your ISP; or, if you created your own DNS server, you can enter that server's IP address.

FIGURE 14-6

Add hosts to /etc/hosts using the Network Configuration window.

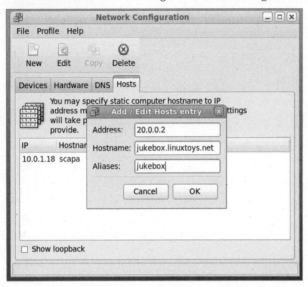

9. Type the name of the domain (probably the name of your local domain) to be searched for hostnames into the DNS Search Path box.

10. Select File ⇨ Save to save the changes.

11. Select File ⇨ Quit to exit.

Now, when you use programs such as lftp, ssh, or other TCP/IP utilities, you can use any hostname that is identified on your local computer; exists in your search path domain; or can be resolved from the public Internet DNS servers. (Strictly speaking, you don't have to set up your /etc/hosts file. You could use IP addresses as arguments to TCP/IP commands, but names are easier to work with.)

Adding Windows computers to your LAN

It is likely that you have other types of computers on your LAN in addition to those running Linux systems (at least for a few more years). If a DHCP server is available on your LAN (or if you have configured one yourself as described in Chapter 21), Windows and most other computer systems can simply start up and begin using the network. In cases where your network card is not properly detected, or you want to set static IP addresses, you need to do some extra configuration.

If you are using Windows Vista or Windows 7, Windows will detect when you connect a network cable. A Set Network Location dialog appears, where you can specify whether the network is a Home, Work, or Public location. After you choose the connection type, you can accept the defaults or select to change or view your network and sharing settings.

For Windows XP or earlier Windows systems, use the following general steps to manually add your Windows computers to the Ethernet LAN you just created:

1. Power down your computer and install an Ethernet card. (Most PC Ethernet cards will run on Windows.)

2. Connect an Ethernet cable from the card to your switch.

3. Reboot your computer. If your card is detected, Windows will either automatically install a driver or ask you to insert a disk that comes with the card to install the driver.

4. Open the window to configure networking. (Select Start ➪ Settings ➪ Control Panel; then double-click the Network icon. If you have Windows XP, you also need to click Set up or change your Internet connection.). A window to change network properties appears.

5. What you do next depends on the version of Windows you are running. If you are using Windows 7, go to the Control Panel and configure networking from the Network and Sharing Center. For Windows 2000 or XP, do the following:

   a. Click Switch to classic view.

   b. Double-click Network connections.

   c. Double-click Local Area Connection. The Local Area Connection Status window appears.

   d. Click Properties. The Local Area Connection Properties window appears.

   e. Select Internet Protocol (TCP/IP) and click the Properties button.

6. From the Properties window, do the following:

   a. Click Use the following IP address to configure your IP address manually.

Note
If you are using a DHCP server to assign IP addresses, click Obtain an IP address automatically instead. See Chapter 21 for information on setting up Linux as a DHCP server. ■

   b. Add the IP address, Subnet mask, and Default gateway for this computer.

   c. Add the IP addresses of up to two DNS servers.

   d. Click OK. You may need to reboot Windows for the settings to take effect.

At this point, your Windows computer knows to listen on the network (via its Ethernet card) for messages addressed to the IP address you just entered.

Setting Up a Wireless LAN

Although you can use wireless LAN cards with other computer systems, you may want to use Linux systems for one or more nodes in your wireless network. For example, the features in Linux can eliminate the need to buy other types of equipment. Some additional features that make Linux a valuable asset on a wireless LAN include:

- **Internet access** — You don't need a separate router or gateway machine to attach your wireless LAN to the Internet. Having wired and wireless Ethernet LAN cards on a Linux system enables your wireless clients to access the Internet through your Linux system.

- **Firewall** — Because of some inherent security weaknesses with wireless encryption protocols, you may want to add an extra measure of security to your network by configuring firewalls. With a Linux firewall (iptables) at the boundary between your wireless LAN and your larger network, you still have a measure of protection for your network if someone cracks your wireless LAN.

- **Monitoring and logging** — All the tools you use for monitoring and logging activity on your wired networks in Linux are also available for your wireless network.

Note
Keep in mind that you don't have to use Fedora to provide Internet access, firewalls, and monitoring. Several Linux firewall distributions were created specifically for this purpose and can run from live CDs or even USB drives. ■

In the past few Fedora releases, support for different wireless cards and tools for connecting to wireless networks have improved tremendously. In most cases, to connect to a wireless network you can just use NetworkManager (described earlier in this chapter) and skip this section altogether. However, if your wireless card isn't properly detected or configured, this section will help you find the drivers you need and perform any manual configuration necessary.

This section describes how to use wireless LAN equipment on computers running Fedora to create a wireless Ethernet LAN. It focuses on configuring two Linux systems for wireless communication; however, after you configure these nodes, you can add Windows, Linux, or other types of systems to your wireless LAN by installing compatible wireless cards on each system.

Understanding wireless networks

Wireless LANs are most appropriate in environments where wires are impractical. Despite some challenges such as security and interference, a wireless LAN provides advantages:

- You don't have to run wires in places that are hard to reach. In many cases, a single wireless LAN can extend your network throughout a building or to another building without the need for wires between each node.

- For the price of a wireless card, you can save the expense of wires, network switches (the air is your switch), and wall repairs (to fix the holes made from pulling wires through).

- You can freely move computers around within the transmission range that your environment allows (distances being limited by such variables as antenna power, obstacles, and rates of transmission).

Although several different wireless networking standards exist, this chapter focuses on the installation of relatively low-cost, standard IEEE 802.11b, 802.11g, and 802.11n wireless-networking equipment. These three wireless networks use space in the spectrum available to the public (in other words, you use space in the air for which no special license is required). The 802.11 standards are often referred to as the *WiFi* standard.

An 802.11 network is characterized by the following:

- It provides transmission rates of up to 11 Mbps (802.11b), 54 Mbps (802.11g), or 160 Mbps (802.11n). Transmission rates can also be set (or autodetected) to lower rates for each standard.

- It uses the 2.4 GHz band of the spectrum. Microwave ovens, Bluetooth devices, and some high-end cordless phones also use this band. (Check local regulations if you are setting up an 802.11 network outside the United States.) To reduce congestion, 14 separate channels are available within the 2.4 GHz range.

- It allows transmission over distances as short as a desktop away to as long as several miles away (using special antennas). Greater distances can be gained at lower transmission speeds.

- It makes connections between multiple clients, or clients and a base station (usually referred to as an *access point*). On the clients, the wireless LAN cards run in Ad hoc mode, while the base station uses infrastructure mode (also called Managed mode).

Other 802.11 standards exist (such as 802.11a, which can operate at higher speeds); but for the most part, wireless-equipment manufacturers originally rallied around the 802.11b standard, and now rally around the 802.11n and 802.11g standards (which can communicate at lower speeds with 802.11b equipment as well). Most wireless cards available today support all three standards.

After your wireless network has been configured, you can use the wireless connections as you would a regular wired Ethernet connection. For example, you can configure TCP/IP on top of your wireless network so that it acts as a gateway to your network's Internet connection. If you are using Linux as a wireless network client as well, you can take full advantage of firewall, masquerading, network proxy, or other networking features to protect and make full use of your wireless network.

Choosing wireless hardware

Getting wireless cards working in Fedora, without some scrambling around, used to be hit-or-miss. Some time ago, the Fedora project made the decision to track down and include firmware drivers for as many wireless LAN cards as they could find (provided they could be legally redistributed with Fedora). You can follow the progress of this effort at `http://fedoraproject.org/wiki/Firmware`

Some of the results of that effort are the following Fedora software packages that include support for different wireless cards:

- **atmel-firmware** — Contains firmware needed for Amtel at76c50x wireless network chips.

- **b43-openfwwf** — Contains firmware needed for some Broadcom 43xx series WLAN chips.

- **ipw2100-firmware** — Contains firmware needed for Intel PRO/Wireless 2100 Network Connection mini PCI adapters in Linux.

- **ipw2200-firmware** — Contains firmware needed for Intel PRO/Wireless 2915ABG Network Connection and Intel PRO/Wireless 2200BG Network Connection mini PCI adapters in Linux.

- **iwl3945-firmware** — Contains firmware needed for Intel xc2 xae PRO/Wireless 3945 A/B/G network adaptors. The project page for the Linux drivers used for these cards is located at `http://intellinuxwireless.org`.

- **iwl4965-firmware, iwl5000-firmware, iwl6000-firmware** — Contain firmware needed for Intel xc2 xae PRO/Wireless 4965/5000/6000 A/G/N network adaptors.

- **zd1211-firmware** — Contains firmware needed to work with wireless LAN USB sticks based on ZyDAS ZD1211 and ZD1211B chips. Source code and docs on the Linux driver for these wireless cards can be found at `http://sourceforge.net/projects/zd1211/`.

- **rt61pci-firmware** — Contains firmware needed for Ralink xc2 xae RT2561/RT2661 A/B/G network adaptors.

- **rt73usb-firmware** — Contains firmware needed for Ralink xc2 xae RT2571W/RT267.1 A/B/G network adaptors.

- **b43-fwcutter** — Contains the `b43-fwcutter` command for extracting firmware from drivers created from Broadcom wireless cards. Because the firmware for these cards cannot be freely distributed, you need to download the driver that comes with the card and extract the firmware to the `/lib/firmware` directory. Although Fedora still ships this tool, it does not ship the bcm43xx driver, as it is considered obsolete.

If you have a wireless card that is supported by any of these packages, you can try to install the package, reboot, and start NetworkManager. If your card isn't supported this way, refer to the next section for information on getting other wireless cards going.

Selecting wireless LAN cards

Wireless LAN card manufacturers haven't shown much interest in providing Linux drivers. Most wireless card drivers that are native to Linux were created without the help of those manufacturers; and in many cases Linux drivers are not available at all.

Another issue related to purchasing a wireless LAN card is that manufacturers often change their hardware without notice. Wireless cards with the same name and model number may include different wireless chipsets. While this may not be a problem for Windows users (because the vendor includes a Windows driver to match), the card may fail on your Linux machine despite that fact that others using a card of the same name in Linux swear it is working just fine.

Now that you know that your wireless card may not work once you get it home, let's talk about how to have the best chance of picking a card that will work. Here are some places to begin looking:

- **Native Linux driver** — Some wireless cards have drivers that were created specifically for Linux systems (see the previous section). Cards with those drivers have a good chance of being detected automatically and working after you install the wireless card. A project called Madwifi (`http://madwifi-project.org/`) has additional Linux wireless drivers, created specifically for wireless LAN cards that use chipsets from Atheros (`www.atheros.com`). Select Compatibility List from the Madwifi Wiki (`http://madwifi-project.org/wiki/Compatibility`) to see supported wireless cards.

- **Windows driver** — In cases where no native Linux driver is available, it's sometimes possible to use an open-source driver called ndiswrapper along with the Windows driver to use a wireless card in Linux. To see which cards are supported by ndiswrapper, refer to the list of ndiswrapper-supported cards. See the NDISwrapper project page (`http://ndiswrapper.sourceforge.net/`). Note that some aspects of this project have become quite controversial. You may need to look in the Internet Archive to find information. Go to `web.archive.org` and search for NDISwrapper to see the old list of supported cards.

Note

It's possible that even if your wireless card isn't listed in one of the sites referenced above, it might still work with drivers included with Fedora. Some wireless cards that include the same chipset (and therefore work with the same driver) may be referred to by different names. Rather than try to keep track of all the various acquisitions and name changes in the wireless industry, I refer you to the Linux Wireless LAN HOWTO (`www.hpl.hp.com/personal/Jean_Tourrilhes/Linux`). The Drivers section provides more insight into which drivers work with which cards. Note, however, that this list is dated as being last updated in July 2007. ∎

Loading nonfree drivers

The RPMFusion.org site maintains a number of wireless drivers provided by vendors or under a variety of licenses that do not meet the Fedora project's definition of a free software license. The `akmods` and `akmod-wl` packages allow you to build these modules for your Linux kernel. For example, Broadcom offers drivers for the wireless card used in MacBook Pro laptops at `www.broadcom.com/support/802.11/linux_sta.php`. The RPMfusion.org site includes nonfree packages for Broadcom cards.

To use this or other nonfree drivers, you need to first add the RPMfusion.org repository to the list of repositories supported by the yum command. Run the following command as the root user:

```
# rpm -Uvh \
http://download1.rpmfusion.org/free/fedora/↵
rpmfusion-free-release-stable.noarch.rpm \
http://download1.rpmfusion.org/nonfree/fedora/↵
rpmfusion-nonfree-release-stable.noarch.rpm
```

See Chapter 5 for more on repositories as well as the rpm and yum commands. After adding this repository, install the following packages for the MacBook Pro:

```
# yum upgrade
# yum install akmod-wl akmods kernel-PAE-devel
```

The first command ensures that all your packages are up to date. This is especially important because in this example I need to build a kernel module. The second command installs the akmod-wl (wireless) package. It should bring in the Broadcom package from the nonfree part of the RPMfusion.org site. Other wireless cards will require different packages. I recommend browsing the RPMfusion.org site, especially the nonfree portion of the repository.

Note

Nonfree packages, obviously, come with nonfree software licenses. Read over each license first to ensure you are OK with it. ■

Next, run the akmods command:

```
# akmods --akmod wl
```

You may need to force akmods to work for a particular kernel with the --kernel option. Use this option if you get an error that a particular directory under /lib/modules does not exist.

Note

You may also be able to get MacBook Pro wireless working by simply installing the latest kmod (compiled kernel module) for wl (wireless) with a command like the following:

```
# yum install mod-wl ■
```

Selecting antennas

If you are setting up your wireless LAN among several computers in close proximity, you may not need an additional antenna. To deal with obstructions and longer distances, however, you can add indoor or outdoor antennas to your wireless hardware. In the sections that follow, I illustrate different types of indoor and outdoor antennas that are compatible with those cards.

Using indoor antennas

The antennas that are built into wireless LAN cards often work well enough to enable communication among computers in an open area. Additional indoor antennas are useful if the direct line of sight between the wireless LAN cards is blocked. A computer may be locked in a storage closet or stuck under a desk. A pile of papers might inhibit transmission, or a sheet of metal might stop it dead. A small antenna that draws the transmission away from the card might be the answer to these problems.

While most wireless LAN cards don't require a completely unobstructed line of sight, an obstacle can certainly slow reception. To get around this problem, an antenna such as the Orinoco IEEE range-extender can plug directly into an Orinoco wireless LAN card. A 1.5-meter extension cable can bring the signal out from behind a closed door or out on top of a desk. When you set up the antenna, the following are recommended:

- Place it in a central location.
- Mount it vertically.
- Locate it away from obstructions (metal surfaces in particular, and, to a lesser extent, solid objects such as concrete walls or stacks of papers).

Refer to the instructions that come with your antenna for specific guidelines regarding placing and mounting the antenna.

Using outdoor antennas

Choosing and setting up outdoor antennas for your wireless LAN can be more difficult and expensive than setting them up indoors. Once the outdoor antennas are in place, however, you can save money because you won't need multiple Internet access accounts (monthly fees, DSL/cable modems, and so on).

Although a complete description of the use of outside antennas with your wireless LAN is outside the scope of this chapter, here are some tips that will help you choose the best antennas for your wireless LAN:

- **Point-to-point versus multipoint** — If you are creating a point-to-point link between two outdoor locations (for example, to share an Internet connection between two buildings), a directional antenna can help you achieve greater distance and transmission speeds. However, if your antenna is providing multipoint access for several other outdoor antennas or wireless clients (such as students working from laptops on the campus lawn), an omnidirectional antenna may be more appropriate.

- **Clearance** — The clearer the line of sight between each outdoor antenna, the greater the distance and transmission speed you can achieve. Placing antennas at the highest possible points can prevent diminished performance caused by trees, cars, buildings, and other objects. The amount of distance between obstacles and the coverage area of your wireless transmission is referred to as the *clearance factor*.

- **Distance** — Although the actual distances over which antennas can send and receive data varies greatly based on different factors, you can achieve distances of many miles with outdoor antennas. For example, two Orinoco 24 dBi directional parabolic-grid antennas can theoretically achieve distances of up to 52 miles at an 11 Mbps transmission speed with a 180-meter clearance. Reduce that transmission rate to 1 Mbps and you can achieve distances of up to 149 miles with a 1,200-meter clearance. Shorter distances are achieved with less expensive equipment, such as the Orinoco 14 dBi directional antenna, which can achieve distances of up to 5.3 miles at 11 Mbps with a 13-meter clearance.

- **Cable factor** — The distances that transmissions travel on the cables between the wireless cards and the antennas can be a factor in choosing the right antenna. The shorter the cables, the greater the distance and speed you will get on your antenna.

The power of an antenna is rated in terms of *gain*. Gain is measured in decibels, based on a *theoretic isotropic radiator* (or *dBi*). Higher gains offer opportunities to reach greater distances at greater speeds. However, the ability of the antenna to focus that power (directional versus omni-directional) greatly affects the speeds and distances that can be achieved. If you want to see some interesting homemade antennas, search the Web for the word *cantenna*.

Getting wireless drivers

If you are using a wireless card that includes a supported driver in Fedora, the system might detect that card and load the proper driver, so you will be able to configure it as described later in this section. As Fedora supports more and more wireless cards, this will be the most common case. In other cases, though, you will need to install the associated firmware for the driver that comes with the hardware (usually intended for Windows systems). If the driver you need for your wireless card is not included with Fedora, you may be able to use ndiswrapper and a Windows driver to configure your wireless card. (NDIS is short for Network Driver Interface Specification.) The following procedure contains an example of configuring ndiswrapper with a Linksys 802.11g wireless PCI adapter card, a common type of wireless card.

If you find you need further information about using ndiswrapper, refer to the Fedora Ndiswrapper project page (ndiswrapper.sourceforge.net/).

Note

There is now a b43 driver available in Fedora, so you can use the bc43-fwcutter command to extract the firmware from the package to use with that native Linux driver. After that, a reboot should properly detect and load the modules needed for the card. You can learn more about your specific card's firmware here: http://linuxwireless.org/en/users/Drivers/b43. ∎

1. Determine the kind of wireless card you are using. If you have a PCI card, type the following:

```
# lspci -v | less
00:0a.0 Network controller: Broadcom Corporation BCM4306 802.11b/g
Wireless LAN Controller (rev 03)
Subsystem: Linksys: Unknown device 0014
Flags: bus master, fast devsel, latency 64, IRQ 5
Memory at ee000000 (32-bit, non-prefetchable) [size=8K]
```

2. In this example, the PCI card is a BCM4306 802.11b/g Wireless Controller from Broadcom Corporation. (If your wireless card is a USB device, type the lsusb command instead.)

3. Check the list of wireless card drivers known to run under ndiswrapper, as mentioned previously.

4. If your card is supported, download the driver recommended. I used the Linksys WMP54GS Wireless-G PCI Adapter (which was reflected by the chipset BCM4306 802.11g, rev 03 shown in the preceding lspci output). You will need to search for the driver for your card.

Note

Be sure to check the ndiswrapper website and your network adapter's driver downloads to see what versions are available. ■

5. Install the kernel-devel and gcc packages. Then link the kernels directory to the modules directory or your current kernel (replacing <kernel-version> with the version of your kernel development package and current kernel, where shown):

```
# yum install kernel-devel gcc
# ln -s /usr/src/kernels/<kernel-version> \
/lib/modules/<kernel-version>/build
```

6. Download the ndiswrapper source code to your Fedora system from the following site: http://sourceforge.net/projects/ndiswrapper.

Note

There are also ndiswrapper RPM packages available for Fedora at rpmfusion.org. **If you decide to go that route, instead of installing the source code, make sure that you find the ndiswrapper package that matches your kernel version. See Chapter 5 for information on enabling the** rpmfusion.org **repository.** ■

7. With the ndiswrapper source code package in the current directory, unzip and untar it as follows:

```
# tar xvfz ndiswrapper-*tar.gz
```

8. As root user, change to the ndiswrapper directory and run the make command as follows:

```
# cd ndiswrapper*
# make install
```

9. Get the INF file from the unzipped driver package. From our example, the file we needed was lsbcmnds.inf. Then run the ndiswrapper -i command to install the driver. For example, with the lsbcmnds.inf file in the current directory, I ran this:

```
# ndiswrapper -i lsbcmnds.inf
```

10. Check that the driver and the hardware are available:

```
# ndiswrapper -l
lsbcmnds          driver present, hardware present
```

11. To load the ndiswrapper module, type the following:

```
# modprobe ndiswrapper
```

12. Type the following command to see your wireless LAN (wlan) entry:

```
# iwconfig
```

13. In this case, eth1 was the device name for the wireless card. Use the device name reported by iwconfig and type the following to see your access point:

```
# iwlist eth1 scan
```

14. Create an alias for your wireless device to eth1, so that the interface is loaded automatically at boot time:

```
# ndiswrapper -m
```

15. To check that the ndiswrapper module loaded properly, check the /var/log/messages file. These messages appeared after the module was loaded:

```
Nov  2 20:28:53 toys kernel: ndiswrapper version 1.54 loaded
         (preempt=no,smp=no)
Nov  2 20:28:53 toys kernel: ACPI: PCI interrupt 0000:00:0a.0[A]->
         GSI 5 (level, low) -> IRQ 5
Nov  2 20:28:53 toys kernel: ndiswrapper: using irq 5
Nov  2 20:28:54 toys udev: creating device node '/dev/ndiswrapper'
Nov  2 20:28:54 toys kernel: eth1: ndiswrapper ethernet
         device 00:0f:66:6f:b9:0a using driver lsbcmnds
Nov  2 20:28:54 toys kernel: eth1: encryption modes supported:
         WEP, WPA with TKIP, AES/CCMP
Nov  2 20:28:54 toys kernel: ndiswrapper: driver lsbcmnds
         (The Linksys Group, Inc.,07/17/2003, 3.30.15.0) added
```

From the output, you can see that the ndiswrapper module was loaded, that it found the wireless PCI card, and that the eth1 interface was assigned to that device using the lsbcmnds driver. With the card properly detected, you can configure TCP/IP to use with that card.

Installing wireless Linux software

For most Fedora install types, the software packages you need to create your wireless LAN will already be installed. Drivers and modules needed to support PCMCIA cards and wireless cards should be in your system. Besides the wireless drivers, the following software packages contain tools for configuring and working with your wireless LAN cards in Fedora:

- **pcmciautils** — Contains commands and configuration files to support your wireless card if it happens to be a PCMCIA or CardBus card.

- **wireless-tools** — Contains commands for setting extensions for your wireless LAN interface. Commands include `iwconfig` (for configuring your wireless interface) and `iwlist` (for listing wireless statistics).

After you have established a wireless LAN interface, you can use a variety of Linux software to monitor and control access to that interface. You will need to install the appropriate software packages as well. Here are some examples of other wireless software packages in Fedora that you might find useful, although some of them have not been updated since Fedora 12:

- **aircrack-ng** — Can be used to audit wireless networks.

- **wifi-radar** — Scans for available wireless networks.

- **kismet** — Sniffs 802.11 wireless networks.

- **wifiroamd** — Lets you search for the best available access point.

- **airsnort** — Has tools for checking the strength of your wireless encryption keys.

Configuring the wireless LAN

Before you begin testing the distances you can achieve with your wireless Linux LAN, I recommend that you configure wireless cards on two computers within direct sight of each other. After the two computers are communicating, you can change wireless settings to tune the connection and begin experimenting with transmission distances.

The following sections describe the steps you need to take to set up a wireless LAN between two Linux systems. Although only two nodes are described, you can add more computers to your wireless LAN once you know how. This procedure describes how to operate your wireless Linux LAN in two different modes:

- **Ad hoc** — Using this mode, all the computers in your wireless LAN are gathered into a single virtual network made up of only one cell. A single cell means that you cannot roam among different groups of wireless nodes and continue your communication invisibly. Doing that requires a managed network.

- **Managed** — As noted earlier, many wireless cards supported in Linux cannot operate as access points; but a Linux wireless card can operate as a node in a managed network. The wireless configuration tools that come with Fedora enable you to identify the access point for Linux to use by indicating the access point's MAC address.

Install your wireless cards per the manufacturer's instructions. Then configure the interface for each card as described in the procedure covered in the next section.

Configuring the wireless interface

If you have NetworkManager enabled (the default), configuring your wireless networks should be easy. Select the NetworkManager icon in your top panel to see available wireless networks that are detected, choose the one you want, and enter any authentication information that's required. If you prefer not to use NetworkManager, however, you can still manually configure wireless interfaces using the Network Configuration window.

The Network Configuration window (system-config-network command) can configure both wireless Ethernet card interfaces and regular wired Ethernet cards. The following procedure describes how to configure a wireless Ethernet card using the Network Configuration window:

Note

If your wireless card driver does not appear in the list of devices when adding a new wireless device, you may need to configure your wireless card manually, as described in this chapter. Step through this procedure and if you are not able to activate the wireless card, refer to the description of the ifcfg-eth1 file at the end of this procedure. ■

1. Start the Network Configuration. From the Desktop menu, click System ➪ Administration ➪ Network, or, as root user from a terminal window, type **system-config-network**. The Network Configuration window appears.

2. Click the New button. The Select Device Type window appears, as shown in Figure 14-7.

FIGURE 14-7

Add a wireless interface using the Network Configuration window.

3. Click Wireless connection, and then click Forward. The Select Wireless Device window appears.

4. Select your wireless card from the list of cards shown, and click Forward. The Configure Wireless Connection window appears.

5. Add the following information and click Forward:

   - **Mode** — Indicates the mode of operation for the wireless LAN card. Because I am setting up a wireless LAN consisting of only one cell (that is, with no roaming to cells set up in other areas), I could set the mode to Ad hoc. Ad hoc mode allows the card to communicate directly with each of its peers. You can use Managed mode if you have multiple cells, requiring your card to communicate directly to an access point. You can use Managed mode for a point-to-point network. You can also use Master mode to have the card behave like a wireless access point device.

   - **Network Name (SSID)** — The network name (or Network ID) that identifies cells that are part of the same network. If you have a group of cells (which might include multiple nodes and repeaters among which a client could roam), this name can identify all of those cells as being under one virtual network. Choose a name and then use that name for all computers in your virtual network. (SSID stands for Service Set ID.)

   - **Channel** — Choose a channel between 1 and 14, or leave the setting at Auto. You can begin with channel 1; if you get interference on that channel, try changing to other channels.

   - **Transmit Rate** — Choose the rate of transmission from the following rates: 11M, 5.5M, 2M, 1M, or Auto. Choosing Auto allows the interface to automatically ramp down to lower speeds as needed, which enables the interface to transmit over greater distances and deal with noisy channels.

   - **Key** — You need the same encryption key for all wireless LAN cards that are communicating with each other. It is critical to get this value right. This key is used to encrypt all data transmitted and to decrypt all data received on the wireless interface. You can enter the number (up to 40 bits, depending on what is supported by your card) as XXXXXXXXXX or XXXX-XXXX-XX (where each X is a number from 0 to 9 or a letter between A and F). For 64-bit encryption, the key must be 10 hexadecimal characters; for 128-bit encryption, the key must be 32 hexadecimal characters.

6. A Configure Network Settings window appears. You can enter the following information:

   - **Automatically obtain IP address settings with** — If you want to get your IP address from a DHCP server, click this box; the rest of the information is obtained automatically. Otherwise, set the IP address statically using the other options.

   - **Hostname** — If you are using DHCP, you can optionally add a hostname to identify this network interface. If none is entered here, the output from the /bin/hostname command is used.

- **Automatically obtain DNS information from provider** — Select this check box to allow the DHCP server to overwrite your /etc/resolv.conf file with DNS server information. (Leave it unchecked to configure that file yourself.)

- **Statically set IP addresses** — Click here to manually set your IP addresses.

- **Address** — If you selected static IP addresses, type the IP address of this computer into the Address text box. This number must be unique on your wireless network.

- **Subnet Mask** — Enter the netmask to indicate what part of the IP address represents the network. (Netmask is described later in this chapter.)

- **Default Gateway address** — If a computer on your wireless LAN is providing routing to the Internet or other network, type the IP address of the computer here.

- **Primary and Secondary DNS** — If you want to manually set which DNS servers to use when this interface is up, enter your DNS information here.

- **MTU and MRU** — You can manually set the maximum transfer and receive units, but in most cases you should leave these settings alone.

7. Click Forward to see a listing of the information you just entered.

8. Click Apply to complete the new wireless network interface.

9. Select File ⇨ Save (on the main window) to save the interface.

This procedure creates an interface configuration file in your /etc/sysconfig/network-scripts directory. The name of the configuration file is ifcfg- followed by the interface name (such as eth0, eth1, and so on). Therefore, if your wireless card is providing your only network interface, it might be called ifcfg-eth0.

Using any text editor, open the ifcfg-eth? file (replacing ? with the interface number) as root user. The following is an example of an ifcfg-eth1 file:

```
ONBOOT=no
USERCTL=no
PEERDNS=no
GATEWAY=10.0.1.1
TYPE=Wireless
DEVICE=eth1
HWADDR=00:02:2d:2e:8c:a8
BOOTPROTO=none
NETMASK=255.255.255.0
IPADDR=10.0.1.2
DOMAIN=
ESSID=
CHANNEL=1
MODE=Ad-Hoc
RATE=11Mb/s
NETWORK=10.0.1.0
BROADCAST=10.0.1.255
```

In this example, the wireless card's hardware (MAC) address is automatically set to
`00:02:2d:2e:8c:a8`. (Your MAC address will be different.) The interface is not yet set
to come up at boot time (`ONBOOT=no`). The interface device is `eth1` (which matches the
interface filename `ifcfg-eth1`) because this particular computer has another Ethernet
card on the `eth0` interface. The interface type is set to `Wireless`.

Other information in the file sets standard TCP/IP address information. The netmask is set to
`255.255.255.0` and the IP address for the card is set to `10.0.1.1`. The broadcast address is
`10.0.1.255`.

You can also set many options that are specific to your wireless network in this file. The following
list explains some additional options you might want to set:

- **NWID** — Identifies the name of this particular computer on the network. The computer's hostname (determined from the `uname -n` command) is used by default if you don't set it with NWID.

- **FREQ** — You can choose a particular frequency in which to transmit. No value is required because selecting a channel implies a certain frequency. If you do enter a frequency, the value must be a number followed by a k (kilohertz), M (megahertz), or G (gigahertz). The default values for the channels you select range from `2.412G` (channel 1) to `2.484G` (channel 14), with other channels occurring at increments of .005G. The default is `2.422G`.

- **SENS** — You can select the sensitivity level of the access point. SENS can be set to 1 (low density), 2 (medium density), or 3 (high density). The default is 1. The `sensitivity threshold` has an impact on roaming.

Caution

The encryption algorithm used with many 802.11 networks is the Wired Equivalent Privacy (WEP) algorithm.
Although using the encryption key is more secure than not using it, experts feel that WEP has some inherent flaws that might allow a drive-by hacker to decrypt your wireless LAN traffic. For that reason, I strongly recommend using additional techniques to protect your wireless LANs, such as firewalls and diligent log-checking. See the section on "Wireless Security" for further information. (If your wireless card supports WPA encryption standards, use those; they are more secure than WEP.) ■

Besides the options just described, you can also pass any valid options to the `iwconfig` command (which actually interprets these values) by adding an `IWCONFIG` option to the configuration file. Display the `iwconfig` man page (`man iwconfig`) to see all wireless options. Also view the `/etc/sysconfig/network-scripts/ifup-wireless` script to see how the options you just added are processed.

Repeat the configuration procedure for each wireless Fedora computer on your LAN. At this point, your wireless network should be ready to go. Restart your network, as described in the following steps, to ensure that it is working.

Checking your wireless connection

Your wireless LAN interface should be operating at this point. If another wireless computer is available on your wireless network, try communicating with it using the `ping` command and its

IP address (as described in the section "Can you reach another computer on the LAN?" later in this chapter).

If you are not able to communicate with other wireless nodes or if transmission is slow, you may have more work to do. For example, if you see messages that say "Destination Host Unreachable" instead of the `ping` output shown in the section "Can you reach another computer on the LAN?" later in this chapter, refer to the section "Troubleshooting a wireless LAN" for help. Some access points will not allow you to communicate with other wireless clients, so double-check your access point's settings or try pinging the access point itself.

Wireless Security

The Wireless Ethernet Compatibility Alliance (WECA) has recommended changes in response to security concerns about wireless networks. They did this because wireless networks, unlike wired networks, which can often be physically protected within a building, often extend beyond physical boundaries that can be protected.

The Wireless Equivalent Privacy (WEP) standard adds encryption to the 802.11 wireless standard. WECA refers to WEP as its way of providing "walls" that make wireless Ethernet as secure as wired Ethernet. However, you need to implement WEP, as well as other security methods that would apply to any computer network, in order to make your wireless network secure. Here are WECA's suggestions:

- Change the default WEP encryption key on a regular basis (possibly weekly or even daily). This prevents casual drive-by hackers from reading your encrypted transmissions.

- Use password protection on your drives and folders.

- Change the default Network Name (SSID).

- Use session keys, if available in your product (session keys are not supported in current Linux wireless drivers).

- Use MAC address filtering (supported in a limited way in Linux).

- Don't broadcast from the access point, if possible.

- Use a VPN (Virtual Private Network) system, which can add another layer of encryption beyond what is available on your wireless network.

For larger organizations requiring greater security, WECA suggests such features as firewalls and user-verification schemes (such as Kerberos). As mentioned earlier in the chapter, features to protect from intrusions and restrict services are already built into Fedora. Refer to the descriptions of security tools in Chapters 13 and 15 for methods to secure your network, its computers, and their services. In particular, consider adding a VPN to further secure all data sent on your wireless LAN.

WiFi Protected Access (WPA) features are available for most wireless cards in Linux. The software for implementing WPA, wpa_supplicant, is used by NetworkManager to connect to a WPA-enabled access point. Choose WPA over WEP if possible.

Setting wireless extensions

After the wireless module is loaded, you can change wireless extensions using the `iwconfig` command. The `iwconfig` command is the command actually used to set the options added to the `ifcfg` configuration script (e.g., for the `eth1` interface, the script would be `/etc/sysconfig/network-scripts/ifcfg-eth1`).

Some of the same options that you set when the module was loaded can be reset using the `iwconfig` command. This command can be useful for testing different settings on an active wireless LAN. The syntax of the `iwconfig` command is as follows:

```
# iwconfig interface parameter value
```

The `interface` is the name of the wireless interface you want to change, such as `eth1` or `wlan0`. The `parameter` is the name of the option, and the `value` is replaced by its value. For example, to set your network name (also called ESSID, or Extended Service Set Identifier) to Homelan, type the following as root user:

```
# iwconfig eth1 essid "Homelan"
```

Table 14-1 contains a list of available options for the `iwconfig` command.

TABLE 14-1

Options for the iwconfig Command

Option	Description
`essid` *name*	Indicates the network name.
`ap` *address*	Indicates that the access point is at a particular MAC address. For low-quality connections, the client driver may return to trying to automatically detect the access point. This setting is useful in Managed mode only.
`channel` #	Picks the channel number to operate on.
`frag` *frag_size*	Sets the fragmentation threshold for splitting up packets before they are transmitted.
`freq` 2.46G	Sets the frequency of the channel to communicate on.
`key` *xxxx-xxxx-xx*	Sets the key used for WEP encryption.
`mode` *option*	Sets the mode used for communications to Ad-hoc, Managed, Master, Repeater, Secondary, or Auto.
`nick` *name*	Sets the station name to define this particular computer.
`rate` *XX*M	Defines the transmission rate to use.
`rts` *number*	Sets the RTS/CTS threshold for packet transmission.

continued

TABLE 14-1	(continued)
Option	**Description**
`retry number`	For cards that support MAC retransmissions, you can use this option to determine how many retries are made before the transmission fails. The value can be a number (indicating number of seconds allotted for retries), or a number followed by an m (for milliseconds) or u (for microseconds). Instead of a number, you can set a number of retries using the limit parameter. For example: `retry limit 100` indicates that the transmission can retry up to 100 times.
`sens number`	Sets the lowest possible sensitivity threshold for which the wireless interface will try to receive a packet. Raising this level can help block interference from other wireless LANs that might weakly encroach on your transmission area.

The best place to add `iwconfig` options permanently in Fedora is the configuration file for your wireless interface in the `/etc/sysconfig/network-scripts` directory.

Options to `iwconfig` are added to the wireless-interface file (such as `ifcfg-eth0` or `ifcfg-eth1`) using the `IWCONFIG` parameter. For example, to add an encryption-key value of 1234-1234-12 for your wireless LAN card, you could add the following line to your wireless-interface file:

```
IWCONFIG="key 1234-1234-12"
```

Understanding Internet Protocol Addresses

Whether your network is wired or wireless, each computer you communicate with (including yours) must have a unique address on the network. In TCP/IP, each computer must be assigned an Internet Protocol (IP) address. This section gives you some background in IP addresses.

There are two basic ways to assign a hostname and IP address to a network interface in Linux:

- **Static addresses** — With static IP addresses, each computer has an IP address that doesn't change each time the computer reboots or restarts its network interface. Its IP address can be entered manually because it's not assigned on-the-fly. You can do this when Fedora is installed, or later using the Network Configuration window.

- **Dynamic addresses** — With dynamic addresses, a client computer's IP address is assigned from a server on the network when the client boots. The most popular protocol for providing dynamic addresses is called DHCP. With this method, a client computer may not have the same IP address each time it boots.

Tip

If you expect to add and remove computers regularly from your LAN or if you have a limited number of IP addresses, you should use DHCP to assign IP addresses. Chapter 21 describes how to set up a DHCP server. ■

An IP address is a four-part number, with each part represented by a number from 0 to 255 (256 numbers total). Part of that IP address represents the network on which the computer exists, while the remainder identifies the specific host on that network. Here's an example of an IP address:

```
192.168.35.121
```

Originally, IP addresses were grouped together and assigned to an organization that needed IP addresses, based on IP address classes. These days, a more efficient method, referred to as Classless Inter-Domain Routing (CIDR), is used to improve routing and waste fewer IP addresses. These two IP address methods are described in the following sections.

IP address classes

Unfortunately, it's not so easy to understand which part of an IP address represents the network and which represents the host without understanding how IP addresses are structured. IP addresses are assigned in the following manner. A network administrator is given a pool of addresses. The administrator can then assign specific host addresses within that pool as new computers are added to the organization's local network. There were originally three basic classes of IP addresses, each representing a different size network:

- **Class A** — Each Class A IP address has a number between 0 and 127 as its first part. Host numbers within a Class A network are represented by any combination of numbers in the next three parts. A Class A network therefore contains millions of host numbers (approximately 256 × 256 × 256, with a few special numbers being invalid). A valid Class A network number is as follows:

```
24.
```

- **Class B** — A Class B IP address has a number between 128 and 191 in its first part. With a Class B network, however, the second part also represents the network. This enables a Class B network to have more than 64,000 host addresses (256 × 256). A valid Class B network number is as follows:

```
135.84
```

- **Class C** — A Class C IP address begins with a number between 192 and 223 in its first part. With a Class C network, the first three parts of an IP address represent the network, while only the last part represents a specific host. Thus, each Class C network can have 254 numbers (the numbers 0 and 255 can't be assigned to hosts). Here is an example of a Class C network number:

```
194.122.56
```

To tell your computer which part of a network address is the network and which is the host, you must enter a number that masks the network number. That number is referred to as the *netmask*.

Understanding netmasks

Suppose you are assigned the Class B address 135.84, but you are only given the pool of numbers available to the address 135.84.118. How do you tell your network that every address beginning with 135.84.118 represents a host on your network, but that other addresses beginning with 135.84 should be routed to another network? You can do it with a netmask.

The netmask essentially identifies the network number for a network. When you assign the IP address that is associated with your computer's interface to the LAN (eth0), you are asked for a netmask. By default, your computer fills in a number that masks the part of your IP address that represents the class of your network. For example, the default netmasks for Class A, B, and C networks are as follows:

- Class A netmask: 255.0.0.0
- Class B netmask: 255.255.0.0
- Class C netmask: 255.255.255.0

If your network were assigned the network number 135.84.118, to tell your computer that 135.84.118 is the network number and not 135.84 (as it normally would be for a Class B address), add a netmask of 255.255.255.0. Therefore, you could use host numbers from 1 to 254 (which go in the fourth part of the number).

To further confuse the issue, you could mask only one or more bits that are part of the IP address. Instead of using the number 255, you could use a variety of other numbers between 0 and 255, including 128, 192, 224, 240, 248, 252, and 254, to mask only part of the numbers in that part of the address.

Note
The reason why only the numbers just mentioned are valid netmasks is that each part is represented by eight binary numbers, but all 1s that are included must be to the left. Therefore, 240 would be allowed (11110000) but 242 would not (11110010). This limitation is what led to the creation of CIDR (see the next section). ∎

Classless Inter-Domain Routing

The class method of allocating IP addresses had a couple of major drawbacks. First, few organizations fell neatly into one class or another. For most organizations, a Class C address (up to 256 IP addresses) was too small, and a Class B address (up to 65,534 IP addresses) was too big. The result was a lot of wasted numbers in a world where IP addresses were running short. Second, IP classes resulted in too many routing table entries. As a result, routers were becoming overloaded with information.

The Classless Inter-Domain Routing (CIDR) addressing scheme set out to deal with these problems. The scheme is similar to IP address classes, but offers much more flexibility in assigning how much of the 32-bit IP address is the network identifier. Instead of the first 8, 16, or 32 bits identifying the network, 13 to 27 bits can identify the network. As a result, groups of assigned IP addresses can contain from 32 to about 524,000 host addresses.

To indicate the network identifier, a CIDR IP address is followed by a slash (/) and then a number from 13 to 27. A smaller number indicates a network containing more hosts. Here's an example of an IP address that uses the CIDR notation:

```
128.8.27.18/16
```

In this example, the first 16 bits (128.8) represent the network number, and the remainder (27.18) represents the specific host number. This network number can contain up to 65,536 hosts (the same as a Class B address). Table 14-2 shows how many hosts can be represented in networks using different numbers to identify the network:

TABLE 14-2

CIDR-Style Addresses and the Number of Supported Hosts

CIDR Notation	Number of Hosts
/13	524,288
/14	262,144
/15	131,072
/16	65,536
/17	32,768
/18	16,382
/19	8,192
/20	4,096
/21	2,048
/22	1,024
/23	512
/24	256
/25	128
/26	64
/27	32

The CIDR addressing scheme also helps reduce the routing overload problem by having a single, high-level route represent many lower-level routes. For example, an ISP could be assigned a single /13 IP network and assign the 500,000-plus addresses to its customers. Routers outside the ISP would only need to know how to reach the ISP for those half-million addresses. The ISP would then be responsible for maintaining routing information for all the host routes with that network address.

Getting IP addresses

What is the impact of assigning IP addresses for the computers on your LAN? Your choice of which IP addresses to use depends on your situation. If you are part of a large organization, you should get addresses from your network administrator. Even if you don't connect to other LANs in your organization at the moment, having unique addresses can make it easier to connect to them in the future.

If you are setting up a network for yourself (with no other networks to consider in your organization), you can use private addresses. However, if you need to connect computers to the Internet as servers, apply for your own domain name (from an Internet domain registrar) and IP addresses (from your ISP).

If you don't need to have your LAN accessible from the Internet, choose IP addresses from the set of available general-purpose IP addresses. Using these private IP addresses, you can still access the Internet from your LAN for such things as Web browsing and e-mail by using IP Masquerading or Network Address Translation (NAT), as described in Chapter 15. Table 14-3 lists the private IP addresses not used on any public part of the Internet.

TABLE 14-3

Private IP Addresses

Network Class	Network Numbers	Addresses per Network Number
Class A	10.0.0.0	167,777,216
Class B	172.16.0.0 to 172.31.0.0	65,536
Class C	192.168.0.0 to 192.168.255.255	256

For a small private LAN, the following numbers are examples of IP addresses that you could assign to the host computers on your network. (You could use any of the network numbers, plus host numbers, from the table. These are just examples.)

- 192.168.1.1
- 192.168.1.2
- 192.168.1.3
- 192.168.1.4
- 192.168.1.5

You could continue that numbering up to 192.168.1.254 on this network, and you could use a network mask of 255.255.255.0.

Troubleshooting Your LAN

After your LAN has been set up, your Ethernet cards installed, and hostnames and addresses added, several methods can be used to check that everything is up and working. Some troubleshooting techniques are described in the following sections.

Did Linux find your Ethernet driver at boot time?

Type the following right after you boot your computer to verify whether Linux found your card and installed the Ethernet interface properly:

```
dmesg | grep eth
```

The dmesg command lists all the messages that were output by Linux at boot time. The grep eth command causes only those lines that contain the word *eth* to be printed. The first message shown here appeared on my laptop computer with the NETGEAR card. The second example is from my computer with the EtherExpress Pro/100 card:

```
eth0: NE2000 Compatible: port 0x300, irq3, hw_addr 00:80:C8:8C:8E:49
eth0: OEM i82557/i82558 10/100 Ethernet at 0xccc0, 00:90:27:4E:67:35, IRQ 17.
```

The message in the first example shows that a card was found at IRQ3 with a port address of 0x300 and an Ethernet hardware address of 00:80:C8:8C:8E:49. In the second example, the card is at IRQ 17, the port address is 0xccc0, and the Ethernet address is 00:90:27:4E:67:35.

Note

If the eth0 interface is not found but you know that you have a supported Ethernet card, confirm that your Ethernet card is properly seated in its slot. ∎

Can you reach another computer on the LAN?

Try communicating with different network interfaces on your LAN. You can use the ping command to send a packet to another computer or local network interface and to ask for a packet in return. You could give ping either a hostname (pine) or an IP address (10.0.0.10). The following is a succession of ping commands you can use to test your local network interfaces and connections to other computers (your external and router IP addresses will probably be different):

```
# ping localhost            Local loopback
# ping 10.0.0.10            Local external interface
# ping 10.0.0.1             Local router to Internet
# ping 208.77.188.166       Remote server
# ping example.com          Remote server by name
```

Note

Ping **is often disabled for security reasons, as it creates an easy way for other computers to find information about your system, while draining networking resources and bandwidth.** ■

If you are able to ping a remote server by name, you know that both name service and routing are working. If the remote server can be reached, the output will look similar to the following:

```
PING example.com (208.77.188.166): 56(84) bytes of data.
64 bytes from www.example.com (208.77.188.166): icmp_seq=1 ttl=255 time=0.351ms
64 bytes from www.example.com (208.77.188.166): icmp_seq=2 ttl=255 time=0.445ms
64 bytes from www.example.com (208.77.188.166): icmp_seq=3 ttl=255 time=0.409ms
64 bytes from www.example.com (208.77.188.166): icmp_seq=4 ttl=255 time=0.457ms
64 bytes from www.example.com (208.77.188.166): icmp_seq=5 ttl=255 time=0.401ms
64 bytes from www.example.com (208.77.188.166): icmp_seq=6 ttl=255 time=0.405ms
64 bytes from www.example.com (208.77.188.166): icmp_seq=7 ttl=255 time=0.443ms
64 bytes from www.example.com (208.77.188.166): icmp_seq=8 ttl=255 time=0.384ms
64 bytes from www.example.com (208.77.188.166): icmp_seq=9 ttl=255 time=0.365ms
64 bytes from www.example.com (208.77.188.166): icmp_seq=10 ttl=255 time=0.367ms

--- example.com ping statistics ---
10 packets transmitted, 10 packets received, 0% packet loss, time 9011ms
rtt min/avg/max/mdev = 0.351/0.402/0.457/0.042 ms, pipe 2
```

A line of output is printed each time a packet is sent and received in return. It shows how much data was sent and how long it took for each package to be received. After you have watched this for a while, press Ctrl+C to stop ping. At that point, you will see statistics on how many packets were transmitted, received, and lost.

If you don't see output that shows packets have been received, it means you are not contacting the other computer. Try to verify that the names and addresses of the computers that you want to reach are in your /etc/hosts file or that your DNS server is accessible. Next, confirm that the names and IP addresses for the other computers you are trying to reach are correct (the IP addresses are the most critical).

Is your Ethernet connection up?

Using the ip command, you can determine whether your Ethernet and other network interfaces are up and running. Type the following command:

```
# ip -s link
```

The output that appears is similar to the following:

```
1: lo: <LOOPBACK,UP,LOWER_UP> mtu 16436 qdisc noqueue state UNKNOWN
    link/loopback 00:00:00:00:00:00 brd 00:00:00:00:00:00
    RX: bytes   packets  errors   dropped overrun mcast
    1756        20       0        0       0       0
    TX: bytes   packets  errors   dropped carrier collsns
```

```
         1756        20       0       0       0       0
2: eth0: <BROADCAST,MULTICAST,UP,LOWER_UP> mtu 1500 qdisc pfifo_fast
state UP qlen 1000
    link/ether 00:11:11:4c:dc:0f brd ff:ff:ff:ff:ff:ff
    RX: bytes  packets  errors  dropped overrun mcast
    672375007  912637   0       0       0       55
    TX: bytes  packets  errors  dropped carrier collsns
    51041835   743940   0       0       0       0
```

In this example, two network interfaces are on the current computer. The second section shows your Ethernet interface (eth0) and its Ethernet hardware address, and that it is UP. The next lines provide information on packets that have been sent, along with the number of errors and collisions that have occurred.

Note

The lo entry is for loopback. This enables you to run TCP/IP commands on your local system without having a physical network up and running. ∎

If your eth0 interface does not have the UP flag, it may still be configured properly, but not running at the moment. Try to start the eth0 interface by typing the following:

```
# ip link set eth0 up
```

After this, type **ip addr** to see if eth0 is now UP and has the correct IP settings. If it is, it may be that eth0 is simply not configured to start automatically at boot time. You can change it so Ethernet starts at boot time (which I recommend), using the Network Configuration window described earlier in this chapter.

Tip

If your network interfaces are not running at all, try to start them from the network initialization script. This interface reads parameters and basically runs ip for all network interfaces on your computer. Type the following to restart your network:

```
# service network restart ∎
```

Another way to see statistics for your Ethernet driver is to list the contents of the process pseudo file system for network devices. To do that, type the following:

```
# cat /proc/net/dev
```

The output should look like this:

```
Inter-|   Receive                                           |Transmit
 face  |bytes packets errs drop fifo frame compressed multicast|bytes
    lo: 5362    64   0   0   0    0       0        5362    64   0   0   0   0
  sit0:    0     0   0   0   0    0       0           0     0   0   0   0   0
  eth0: 3083    35   0   0   0    0       0        3876    31   0   0   0   0
```

The output is a bit hard to read. (This book isn't wide enough to show it without wrapping around, so the output was truncated at the right.) With this output, you can see Receive and Transmit statistics for each interface. This output also indicates how many Receive and Transmit errors occurred in communication. (Transmit information is cut off in this example.)

The GNOME netspeed applet, available starting with Fedora 14, provides a nicely formatted view of your network interface's performance. This applet can show a graph of network activity for a particular interface such as your wireless card. It also provides a list on the GNOME panel, showing the amount of data sent and received over the network.

To install this applet, you need to install the gnome-applet-netspeed package. Once installed, add the Network Monitor applet to a GNOME panel. Right-click on the applet to see the menu, which enables you to select the interface to view as well as see a graph of the data (choose Device Details to see the data graph).

For a more detailed look at your network, you can use the Wireshark window. Wireshark is described in the section "Watching LAN traffic with Wireshark" later in this chapter.

Troubleshooting a wireless LAN

If you set up your two (or more) wireless LAN cards to enable Fedora systems to communicate, and they are not communicating, you can troubleshoot the problem in several different ways.

Checking wireless settings

You can use the `iwlist` and `iwconfig` commands to check your wireless settings. The `iwconfig` command provides a quick overview of your wireless settings, while the `iwlist` command shows you information about parameters that you specify.

Use the `iwconfig` command, along with the name of the wireless LAN interface, to see information about that interface. For example, if the wireless interface were eth1, you could type the following:

```
# iwconfig eth1
eth1    IEEE 802.11-DS  ESSID:"Homelan"  Nickname:"pine"
        Mode:Ad-Hoc  Frequency:2.412GHz  Cell: 02:02:2D:2D:3B:30
        Bit Rate=11Mb/s   Tx-Power=15 dBm   Sensitivity:1/3
        RTS thr:off   Fragment thr:off
        Encryption key:7365-6375-31
        Power Management:off
        Link Quality:0/92  Signal level:-102 dBm  Noise level:-102 dBm
        Rx invalid nwid:0  invalid crypt:0  invalid misc:0
```

With `iwconfig`, you can see details about the wireless aspects of the Ethernet interface. In this example, the network name (ESSID) is Homelan, and the station name (Nickname) is pine. The interface is operating in Ad hoc mode on channel 1 (frequency of 2.412 GHz). Transmission rates are at the maximum speed of 11 Mbps. The encryption key that must be used by every node the card connects with is 7365-6375-31. Other settings describe the link and signal quality.

You can use the `iwlist` command to request specific information about the wireless LAN interface. The syntax is to follow the `iwlist` command with the interface name and the information you are interested in. For example:

```
# iwlist eth1 freq
eth1      14 channels in total; available frequencies :
          Channel 01 : 2.412 GHz
          Channel 02 : 2.417 GHz
          Channel 03 : 2.422 GHz
          Channel 04 : 2.427 GHz
          Channel 05 : 2.432 GHz
          Channel 06 : 2.437 GHz
          Channel 07 : 2.442 GHz
          Channel 08 : 2.447 GHz
          Channel 09 : 2.452 GHz
          Channel 10 : 2.457 GHz
          Channel 11 : 2.457 GHz
          Channel 12 : 2.457 GHz
          Channel 13 : 2.457 GHz
          Channel 14 : 2.462 GHz
          Current Frequency:2.412GHz (Channel 1)
```

The `freq` parameter displays the frequencies (and channels) available for communication. Note that all the available frequencies are in the 2.4 GHz range. The `rate` parameter displays the transmission rates available for the wireless interface:

```
# iwlist eth1 rate
eth1      6 available bit-rates :
          1Mb/s
          2Mb/s
          5.5Mb/s
          11Mb/s
          58Mb/s
          39.5Mb/s
          Current Bit Rate=54Mb/s
```

You can see that 1, 2, 5.5, 11, 58, and 39.5 Mbps rates are available for the current interface. The `key` parameter lets you see the encryption keys available with the interface:

```
# iwlist eth1 key
eth1      2 key sizes : 40, 104bits
          4 keys available :
                [1] 7365-6375-31 (40 bits)
                [2] off
                [3] off
                [4] off
          Current Transmit Key: [1]
```

It also shows the key sizes currently available. Because the card reflected in the preceding example supports 64- and 128-bit encryption, the key sizes available are 40 and 104 bits. (The encryption algorithm automatically generates the last 24 bits of each key.)

If you are troubleshooting your wireless LAN connection, some settings are more likely than others to cause problems. It is important to set the following wireless LAN settings properly — if you don't, they may prevent your network from working:

- **Network ID (ESSID)** — You may not be able to communicate among peer computers if the Network ID, also called network name or ESSID, doesn't match each of them. Network IDs are case sensitive — for example, Mylan is not the same as MyLAN.

- **Encryption key** — Having encryption keys that don't match is like trying to log in to Linux with the wrong password. Check that all nodes are using the same key. (If nodes were unable to connect, check the encryption key first because typing long hexadecimal keys can be prone to error.)

- **Mode** — If you are communicating through an access point, your mode should be set to Managed and you must provide the MAC address for that access point. In most single-cell networks, you should set all nodes to Ad hoc. The Ad hoc mode allows all nodes to communicate directly to each other as peers.

- **Channel or frequency** — The channel and frequency options are just two different means of setting the same value. For example, setting the channel to 1 is the same as setting the frequency to 2.412G (GHz). Ensure that the nodes on your network are able to communicate on the same frequency.

Checking TCP/IP

To ensure that your wireless LAN is communicating with its peers, use the `ping` command (described earlier in this chapter). If you believe that your cards are working properly but the `ping` command continues to give you a `Network Unreachable` message, you may have a problem with your TCP/IP configuration. Check the following from the Network Configuration window:

- **IP address** — Know the correct IP address of the peer you are trying to reach.

- **Hostname** — If you ping the peer computer by name, make sure that your computer can properly resolve that name into the correct IP address, or have the peer's hostname and IP address properly listed in the `/etc/hosts` file locally. The former option will probably require that you have one or more DNS servers identified to resolve the name.

If you can reach another computer on the wireless LAN but not computers outside of that LAN (such as Internet addresses), confirm that you have properly identified your gateway location. If the gateway address is correct, and you can reach that gateway, the gateway itself might not be configured to allow packet forwarding.

Note

On the computer that is acting as a gateway from your wireless network to the Internet, you need to turn on IP packet forwarding. Change the value of `net.ipv4.ip_forward` **to 1 in** `/etc/sysctl.conf`**. Open that file as the root user with a text editor and change the line as follows:**

```
net.ipv4.ip_forward = 1 ■
```

If any of the preceding information needed to be changed and you changed it, restart the wireless LAN interface. One way to do that is to restart the network interface as follows:

```
# service network restart
```

Adapting to poor reception

Your wireless LAN might be working fine while your two wireless computers are sitting on the same desk; but if performance degrades when you separate the computers, you may need to identify any potential obstructions. Then you must decide how to get around them. For desktop systems, a small indoor antenna can bring the signal out from under a desk or out of a closet. For adjacent buildings, a roof antenna might be the answer.

In cities or other congested areas, many people and pieces of equipment can be competing for the 2.4 GHz range. If applicable, try moving a microwave oven or high-end remote phone that might be interfering with your wireless LAN. These settings might help adapt to poor reception:

- **Reduce transmission rate** — Instead of using 11 Mbps, you can explicitly ramp down to 5.5, 2, or 1 Mbps. Slower rates can mean more efficient operation in noisy places.

- **Use smaller fragment sizes** — Although there is more total overhead associated with transmitting packets broken up into smaller fragments, they can often provide better overall performance in noisy environments. Change the `frag` parameter to reduce fragment sizes.

- **Use different frequencies** — By specifically requesting that certain frequencies (or channels) be used for transmission, you can avoid congested channels.

Using debugging tools

Because most wireless LAN cards were created for Windows systems, debugging tools from the manufacturers are available only on those systems. If your computer is a dual-boot system (Windows and Linux), try booting in Windows to test the quality of your wireless network.

In Fedora, you can use many of the tools you use for wired Ethernet networks and other TCP/IP network interfaces. Here are a couple of examples:

- **Wireshark** — The Wireshark window (type **wireshark** as the root user from a terminal window) enables you to watch Ethernet frames being sent and received by your wireless LAN interface. For example, the output of Wireshark can tell you whether a failed connection reflects a lack of reception or rejected requests. (Wireshark is described in the next section.)

- **/var/log/messages** — When the wireless LAN interface starts, messages related to that startup are sent to the `/var/log/messages` file. In some cases, these messages reflect improper options being set for the wireless LAN module.

Watching LAN traffic with Wireshark

To truly understand the coming and going of information on your LAN, you need a tool that analyzes network traffic. Wireshark (formerly called Ethereal) is a graphical tool for capturing and displaying the packets sent across your network interfaces. Using filters to select particular hosts, protocols, or direction of data, you can monitor activities and track problems on your network.

In addition to reading Ethernet packet data gathered by Wireshark, the Wireshark window can be used to display captured files from LanAlyzer, Sniffer, Microsoft Network Monitor, Snoop, and a variety of other tools. These files can be read from their native formats or after being compressed with gzip (.gz).

Wireshark can track more than 100 packet types (representing different protocols). It can also display specific fields related to each protocol, such as various data sizes, source and destination addresses, port numbers, and other values.

To install Wireshark, type the following as root user:

```
# yum install wireshark-gnome
```

Starting Wireshark

To start Wireshark from the Applications menu, select Internet ⇨ Wireshark Network Analyzer. Alternately, type the following (as root user) from a terminal window:

```
# wireshark &
```

The Wireshark window appears. (If the `wireshark` command is not found, the package is probably not installed. You can install the `wireshark` and `wireshark-gnome` packages from the Internet by typing **yum install wireshark wireshark-gnome**, or you can use the `rpm` command to install them from the installation DVD.) Figure 14-8 shows the Wireshark interface while capturing network packets.

The primary function of Wireshark is to take a snapshot of the packets coming across your network interfaces and display that data in the Wireshark window. You can filter the data based on a variety of filter primitives. When the capture is done, you can step through and sort the data based on the values in different columns. Optionally, you can save the captured data to a file to study the data later.

FIGURE 14-8

Wireshark captures and displays packets on a network interface after you select which interface to monitor.

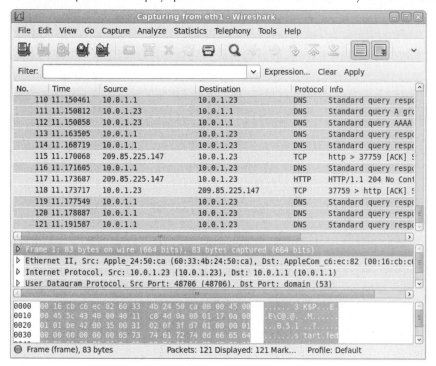

Tip

If you can't use Wireshark because you don't have a GUI available, you can use the `tcpdump` command from the shell. It is not as friendly as Wireshark, but it supports the same filtering syntax. Because `tcpdump` can produce a lot of output, you will probably want to use some form of filtering or direct the output of the command to a file. (Type `man tcpdump` for information on filter options.) ∎

Capturing Ethernet data

With the Wireshark window displayed, you can capture data relating to packet activities on any of your Ethernet network interfaces by doing the following:

1. Click Capture ➪ Interfaces. You will see a list of network interfaces available on your computer.

2. Click Options next to the interface you want to capture from (probably `eth0` for a wired Internet or `wlan0` for a wireless interface). A Wireshark Capture Options window appears.

3. Choose options relating to what data is captured:

- **Capture packets in promiscuous mode** — Any computer on a LAN can see all packets that traverse the LAN, except those packets intended for switched portions of the LAN. With this on, all packets seen by your network interface are captured. With this mode off, only packets intended specifically for your network interface (including multicast and broadcast packets) are captured. In other words, turn on promiscuous mode to monitor the whole LAN; turn it off to monitor only your interface.

- **Limit each packet to** — Limits the size of each packet to a maximum number of bytes

- **Capture Filter** — This optional field lets you enter a filter that can be used to filter capture data. You can type in filters individually or click the Filter button to use a filter you have stored earlier.

Cross-Reference
Filtering is one of the most powerful features of Wireshark. See the sidebar "Using Wireshark Filters" for more information on how to enter filters into the Filter field. ■

- **Capture file(s)** — Enter the name of a file in which you want to capture the data gathered. If you don't enter a filename, the information is displayed on the Wireshark window without being saved to a file.

- **Ring buffer (Number of files)** — Select this option to have packets captured in a set number of files. To use this feature, you must also specify a filename (such as /tmp/abc) and a file size. Data will be put into files you chose, named from the root filename you have provided. Once the files fill up, Wireshark will go back and write to the first file again and continue filling up the files. When you stop the capture, you are left with the number of capture files you chose, containing the most recent data.

- **Update list of packets in real time** — Select this option to have packet information appear in the Wireshark window as each packet crosses the interface. With this option off, the information is displayed after you stop capturing it.

- **Automatic scrolling in live capture** — If you are updating packets in real time, select this option to have packet information scroll up after the screen fills. With this off, you see only the first screen of packets and have to scroll down manually to see the rest.

- **Hide capture info dialog** — This prevents the Capture Info box from appearing to display the number and types of packets being captured.

- **Stop Capture after . . .** — By default, Wireshark will capture data from the moment you click OK until you click Stop (with this value set to 0). Alternately, select one of the three Stop Capture fields and type a number to capture only that number of packets; a number to stop capture after a set number of bytes, kilobytes, megabytes, or gigabytes of data; or a number to indicate the number of seconds, minutes, hours or days to capture data. When the limit is reached, capture stops and the file is stored in /tmp/etherXXXX???????, where ??????? is replaced by a string of characters.

- **Enable MAC/network/transport name resolution** — With any of these three options on, names are displayed instead of addresses (if possible). For example, for transport names, Source and Destination IP addresses are displayed as hostnames (if they can be resolved from /etc/hosts or DNS). With this option off, IP addresses appear in the Source and Destination columns.

4. Click Start. Wireshark begins gathering data on packets encountered by the interface. The Wireshark Capture window displays information on how many incoming and outgoing packets have crossed the interface since the capture began. The number of packets that are associated with each protocol Wireshark monitors is displayed, along with the percentage of total packets associated with each protocol.

5. Click Stop (or the capture might stop automatically, if it has reached a size or time limit set by you). The snapshot of data you just took will appear on the Wireshark window. Packets are displayed in the order in which they traversed the interface.

6. You can choose to save the data to your hard disk by selecting File ⇨ Save As.

At this point, you can start interpreting the data.

Using Wireshark Filters

If you are monitoring a busy server or a busy network, Wireshark can gather so much data that it can become almost unusable. If you know what you are looking for, however, you can filter what packets are captured based on values you enter.

Filters in Wireshark are implemented using the pcap library (type **man pcap-filter** to read about it). The filter expressions you can use with Wireshark are described on the tcpdump man page. Here are some examples of filters that you could enter into the Capture Filter dialog when you capture Ethernet data with Wireshark:

```
host 10.0.0.15
```

Use the host primitive to capture only packets that are either to or from a particular host computer (by IP address or hostname). By preceding host with src or des, you can indicate that you want only packages sent from a particular source or to a particular destination host.

```
tcp port 80
```

You can enter a protocol name (such as tcp, ether, udp, or ip) to limit captured packets to those assigned to that protocol. As shown in the previous example, with tcp you could also indicate a port number (such as 80, to monitor traffic to and from your Web server).

You can filter for certain special activities on the network, using the gateway, broadcast, or multicast primitives. Entering gateway host lets you find packets sent to a gateway host that is neither a source nor a destination for the packet (which is determined because the Ethernet address doesn't match either of those IP addresses). Enter ether broadcast to monitor broadcast packets on your Ethernet network, such as announcements from name servers announcing availability. Likewise, you could filter for multicast packets on ether or ip protocols (ether multicast).

Interpreting captured Ethernet data

With the captured data displayed in your Wireshark window, you can get a detailed view of the network traffic that your computer is exposed to. The Wireshark window is divided into three parts: The top part contains a scrollable list of packets; the protocol tree for the current packet appears in the middle part of the display; a hexadecimal dump of the entire contents of the packet appears in the bottom part.

You can sort data in different ways from the top part of the window by clicking the column headings. To see more details relating to different items in the protocol tree for the current packet, click the triangle-shaped icon next to the protocol information that interests you.

The following tips will help you interpret what the data means:

- The Source and Destination columns show where each packet came from and where it went. If the Enable name resolution option is on (which is recommended), the hostname associated with IP packets is displayed. This makes it much easier to see which computer is communicating with you.

- To see all activity associated with a particular location, click the Source or Destination column. Packets will be sorted alphabetically, making it easy for you to scroll through the activity list for the location that interests you.

- If you are trying to debug a particular feature, click the Protocol column to gather activities based on protocol. For example, if you were trying to get Samba to work (for Windows file or printer sharing), sorting by protocol would enable you to see all NetBIOS and NBNS (NetBIOS name server) requests that arrived at your computer.

- To mark a packet of interest to you, click the middle mouse button. This will highlight the packet, making it easy to find later. (If you have only a two-button mouse, and you indicated during installation that it should emulate a three-button mouse, you can click both mouse buttons together to emulate the middle mouse button.)

The Info column provides details about the intention of the packet. For example, you can see the type of service that was requested (such as HTTP for Web service or FTP for file transfer). You can see what information is being broadcast and determine when attempts to find particular host computers are failing. If you believe someone is using your network improperly, you can see which sites they are visiting and the services they are requesting.

Another handy option is one that lets you follow the stream of TCP information. Click Analyze ⇨ Follow TCP Stream. The Contents of TCP stream window that appears enables you to see the total output of the HTTP, SMTP, or other protocol being used. Of course, viewing data being transmitted by protocols is useful only if it is in plain text. Although an increasing number of encrypted data and service requests makes it more difficult to debug using Wireshark, it also makes it harder for bad guys on your network to steal your data.

Summary

Linux is at its best when it is connected to a network. Configuring a LAN enables you to share resources with other computers in your home or organization. These resources can include files, printers, CD-ROM drives, and backup media.

In this chapter you learned how to connect to wired and wireless networks and create a LAN with a Fedora system on one of the computers on that LAN. You should also be able to determine the kind of equipment you need to obtain, and the layout (topology) of the network. In particular, the chapter describes how to use NetworkManager for making network connections, and Network Configuration for manually configuring your network interfaces.

If something isn't working with your network interface to the LAN, you can use utilities such as ip to confirm that your Ethernet interface is configured and running properly. You can also verify that Linux found and installed the proper driver for your Ethernet card. After an Ethernet interface is working, you can use the Wireshark window to monitor the packets coming and going across the interface between your computer and the network.

If a wired network is not possible or convenient, Linux includes support for wireless LAN cards. A wireless LAN can be an effective means of extending your network to areas that are difficult or expensive to reach with wired connections. Using ndiswrapper, you can also get drivers working for many Windows wireless cards.

Connecting to
the Internet

This chapter demonstrates how to connect Fedora to a TCP/IP-based network, such as the Internet, a private LAN, or a company WAN. The differences in how you connect have more to do with the network medium you use (that is, telephone lines, LAN router, and so on) than they do with whether you are connecting to the public Internet or a company's private network.

The instructions in this chapter build on the procedures in Chapter 14 for creating your own Local Area Network (LAN) by describing how to connect your LAN to the Internet. For those who want to connect a LAN to the Internet, the chapter describes how to use Linux as a router and set it up to do IP masquerading (to protect your private LAN addresses). It also explains how to configure Linux as a proxy server, including how to configure client applications such as Firefox.

Connecting Your LAN to the Internet

The users on your LAN are happy that they can share files and printers with one another. With your users already connected on a LAN, the next logical step is to set up a connection to the Internet that everyone can share. The advantages of doing this are obvious:

- **Central maintenance** — If information related to your Internet connection changes (such as your cable provider or IP addresses), you can administer those changes in one location instead of having to change it on every computer.

- **Central security** — You can better control the Internet traffic that comes into and goes out of your network.

The procedures in this section assume that you have already set up a LAN, as described in Chapter 14. It is also assumed that you have an outgoing connection from your Linux system to the Internet through which all traffic between the computers on your LAN and the Internet can pass. That outgoing connection is typically a wired or wireless LAN (WLAN) card connected to a DSL router, cable modem, or other LAN. This section describes two ways to set up your Linux system so clients on the LAN can access the Internet:

- **As a router** — If you configure Linux as a router, it can route IP packets from clients on the LAN to the Internet through the dial-up connection.

- **As a proxy server** — You can configure Linux as a proxy server. In this way, client computers on your LAN can access the Internet as though the connection were coming from the Linux computer.

Setting Up Linux as a Router

There are several different ways to set up routing from your LAN to the Internet. You can have a dedicated router or you can have a computer already connected to your LAN that will act as a router. This section describes how to use your Linux system as a router.

A computer may have several network interfaces, such as a loopback, an Ethernet LAN, a direct line to another computer, or a dial-up interface. For a client computer to use a router to reach the Internet, it may have a private IP address assigned to it on the LAN. A connection to a routing computer would act as the gateway to all other addresses.

Here's an example of Linux being used as a router between a LAN and the Internet:

- The Linux system has at least two network interfaces: one to the office LAN and one to the Internet. The interface to the Internet may be a DSL or cable modem connection.

- Packets on the LAN that are not addressed to a known computer on the LAN are forwarded to the router (that is, the Linux system acting as a router). Therefore, each client identifies that Linux system as the gateway system.

- The Linux router/firewall is set up to receive packets from the local LAN, then forwards those packets to its other interface (possibly a DSL or cable modem to the Internet). If the LAN uses private IP addresses, the firewall is also configured to use IP masquerading or network address translation (NAT).

The following sections describe how to set up the Linux router, as well as the client computers from your LAN (Linux and MS Windows clients) that will use this router. Using Linux as a router also provides an excellent opportunity to improve the security of your Internet connection by setting up a firewall to filter traffic and hide the identity of computers on your LAN (IP masquerading).

Configuring the Linux router

To configure your Linux computer as a router, you need to have completed a few tasks:

- **Connect to your LAN** — Add a network card and configure the computers on your LAN (as described in Chapter 14).

- **Connect to the Internet** — Set up a connection from your Linux computer to your ISP. Your ISP typically supplies instructions and equipment to do this.

- **Configure your Linux computer as a router** — See the rest of this section.

Selecting IP addresses

The type of IP addresses you are using on your LAN will have an impact on a couple of steps in this procedure. Here are the differences:

- **Private IP addresses** — If the computers on your LAN use private IP addresses (described in Chapter 14), you need to set up Linux as a firewall to do IP masquerading or NAT (as described in Chapter 13). Because those numbers are private, they must be hidden from the Internet when the Linux router forwards their requests. To the outside world, packets forwarded with IP masquerading or NAT look as though they came from the Linux computer forwarding the packets.

- **Valid IP addresses** — If your LAN uses addresses that were officially assigned by your ISP or other registration authority, you don't need to do IP masquerading or NAT. (Actually, for any machine you want to expose to the world, such as a public server, you will want to have a valid, public IP address.)

In most cases, when you are not configuring the computers on your LAN as servers, you will probably want to use private IP addresses.

Enabling forwarding and masquerading

With your Linux computer's LAN and Internet interfaces in place, use the following procedure to set up Linux as a router. After this procedure is completed, any client computer on your LAN can identify your Linux computer as its gateway so it can use Linux to get to the Internet.

1. Open the /etc/sysconfig/network file in a text editor as the root user. Then add either a default gateway or default gateway device as described in the following bullets.

   Your default gateway is where traffic destined for networks outside of your own is sent. This is where you would identify your Internet connection. Here is how you choose which one to enter:

   - **Default gateway** — If you use a static IP address to reach the Internet, enter that IP address here. For example, if your Internet connection goes through a DSL modem connected to your NIC at address 192.168.0.1, enter that address as follows:

   GATEWAY=192.168.0.1

- **Default gateway device** — If you reach the Internet using a dynamic address that is assigned when you connect to a particular interface, enter that interface here. For example, if you have a dial-up interface to the Internet on the first PPP device, you would enter ppp0 as the default gateway device as follows:

  ```
  GATEWAYDEV=ppp0
  ```

  When you are done, the contents of this file should look similar to the following:

  ```
  NETWORKING=yes
  HOSTNAME='maple.handsonhistory.com'
  DOMAINNAME='handsonhistory.com'
  #GATEWAY=
  GATEWAYDEV=ppp0
  ```

  In this case, the computer is configured to route packets over a dial-up connection to the Internet (ppp0). If the gateway device were an Ethernet NIC, instead of ppp0 you would probably use eth0 or eth1 (depending on which of your NICs were connected to your DSL, cable modem, or other device set up to reach your ISP).

2. Turn on IP packet forwarding. One way to do this is to change the value of net.ipv4 .ip_forward to 1 in the /etc/sysctl.conf file. Open that file as root user with any text editor and change the line to appear as follows:

   ```
   net.ipv4.ip_forward = 1
   ```

Note

You can restart your network for this change to take effect (with the command service network restart). To have the change take place without a network restart, run this command:

```
echo 1 > /proc/sys/net/ipv4/ip_forward
```

As an alternative, you could run this command as root:

```
sysctl -p    ■
```

3. If the computers on your LAN have valid IP addresses, skip ahead to the "Configuring network clients" section. If you have configured your computers to have private IP addresses, continue with this procedure.

Caution

The lines shown in Step 4 for configuring your iptables firewall to do IP masquerading should be used in addition to your other firewall rules. They do not, in themselves, represent a secure firewall, but merely describe how to add masquerading to your firewall. See Chapter 13 for details about how to configure a more complete firewall and when to use NAT versus IP masquerading. ■

4. To get IP masquerading going on your Linux router, you need to define which addresses will be masqueraded and forwarded, using iptables.

The following examples assume that you are masquerading all computers on your private LAN 10.0.0 (that is, 10.0.0.1, 10.0.0.2, and so on) and routing packets from that LAN to the Internet over your second Ethernet interface (eth1).

Type the following as root user:

```
# iptables -t nat -A POSTROUTING -o eth1 -j MASQUERADE
# iptables -A FORWARD -s 10.0.0.0/24 -j ACCEPT
# iptables -A FORWARD -d 10.0.0.0/24 -j ACCEPT
# iptables -A FORWARD -s ! 10.0.0.0/24 -j DROP
```

The previous commands turn on masquerading in the NAT table by appending a POSTROUTING rule (-A POSTROUTING) for all outgoing packets on the second Ethernet interface (-o eth1). The next two lines accept forwarding for all packets from (-s) and to (-d) the 10.0.0 network (10.0.0.0/24). The last line drops packets that don't come from the 10.0.0 network.

The previous lines add rules to your running iptables firewall in the Linux kernel. To make the current rules permanent, save them as follows:

```
# service iptables save
```

This copies all the current rules to the /etc/ sysconfig /iptables file, from which the rules are read each time you reboot your system. If the new rules don't work, just copy the iptables.save file back to the original iptables file.

5. At this point, you may want to restart your network as follows:

```
# service network restart
```

6. Then, to reload your firewall rules, type the following:

```
# service iptables restart
```

7. To see if your new rules have taken effect, type **iptables -L**. To view NAT rules, type **iptables -L -t nat**.

At this point, your Linux system is configured to route packets from the IP addresses you configured to another network (typically the Internet).

Configuring network clients

In this example, there are a variety of Linux and Windows operating system clients on a LAN. One Linux computer has a connection to the Internet and is set up to act as a router between the Internet and the other computers on the LAN (as described previously). To be able to reach computers on the Internet, each client must be able to do the following:

- Resolve the names it requests (for example, www.redhat.com) into IP addresses.
- Find a route from the local system to the remote system, using its network interfaces.

Each Linux client computer determines another computer's address based on the contents of the /etc/nsswitch.conf, /etc/host.conf, /etc/hosts, and /etc/resolv.conf files. The contents of the host.conf file, by default, are as follows:

```
multi on
order hosts,bind
```

The order setting tells your system to check for any hostnames (hosts) that you request by first checking the contents of the /etc/hosts file and then checking with name servers that are identified in the /etc/resolv.conf file. In our case, we will put the addresses of the few hosts we know about on our private network (whether on the LAN, direct connection, or other network interface) in the /etc/hosts file. Then, the system knows to resolve addresses using a DNS server (bind) based on addresses of name servers added to the /etc/resolv.conf file.

The /etc/nsswitch.conf file provides similar functionality for hostnames as well as other information. Be sure to verify that both /etc/host.conf and nsswitch.conf have the correct settings for your environment. Similar to /etc/host.conf, hostname resolution first checks /etc/hosts (files) and then /etc/resolv.conf (dns). The relevant line for hostname resolution in /etc/nsswitch.conf is as follows:

```
hosts: files mdns4_minimal dns
```

Next, each client machine must know how to get to the Internet. If you have more than one or two computers on your local network, you could configure your router as a Dynamic Host Configuration Protocol (DHCP) server. That server can provide the address of your router, client IP addresses, and other information to each client.

Cross-Reference
See Chapter 22 for information on setting up a DHCP server. ∎

Whether you set up a DHCP server or configure each client separately, you need to identify the default route (sometimes called a *gateway*) for each client. To add a default route directly to a client Linux system, do the following:

1. Set the default route to point to the router. This entails setting the GATEWAY or GATEWAYDEV value in the /etc/sysconfig/network file as described in the previous procedure. (This time, the address will point to the LAN interface of the router.) For example:

```
GATEWAY=10.0.0.1
```

2. Restart your network interfaces by typing the following as root user:

```
# service network restart
```

3. When the computer comes back up, type the following:

```
# ip route
10.0.0.0/24 dev eth0  proto kernel  scope link  src 10.0.0.2
default via 10.0.0.1 dev eth0
```

You can see that the default gateway was set to the host at the IP address 10.0.0.1 on the eth0 Ethernet interface. Assuming that router is configured to route your packets to the Internet, your Linux client is set up to use that router to find any addresses for which it doesn't have a specific route.

Configuring a Virtual Private Network Connection

There are several ways to go about setting up virtual private network (VPN) connections in Linux:

- **Internet Protocol SECurity (IPsec)** — IPsec is a standard developed by the Internet Engineering Task Force (IETF) as the required method of encryption when the IP version 6 becomes the standard Internet protocol (right now IPv4 is the standard in North America and Europe). There are several implementations of IPsec over IPv4 in Linux these days. Linux includes IPsec support by including the Linux 2.6 kernel and offering an administrative interface for configuring it (via the ipsec-tools package).

- **PPP over OpenSSH** — With this method, using software already in Linux, you can configure a PPP interface (as you would a regular dial-up connection) to use SSH to encrypt all data that goes across the PPP interface. While this method is not too difficult to configure, it can provide poor performance. To see how to create a PPP over OpenSSH VPN, refer to the VPN PPP-SSH HOW-TO (search www.tldp.org).

- **OpenVPN** — With OpenVPN (http://openvpn.net), you can use all OpenSSL encryption and authentication features to create a tunnel to remote systems over public networks (such as the Internet). An OpenVPN package for Fedora is available from the Fedora software repository (type **yum install openvpn**).

- **Openswan** — The Openswan project (www.openswan.org) produces an implementation of IPsec that was originally based on code from the FreeS/WAN project (www.freeswan.org). Openswan is included in the Fedora software repository (to install it, type **yum install openswan**).

- **Crypto IP Encapsulation (CIPE)** — Using this method, IP packets are routed across selected IP interfaces as encrypted UDP packets. CIPE is easy to set up and carries less overhead than PPP over OpenSSH, so you should get better performance. One drawback is that because it is not a standard VPN, CIPE is not available on all platforms and was dropped from Fedora.

Chapter 14 explains the basic idea behind using a VPN and describes how to configure NetworkManager to communicate with a remote openvpn server. This chapter provides an overview of the features and tools in IPsec and a detailed description of configuring an OpenVPN server in Fedora.

Understanding IPsec

To provide more secure transmission of TCP/IP data in the new Internet Protocol version 6 (IPv6) standard, developers of that standard created the Internet Protocol Security (IPsec) architecture. With IPsec, encrypted communication is possible right at the IP level, and methods to provide access control, data integrity, authentication, and traffic flow confidentiality are standardized.

In practical terms, organizations with computers that need to communicate on public networks in ways that are secure and private can create VPNs with IPsec. Unlike other VPN implementations (such as CIPE), which require a manual exchange of keys to work, IPsec offers an automated way to create security associations between communications endpoints and managing keys.

With slow adoption of IPv6 in the United States and other places, IPsec has been included (backported) into the IPv4 protocol, which is still the most common IP version used on the Internet. That backport was added into the IP networking stack included with the Linux 2.6 kernel that comes with Fedora starting with version 2. The Internet standard RFC 2401 document describes the IPsec architecture.

Using IPsec protocols

IPsec consists of two primary protocols: Authentication Header (AH) and Encapsulating Security Payload (ESP). Look in the /etc/protocols file and you'll see that AH is assigned to protocol number 51 and ESP is assigned to protocol number 50.

To authenticate peer computers and exchange symmetric keys, IPsec uses the Internet Key Exchange (IKE) protocol. At the beginning of communication between two host computers using IPsec, IKE does the following:

- Authenticates that the peer computers are who they say they are
- Negotiates security associations
- Chooses secret symmetric keys (using Diffie-Hellmann key exchange)

The security associations established by IKE are stored in a security association database (SAD). A security association holds information about the communications endpoints (possibly public Internet IP addresses), whether AH or Encapsulating Security Payload (ESP) protocols are being used with IPsec, and the secret key/algorithm being used.

IPsec itself has two possible modes of operation: tunnel mode and transport mode:

- **Tunnel mode** — The entire IP datagram is encapsulated into the new IP datagram by IPsec. This protects both the data and the control information, such as the source and destination addresses, from being seen by anyone except the communications endpoint that is allowed to decrypt the communication.

- **Transport mode** — Only the data (the payload intended for the client receiving the data) is encrypted. To do this, IPsec inserts its own header between the Internet Protocol header and the protocol header for the upper layer.

Included in the protocol header of each packet transmitted is information referred to as Hash Message Authentication Codes (HMAC). Including these codes with transmitted data in IPsec offers the following advantages:

- **Data integrity** — By using a hash algorithm to create a hash from a secret key and the data in the IP datagram, the resulting HMAC is added to the IPsec protocol header. The receiver can then confirm that the HMAC is correct using its own copy of that secret key. Supported authentication algorithms include MD5, SHA1, and SHA2 (256, 384, and 512).

- **Data privacy** — By using symmetric encryption algorithms (such as DES, NULL, AES, 3DES, and Blowfish), datagrams are encrypted so their contents cannot be seen by outsiders.

By recording a sequence of packets during data communications, an intruder can attempt denial-of-service attacks by replaying that sequence of packets. IPsec combats that type of attack by accepting packets that are within a "sliding window" of sequence numbers or higher. Packets using older sequence numbers are dropped.

Using IPsec in Fedora

Using IPsec in Fedora, you can configure VPNs between Fedora and other systems that support IPsec. Hosts at both ends of the IPsec VPN must be configured in the same way. In fact, you may have the best results by using the same operating system version and IPsec software. In Fedora, you have the choice of using OpenVPN, Openswan, or IPsec-Tools.

By default, the necessary modules to use IPsec are already available in Fedora. If you choose to use IPsec, all the tools you need to configure a VPN are contained in the ipsec-tools packages. You set up IPsec in the kernel in much the same way that you set up firewalls with iptables: You run commands that load settings into the kernel, either from command-line options (standard input) or from a file containing your preconfigured options.

The commands you use to set up a VPN with IPsec include the following:

- `setkey` — Use this command to load the data about your VPN connections into the kernel. It can add, change, flush, or dump information in the Security Association

Database (SAD) and the Security Policy Database (SPD) for your IPsec VPN. Typically, you would create a configuration file in the format described on the `setkey` man page, and then run `setkey -f filename` to load that data into the kernel.

- `racoon` — Use this command to create IKE security associations between host computers communicating together over an IPsec VPN. Security data are loaded into `racoon` from the `/etc/racoon/racoon.conf` file (unless that file is overridden from the `racoon` command line using the `-f` option).

Sample configuration files to use with `setkey` are available from the IPsec-HOWTO (`www.ipsec-howto.org`). A sample `racoon.conf` file is included with the ipsec-tools package (in the `/usr/share/doc/ipsec-tools-*` directory). For an in-depth description of the tools used with IPsec, refer to the IPsec-Tools website (`http://ipsec-tools.sourceforge.net/`).

Configuring an OpenVPN Server

VPNs were created to enable computer systems to have secure connections using insecure public networks. Setting up an OpenVPN server at your place of business can provide an inexpensive way for branch offices or telecommuters to securely access your company's private network.

Because VPN technologies, such as OpenVPN, provide encrypted connections between two transport-level network interfaces, any applications communicating between those two systems are secure. This is unlike user-space applications, such as SSL, that must implement features from every application they want to offer to users.

For Linux systems, OpenVPN provides a very good option for configuring a VPN server. The following are some of OpenVPN's features:

- A single port can provide access to up to 128 clients.
- The server can control client setup, doing tasks such as pushing configuration data to clients through the VPN tunnel.
- You can use telnet to access the server.
- OpenVPN includes TUN/TAP virtual network interface drivers at the networking layer, with device names like `/dev/tunX` and `/dev/tapX`. Applications can use the TUN devices as a virtual point-to-point interface to VPN partner (routed mode). TAP devices provide a virtual Ethernet adapter, so daemons listening on TAP can capture Ethernet frames.

The OpenVPN procedure in this chapter describes how to set up an OpenVPN server. This includes the following:

- Setting up information needed to create certificate authority certificates and keys. In the process, you create a root RSA Private Key (`ca.key`) that you need to keep confidential and a root certificate (`ca.crt`) that you share.
- Setting up configuration files and starting the OpenVPN service.

To use OpenVPN in Fedora, you need have the openvpn package installed. If it is not yet installed, type the following:

```
# yum install openvpn
```

Before configuring OpenVPN

You need to make a few decisions before setting up your OpenVPN connection:

- **Do you want a public key infrastructure or static key?** If you have a single VPN client connection to a single server, you can use a static key. That way, you don't have to maintain a key infrastructure. See the OpenVPN HOWTO for more information:

  ```
  http://openvpn.net/index.php/open-source/documentation/howto.html
  ```

- **Will your VPN do routing or bridging?** Routing, whereby data is routed from the VPN server to the LAN (instead of just being passed through), is usually a better choice than bridging. Routing is easier to set up and provides more control for specific client features.

The following assumes you decided to set up a public key infrastructure and are using a routing OpenVPN server. For information on using OpenVPN to do bridging, refer to the OpenVPN FAQ (`http://openvpn.net/index.php/open-source/faq.html`).

Creating a public key infrastructure

Using certificates and private keys, you can create a safe environment for allowing multiple clients to access your private networks over the Internet. The following procedure is done on a Fedora system that doesn't necessarily have to be the same one that you use for your VPN server. In this example, however, the entire procedure is run on the OpenVPN server.

To begin setting up your public key infrastructure, open a terminal window as root and do the following:

1. **Copy the sample configuration files.**

   ```
   # cp -r /usr/share/openvpn/easy-rsa/ /etc/openvpn/
   # cd /etc/openvpn/easy-rsa/2.0
   ```

2. **Choose variables:** Edit the vars file (in this example, the vars file is located in /etc/openvpn/easy-rsa/2.0). Most of the defaults will work, as long as you work from this configuration directory. However, you need at least to set the key values that are placed in your certificate. Replace the examples in quotes with your own values:

   ```
   export KEY_COUNTRY="US"
   export KEY_PROVINCE="WI"
   ```

```
export KEY_CITY="Madison"
export KEY_ORG="Reedsburg-LUG"
export KEY_EMAIL="chris@linuxtoys.net"
```

In the `vars` file, you can also change such values as the default key size (1024) and days to certificate expiration (3650 days).

3. **Set variables.** Export the variables in the `vars` file to the current shell so they can be used by commands you run later:

```
# source ./vars
```

4. **Prepare to create new keys.** If there are any keys in your KEY_DIR directory (probably named keys/ in the current directory), this command removes them and creates `index.txt` and `serial` files in that directory:

```
# ./clean-all
```

Next you will create the server certificates and keys.

5. **Build root certificate authority certificate and key.** Run the following script, which in turn uses the `pkitool` command to create a 1024-bit RSA private key:

```
# ./build-ca
Generating a 1024 bit RSA private key
.....................++++++
....++++++
writing new private key to 'ca.key'
    .

    .

    .
Country Name (2 letter code) [US]:
State or Province Name (full name) [WI]:
Locality Name (eg, city) [Madison]:
Organization Name (eg, company) [Reedsburg-LUG]:
Organizational Unit Name (eg, section) []:
Common Name (eg, your name or your server's hostname) [Reedsburg-LUG CA]:
Email Address [chris@linuxtoys.net]:
```

You should have two new files in the keys directory. The `ca.key` file holds the private key and the `ca.crt` key holds the new certificate generated from your KEYS values.

6. **Create parameters for SSL/TLS.** Type the following to build the server-side Diffie-Hellman parameters needed for SSL/TLS connection:

```
# ./build-dh
Generating DH parameters, 1024 bit long safe prime, generator 2
This is going to take a long time
```

```
.....+....................+.........+
```
This creates a file named dh1024.pem in the keys directory.

7. **Create server keys and certificates.** Run the following command to create the keys and certificates needed on the OpenVPN server, replacing server1 with your server's hostname or other common name to identify it:

```
# ./build-key-server server1
Generating a 1024 bit RSA private key
..++++++
.....................++++++
writing new private key to 'server1.key'
    .

    .

    .
A challenge password []: chzypassw77
An optional company name []:
Using configuration from /etc/openvpn/easy-rsa/2.0/openssl.cnf
    .

    .

    .
Sign the certificate? [y/n]:y
1 out of 1 certificate requests certified, commit? [y/n]  y
Write out database with 1 new entries
Data Base Updated
```

The command just run produces the *server1*.crt, *server1*.csr, and *server1*.key files in the keys directory. The *server1*.key file must be kept secret! Next you need to create client certificates and keys for each client you want to connect to your OpenVPN server.

8. **Create client certificates and keys.** Run the build-key (or build-key-pass) script for every client that you want to use the OpenVPN server. Here is an example running the build-key script for a client named client01:

```
# ./build-key client01
    .

    .

    .
A challenge password []: my67ChvyB
An optional company name []:
Sign the certificate? [y/n] y
1 out of 1 certificate requests certified, commit? [y/n]  y
```

After you have run build-key for every client, you will have a crt (client01.crt), csr (client01.csr), and key (client01.key) file in the keys/ directory for each client. The next step is to ensure that each of those keys is transported to the appropriate computer.

For this example, we will copy the keys to a directory on the Fedora client machine we are call-ing client01 in the /etc/openvpn/keys/ directory on that machine. (See the section "Creating the OpenVPN client configuration" later in this chapter.)

Creating the OpenVPN server configuration

Before starting the OpenVPN service on the server, you need to create a server.conf file in the /etc/openvpn directory. You can do this by copying a sample server.conf file and editing it. Here is an example of one you can use:

```
# cd /usr/share/doc/openvpn-2.1.1/sample-config-files
# cp server.conf /etc/openvpn/
```

As root user, open the server.conf file in any text editor. This is an example for a multi-client server that is doing routing (not bridging). The locations of key files should match those you cre-ated earlier in this section. Many of the comments have been left out of this example, but you should read them in the server.conf file to guide your configuration.

```
port 1194
proto udp
dev tun

ca /etc/openvpn/easy-rsa/2.0/keys/ca.crt
cert /etc/openvpn/easy-rsa/2.0/keys/server1.crt
key /etc/openvpn/easy-rsa/2.0/keys/server1.key # This file should be kept secret
dh /etc/openvpn/easy-rsa/2.0/keys/dh1024.pem

server 10.8.0.0 255.255.255.0

keepalive 10 120
comp-lzo

persist-key
persist-tun

status openvpn-status.log

verb 3
```

In this configuration, the OpenVPN server listens on port 1194, UDP protocol, as a routing VPN server (dev tun). You can use a different port number to make the service more obscure, but the clients must use that port number as well. The private network that OpenVPN clients will be able to reach from this VPN connection is on the subnetwork 10.8.0 (identified by 10.8.0.0 255.255.255.0). With the configuration file completed, you can start the OpenVPN service on the server by typing the following:

```
# service openvpn start
```

The last step you need to do to make your OpenVPN server ready to accept connections is to open your firewall to accept connections on port 1194 and to allow your system to route packets for your private subnetwork. In this example, we used a private subnetwork with IP addresses 10.8.0.1 through 10.8.0.254. See "Securing Linux with the iptables Firewall" in Chapter 13 for details.

Creating the OpenVPN client configuration

To configure an OpenVPN client to connect to the OpenVPN server you just configured, you need to copy the key files to the client, create a client configuration file, and start the service. Here is an example of how you might copy the keys from the server:

```
# cd /etc/openvpn
# mkdir keys
# scp root@server1:/etc/openvpn/easy-rsa/2.0/keys/ca.crt keys
# scp root@server1:/etc/openvpn/easy-rsa/2.0/keys/client01.crt keys
# scp root@server1:/etc/openvpn/easy-rsa/2.0/keys/client01.key keys
```

Copy a client configuration file to your /etc/openvpn directory and edit it as appropriate. For example, type the following:

```
# cd /usr/share/doc/openvpn-2.1.1/sample-config-files
# cp client.conf /etc/openvpn/
```

Here is an example of an edited client.conf file:

```
client

dev tun
proto udp

ns-cert-type server

remote example.com 1194

resolv-retry infinite

nobind

persist-key
persist-tun

ca /etc/openvpn/keys/ca.crt
cert /etc/openvpn/keys/client01.crt
key /etc/openvpn/keys/client01.key

comp-lzo
verb 3
```

To test that your VPN client configuration is working, type the following:

```
# openvpn --config client.conf
```

The output from this command will help you debug any problems you have connecting to the OpenVPN server. If you use a GUI to start your OpenVPN client, be sure to identify the location of your client configuration file and keys.

Enhancing OpenVPN security with eurephia

Starting with Fedora 14, you can use eurephia to enhance the security of your OpenVPN server. Eurephia adds the ability to support individual user names and passwords to access the server. In addition, eurephia will lock out not only users, but IP addresses if too many failed attempts come from a particular system. You can also use eurephia's administration to quickly disable individual accounts if needed.

To install eurephia, run the following command:

```
# yum install eurephia eurephia-init eurephia-admin
```

With the eurephia-iptables package, you can add the capability to provide user-specific firewall rules. As of the current release, you need to recompile OpenVPN. See the eurephia documentation for details at www.eurephia.net/documentation/eurephia/1.0/html/ Administrators_Tutorial_and_Manual/.

Read more on eurephia at http:// eurephia.sourceforge.net/.

Setting Up Linux as a Proxy Server

You have a LAN set up, and your Linux computer has both a connection to the LAN and a connection to the Internet. One way to provide Web-browsing services to the computers on the LAN without setting up routing is to configure Linux as a proxy server.

The Squid Web proxy and caching server software are included with Fedora. In a basic configuration, you can get the software going very quickly.

However, the package is full of features that enable you to adapt it to your needs. You can control which hosts have access to proxy services, how memory is used to cache data, how logging is done, and a variety of other features. Here are the basic proxy services available with Squid:

- **HTTP** — Allowing HTTP proxy services is the primary reason to use Squid. This is what lets client computers access Web pages on the Internet from their browsers (through your Linux computer). In other words, HTTP proxy services will find and return the content to you for addresses that look similar to this: www.ab.com. Note that Squid remains only HTTP 1.0 compliant.

- **FTP** — This represents File Transfer Protocol (FTP) proxy services. When you enable HTTP for a client, you enable FTP automatically (e.g., `ftp://ftp.ab.com`).

- **Gopher** — The gopher protocol proxy service was one of the first mechanisms for organizing and searching for documents on the Internet (it predates the Web by more than a decade). Nobody uses gopher anymore. However, gopher is automatically supported when you enable HTTP for a client.

Besides allowing proxy services, Squid can also be part of an Internet cache hierarchy. Internet caching occurs when Internet content is taken from the original server and copied to a caching server that is closer to you. When you, or someone else in the caching hierarchy, requests that content again, it can be taken from the caching server instead of from the original server.

You don't have to cache Internet content for other computers to participate in caching with Squid. If you know of a parent caching-computer that will allow you access, you can identify that computer in Squid and potentially speed your Web browsing significantly.

Caching services in Squid are provided through your Linux system's ICP port. Besides ICP services, you can also enable Simple Network Management Protocol (SNMP) services. SNMP enables your computer to provide statistics and status information about itself to SNMP agents on the network. SNMP is a feature for monitoring and maintaining computer resources on a network.

Caution

SNMP poses a potential security risk if it is not configured properly because it allows an outside system to gain knowledge of your system's hardware, installed software, and which applications are running, as well as the ability to modify your system. Use caution when configuring SNMP with Squid. ■

The `squid` daemon process (`/usr/sbin/squid`) can be started automatically at system boot time by enabling the `squid` service (`chkconfig squid on`). After it is set up, most of the configuration for Squid is done in the `/etc/squid/squid.conf` file. The example configuration file `/usr/share/doc/squid-*/squid.conf.documented` contains a lot of information about configuring Squid. The file contains more than 5,600 lines of comments and examples, although there are only 32 lines of active settings. Those active settings are already copied to your default `/etc/squid.conf` file.

For further information about the Squid proxy server, refer to the Squid Web Proxy Cache home page (`www.squid-cache.org`).

Starting the squid daemon

When you install Fedora you have an opportunity to install Squid (`squid` package). If you are not sure whether or not Squid was installed, type the following:

```
# rpm -q squid
squid-3.1.8-1.fc14.i686
```

If Squid is not installed, you can install it from the DVD that comes with this book or by typing **yum install squid** to install it over the network. Next you can check whether or not Squid is configured to run. To do that, type the following:

```
# chkconfig --list squid
squid           0:off  1:off  2:off  3:off  4:off  5:off  6:off
```

If the `squid` service is off for run levels 3, 4, and 5 (it's off at all run levels by default), you can set it to start automatically at boot time. To set up the `squid` daemon to start at boot time, type the following:

```
# chkconfig squid on
```

At this point, the `squid` daemon should start automatically when your system boots. If you want to add other options to the `squid` daemon, you can edit the `/etc/sysconfig/squid` configuration file. Look for the line that looks similar to the following:

```
SQUID_OPTS=""
```

You can add any options between the quotes. Most of these options are useful for debugging Squid:

- **-a port#** — Substitute for *port#* a port number that will be used instead of the default port number (3128) for servicing HTTP proxy requests. This is useful for temporarily trying out an alternative port.
- **-f squidfile** — Use this option to specify an alternative `squid.conf` file (other than `/etc/squid/squid.conf`). Replace *squidfile* with the name of the alternative `squid.conf` file. This is a good way to try out a new `squid.conf` file before you replace the old one.
- **-d level** — Change the debugging level to a number indicated by `level`. This also causes debugging messages to be sent to `stderr`.
- **-X** — Use this option to confirm that the values are set properly in your `squid.conf` file. It turns on full debugging while the `squid.conf` file is being interpreted.

You can restart the `squid` service by running the command `service squid restart`. While the `squid` daemon is running, there are several ways you can run the `squid` command to change how the daemon works:

- `squid -k reconfigure` — Causes Squid to again read its configuration file.
- `squid -k shutdown` — Causes Squid to exit after waiting briefly for current connections to exit.
- `squid -k interrupt` — Shuts down Squid immediately, without waiting for connections to close.
- `squid -k kill` — Kills Squid immediately, without closing connections or log files. (Use this option only if other methods don't work.)

With the `squid` daemon ready to run, you need to set up the `squid.conf` configuration file.

Using a simple squid.conf file

You can use the /etc/squid/squid.conf file that comes with Squid to get started. Although the file contains a lot of comments, the actual settings in it are quite manageable. The following paragraphs describe the contents of the default squid.conf file. The http_port tag identifies the port on which Squid listens for HTTP client requests:

```
http_port 3128
```

The normal port to use (which is the default) is 3128. Optionally, you can add a hostname (such as example.com:3128) or IP address (such as 10.0.0.1:3128) to limit allowed incoming requests to those made to a particular hostname or IP address.

The hierarchy_stoplist tag indicates that when a certain string of characters appears in a URL, the content should be obtained from the original server and not from a cache peer:

```
hierarchy_stoplist cgi-bin ?
```

In this example, requests for the string cgi-bin and the question mark character (?) are all forwarded to the originating server:

```
refresh_pattern -i (/cgi-bin/|\?)  0    0%    0
```

The preceding line can be used to cause URLs containing certain characters to never be cached. These go along with the previous line by not caching URLs containing the same strings (cgi-bin and ?) that are always sought from the original server. The acl tags are used to create access control lists:

```
acl manager proto cache_object
acl to_localhost src 127.0.0.1/32 ::1
```

The first acl line assigns the manager acl to handle the cache_object protocol. The local-host source is assigned to the IP address of 127.0.0.1.

Squid includes default settings for how long different types of content in cache are still considered to be fresh. The following refresh_pattern values are included in the squid.conf file:

```
refresh_pattern   ^ftp:       1440    20%    10080
refresh_pattern   ^gopher:    1440     0%    1440
refresh_pattern   .              0    20%    4320
```

In the preceding code, all lines that begin with (^) ftp or gopher are set to expire in 1,440 minutes. The percentage of the object's age during which it is considered to be fresh is shown in the next column (20%, 0%, and 20%). The last column indicates the maximum number of minutes during which the object is considered fresh. The next several entries define how particular ports are handled and how access is assigned to HTTP and ICP services:

```
acl SSL_ports port 443
acl Safe_ports port 80          # http
acl Safe_ports port 21          # ftp
```

```
acl Safe_ports port 443       # https
acl Safe_ports port 70        # gopher
acl Safe_ports port 210       # wais
acl Safe_ports port 1025-65535 # unregistered ports
acl Safe_ports port 280       # http-mgmt
acl Safe_ports port 488       # gss-http
acl Safe_ports port 591       # filemaker
acl Safe_ports port 777       # multiling http
acl CONNECT method CONNECT
http_access allow manager localhost
http_access deny manager
http_access deny !Safe_ports
http_access deny CONNECT !SSL_ports
http_access allow localnet # localnet is defined as private ip networks
http_access allow localhost
http_access deny all
```

The following sections describe these settings in more detail, as well as other tags you might want to set in your squid.conf file. By default, no clients can use the Squid proxy server, so you at least want to define which computers can access proxy services.

To ensure that this simple Squid configuration is working, follow this procedure:

1. On the Squid server, restart the squid daemon. To do this, type **service squid restart.** (If Squid isn't running, use **start** instead of **restart.**)

2. On the Squid server, start your connection to the Internet (if it is not already up).

3. On a client computer on your network, set up Firefox (or another Web browser) to use the Squid server as a proxy server (described later in this chapter). In Firefox, select Edit ➪ Preferences ➪ Advanced and click the Network tab; then choose Settings. From the Connection Setting window that pops up, select Manual proxy configuration. Then add the Squid server's computer name and, by default, port 3128 to each protocol. You can also check the "Use this proxy server for all protocols" option to use the same proxy for all service requests from the browser.

4. On the client computer, try to open any Web page on the Internet with the browser you just configured.

If the Web page doesn't appear, see the "Debugging Squid" section for details about how to fix the problem.

Modifying the Squid configuration file

If you want to set up a more complex set of access permissions for Squid, you should start with a copy of the /usr/share/doc/squid-*/squid.conf.documentation configuration file (described earlier).

After copying the file to /etc/squid/squid.conf, edit the file as the root user. You will see a lot of information describing the values that you can set in this file. Most of the tags that you need to configure Squid are used to set up caching and provide host access to your proxy server.

Tip

Don't change the squid.conf.default **file! If you really mess up your** squid.conf **file, you can start again by making another copy of the default file,** squid.conf.default, **to** squid.conf. **If you want to recall exactly what changes you have made so far, type the following from the** /etc/squid **directory:**

```
# diff squid.conf squid.conf.default | less
```

or

```
# diff squid.conf /usr/share/doc/squid-*/squid.conf.documentation
```

This will show you the differences between your actual squid.conf **and the version you started with.** ∎

Configuring access control in squid.conf

To protect your computing resources from being used by anyone, Squid requires that you define which host computers have access to your HTTP (Web) services. By default, all hosts are denied access to Squid HTTP services except for the local host. With the acl tag, you can create access lists. Then, with the http_access tag, you can authorize access to HTTP (Web) services for the access lists you create.

The form of the access control list tag (acl) is as follows:

```
acl   name   type   string
acl   name   type   file
```

The *name* is any name you want to assign to the list. A *string* is a string of text, and *file* is a file of information that applies to the particular *type* of acl. Valid acl types include dst, src, dstdomain, srcdomain, url_path_pattern, url_pattern, time, port, proto, method, browser, and user.

Several access control lists are set up by default. You can use these assigned acl names to assign permissions to HTTP or ICP services. You can also create your own acl names to assign to those services. Here are some of the default acl names from the /etc/squid/squid.conf file that you can use or change:

```
acl manager proto cache_object
acl localhost src 127.0.0.1/32 ::1
acl localnet src 10.0.0.0/8          # RFC1918 possible internal network
acl localnet src 172.16.0.0/12       # RFC1918 possible internal network
acl localnet src 192.168.0.0/16      # RFC1918 possible internal network
acl SSL_ports port 443
acl Safe_ports port 80               # http
```

```
acl Safe_ports port 21              # ftp
acl Safe_ports port 443             # https
acl Safe_ports port 70              # gopher
acl Safe_ports port 210             # wais
acl Safe_ports port 1025-65535      # unregistered ports
acl Safe_ports port 280             # http-mgmt
acl Safe_ports port 488             # gss-http
acl Safe_ports port 591             # filemaker
acl Safe_ports port 777             # multiling http
acl CONNECT method CONNECT
```

Squid tries to determine which class a particular computer falls in by going from top to bottom. In the first line, you create a manager group called `manager` that has access to your `cache_object` (the capability to get content from your cache). The group `localhost` is assigned to your loopback address. Secure socket layer (SSL) ports are assigned to the number 443, whereas `Safe_ports` are assigned to indicate ports that are safe to use. The last line defines a group called `CONNECT` (which you can use to allow access to SSL ports).

To deny or enable access to HTTP services on the Squid computer, the following definitions are set up:

```
http_access allow manager localhost
http_access deny manager
http_access deny !Safe_ports
http_access deny CONNECT !SSL_ports
http_access allow localnet
http_access allow localhost
http_access deny all
```

These definitions are quite restrictive. The first line allows someone requesting cache objects (`manager`) from the local host to do so, but the second line denies anyone else making such a request. Access is not denied to ports defined as safe ports. Also, secure socket connections via the proxy are denied on all ports, except for SSL ports (`!SSL_ports`). HTTP access is permitted only from the local host and is denied to all other hosts.

To allow the client computers on your network access to your HTTP service, you need to create your own `http_access` entries. You probably want to do something more restrictive than simply saying `http_access allow all`. Here is an example of a more restrictive acl group and how to assign that group HTTP access:

```
acl ourlan src 10.0.0.1-10.0.0.100
http_access allow ourlan
```

In this example, all computers at IP addresses `10.0.0.1` through `10.0.0.100` are assigned to the `ourlan` group. Access is then allowed for `ourlan` with the `http_access` line. Make sure you put the new `http_access allow` rule before the existing `http_access deny all` rule.

Configuring caching in squid.conf

Caching, as it relates to a proxy server, is the process of storing data on an intermediate system between the Web server that sent the data and the client that received it. The assumption is that subsequent requests for the same data can be serviced more quickly by not having to go all the way back to the original server. Instead, the proxy server can simply send you the content from its copy in cache. Another benefit of caching is that it reduces demands on network resources and the information servers.

You can arrange caching with other caching proxy servers to form a cache hierarchy. The idea is to have a *parent cache* exist close to an entry to the Internet backbone. When a *child cache* requests an object, if the parent doesn't have it, the parent gets the object, sends a copy to the child, and keeps a copy itself. That way, if another request for the data comes to the parent, it can probably service that request without making another request to the original server. This hierarchy also supports *sibling caches*, which can, in effect, create a pool of caching servers on the same level.

Caution

Caching can consume a lot of your hard disk space if you let it. If you have separate partitions on your system, make sure that you have enough space in /var to handle the added load. ■

Here are some cache-related tags that you should consider setting:

- `cache_peer` — If there is a cache parent whose resources you can use, you can add the parent cache using this tag. You would need to obtain the parent cache hostname, the type of cache (parent), the proxy port (probably 3128), and the ICP port (probably 3130) from the administrator of the parent cache. (If you have no parent cache, you don't have to set this value.) Here's an example of a `cache_peer` entry:

  ```
  cache_peer parent.handsonhistory.com parent 3128 3130
  ```

  You can also add options to the end of the line. Use the `proxy-only` option so that what you get from the parent isn't stored locally and `weight=n` (where *n* is replaced by a number above 1 to indicate that the parent should be used before other parents). Add `default` if the parent is used as a last resort (when all other parents don't have the requested data).

- `cache_mem` — Specifies the amount of cache memory (RAM) used to store in-transit objects (those currently being used), hot objects (those used often), and negative-cached objects (recent failed requests). The default is 8MB, although you can raise that value. To set `cache_mem` to 16MB, enter the following:

  ```
  cache_mem  16 MB
  ```

Note

Because Squid will probably use a total of three times the amount of space you give it for all its processing, Squid documentation recommends that you use a `cache_mem` one-third the size of the space that you actually have available for Squid. ■

- `cache_dir` — Specifies the directory (or directories if you want to distribute cache across multiple disks or partitions) in which cache swap files are stored. The default is `/var/spool/squid`. You can also specify how much disk space to use for cache in megabytes (100 is the default), the number of first-level directories to create (16 is the default), and the number of second-level directories (256 is the default). Here's an example:

```
cache_dir  ufs /var/spool/squid 100 16 256
```

Note

The cache directory must exist. Squid won't create it for you. It will, however, create the first- and second-level directories. ■

- `cache_mgr` — Add the e-mail address of the user who should receive e-mail if the cache daemon dies. By default, e-mail is sent to root. To explicitly set `cache_mgr` to the root user, use the following:

```
cache_mgr  root
```

- `cache_effective_user` — After the squid daemon process is started as root, subsequent processes are run as `squid` user and group (by default). To change that subsequent user to a different name (e.g., to `nobody`) set the `cache_effective_user` as follows:

```
cache_effective_user nobody
```

Note

When I changed the `cache_effective_user` name so that a user other than `squid` ran the `squid` daemon, the messages log recorded several failed attempts to initialize the Squid cache before the process exited. When I changed the user name back to `squid`, the process started properly. To use the `cache_effective_user` feature effectively, you must identify which files are not allowing access. ■

Configuring port numbers in squid.conf

When you configure client computers to use your Squid proxy services, the clients need to know your computer's name (or IP address) and the port numbers associated with the services. For a client that wants to use your proxy to access the Web, the HTTP port is the needed number. Here are the tags you use to set port values in Squid for various services, along with their default values:

- `http_port 3128` — The `http_port` is set to 3128 by default. Client workstations need this number (or the number you change this value to) to access your proxy server for HTTP services (that is, Web browsing).
- `icp_port 3130` — ICP requests are sent to and from neighboring caches through port 3130 by default.
- `htcp_port 4827` — ICP sends HTCP requests to and from neighboring caches on port 4827 by default.

Debugging Squid

If Squid isn't working properly when you set it up, or if you just want to monitor Squid activities, several tools and log files can help you.

Checking the squid.conf file

By running the squid daemon with the `-X` option (described earlier), you can check what is being set from the `squid.conf` file. You can add an `-X` option to the `SQUID_OPTS` line in the `/etc/sysconfig/squid` file. Then run `service squid restart`. A lot of information is output, which details what is being set from `squid.conf`. If there are syntax errors in the file, they appear here.

Checking Squid log files

Squid log files (in Fedora) are stored in the `/var/log/squid` directory by default. The following are the log files created there, descriptions of what they contain, and how they might help you debug potential problems:

- `access.log` — Contains entries that describe each time the cache has been hit or missed when a client requests HTTP content. Along with that information is the identity of the host making the request (IP address) and the content requested. Use this information to determine when content is being used from cache and when the remote server must be accessed to obtain the content. The following are possible access result codes:

  - `TCP_DENIED` — Squid denied access for the request.
  - `TCP_HIT` — Cache contained a valid copy of the object.
  - `TCP_IMS_HIT` — A fresh version of the requested object was still in cache when the client asked if the content had changed.
  - `TCP_IMS_MISS` — An If-Modified-Since request was issued by the client for a stale object.
  - `TCP_MEM_HIT` — Memory contained a valid copy of the object.
  - `TCP_MISS` — Cache did not contain the object.
  - `TCP_NEGATIVE_HIT` — The object was negatively cached, meaning an error was returned (such as the file not being found) when the object was requested.
  - `TCP_REF_FAIL_HIT` — A stale object was returned from cache because of a failed request to validate the object.
  - `TCP_REFRESH_UNMODIFIED` — A stale copy of the object was in cache, but a request to the server returned information that the object had not been modified.
  - `TCP_REFRESH_MODIFIED` — A stale cache object was replaced by new, updated content.
  - `TCP_SWAPFAIL` — An object could not be accessed from cache, despite the belief that the object should have been there.

- `cache.log` — Contains valuable information about your Squid configuration when the `squid` daemon starts. You can see available memory (Max Mem), available swap space (Max Swap), location of the cache directory (`/var/spool/squid`), types of connections being accepted (HTTP, ICP, and SNMP), and the port on which connections are being accepted. You can also see a lot of information about cached objects (such as how many are loaded, expired, or canceled).

- `store.log` — Contains entries that show when content is being swapped out from memory to the cache (`SWAPOUT`), swapped back into memory from cache (`SWAPIN`), or released from cache (`RELEASE`). You can see where the content comes from originally and where it is being placed in the cache. Time is logged in this file in raw Unix time (in milliseconds).

You might also be interested in another log file: `/var/log/messages`. This file contains entries describing the startup and exit status of the `squid` daemon.

Using the top command

Run the `top` command to see information about running processes, including the Squid process. If you are concerned about performance hits from too much Squid activity, type **M** from within the top window. The M option displays information about running processes, sorted by the percentage of memory each process is using. If you find that Squid is consuming too large a percentage of your system memory, you can reduce memory usage by resetting the `cache_mem` value in your `squid.conf` file.

Setting Up Proxy Clients

In order for your Linux proxy server to provide Web-browsing access (HTTP) to the Windows and Linux client computers on your network, each client needs to do a bit of setup within the Web browser. The beauty of using proxy servers is in what your client computers don't need to know, such as the following:

- Addresses of DNS servers
- Telephone numbers of ISPs
- Chat scripts to connect to the ISP

There are probably other things that clients don't need to know, but you get the idea. After the proxy server has a connection to the Internet and has allowed a client computer on the LAN access to that service, all the client needs to know is the following:

- **Hostname** — The name or IP address of the proxy server. (This assumes that the client can reach the proxy over the company's LAN or other IP-based network.)
- **Port numbers** — The port number of the HTTP service (3128 by default). That same port number can be used for FTP service as well.

How you set up proxy service on the client has more to do with the browser you are using than with the operating system you are using. Follow the procedures outlined in the following sections for setting up Firefox or Microsoft Internet Explorer browsers.

Configuring Firefox to use a proxy

Normally, you would set up Firefox to browse the Web directly over a TCP/IP connection to the Internet (over telephone lines or via a router on your LAN). Follow this procedure to change Firefox to access the Web through your proxy server:

1. Open Firefox.
2. Choose Edit ➪ Preferences. The Preferences window appears.
3. Select the Advanced category and select the Network tab.
4. Click the Settings button. The Connection Settings window appears.
5. Click Manual proxy configuration to enable proxy configuration (see Figure 15-1 for an example of the Firefox Connection Settings page).
6. Type the proxy server's name or IP address in the address boxes for HTTP, FTP, and Gopher services.

FIGURE 15-1

The Connection Settings window identifies proxy servers and port numbers in Firefox.

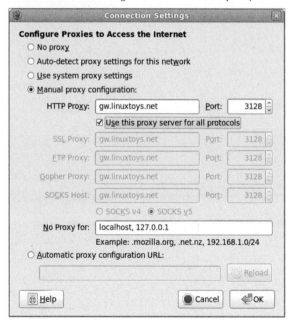

7. Type the port number for HTTP services on your proxy server (commonly 3128) in the Port boxes for HTTP, FTP, and Gopher services. (You can just fill in the information for the HTTP Proxy and check the "Use this proxy server for all protocols" option to have the other services filled in automatically.)

8. Click OK.

The next time you request a Web address from Firefox, it will contact the proxy server to try to obtain the content.

Configuring other browsers to use a proxy

There are different methods for indicating a proxy server to other browsers available with Linux. Many Linux browsers honor environment variable settings for proxies, based on old Mozilla conventions. Here's how you would set the environment variables for HTTP and FTP proxy services to a proxy computer named maple using a `ksh` or `bash` shell:

```
export http_proxy=http://maple:3128
export ftp_proxy=http://maple:3128
```

If you are using a `csh` or `tcsh` shell, type the following:

```
setenv http_proxy http://maple:3128/
setenv ftp_proxy http://maple:3128/
```

You can add any of these values to your startup scripts. Or, to make them available on a system-wide basis, you could add them to a system configuration file, such as `/etc/profile` or `/etc/skel/.bash_profile`.

For the `elinks` and `links` browsers, you can indicate to use a proxy server in the `/etc/elinks.conf` file. For example, here are the lines you would add to the `/etc/elinks.conf` file to have `elinks` and `links` use the computer named maple act as a proxy for FTP and HTTP services:

```
protocol.ftp.proxy.host maple:3128
protocol.http.proxy.host maple:3128
```

Note

It is possible to set up your Linux router (usually the same server as your gateway and firewall) to enable a transparent `squid` proxy. A transparent proxy forces the client's network traffic to use your proxy server and does not require any setup on the client. You can read more about transparent squid proxies at `http://tldp.org/HOWTO/TransparentProxy.html`. ∎

Summary

Connecting to the Internet opens a whole world of possibilities for your Fedora computer. Using Fedora as a public Web server, mail server, or FTP server depends on its capability to connect to the Internet. Likewise, if your computers are already connected in a LAN, adding an Internet connection can provide Internet access to everyone on the LAN in one stroke.

This chapter discussed several different techniques for connecting your LAN to the Internet. You can set up your Linux computer as a router or as a Squid proxy server. To use your Internet connection to transport sensitive data to another location in your company's private network, you can configure a VPN. You also learned how to use IPsec in Fedora to create a VPN connection between two locations.

Setting Up Printers and Printing

Very few people need to print all the time, but when they do want to print something, they usually need it quickly. Setting up a print server and sharing printers can save you money by eliminating the need for a printer at every workstation. Some of those savings can be used to buy printers that can output more pages per minute or provide higher-quality output.

You can attach printers to your Fedora system to make them available to users of that system or to other computers on the network. You can configure your Fedora printer as a remote CUPS printer or Samba printer (emulating a Windows print server).

This chapter describes configuring and using printers in Fedora. It focuses on Common Unix Printing Service (CUPS), which is the recommended print service for the current versions of Fedora. To configure CUPS printers, this chapter focuses on the Printer Configuration window (`system-config-printer` command).

When a local printer is configured, print commands (such as `lpr`) are available for carrying out the actual printing. Commands also exist for querying print queues (`lpq`), manipulating print queues (`lpc`), and removing print jobs (`lprm`). A local printer can also be shared to users on other computers on your network if you set up your Linux system as a print server.

IN THIS CHAPTER

Understanding printing in Linux

Setting up printers

Using printing commands

Managing document printing

Sharing printers

Common Unix Printing Service

CUPS has become the standard for printing from Linux and other Unix-like operating systems, including Mac OS X. Instead of being based on older, text-based line printing technology, CUPS was designed to meet today's needs for standardized printer definitions and sharing on IP-based networks (as most computer networks are today). Here are some features of CUPS:

- **IPP** — At its heart, CUPS is based on the Internet Printing Protocol (www.pwg.org/ipp), a standard created to simplify how printers can be shared over IP networks. In the IPP model, print servers and clients that want to print can exchange information about the model and features of a printer using HTTP. A server can also broadcast the availability of a printer, so a printing client can easily find a list of locally available printers.

- **Drivers** — CUPS also standardized how printer drivers are created. The idea was to have a common format for printer manufacturers that could be used across all different types of Unix systems.

- **Printer classes** — Using printer classes, you can create multiple print server entries that point to the same printer or one print server entry that points to multiple printers. In the first case, multiple entries could each allow different options (such as pointing to a particular paper tray or printing with certain character sizes or margins). In the second case, you could have a pool of printers to distribute printing.

- **Unix print commands** — To integrate into Linux and other Unix environments, CUPS offers versions of standard commands for printing and managing printers that have been traditionally offered with Unix systems.

The Printer Configuration window (system-config-printer command) lets you configure printers in Fedora that use the CUPS facility. However, CUPS also offers a Web-based interface for adding and managing printers. Configuration files for CUPS are contained in the /etc/cups directory. In particular, you might be interested in the cupsd.conf file (which identifies permission, authentication, and other information for the printer daemon) and printers.conf (which identifies addresses and options for configured printers).

Setting Up Printers

Starting with Fedora 13, print setup has never been easier. Just plug in a USB printer; Fedora should not only detect the printer's make and model, but also download the appropriate driver. In addition, most parallel printers and USB printers can be detected and set up using the Printer Configuration window. However, the Printer Configuration window also lets you configure Fedora so that you can use printers that are available on your LAN as a Windows printer (Samba), AppSocket or HP JetDirect, Internet Printing Protocol (IPP) printer, or Unix printer (LPD or LRP daemons).

Choosing a Printer

If you are choosing a new printer to use with your Fedora system, look for one that is PostScript-compatible. The PostScript language is the preferred format for Linux and Unix printing and has been for many years. Every major word and image-processing application that runs on Fedora, Red Hat Enterprise Linux (RHEL), and most other Unix/Linux systems supports PostScript printing.

If you get a PostScript printer and it is not explicitly shown in the list of supported printers, simply select the PostScript filter when you install the printer locally. No special drivers are needed. Your next best choice is to choose a printer that supports PCL (Hewlett Packard's Printer Control Language). In either case, make sure that the PostScript or PCL is implemented in the printer hardware, not in the Windows driver.

When selecting a printer, avoid those that are referred to as *Winprinters*. These printers use nonstandard printing interfaces (those other than PostScript or PCL). Support for these low-end printers is hit-or-miss. For example, some low-end HP DeskJet printers use the pnm2ppa driver to print documents in Printing Performance Architecture (PPA) format. Some Lexmark printers use the pbm217k driver to print. Although drivers are available for many of these Winprinters, many of them are not fully supported.

Ghostscript may also support your printer; if it does, you can use that tool to do your printing. Ghostscript (www.ghostscript.com) is a free PostScript and PDF file interpreter program. It can convert PostScript and PDF content to output that can be interpreted by a variety of printers. With the ghostscript package installed, type **gs -h** to see a list of available output device formats.

You'll find an excellent list of printers supported in Linux at the Free Standards Group OpenPrinting site (www.linuxfoundation.org/collaborate/workgroups/openprinting). I strongly recommend that you visit that site before you purchase a printer to work with Linux. The site offers a printer compatibility database, so you can find out if your printer is supported and, if so, what print driver is needed to get your printer working in Linux. For useful information on purchasing a printer that will work in Linux, look at the Supported Printers section of the Printing HOWTO (www.tldp.org/HOWTO/Printing-HOWTO/printers.html).

Using the Printer Configuration window

Fedora's easy printer setup facility takes advantage of the fact that printers identify themselves using an IEEE 1284 Device ID string. This ID string identifies the make and model of the printer.

Fedora can detect most Bluetooth, USB, network, or parallel printers. To begin, connect your printer to your Fedora system and then power up the printer. In a few moments, you should see a window like that shown in Figure 16-1, notifying you that your printer has been installed.

You may be asked to install additional packages, such as hplip for Hewlett-Packard printers. See http://hplipopensource.com for more on the hplip package, especially if you have a Hewlett-Packard printer that is not automatically detected. For HP printers, you can also run the following command to see a listing of connected printers:

```
# /usr/lib/cups/backend/hp
```

FIGURE 16-1

Fedora detects most printers automatically.

Once the printer is installed, you can configure your printer using the Printer Configuration window (`system-config-printer` command or select System ➪ Administration ➪ Printing from the GNOME desktop). This tool enables you to add printers, delete printers, and edit printer properties. It also lets you send test pages to those printers to ensure that they are working properly.

The key here is that you are configuring printers that are managed by your print daemon (`cupsd` for CUPS). After a printer is configured, users on your local system can use it. Refer to the "Configuring Print Servers" section to learn how to make the server available to users from other computers on your network.

The printers that you set up can be connected locally to your computer (as on a parallel or USB port) or to another computer on the network (for example, from another Unix system or Windows system).

Configuring local printers

After you have added a local printer, you can edit the printer definitions to change how that printer behaves. Right-click the icon for the printer you want to edit and select Properties from the menu to see the screen shown in Figure 16-2.

FIGURE 16-2

Change printer settings, policies, and access from the Printer Properties window.

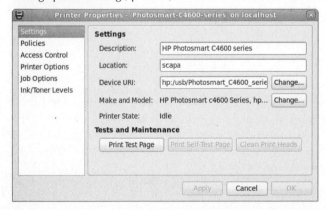

With the printer you want to configure selected, choose from the following sections on the left to change its configuration:

- **Settings** — The Description, Location, Device URI, and Make and Model information you created earlier are displayed on this pane. You can also send a test page to the printer from this pane.

- **Policies** — Click the Policies item. From this pane, you can set the following:

  - **State** — Select check boxes to indicate whether the printer will print jobs that are in the queue (Enabled), accept new jobs for printing (Accepting Jobs), or be available to be shared with other computers that can communicate with your computer (Shared).

Tip

If the print job is rejected when you send it to test the printer, the print server computer may not have allowed you access to the printer. Ask the remote computer's printer administrator to add your hostname to the /etc/ lpd.perms **file. (Type lpq -P** printer, **using the name of the printer to see the status of your print job.)** ■

  - **Policies** — In case of error, the stop-printer selection causes all printing to that printer to stop. You can also select to have the job discarded (abort-job) or retried (retry-job) in the event of an error condition.

  - **Banner** — Add banner pages at the beginning or end of a job. This is good practice for a printer that is shared by many people. The banner page helps you sort who gets which print job.

- **Access Control** — If your printer is a shared printer, you can select this item to create a list of users who are either allowed access to the printer (with all others denied) or denied access to the printer (with all others allowed).

- **Printer Options** — Click Printer Options to set defaults for options related to the printer driver. The available options vary for different printers. Many of these options can be overridden when someone prints a document. Here are a few of the options you might have available to set (depending on the type of printer and its capabilities):

  - **Media Size** — The default is U.S. letter size, but you can also ask the printer to print legal size, envelopes, ISO A4 standard, or several other page sizes.

  - **Media Source** — Choose which tray to print from. Select Tray 1 to insert pages manually.

  - **Print Quality** — Either use the printer's current setting or choose a mode that enables you to save toner or obtain the highest possible quality.

- **Job Options** — Click Job Options to set common default options that will be used for this printer if the application printing the job doesn't already set them. These include Common Options (number of copies, orientation, scale to fit, and pages per side), Image Options (scaling, saturation, hue, and gamma), and Text Options (characters/inch, lines/inch, and margin settings).

  - **Ink/Toner Levels** — Some printers can report back to your Linux system when the levels of ink or toner are low.

Note

For a description of other driver options, refer to the CUPS documentation at `www.cups.org/documenta-tion.php/options.html.` ∎

Click Apply or OK when you are satisfied with the changes you made to the local printer. To make this printer the default printer, right-click on the printer icon in the main Printer Configuration window and select Set As Default. The default printer's icon shows a green check mark.

You can right-click any printer in the Printer Configuration window and then set that printer as the default from the Properties menu option.

Tip

If you have problems seeing your changes applied to your printer or printing the test page, double-check that the cups service is running by entering the following command:

`# service cups restart` ∎

Configuring remote printers

To use a printer that is available on your network, you must identify that printer to your Fedora system. Supported remote printer connections include Networked CUPS (IPP) printers, Networked Unix (LPD) printers, Networked Windows (Samba) printers, and AppSocket/JetDirect printers. (Of course, both CUPS and Unix print servers can be run from Linux systems, as well as other Unix systems.) In each case, you need a network connection from your Fedora system that enables you to reach the servers to which those printers are connected.

You can use the Printer Configuration window to configure each of the remote printer types:

1. From the GNOME desktop, select System ➪ Administration ➪ Printing.
2. Click Add. The New Printer window appears.
3. In addition to the local printers, you can select one of the following types of network printers:
   - **Find Network Printer** — Enables you to try to detect remote printers given a hostname. This is the easiest option.
   - **AppSocket/HP JetDirect** — For a JetDirect printer.
   - **Internet Printing Protocol (ipp)** — For a CUPS or other IPP printer.
   - **Internet Printing Protocol (https)** — For a CUPS printer using HTTPS protocol.
   - **LPD/LPR Host or Printer** — For a Unix printer.
   - **Windows Printer via SAMBA** — For a Windows system printer.
4. Continue following the steps in whichever of the following sections is appropriate.

I suggest selecting Find Network Printer. Fill in the hostname and select Find to find the available network printers from that host. After selecting the printer from a list, the Host and Queue information is automatically filled in. Click the Verify button to make sure the printer is accessible. Click Forward and complete the rest of the procedure as you would for a local printer.

The two most common types of remote printers you will come across are CUPS and Windows printers.

Adding a remote CUPS printer

After choosing to add an Internet Printing Protocol (IPP) CUPS printer, you must add the following information to the window that appears:

- **Host** — The host of the computer to which the printer is attached (or otherwise accessible). This can be an IP address or TCP/IP hostname for the computer (the TCP/IP name is typically accessible from your /etc/hosts file or through a DNS name server).

- **Queue** — The printer name on the remote CUPS print server, which might look something like /printers/HP722C. CUPS supports the concept of printer instances, which allows each printer to have several sets of options. Therefore, if the remote CUPS printer is configured this way, you might be able to choose a particular path to a printer, such as hp/300dpi or hp/1200dpi. A slash character separates the print queue name from the printer instance.

Adding a Windows (SMB) printer

Enabling your computer to access a Server Message Block (SMB) printer (the Windows printing service) involves adding an entry for that printer in the New Printer window.

Note

Before you can add an SMB printer queue to Linux, you must first have configured that printer to work on the Windows machine. You must also indicate that the printer can be shared and is accessible to your Linux machine on your LAN. ■

After you have selected Windows Printer via SAMBA in the New Printer window (described previously), you can browse for computers on your network that offer SMB services (file or printing service) by clicking the Browse button. Drill down from groups to servers to the actual printer.

Alternatively, you could identify a server that does not appear on the list of servers. Type a server name and share into the smb:// box at the top of the page. For example:

```
smb://MYGROUP/EINSTEIN/hp2100m
```

Tip

To find a remote printer name on most Windows systems, first go to the Printers folder (Start ⇨ Settings ⇨ Printers), and double-click the printer being shared. From the printer queue window that appears, choose Printer ⇨ Properties, and then select the Sharing tab. The Sharing tab indicates whether the printer is shared and, if so, the name under which it is shared. ■

Next, select the "set authentication details now" check box, if authentication is required to access the shared printer, and enter the following details:

- **User name** — The user name is the name required by the SMB server system to give you access to the SMB printer. A user name is not necessary if you are authenticating the printer based on share-level, rather than user-level, access control. With share-level access, you can add a password for each shared printer or file system.

- **Password** — The password associated with the SMB user name or the shared resource, depending on the kind of access control being used. Click the Verify button to confirm that the User name and Password are correct.

Caution

When you enter a User name and Password for SMB, that information is stored unencrypted in the /etc/cups/printers.conf file. Be sure that the file remains readable only by root. ■

You can also leave the default selected, which prompts the user for the authentication details as needed.

Click Forward and complete the configuration as you would for a local printer.

If everything is set up properly, you should be able to use the standard lpr command to print the file to the printer. With this example, you could use the following form for printing:

```
$ cat file1.ps | lpr -P hp2100m
```

Tip

If you are receiving failure messages, make sure that the computer to which you are printing is accessible. For the previous example, you could type smbclient -L NS1 -U *username*, but replace *username* with the name of a valid Samba user. Type the password. If you get a positive name query response after you enter a password, you should see a list of shared printers and files from that server. Check the names, and try printing again. ■

Using Printing Commands

To remain backward compatible with older Unix and Linux printing facilities, CUPS supports many of the old commands for working with printing. Most command-line printing with CUPS can be performed with the lpr command. Word processing applications for Linux, such as OpenOffice.org and AbiWord, are set up to use this facility for printing.

With the Printer Configuration window, you can define the filters needed for each printer so that the text can be formatted properly. Options to the lpr command can add filters to process the text properly. Other commands for managing printed documents include lpq (to view the contents of print queues), lprm (to remove print jobs from the queue), and lpc (to control printers).

Cross-Reference

Chapter 6 provides examples of how to format and print documents in several different formats, including troff and TeX. ■

Using lpr to print

With the `lpr` command, you can print documents to both local and remote printers. Document files can be either added to the end of the `lpr` command line or directed to the `lpr` command using a pipe (|). Here is an example of a simple `lpr` command:

```
$ lpr doc1.ps
```

When you just specify a document file with `lpr`, output is directed to the default printer. As an individual user, you can change the default printer by setting the value of the PRINTER environment variable. Typically, you would add the PRINTER variable to one of your startup files, such as $HOME/.bashrc. Here is a line to add to your .bashrc file to set your default printer to lp3:

```
export PRINTER=lp3
```

For the new PRINTER value to take effect immediately, source the .bashrc file (type **source $HOME/.bashrc**). To override the default printer, specify a particular printer on the `lpr` command line. The following example uses the -P option to select a different printer:

```
$ lpr -P canyonps doc1.ps
```

The `lpr` command has a variety of options that enable `lpr` to interpret and format several different types of documents. These include -# *num*, where *num* is replaced by the number of copies to print (from 1 to 100) and -l (ell, which causes a document to be sent in raw mode, presuming the document has already been formatted). The -P option names the printer to use, canyonps in this case.

Listing status with lpc

The `lpc` command in CUPS has limited features. You can use `lpc` to list the status of your printers. Here is an example:

```
$ lpc status
hp:
        printer is on device 'parallel' speed -1
        queuing is enabled
        printing is disabled
        no entries
        daemon present
deskjet_5550:
        printer is on device 'usb' speed -1
        queuing is enabled
        printing is enabled
        no entries
        daemon present
```

This output shows two active printers. The first (hp) is connected to the parallel port. The second (deskjet_5550) is a USB printer (shown as usb). The hp printer is currently disabled (offline), although the queue is enabled so people can continue to send jobs to the printer.

Removing print jobs with lprm

Users can remove their own print jobs from the queue with the lprm command. Used alone on the command line, lprm removes the user's current print job from the default printer. To remove jobs from a specific printer, use the -P option and a printer name, lp0 in this example, as follows:

```
$ lprm -P lp0
```

To remove all print jobs for the current user, type the following:

```
$ lprm -
```

To remove an individual print job from the queue, indicate the job number of that print job on the lprm command line. To find the job number, type the lpq command. Here's what the output of that command may look like:

```
$ lpq
printer is ready and printing
Rank    Owner             Job Files               Total Size Time
active  root              133 /home/jake/pr1          467
2       root              197 /home/jake/mydoc      23948
```

The output shows two printable jobs waiting in the queue. Under the Job column, you can see the job number associated with each document. To remove the first print job, type the following:

```
# lprm 133
```

Configuring Print Servers

You've configured a printer so that you and the other users on your computer can print to it. Now you want to share that printer with other people in your home, school, or office. Basically, that means configuring your computer as a print server.

The printers configured on your Linux system can be shared in different ways with other computers on your network. Not only can your computer act as a Linux print server, it can also look to client computers like an SMB print server. In other words, a Windows client would just see your printer as a printer from another Windows machine.

After a local printer is attached to your Linux system, and your computer is connected to your local network, you can use the procedures in this section to share the printer with client computers using a Linux (Unix) or SMB interface.

Configuring a shared CUPS printer

After a local printer is added to your Linux computer, making it available to other computers on your network is fairly easy. If a TCP/IP network connection exists among the computers sharing the printer, you can simply grant permission to individual hosts or users from remote hosts to access your computer's printing service. The procedures for setting up local printers are discussed earlier in this chapter.

To share a local printer as a print server with other computers on your network, do the following:

1. From the desktop panel, select System ➪ Administration ➪ Printing. The Printer Configuration window appears.

2. Right-click the icon of the printer you want to share. (If the printer is not yet configured, refer to the "Setting Up Printers" section earlier in this chapter.)

3. Select the Shared box on the menu so that a checkmark appears in the box.

4. If you want only selected users to access your printer, select Properties from the menu and then click the Access Control item. Select "Deny printing for everyone except these users," type each user you want to allow to use the printer, and click Add to add each user. Likewise, you could select "Allow printing for everyone except these users" and add selected users to be excluded from those allowed to print. Click Cancel or OK on the Printer Properties window and go back to the Printer Configuration window.

5. Select Settings from the Server menu at the top of the Printer Configuration window. (This is not the Settings option in the Printer Properties window. Instead, look at the Server menu in the Printer Configuration window.) From the Basic Server Settings screen that appears, select the Publish shared printers connected to this system check box. (You will likely need to enter the root password to configure the server settings.)

6. Click OK to make the changes permanent.

At this point, you can configure other computers to use your printer. If you try to print from another computer and it doesn't work, here are a few things to try:

- **Open your firewall** — If you have a restrictive firewall, it may not permit remote users to access your printers. You must allow access to port 513 (UDP and TCP) and possibly port 631 to allow access to printing on your computer. See Chapter 13 for information on configuring your firewall.

- **Check names and addresses** — Make sure that you entered your computer's name and print queue properly when you configured it on the other computer. Try using the IP address instead of the hostname (if that worked, it would indicate a DNS name resolution problem). A tool such as wireshark enables you to watch where the transaction fails.

Access changes to your shared printer are made in the /etc/cups/cupsd.conf file.

Configuring a shared Samba printer

Your Linux printers can be configured as shared SMB printers. To share your printer as a Samba (SMB) printer, all you need to do is configure basic Samba server settings as described in Chapter 17. All your printers should be shared on your local network by default. The next section shows what the resulting settings look like and how you might want to change them.

Understanding smb.conf for printing

When you configure Samba, as described in Chapter 17, the /etc/samba/smb.conf file is configured to allow all your configured printers to be shared. Here are a few lines you might find in the [global] and [printers] sections of the smb.conf file that relate to printer sharing:

```
[global]
    workgroup = MYGROUP
    serverstring = Samba Server Version %v
    security = share
    printcap name = /etc/printcap
    load printers = yes
    printing = cups
    encrypt passwords = yes
    smb passwd file = /etc/samba/smbpasswd
    unix password sync = Yes

[printers]
        comment = All Printers
        path = /var/spool/samba
        guest ok = yes
        browseable = no
        writeable = no
        printable = yes
```

The settings shown resulted from configuring Samba from the Samba Server Configuration window (System ➪ Administration ➪ Samba). You need to install the system-config-samba package to use the Samba Server Configuration window. In this case, I selected to use encrypted passwords. The lines show that printers from /etc/printcap were loaded and that CUPS is being used. The /etc/samba/smbpasswd file stores the encrypted passwords. Because password sync is on, each user's Samba password is synchronized with the local Unix password for the user.

The [printers] section determines the defaults for how printers are shared in Samba. The final line (printable = yes) defines that users can print to all printers.

Summary

Sharing printers is an economical and efficient way to use your organization's printing resources. A centrally located printer can make it easier to maintain a printer, while still allowing everyone to get their printing jobs done.

You configure your printer through the Printer Configuration window. A variety of filters make it possible to print to different kinds of printers, as well as to printers that are connected to computers on the network.

The default printing service in Fedora is the Common Unix Printing Service (CUPS). Besides being able to set up your computer as a Linux print server, you can also have your computer emulate an SMB (Windows) print server. After your network is configured properly and a local printer is installed, sharing a printer over the network as a Unix or SMB print server is not very complicated.

Setting Up a File Server

## 17

Whenen groups of people need to work together on projects, they usually need to share documents. Likewise, it can be efficient for groups of people on a computer network to share common applications and directories of information needed to do their jobs. A common way to store files centrally and share them on a network is by setting up a file server.

Fedora systems include support for each of the most common file server protocols in use today. The Network File System (NFS) has been a file-sharing protocol for decades on Unix and Linux systems. Networks with many Windows computers tend to use Samba, or SMB/CIFS (Server Message Block/Common Internet File System) protocol. Samba can help make your Linux systems fit seamlessly, or near seamlessly, into Windows-centric networks. This chapter describes how to set up file servers and clients associated with NFS and Samba in Linux.

Cross-Reference

One other type of file server is also described in this book: FTP (using vsFTPd). To set up public FTP file servers, refer to Chapter 19. ■

Goals of Setting Up a File Server

By centralizing data and applications on a *file server*, you can accomplish several goals:

- **Centralized distribution** — You can add documents or applications to one location where they will be accessible to any authorized computer or user. This way, you don't have to be responsible for placing necessary files on every computer.

IN THIS CHAPTER

Setting up an NFS file server in Linux

Setting up a Samba file server in Linux

- **Transparency** — Using protocols such as NFS, clients of your file server (Windows, Linux, or Unix systems) can connect your file systems to their local file systems as if your file systems existed locally. (In other words, no drive letters on the Linux or Unix systems. Just change to the remote system's mount point and you are there.)

Setting Up an NFS File Server

Instead of representing storage devices as drive letters (A, B, C, etc.), as they traditionally are in Microsoft operating systems, Linux systems connect file systems from multiple hard disks, USB drives, CD-ROMs, and other local devices invisibly to form a single Linux file system. The Network File System (NFS) facility enables you to extend your Linux file system in the same way, to connect file systems on other computers to your local directory structure.

Cross-Reference

See Chapter 9 for a description of how to mount local devices on your Linux file system. The same command (mount) is used to mount both local devices and NFS file systems. ■

Creating an NFS file server is an easy way to share large amounts of data among the users and computers in an organization. An administrator of a Linux system that is configured to share its file systems using NFS has to perform the following tasks to set up NFS:

1. **Set up the network** — If a LAN or other network connection is already connecting the computers on which you want to use NFS (using TCP/IP as the network transport), you already have the network you need.

2. **On the server, choose what to share** — Decide which file systems on your Linux NFS server to make available to other computers. You can choose any point in the file system and make all files and directories below that point accessible to other computers. However, it is most secure to share directories from the root of a file system partition.

3. **On the server, set up security** — You can use several different security features to suit the level of security with which you are comfortable. Mount-level security lets you restrict the computers that can mount a resource; and for those allowed to mount it, it lets you specify whether it can be mounted read/write or read-only. With user-level security, you map users from the client systems to users on the NFS server. This way, users can rely on standard Linux read/write/execute permissions, file ownership, and group permissions to access and protect files.

4. **On the client, mount the file system** — Each client computer that is allowed access to the server's NFS shared file system can mount it anywhere the client chooses. For example, you may mount a file system from a computer called oak on the /mnt/oak directory in your local file system. After it is mounted, you can view the contents of that directory by typing **ls /mnt/oak**. Then you can use the cd command below the /mnt/oak mount point to see the files and directories it contains.

Although Linux is often used as a file server (or other type of server), it is a general-purpose operating system. Therefore, any Fedora system can share file systems (export) as a server or use another computer's file systems (mount) as a client. Contrast this with dedicated file servers, such as NetWare, which was created to share files with client computers (such as Windows workstations) but was not intended to act as a client.

Many people use the term *file system* rather loosely. A file system is usually a structure of files and directories that exists on a single device (such as a hard disk partition or CD-ROM). When I talk about the Linux file system, however, I am referring to the entire directory structure (which may include file systems from several disks or NFS resources), beginning from root (/) on a single computer. A shared directory in NFS may represent all or part of a computer's file system, which can be attached (from the shared directory down the directory tree) to another computer's file system.

Sharing NFS file systems

To share an NFS file system from your Linux system, you need to export it from the server system. Exporting is done in Fedora by adding entries to the /etc/exports file. Each entry identifies the directory in your local file system that you want to share with other computers. The entry identifies the other computers that can share the resource (or opens it to all computers) and includes other options that reflect permissions and mount settings associated with the directory.

Remember that when you share a directory, you are sharing all files and subdirectories below that directory as well (by default). Therefore, you need to be sure that you want to share everything in that directory structure. (There are still ways to restrict access within that directory structure. Those methods are described later).

Fedora provides a graphical tool for configuring NFS called the NFS Server Configuration window (system-config-nfs command). The following sections explain how to use the NFS Server Configuration window to share directories with other computers and describe the underlying configuration files that are changed to make that happen.

Using the NFS Server Configuration window

The NFS Server Configuration window (system-config-nfs command from the package of the same name) enables you to share your NFS directories using a graphical interface. Start this window from the Desktop menu by clicking System ➪ Administration ➪ Server Settings ➪ NFS. (If it's not there, type **yum install system-config-nfs** to install it.)

To share a directory with the NFS Server Configuration window, do the following:

1. From the NFS Server Configuration window, click File ➪ Add Share, or click the Add button. The Add NFS Share window appears, as shown in Figure 17-1.

FIGURE 17-1

Identify a directory to share and access permissions with the Add NFS Share window.

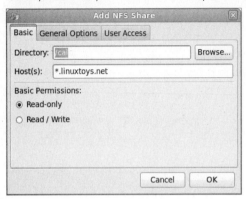

2. In the Basic tab, enter the following information:

   - **Directory** — Type the name of the directory you want to share. (The directory must exist before you can add it.)

   - **Host(s)** — Enter one or more hostnames to indicate which hosts can access the shared directory. Hostnames, domain names, and IP addresses are allowed here. Separate each name with a space. (See the "Hostnames in /etc/exports" section later in this chapter for valid hostnames.) Add an asterisk (*) to place no restrictions on which hosts can access this directory.

   - **Basic permissions** — Click Read-only or Read/Write to let remote computers mount the shared directory with read-only access or read/write access, respectively.

3. Click the General Options tab. This tab lets you add options that define how the shared directory behaves when a remote host connects to it (mounts it):

   - **Allow connections from ports 1024 and higher** — Normally, an NFS client will request the NFS service from a sender port number under 1024. Select this option if you need to allow a client to connect to you from a higher port number. (This sets the insecure option.) To allow a Mac OS X computer to mount a shared NFS directory, you must have the insecure option set for the shared directory.

   - **Allow insecure file locking** — If this is checked, NFS will not authenticate any locking requests from remote users of this shared directory. Older NFS clients may not deliver their credentials when they ask for a file lock. (This sets the insecure_locks option.)

   - **Disable subtree checking** — By selecting this option, NFS won't verify that the requested file is actually in the shared directory (only that it's in the correct file system). You can disable subtree checking if an entire file system is being shared. (This sets the no_subtree_check option.)

- **Sync write operations on request** — On by default, this forces a write operation from a remote client to be synced on your local disk when the client requests it. (This sets the `sync` option.)

- **Force sync of write operations immediately** — If keeping the shared data immediately up-to-date is critical, select this option to force the immediate synchronization of writes to your hard disk. (This sets the `no_wdelay` option.)

- **Hide filesystems beneath** — By default, the `hide` option is checked. If a shared NFS file system has another local file system mounted on it, the second file system will not appear when the client mounts the original file system. If this box is not checked, the `nohide` option is set instead, causing the second mounted file system to be accessible from clients.

- **Export only if mounted** — If a file system that is set to be shared is a mount point that is currently not mounted, the file system will not be exported if this option is on (represented by the `mp` option). This can prevent NFS from sharing empty directories and having contents stored to the empty directory disappear the next time the resource is mounted.

- **Optional mount point** — You can also identify the mount point directly by checking this box and setting the file system mount point. For example, if you are sharing the `/mnt/files/isos` directory and you identify `/mnt/files` as the mount point (mp=`/mnt/files`), the `/mnt/files/isos` directory will not be shared if the `/mnt/files` directory isn't mounted.

- **Set explicit Filesystem ID** — Because not all file systems have UUIDs to identify them, you can identify a further file system you want to share using its file system ID. As a result, the `fsid` option is set to that value (`fsid=???`). If you prefer, you can identify a file system as the root of your shared file systems (`fsid=0`).

4. Click the User Access tab, and then select any of the following options:

   - **Treat the remote root user as local root** — If this option is on, it enables the remote root user host accessing your shared directory to save and modify files as though he or she were the local root user. Enabling this is a security risk because the remote user can potentially modify critical files. (This sets the `no_root_squash` option.)

   - **Treat all client users as anonymous users** — When this option is on, all users are assigned the default anonymous user and group ID of 65534 (`nfsnobody`). (This sets the `all_squash` option.) You can also indicate that particular user and group IDs be assigned to every user accessing the shared directory from a remote computer by entering the user ID and group ID you want assigned to all remote users. (This sets the `anonuid` and `anongid` options to the numbers you choose.)

5. Click OK. The newly shared directory appears in the NFS Server Configuration window.

6. Click the Server Settings button. If your system is configured to use a firewall, the pop-up window that appears lets you set static ports for NFS-related services. Once you set specific numbers for those ports, you need to set firewall rules to allow access to those ports through your firewall. (See Chapter 13 for information on configuring your firewall.)

At this point, the configuration file (/etc/exports) should have the shared directory entry created in it. The /etc/sysconfig/nfs file should have the static ports assigned to NFS services, if you set them in the previous step. To turn on the NFS service and make the shared directory available, type the following from a terminal window as root user:

- To immediately turn on NFS, type this:

```
# service nfslock start; service nfs start
```

- To permanently turn on the NFS service, type this:

```
# chkconfig nfslock on; chkconfig nfs on
```

The next few sections describe the /etc/exports file you just created. At this point, clients can use your shared directory if they mount it on their local file system. Refer to the "Using NFS file systems" section later in this chapter.

Configuring the /etc/exports file

The shared directory information you entered into the NFS Server Configuration window is added to the /etc/exports file. As root user, you can use any text editor to configure the /etc/exports file to modify shared directory entries or add new ones. To see available options, type **man exports**. Here's an example of an /etc/exports file, including some entries that it could include:

```
/cal          *.linuxtoys.net(rw,sync)                # Company events
/public       * (ro,insecure,all_squash)              # Public dir
/home     maple(rw,root_squash) spruce(rw,root_squash)
```

The following text describes the /etc/exports entries just shown:

- **/cal** — Represents a directory that contains information about events related to the company. It is made accessible to everyone with accounts to any computers in the company's domain (*.linuxtoys.net). Users can write files to the directory and read them (indicated by the rw option).

  The sync option, which is the default behavior, is explicitly entered here to indicate that NFS will only reply to new requests after changes have been committed to storage. (The alternative is to enter async, which allows new requests before changes are committed to improve performance but can result in data corruption.) The comment (# Company events) simply serves to remind you what the directory contains.

- **/public** — Represents a public directory. It allows any computer and user to read files from the directory (indicated by the ro option), but not to write files. The insecure option enables any computer, even one that doesn't use a secure NFS port, to access the directory. The all_squash option causes all users (UIDs) and groups (GIDs) to be mapped to the nfsnobody user, giving them minimal permissions to files and directories.

- **/home** — This entry enables a set of users to have the same /home directory on different computers. Say, for example, that you are sharing /home from a computer named oak. The computers named maple and spruce could each mount that directory on their own /home directory. If you gave all users the same user name/UIDs on all machines, you could have the same /home/user directory available for each user, regardless of which computer they logged into. The root_squash is used to exclude the root user login from another computer from changing any files in the shared directory. (See the description of user mapping options in /etc/exports later in this chapter to change that behavior.)

Of course, you can share any directories that you choose (these were just examples), including the entire file system (/). There are security implications of sharing the whole file system or sensitive parts of it (such as /etc). Security options that you can add to your /etc/exports file are described throughout the sections that follow.

The format of the /etc/exports file is as follows:

```
Directory   Host(Options)   # Comments
```

Directory is the name of the directory that you want to share. Host indicates the host computer to which the sharing of this directory is restricted. Options can include a variety of options to define the security measures attached to the shared directory for the host. (You can repeat Host/Option pairs.) Comments are any optional comments you want to add (following the # sign).

Hostnames in /etc/exports

You can indicate in the /etc/exports file which host computers can have access to your shared directory. Be sure to include a space between each hostname. Here are ways to identify hosts:

- **Individual host** — You can enter one or more TCP/IP hostnames or IP addresses. If the host is in your local domain, you can simply indicate the hostname. Otherwise, you can use the full host.domain format. These are valid ways of indicating individual host computers:

```
maple
maple.handsonhistory.com
10.0.0.11
```

- **IP network** — To allow access to all hosts from a particular network address, indicate a network number and its netmask, separated by a slash (/). These are valid ways of indicating network numbers:

```
10.0.0.0/255.0.0.0
172.16.0.0/255.255.0.0
192.168.18.0/24
192.168.18.0/255.255.255.0
```

- **TCP/IP domain** — Using wildcards, you can include all or some host computers from a particular domain level. Here are some valid uses of the asterisk and question mark wildcards:

```
*.handsonhistory.com
*craft.handsonhistory.com
???.handsonhistory.com
```

The first example matches all hosts in the handsonhistory.com domain. The second example matches woodcraft, basketcraft, or any other hostnames ending in craft in the handsonhistory.com domain. The final example matches any three-letter hostnames in the domain.

Note

You can also separate multiple hostnames with spaces, but if you add options after each hostname, leave no spaces between the hostname and the parentheses. For example:

```
*.handsonhistory.com(rw) *.example.net(ro) ■
```

- **NIS groups** — You can allow access to hosts contained in an NIS group. To indicate an NIS group, precede the group name with an at (@) sign (for example, @group).

Access options in /etc/exports

You don't have to just give away your files and directories when you export a directory with NFS. In the options part of each entry in /etc/exports, you can add options that allow or limit access by setting read/write permissions. These options, which are passed to NFS, are as follows:

- **ro** — Only allow the client to mount this exported file system read-only. The default is to mount the file system read/write.

- **rw** — Explicitly ask that a shared directory be shared with read/write permissions. (If the client chooses, it can still mount the directory read-only.)

User mapping options in /etc/exports

Besides options that define how permissions are handled generally, you can also use options to set the permissions that specific users have to NFS shared file systems.

One method that simplifies this process is to have each user with multiple user accounts have the same user name and UID on each machine. This makes it easier to map users so that they have the same permissions on a mounted file system as they do on files stored on their local hard disk. If that method is not convenient, user IDs can be mapped in many other ways. Here are some methods of setting user permissions and the /etc/exports option that you use for each method:

- **root user** — Normally, the client's root user is mapped into the nfsnobody user name (UID 65534). This prevents the root user from a client computer from being able to change all files and directories in the shared file system. If you want the client's root user to have root permissions on the server, use the `no_root_squash` option.

- **nfsnobody user/group** — By using the `nfsnobody` user name and group name, you essentially create a user/group whose permissions will not allow access to files that belong to any real users on the server (unless those users open permission to everyone). However, files created by the `nfsnobody` user or group will be available to anyone assigned as the `nfsnobody` user or group. To set all remote users to the `nfsnobody` user/group, use the `all_squash` option.

  The `nfsnobody` user is assigned to UIDs and GIDs of 65534. This prevents the ID from running into a valid user or group ID. Using the `anonuid` or `anongid` options, you can change the `anonymous` user or group, respectively. For example, `anonuid=175` sets all `anonymous` users to UID 175, and `anongid=300` sets the GID to 300. (Only the number is displayed when you list file permissions, however, unless you add entries with names to `/etc/password` and `/etc/group` for the new UIDs and GIDs.)

- **User mapping** — If the same users have login accounts for a set of computers (and they have the same IDs), NFS, by default, will map those IDs. This means that if the user named mike (UID 110) on maple has an account on pine (`mike`, UID 110), he could use his own remotely mounted files from either computer.

  If a client user who is not set up on the server creates a file on the mounted NFS directory, the file is assigned to the client's UID and GID. (An `ls -ln` on the server would show the UID of the owner.)

Exporting the shared file systems

After you have added entries to your `/etc/exports` file, you can actually export the directories listed using the `exportfs` command. If you reboot your computer or restart the NFS service, the `exportfs` command is run automatically to export your directories. However, if you want to export them immediately, you can do so by running `exportfs` from the command line (as root).

Tip

It's a good idea to run the `exportfs` command after you change the exports file. If any errors are in the file, `exportfs` will identify those errors for you. If you are not able to immediately access changed NFS shares from clients, you might need to restart the NFS and portmap services. ∎

Here's an example of the `exportfs` command:

```
# /usr/sbin/exportfs -a -r -v
exporting maple:/public
exporting spruce:/public
exporting maple:/home
exporting spruce:/home
exporting *:/mnt/win
```

The -a option indicates that all directories listed in /etc/exports should be exported. The -r option will cause any previously existing exports to pick up new options. The -v option says to print verbose output. In this example, the /public and /home directories from the local server are immediately available for mounting by those client computers that are named (maple and spruce). The /mnt/win directory is available to all client computers.

Running the exportfs command makes your exported NFS directories immediately available. Any changes to your /etc/export file will be used again the next time you reboot or otherwise restart the NFS service.

Starting the nfsd daemons

For security purposes, the NFS service is turned off by default on your Fedora system. You can use the chkconfig command to turn on the NFS service so that your files are exported and the nfsd daemons are running when your system boots.

There are two startup scripts you want to turn on for the NFS service to work properly. The nfs service exports file systems (from /etc/exports) and starts the nfsd daemon that listens for service requests. The nfslock service starts the lockd daemon, which helps allow file locking to prevent multiple simultaneous use of critical files over the network.

Note
If you see the message "Cannot register service: RPC: Unable to receive; errno= connection refused," you probably need to start the portmap service on the client machine. ∎

You can use the chkconfig command to turn on the nfs service by typing the following commands (as root user):

```
# chkconfig nfslock on; chkconfig nfs on
```

The next time you start your computer, the nfs service will start automatically and your exported directories will be available. If you want to start the service immediately, without waiting for a reboot, you can type the following:

```
# service nfslock start; /etc/init.d/nfs start
```

The nfs service should now be running and ready to share directories with other computers on your network.

Using NFS file systems

After a server exports a directory over the network using NFS, a client computer connects that directory to its own file system using the mount command. The mount command is the same one used to mount file systems from local hard disks, CDs, and USB flash drives; however, the available options are slightly different.

Mount can automatically mount NFS directories at boot that are added to the /etc/fstab file, just as it does with local disks. NFS directories can also be added to the /etc/fstab file in such a way that they are not automatically mounted. With a `noauto` option, an NFS directory listed in `/etc/fstab` is inactive until the `mount` command is used, after the system is up and running, to mount the file system.

Manually mounting an NFS file system

If you know that the directory from a computer on your network has been exported (that is, made available for mounting), you can mount that directory manually using the `mount` command. This is a good way to ensure that it is available and working before you set it up to mount permanently. Here's an example of mounting the `/home/chris/files` directory from a computer named maple on your local computer:

```
# mkdir /mnt/maple
# mount maple:/home/chris/files /mnt/maple
```

The first command (`mkdir`) creates the mount point directory (`/mnt` is a common place to put temporarily mounted disks and NFS file systems). The `mount` command then identifies the remote computer and shared file system, separated by a colon (`maple:/home/chris/files`). Then, the local mount point directory follows (`/mnt/maple`).

Note

If the mount failed, make sure the NFS service is running on the server and that the server's firewall rules don't deny access to the service. From the server, type `ps ax | grep nfsd`. You should see a list of `nfsd` server processes. If you don't, try to start your NFS daemons as described in the previous section. To view your firewall rules, type `iptables -L` (see Chapter 13 for a description of firewalls). NFS requires a number of server processes, including `nfsd`, `statd`, `lockd`, and `rquotad`, each of which listens on a different port. For security reasons, some port numbers are below 1024 and therefore require root privileges to run, and others listen on higher port numbers. By default, the `nfsd` daemon listens for NFS requests on port number 2049. Your firewall must accept udp requests on ports 2049 (nfs) and 111 (rpc). The rpc portmapper helps clients find the right server processes. Also, set static NFS ports in the `/etc/sysconfig/nfs` file for related NFS services and be sure those ports are open as well. ■

To ensure that the mount occurred, type **mount**. This command lists all mounted disks and NFS file systems. Here is an example of the `mount` command and its output:

```
# mount | grep nfs
/dev/sda3 on / type ext3 (rw)
none on /proc type proc (rw)
none on /sys type sysfs (rw)
none on /dev/pts type devpts (rw,gid=5,mode=620)↵
usbdevfs on /proc/bus/usb type usbdevfs (rw)
/dev/sda1 on /boot type ext3 (rw)
none on /dev/shm type tmpfs (rw)
maple:/home/chris/files on /mnt/maple type nfs (rw,addr=10.0.0.11)
```

The output from the `mount` command shows your mounted disk partitions, special file systems, and NFS file systems. The first output line shows your hard disk (`/dev/sda3`), mounted on the root file system (`/`), with read/write permissions (`rw`), with a file system type of `ext3` (the standard Linux file system type). The small /boot file system is also of type ext3. The /proc, /sys, /dev/shm, /dev/pts, and usbdevfs mount points represent special file system types. The just-mounted NFS file system is the /home/chris/files directory from maple (maple:/home/chris/files). It is mounted on /mnt/maple and its mount type is nfs. The file system was mounted read/write (rw) and the IP address of maple is 10.0.0.11 (addr=10.0.0.11).

That's a simple case of using mount with NFS. The mount is temporary and is not remounted when you reboot your computer. You can also add options to the mount command line for NFS mounts:

- -a — Mounts all file systems in /etc/fstab (except those indicated as noauto).
- -f — This goes through the motions of (fakes) mounting the file systems on the command line (or in /etc/fstab). Used with the -v option, -f is useful for seeing what mount would do before it actually does it.
- -F — When used with -a, you tell mount to fork off a new incarnation of mount for each file system listed to be mounted in the /etc/fstab file. An advantage of using this option, as it relates to NFS shared directories, is that other file systems can be mounted if an NFS file system isn't immediately available. This option should not be used, however, if the order of mounting is important (e.g., if you needed to mount /mnt/pcs and then /mnt/pcs/arctic).
- -r — Mounts the file system as read-only.
- -w — Mounts the file system as read/write. (For this to work, the shared file system must have been exported with read/write permissions.)

The next section describes how to make the mount more permanent (using the /etc/fstab file) and how to select various options for NFS mounts.

Automatically mounting an NFS file system

To set up an NFS file system to mount automatically each time you start your Fedora system, you need to add an entry for that NFS file system to the /etc/fstab file. The /etc/fstab file contains information about all different kinds of mounted (and available to be mounted) file systems for your Fedora system.

The format for adding an NFS file system to your local system is as follows:

```
host:directory     mountpoint     nfs     options     0     0
```

The first item (host:directory) identifies the NFS server computer and shared directory. mountpoint is the local mount point on which the NFS directory is mounted, followed by the file system type (nfs). Any options related to the mount appear next in a comma-separated list. (The last two zeros just tell Fedora not to do dump backups of the contents of the file system and not to run fsck on the file system.)

Note

System-created entries in /etc/fstab for hard disk mounts will likely show a UUID, or Universal Unique
Identifier, in place of the *host:directory* entry — for example, UUID=8366237bb-d845-4117-a1b2-
e286d0f56f15. You can view these entries under /dev/disk/by-uuid. ∎

The following are two examples of NFS entries in /etc/fstab:

```
maple:/home/chris/files /mnt/maple nfs    rsize=8192,wsize=8192  0 0
oak:/apps    /oak/apps  nfs   noauto,ro              0 0
```

In the first example, the remote directory /home/chris/files from the computer named maple
(maple:/home/chris/files) is mounted on the local directory /mnt/maple (the local directory must already exist). The file system type is nfs, and read (rsize) and write (wsize) buffer
sizes are set at 8192 to speed data transfer associated with this connection. In the second example, the remote directory is /apps on the computer named oak. It is set up as an NFS file system
(nfs) that can be mounted on the /oak/apps directory locally. This file system is not mounted
automatically (noauto), however, and can be mounted only as read-only (ro) using the mount
command after the system is already running.

Tip

The default is to mount an NFS file system as read/write, but the default for exporting a file system is
read-only. If you are unable to write to an NFS file system, confirm that it was exported as read/write
from the server. ∎

Mounting noauto file systems

In your /etc/fstab file there can also be devices for other file systems that are not mounted
automatically. For example, you might have multiple disk partitions on your hard disk or an
NFS shared file system that you want to mount only occasionally. A noauto file system can be
mounted manually. The advantage is that when you type the mount command, you can type less
information and have the rest filled in by the contents of the /etc/fstab file. So, for example,
you could type

```
# mount /oak/apps
```

With this command, mount knows to check the /etc/fstab file to get the file system to mount
(oak:/apps), the file system type (nfs), and the options to use with the mount (in this case ro
for read-only). Instead of typing the local mount point (/oak/apps), you could have typed the
remote file system name (oak:/apps) instead, and had other information filled in.

Tip

When naming mount points, including the name of the remote NFS server in that name can help you remember where the files are actually being stored. This may not be possible if you are sharing home directories
(/home) or mail directories (/var/spool/mail). ∎

Using mount options

You can add several mount options to the /etc/fstab file (or to a mount command line itself) to affect how the file system is mounted. When you add options to /etc/fstab, they must be separated by commas. The following are some options that are valuable for mounting NFS file systems:

- **hard** — With this option on, if the NFS server disconnects or goes down while a process is waiting to access it, the process will hang until the server comes back up. This option is helpful if it is critical that the data you are working with not get out of sync with the programs that are accessing it. (This is the default behavior.)

- **soft** — If the NFS server disconnects or goes down, a process trying to access data from the server will time out after a set period of time when this is on.

- **rsize** — The number of bytes of data read at a time from an NFS server. Using a large number (such as 8192) will get you better performance on a network that is fast (such as a LAN) and relatively error-free (that is, one without a lot of noise or collisions).

- **wsize** — The number of bytes of data written at a time to an NFS server. Performance issues are the same as with the rsize option.

- **timeo=#** — Sets the time after an RPC timeout occurs that a second transmission is made, where # represents a number in tenths of a second. The default value is 600, sixty seconds. If you set a value below 600, each successive timeout causes the timeout value to be doubled (up to 60 seconds maximum).

- **retrans=#** — Sets the number of minor retransmission timeouts that occur before a major timeout. When a major timeout occurs, the process is either aborted (soft mount) or a Server Not Responding message appears on your console.

- **retry=#** — Sets how many minutes to continue to retry failed mount requests, where # is replaced by the number of minutes to retry. The default is 10,000 minutes (about one week).

- **bg** — If the first mount attempt times out, try all subsequent mounts in the background. This option is very valuable if you are mounting a slow or sporadically available NFS file system. By placing mount requests in the background, Fedora can continue to mount other file systems, rather than wait for the current one to complete.

Note

If a nested mount point is missing, a timeout to allow for the needed mount point to be added occurs. For example, if you mount /usr/trip and /usr/trip/extra as NFS file systems, if /usr/trip is not yet mounted when /usr/trip/extra tries to mount, /usr/trip/extra will time out. With any luck, /usr/trip will come up and /usr/trip/extra will mount on the next retry. ■

- **fg** — If the first mount attempt times out, try subsequent mounts in the foreground. This is the default behavior. Use this option if it is imperative that the mount be successful before continuing (for example, if you were mounting /usr).

Any of the options that don't require a value can have no prepended to have the opposite effect. For example, nobg indicates that the mount should not be done in the background.

Using autofs to mount NFS file systems on demand

Recent improvements to autodetecting and mounting removable devices have meant that you can simply insert or plug in those devices to have them detected, mounted, and displayed. However, to make the process of detecting and mounting remote NFS file systems more automatic, you still need to use a facility such as autofs. If it is not installed, you can install the autofs package with the yum install autofs command.

With the autofs facility configured and turned on, you can cause any NFS shared directories to mount on demand. If you know the hostname and directory being shared by another host computer, you can simply change (cd) to the autofs mount directory (/net by default) and have the shared resource automatically mount and be accessible to you.

The following steps explain how to turn on the autofs facility:

1. As root user from a terminal window, open the /etc/auto.master file and look for a line that appears as follows:

   ```
   /net    -hosts
   ```

   This causes the /net directory to act as the mount point for the NFS shared directories you want to access on the network. (If there is a comment character at the beginning of that line, remove it.)

2. Start the autofs service by typing the following as root user:

   ```
   # service autofs start
   ```

3. Set up the autofs service to restart every time you boot your system:

   ```
   # chkconfig autofs on
   ```

Believe it or not, that's all you have to do. Provided that you have a network connection to the NFS servers from which you want to share directories, you can try to access a shared NFS directory. For example, if you know that the /usr/local/share directory is being shared from the computer on your network named shuttle, do the following:

1. Type the following:

   ```
   $ cd /net/shuttle
   ```

   If the computer named shuttle has any shared directories that are available to you, you will be able to successfully change to that directory. Another thing to note is that you could use an IP address instead of a hostname (for example, cd /net/10.0.0.1).

2. Type the following:

   ```
   $ ls
   ```

633

You should see the root directory of any file systems the server is exporting. If you do a directory listing on a root directory, it may be empty unless you specify the full path of the export. Once you change to a directory that is part of a shared NFS resource, that directory and shared contents associated with it will be mounted and become visible.

3. Try going straight to any point in a shared directory from the host within the /net/ *host* directory. For example:

```
$ cd /net/shuttle/usr/local/share
$ ls
info man music television
```

At this point, the ls should reveal the contents of the /usr/local/share directory on the computer named shuttle. What you can do with that content depends on how that content was configured for sharing by the server.

There are ways to configure autofs to connect shared NFS directories to any point in your file system. Refer to the autofs man page (type **man 5 autofs**) to learn how to do such things as mount shared home directories using wildcards, do direct maps, and even mount removable media with autofs.

Unmounting NFS file systems

After an NFS file system is mounted, unmounting it is simple. You use the umount command with either the local mount point or the remote file system name. For example, here are two ways you could unmount maple:/home/chris/files from the local directory /mnt/maple:

```
# umount maple:/home/chris/files
# umount /mnt/maple
```

Either form will work. If maple:/home/chris/files is mounted automatically (from a listing in /etc/fstab), the directory will be remounted the next time you boot Fedora. If it was a temporary mount (or listed as noauto in /etc/fstab), it will not be remounted at boot time.

Tip

The command is not unmount, it is umount. This is easy to get wrong. ∎

If you get the message device is busy when you try to unmount a file system, it means the unmount fails because the file system is being accessed. Most likely, one of the directories in the NFS file system is the current directory for your shell (or the shell of someone else on your system). The other possibility is that a command is holding a file open in the NFS file system (such as a text editor). Check your terminal windows and other shells, and cd out of the directory if you are in it, or just close the terminal windows.

You can find out what processes are holding a file system open using the fuser command (e.g., fuser -v /home). If you can't close those processes gracefully (which is preferred), you can kill them all immediately using the -k option (e.g., fuser -k /home). If an NFS file system still won't unmount, you can force unmount it (umount -f /mnt/maple) or unmount and clean up later (`umount -l /mnt/maple`). The `-l` option is usually the better choice because a forced unmount can disrupt a file modification that is in progress.

If you are working exclusively with Fedora and other Linux and Unix systems, NFS is probably your best choice for sharing file systems. If your network consists primarily of Microsoft Windows computers or a combination of systems, you may want to look into using Samba for file sharing.

Setting Up a Samba File Server

Samba is a software package that comes with Fedora and most other Linux systems. Samba enables you to share file systems and printers on a network with computers that use the Server Message Block (SMB) or Common Internet File System (CIFS) protocols. SMB is the Microsoft protocol that is delivered with Windows operating systems for sharing files and printers. CIFS is an open, cross-platform protocol that is based on SMB. Samba contains free implementations of SMB and CIFS.

On Fedora, the Samba software package contains a variety of daemon processes, administrative tools, user tools, and configuration files. (If Samba is not currently installed on Linux, refer to the "Getting and Installing Samba" section later in this chapter.) To do basic Samba configuration, you can start with the Samba Server Configuration window. This window provides a graphical interface for configuring the server and setting directories to share.

Most of the Samba configuration you do ends up in the `/etc/samba/smb.conf` file. If you need to access features that are not available through the Samba Server Configuration window, you can edit `/etc/samba/smb.conf` by hand or use SWAT, a Web-based interface to configure Samba.

Daemon processes consist of `smbd` (the SMB daemon) and `nmbd` (the NetBIOS name server). The `smbd` daemon makes the file sharing and printing services you add to your Linux system available to Windows client computers. The client operating systems this package supports include most versions of Windows, Mac OS X, Linux, and Unix.

As for administrative tools for Samba, you have several shell commands at your disposal. You can check your configuration file using the `testparm` command. The `smbstatus` command tells you which computers are currently connected to your shared resources. Using the `nmblookup` command, you can query for NetBIOS names (the names used to identify host computers in Samba).

Because SMB is considered a Windows system technology, some of the terms used to describe Samba sound more familiar to Windows users than to Linux users. For example, a shared directory or file system is often referred to as a *share*.

Although Samba uses the NetBIOS service to share resources with SMB clients, the underlying network must be configured for TCP/IP. Although other SMB hosts can use TCP/IP, NetBEUI, and IPX/SPX to transport data, Samba for Linux supports only TCP/IP. Messages are carried between host computers with TCP/IP and are then handled by NetBIOS.

Getting and installing Samba

To see if Samba is installed on your Fedora system, type the following:

```
# rpm -qa | grep samba
samba-*
system-config-samba
samba-swat-*
samba-common-*
samba-client-*
samba-winbind-*
```

You should see the name of each of these packages, followed by the version number (above, version numbers are represented with an asterisk). The samba-swat package is not installed by default when you install Samba.

If you have an Internet connection, you could try yum install samba to start using Samba. You can install any of the other packages as well. Before you start trying to configure Samba, read the README file (located in /usr/share/doc/samba-common-*). It provides a good overview of Samba.

Note

With the expanded Fedora software repository, other useful tools for working with Samba are now available. The smb4k **package enables you to search for available shared SMB/CIFS resources and mount them on your computer. The** fuse-smb **package enables you to find and browse available SMB shares on your network.** ■

Configuring a simple Samba server

Using the Samba Server Configuration window, you can do a basic Samba configuration and then identify which directories you want to share.

The following procedure describes how to configure Samba and create a shared directory in Samba:

1. To open the Samba Server Configuration window, click System ➪ Administration ➪ Samba. When the window opens, you will likely need to enter the root password. (If you do not see the Samba choice on the Administration menu, install the system-config-samba package.)

2. Click Preferences ➪ Server Settings. The Server Settings window appears.

3. Type the workgroup name (to match that of other computers with which you want to share files) and a short description.

4. Click the Security tab. A window appears like the one shown in Figure 17-2.

5. Provide the following information for the fields on the Security tab and click OK:

   - **Authentication Mode** — Select User, Share, Server, ADS (Active Directory Server), or Domain. For this example, I selected User. (See the "Security options" section later in this chapter for details on each of the authentication modes.)

- **Authentication Server** — This field is valid only if your Samba server is configured to use Server or Domain security. It identifies the server (NetBIOS name) that will be used to authenticate the user name and password the Samba client enters to gain access to this Samba server. With user authentication, passwords are checked on the Samba server (in this example, therefore, this field is blank).

- **Kerberos Realm** — If your network uses Kerberos for user authentication, enter the name of your Kerberos realm here.

- **Encrypt Passwords** — Select Yes (to expect clients to send encrypted passwords) or No (to expect clear-text passwords). See the section "Setting up Samba clients" later in this chapter to learn how to configure clients to use encrypted passwords.

- **Guest Account** — Set this field to a user name that you want assigned to requests from anonymous users. Even with User mode security set globally, you can assign guest access to particular Samba shares (such as printers).

6. With User mode security, any user who wants to access a Samba share must have a regular user account on the Linux system. (Refer to Chapter 10 for information on adding user accounts.)

FIGURE 17-2

Fill in security information for your Samba server.

7. To add a user as a Samba user (that is, one who can access your Samba server), select Preferences ➪ Samba Users. The Samba Users window appears.

8. Click Add User. The Create New Samba User window appears.

9. Provide information for the following fields in the Create New Samba User window and click OK:

- **Unix Username** — Select the Linux user name to which you want to give access to the Samba server.

- **Windows Username** — This is the user name provided by the user when he or she requests the shared directory. (Often, it is the same as the Unix Username.)

- **Samba Password** — Type the Samba password, and then retype it into the Confirm Samba Password field.

10. Repeat the previous step for each user you want to be able to access the Samba shared directory.

11. Now that you have configured the default values for your Samba server, add a directory to share by clicking File ⇨ Add Share. Figure 17-3 shows the Create Samba Share window that appears.

FIGURE 17-3

The Create Samba Share window allows you to share a directory on your Linux system with other computers.

12. In the Create Samba Share window, fill in the following fields:

   - **Folder** — Type the name of the directory you want to share.

   - **Share name** — Enter the name of the share (shared file system) that clients will use to mount the Samba file system.

   - **Description** — Type any description you like of the shared directory.

   - **Basic Permissions** — Select either Writable (read-write) or Visible (read-only). For Visible, files can be viewed but not changed on the shared directory. For Writable, users are free to add, change, or delete files, provided they have Linux file access to the particular file. If you don't make a share Visible, it will not show up as being shared but will still be able to be used if the client specifies the hidden share name.

13. Click the Access tab, select one of the following options for access to the share, and then click OK:

   - **Give access to these users** — Click here and then choose which users will be allowed to access the shared directory. For example, if you are sharing a user's directory (such as /home/chris), you probably want to restrict access to that directory to the directory's owner (i.e., chris). Read and write access to particular files and directories are determined by the Linux ownership and group assigned to them.

   - **Give access to everybody** — Choose this option if you want to allow anyone to access this directory. (All users will have the same privileges assigned to the guest user when accessing the directory.)

14. After you click OK, Samba is started and the new directory is immediately available. You can close the Samba Server Configuration window.

15. Although Samba should be running at this point, you probably need to set Samba to start automatically every time you reboot Linux. To do that, type the following as root user in a terminal window:

```
# chkconfig smb on
```

If Samba isn't running yet, type **service smb start** to start it right now. You can repeat the steps for adding a Samba shared directory for every directory you want to make available on your network. At this point, you can do one of the following:

- Go through your Samba server settings in more detail (as described in the "Configuring Samba with SWAT" section) to understand how you might want to further tune your Samba server.

- Try accessing the shared directories you just created from a client computer on your network. To do that, refer to the section "Mounting Samba directories in Linux" later in this chapter.

If you cannot open the shared directory you just configured from a Windows computer or other Linux computer on your LAN, you are probably experiencing one of the following problems:

- The client isn't supplying a valid user name and password.
- The client isn't supplying an encrypted password.

The quick way around these problems is to use only share-level security (which, of course, throws your security right out the window). The other solution is to update passwords and ensure that clients are using encrypted passwords (as described in the "Setting up Samba clients" section later in this chapter).

Configuring Samba with SWAT

The Samba Web Administration Tool (SWAT) is a Web-based interface for configuring Samba. While it's not quite as easy to use as the Samba Server Configuration window, it offers more options for tuning Samba, and Help descriptions for each option. In addition, because SWAT is Web-based, you can configure your system remotely from any Web browser.

Caution

Both SWAT and the Samba Server Configuration window configure Samba by modifying the /etc/samba/ smb.conf **file. Different GUI tools can overwrite each other's settings, sometimes in a way that causes the other tool not to work.**

In general, it's best to make a backup copy of your files before switching GUI tools. Eventually, you should choose one tool and stick with it. ■

Turning on SWAT

Before you can use SWAT, you must have the samba-swat package installed (type **yum install samba-swat**) and start the swat service. To set up SWAT to run from your browser, follow these steps:

1. To turn on the swat service, type the following, as root user, from a terminal window:

   ```
   # chkconfig swat on
   ```

2. To pick up the change to the swat service, reload data for the running xinetd startup script as follows:

   ```
   # service xinetd reload
   ```

If xinetd is not yet installed, you should install it (type **yum install xinetd**). If it is not already running, use start instead of reload. When you have finished this procedure, use the SWAT program, described in the next section, to configure Samba.

Starting with SWAT

You can access SWAT by typing the following URL in your local browser:

```
http://127.0.0.1:901/
```

At this point, the browser will prompt you for a user name and password. Enter the root user name and password. The SWAT page should appear.

Tip

Instead of accessing SWAT from your local browser, you can run it from another computer on the network by substituting the server computer's name for 127.0.0.1. (To allow computers besides the local computer to access the swat service, you must change or remove the only_from = 127.0.0.1 line from the /etc/xinetd.d/ swat file and reload the xinetd service.) Keep in mind that you are entering clear-text passwords when you connect to the swat service, so using this feature outside of the local computer is not particularly secure. ■

The rest of this section describes how to use SWAT to create your configuration entries (in /etc/ samba/smb.conf) and to work with that configuration.

Caution

Anytime you use a GUI to change a plain-text configuration file (as you do with SWAT), you may lose some of the information that you added by hand. In this case, SWAT deletes comment lines and rearranges other entries. To protect changes you have made manually, make a backup copy of your /etc/samba/smb.conf file before you edit it with SWAT. ■

Creating global Samba settings in SWAT

A group of global settings affects how file and print sharing are generally accomplished on a Samba server. They appear under the [global] heading in the /etc/samba/smb.conf file. To view and edit global variables, click the GLOBALS option on the SWAT window.

The following sections describe the most useful options available from SWAT:

Note

Each option shown relates to the exact parameters used in the /etc/samba/smb.conf **file. You can refer to the** smb.conf **man page (type** man smb.conf**) to get more information on these parameters.** ∎

Base options

The following are some general Samba server options:

- **workgroup** — The name of the workgroup associated with the group of SMB hosts. By default in Fedora, the value for this field is MYGROUP.

- **realm** — If you are using Kerberos authentication, this value indicates which Kerberos realm to use. Typically, that is reflected by the hostname of the server providing the service.

- **netbios name** — The name assigned to this Samba server. You can use the same name as your DNS hostname or leave it blank, in which case the DNS hostname is used automatically.

- **netbios alias** — This enables you to specify a way of referring to a host computer (an alias) that is different from the host's TCP/IP DNS name.

- **server string** — A string of text identifying the server. This name appears in places such as the printer comment box. By default, it says Samba and the version number.

- **interfaces** — Enables you to set up more than one network interface. This enables Samba to browse several different subnetworks. The form of this field can be *IP Address/Subnetwork Mask*. Or, you can identify a network interface (such as eth0 for the first Ethernet card on your computer). For example, a Class C network address may appear as 192.168.24.11/255.255.255.0.

Security options

Of the security options settings, the first option (security) is the most important one to get right. It defines the type of security used to provide access to the shared file systems and printers to the client computers. (To see some of the fields described here, you need to click the Advanced view.)

- **security** — Sets how password and user information is transferred to the Samba server from the client computer. As noted earlier, it's important to get this value right. The default value for security (security=user) is different from the default value for security (security=share) in pre-2.0 versions of Samba.

- **auth methods** — Sets the authentication method used by the Samba server (smbd). Leave the default in most cases. Authentication methods you can choose include anonymous access (guest), relay authentication through winbind (winbind), pre-winbind NT authentication (ntdomain), local lookups based on netbios or domain name (sam), or remote DC authentication of trusted users (trustdomain).

- **encrypt passwords** — Controls whether encrypted passwords can be negotiated with the client. This is on (Yes) by default. For *domain* security, this value must be Yes.

- **client schannel** — Indicates whether the client should require the use of netlogin schannel (yes), offer schannel but not enforce it (auto), or not even offer schannel (no).

- **server schannel** — Specifies whether the server should require clients to use netlogin schannel (yes), offer schannel but not enforce it (auto), or not even offer schannel (no). If you set this to no, you must apply the Windows XP WinXP_SignOrSeal.reg patch available from the Samba project.

- **guest account** — Specifies the user name for the guest account. When a service is specified as Guest OK, the user name entered here will be used to access that service. The account is usually the *nobody* user name.

Tip
Make sure that the guest account is a valid user. (The default of *nobody* should already be set up to work.) With an invalid user as the guest account, the IPC$ connection that lists the shared resources fails. ∎

Assigning Guest Accounts

Samba always assigns the permissions level of a valid user on the Linux system to clients who use the server. In the case of share security, the user is assigned a guest account (the *nobody* user account by default).

If the guest account value isn't set, Samba goes through a fairly complex set of rules to determine which user account to use. As a result, it can be hard to ensure which user permissions will be assigned in each case. This is why it is recommended to use *user* security if you want to provide more specific user access to your Samba server.

- **invalid users** — Can contain a list of users who should not be allowed to log in for Samba service. Add an at sign (@) before a name to have it interpreted as a group name.

- **valid users** — Add a list of user names that should be allowed to log in to the Samba service. If nothing is entered here or in the invalid users field, any user is allowed to log in.

- **admin users** — Can contain a list of users who have administrative privileges associated with a Samba share.

- **read list** — Can contain a list of users who have only read-only access to a service.

- **write list** — Can contain a list of users who have read/write access to a service.

- **printer admin** — Add users to this list who you want to allow remote administrative privilege to control Samba printers using the MS-RPC service, typically from a NT workstation.

- **hosts allow** — Contains a list of one or more hosts that are allowed to use your computer's Samba services. By default, users from any computer can connect to the Samba server (of course, they still have to provide valid user names and passwords). Usually, you use this option to allow connections from specific computers (such as 10.0.0.1) or computer networks (such as 10.0.0.) that are excluded by the `hosts deny` option.

- **hosts deny** — Contains a list of one or more hosts from which users are not allowed to use your computer's Samba services. You can make this option fairly restrictive, and then add the specific hosts and networks you want to use the Samba server. By default, no hosts are denied.

- **preload modules** — Contains a list of modules you want to be loaded into the `smbd` daemon before any clients can connect to the service.

Logging options

The following options help define how logging is done on your Samba server:

- **log file** — Defines the location of the Samba smb log file, such as `/var/log/samba/log.%m`. By default, Samba log files are contained in `/var/log/samba`. In this option, the `%m` is replaced by the name of each host that tries to connect to the local Samba server. For example, for a client computer named maple, the smb log file would be `/var/log/samba/log.maple`. Samba will log additional information to `nmbd.log`, `smbd.log`, and `smb.log`.

- **max log size** — Sets the maximum amount of space, in kilobytes, that the log files can consume.

Protocol options

The `svcctl list` option lets you create a list of Linux init scripts (from the `/etc/init.d` directory) that the Samba service can start and stop via the Win32 Service Control API. This feature enables you to use the Microsoft Management Console plugins to manage Linux services through the Samba facility.

Tuning options

Set the clustering option to `yes` to enable a clustered TDB database to store temporary data in Samba. See the CTDB site (`http://ctdb.samba.org`) for details on configuring a clustered TDB database in Samba.

Printing options

The `cups` options field is used to define options that are passed to the CUPS, or Common Unix Printing Service. By default, only the raw option is set (which causes printing data to be passed directly to the Samba printer).

Browse options

A browse list is a list of computers that are available on the network to SMB services. Clients use this list to find computers that are on their own LAN, and computers in their workgroups that may be on other reachable networks.

In Samba, browsing is configured by the following options and implemented by the nmbd daemon. If you are using Samba for a workgroup within a single LAN, you probably don't need to concern yourself with the browsing options. If, however, you are using Samba to provide services across several physical subnetworks, you might want to consider configuring Samba as a domain master browser. Here are some points to think about:

- Samba can be configured as a master browser. This allows it to gather lists of computers from local browse masters to form a wide-area server list.

- If Samba is acting as a domain master browser, Samba should use a WINS server to help clients resolve the names from this list.

- Samba can be used as a WINS server, although it can also rely on other types of operating systems to provide that service.

- There should be only one domain master browser for each workgroup. Don't use Samba as a domain master for a workgroup with the same name as an NT domain.

If you are working in an environment that has a mix of Samba and Windows NT servers, use an NT server as your WINS server. If Samba is your only file server, choose a single Samba server (nmbd daemon) to supply the WINS services.

Note

A WINS server is basically a name server for NetBIOS names. It provides the same service that a DNS server does with TCP/IP domain names: It can translate names into addresses. A WINS server is particularly useful for allowing computers to communicate with SMB across multiple subnetworks where information is not being broadcast across the subnetworks' boundaries. ■

To configure the browsing feature in Samba, you must have the workgroup named properly (described earlier in this section). Here are the global options related to SMB browsing:

Note

If browsing isn't working, check the nmbd log file (/var/log/samba/nmbd.log). To get more detail, increase the debug information level to 2 or 3 and restart Samba. The log should indicate whether your Samba server is the master browser, and if so, which computers are on its list. ■

- **os level** — Set a value to control whether your Samba server (nmbd daemon) may become the local master browser for your workgroup. Raising this setting increases the Samba server's chance to control the browser list for the workgroup in the local broadcast area. If the value is 0, a Windows machine will probably be selected. A value of 65 will probably ensure that the Samba server is chosen over an NT server. The default is 20.

- **preferred master** — Set this to Yes if you want to force selection of a master browser. By setting this to Yes, the Samba server has a better chance of being selected. (Setting Domain Master to Yes along with this option should ensure that the Samba server is selected.) This is set to Auto by default, which causes Samba to try to detect the current master browser before taking that responsibility.

- **local master** — Set this to Yes if you want the Samba server to become the local browser master. (This is not a guarantee but gives it a chance.) Set the value to No if you do not want your Samba server selected as the local master. Local master is Auto by default.

- **domain master** — Set this to Yes if you want the Samba server (nmbd daemon) to identify itself as the domain master browser for its workgroup. This list will then allow client computers assigned to the workgroup to use SMB-shared files and printers from subnetworks that are outside of their own subnetwork. The default is No.

WINS options

Use the WINS options if you want a particular WINS server to provide the name-to-address translation of NetBIOS names used by SMB clients. As noted earlier, you probably don't need to use a WINS server if all the clients and servers in your SMB workgroup are on the same subnetwork. That's because NetBIOS names can be obtained through addresses that are broadcast. It is possible to have your Samba server provide WINS services.

- **wins server** — If you want to use a WINS server on your network to resolve the NetBIOS names for your workgroup, you can enter the IP address of that server here. Again, you probably want to use a WINS server if your workgroup extends outside of the local subnetwork.

- **wins support** — Set this value to Yes if you want your Samba server to act as a WINS server. (It's No by default.) Again, this is not needed if all the computers in your workgroup are on the same subnetwork. Only one computer on your network should be assigned as the WINS server.

Besides the values described here, you can access dozens more options by clicking the Advanced View button. When you have filled in all the fields you need, click Commit Changes to have the changes written to the /etc/samba/smb.conf file.

Configuring shared directories with SWAT

To make your Samba share (shared directory) available to others, you can add an entry to the SWAT window. To use SWAT to set up Samba to share directories, do the following:

Note

You may see one or more security warnings during the course of configuring shared directories with SWAT. These messages warn you that someone can potentially view the data you are sending to SWAT. If you are working on your local host or on a private LAN, the risk is minimal. ■

1. From the main SWAT window, click the SHARES button.

2. Type the name of the directory that you want to share in the Create Share box, and then click Create Share.

3. Click Advanced if you would like to change to the Advanced view.

4. There are a few dozen options to choose from. Here are a few that might particularly interest you:

- **comment** — A few words to describe the shared directory (optional).

- **path** — The path name of the directory you are sharing.

- **invalid users** — Enables you to add a list of users who are not allowed to log in to the Samba service.

- **valid users** — Add names here to identify which Linux user accounts can access the Samba service. Names can be preceded with +, &, or @ characters, which tell Samba to respectively refer to a Linux group, an NIS netgroup, or check the Linux group and then the NIS netgroup.

- **admin users** — Lets you identify users who have administrative privilege on a particular share. This is available with the `security = share` type of security only.

- **read list** — Add users to this list to grant read access only to shares (even if a share is available with read-write access). This is available with the `security = share` type of security only.

- **write list** — Add users to this list to grant write access for those users to a shared directory, even if the shared directory is available with read-only access to all others. This is available with the `security = share` type of security only.

- **read only** — If Yes, then files can only be read from this file system, but no remote user can save or modify files on the file system. Select No to allow users to save files to this directory over the network.

- **guest ok** — Select Yes to enable anyone access to this directory without requiring a password.

- **hosts allow** — Add the names of the computers that will be allowed to access this file system. You can separate hostnames by commas, spaces, or tabs.

- **hosts deny** — Deny access to specific computers by placing their names here. By default, no particular computers are excluded. Enter hostnames in the same forms you used for hosts allow.

- **browseable** — Indicates whether you can view this directory on the list of shared directories. This is on (Yes) by default.

- **available** — Enables you to leave this entry intact, but turns off the service. This is useful if you want to close access to a directory temporarily. This is off (No) by default. Select Yes to turn it on.

5. Select Commit Changes.

At this point, the shared file systems should be available to the Samba client computers that have access to your Linux Samba server. Before you try that, however, you can check a few things about your Samba configuration.

Checking your Samba setup with SWAT

From the SWAT window, select the Status button.

From this window, you can restart your smbd and nmbd processes. Likewise, you can see lists of active connections, active shares, and open files.

The preferred way to start the smbd and nmbd daemons is to set up the smb service to start automatically. Type **chkconfig smb on** in a terminal window to set the service to start at boot time.

Working with Samba files and commands

Although you can set up Samba through the Samba Server Configuration window or SWAT, many administrators prefer to edit the /etc/samba/smb.conf directly. As root user, you can view the contents of this file and make needed changes. If you selected *user* security (as recommended), you will also be interested in the smbpasswd command and the passdb.tdb and secrets.tdb files. These files, as well as commands such as testparm and smbstatus, are described in the following sections.

Editing the smb.conf file

Changes you make using the Samba Server Configuration window or SWAT Web interface are reflected in your /etc/samba/smb.conf file. Listing 17-1 shows an example of an smb.conf file (with comments removed):

LISTING 17-1

A Sample smb.conf File

```
[global]
workgroup = ESTREET
server string = Samba Server on Maple
hosts allow = 192.168.0.
printcap name = /etc/printcap
load printers = yes
printing = cups
log file = /var/log/samba/log.%m
max log size = 0
security = user
encrypt passwords = Yes
unix password sync = Yes
passwd program = /usr/bin/passwd %u
passwd chat = *New*password* %n\n *Retype*new*password* %n\n *passwd:
        *all*authentication*tokens*updated*successfully*
pam password change = yes
obey pam restrictions = yes
socket options = TCP_NODELAY SO_RCVBUF=8192 SO_SNDBUF=8192
dns proxy = no
```

continued

LISTING 17-1 *(continued)*

```
[homes]
comment = Home Directories
browseable = no
writable = yes
valid users = %S
create mode = 0664
directory mode = 0775

[printers]
comment = All Printers
path = /var/spool/samba
browseable = no
guest ok = no
writable = no
printable = yes
```

In the [global] section, the workgroup is set to ESTREET, the server is identified as the Samba Server on Maple, and only computers on the local network (192.168.0.) are allowed access to the Samba service. You must change the 'hosts allow =' parameter to match your network.

Definitions for the local printers that will be shared are taken from the /etc/printcap file, the printers are loaded (yes), and CUPS (the default print service used by Fedora) is used.

Separate log files for each host trying to use the service are created in /var/log/samba/log.%m (with %m automatically replaced with each hostname). There is no limit to log file size (0).

In this case, we are using user-level security (security = user). This allows a user to log in once and then easily access the printers and the user's home directory on the Linux system. Password encryption is on (encrypt passwords = yes) because most Windows systems have password encryption on by default. User mappings and passwords are stored in the /var/lib/samba/passdb.tdb and secrets.tdb files on your Linux system.

The dns proxy = no option prevents Linux from looking up system names on the DNS server (used for TCP/IP lookups) when they can't be found among registered NetBIOS names.

The [homes] section allows each user to access his or her Linux home directory from a Windows system on the LAN. Users will be able to write to their home directory, but other users will not be able see or share this directory. The [printers] section allows all users to print to any printer configured on the local Linux system.

Adding Samba users

User-style Samba security means assigning a Linux user account to each person using the Linux file systems and printers from his or her Windows workstation. (You could assign users to a guest account instead, but in this example all users have their own accounts.) Then you need to add SMB passwords for each user. For example, here is how you would add a user whose Windows login is chuckp:

1. Type the following as root user from a terminal window to add a Linux user account:

   ```
   # useradd -c "Charles Perkins" chuckp
   ```

2. Add a Linux password for the new user as follows:

   ```
   # passwd chuckp
   Changing password for user chuckp
   New UNIX password: ********
   Retype new UNIX password: ********
   ```

3. Repeat the previous steps to add user accounts for all users from Windows workstations on your LAN to whom you want to allow access to your Linux system.

4. Add an SMB password for each user as follows:

   ```
   # smbpasswd chuckp
   New SMB password: ********
   Retype new SMB password: ********
   ```

   (The smbpasswd -a *user* command can be used to create the passdb.tdb and secrets.tdb files at the same time you set a user password.) Repeat this step for each user. Later, each user can log in to Linux and rerun the passwd and smbpasswd commands to set private passwords.

Note

In the most recent versions of Samba, options are available in the smb.conf **file that cause SMB and Linux passwords to be synchronized automatically.** ■

Starting the Samba service

To start the Samba SMB and NMB daemons, you can run the /etc/init.d/smb startup script by typing the following as the root user:

```
# service smb start
```

This runs the Samba service during the current session. To set up Samba to start automatically when your Linux system starts, type the following:

```
# chkconfig smb on
```

This turns on the Samba service to start automatically in run levels 2, 3, 4, and 5. You can now check SMB clients on the network to see if they can access your Samba server.

Testing your Samba permissions

You can run several commands from a shell to work with Samba. One is the `testparm` command, which you can use to check the access permissions you have set up. It lists global parameters that are set, along with any shared directories or printers.

Checking the status of shared directories

The `smbstatus` command enables you to view who is currently using Samba shared resources offered from your Linux system. The following shows example output from `smbstatus`:

```
# smbstatus

Samba version 3.5.5-68.fc14
PID     Username      Group           Machine
-------------------------------------------------------------------
25770   chris         chris           booker        (10.0.0.50)
25833   chris         chris           10.0.0.50     (10.0.0.50)


Service      pid     machine      Connected at
-------------------------------------------------------------
IPC$         25729   booker       Thu Jan 20 12:06:29 2011
mytmp        25770   booker       Thu Jan 20 12:16:03 2011
mytmp        25833   10.0.0.50    Thu Jan 20 12:25:52 2011
IPC$         25730   booker       Thu Jan 20 12:06:29 2009


Locked files:
Pid   Uid DenyMode  Access   R/W  Oplock SharePath    Name    Time
-------------------------------------------------------------------------------
25833 501 DENY_NONE 0x12019f RDWR NONE   /home/chris/files/.b.txt.swp Thu ↵
Jan 20 12:26:18 2011
```

This output shows that from your Linux Samba server, the `mytmp` service (which is a share of the `/home/chris/files` directory) is currently open by the computer named booker. PID 25833 is the process number of the `smbd` daemon on the Linux server that is handling the service. The open file is `/home/chris/files/.b.swap`, which happens to be opened by a `vi` command. It has read/write access.

Setting up Samba clients

Once you have configured your Samba server, you can try using the shared directories from a client computer on your network. The following sections describe how to use your Samba server from another Linux system or from various Windows systems.

Using Samba shared directories from Linux

There are several methods for connecting to shared directories from your Samba client. The following sections address these methods.

Using Samba from Nautilus

To connect to a Samba share from Nautilus, use the Open Location box by clicking Go ⇨ Location. Then type **smb:** into your Nautilus file manager Open Location box.

A list of SMB workgroups on your network appears in the window. You can select a workgroup, choose a server, and then select a resource to use. This should work for shares requiring no password.

The Nautilus interface requires you to either send clear-text passwords or type the user and password into your Location box. For example, to get to my home directory (/home/chris) through Nautilus, I can type my user name, password, server name, and share name as follows:

```
smb://chris:a72mg@toys/chris
```

Rather than type this information into the Location box, you can use the Connect to Server feature of Nautilus. Select File ⇨ Connect to Server. From the Connect to Server window that appears, select the Service Type as Windows Share and type the server name to see all available shares from that window. Optionally, you can request a specific Share, Folder, or User Name. Then you can also choose a particular name to use for the connection. You can also drop the password portion (such as smb://chris@toys/chris) and be prompted for the password.

Mounting Samba directories in Linux

Linux can view your Samba shared directories as it does any other medium (hard disk, NFS shares, CD-ROM, and so on). Using the mount command, you can mount a Samba shared file system so that it is permanently connected to your Linux file system.

The following example of the mount command shows how I would mount my home directory (/home/chris) from a computer named toys on a local directory (/mnt/toys). As root user, from a terminal window, type the following:

```
# mkdir /mnt/toys
# mount -t cifs -o username=chris,password=a72mg //toys/chris /mnt/toys
```

The file system type for a Samba share is cifs (-t cifs). I pass the user name (chris) and password (a72mg) as options (-o). The remote share of my home directory on toys is //toys/chris. (The two slashes in front of the hostname, toys, follows the syntax used for Windows shares with forward slashes instead of the Windows backslashes.) The local mount point is /mnt/toys. At this point, you can access the contents of /home/chris on toys as you would any file or directory locally. You will have the same permission to access and change the contents of that directory (and its subdirectories) as you would if you were the user chris using those contents directly from toys.

To mount the Samba shared directory permanently, you can add an entry to your /etc/fstab file. For the example just described, you could add the following line (as root user):

```
//toys/chris    /mnt/toys    cifs    username=chris,password=a72mg  0  0
```

You can add a credentials file readable only by root and use that to contain your user name and password, rather than expose that information to the command line. That way, someone running the ps command or looking at the world-readable /etc/fstab file on your system won't be able to see that information. For example, you could create a file named /etc/samba/creds.smb-pub containing the following two lines:

```
username=chris
password=a72mg
```

You could then change the mount command shown earlier to appear as follows:

```
# mount -t cifs -o credentials=/etc/samba/creds.smbpub //toys/chris
```

Troubleshooting your Samba server

A lot can go wrong with a Samba server. If your Samba server isn't working properly, the descriptions in this section should help you pinpoint the problem.

Basic networking in place?

In Samba, your Samba server can use the TCP/IP name as the NetBIOS name (used by Windows networks for file and printer sharing), or a separate NetBIOS name can be set in the smb.conf file. It is critical, however, that the broadcast address be the same as those for all clients communicating with your Samba server. To see your broadcast address, type the following:

```
$ /sbin/ifconfig -a
eth0        Link encap:Ethernet  HWadd 00:D1:B3:75:A5:1B
            inet addr:10.0.0.1  Bcast:10.0.0.255  Mask:255.255.255.0
```

The broadcast address (Bcast: 10.0.0.255) is determined by the netmask (Mask:255.255.255.0). If the broadcast address isn't the same for the Samba server and the clients on the LAN, the clients cannot see that the Samba server has directories or printers to share.

Cross-Reference

Before computers can share directories and printers from Samba, they must be able to communicate on your LAN. Refer to Chapter 14 for information on setting up a LAN. ■

Samba service running?

First, try the smbclient command from your Linux system to confirm that everything is running and being shared as expected. The smbclient command is a great tool for getting information about a Samba server and even accessing shared directories from both Linux and Windows computers. While logged in as root or any user who has access to your Samba server, type the following:

```
$ smbclient -L localhost
Password: **********
Domain=[ESTREET] OS=[Unix] Server=[ Samba 3.5.5-68.fc14]
```

```
Sharename      Type      Comment
---------      ----      -------
homes          Disk      Home Directories
IPC$           IPC       IPC Service (Samba Server Version 3.5.5-68.fc14)
hp-ns1         Printer
Domain=[ESTREET] OS=[Unix] Server=[Samba 3.5.5-68.fc14]

Server                   Comment
---------                -------
PINE                     Samba Server Version 3.5.5-68.fc14
MAPLE                    Windows XP


Workgroup                Master
---------                -------
ESTREET                  PINE
```

This shows that the Samba server is running on the local computer. Shared directories and printers, as well as servers in the workgroup, appear here. If the Samba server is not running, you will see Connection refused messages. If this is the case, you need to start the Samba service as described in the "Starting the Samba service" section earlier in this chapter.

Firewall or SELinux restricting access?

If the Samba server is running, it should begin broadcasting its availability on your LAN. If you try to access the server from a Windows or Linux client on your LAN but get a Connection refused error, the problem may be that the firewall on your Linux Samba server is denying access to the NetBIOS service. If you have a secure LAN, you can type the following (as root user) to turn off the firewall temporarily:

```
# service iptables stop
```

Then, try to connect to the Samba server from a Windows or Linux client. If you can connect to the server, turn the firewall back on:

```
# service iptables restart
```

You then need to open access to ports 137, 138, and 139 in your firewall so that the Samba server will be able to accept connections for services. (See Chapter 13 for information on modifying your firewalls.)

If you suspect that SELinux may be blocking access to your Samba service, type this:

```
# setenforce 0
```

This changes your SELinux service from Enforcing mode to Permissive mode. If you are then able to access your Samba service, make sure the file contexts for all your Samba configuration files are correct and that Samba-related SELinux booleans that are required are on. Then set SELinux back to Enforcing mode (setenforce 1).

User passwords working?

Try accessing a shared Samba directory as a particular user (from the local host or other Linux system on your LAN). You can use the smbclient command to do this. Here's an example:

```
# smbclient //localhost/home/ -U chris

Password: *******
Domain=[ESTREET] OS=[Unix] Server=[Samba 3.5.5-68.fc14]
smb: \>
```

In this example, smbclient connects to the directory share named home as the Samba user named chris. If the password is accepted, you should see information about the server and an smb:\> prompt. If you cannot access the same shared directory from a Windows client, it's quite possible that the client is passing an improper user name and password. Part of the problem may be that the Windows client is not providing encrypted passwords.

For certain Windows clients, using encrypted passwords requires that you change a Windows registry for the machine. One way to change the registry is with the Windows regedit command. Registry changes required for different Windows systems are contained within the /usr/share/doc/samba-*/docs/registry directory.

Tip

The smbclient **command, used here to list server information and test passwords, can also be used to browse the shared directory and copy files after you are connected. When you see the** smb:\> **prompt, type help to see the available commands. The interface is similar to command-line ftp clients. ∎**

Summary

By providing centralized file servers, an organization can efficiently share information and applications with people within the organization, with customers, or with anyone around the world. Several different technologies are available in Fedora to enable you to make your Linux computer a file server.

The Network File System (NFS) protocol was one of the first file server technologies available. It is particularly well suited for sharing file systems among Fedora and other Linux/Unix systems. NFS uses standard mount and umount commands to connect and disconnect file systems to the directory structures of client computers.

The Samba software package included with Fedora contains protocols and utilities for sharing files and printers among Windows, Unix and Linux operating systems. It uses SMB and CIFS protocols that are included with all Microsoft Windows systems, and therefore provides a convenient way to share resources on LANs containing many Windows systems.

## 18

Setting Up a Mail Server

Today, electronic messaging is part of the communication backbone and the core of information dissemination within companies of all sizes. Everyone uses e-mail — from companies to your grand-mother — and if you're in charge of an organization's mail server, you'll be notified (incessantly) when it stops working.

This chapter explains how to set up a mail server in Fedora to send and receive messages. In particular, it focuses on configuring a sendmail mail server, but it also explains how to configure a Postfix mail server (which is also in the Fedora distribution). Once the mail server is configured, Fedora provides your mail server's users with different ways to get their e-mail from your server, such as downloading it to their mail clients (with IMAP or POP).

Fedora also introduced Zarafa, which acts as a replacement for Microsoft Exchange, proving especially useful for business users. Zarafa can help your organization migrate away from Exchange and its expensive licenses.

Note

Although the primary aspects of mail server configuration are discussed in this chapter, many configuration aspects are beyond its scope and thus are not addressed. Because security is an important concern when you're con-nected to the Internet, I give it considerable focus here. ■

Introducing SMTP and sendmail

Even with multimedia attachments and HTML encoding prevalent in e-mail messages today, the technology behind message transfer hasn't changed significantly since the early 1980s. The framework for the Simple Mail

Transfer Protocol (SMTP) was initially described in RFC 821 in 1982. The protocol itself was extended in 1993 (RFC 1425), yielding the Extended Simple Mail Transfer Protocol (ESMTP), which provides more commands and new delivery modes.

The three primary parts to message transfer are the mail transfer agent (MTA), the mail delivery agent (MDA), and the mail user agent (MUA). The MTA, commonly referred to as the mail server (of which sendmail and Postfix are examples), actually handles distributing outgoing mail and listening for incoming mail from the Internet. The MDA accepts messages from the MTA and copies the message into a user's mailbox. Fedora uses procmail as the default MDA, as specified in the sendmail configuration file (sendmail.cf). Other MDAs (also referred to as local delivery agents, or LDAs) include maildrop and postdrop.

End users, for whom the mail is ultimately intended, use MUAs to get mail from the server and read it from their desktops. Most MUAs support Post Office Protocol (POP3) and Internet Message Access Protocol (IMAPv4) features for getting mail from the server so it can be read and managed from the user's desktop computer. When possible, you should use the more secure versions of POP and IMAP (pop3s and imaps, respectively).

Cross-Reference

See Chapter 8 for details on Mail User Agents available with Fedora. ∎

This chapter focuses on the sendmail MTA, the most common mail server on the Internet. Nearly 70 percent of all e-mail messages on the Internet are delivered by sendmail. With the growing Internet population, billions of e-mail messages are sent and received each day. This chapter also includes a short description of Postfix, an alternative to sendmail.

For getting mail from the server, this chapter describes the dovecot software package, which includes POP3 and IMAPv4 server software.

There have been three major releases of sendmail. The original sendmail (sendmail version 5) was written in 1983 by Eric Allman, a student at the University of California at Berkeley. He maintained the code until 1987, when Lennart Lövstrand enhanced the program and developed IDA sendmail. Eric Allman returned to Berkeley in 1991 and embarked on a major code revision, releasing sendmail v8 in 1993, which incorporated the extensions from IDA sendmail. The current version (8.14) is based on this "version 8" code.

Installing and Running sendmail

In Fedora, the sendmail distribution consists of three RPM packages: sendmail, sendmail-cf, and sendmail-doc. Only the first package is truly necessary to send and receive mail on your machine. The second package includes configuration macros and other files that can help you reconfigure your site's sendmail installation if the defaults are insufficient. The third package contains documentation files that help to explain some of the details of the current version.

The sendmail binary packages are included in the Fedora distribution. The sendmail and sendmail-cf packages are on the Fedora DVD that comes with this book. To install all three packages from Fedora, run the following command:

```
# yum install sendmail sendmail-cf sendmail-doc
```

Because sendmail is a common target of intruders, it's a good idea to immediately apply any updates that are available for sendmail before proceeding. You can do that using the `yum` command or the PackageKit utility. To update sendmail using `yum`, type the following:

```
# yum update "sendmail*"
```

Other Mail Servers for Fedora

The open-source version of sendmail is not the only mail server available for Fedora systems, but it is definitely the most common. The following list describes other servers and provides URLs for further information:

- **Postfix** — As with sendmail, the Postfix MTA is also included with Fedora. Written by Wietse Venema (of tcp_wrappers fame), this free mail server was designed with security in mind and executes most functions as an unprivileged user in a restricted chroot environment. The server encompasses more than a dozen small programs (each performing a simple, distinct task) and several single-purpose queues. You can find more information and source code at `www.postfix.org`.

- **Exim** — The Exim MTA is a free mail server (under GPL) that runs on Linux and Unix systems. Exim is included in the Fedora distribution. This MTA includes flexible features for checking and routing mail. Find out more about Exim from the Exim Home Page (`www.exim.org`). Exim follows a lot of conventions from an earlier MTA called Smail.

- **Qmail** — Also conceived with security as a high priority, this mail server (written by Daniel J. Bernstein) offers secure and reliable message transfer, mailbox quotas, virtual domains, and antispam features. More information is available from `www.qmail.org/top.html`.

Starting sendmail

Once installed, the sendmail service is turned on by default, although it only accepts incoming mail sent on the local system. To start sendmail immediately, you can either reboot the machine or just run `service sendmail start` to start the server. The procedure for starting and stopping sendmail is similar to that of any other server process.

By default, incoming messages received by sendmail are processed and stored in the `/var/spool/mail` directory. Each file in this directory represents a valid user name on the local machine. The file is created automatically the first time e-mail is sent to the user (or if it's otherwise missing). People with login accounts use this directory and their user account name as their incoming mailboxes (for example, `/var/spool/mail/johnq`).

Outgoing messages go in the /var/spool/mqueue directory while waiting to be sent. Filenames in this directory follow a consistent naming scheme. The first two characters indicate what type of data is stored in the file (see Table 18-1). Subsequent characters form a unique random identifier based on the process ID of the sendmail process that is handling that message.

TABLE 18-1

File Prefixes in /var/spool/mqueue

Filename Prefix	Type of Data Stored
df	The data that constitutes the body of an e-mail message
qf	The queue control file that contains the message headers and other administrative details
tf	A temporary copy of the qf file, created if delivery errors occur
xf	Any error messages generated while trying to send the message

Other programs

Several other executable programs are included in the distribution. These are described in Table 18-2.

TABLE 18-2

Other Related sendmail Programs

Program	Description
mailq	Displays a summary of the messages awaiting processing in the mail queue (the command is equivalent to sendmail -bp).
mailstats	Displays message quantity and byte count statistics.
makemap	Translates text files (/etc/mail/virtusertable) to hashed Berkeley databases (/etc/mail/virtusertable.db). This command runs each time the sendmail script starts.
newaliases	Translates the plain-text /etc/aliases file into the hashed Berkeley database file /etc/aliases.db (the command is equivalent to sendmail -bi).
praliases	Prints out all aliases defined in /etc/aliases.
procmail	Not included with the sendmail package but used as an MDA for sendmail. (It is included in Fedora in the procmail package.)

Program	Description
purgestat	Clears the directory where host status information is stored. The command is equal to `sendmail -bH`, which is disabled by default.
rmail	Handles incoming mail via UUCP (Unix to Unix Copy).
smrsh	Implements a restricted shell for running programs from sendmail.

Logging performed by sendmail

The amount of logging performed by sendmail is configurable in the `sendmail.mc` file, but the default level provides good coverage of informational notices and error messages. By default, the syslog facility configuration file (`/etc/rsyslog.conf`) tells rsyslog to store logging information from sendmail in the `/var/log/maillog` file. A few examples from this file are shown in this section.

An informational message similar to the following is written in the `/var/log/maillog` file each time the daemon starts (which also causes the hashed alias database to be regenerated):

```
May 16 12:52:40 toys sendmail[1787]: starting daemon (8.14.4):
        SMTP+queueing@01:00:00
```

Each time a message is sent or received, a log file entry is created:

```
May 16 12:54:34 toys sendmail[1120]: OAA01120: from=root, size=161,
  class=0, pri=3 0161, nrcpts=1,
  msgid=<199907191254.OAA01120@toys.linuxtoys.net>, relay=root@localhost
May 16 12:54:35 toys sendmail[1127]: OAA01120: to=jkpat, ctladdr=root
  (0/0), delay=00:00:01, xdelay=00:00:00, mailer=local, stat=Sent
```

Besides showing normal mail server activity, the logs also show when people attempt to break into your mail server. The `wiz` and `debug` commands implemented in earlier versions of sendmail were found to be a huge security problem. You may see log file entries, such as those shown in the following code examples, as people with malicious intent check whether you're running a vulnerable sendmail daemon. Also, the `expn` and `vrfy` commands (which can be disabled via a configuration option) can return more information than you'd care to distribute.

```
May 16 13:03:27 toys sendmail[699]: NOQUEUE: "wiz" command from localhost
  [127.0.0 .1] (127.0.0.1)
May 16 13:03:29 toys sendmail[699]: NOQUEUE: "debug" command from
  localhost [127.0 .0.1] (127.0.0.1)
May 16 13:03:37 toys sendmail[701]: NOQUEUE: localhost [127.0.0.1]:
  expn oracle
May 16 13:03:43 toys sendmail[702]: NOQUEUE: localhost [127.0.0.1]:
  vrfy oracle
```

Configuring sendmail

To configure the sendmail facility, you edit configuration files in /etc/mail and /etc that are then used by the sendmail startup script to generate database files. Those database files are, in turn, used by the sendmail daemon to control the behavior of your sendmail server. Once sendmail is configured, you can begin adding user accounts to have mailboxes on your server. The general steps described in this section for configuring sendmail are as follows:

1. **Getting a domain name:** You need a unique Internet domain name to assign to your mail server. You can purchase an Internet domain name from one of many different places, and then have DNS mail exchange (MX) records for your domain point to the mail server you are creating.

2. **Configuring basic sendmail settings:** In this step, you edit the /etc/mail/sendmail .mc file. That file defines such things as the locations of other configuration and log files, and enables you to configure the sendmail daemon.

3. **Defining outgoing mail access:** The most critical security issue associated with your mail server is which mail messages it will accept to relay to other mail servers. By editing the /etc/mail/access file, you can indicate the hosts and users from which your server will accept mail for local delivery or relay.

4. **Configuring virtual servers:** By default, sendmail assumes that you are setting up the mail server for the domain of which the server is a member. To have sendmail on a single computer be the mail server for multiple domains (referred to as virtual servers), you need to define each domain name in the /etc/mail/local-host-names file. (The local-host-names file is in the sendmail package, but it starts out empty.)

5. **Configuring virtual users:** Using the /etc/mail/virtusertable configuration file, you can instruct the sendmail daemon what to do with the mail it receives for the users and domains it's configured to handle. This file gives you a lot of flexibility to take mail addressed to a particular user and direct it to a particular mailbox, forward it to a different mail address, or reject that mail in various ways. The virtusertable file is in the sendmail package, although it only includes comments at first.

6. **Adding user accounts:** For the default sendmail installation, you need to add a user account for every user who has a mailbox on your mail server.

7. **Starting sendmail and generating database files:** Starting the sendmail service causes two major actions to occur: It runs the sendmail server daemon and, if you have the sendmail-cf package installed, it compiles your configuration files into database files that can be used by sendmail. If the server is already running, you can simply compile the configuration files and have any new settings take effect without restarting the server.

The following subsections provide details about each of these steps.

Getting a domain name

In order for people to be able to send mail to the users on your mail server, you must have your own domain name. In particular, you want to ensure that the MX record for your domain on the DNS server points to the hostname of your mail server.

Note

Your ISP might not allow you to have a private mail server on your residential Internet account. To enforce this, the ISP may block packets from being addressed to port 25. You may need to contact them to open that port before you can set up a mail server on that connection. Because many spamming and otherwise evil (or at least poorly controlled) e-mail servers try to hide behind dynamic IP addresses, many ISPs will neither allow e-mail addresses from dynamic IP addresses nor accept e-mail sent from those servers. ■

Configuring basic sendmail settings (sendmail.mc)

Much of the configuration of your sendmail server comes from information in your /etc/mail/sendmail.mc file. Because this file sets sendmail default values that can be used in most cases, you may not have to do much with sendmail.mc. However, I recommend you step through this section so you understand how your mail server is configured. Also, you must edit this file for sendmail to function as a public server (it listens only on local ports by default).

Changes you make to the sendmail.mc file do not immediately take effect. First you must compile the sendmail.mc settings to generate the /etc/mail/sendmail.cf file. I describe how to do that in the section "Starting sendmail and generating database files."

The resulting /etc/mail/sendmail.cf file contains over 1,800 lines of settings and comments that are used to direct the behavior of your sendmail daemon. The m4 macros you use in the sendmail.mc file are different from the resulting settings in the sendmail.cf file.

Note

The m4 utility can be used to process text files containing macros in IEEE Standard 1003.1-2001 format (Section 12.2, Utility Syntax Guidelines). This compiler is particular about how you use single quotes versus backticks, so be careful when editing sendmail.mc. For details on the m4 utility, enter the info m4 command. ■

To find out which macros to use for a setting you find in the sendmail.cf file, refer to the /usr/share/doc/sendmail*/README.cf file. (You must install the sendmail-doc package to get this file.)

Caution

Because of the way sendmail is configured in Fedora, you should not directly modify the sendmail.cf file. If you have the sendmail-cf package installed, the sendmail.cf file is regenerated automatically when sendmail restarts if sendmail.mc changes. As a result, any modifications made directly to sendmail.cf will be lost. ■

The following code samples are from the /etc/mail/sendmail.mc file that accompanies the Fedora version of sendmail. In these examples, the marker dnl means delete to new line. Lines that begin with dnl are comments. Also, notice that sendmail uses backticks as opening quotes and straight quotes as ending quotes.

```
 divert(-1)dnl
include(`/usr/share/sendmail-cf/m4/cf.m4')dnl
VERSIONID(`setup for linux')dnl
OSTYPE(`linux')dnl
```

The first few lines of the sendmail.mc file do some housekeeping. The divert line removes extra output when the configuration file is generated. The include line causes rule sets needed by sendmail to be included. The VERSIONID line identifies the configuration file as being for Linux systems, such as Fedora (although this setting is not checked, so it could be anything you like). The OSTYPE, however, must be set to linux to get the proper location of files needed by sendmail. You can choose to uncomment (remove the dnl string) the following two lines:

```
dnl define(`confSMTP_LOGIN_MSG', `$j Sendmail; $b')dnl
dnl define(`SMART_HOST', `smtp.your.provider')dnl
```

The confSMTP_LOGIN_MSG definition can be used to disguise the mail server you are using (change Sendmail to whatever). As for the second line, by default, the sendmail daemon tries to send your outgoing e-mails directly to the mail server to which they are addressed. If you want all e-mail to be relayed through a particular mail server instead, you can remove the comment marker, dnl, from the beginning of the SMART_HOST line above (leave the dnl at the end). Then, change smtp.your.provider to the fully qualified domain name of the mail server you want to use. Of course, you need to ensure that the SMART HOST you define will accept relays from your mail server.

```
define(`confDEF_USER_ID', ``8:12'')dnl
```

Instead of running as the root user, the daemon runs as the mail user (UID 8) and mail group (GID 12) based on the confDEF_USER_ID line set previously. This is a good policy because it prevents someone who might compromise your mail server from gaining root access to your machine.

```
dnl define(`confAUTO_REBUILD')dnl
define(`confTO_CONNECT', `1m')dnl
```

If you remove the initial dnl, the confAUTO_REBUILD line tells sendmail to automatically rebuild the aliases database, if necessary. The confTO_CONNECT line sets the amount of time sendmail will wait for an initial connection to complete to one minute (1m).

```
define(`confTRY_NULL_MX_LIST', `True')dnl
define(`confDONT_PROBE_INTERFACES', `True')dnl
```

With confTRY_NULL_MX_LIST true, if a lookup returns no mail exchange (MX) for a host, sendmail will try connecting to that host directly. If confDONT_PROBE_INTERFACES is true, the sendmail daemon will not insert local network interfaces into the list of known equivalent addresses.

```
define(`PROCMAIL_MAILER_PATH', `/usr/bin/procmail')dnl
define(`ALIAS_FILE', `/etc/aliases')dnl
dnl define(`STATUS_FILE', `/var/log/mail/statistics')dnl
```

The previous three lines (PROCMAIL_MAILER_PATH, ALIAS_FILE, and STATUS_FILE) set locations for the program that distributes incoming mail (procmail, by default), the mail aliases file, and the mail statistics file, respectively. The mail statistics line is commented out with a leading dnl. The following lines relate to the user database file, and mail protocols:

```
define(`confUSERDB_SPEC', `/etc/mail/userdb.db')dnl
define(`confPRIVACY_FLAGS', `authwarnings,novrfy,noexpn,restrictqrun')dnl
define(`confAUTH_OPTIONS', `A')dnl
```

The confUSERDB_SPEC line sets the location of the user database (where you can override the default mail server for specific users). The confPRIVACY_FLAGS line causes sendmail to insist on certain mail protocols. For example, authwarnings causes X-Authentication-Warning headers to be used and noted in log files. The novrfy and noexpn settings prevent those services from being requested. The restrictqrun option prevents the -q option to sendmail. The following are a few lines you can consider uncommenting:

```
dnl define(`confAUTH_OPTIONS', `A p')dnl
dnl TRUST_AUTH_MECH(`EXTERNAL DIGEST-MD5 CRAM-MD5 LOGIN PLAIN')dnl
dnl define(`confAUTH_MECHANISMS', `EXTERNAL GSSAPI DIGEST-MD5 CRAM-MD5
     LOGIN PLAIN')dnl

dnl define(`confCACERT_PATH', `/etc/pki/tls/certs')dnl
dnl define(`confCACERT', `/etc/pki/tls/certs/ca-bundle.crt')dnl
dnl define(`confSERVER_CERT', `/etc/pki/tls/certs/sendmail.pem')dnl
dnl define(`confSERVER_KEY', `/etc/pki/tls/certs/sendmail.pem')dnl
dnl define(`confDONT_BLAME_SENDMAIL', `groupreadablekeyfile')dnl
```

Some of the preceding groups of lines that begin with dnl (so they are commented out) can be uncommented (remove the initial dnl) to provide certain features. Others are set explicitly. The confAUTH_OPTIONS line can be used to set options used with SMTP authentication. This example (with A and p options) would allow authenticated users with plain-text logins to send mail. The TRUST_AUTH_MECH line would cause sendmail to allow authentication mechanisms other than plain passwords (if dnl were removed). The confAUTH_MECHANISMS line configures the types of authentication mechanisms that can be used (if dnl were removed). The next few lines above set the location of the certificates directory for sendmail to /etc/pki/tls/certs, and then identify different files in that directory that hold the certificates and keys needed for authentication. The confDONT_BLAME_SENDMAIL line should be uncommented if the key file needs to be readable by applications other than sendmail. (Typically, you don't want the file to be readable by everyone.)

The next few lines reflect several default values used by sendmail:

```
dnl define(`confTO_QUEUEWARN', `4h')dnl
dnl define(`confTO_QUEUERETURN', `5d')dnl
dnl define(`confQUEUE_LA', `12')dnl
dnl define(`confREFUSE_LA', `18')dnl
define(`confTO_IDENT', `0')dnl
```

The preceding commented lines actually show the default values set for certain timeout conditions. You can remove comments and change these values if you like. The confTO_QUEUEWARN option sets how long after delivery of a message has been deferred that a warning message to the sender should be sent. Four hours (4h) is the default. The confTO_QUEUERETURN option sets how long before an undeliverable message is returned. The confQUEUE_LA and confREFUSE_LA options set the system load average levels at which mail received is queued or refused, respectively. The confTO_IDENT option sets the timeout when waiting for a response to an IDENT query to be received (by default it is 0, which means no timeout).

Next are a few FEATURE lines:

```
FEATURE(`no_default_msa', `dnl')dnl
FEATURE(`smrsh', `/usr/sbin/smrsh')dnl
FEATURE(`mailertable', `hash -o /etc/mail/mailertable.db')dnl
FEATURE(`virtusertable', `hash -o /etc/mail/virtusertable.db')dnl
FEATURE(redirect)dnl
FEATURE(always_add_domain)dnl
FEATURE(use_cw_file)dnl
FEATURE(use_ct_file)dnl
FEATURE(local_procmail, `',`procmail -t -Y -a $h -d $u')dnl
FEATURE(`access_db', `hash -T<TMPF> -o /etc/mail/access.db')dnl
FEATURE(`blacklist_recipients')dnl
```

The FEATURE macro is used to set some special sendmail features. The no_default_msa feature tells sendmail not to generate a default MSA daemon (which normally is set to listen on port 587). The smrsh feature defines /usr/sbin/smrsh as the simple shell used by sendmail to receive commands. The mailertable and virtusertable options set the locations of the mailertable and virtusertable databases. The redirect option allows you to reject mail for users who have moved and provide new addresses. The always_add_domain option causes the local domain name to be added to the hostname on all delivered mail. The use_cw_file and use_ct_file options tell sendmail to use the file /etc/mail/local-host-names for alternative hostnames for this mail server and /etc/mail/trusted-users for trusted user names, respectively. (A trusted user can send mail as another user without resulting in a warning message.)

The local_procmail option sets the command used to deliver local mail (procmail), as well as options to that command (including the $h hostname and $u user name). The access_db option sets the location of the access database, which identifies which hosts and users are allowed to relay mail through the server. The blacklist_recipients option turns on the server's capability to block incoming mail for selected users, hosts, or addresses. (The access_db and blacklist_recipients features are useful for blocking spam.)

The following two lines affect how the root user name is exposed and on which interfaces the sendmail daemon listens:

```
EXPOSED_USER(`root')dnl
DAEMON_OPTIONS(`Port=smtp,Addr=127.0.0.1, Name=MTA')dnl
```

The EXPOSED_USER line allows the root user name to be displayed instead of a masquerade name. As it stands, the DAEMON_OPTIONS line allows only incoming mail created by the local host to be accepted. Be sure to comment this line out if you want to allow incoming mail from the Internet or other network interface (such as the local LAN).

```
FEATURE(`accept_unresolvable_domains')dnl
```

The `accept_unresolvable_domains` option is on, meaning mail is accepted from host computers that don't have resolvable domain names. For most public mail servers, you should comment out this line, so that mail from unresolvable domains will not be accepted (this is a good way to cut down on spam).

The `LOCAL_DOMAIN` option that follows causes the name `localhost.localdomain` to be accepted as a name for your local computer:

```
LOCAL_DOMAIN(`localhost.localdomain')dnl
MAILER(smtp)dnl
MAILER(procmail)dnl
```

The last lines in your `sendmail.mc` file define the mailers to use on your server. The `/usr/share/sendmail-cf/mailer` directory contains definitions for smtp, procmail, and other mailers. After you have made the changes you want to the `sendmail.mc` file, you can regenerate the `sendmail.cf` file as described in the section "Starting sendmail and generating database files."

Defining outgoing mail access

Every time an e-mail message intended for outgoing mail is received by your sendmail server, the server needs to decide if it will accept or reject relaying of that message. Policies that are too restrictive might prevent legitimate mail from getting out. Policies that are too loose can leave your server open to spammers.

With e-mail abuse as bad as it is, you should not run an open relay (whereby your server simply relays all messages it receives to the requested mail servers). Spammers can use software referred to as *spiders* to look for open relays. If you leave your mail server open, they will find you quickly and use your machine to relay their spam. If this happens, you might end up on a blacklist. Some e-mail blacklist maintainers look for open relays themselves and block them before abuse is even reported. Servers that use those blacklists will block all mail from you, even legitimate e-mail. Furthermore, you won't be acting as a good citizen of the Internet.

This section describes how to set up the sendmail access file (`/etc/mail/access`) to include a sensible set of rules defining for whom your server will relay mail. Using the `access` file, sendmail can make decisions about whether or not to relay a message based on the sender's host/domain name, IP address, or e-mail address. You can further refine the match by checking for those addresses in Connect, From, or To data associated with the message.

There are four basic actions you can have the server take on a match:

- **RELAY** — Your mail server simply sends the message on to the mail server requested in the mail message.

- REJECT — The message is rejected (not relayed) and the sender is told it was rejected.

- DISCARD — The message is silently discarded and the sender is not told.

- ERROR: text you choose — You can add some informative text here to give the sender a reason why the relay did not occur.

The /etc/mail/access file, by default, relays messages only from users who are directly logged into the mail server (localhost). Without being explicitly allowed, users from all other machines are not allowed to relay messages. Here's how the access file is set up by default:

```
Connect:localhost.localdomain        RELAY
Connect:localhost                    RELAY
Connect:127.0.0.1                    RELAY
```

With these defaults set, only mail sent from the local machine is relayed. Therefore, if the only outgoing mail you send is done while you are logged in directly to the server, you don't need to change this file. The following examples illustrate how you can selectively choose to relay or reject mail received by your sendmail server:

```
Connect:192.168                      RELAY
Connect:linuxtoys.net                RELAY
Connect:spammer-domain.com           REJECT

From:chris@linuxtoys.net             RELAY
To:spidermaker.com                   RELAY
To:former-user@linuxtoys.net         ERROR: User no longer works here
```

On the Connect:192.168 line, the network address (presumably the first part of the IP addresses used on your LAN) is allowed to relay mail. This is a good way to allow everyone sending mail from a machine on the LAN to have their mail relayed. On the next line (Connect:linuxtoys.net), mail coming from any machine in the named domain is allowed to be relayed. The third line represents a domain that you know to be a spam relay, so you reject messages originating from that domain.

The next three lines indicate how to treat mail received for relaying, based on the From and To names associated with the message. As you can see, the first example allows relay of any messages from chris@linuxtoys.net. In the last example, mail being forwarded to a particular person (*former-user*@linuxtoys.net) is rejected, and a custom error message (in this case User no longer works here) is sent back to the sender.

Caution

Use some caution when you are creating relay rules based on user e-mail address. Because those values are reported by the users themselves, they are vulnerable to being spoofed. ■

Once you have adjusted this file to suit you, you must rebuild the access database (access.db file) for the changes to take effect. See "Starting sendmail and generating database files" for information on this topic.

Configuring virtual servers

If you have set up a sendmail server for one domain, it's quite possible that you will someday want to have multiple domains served from that same computer. To create virtual servers on the same computer, you must add the name of every domain being served to the `/etc/mail/local-host-names` file.

For example, if your sendmail server were handling e-mail accounts for `linuxtoys.net`, `example.com`, and `example.net` domains, the `local-host-names` file would appear as follows:

```
# local-host-names - include all aliases for your machine here.
linuxtoys.net
example.com
example.net
```

Even if you are serving only one domain with your mail server, it is a good idea to identify that domain in this file. When messages arrive at the server for the domains listed here, sendmail knows to try to deliver the messages locally. Sendmail interprets messages for domains not listed here as needing to be relayed.

Note

If you want to off-load the processing of mail for a particular domain that is currently being directed to your sendmail server, you can use the `/etc/mail/mailertable` file. After setting up a DNS MX record to point to your sendmail server for this domain, and listing that domain name in the `mailertable` file, you can identify another computer to which sendmail will forward all the traffic for that domain. For example, the following indicates that all messages destined for example.com that are received by your sendmail server should be forwarded to the server named `mx1.linuxtoys.net`:

```
example.com        smtp:mx1.linuxtoys.net
```

The `smtp` indicates that the server supports Simple Mail Transfer Protocol. ∎

Configuring virtual users

Incoming mail to your sendmail server will be directed to your machine with a request to deliver the message to a particular person at a particular domain name. For each domain that the sendmail server supports, you can identify how e-mail to mail recipients of that domain is treated.

With sendmail, you set up virtual user definitions in the `/etc/mail/virtusertable` file. Essentially, you are telling sendmail to redirect messages addressed to particular user names or domain names based on definitions you set up.

Configuring the `virtusertable` file is particularly important if your server is handling mail for multiple domains. That's because, by default, mail for the same user name (regardless of the domain name) is stored in the same mailbox. For example, if your server handles mail for `example.com` and `linuxtoys.net` domains, mail for `chris@example.com` and `chris@linuxtoys.net` would all be directed to the `/var/spool/mail/chris` mailbox. With the `virtusertable` file, you can change that behavior in a lot of ways.

The virtusertable file is empty by default. Following are some examples that illustrate how incoming messages can be directed in different ways based on virtusertable definitions:

```
chris@linuxtoys.net          chris
cnegus@linuxtoys.net         chris
francois@linuxtoys.net       francois@spidermaker.com
info@linuxtoys.net           info-list
bogus@linuxtoys.net          error:nouser No such user here
@example.net                 example-catchall
@example.com                 %1@linuxtoys.net
```

In the first two lines, incoming mail destined for chris or cnegus at linuxtoys.net is directed to the mailbox for the local mail server user named chris. In the next line, any e-mail directed to francois in the same domain goes to francois@spidermaker.com. After that, e-mail sent to the info user name is saved to the local info-list mail account.

The line beginning with bogus@linuxtoys.net illustrates an error condition. Here, e-mail destined for the user named bogus will be rejected, with the error message No such user here directed back to the sender. Besides creating custom error messages, you can also use any Enhanced Mail System Status codes that are compliant with RFC 1893.

Note

In general, it's not a good idea to tell a potential spammer that a user account doesn't exist. Spammers often query mail servers looking for such information, often addressing e-mail to common names in an attempt to determine what real users exist on the server. Try to provide as little information as possible to someone phishing for information on your mail server. ∎

The last two lines (beginning with @example.net and @example.com) illustrate how e-mail for all recipients for a given domain can be directed to the same place. In the first case, all example.net messages go into the mailbox for the user named example-catchall. The last line shows how the users from a particular domain can all be mapped into their same user name (%1) on a selected domain name.

Once you have made changes to this file as desired, you must rebuild the virtusertable database (virtusertable.db file) for the changes to take effect. See the section "Starting sendmail and generating database files" for information on this topic.

Adding user accounts

Ultimately, the e-mail received by your mail server is placed in users' mailboxes, where they can pick it up and read it at their leisure. Each of those user names must be added as a real user on your Fedora system. For example, to add the user chris to your Fedora sendmail server, you could type (as root user) the following:

```
# useradd -s /sbin/nologin chris
```

This action creates a user account named chris in the /etc/passwd file, sets the shell to /sbin/nologin, and creates a mailbox for that user in /var/spool/mail/chris. The /sbin/nologin shell prevents the user from logging in to a shell (which is a good security practice when you want a user to have only mail or FTP access, for example). Now, sendmail can direct e-mail to that user's mailbox.

In order for that user to be able to access his e-mail later from his POP3 or IMAP client, he needs a password for his user account. Set the password for that user with the `passwd` command as follows:

```
# passwd chris
Changing password for user chris
New password: ********
Retype new password: ********
passwd: all authentication tokens updated successfully
```

Make sure that the user has this user account name and password so it can be configured into the user's e-mail client.

Starting sendmail and generating database files

The configuration that you just did to your `sendmail.mc`, `virtusertable`, `access`, `domaintable`, and `mailertable` configuration files doesn't take effect until those files are regenerated into database (.db) files. There are a few different ways you can go about loading your configuration files into database files:

- **Restarting sendmail** — Each time you reboot your computer or restart the sendmail daemon (`service sendmail restart`), all sendmail configuration files (including `sendmail.mc`) are compiled into database files that are ready to be used by the sendmail server. You can also just rebuild the databases without stopping the sendmail daemon (including the `/etc/aliases.db` file) using the sendmail startup script. To simply rebuild the database type, use this command:

  ```
  # service sendmail reload
  ```

  This command rebuilds all the database files, including the `/etc/aliases` file. (If the reload doesn't update your `sendmail.cf` file, ensure that the sendmail-cf package is installed: `yum install sendmail-cf`.)

- **Making the configuration files** — Using the `make` command, you can have some or all of the configuration files made into database files so they become immediately usable by the sendmail daemon. To do that, change to the `/etc/mail` directory, and then type either **make all** or **make** with the target database file you are creating. For example:

  ```
  # cd /etc/mail
  # make virtusertable.db
  ```

  You can replace `virtusertable.db` with `access.db`, `domaintable.db`, `mailertable.db`, or `sendmail.db`. (Note that you use the .db target name, not the name of the original configuration file.) As mentioned, you can also use the `make all` command to rebuild all database files.

At this point, your sendmail server should be up and running. You can test your server by sending mail to it and checking log files to see how the server reacted. Make sure that your firewall allows requests on TCP port 25. Then confirm that your mail server is responding to requests by typing the following:

```
# telnet 127.0.0.1 25
Trying 127.0.0.1...
Connected to 127.0.0.1.
Escape character is '^]'.
220 toys.linuxtoys.net ESMTP Sendmail 8.14.4/8.14.4;
     Sat, 20 Nov 2010 03:34:02 -0500
```

You can see that the sendmail daemon is running and responding to port number 25. Try typing **HELO** (not HELLO.) When you are done, type **QUIT** to exit.

Note

For more information on troubleshooting your mail server, refer to the *Linux Troubleshooting Bible* (Wiley, 2004). ∎

Redirecting mail

At times, your e-mail users may want to redirect mail to somewhere other than their own mailboxes on the local server. Each user can redirect his or her mail using the .forward file. System-wide, you as the administrator can set aliases to redirect mail in the /etc/aliases file.

The .forward file

One way for users to redirect their own mail is through the use of the .forward file, which users can place in their own home directories (for example for a user with a username of jkpat, the file is /home/jkpat/.forward). The format of a plain-text .forward file is a comma-separated list of mail recipients. Common uses of the .forward file include the following:

- Piping mail to a program to filter the mailbox contents:

  ```
  "| /usr/bin/procmail"
  ```

- Sending mail destined for one user (e.g., jkpat in this example) to another (e.g., cht09), on a different machine in this case:

  ```
  cht09@other.mybox.com
  ```

- Delivering mail to the local user (jkpat again) *and* sending it to two others (cht09 and brannigan):

  ```
  \jkpat, cht09@other.mybox.com, \brannigan
  ```

Tip

You are not allowed to have a .forward **file in a directory that can be read by all users. If you leave permissions open on a** .forward **file, sendmail will ignore that file and not forward mail as you want. To allow** .forward **files with open permissions to be used by sendmail, you can remove the** dnl **from the** confDONT_BLAME_SENDMAIL **line in the** sendmail.mc **file.** ∎

The aliases file

A more flexible method of handling mail delivery (system-wide rather than being specific to one particular user) involves the /etc/aliases file, which is also a plain-text file. The aliases file contains a name followed by a colon, and then a user name, another alias, a list of addresses, a file, or a program to which mail will be delivered. The name to the left of the colon (which can be a valid user name or just an alias) can then be used as an e-mail recipient on the local machine or a remote machine.

Some aliases are already set by default in /etc/aliases. For example, because a lot of administrative users are defined in Fedora (bin, adm, lp, and so on), instead of having separate mailboxes for each one, messages for all of them are directed to the root user's mailbox as follows:

```
bin:        root
daemon:     root
adm:        root
lp:         root
```

Using the aliases file for mail-aliasing allows for several extensions to normal mail-handling behavior:

- You can use the aliases file yourself to create mini-mailing lists. Here's an example:

  ```
  info-list:  chris, tweeks, francois@spidermaker.com
  ```

  In this example, any messages sent to info-list are distributed to chris, tweeks, and francois@spidermaker.com. Notice that the user list can be a combination of local users and outside mail addresses.

- One account can receive mail under several different names:

  ```
  patterson: jkpat
  ```

  This indicates that any mail addressed to patterson@mybox.com (just an alias) will arrive in the mailbox of jkpat (an actual user account).

- Mail can be received under a name that isn't a valid (or reasonable) user name:

  ```
  eric.foster-johnson@example.com: efjohnson
  ```

  He may not want to type eric.foster-johnson as a user name, but that doesn't mean he can't receive mail as such.

- Messages intended for one user can be redirected to another account (or to several accounts):

```
oldemployee: bradford
consultant: bradford, jackson, patterson
users: :include:/root/mail/lists/users
```

Here, any message for oldemployee@mybox.com would be delivered to the mailbox of user bradford. Also, the users bradford, jackson, and patterson would receive any mail addressed to consultant. The third line indicates that the recipients of the "users" alias are specified in the file /root/mail/lists/users.

- Mail can be sent directly to a file on the local machine:

```
acsp-bugs: /dev/null
trouble-ticket: /var/spool/trouble/incoming
```

In the first line, because the fictional ACSP program is no longer used on the machine, there's no need to track its errors, so the mail is effectively ignored. The second line stores incoming trouble tickets in the /var/spool/trouble/incoming file. Remember that if you enable this, anyone anywhere can send you a sufficiently large message to fill up the partition on which that directory resides. This is a security risk, so it should be carefully evaluated before being implemented.

When you are done adding new aliases, type the following to have those changes take effect:

```
# newaliases
```

Tip

When resolving addresses, sendmail doesn't actually use the /etc/aliases text file. For faster access, the text file is turned into a Berkeley database file, /etc/aliases.db, which resolves aliased addresses. For this reason, the newaliases command (equivalent to sendmail -bi) must be run to rebuild the database file each time the /etc/aliases text file is modified. This happens automatically each time sendmail is restarted. ∎

Introducing Postfix

Postfix is a mail transfer agent (MTA) that you can use in place of sendmail to handle mail service on your Fedora system. Postfix proponents offer several reasons for using Postfix instead of sendmail for their mail service, including the following:

- Postfix is designed to be easier to administer. Instead of using m4 syntax in the sendmail.mc file, Postfix uses the same types of directives used in the Apache Web server.
- Postfix has multiple layers of security built in, including the capability to run in a chroot jail, which locks the program into a certain set of directories. It also filters any sender-provided information before exporting that information into the Postfix environment.

Although some of the configuration files and other components are different from those in send-mail, many are meant to replace sendmail components (such as `aliases`, `access`, and `.for-ward` files, as well as the `/var/mail` directory structure). To get Postfix, you need to install the postfix package. To help you make the transition to Postfix from sendmail, Fedora has configured the two packages to use the alternatives system. Chapter 9 describes how to use the `system-switch-mail` application to change from one transport to the other.

When you switch to Postfix and start the Postfix daemon, as described in Chapter 9, Postfix takes over as the MTA, replaces sendmail components with Postfix components, and uses some of the same locations for mailboxes and log files. Postfix takes over mail transport based on configuration files set in the `/etc/postfix` directory. The following is an overview of the default locations used by the Postfix service:

- **Mail configuration** (`/etc/postfix/main.cf`) — The primary configuration file for Postfix. Identifies the locations of Postfix queues, commands, and aliases, and defines the host and domain names that Postfix is serving. If you do not add a fully qualified domain name to this file, Postfix will use your local hostname as the name of the mail service it represents.

- **Mailboxes** (`/var/spool/mail`) — Directory containing incoming mail files, with each user's mailbox represented by a file of the user's name. (This is the same default spool directory used by sendmail.)

- **Mail queue** (`/var/spool/postfix`) — Location of directories where mail messages are queued for delivery.

- **Mail log** (`/var/log/mail` and `/var/log/maillog`) — Location of mail log files.

Although most options you need for Postfix are described in the `/etc/postfix/main.cf` file, you can see many more available options in the `main.cf.default` file in `/usr/share/doc/postfix-*/`. Based on the default configuration in the `main.cf` file, here is how Postfix handles outbound and incoming mail:

- **Outbound mail** — The local hostname is added as the sending host for the mail posted from this computer. You might want to change it to the local domain name (set `myorigin = $myhostname`).

- **Incoming mail** — Only mail destined for the local hostname is kept on the local server by default. Other mail is forwarded. To have all mail for your domain kept on the local server, add $myhostname to the `mydestination` line. You must also change the `inet_interfaces` line to not merely listen for incoming mail sent from the local host. For example, the line could appear as follows to listen on all interfaces:

  ```
  inet_interfaces = all
  ```

For complete information on configuring Postfix, refer to `www.postfix.org/docs.html`.

Stopping Spam with SpamAssassin

Despite the fact that it is rude and antisocial, there are people who send out thousands of unsolicited e-mail messages (referred to as spam), hoping to get a few responses. Due to the economics of the Internet, spammers can send out literally millions of messages. Just a very small number of respondents is enough to make a profit for the spammers. Furthermore, modern spam can be dangerous, including messages designed to fool users into entering user names and passwords (called *phishing*) or messages that try to exploit vulnerable systems (particularly Windows systems).

Because Linux systems are often used as mail servers, tools for scanning mail messages for spam and viruses have become quite sophisticated over the years. This section describes how to use a tool called SpamAssassin to deal with spam and viruses on your mail server. If this doesn't meet your needs, you might add the ClamAV virus scanner to test mail messages for actual malware attachments. You can learn about ClamAV and how to use it with different mail software by using the following links:

- **ClamAV (`www.clamav.net`)** — Command-line virus scanner with database update features. The clamav package is in the Fedora repository (`yum install clamav`).

- **Klamav (`http://klamav.sourceforge.net/klamavwiki/index.php`)** — The KDE version of ClamAV (`yum install klamav`).

- **Third-party ClamAV Apps (`www.clamav.net/lang/en/download/third-party-tools/`)** — Find links to third-party software that works with ClamAV.

Using SpamAssassin

With SpamAssassin, you can configure your incoming mail service to tag messages it believes to be spam so you and your users can deal with those messages as you choose.

SpamAssassin uses several methods to identify spam:

- **Checking mail headers** — Examines the headers of your incoming mail to look for well-known tricks used to make the e-mail look valid.

- **Checking mail text** — Looks for text style, content, and disclaimers in message bodies that are commonly used in spam.

- **Checking blacklists** — Checks blacklists to find e-mail sent from sites previously known to relay spam. (The `mail-abuse.com` site provides a search tool for checking whether a server at a particular IP address has been blacklisted. To use that tool, go to `www.mail-abuse.com/cgi-bin/lookup`.)

- **Checking spam signatures** — Compares e-mail signatures. Because spam often consists of the exact same message sent thousands of times, taking signatures of spam messages enables SpamAssassin to compare your message to a database of known spam messages. SpamAssassin uses Vipul's Razor (see `http://razor.sourceforge.net`).

There are many different ways to deal with spam (or rather, e-mail that *might* be spam), but most of the experts I have consulted like to configure SpamAssassin to simply tag incoming e-mail messages that appear to be spam. Then they encourage each user of the e-mail server to create his or her own rules for filtering the spam.

Note

Although the procedure here describes how to use SpamAssassin from the RPM package that's included with the latest version of Fedora, many people get their version of SpamAssassin directly from the SpamAssassin **website. Because anti-spam software is evolving so quickly (to keep ahead of spammers), some people like to ensure that they have the very latest software. Instructions for installing the spamassassin package from source code are available from the SpamAssassin download page:** http://spamassassin.apache.org/ downloads.cgi. **Typically, you can simply run the** rpmbuild -tb **command on the Mail-Spamassassin tar file to create a new RPM.** ■

Setting up SpamAssassin on your mail server

Here's a quick procedure for enabling SpamAssassin and having your users choose what to do with spam messages that are encountered:

1. Configure your mail transport agent (sendmail or Postfix, for example) to use the procmail command as its mailer. For sendmail, it is already configured as the default mailer, based on the following line in the /etc/mail/sendmail.mc file:

    ```
    FEATURE(local_procmail,`',`procmail -t -Y -a $h -d $u')dnl
    ```

2. Ensure that the SpamAssassin spamd daemon is running. If it isn't, start it by typing the following (as root user):

    ```
    # chkconfig spamassassin on
    # chkconfig --list spamassassin
    spamassassin   0:off   1: off   2:on   3:on   4:on   5:on   6:off
    # service spamassassin start
    ```

3. Create an /etc/procmailrc file (using any text editor, as root user). This procmailrc file example pipes all mail messages received by procmail through spamc (which is the client side of the spamd daemon turned on in the previous step):

    ```
    :0fw
    | /usr/bin/spamc
    ```

4. If you like, you can do a lot more in the procmailrc file to deal with spam on a system-wide basis. You could, for example, create procmail recipes that take reported spam e-mail messages and sort them into a system-wide spam folder or delete them completely. Likewise, each user can create an individual $HOME/.procmailrc file to create personal procmail recipes. (Type **man procmailex** for examples of rules in a procmailrc file.)

5. Check the /etc/mail/spamassassin/local.cf file. This file contains rules that are used system-wide by SpamAssassin, unless they are overridden by a user's individual $HOME/.spamassassin/user_prefs.cf file. Here are the contents of the local.cf file:

```
required_hits 5
report_safe 0
rewrite_header Subject [SPAM]
```

6. In SpamAssassin, a scoring system is used to try to determine whether a particular message is spam or not. The required_hits line shows that a score of 5 is needed to flag the message as spam. You should set that higher (such as 8 or 10) for a public mail server. Setting rewrite_header to [SPAM] has SpamAssassin add the text [SPAM] to the Subject line of spam it finds. (Type **man Mail::SpamAssassin::Conf** to see other settings you can use in the local.cf file.)

Because false positives sometimes occur, you risk preventing your users from seeing an e-mail they need if you do system-wide filtering. To avoid this problem, the approach shown here lets the user decide what to do with e-mail tagged as spam. Users can even adjust their own threshold for determining when a message is believed to be spam.

Next, you should have the users of that mail server set up their own user preferences in their home directories. The preferences set in each user's $HOME/.spamassassin/user_prefs. cf file tell SpamAssassin how to behave for that user's e-mail. Here are examples of lines a user might want to have in that file:

```
required_score        3
whitelist_from        jsmith@example.com bjones@example.net
blacklist_from        *.example.org
```

The required_score line (which is set to 5 by default, but set to 3 here) sets the score needed to consider the message as spam. Scores are based on matching or not matching criteria in the tests SpamAssassin performs. (See http://spamassassin.apache.org/tests.html.)

The whitelist_from and blacklist_from lines let you set addresses for people, individual hosts, or entire domains that should not be considered spam (whitelist_from) or should always be considered spam (blacklist_from). For other ways to modify SpamAssassin behavior, type the following command:

```
man Mail::SpamAssassin::Conf
```

At this point, SpamAssassin should be running and identifying spam based on input from you and the people using your e-mail server. Next, each user needs to decide what to do with the messages that are marked as spam, as described in the following section.

Tip

Techniques you can use along with SpamAssassin include services such as SpamCop. SpamCop (www.spamcop .net) provides a service that enables you to enter spam messages you receive into a database that helps others block the same spam messages. ∎

Setting e-mail readers to filter spam

Each user can turn on filtering in his or her e-mail reader to decide what to do with messages tagged as spam by SpamAssassin. A common practice is to direct e-mail marked as spam to a separate folder. Because some real mail can occasionally be mistakenly marked as spam, you can check the spam folder every week or two, just to ensure you don't miss anything.

Here's an example of how to add a filter rule from Evolution Email:

1. Create a folder labeled SPAM under your incoming mailbox.
2. Click Edit ⇨ Message Filters.
3. From the Filters window, click Add. An Add Rule window appears.
4. Identify a rule name (such as Spam) that adds a criterion that looks for a specific header (X-Spam-Flag) containing specific text (YES). Then under Add Action, select an action (Move to Folder) and identify the folder to contain the spam messages (SPAM).

When you ask to receive mail from your mail server, all messages with the X-Spam-Flag set to yes are sorted into your SPAM folder. As an alternative, you can check for the text [SPAM] to appear in the subject line as the criterion for sorting the spam messages.

Other mail readers (Thunderbird, pine, , and others) also include features for filtering and sorting e-mail based on criteria you enter.

Evolution includes some SpamAssassin features within its framework. Evolution runs a daemonized version of SpamAssassin using the spamd daemon. The spamd daemons automatically filter your mail to find junk mail. When it finds junk mail, it automatically puts it into the Junk folder in the Evolution window. You can ignore those messages or simply scan through them quickly and delete them.

Getting Mail from the Server (POP3 or IMAPv4)

After you have set up your mail server, you want to enable users to access their e-mail from that server. That means either having the users log in to the mail server to read their e-mail or, more likely, configuring POP3 or IMAPv4 to let users access their mail from their workstations. Here are descriptions of POP3 and IMAPv4:

- **POP3** — With POP3, users download and manage their e-mail messages on their local workstations. POP3 is simpler and requires fewer server resources.
- **IMAPv4** — With IMAPv4, messages stay on the server, although you can manipulate those messages from the mail client. Because the messages stay on the server, an IMAPv4 server requires more disk space and uses more CPU, but you can log in to different workstations to read your mail and the mail and folders you have set up appear the same. With

all the e-mail on the server, an administrator needs to back up only one machine to keep permanent records of everyone's e-mail.

Fedora comes with software that is able to provide POP3 and IMAPv4 service. The dovecot package is primarily an IMAPv4 server that also contains a small POP3 server. It supports mail in both maildir (each message is a single file and folders are directories on disk) and mbox (all messages are in a single file) formats.

This section describes how to use POP3 to allow the users of your mail server to download their mail messages from your server over the network. POP3 is the simpler of the two protocols for accessing mailboxes over networks.

Accessing mailboxes in Linux

When e-mail messages are received on your sendmail or Postfix mail server, they are sorted to separate files, each of which represents a user's mailbox. The default location of mailbox files is the /var/spool/mail directory. For example, the login account jsmith would have the following mailbox:

```
/var/spool/mail/jsmith
```

While logged into the mail server, jsmith could simply type **mail** from a terminal window to read his e-mail (using the simple, text-based mail command). However, because most people prefer to get their e-mail from the comfort of their own desktop computer, you can set up either Post Office Protocol (POP3) or Internet Message Access Protocol (IMAPv4).

POP3 and IMAPv4 servers listen on the network for requests for a user's e-mail, and then either download the entire contents of the mailbox to the user's mail reader (as with POP3) or let the user manage the messages while the messages stay on the server (as with IMAPv4).

Typically, your mail server will be configured to use either POP3 or IMAPv4 to provide e-mail messages to your users (although it is possible to have both running on the same machine). The next section explains how to set up an IMAPv4 or POP3 service to allow access to e-mail accounts.

Tip

At times, you may want to check your e-mail on a computer that is not your regular computer but be able to save messages for later. In that case, most mail readers let you choose a setting that copies the e-mail messages without deleting them from your POP3 server. That way, when you get back to your regular computer, you can copy the messages again. IMAPv4 avoids that problem by always keeping the mail messages on the server and letting the user create and work with additional folders on the server. ∎

Configuring IMAPv4 and POP3 with dovecot

When a user is added to Fedora, a mailbox is configured under that user name in the /var/spool/mail directory (such as /var/spool/mail/chris). The format of that file, by default, is the traditional mbox format, with all messages and attachments stored in that one file. By configuring the POP3 service on your mail server, users will be able to download their e-mail messages from e-mail clients on other machines. By configuring IMAPv4, users can work with messages and folders directly on the server.

The following procedure describes how to configure the IMAPv4 or POP3 service in Fedora using dovecot:

1. Review the values set in the /etc/dovecot/dovecot.conf file. For the purpose of this example, the POP3 protocol is enabled, plain-text passwords are enabled from the standard /etc/passwd file, and PAM is used for authentication. To make that happen, at the very least, you should uncomment the protocols line in this file so that dovecot is configured to listen for pop3 and/or imap. Read through the comments in the file to see if you want to change any other settings.

2. Turn on the dovecot service by typing the following (as root user):

   ```
   # chkconfig dovecot on
   ```

   (If dovecot is not installed, install it by typing **yum install dovecot**.)

3. Start the POP3 service immediately by starting the dovecot service as follows:

   ```
   # service dovecot start
   ```

4. Open port 110 on your firewall to allow other computers to request POP3 service on your mail server. If you were using POP3 with SSL support, you would open port 995 instead (or port 993 for IMAPv4 over SSL). An easy way to open a port is through the Security Level and Firewall window (select System ➪ Administration ➪ Firewall). Select Other ports and click the Add button to add 110 as the port and TCP and UDP as the protocols.

All users who have user accounts on your mail server are configured, by default, to accept e-mail. For example, if e-mail comes in to the mail.handsonhistory.com server for a user named jsmith, the message is copied to the /var/spool/mail/jsmith file on the server. Continuing the example, the user named jsmith could set up his mail reader as follows:

- **Mail server:** mail.handsonhistory.com
- **User name:** jsmith
- **Password:** *theuserspassword*
- **Protocol:** POP3

After the mail reader is configured, when jsmith clicks Send & Receive from his mail reader, all e-mail messages in the /var/spool/mail/jsmith file are downloaded to his local mail reader. The messages are then erased from the server.

Keep in mind that regular POP3 (pop3) and IMAPv4 (imap) services use plain-text protocols to carry user names and passwords across the network. Depending on your network environment, this may pose a security threat. To use the more secure pop3s and imaps protocols, you must provide a key and certificate to dovecot. The following procedure describes how to do that by creating a self-signed certificate:

1. Remove any old `dovecot.pem` files that exist within your `/etc/pki` directory structure. (You can find them by running `find /etc/pki -name dovecot.pem`.)

2. Run the following commands to create a `dovecot.pem` file that includes both a key and a self-signed certificate. In the process, answer questions about your organization that are included in your certificate to present to users who try to access your dovecot server:

   ```
   # cd /etc/pki/tls/certs
   # make dovecot.pem
       .
       .
       .
   Country Name (2 letter code [XX]:
   ```

3. Open the `/etc/dovecot/dovecot.conf` file. Then enable at least the secure protocols you want to allow:

   ```
   protocols = imaps pop3s
   ```

4. Edit `/etc/dovecot/conf.d/10-ssl.conf` by changing the lines that identify the file containing the certificate and private key you just created. You need to uncomment the `ssl` line to turn on SSL. With this example, be sure to use the same file for both the certificate and the key:

   ```
   ssl = yes
   ssl_cert = </etc/pki/tls/certs/dovecot.pem
   ssl_key = </etc/pki/tls/certs/dovecot.pem
   ```

5. Reload or restart the dovecot service by typing the following (as root user):

   ```
   # service dovecot reload
   ```

If you set the protocols as described in the `dovecot.conf` file, users should now be able to connect to your dovecot service using imaps or pop3s. They will be presented with the certificate you created when they try to get their mail and will need to accept that certificate to proceed.

Managing e-mail, tasks, and calendars with Zarafa

Starting with Fedora 13, Fedora includes the Zarafa Collaboration Platform Community Edition. Zarafa aims to act much like Microsoft Exchange. It supports e-mail, contacts, calendars, and tasks with a sophisticated Web interface. Zarafa also supports Microsoft Outlook, which means you can use Zarafa as a drop-in replacement for Exchange.

The community edition is available under an open-source license (Affero GPLv3). You can also purchase commercial versions from zarafa.com.

To install Zarafa, you need to install the zarafa and zarafa-webaccess packages. (These will also add a number of other packages.) Next, edit the file /etc/zarafa/server.cfg by entering the MySQL username and password. (See Chapter 22 for more on installing the MySQL database.) Check over the configuration. You may need to edit other values.

You can then start the services with the following commands:

```
# service zarafa-server start
# service zarafa-gateway start
# service zarafa-spooler start
```

See www.zarafa.com/content/documentation for more information and manuals for Zarafa. The Zarafa wiki at www.zarafa.com/wiki has a good set of information on topics such as installation, integration with mail transport agents such as Postfix, as well as working with SELinux.

Summary

Fedora includes a full range of tools for configuring and managing mail servers. For mail transfer agents, Fedora includes the sendmail and Postfix software packages. Both are considered to be excellent, professional-quality mail servers.

To allow users to access their mailboxes from the server, Fedora includes the dovecot package. That package implements POP3 and IMAPv4 protocols to enable e-mail to be downloaded or manipulated on the server.

Information is included to help keep your mail service safe from intruders. In particular, filtering software such as SpamAssassin and virus scanner software such as ClamAV are critical to keeping your mail service clients safe from harm.

Zarafa provides a replacement for Microsoft Exchange for e-mail and groupware functions. You can use Zarafa to support Windows clients as well as Linux or Mac OS X systems.

Setting Up an FTP Server

F ile Transfer Protocol (FTP) has been the standard method for sharing files over the Internet for many years. Even with the popularity of the Web, which made document database services such as Gopher and WAIS obsolete, FTP servers are still the most common way to make directories of documents (especially large files) and software available to the public over the Internet.

File-sharing applications, such as NFS and Samba, are excellent tools for sharing files and directories over a private network. For organizations that need to share large numbers of files over public networks, however, FTP server software provides more robust tools for sharing files and protecting your computer systems. Also, FTP client software (for accessing FTP servers) is available for any type of computer that can access a network. Most Web browsers support FTP file downloads as well.

This chapter describes how to set up and maintain an FTP server using the Very Secure FTP Daemon package (vsFTPd).

Configuring your FTP server to enable users to upload files to it involves more risk than just allowing downloads. Anyone could upload a malicious file, overwrite other files, or, depending on the configuration, place a file in an undesired location. To help mitigate this risk, you can set up your server in a chrooted environment to limit access to the file system or allow only read-only access to anonymous users.

Also, keep in mind that authentication information and file transfers are sent in plain text across the network. If this traffic contains sensitive information, you might want to configure encryption. One way to do that is to use FTPS (also sometimes called FTP/SSL), the combination of the File Transfer Protocol (FTP) over a Secure Sockets Layer (SSL) connection.

IN THIS CHAPTER

Understanding FTP servers

Using the vsFTPd FTP server

Getting more information about FTP servers

Note

In discussing secure file transfer options, you may come across both SFTP and FTPS. FTPS, a newer protocol designed by the Internet Engineering Task Force (IETF), offers more features than traditional FTP, including secure transfers. FTPS is FTP transacted over an encrypted SSL connection, whereas SFTP is File Transfer Protocol over Secure Shell (SSH). ∎

Understanding FTP Servers

The first implementations of FTP date back to 1971, predating the Web by almost two decades. FTP was created at a time when most computing was done on large mainframe computers and minicomputers. The predominant platforms using FTP were Unix systems.

FTP set out to solve the need to publish documents and software so that people could get them easily from other computer systems. On the FTP server, files were organized in a directory structure. Users could connect to the server over the network (originally ARPANET, and now the Internet), move up and down the directory structure to find the desired files, and download files from (and possibly upload files to) the server.

Originally, one drawback with FTP servers was that when people looked for a file or a document on the Internet, they had to know which FTP server held the file they were looking for. Tools such as Gopher and WAIS helped in searches. With the advent of the Web, however, users now rely on a variety of search engines and links from Web pages to help identify FTP servers that have the files they want. In fact, because most modern Web browsers have integrated multiple protocols to access content, when you download files by clicking a link on a Web page, you may not even be aware that the file is being downloaded from an FTP server.

Attributes of FTP servers

That FTP was originally implemented on large, multiuser Unix systems accounts for many of the design decisions that remain a part of FTP today. FTP servers in Linux draw on FTP features that have resulted from years of testing and experience gained from other Unix versions of FTP. Some attributes of FTP servers follow:

- Because FTP was originally used on multiuser systems, only limited parts of the file system in Fedora are devoted to public FTP access. Those who access FTP from a public user account (by default, the anonymous or ftp user name) are automatically given an FTP directory (by default, /var/ftp) as their root directory. From there, the anonymous user can access only files and directories below that point in the file system.

- Non-anonymous access to the FTP server relies on a login process that uses standard Unix login names and passwords (by default, those user names are found in /etc/passwd). Although strangers to the system can log in using anonymous as a user name, users with their own accounts on the system can log in with their own user names through FTP and most likely have access to a greater part of the file system (in particular, their own private files and directories).

- The ftp and lftp commands, along with other FTP client programs let you log in and then operate from a command interpreter (similar to a very simple shell). Many of the commands that you use from that command interpreter are familiar Unix commands. You change directories with cd, list files with ls, change permissions with chmod, and check your location with pwd (to name a few). Some commands are unique to ftp, such as the lcd (local cd) command, which changes the current working directory on the client. When you find where you want to be, you use the get command to download a file, or the put command to upload one.

As an administrator of an FTP server, it is your responsibility to ensure that you share your files in a way that gives people access to the information you want them to have without compromising your system's security. This means implementing a strong security policy and relentlessly monitoring the system to prevent abuse.

Cross-Reference
See Chapter 13 for information on computer security issues. ∎

FTP user types

Several different types of users can log in to and use an FTP server. *Real users* represent the category of users who have login accounts to the Fedora system that contains your FTP server (that is, you know them and have given them permission for other uses besides FTP). With vsFTPd (described in the following section), you can configure settings for each real user separately, if you choose.

A *guest user* is similar to a real user account, except that guest user access to the computer's file system is more restricted. The user name anonymous is the most common for providing public (guest type) access.

The vsFTPd server also supports the concept of virtual users. The recommended method for creating virtual users for vsFTPd is to configure PAM (pluggable authentication modules) to point to per-user configuration files. Sample files for configuring virtual users are included with the vsftpd package. Refer to the /usr/share/doc/vsftpd*/EXAMPLE directory for directories containing virtual user example configuration files.

Cross-Reference
See Chapter 10 for information on creating user accounts that have restricted access to your server. ∎

Using the Very Secure FTP Server

The Very Secure FTP Server (vsFTPd) is a general-purpose FTP server project included in Fedora. vsFTPd is becoming the FTP server of choice for sites that need to support thousands of concurrent downloads. It was also designed to secure your systems against many common attacks.

Note

The Trivial File Transfer Protocol server (tftp-server package), which is distributed with Fedora, can also be used to provide file transfer service. The tftpd daemon is used primarily to provide support for diskless devices, which gather the files they need to boot and run from a TFTP server. Because FTP uses TCP, and TFTP uses UDP, FTP is considered safer to use over the Internet because it can be deployed with TCP/IP-related security features. Because TFTP is not securable, it is not intended for general, public FTP service and is generally used only on private LANs that are not accessible to public networks. Other FTP server packages available from the Fedora software repository include ProFTPD (http://proftpd.org) and Pure-FTPD (http://pureftpd.org). ■

Besides security and scalability, vsFTPd was designed for simplicity. Therefore, you are expected to rely on standard Linux file and directory permissions to provide refined access to your server. Getting started with vsFTPd is fairly straightforward.

Note

Although vsFTPd is the recommended FTP server software in Fedora, the WU-FTPD FTP server software, which was once part of Red Hat Linux, is still available on the Web. However, WU-FTPD is considered by most to be far less secure than vsFTPd; therefore, it should not be used in most cases. ■

Quick-starting vsFTPd

By enabling the vsFTPd service, you can almost instantly have an FTP service running with the default values (set in the /etc/vsftpd/vsftpd.conf file). The following is a quick procedure for getting your vsFTPd server up and running. In case you didn't install vsFTPd when you originally installed Fedora, install it now by typing the following:

```
# yum install vsftpd
```

Here's how to start and try out the vsFTPd service:

1. To use the vsFTPd server, you must ensure that the vsFTPd software package is installed:

   ```
   # rpm -q vsftpd
   ```

2. Enable the vsFTPd server by typing the following line (as root user):

   ```
   # chkconfig vsftpd on
   ```

3. Start the vsFTPd server as follows:

   ```
   # service vsftpd start
   ```

4. Try to log in to the FTP server as anonymous (using any password):

   ```
   $ ftp localhost
   Connected to yourhost (127.0.0.1)
   ```

```
220 (vsFTPd 2.2.2)
Name (localhost:chris): anonymous
331 Please specify the password.
Password:
230 Login successful.
Remote system type is UNIX.
Using binary mode to transfer files.
ftp>
```

If you see messages similar to the preceding, your vsFTPd server is now up and running. Next, try to access the server from another computer on the network to ensure that it is accessible.

Securing vsFTPd

If your FTP server is not accessible to the outside world, you may need to ensure that your network is configured properly and that vsFTPd is secured using one or more security features in Fedora. Security features and/or services that can be configured to allow or block access to vsFTPd include firewalls, TCP wrappers, and Security Enhanced Linux (SELinux).

- **Firewalls** — If your firewall is enabled, it must be set to allow access to port 21 and possibly port 20. The quick way to do that is to run system-config-firewall and add FTP as a trusted service. To allow passive FTP from the server, load the nf_conntrack_ftp module. The best way to do that is to edit the /etc/sysconfig/iptables-config file, changing the IPTABLES_MODULES line so it looks as follows:

  IPTABLES_MODULES="nf_conntrack_ftp"

- **TCP wrappers** — You can use TCP wrappers to restrict access to vsFTPd by adding entries to the /etc/hosts.allow and/or /etc/hosts.deny files (type **man hosts_access** for information). The daemon name to use is vsftpd.

- **SELinux** — If SELinux is enabled, it may prevent access to your FTP server that you might normally expect to work. To set SELinux to permissive mode, type setenforce 0 as root. Note that this setting has security implications. Alternately, type **man ftpd_selinux** to learn how to use SELinux with vsftpd. In particular, make sure that proper SELinux file contexts are set on files and directories you want to share from vsFTPd and that SELinux booleans are set to allow such features as access to home directories and file uploads.

The next section explains the /etc/vsftpd/vsftpd.conf configuration file.

Configuring vsFTPd

Most of the configuration of vsFTPd is done in the /etc/vsftpd/vsftpd.conf file. Although many values are not set explicitly in vsftpd.conf, you can override the defaults by setting *option=value* statements in this file. You can set such things as which users have access to your vsFTPd server, how logging is done, and how timeouts are set.

The following sections provide more information about how vsFTPd is configured by default and how you can further configure your vsFTPd server.

Enabling user access

Users who can access your vsFTPd server are, by default, the anonymous user and any users with real user accounts on your system. (A *guest* user is simply a real user account that is restricted to its own home directory.) The following lines set these user access features:

```
anonymous_enable=YES
local_enable=YES
```

The anonymous_enable line lets users log in anonymously using either the anonymous or the ftp user name. If you want to disable access by anonymous users, don't just comment out anonymous_enable by placing a # character at the start of the line. Anonymous access is on by default, so you must set anonymous_enable=NO to disable it.

Any users with local accounts (in /etc/passwd) and valid passwords can log into the FTP server with local_enable set to YES. By default, local_enable is off and disallowed by SELinux. Even with this feature enabled, all user accounts listed in the /etc/vsftpd/user_list file are denied access.

When you test FTP and try to log in with your user account, you may see an error like the following:

```
500 OOPS: Cannot change directory:/home/chris
```

This is because SELinux stops what it sees as a security concern. You can enable user account access by running the following command:

```
# /usr/sbin/setsebool -P ftp_home_dir=1
```

Cross-Reference
See Chapter 13 for more on SELinux. ■

There is another file called /etc/vsftpd/ftpusers that is also a list of users who are not allowed to log in. By default, it has the same contents as the user_list file, but the functionality is provided by the PAM facility. If you make changes to user_list you may also want to edit ftpusers and/or /etc/pam.d/vsftpd.

Note
Before you start logging into an FTP server with your personal user name and password, keep in mind that the FTP login service uses clear-text passwords. Therefore, a network sniffer is capable of seeing this information. If you want to use an FTP-type interface to access files on an FTP server using your personal account, consider using the OpenSSH (www.openssh.org/) sftp command instead of a normal FTP client. If the server running FTP includes an SSH service, you can use sftp to connect to that server using encrypted passwords. ■

Check the user_list file to see which users are denied access to the vsFTPd server. Note that root and other administrative logins are excluded. You can add other users to this list or change the location of the list by setting the `userlist_file` parameter to the file you want. To add a user to the `user_list` or use the `userlist_file` parameter to create a new list, you must also have `userlist_enable` set to `YES` (as it is by default). For example:

```
userlist_file=/etc/vsftpd/user_list_local
userlist_enable=YES
```

If you like, you can change the meaning of the `/etc/vsftpd/user_list` file so that only the users in that list are allowed to use the vsFTPd service. Set `userlist_deny=NO` and change the `/etc/vsftpd/user_list` to include only names of users to whom you want to grant access to the server. All other users, including `anonymous` and the system-defined user `ftp` (which is often used for running FTP services), will be denied access.

Setting FTP access

The vsFTPd server software provides a simple and seemingly secure approach to access permissions. Instead of using settings in the FTP service to selectively prevent downloads and uploads from particular directories (as older FTP servers such as WU-FTPD do), you can use standard Linux file and directory permissions to limit access. However, the following general settings in the `/etc/vsftpd/vsftpd.conf` file let users get files from and put files onto your vsFTPd server.

Downloading files

Anonymous users can download files from the vsFTPd server by default. Real users, excluding some administrative logins, can download and upload files if enabled, as described in the previous section. The ability to download a particular file or a file from a particular directory is governed by the following basic Linux features:

- **File and directory permissions** — Standard file and directory permissions apply as a means of limiting access to particular files, even in accessible file systems. Therefore, if the root user puts a file with 600 permission (read/write to root only) in the `/var/ftp` directory, an anonymous user cannot download that file.

- **Root directory** — The root directory (chroot) for anonymous users is `/var/ftp`. The root directory for regular users is the entire computer's root directory (`/`), although their current directory after connecting to FTP is the user's home directory, or typically `/home/user`, where `user` is the user name. Therefore, an anonymous user is restricted to downloads from the `/var/ftp` directory structure, whereas a regular user potentially has access to the whole file system. Another possibility is to create *guest* accounts by restricting some or all users to their home directories.

You can use the `chroot_local_user` option to change the root directory for regular users so that they are restricted to their home directory. To restrict all regular users to their home directory when using vsFTPd, add this line to the `vsftpd.conf` file:

```
chroot_local_user=YES
```

689

To enable the concept of *guest users*, you can choose to limit only selected users to their home directories. (As mentioned previously, a *guest* user in FTP parlance is simply a real user account that is restricted to its own home directory.) You do this by setting chroot_list_enable to YES and then adding a list of guest users to a file noted with the chroot_list_file option. The following example lets you add such a list (one user name per line) to the /etc/vsftpd/ chroot_list file:

```
chroot_list_enable=YES
chroot_list_file=/etc/vsftpd/chroot_list
```

Tip

To restrict a user to FTP access only, set the user's shell to /sbin/nologin **in the** /etc/passwd **file. Do this by running the** system-config-users **command or** usermod **command and changing properties for the user, as described in Chapter 10.** ■

You can add a setting to the vsftpd.conf file to affect how files are downloaded. To enable ASCII downloads, use the following:

```
ascii_download_enable=YES
```

Without making that change, all downloads are done in binary mode. Although vsFTPd will seem to allow the user to change to ascii mode, ascii mode will not work if this setting is NO. With ASCII downloads disabled, it is up to the client side to handle ASCII mangling when required.

Uploading (writing) files from local users

Two values set in the vsftpd.conf file allow the uploading of files during a vsFTPd session. The following defaults allow any users with regular, local user accounts to upload files:

```
write_enable=YES
local_umask=022
```

The write_enable value must be YES if you intend to allow any users to write to the FTP server. The umask=022 value sets the default file permission used when a local user creates a file on the server. (The 022 value causes created files to have 644 permission, which gives the user read and write permission and everyone else only read permission.)

As with downloading, uploading in ascii mode is disabled by default. To allow ascii uploads, add the following line:

```
ascii_upload_enable=YES
```

Uploading (writing) files from anonymous users

The ability to upload files is turned off for anonymous FTP users. If you want to enable it, add the following line to the vsftpd.conf file:

```
anon_upload_enable=YES
```

To use anonymous upload, the global write enable must be activated. You must also ensure that the /var/ftp directory contains one or more directories with write permissions open to anonymous users. For example, you might want to create an incoming directory and open its permissions (chmod 777 /var/ftp/incoming).

Files uploaded by anonymous users will be created with 600 permission by default (read/write permission for the ftp user, not accessible to any other users, so that even the user who uploaded the files can't remove them or even see them). To allow 644 permission, for example, you can add the following line:

```
anon_umask=022
```

When you allow the anonymous user to upload files, you can grant limited ability to change the files he or she uploads. By adding the following line, you can allow anonymous users to rename or delete any files owned by anonymous users (provided that the files are in directories for which the users have write permission):

```
anon_other_write_enable=YES
```

If you also want to allow anonymous users to create their own directories, add the following:

```
anon_mkdir_write_enable=YES
```

By default, the ftp user is given ownership of uploaded files from anonymous users. If you want to specify that anonymous uploads be owned by a different user (of your choice), you can use the chown_uploads and chown_username options. For example, if you have a user account named mynewuser, you can set these options as follows:

```
chown_uploads=YES
chown_username=mynewuser
```

Of course, you can create and use any user name you want. However, for security reasons you should not use the root login or any other administrative login for this purpose.

If SELinux is in enforcing mode, you must specifically allow anonymous writing. In particular, you need to enable the allow_ftpd_anon_write boolean and make sure that any directory you want open for writing has the public_content_rw_t file context set.

Adding message files

Although vsFTPd doesn't support the arrangement of README and welcome files that FTP servers such as WU-FTP support, you can add .message files to any accessible directory on your vsFTPd server. Then, if you use the default dirmessage_enable option as follows, the text from the .message file will be displayed when the user enters the directory:

```
dirmessage_enable=YES
```

You will probably at least want to add a .message file to the root directory of the FTP server for anonymous users. By default, that location is /var/ftp/.message. If you want to use files other than .message files, you can set the message_file option. For example, to have text from the .mymessage file displayed when you enter a directory, you can add the following line:

```
message_file=.mymessage
```

A .message file provides an opportunity for you to add information about the contents of your server, copyright or compliance information, or instructions about how to use the software. By allowing different message files, you can tailor what you want to say to visitors, depending on where they are located on your file server.

You can also set a one-line message to appear before the login prompt. To do so, enter the following line, replacing the text with anything you want to say:

```
ftpd_banner=Welcome to My FTP service.
```

As a security measure, don't mention the software or operating system that you have running. Any information that can slow down a potential intruder from finding out what software you are running makes it easier for you to keep that intruder out.

Logging vsFTPd activities

Logging is enabled in vsFTPd by default, and the activities of your vsFTPd site are written to the /var/log/xferlog file. The following options enable logging and change the log file to /var/log/vsftpd.log:

```
xferlog_enable=YES
xferlog_file=/var/log/vsftpd.log
```

You can turn off logging if you like by changing YES to NO. (Note, however, that logging enables you to watch for potential break-ins, so turning it off is not recommended.) Or, you can change the location of the log file by changing the value of the xferlog_file option. Keep in mind that with a lot of usage, your FTP server can produce a lot of log messages. Therefore, to be useful, the logs should be monitored fairly often.

If you want to be able to use tools that generate transfer statistics, you can have vsFTPd log data written in the standard xferlog format that is used by WU-FTPD and other FTP servers. To store your transfer data in xferlog format, set the following option:

```
xferlog_std_format=YES
```

Setting timeouts

The following timeouts are set by default in vsFTPd (these values are built in, so you don't have to make any changes to the /etc/vsftpd/vsftpd.conf file for them to take effect):

```
accept_timeout=60
connect_timeout=60
```

```
idle_session_timeout=300
data_connection_timeout=300
```

The `accept_timeout=60` and `connect_timeout=60` values determine how long the client has to establish a PASV- or PORT-style connection, respectively, before the connection times out. Both are set to 60 seconds. (Note that these two lines are not automatically included in the configuration file; you can add them by hand if you want to change their values.) The `idle_session_timeout=300` option causes the FTP session to be dropped if the user has been inactive for more than five minutes (300 seconds). The `data_connection_timeout` value sets the amount of time, during which no progress occurs, that the server will wait before dropping the connection (the default here is 300 seconds).

Navigating a vsFTPd site

Most shell wildcard characters that a user might expect to use, such as question marks and brackets, are supported by vsFTPd. There is one particularly useful wildcard character you can use with the `ls` command, and one option you can turn on. The asterisk (`*`) wildcard can be used with the `ls` command. Multiple asterisks in the same line are supported. You can add support for the `-R` option of `ls` so that a user can recursively list the contents of the current directory and all subdirectories. To enable this feature (it is off by default), add the following line to the `vsftpd.conf` file:

```
ls_recurse_enable=YES
```

Setting up vsFTPd behind a firewall

If you are configuring an FTP server behind a firewall, you need to do some special configuration to allow communications to pass through that firewall to anyone you want to allow access to your server. To do that, you can use *ephemeral port numbers*, which provide random, temporary port numbers, within a range of numbers, as needed.

Note

For information setting up vsFTPd behind a firewall, refer to the FTP and Your Firewall pages at `www.linux-homenetworking.com/wiki/index.php/Quick_HOWTO_:_Ch15_:_Linux_FTP_Server_Setup`. ∎

Getting More Information About FTP Servers

You can find plenty of resources for gaining more information about FTP servers. Here are two options:

- **FAQ** — To check out the vsFTPd FAQ, go to `/usr/share/doc/vsftpd*/FAQ`.
- **RFCs** — Requests For Comments are the documents that define standard protocols used with the Internet. The main RFC for FTP is RFC959. You can obtain RFCs from a variety of locations on the Internet, including the Internet RFC/FYI/STD/BCP Archives (`www.faqs.org/rfcs`).

Summary

The FTP service is the primary method of offering archives of document and software files to users over the Internet or other TCP/IP-based networks. The most popular FTP server package delivered with Fedora is the Very Secure FTP (vsFTPd) Server package. The vsFTPd server relies on standard Linux file and user permissions to provide a simple, yet secure, FTP environment to run in Fedora.

Setting Up a Web Server

20

pproximately 58 percent of all websites today are powered by the open-source Apache Web Server Project (compared with about 23 percent for Microsoft Web servers). In October 2010, Netcraft (www.netcraft.com) reported receiving responses from more than 232 million sites, more than 135 million of which were running Apache. As registration of Internet domain names continues to grow at an average rate of more than 6 million per month, Apache is getting the lion's share of new websites being launched.

The Web has also been a boon to organizations seeking an inexpensive means to publish and distribute information. Using the Fedora distribution included with this book, you can launch your own website using software available from the Apache project. Combine your own domain name, Internet connection, and Fedora to create your own presence on the World Wide Web.

This chapter shows you how to install and configure the Apache Web server. Each of the server's configuration files is described and explained in detail. You learn about various options for starting and stopping the server, as well as how to monitor the activity of a Web server. Related security concerns and practices are addressed throughout the chapter in the descriptions and examples (as well as in a special Web server security section, "Protecting Web Servers with Certificates and Encryption," in Chapter 13).

Note
The current version of Fedora comes with Apache version 2.2.16. If you have been using a pre-2.0 version of Apache, note that the package names apache and apache-manual have changed to httpd and httpd-manual, respectively. ■

Introducing Web Servers

The World Wide Web, as it is known today, began as a project of Tim Berners-Lee at the European Organization for Nuclear Research (CERN). The original goal was to provide one consistent interface for geographically dispersed researchers and scientists who needed access to information in a variety of formats. From this idea came the concept of using one client (the Web browser) to access data (text, images, sounds, video, and binary files) from several types of servers (HTTP, FTP, SMTP, Gopher, NNTP, WAIS, Finger, and streaming-media servers).

The Web server usually has a simpler job: to accept HyperText Transfer Protocol (HTTP) requests and send a response to the client. However, this job (and the server) can get much more complex, executing functions such as the following:

- Performing access control based on file permissions, username/password pairs, and hostname/IP address restrictions

- Parsing a document (substituting appropriate values for any conditional fields within the document) before sending it to the client

- Spawning a Common Gateway Interface (CGI) script or custom application programming interface (API) program to evaluate the contents of a submitted form, presenting a dynamically created document, or accessing a database

- Logging any successful accesses and errors

The Apache Web server

The Apache Web server was originally based on HTTPd, a free server from the National Center for Supercomputing Applications (NCSA). HTTPd was the first, and at one time the only, Web server on the Internet. Unfortunately, the server's development wasn't keeping up with the needs of Webmasters, and several security problems were discovered. Many Webmasters had been independently applying their own features and fixes to the NCSA source code.

In early 1995, a group of these developers pooled their efforts and created a new project, called Apache, from this code base. Since then, what is now the Apache Software Foundation (www .apache.org) has largely rewritten the code and created a stable, multiplatform Web server daemon. The Apache Software Foundation sponsors more than two dozen related projects. Those projects include mod_perl (to create dynamic websites with the Perl language), Jakarta (to provide server-side Java content), DB (to create and maintain commercial-quality database solutions), and SpamAssassin (to identify and deal with junk e-mail).

The main features of the Apache Web server are as follows:

- The stability and rapid development cycle associated with a large group of cooperative volunteer programmers

- Full source code, downloadable at no charge (there are no restrictions by End User License Agreements [EULAs] and no caps on the number of servers you can run)

- Ease of configuration using plain-text files

- Access control based on client hostname/IP address or username/password combinations

- Support for server-side scripting as well as CGI scripts; this includes the capability to have different users controlling script execution (to limit the vulnerability of an entire Web server if a single script is compromised)

- A custom API that enables external modules (e.g., for extended logging capabilities, improved authentication, caching, connection tracking, and so on) to be used by the server daemon

Apache is not the only Web server for Fedora systems, but it is the one most often used with Linux, and it is still the most popular server used on the Internet according to Netcraft (`http://news.netcraft.com/archives/web_server_survey.html`).

Other Web servers available for Fedora

Other Web servers that can run on Fedora and other Linux distributions are described in the following list, with URLs that provide more detailed information:

- **lighttpd** — The lighttpd Web server (`www.lighttpd.net`) is built for security, speed, compliance, and flexibility, hence its nickname, "Lighty." It is particularly optimized for high-performance environments because it has a low-memory footprint and balances CPU load. Sites such as YouTube, Wikipedia, and meebo have used lighttpd for some specialty Web applications.

- **tclhttpd** — TheTclHttpd Web server (`tclhttpd` package) is created in the Tool Command Language (TCL). Besides acting as a Web server, TclHttpd can also be used as a TCL application server.

- **thttpd** — The thttpd HTTP server (`http://acme.com/software/thttpd`) was designed to be simple, small, portable, fast, and secure. Its creators call it a tiny, turbo, throttling HTTP server. It implements little more than the minimum needed to be HTTP/1.1 compliant, so it can run much faster than many larger Web servers under extreme loads.

Quick-Starting the Apache Web Server

If Apache wasn't installed during the Fedora installation, you can install it later. You need the httpd package and optionally the httpd-manual package (named apache and apache-manual, respectively, in earlier versions).

Here's a quick way to get your Apache Web server going. From here, you'll want to customize it to match your needs and your environment (as described in the section that follows).

1. Make sure that Apache is installed by typing the following from a terminal window:

```
$ rpm -qa | grep httpd
system-config-httpd-1.5.2-2.fc14.noarch
httpd-tools-2.2.16-1.fc14.i686
http-devel-2.2.16-1.fc14.i686
httpd-2.2.16-1.fc14.i686
httpd-manual-2.2.16-1.fc14.i686
```

2. The version number you see may be different. You need only the `httpd` package to get started. I recommend `httpd-manual` because it has excellent information on the whole Apache setup. The `httpd-devel` package includes the `apxs` tool for building and installing extension modules. The `httpd-tools` package includes tools for running benchmarks and managing passwords for Apache.

3. The `system-config-httpd` package contains a GUI-based Apache configuration tool. Depending on the type of content you are serving, you might also add packages containing modules to run that code within the Apache server (such as `mod_perl`, `mod_python`, and `mod_mono`).

4. A valid hostname is recommended if you're planning a public Apache server (e.g., `www.handsonhistory.com`). If you don't have a real, fully qualified domain name, you can edit the `/etc/httpd/conf/httpd.conf` file to define the `ServerName` as your computer's IP address. Open the `httpd.conf` file (as the root user) in any text editor, search for the line containing `ServerName www.example.com:80`, and uncomment it. It should appear as follows:

```
ServerName www.example.com:80
```

5. If you don't provide a name for `ServerName`, the server will do a reverse lookup on your IP address to try to find the name. Failing that, it uses your loopback address (`127.0.0.1`). The `:80` represents the port number (which is the default). For a public Web server, get a real DNS hostname. No changes are required to this file to make Apache available on the local host.

6. Add an administrative e-mail address where someone can contact you in case an error is encountered with your server. In the `/etc/httpd/conf/httpd.conf` file, the default administrative address appears as follows:

```
ServerAdmin root@localhost
```

7. Change `root@localhost` to the e-mail address of your Apache administrator.

8. Start the `httpd` server. As root user, type the following:

```
# service httpd start
```

9. If all goes well, the following message should appear:

```
Starting httpd: [OK]
```
Now you're ready to go.

10. To have `httpd` start every time you boot your system, run this command as root user:

```
# chkconfig httpd on
```

11. To ensure that the Web server is working, open Firefox (or another Web browser), type the following into the location box, and press Enter:

```
http://localhost/
```

12. You should see the Test Page for the Apache Web server, as shown in Figure 20-1. To access this page from another computer, you need to enter your Apache server's host-name or IP address.

FIGURE 20-1

Appearance of the Test Page indicates that the Apache installation succeeded.

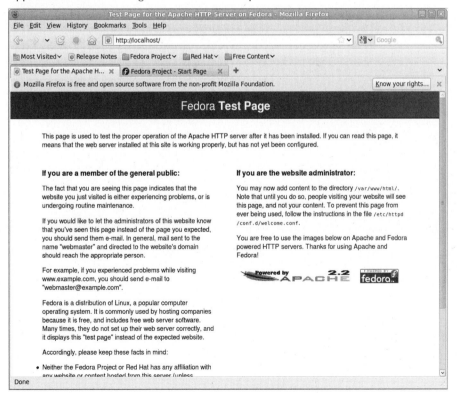

Tip

It is not necessary to be connected to a network (or even to have a network connection) just to test the server or to view the files on your local Apache machine. Rather than specify the server's real name in the URL, just use "localhost" (that is, `http://localhost/`**) from a browser on the same computer. In fact, it's best to fully test the configuration before making the server accessible on an unprotected network.** ■

13. The Test Page is actually an error condition, indicating that you haven't added any content to your website yet. To get started, you can create an `index.html` file that contains your own home page content in the `/var/www/html` directory. Then you can continue to add your own content to that directory structure.

Now that your Web server is working (at least, I hope it is), step through the next section. It helps you understand how to set up more complex Web server arrangements and protect your server from misuse. Stepping through that section will also help you troubleshoot your Web server if it isn't working.

Tip

If your Web server is accessible from your local host but not available to others from your LAN or the Internet, you may need to change your firewall rules to allow greater access. In particular, you need to open tcp port 80 and possibly tcp port 443 (if you offer https content). Also, if SELinux is enabled, it may prevent access to your Web server that you might otherwise expect to work. To disable SELinux, type `setenforce 0` **as root. Or type** `man httpd_selinux` **to learn how to use SELinux with httpd. In particular, ensure that all booleans are set properly to allow the services you want and that all file context labels are correct for your content and configuration files.** ■

Configuring the Apache Server

The primary file for configuring your Apache Web server is `httpd.conf` (located in the `/etc/httpd/conf` directory). A few years ago, the Apache project began recommending not using additional configuration files, such as `srm.conf` and `access.conf`, but rather simply putting everything in `httpd.conf`. In recent releases, however, the trend is toward having modules and other components that are used with Apache to have their own configuration files (usually located in the `/etc/httpd/conf.d/` directory).

All Apache configuration files are plain-text files and can be edited with your favorite text editor. The `/etc/httpd/conf/httpd.conf` file is reproduced in its entirety in the following section, with explanations inserted after related blocks of options (intended to supplement the comments provided with each file).

Some individual modules, scripts, and other services related to Apache, such as perl, php, ssl, and webalizer, have individual configuration files that may interest you. Those files are contained in the `/etc/httpd/conf.d/` directory. See "Configuring Modules and Related Services (/etc/httpd/conf.d/*.conf)" later in this chapter.

Note

More information on Apache can be obtained on your own Web server, from `http://localhost/manual/` (if the `httpd-manual` **package is installed).** ∎

Configuring the Web server (httpd.conf)

The `httpd.conf` file, the primary configuration file for the Apache Web server, contains options that pertain to the general operation of the server. The default filename (`/etc/httpd/conf/httpd.conf`) can be overridden by the `-f` *filename* command-line argument to the httpd daemon or the `ServerConfigFile` directive. The following sections list the contents of the `httpd.conf` file and describe how to use the file.

The first section contains comments about the `httpd.conf` file:

```
# This is the main Apache server configuration file. It contains the
# configuration directives that give the server its instructions.
# See <URL:http://httpd.apache.org/docs/2.2/> for detailed information.
# In particular, see
# <URL:http://httpd.apache.org/docs/2.2/mod/directives.html>
# for a discussion of each configuration directive.
#
# Do NOT simply read the instructions in here without understanding
# what they do.  They're here only as hints or reminders.  If you are
# unsure consult the online docs. You have been warned.
            .
            .
            .
```

This section consists entirely of comments. It basically tells you how information is grouped in this file and how the httpd daemon accesses the file. By default, log files are in the `/var/log/httpd` directory.

Setting the global environment

In "Section 1: Global Environment" of the `httpd.conf` file, you set directives that affect the general workings of the Apache server:

```
### Section 1: Global Environment
#
# The directives in this section affect overall operation of Apache,
# such as the number of concurrent requests it can handle or where it
# can find its configuration files.
#
```

Most of the global directives can be overridden for specific virtual domains, if you are providing Web service for more than one domain. The following subsections describe what the different directives are for.

Revealing subcomponents

The `ServerTokens` directive enables you to prevent remote computers from finding out what subcomponents you are running on your Apache server. Comment out this directive if you don't mind exposing this information. To prevent exposure, `ServerTokens` is set as follows:

```
#
# Don't give away too much information about all the subcomponents
# we are running.  Comment out this line if you don't mind remote sites
# finding out what major optional modules you are running
ServerTokens OS
```

Setting `ServerTokens` to `ProductOnly` minimizes the connection information a potential cracker could see.

Setting the server root directory

The `ServerRoot` directive specifies the directory that contains the configuration files, a link to the log file directory, and a link to the module directory. An alternative `ServerRoot` path name can be specified using the `-d` command-line argument to `httpd`.

```
ServerRoot "/etc/httpd"
```

Storing the server's PID file

The Apache Web server keeps track of the PID for the running server process. You can change the locations of this file using the entry following:

```
PidFile run/httpd.pid
```

Apache uses the `PidFile` to store the process ID of the first (root-owned) master daemon process. This information is used by the `/etc/init.d/httpd` script when shutting down the server and by the server-status handler (as described later in this chapter).

Configuring timeout values

You can set several values that relate to timeout. Some of these values are described in the text following the code:

```
Timeout 60
KeepAlive Off
MaxKeepAliveRequests 100
KeepAliveTimeout 5
```

The `Timeout` directive determines the number of seconds that Apache will hold a connection open between the receipt of packets, between the receipt of acknowledgments on sent responses, or while receiving an incoming request. You can reduce the default of one minute (60 seconds) if you find an excessive number of open, idle connections on your machine.

The `KeepAlive` directive instructs Apache to hold a connection open for a period of time after a request has been handled. This enables subsequent requests from the same client to be processed faster, as a new connection doesn't need to be created for each request.

The `MaxKeepAliveRequests` directive sets a limit on the number of requests that can be handled with one open connection. The default value is certainly reasonable because most connections will hit the `KeepAliveTimeout` before `MaxKeepAliveRequests`.

The `KeepAliveTimeout` directive specifies the number of seconds to hold the connection while awaiting another request. You might want to increase the default (5 seconds). Reasons for having a longer timeout could be to allow all the images on the page to be downloaded on the same connection or to account for how long it may take a client to peruse your average page and select a link from it. The Web application you are using may also need a longer persistent connection. (Of course, a longer `KeepAliveTimeout` prevents each server from moving on to another client during this time period, so you may find that you need to add more request processes to account for that.)

Setting the number of server processes

To operate efficiently, a Web server has to be able to handle numerous incoming requests for content simultaneously. To be ready for requests for Web content, Apache (as it is set up in Fedora) has multiple server processes (`httpd` daemons) running and listening to service requests. Those servers can, in turn, direct requests to multiple threads to service the content requests.

With the Multi-Processing Module (MPM) feature (introduced in Apache 2.0), support for threads was added to Apache. On an operating system that supports Native POSIX Thread Libraries (which Fedora does), threading enables Apache to improve performance by using fewer process slots and less memory for the number of servers it needs. Adding threads consumes fewer resources than adding processes.

For a low-volume Web server, you can probably leave alone the parameters that support the MPM feature. You will probably have enough processes to handle your incoming requests, but not so many that they will be a drain on your server. However, if your server needs to serve up a lot of content consistently, or needs to respond occasionally to large spikes of requests, consider tuning the MPM-related parameters in the `httpd.conf` file.

Here are a few issues to consider if you want to change any of the MPM-related parameters:

- **Get enough RAM** — RAM is critical. Every active process and thread consumes some amount of memory. If the number of active processes and threads exceeds the amount of available RAM, your computer will begin to use swap space, and performance will degrade quickly. Make sure your system has enough RAM to handle the maximum number of server processes and threads you expect to run on your Apache Web server.

- **Configure for maximum load** — Apache can create new server processes and threads as they are needed. You don't need the maximum number of processes and threads available at all times. Instead, you can configure the maximum number of servers and threads that Apache can dynamically add as demand on the server requires.

- **Configure for performance** — Performance degrades (small amount) when Apache has to start a new thread, start a server process (greater amount), or use swap space (greatest amount). The actual amount depends on server hardware, configuration, and load, but these relative values will hold. In a perfect world, the exact number of servers you need should be the default number of servers running, with a few spares to handle reasonable spikes. If response is critical, you might opt to have more servers running than you need so that performance isn't hurt when spikes occur.

When Apache starts up, it launches a set number of httpd server processes (one parent and multiple child httpd processes) to handle incoming requests for Web server content. Parameters for defining how many httpd server processes are available include those that set the following:

- How many child server processes should be started by the parent httpd server (StartServers)
- The minimum number of idle server processes kept spare (MinSpareServers)
- The maximum number of idle server processes kept spare (MaxSpareServers)
- The maximum number of server processes allowed to start (MaxClients)
- The maximum value MaxClients can have over the life of the server (ServerLimit)
- The maximum number of requests a process can serve (MaxRequestsPerChild)

Parameters for defining how many threads are available for each httpd server process include those that set the following:

- The minimum number of spare threads that should always be available, after which more will be created (MinSpareThreads)
- The maximum number for spare threads, after which active threads are deleted to get back to the number of threads per child (MaxSpareThreads)
- The number of threads always available to each child process (ThreadsPerChild)

The following code example shows how MPM-specific parameters in the httpd.conf file are set for the prefork.c module (nonthreaded module for managing servers processes) and the worker.c module (multithread, multiprocess Web server module):

```
<IfModule prefork.c>
StartServers         8
MinSpareServers      5
MaxSpareServers     20
ServerLimit        256
MaxClients         256
MaxRequestsPerChild  4000
</IfModule>

<IfModule worker.c>
StartServers         4
MaxClients         300
MinSpareThreads     25
MaxSpareThreads     75
```

```
ThreadsPerChild     25
MaxRequestsPerChild  0
</IfModule>
```

Apache starts a master daemon process owned by root that binds to the appropriate port and then switches to a nonprivileged user. More servers (equivalent to the value of the `StartServers` directive in `prefork.c`) are then started as the same nonprivileged user (the `apache` user in this case).

Apache attempts to start and kill servers intelligently based on the current load. If the amount of traffic decreases and too many servers are idle, some will be killed (down to the number of servers specified in `MinSpareServers`). Similarly, if many requests arrive in close proximity and too few servers are waiting for new connections, more servers will be started (up to the number of servers specified in `MaxClients`).

Caution

Getting the value of `MaxClients` right is critical because it puts a lid on the total number of client connections that can be active at the same time. If the full number of `MaxClients` servers are in use, no more will be created, and subsequent requests to the server will fail until one is freed up. Failing requests becomes bad for an organization if your business depends on users getting access to the site. If you increase `MaxClients` from the defaults, you need to increase `ServerLimit` as well. ■

Using the values specified above, when the daemon is started, the parent and eight child server processes will run, waiting for connections (as defined by `StartServers`). As more requests arrive, Apache ensures that at least five server processes are ready to answer requests. When requests have been fulfilled and no new connections arrive, Apache will begin killing processes until the number of idle Web server processes is below 20. The value of `StartServers` should always be somewhere between `MinSpareServers` and `MaxSpareServers`.

Apache limits the total number of simultaneous threads with the `MaxClients` directive. The default value is 256, which should be sufficient. However, if you find that you frequently have nearly that many threads running, remember that any connection beyond the 256th will be rejected. In such cases, if your hardware is sufficiently powerful (and your network connection can handle the load), increase the value of `MaxClients`.

Note

You can see the state of your Apache server processes and get a feel for the server's activity by viewing the `server-status` page for your server, as described later in this chapter. The `ps -fU apache` command shows you if the Apache server processes (httpd daemon) are currently running. ■

To minimize the effect of possible memory leaks (and to keep the server pool "fresh"), each server process is limited in the number of requests that it can handle (equal to the value of `MaxRequestsPerChild`). After servicing 4,000 requests (the value specified in the previous example), the process will be killed. It is more accurate to say that each process can service 4,000 *connections* because all `KeepAlive` requests (occurring prior to the keep-alive requests timeout, as specified by the `KeepAliveTimeout`) are calculated as just one request.

In a multiprocessor environment, setting thread values as described previously can both limit the number of threads that servers can consume and supply as many threads as you will allow to handle server processing. `MinSpareThreads` and `MaxSpareThreads` control the number of threads available that are not being used. More are added if available threads fall below `MinSpareThreads`. If spare threads exceed `MaxSpareThreads`, some are dropped.

Binding to specific addresses

You can bind to specific IP addresses using the `Listen` directive. `Listen` directives can be used to add to the default bindings you already have:

```
Listen 80
```

The `Listen` directive is more flexible than the `BindAddress` directive. You can specify multiple `Listen` commands, which enables you to specify several IP address/port number combinations. They can also be used to specify just IP addresses or just port numbers.

By default, Apache listens to port 80 (for standard http services) and port 443 (for secure https services) on all interfaces on the local computer (which is where Web browsers expect to find Web content). Listening on only `localhost:80` restricts access only to users on the local machines. A Web server run by a nonprivileged user often will bind to port 8080 (only root can bind to ports lower than 1024). If you have multiple network interface cards, you can limit which interfaces Apache will listen on (for example, you can have a Web server intended only for the company LAN, which is not exposed to your Internet interface).

Selecting modules in httpd.conf

During the compilation process, individual Apache modules can be selected for dynamic linking. Dynamically linked modules are not loaded into memory with the httpd server process unless `LoadModule` directives explicitly identify those modules to be loaded. The blocks of code that follow select several modules to be loaded into memory by using the `LoadModule` directive with the module name and the path to the module (relative to `ServerRoot`, typically `./etc/httpd`). The following code shows a partial listing of these modules:

```
#
# Dynamic Shared Object (DSO) Support
# Example:
# LoadModule foo_module modules/mod_foo.so
#
LoadModule auth_basic_module modules/mod_auth_basic.so
LoadModule auth_digest_module modules/mod_auth_digest.so
LoadModule authn_file_module modules/mod_authn_file.so
        .
        .
        .
LoadModule suexec_cache_module modules/mod_suexec.so
LoadModule disk_cache_module modules/mod_disk_cache.so
LoadModule cgi_module modules/mod_cgi.so
```

Apache modules are included in the list of active modules via the LoadModule directive. The ClearModuleList directive removes all entries from the current list of active modules. Each of the standard modules included with Apache on Fedora is described in Table 20-1.

Dynamic Shared Object (DSO) Modules

Module	Description
mod_actions	Conditionally executes CGI scripts based on the file's MIME type or the request method.
mod_alias	Allows for redirection and mapping parts of the physical file system into logical entities accessible through the Web server.
mod_asis	Enables files to be transferred without adding any HTTP headers (e.g., the Status, Location, and Content-type header fields).
mod_auth_basic	Provides HTTP Basic Authentication. It is used in combination with authentication modules (such as mod_authn_file) and authorization modules (such as mod_authz_user).
mod_auth_digest	Provides MD5 Digest user authentication.
mod_authn_alias	Lets you create extended authentication providers that are assigned to aliases. Later you can reference the aliases through AuthBasicProvider or AuthDigestProvider directives.
mod_authn_anon	Similar to anonymous FTP, enables predefined usernames access to authenticated areas by using a valid e-mail address as a password.
mod_authn_dbd	Provides access to SQL tables to authenticate users. It enables you to use mod_auth_basic and mod_auth_digest front ends.
mod_authn_dbm	Provides access control based on username/password pairs. The authentication information is stored in a DBM binary database file, with encrypted passwords.
mod_authn_default	Offers a fallback authentication module, if no other is in use. Any credentials presented by the user are rejected.
mod_authn_file	Provides access control by user lookup in plain-text password files (similar to mod_authn_dbm, but without encryption).
mod_authnz_ldap	Lets you use an LDAP directory to store the HTTP Basic authentication database.
mod_authz_dbm	Provides access control to authenticated users based on group name. The authentication information is stored in a DBM binary database file.

continued

TABLE 20-1 *(continued)*

Module	Description
mod_authz_default	If modules such as mod_authz_user or mod_authz_groupfile are not configured, this provides a fallback (simply rejecting authorization requests).
mod_authz_groupfile	Provides access control based on group membership.
mod_authz_host	Provides access control based on client hostname, IP address, or other environment variable characteristics.
mod_authz_owner	With a verified username and password, allows access to files based on ownership.
mod_authz_user	Allows access to files based on whether an authenticated user is listed in a Required User directive.
mod_autoindex	Implements automatically generated directory indexes.
mod_cache	Allows local or proxied Web content to be cached. Used with the mod_disk_cache or mod_mem_cache modules.
mod_cern_meta	Offers a method of emulating CERN HTTPD meta file semantics.
mod_cgi	Controls the execution of files that are parsed by the "cgi-script" handler or that have a MIME type of x-httpd-cgi. ScriptAlias sets the default directory.
mod_cgid	Similar to mod_cgi with the exception that this module offers a ScriptSock directive to name the socket used with the cgi daemon.
mod_dav	Provides Web-based Distributed Authoring and Versioning (WebDAV) to upload Web content using copy, create, move, and delete resources.
mod_dav_fs	Provides file system features to the mod_dav module, used with Web-based Distributed Authoring and Versioning (WebDAV).
mod_dbd	Uses apr_dbd to manage SQL database connections. (The apr_dbd framework offers a common API for different SQL database engines.)
mod_deflate	Includes the DEFLATE output filter, to compress data before it is sent to the client.
mod_dir	Sets the list of filenames that may be used if no explicit filename is selected in a URL that references a directory.
mod_disk_cache	Enables a disk-based storage manager to use with mod_proxy.
mod_dnssd	Adds ZeroConf support to Apache.
mod_dumpio	Lets you log all input received by or sent from Apache. Because this can involve a lot of data, it is used mostly for debugging purposes.
mod_env	Controls environment variables passed to CGI scripts.

Module	Description
mod_expires	Implements time limits on cached documents by using the Expires HTTP header.
mod_ext_filter	Before delivering a response to the client, passes it through an external filter.
mod_filter	Allows you to configure context-sensitive output filtering.
mod_headers	Enables the creation and generation of custom HTTP headers.
mod_ident	Lets you query an RFC 1413–compatible daemon on a remote host to request information about the owner of a connection.
mod_include	Implements Server-Side Includes (SSI), which are HTML documents that include conditional statements parsed by the server prior to being sent to a client. This module also has the ability to include files one into another.
mod_info	Provides a detailed summary of the server's configuration, including a list of actively loaded modules and the current settings of every directive defined within each module.
mod_ldap	Used to speed performance of websites using LDAP servers.
mod_logio	Can be used to log bytes of data that are sent and received.
mod_log_config	Enables a customized format for information contained within the log files.
mod_log_forensic	Provides the capability to do forensic logging of client requests.
mod_mime	Alters the handling of documents based on predefined values or the MIME type of the file.
mod_mime_magic	Similar to the Unix file command, attempts to determine the MIME type of a file based on a few bytes of the file's contents.
mod_negotiation	Provides for the conditional display of documents based on the Content-Encoding, Content-Language, Content-Length, and Content-Type HTTP header fields.
mod_perl	Integrates Perl scripting with the Apache server.
mod_proxy	Implements an HTTP 1.1 proxy/gateway server.
mod_proxy_ajp	Uses mod_proxy to provide support for Apache JServ Protocol (version 1.3).
mod_proxy_balancer	Extension to mod_proxy to handle load balancing.
mod_proxy_connect	Extension to mod_proxy to handle CONNECT requests.
mod_proxy_ftp	Extension to mod_proxy to handle FTP requests.
mod_proxy_http	Extension to mod_proxy to handle HTTP requests.

continued

TABLE 20-1 *(continued)*

Module	Description
mod_proxy_scgi	Depends on mod_proxy and supports the SCI protocol.
mod_python	Embeds an interpreter for the Python scripting language into the Apache server.
mod_reqtimeout	Sets the timeout and minimum data rate for network requests.
mod_rewrite	Provides a flexible and extensible method for redirecting client requests and mapping incoming URLs to other locations in the file system.
mod_setenvif	Conditionally sets environment variables based on the contents of various HTTP header fields.
mod_speling	Attempts to correct misspellings automatically in requested URLs. (Yes, this module name spells *speling* incorrectly.)
mod_ssl	Integrates Apache with OpenSSL to support https connections.
mod_status	Provides a summary of the activities of each individual httpd server process, including CPU and bandwidth usage levels.
mod_substitute	Provides a way to do fixed-string and regular expression substitutions on response bodies.
mod_suexec	Lets CGI scripts run with permissions of a particular user or group.
mod_unique_id	Assigns the UNIQUE_ID environment variable to provide a unique identifier for each request.
mod_userdir	Specifies locations that can contain individual users' HTML documents.
mod_usertrack	Uses cookies to track the progress of users through a website.
mod_version	Allows you to use <IFVersion> containers to permit version-dependent configuration.
mod_vhost_alias	Contains support for dynamically configured mass virtual hosting.

If a particular module contains features that are not necessary, it can easily be commented out of the preceding list. In fact, it is a good security practice to comment out unused modules. Similarly, you might want to add the features or functionality of a third-party module (e.g., mod_perl, which integrates the Perl run-time library for faster Perl script execution, or mod_php, which provides a scripting language embedded within HTML documents) by including those modules in the list.

Note

Some modules, including core, prefork, http_core, and mod_so, are compiled into the httpd daemon in Fedora. To see the list of modules compiled into the daemon, type the httpd -l command. ■

More information about each module (and the directives that can be defined within it) can be found on your server at `http://localhost/manual/mod/` (provided that you have installed the `httpd-manual` package).

Including module-specific configuration files

The following line causes Apache to load configuration files from the `/etc/httpd/conf.d/` directory. This directory contains configuration files associated with specific modules.

```
Include conf.d/*.conf
```

Cross-Reference

The "Configuring Modules and Related Services (/etc/httpd/conf.d/*.conf)" section, later in this chapter, describes some of the configuration files in the `conf.d` **directory that may interest you. ■**

Choosing the server's user and group

The `httpd` daemon doesn't have to run as the root user; the fact that it doesn't run as root by default makes your system more secure. By setting `User` and `Group` entries, you can have the `httpd` daemon run using the permissions associated with a different user and group:

```
User apache
Group apache
```

By default, `apache` is defined as both the user and group for the server. If you change the `User` and `Group` directives, you should specify a nonprivileged entity. Doing so minimizes the risk of damage if your site is compromised. The first daemon process that is started runs as root. This is necessary to bind the server to a low-numbered port and to switch to the user and group specified by the `User` and `Group` directives. All other processes run under the user ID (UID) and group ID (GID) defined by those directives.

Setting the main server's configuration

The second section of the `http.conf` file relates to directives handled by your main server (the one defined by the `ServerName` directive). In other words, these values are used by the default server and for all virtual hosts, unless they are explicitly changed for a virtual host. To change the same directives for particular virtual hosts, add them within virtual host containers.

Setting an e-mail address

You can identify an address where users can send e-mail if they encounter a problem with your server. This is done with the `ServerAdmin` directive:

```
ServerAdmin you@your.address
```

The `ServerAdmin` directive can be set to any valid e-mail address. The default is `root@localhost`.

Setting the server name

If your server name is anything but your exact registered host or domain name, you should identify your server name here. As the comments point out, the ServerName directive can be set to a value other than the actual hostname of your machine. However, this other name should still point to your machine in DNS if the server is to be a public Internet server. Frequently, www is just an alias for the real name of the machine (e.g., a machine may respond to www.linuxtoys .net, but its real name may be a1.linuxtoys.net).

```
ServerName jukebox.linuxtoys.net
```

Apache tries to use your hostname as the ServerName if you don't enter a valid server name. I recommend that you explicitly enter a ServerName here.

Setting canonical names

There may be times when you need to configure how the server determines its own name and port. To do this, you can alter the UseCanonicalName directive to create a self-referencing URL. This allows Apache to use the hostname and port specified to construct the canonical name for the server. The value resulting from UseCanonicalName is used in all self-referential URLs and for the values of SERVER_NAME and SERVER_PORT in CGIs. You can set the UseCanonicalName directive to On, Off, or DNS.

To allow Apache to form self-referential URLs using the hostname and port, set the UseCanonicalName directive as follows:

```
UseCanonicalName Off
```

Using the UseCanonicalName directive can make the names that identify the server more consistent. When the directive is set to On, Apache uses ServerName and Port directives to create URLs that reference files on the same machine (e.g., http://www.linuxtoys.net/docs/). When UseCanonicalName is set to Off, the URL consists of whatever the client specified (e.g., the URL could be http://abc.linuxtoys.net/docs/ or http://abc/docs/ if the client is within the same domain).

This can be problematic, particularly when access-control rules require username and password authentication: If the client is authenticated for the host abc.linuxtoys.net but a link sends him or her to www.linuxtoys.net (physically the same machine), the client will be prompted to enter a username and password again. I recommend setting UseCanonicalName to On so that in a situation like the one just described, the authentication would not need to be repeated because any reference to the same server would always be interpreted as www.linuxtoys.net.

The last option, UseCanonicalName DNS, can be configured when you want to deploy a virtual hosting environment to support older clients that do not provide a Host: header. With this option, Apache does a reverse DNS lookup on the server's IP address that the client connected to in order to figure out self-referential URLs.

Identifying HTTP content directories

There are several directives for determining the location of your server's Web content. The main location for your Web content is set to /var/www/html by the DocumentRoot directive. Notice that the trailing slash is not used on the path name.

```
DocumentRoot "/var/www/html"
```

(Note that this location has changed from early versions of Red Hat Linux. The location was formerly /home/http. Moving the Web content out of /home has helped keep user directories in /home separate from system files.)

Setting access options and overrides

You can set individual access permissions for each directory in the Web server's directory structure. The default, shown here, is fairly restrictive:

```
<Directory />
    Options FollowSymLinks
    AllowOverride None
</Directory>
```

This segment sets up a default block of permissions for the Options and AllowOverride directives. The <Directory /> ... </Directory> tags enclose the directives that are to be applied to the / directory (which is /var/www/html by default, as defined by DocumentRoot).

The Options FollowSymLinks directive instructs the server that symbolic links within the directory can be followed to allow content that resides in other locations on the computer. None of the other special server features will be active in the / directory, or in any directory below that, without being explicitly specified later. Next, the following access options are specifically set for the root of your Web server (/var/www/html). (I removed the comments here for clarity.)

```
<Directory "/var/www/html">
    Options Indexes FollowSymLinks
    AllowOverride None
    Order allow,deny
    Allow from all
</Directory>
```

If you have changed the value of DocumentRoot earlier in this file, you need to change /var/www/html to match that value. The Options set for the directory are Indexes and FollowSymLinks. Those and other special server features are described in Table 20-2. The AllowOverride None directive instructs the server that an .htaccess file (or the value of AccessFileName) cannot override any of the special access features. You can replace None with any of the special access features described in Table 20-3.

TABLE 20-2

Special Server Features for the Options Directive

Feature	Description
ExecCGI	The execution of CGI scripts is permitted.
FollowSymLinks	The server will traverse symbolic links.
Includes	Server-Side Includes are permitted.
IncludesNOEXEC	Server-Side Includes are permitted, except the #exec element.
Indexes	If none of the files specified in the DirectoryIndex directive exists, a directory index will be generated by mod_autoindex.
MultiViews	The server allows content negotiation based on preferences from the user's browser, such as preferred language, character set, and media type.
SymLinksIfOwnerMatch	The server will traverse symbolic links only if the owner of the target is the same as the owner of the link.
None	None of the features above are enabled.
All	All the features above are enabled, with the exception of MultiViews. This must be explicitly enabled.

TABLE 20-3

Special Access Features for the AllowOverride Directive

Feature	Description
AuthConfig	Enables authentication-related directives (AuthName, AuthType, AuthUserFile, AuthGroupFile, Require, and so on)
FileInfo	Enables MIME-related directives (AddType, AddEncoding, AddLanguage, LanguagePriority, and so on)
Indexes	Enables directives related to directory indexing (FancyIndexing, DirectoryIndex, IndexOptions, IndexIgnore, HeaderName, ReadmeName, AddIcon, AddDescription, and so on)
Limit	Enables directives controlling host access (Allow, Deny, and Order)
Options	Enables the Options directive (as described in Table 20-2)

Note

Remember that unless you specifically enable a feature described in Tables 20-2 and 20-3, that feature is not enabled for your server (with the exceptions of Indexes and FollowSymLinks). ■

Identifying user directories

If you have multiple users on your server and you want them to be able to publish their own Web content, it is common practice to identify a directory name that users can create in their own home directories to store that content. When you identify the name that is appended to a user's home directory, that directory is used to respond to requests to the server for the user's name (~$user$). This directory name used to be set to public_html by default; however, it is now turned off by default.

To allow access to your users' personal Web pages, add a comment character (#) to the UserDir disable line. Then remove the # from the UserDir public_html line to make users' personal public_html directories accessible through the Web server. The following code shows what the enabled section looks like after extra comment lines have been removed:

```
<ifModule mod_userdir.c>
#  UserDir disable
UserDir public_html
</IfModule>
```

In addition to uncommenting the UserDir public_html line shown in the previous example, you must make both the user's home directory and the public_html directory executable by everyone in order for the UserDir directive to allow access to a particular user's public_html directory. For example, the user cjb could type the following to make those directories accessible:

```
$ chmod 711 /home/cjb
$ mkdir /home/cjb/public_html
$ chmod 755 /home/cjb/public_html
```

Cross-Reference
See Chapter 4 for more on setting permissions. ∎

In order for UserDir to work, the mod_userdir module must also be loaded (which it is by default).

Note
By default in Fedora, SELinux will prevent Apache from sharing content contained anywhere but in the /var/www/html directory structure. Because SELinux is in Enforcing mode by default, you have to either set SELinux to Permissive mode (setenforce 0) or cause all the content you are sharing outside of /var/www/html to be given proper file contexts. See the httpd_selinux man page for details. ∎

There are two ways in which the UserDir directive can handle an incoming request that includes a username (e.g., ~cjb). One possible format identifies the physical path name of the individual user's publicly accessible directories. The other can specify a URL to which the request is redirected. A few examples are presented in Table 20-4, using the URL http://www.mybox.com/~cjb/proj/c004.html as a sample request.

TABLE 20-4

UserDir Path Name and URL Examples

UserDir Directive	Referenced Path or URL
UserDir public_html	~cjb/public_html/proj/c004.html
UserDir /public/*/WWW	/public/cjb/WWW/proj/c004.html
UserDir /usr/local/web	/usr/local/web/cjb/proj/c004.html
UserDir http://www.mybox.com/users	http://www.mybox.com/users/cjb/proj/c004.html
UserDir http://www.mybox.com/~*	http://www.mybox.com/~cjb/proj/c004.html
UserDir http://www.mybox.com/*/html	http://www.mybox.com/cjb/html/proj/c004.html

The UserDir directive can also be used to explicitly allow or deny URL-to-pathname translation for particular users. For example, it is a good idea to include the following line to avoid publishing data that shouldn't be made public:

```
UserDir disable root
```

Alternatively, use the following lines to disable translations for all but a few users:

```
UserDir disable
UserDir enable wilhelm cjb jsmith
```

Note

Be careful about content you publish about yourself on the Internet (names, addresses, personal information, and so on) and keep in mind that you can be held accountable for the content you publish on your Web server. When you allow others to publish on your Web server, your liability can extend to what those users publish as well. Be sure to have a clear policy about what is acceptable (and legal) to publish on your Web server and make that policy known to those you allow to use the server. ■

Setting default index files for directories

The DirectoryIndex directive establishes a list of files that is used when an incoming request specifies a directory, rather than a file. For example, say a client requests the URL http://www.mybox.com/~jsmith. Because it's a directory, it is automatically translated to http://www.mybox.com/~jsmith/. Now that directory is searched for in any of the files listed in the DirectoryIndex directive. The first match (from the default list of index.html and index.html.var) is used as the default document in that directory. If none of the files exist and the `Indexes` option (as in the `httpd.conf` file) is selected, the server will automatically generate an index of the files in the directory.

```
DirectoryIndex index.html index.html.var
```

Sometimes dynamic content (such as `index.php` or `index.cgi`) will be added to the `DirectoryIndex` to ensure that dynamic content is accessed before static content when a user simply requests a domain name or directory.

Setting directory-access control

You and your users can add an access file to each directory to control access to that directory. By default, the `AccessFileName` directive sets `.htaccess` as the file containing this information. The following lines set this filename and prevent the contents of that file from being viewed by visitors to the website. If you change the file to a name other than `.htaccess`, be sure to change the line (`"^\.ht"`) that denies access to that file.

```
AccessFileName .htaccess

<Files ~ "^\.ht">
    Order allow,deny
    Deny from all
</Files>
```

You can add the same access directives to an `.htaccess` file as you do to the `httpd.conf` file. In general, it is more efficient to use a `<Directory>` directive in the `httpd.conf` file than it is to create an `.htaccess` file. With a `<Directory>` directive, you can specifically identify the access associated with that directory alone. Because directives you put in `.htaccess` apply to all directories below the current directory, anytime you add an `.htaccess` file to a directory, Apache must search all directories above that point (e.g., /, /var, /var/www, and so on) to include settings from possible `.htaccess` files in those directories as well.

Setting MIME type defaults

The location of the MIME type definitions file is defined by the `TypesConfig` directive. The `DefaultType` directive sets the MIME type:

```
TypesConfig /etc/mime.types
DefaultType text/plain
```

With the mod_mime_magic module, a server can look for hints to help determine what type of file is being requested. You must ensure that this module is loaded to Apache for it to be used (it is loaded by default). The module can use hints from the files `/usr/share/magic.mime` (off by default) and `/etc/httpd/conf/magic` (on by default) to determine the contents of a requested file.

The name "magic" comes from the list of magic numbers used by the Linux `file` command to determine a file's type. Many files have a *magic* number in the first few bytes that identifies whether the file is a compiled executable, compiled object code, and so on. Here are the directives that cause that module to be used:

```
<IfModule mod_mime_magic.c>
#   MIMEMagicFile /usr/share/magic.mime
    MIMEMagicFile conf/magic
</IfModule>
```

Setting hostname lookups

With the Apache Web server, you can have the server look up addresses for incoming client requests. Turning on the HostnameLookups directive can do this:

```
# HostnameLookups: Log the names of clients or just their IP addresses
HostnameLookups Off
```

If the HostnameLookups directive is enabled, every incoming connection generates a DNS lookup to translate the client's IP address into a hostname. If your site receives many requests, the server's response time could be adversely affected. The HostnameLookups directive should be turned off unless you use a log file analysis program or statistics package that requires fully qualified domain names and cannot perform the lookups on its own. The logresolve program installed with the Apache distribution can be scheduled to edit log files by performing hostname lookups during off-peak hours.

Configuring HTTP logging

You can set several values related to logging of Apache information. When a relative path name is shown, the directory set by ServerRoot (/etc/httpd/ by default) is appended (e.g., /etc/httpd/logs/error_log). As shown in the following example, you can set the location of error logs, the level of log warnings, and some log nicknames:

```
ErrorLog logs/error_log
LogLevel warn
LogFormat "%h %l %u %t \"%r\" %>s %b \"%{Referer}i\" \"%{User-    ↵
Agent}i\"" combined
LogFormat "%h %l %u %t \"%r\" %>s %b" common
LogFormat "%{Referer}i -> %U" referer
LogFormat "%{User-agent}i" agent
# CustomLog logs/access_log common

# If you would like to have separate agent and referer logfiles,
# uncomment the following directives.
#CustomLog logs/referer_log referer
#CustomLog logs/agent_log agent
# For a single logfile with access, agent, and referer information
# (Combined Logfile Format), use the following directive:
#
CustomLog logs/access_log combined
```

These lines deal with how server errors, client tracking information, and incoming requests are logged. The `ErrorLog` directive, which can specify an absolute path name or a path name relative to the `ServerRoot` (which is `/etc/httpd` by default), indicates where the server should store error messages. In this case the specified file is `logs/error_log`, which expands to `/etc/httpd/logs/error_log`. The `/etc/httpd/logs` directory is a symlink to the `/var/log/httpd` directory, so you can view the files in both places.

The `LogLevel` directive controls the severity and quantity of messages that appear in the error log. Messages can range from the particularly verbose `debug` log level to the particularly silent `emerg` (short for *emergency*) log level. With `debug`, a message is logged anytime the configuration files are read, when an access-control mechanism is used, or if the number of active servers has changed. With `emerg`, only critical system-level failures that create panic conditions for the server are logged.

The level specified by the `LogLevel` directive indicates the least-severe message that will be logged — all messages at that severity and greater are recorded. For example, if `LogLevel` is set to `warn`, the error log will contain messages at the `warn`, `error`, `crit`, `alert`, and `emerg` levels. The default value of `warn` is a good choice for normal use (it will log only significant events that may eventually require operator intervention), but `info` and `debug` are sufficient for testing a server's configuration or tracking down the exact location of errors.

The four `LogFormat` lines define (for later use) four types of log file formats: combined, common, referer, and agent. You can also add a fifth format called *combinedio*. The tokens available within the `LogFormat` directive are described in Table 20-5. You can modify the `LogFormat` definitions per your own personal preference, and other custom formats can be created as needed.

TABLE 20-5

Available Tokens within LogFormat

Token	Description
%a	IP address of the client machine.
%b	Number of bytes sent to the client (excluding header information).
%{VAR}e	Contents of the environment variable VAR.
%f	The filename referenced by the requested URL.
%h	The hostname of the client machine or IP address.
%{Header}i	Contents of the specified header line in the HTTP request.
%l	As reported by the identd daemon (if available), the user on the client machine who initiated the request.
%{Note}n	Contents of the message Note from a different module.

continued

TABLE 20-5 *(continued)*

Token	Description
%m	The request method.
%{Header}o	Contents of the specified header line in the HTTP response.
%p	Port number on which the request was received.
%P	PID of the server process that handled the request.
%q	Query string part of the HTTP request.
%r	First line of the full HTTP request from the client.
%s	Server response code generated by the request.
%t	Current local time and date. The time format can be altered using %{Format}t, where Format is described in the strftime(3) man page.
%T	Number of seconds required to fulfill the client request.
%u	If access-control rules require username and password authentication, this represents the username supplied by the client.
%U	URL requested by the client.
%v	Canonical name of the server according to the Domain Name System (DNS).
%V	Canonical name of the server handling the request according to the UseCanonicalName directive.
%X	Connection status after the response is finished. A status of X means the connection was closed before the response was completed, + means the connection may be kept open (alive) after the response, and - means the connection will be closed after the response is sent to the client.

The *common* format includes the client host's name or IP address, the username as reported by the ident daemon and the server's authentication method (if applicable), the local time when the request was made, the actual HTTP request, the server response code, and the number of bytes transferred. This format is a de facto standard among Web servers (and lately even among FTP servers).

For the purpose of connection tracking, the *referer* format stores the URL (from the same site or an external server) that linked to the document just delivered (relative to the ServerRoot). For example, if the page http://www.example.com/corp/about_us.html contains a link to your home page at http://www.mybox.com/linuxguy/bio.html, when a client accesses that link, the referer log on www.mybox.com would look like the following:

```
http://www.example.com/corp/about_us.html -> /linuxguy/bio.html
```

This information can be used to determine which path each client took to reach your site.

The *agent* format stores the contents of the User-agent: HTTP header for each incoming connection. This field typically indicates the browser name and version, the language, and the operating system or architecture on which the browser was run. Accessing an Apache server from a Firefox browser on a Linux system running on a PC produces the following entry:

```
Mozilla/5.0 (X11; U; Linux i686; en-US; rv:1.9.2.10) ↵
Gecko/20101005 Fedora/3.6.10-1.fc14 Firefox/3.6.10
```

The *combined* format concatenates all the information from the other three log file formats into one line. This format is useful for storing all connection-related log entries in one centralized file. The *combinedio* format, which is commented out by default, can be enabled (by removing the # character) to log the actual number of bytes received (%I) and sent (%O), provided the mod_logio module is loaded.

The CustomLog directive assigns one of the defined LogFormat formats to a filename (again, specified as an absolute path name or a path name relative to ServerRoot). The only uncommented definition assigns combined format to the /etc/httpd/logs/access_log file. To retain the agent or referer information separately, uncomment the definitions. You could also choose to comment out the CustomLog logs/access_log combined line and use the definition for the common format instead.

Adding a signature

Any page that is generated by the Apache server can have a signature line added to the bottom of the page. Examples of server-generated pages include a directory listing, an error page, a status page, or an info page. The ServerSignature directive can be set to On, Off, or EMail. Here is how ServerSignature appears by default:

```
ServerSignature On
```

With ServerSignature On, a line similar to the following appears at the bottom of server-generated pages:

```
Apache/2.2.16 (Fedora) Server at toys.linuxtoys.net Port 80
```

With ServerSignature set to EMail, a mailto link to the Web page's administrative e-mail account is added to the signature line (the server name becomes the link). If the directive is set to Off, the line doesn't appear at all. With SSL or WebDAV enabled, this information appears in the server signature as well. In general, it's best to reveal as little information as possible on Internet-facing servers, so it may be best to leave these directives off.

Aliasing relocated content

There are various ways to define alias content, including the Alias and the ScriptAlias directives. Here are alias-related settings in httpd.conf (with comments removed):

```
Alias /icons/ "/var/www/icons/"
```

```
<Directory "/var/www/icons">
    Options Indexes MultiViews FollowSymLinks
    AllowOverride None
    Order allow,deny
    Allow from all
</Directory>

ScriptAlias /cgi-bin/ "/var/www/cgi-bin/"

<Directory "/var/www/cgi-bin">
    AllowOverride None
    Options None
    Order allow,deny
    Allow from all
</Directory>
```

The Alias directive points to a file system location (not necessarily within DocumentRoot). For example, with the following line in place, requests for documents in /bigjob (http://www.mybox.com/bigjob/index.html) would result in the retrieval of /home/newguy/proj/index.html:

```
Alias /bigjob /home/newguy/proj
```

The icons alias allows access to the Apache icons used by the Web server for your website. The icons directory is accessible from the /var/www directory.

The ScriptAlias directive performs a related function, but directories that it aliases contain executable code (most likely CGI scripts). The syntax is the same as for the Alias directive. Pay special attention whenever you use ScriptAlias. Because ScriptAlias defines the location of scripts that can be run from Web content on the server, be sure you assign only directories that contain scripts that are secured and won't open security holes in your system.

Redirecting requests for old content

As content changes on your Web server, some of it will become obsolete, while other content may move to a different place in the file system or to a different server. Using the Redirect directive, you can redirect requests for old content to new locations.

By default, there are no Redirect directives set for your Apache server, but you can uncomment the following example and tailor it to your needs:

```
# Redirect permanent /foo http://www.example.com/bar
```

Redirect can be used to instruct clients that the document they seek has moved elsewhere (to the same server or to an external location) by simply indicating the old and new locations. If the previous Redirect option were in place, a client's attempt to access http://www.mybox.com/foo would redirect to http://www.example.com/bar.

Besides using permanent as the service for Redirect (which results in a redirect status 301), you could instead use temp (a redirect status of 302), seeother (a replaced status of 303), or gone (a permanently removed status of 401). You could also provide any status code between 300 and 399 as the service, which represent different error responses. (These numbers are HTTP status codes.)

Note

The HTTP status codes are defined as part of the HTTP protocol in RFC 2616. Refer to that document at www.w3.org/Protocols/rfc2616/rfc2616.txt. ■

Defining indexing

It's possible to have your Apache server show different icons for different types of files. To use this feature, IndexOptions should be set to FancyIndexing, and AddIconByEncoding, AddIconByType, and AddIcon directives should be used:

```
IndexOptions FancyIndexing VersionSort NameWidth=* HTMLTable Charset=UTF-8

AddIconByEncoding (CMP,/icons/compressed.gif) x-compress x-gzip

AddIconByType (TXT,/icons/text.gif) text/*
AddIconByType (IMG,/icons/image2.gif) image/*
AddIconByType (SND,/icons/sound2.gif) audio/*
AddIconByType (VID,/icons/movie.gif) video/*

AddIcon /icons/binary.gif .bin .exe
AddIcon /icons/binhex.gif .hqx
AddIcon /icons/tar.gif .tar
AddIcon /icons/world2.gif .wrl .wrl.gz .vrml .vrm .iv
AddIcon /icons/compressed.gif .Z .z .tgz .gz .zip
AddIcon /icons/a.gif .ps .ai .eps
AddIcon /icons/layout.gif .html .shtml .htm .pdf
AddIcon /icons/text.gif .txt
AddIcon /icons/c.gif .c
AddIcon /icons/p.gif .pl .py
AddIcon /icons/f.gif .for
AddIcon /icons/dvi.gif .dvi
AddIcon /icons/uuencoded.gif .uu
AddIcon /icons/script.gif .conf .sh .shar .csh .ksh .tcl
AddIcon /icons/tex.gif .tex
AddIcon /icons/bomb.gif core

AddIcon /icons/back.gif ..
AddIcon /icons/hand.right.gif README
AddIcon /icons/folder.gif ^^DIRECTORY^^
AddIcon /icons/blank.gif ^^BLANKICON^^

DefaultIcon /icons/unknown.gif
```

```
ReadmeName README.html
HeaderName HEADER.html

IndexIgnore .??* *~ *# HEADER* README* RCS CVS *,v *,t
```

The previous block of options deals with how server-generated directory indexes are handled. The `IndexOptions FancyIndexing VersionSort NameWidth=*` directive enables an autogenerated directory index to include several bits of information about each file or directory, including an icon representing the file type, the filename, the file's last modification time, the file's size, and a description of the file. Figure 20-2 shows an example of a directory using default `FancyIndexing` settings.

FIGURE 20-2

Change how directories are displayed from Apache using IndexOptions.

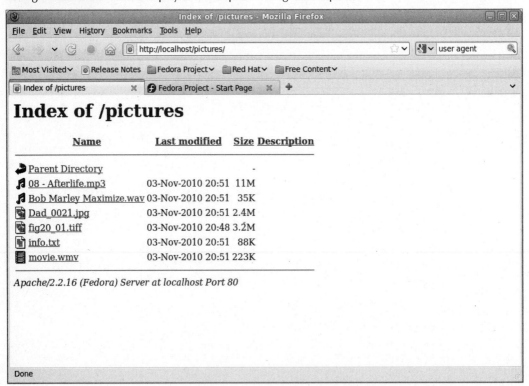

The `VersionSort` option enables files that include version numbers to be sorted as would be most natural (so, for example, version-2 would come before version-10 with this option on). The `NameWidth=*` option enables filenames of any length to be displayed. You change the `asterisk`

to a number representing the maximum number of characters that can be displayed in the Name column. If `IndexOptions` is not set to `FancyIndexing`, the index lists only the file's name.

The `AddIconByEncoding` directive is used to configure the output of `FancyIndexing`. It causes a particular icon to be displayed for files matching a particular MIME encoding. In the `AddIconByEncoding` line in the previous example, `compressed.gif` (with an alternative image tag of `CMP` for browsers that don't load images) will be displayed for files with a MIME encoding of x-compress and x-gzip. The `AddIconByType` directive has the same syntax but matches files based on their MIME type.

The `AddIcon` directive performs a similar function, but the icons are displayed based on a pattern in the filename. In the preceding lines, for example, `bomb.gif` will be displayed for files ending with `core`, and `binary.gif` will be displayed for files ending in `.bin` and `.exe`. The `folder.gif` icon represents a subdirectory.

If there is a conflict among the `AddIcon`, `AddIconByEncoding`, or `AddIconByType` directives, the `AddIcon` directive has precedence. The `DefaultIcon` directive specifies the image to be displayed (`unknown.gif`, according to the line above) if no previous directive has associated an icon with a particular file.

The `HeaderName` and `ReadmeName` directives specify files that will be inserted at the top and bottom of the autogenerated directory index, if they exist. Using the default values, the server first looks for `HEADER.html`, then `HEADER`, to include at the top of the "fancy index." At the end of the index, `README.html` or `README` (whichever is located first) is inserted.

The `IndexIgnore` directive specifies files that should not appear in an autogenerated directory index. The line above excludes the following:

- Any filename starting with a dot and containing at least two additional characters
- Any filename ending with a tilde (~) or what is commonly called a hash mark (#) (typically used by text editors as temporary files or backup files)
- Filenames beginning with `HEADER` or `README` (the files displayed at the top and bottom of the directory listing, according to the `HeaderName` and `ReadmeName` directives)
- The RCS (Revision Control System) or CVS (Concurrent Versions System) directories

Defining encoding and language

The `AddEncoding` directive enables you to set compression definitions that can be used by browsers to encode data as it arrives. The `AddLanguage` directive enables you to indicate the language of a document, based on its file extension:

```
# AddEncoding x-compress Z
# AddEncoding x-gzip gz tgz

AddLanguage ca .ca
AddLanguage cs .cz .cs
```

```
AddLanguage da .dk
AddLanguage nl .nl
AddLanguage en .en
AddLanguage et .et
AddLanguage es .es
AddLanguage fr .fr
       .
       .
       .
LanguagePriority en ca cs da de el eo es et fr he hr it ja ko ltz ↵
nl nn no pl pt pt-BR ru sv zh-CN zh-TW
```

The `AddEncoding` directive supplements or overrides mappings provided by the `TypesConfig` file (`/etc/mime.types` by default). Knowledge of the MIME type/encoding may allow certain browsers to manipulate files automatically as they are being downloaded or retrieved.

The `AddLanguage` directive performs similar mappings, associating a MIME language definition with a filename extension. The `LanguagePriority` directive determines the precedence if a particular file exists in several languages (and if the client does not specify a preference). Using the preceding definition, if the file `index.html` were requested from a directory containing the files `index.html.de`, `index.html.en`, `index.html.fr`, and `index.html.it`, the `index.html.en` file would be sent to the client.

Using `LanguagePriority`, you can set which language is used in case a determination about what language to use can't be made during content negotiation. If you are expecting multi-language use of your Web content, check (and probably change) the priority here.

Choosing character sets

The default character set to use and the character sets to use for files with particular file extensions are set using the `AddDefaultCharset` and `AddCharset` directives, respectively. The default character set of UTF-8 (shown in the following code example) is a good choice. Other standard ISO fonts, as well as some nonstandard fonts, can be set using `AddCharset` directives.

```
AddDefaultCharset UTF-8
```

You can retrieve an official list of character sets and the file extensions that are assigned to them at `www.iana.org/assignments/character-sets`.

Adding MIME types and handlers

With the `AddType` directive, you can enhance the MIME types assigned for your Apache Web server without editing the `/etc/mime.types` file. With the `AddHandler` directive, you can map selected file extensions to handlers (which results in certain actions being taken):

```
# AddType application/x- gzip .gz .tgz

AddHandler type-map var
```

Defining actions and headers

Some types of media can be set to execute a script when they are opened. Likewise, certain handler names, when opened, can be set to perform specified scripts. The `Action` directive can be used to configure these scripts:

```
# Action lets you define media types that execute a script whenever
# a matching file is called. This eliminates the need for repeated URL
# pathnames for oft-used CGI file processors.
# Format: Action media/type /cgi-script/location
# Format: Action handler-name /cgi-script/location
```

The `Action` directive maps a CGI script to a handler or a MIME type, whereas the `Script` directive maps a CGI script to a particular HTTP request method (`GET`, `POST`, `PUT`, or `DELETE`). These options allow scripts to be executed whenever a file of the appropriate MIME type is requested, a handler is called, or a request method is invoked.

Customizing error responses

For different error conditions that occur, you can define specific responses. The responses can be in plain text, redirects to pages on the local server, or redirects to external pages:

```
#
# Customizable error responses come in three flavors:
# 1) plain text 2) local redirects 3) external redirects
#
# Some examples:
#ErrorDocument 500 "The server made a boo boo."
#ErrorDocument 404 /missing.html
#ErrorDocument 404 "/cgi-bin/missing_handler.pl"
#ErrorDocument 402 http://www.example.com/subscription_info.html
#
```

As the comments suggest, the `ErrorDocument` directive can customize any server response code, redirecting it to an external page, a local file or CGI script, or a simple text sentence. Table 20-6 lists and describes the most common server response codes.

TABLE 20-6

HTTP Response Codes

Response Code	Description
200 OK	The request was successfully processed.
201 Created	Using the `POST` request method, a new file was successfully stored on the server.
202 Accepted	The request has been received and is currently being processed.

continued

TABLE 20-6 *(continued)*

Response Code	Description
204 No Content	The request was successful, but there is no change in the current page displayed to the client.
301 Moved Permanently	The requested page has been permanently moved, and future references to that page should use the new URL that is displayed.
302 Moved Temporarily	The requested page has been temporarily relocated. Future references should continue to use the same URL, but the current connection is being redirected.
304 Not Modified	A cached version of the page is identical to the requested page.
400 Bad Request	The client's request contains invalid syntax.
401 Unauthorized	The client specified an invalid username/password combination.
402 Payment Required	The client must provide a means to complete a monetary transaction.
403 Forbidden	Access-control mechanisms deny the client's request.
404 Not Found	The requested page does not exist on the server.
500 Internal Server Error	Usually encountered when running a CGI program, this response code indicates that the program or script contains invalid code or was given input that it cannot handle.
501 Not Implemented	The request method (e.g., `GET`, `POST`, `PUT`, `DELETE`, `HEAD`) is not understood by the server.
502 Bad Gateway	With the Web server acting as a proxy server, an error was encountered when trying to fulfill the request to an external host.
503 Service Unavailable	The server is currently processing too many requests.
505 HTTP Version Not Supported	The request version (e.g., HTTP/1.0, HTTP/1.1) is not understood by the server.

To make it easier to internationalize error messages and to standardize how these messages are presented, the latest version of Apache includes what are referred to as *variant pages* (ending in a .var extension). These variant pages, which offer variable output based on language, are stored in the /var/www/error directory.

```
Alias /error/ "/var/www/error/"

<IfModule mod_negotiation.c>
<IfModule mod_include.c>
    <Directory "/var/www/error">
        AllowOverride None
```

```
        Options IncludesNoExec
        AddOutputFilter Includes html
        AddHandler type-map var
        Order allow,deny
        Allow from all
        LanguagePriority en es de fr
        ForceLanguagePriority Prefer Fallback
    </Directory>

    ErrorDocument 400 /error/HTTP_BAD_REQUEST.html.var
    ErrorDocument 401 /error/HTTP_UNAUTHORIZED.html.var
    ErrorDocument 403 /error/HTTP_FORBIDDEN.html.var
    ErrorDocument 404 /error/HTTP_NOT_FOUND.html.var
    ErrorDocument 405 /error/HTTP_METHOD_NOT_ALLOWED.html.var
        .
        .
        .
```

The ErrorDocument directive associates a particular error code number with a particular .var file that contains multiple possible responses based on language.

Setting responses to browsers

If file extensions are not enough to determine a file's MIME type, you can define hints with the MimeMagicFile directive. With the BrowserMatch directive, you can set responses to conditions based on particular browser types:

```
BrowserMatch "Mozilla/2" nokeepalive
BrowserMatch "MSIE 4\.0b2;" nokeepalive downgrade-1.0 force-response-1.0
BrowserMatch "RealPlayer 4\.0" force-response-1.0
BrowserMatch "Java/1\.0" force-response-1.0
BrowserMatch "JDK/1\.0" force-response-1.0

BrowserMatch "Microsoft Data Access Internet Publishing Provider"
    redirect-carefully
BrowserMatch "MS FrontPage" redirect-carefully
BrowserMatch "^WebDrive" redirect-carefully
BrowserMatch "^WebDAVFS/1.[0123]" redirect-carefully
BrowserMatch "^gnome-vfs/1.0" redirect-carefully
BrowserMatch "^XML Spy" redirect-carefully
BrowserMatch "Dreamweaver-WebDAV-SCM1" redirect-carefully
```

The BrowserMatch directive enables you to set environment variables based on the contents of the User-agent: header field. The force-response-1.0 variable causes an HTTP/1.0 response, indicating that Apache will respond to the browser in basic HTTP 1.0 operations.

Note

If you are following the `httpd.conf` file, notice that we are skipping descriptions of the `server-status` lines and `server-info` lines. They are described in the section "Monitoring Server Activities" later in this chapter. ■

Enabling proxy and caching services

Proxy and caching services are turned off by default. You can turn them on by uncommenting the following directives:

```
#
# Proxy Server directives. Uncomment the following lines to
# enable the proxy server:
#
#<IfModule mod_proxy.c>
#     ProxyRequests On
#
#<Proxy:*>
#     Order deny,allow
#     Deny from all
#     Allow from .example.com
#</Proxy>

#
# Enable/disable the handling of HTTP/1.1 "Via:" headers.
# ("Full" adds server version; "Block" removes outgoing Via: headers)
# Set to one of: Off | On | Full | Block
#
#ProxyVia On

# To enable a cache of proxied content, uncomment the following lines.
# See http:/httpd.apache.org/docs/2.2/mod/mod_cache.html for more
details.
#
#<IfModule mod_disk_cache.c>
# CacheEnable disk /
# CacheRoot "/var/cache/mod_proxy"
#</IfModule>

#</IfModule>
# End of proxy directives.
```

Apache can function as a proxy server, a caching server, or a combination of the two. If `ProxyRequests` is set to `Off`, the server will simply cache files without acting as a proxy. If `CacheRoot` (which specifies the directory used to contain the cache files) is undefined, no caching will be performed. Both proxy and caching services are `Off` (commented out) by default.

Note

If you use Apache with the Tomcat Java application server, you also need to set the ProxyPass and ProxyPassReverse values. See `http://tomcat.apache.org/tomcat-6.0-doc/proxy-howto.html` **for more on this topic. If you turn on caching, the** `CacheRoot` **should exist on a file system with enough free space to accommodate the cache, which is limited by the** `CacheSize` **directive. However, you should have 20 to 40 percent more space available in the file system because cache cleanup (to maintain the** `CacheSize`, **in kilobytes) occurs only periodically (you can set this using the** `CacheGcInterval` **directive). ■**

You can add other directives to this example to enable other caching features. The `CacheMaxExpire` directive can indicate the maximum number of hours that a document will exist in the cache before Apache checks the original document for modifications. `CacheLastModifiedFactor` applies to documents that do not have an expiration time, even though the protocol would support one. To formulate an expiration date, the factor (a floating-point number) is multiplied by the number of hours since the document's last modification. For example, if the document were modified three days ago and `CacheLastModifiedFactor` were 0.25, the document would expire from the cache in 18 hours (as long as this value was still below the value of `CacheMaxExpire`).

The `CacheDefaultExpire` directive (specifying the number of hours before a document expires) applies to documents received via protocols that do not support expiration times. The `NoCache` directive contains a space-separated list of IP addresses, hostnames, or keywords in hostnames that should not have documents cached.

Here's how the caching server behaves if you uncomment the previous `Cache` lines:

- The cached files exist in `/var/cache/mod_proxy`.
- Cache size is limited to 500KB.

You might want to allow a much larger `CacheSize`, and possibly set a short `CacheGcInterval`, but otherwise the supplied values are reasonable. The `CacheGcInterval` value can be a floating-point number (e.g., 1.25 indicates 75 minutes).

Configuring virtual hosting

If you have one Web server computer but more than one domain that you want to serve with that computer, you can set up Apache to do virtual hosting. With name-based virtual hosting, a single IP address can be the access point for multiple domain names on the same computer. With IP-based virtual hosting, you have a different IP address for each virtual host, which you achieve by having multiple network interfaces to a machine.

With virtual hosting, when a request comes into your Apache server from a Web browser through a particular IP address on your computer, Apache checks the domain name being requested and displays the content associated with that domain name. As administrator of a Web server that supports virtual hosting, you must ensure that everything that needs to be configured for that virtual server is set up properly (by defining such things as locations for the Web content, log files, administrative contact, and so on).

Virtual hosting is defined with the `VirtualHost` tags. Information related to virtual hosts in the `/etc/httpd/conf/httpd.conf` file is shown in the following code:

```
### Section 3: Virtual Hosts
...
# VirtualHost example:
# Almost any Apache directive may go into a VirtualHost container.
# The first VirtualHost section is used for requests without a known
# server name.
#
#<VirtualHost *:80>
#    ServerAdmin webmaster@dummy-host.example.com
#    DocumentRoot /www/docs/dummy-host.example.com
#    ServerName dummy-host.example.com
#    ErrorLog logs/dummy-host.example.com-error_log
#    CustomLog logs/dummy-host.example.com-access_log common
#</VirtualHost>
```

The following example lists virtual host directives that would allow you to host the domains `handsonhistory.com` and `linuxtoys.net` on the same computer:

```
NameVirtualHost *:80

<VirtualHost *:80>
    DocumentRoot /var/www/handsonhistory
    ServerName www.handsonhistory.com
    ServerAlias handsonhistory.com
    ServerAdmin webmaster@handsonhistory.com
    ErrorLog logs/handsonhistory.com-error_log
    CustomLog logs/handsonhistory.com-access_log common
</VirtualHost>

<VirtualHost *:80>
    DocumentRoot /var/www/linuxtoys
    ServerName www.linuxtoys.net
    ServerAlias linuxtoys.net
    ServerAdmin webmaster@linuxtoys.net
    ErrorLog logs/linuxtoys.net-error_log
    CustomLog logs/linuxtoys.net-access_log common
</VirtualHost>
```

To experiment with virtual hosts, you can add the new hostname to your local `/etc/hosts` file and define it with your localhost IP address. For example:

```
127.0.0.1        www.linuxtoys.net
```

If you see the content you set up for your virtual host, and not the Fedora error page or default content you set up, then you've probably set up your virtual host properly.

Configuring modules and related services (/etc/httpd/conf.d/*.conf)

Any module that requires special configuration typically has a configuration file (`.conf`) in the `/etc/httpd/conf.d/` directory. Here are modular configuration files that might be contained in that directory, along with some ways to use those files and the packages associated with them (use **yum install package** to install each package you want):

- **auth_kerb.conf** — Configure Kerberos authentication over a Web (HTTP) connection. The example in this file suggests using Kerberos authentication over an SSL connection. (Install the mod_auth_kerb package.)

- **auth_mysql.conf** — Configure authentication based on data you add to a MySQL database. Comments in the file describe how to set up the database and then use it for user or group authentication before allowing a client to access your Web content. (Install the mod_auth_mysql package.)

- **auth_pgsql.conf** — Configure authentication based on data in a PostgreSQL database. (Install the mod_auth_pgsql package.)

- **authz_ldap.conf** — Configure authentication to access an LDAP database to authenticate users. (Install the mod_authz_ldap package.)

- **htdig.conf** — Identify the location of the `htdig` search content that can be used on your website (`/usr/share/htdig` is the default location). To see the `htdig` search screen from a Web browser, type **http://localhost/htdig**. The `htdig` system lets you set up tools for indexing and searching your website or company intranet. It is optional for your Web server. (Install the htdig-web package.)

- **mailman.conf** — Set up mailman list server software to allow features such as making mailing-list archives available from Apache. (Install the mailman package.)

- **manual.conf** — Defines the location of Apache manuals (`/var/www/manual`) on the server for different languages. Type **http://localhost/manual** in a browser window. (Install the httpd-manual package.)

- **mrtg.conf** — Defines the location of daily `mrtg` output (`/var/www/mrtg`), which tracks network traffic. Type **http://localhost/mrtg** in a browser window. (Install the mrtg package.)

- **perl.conf** — Identifies and loads the `mod_perl` module so that your Web pages can include Perl code. (Install the mod_perl package.)

- **php.conf** — Identifies and loads the `libphp5` module so that your Web pages can include PHP scripting language. There is also a `DirectoryIndex` setting that allows an `index.php` file you add to a directory to be served as a directory index. (Install the php package.)

- **python.conf** — Identifies and loads the `mod_python` module so Web pages can include Apache handlers written in Python. (Install the mod_python package.)

- **squirrelmail.conf** — Identifies the location of the SquirrelMail Web-based mail interface so that it can be incorporated into your Apache Web server. To see the SquirrelMail login screen, type http://localhost/webmail into a browser window. (Install the squirrelmail package.)

- **ssl.conf** — Configures SSL support so that Apache knows how to serve pages requested over a secure connection (https). (Install the mod_ssl package.)

- **subversion.conf** — Loads the mod_dav_svn and mod_authz_svn modules to enable you to access a Subversion repository from Apache. By uncommenting lines in this file, you can set /home/svnroot as the location where you hold authorization files. (Install the mod_dav_svn package.)

- **webalizer.conf** — Enables you to identify who can access the Webalizer data (statistics about your website). (Install the webalizer package.)

- **wordtrans.conf** — Identifies the location of the WordTrans language translation window so that it can be incorporated into your Apache Web server. To see the WordTrans login screen, type http://localhost/wordtrans into a browser window. (Install the wordtrans package.)

These configuration files are read when the httpd server starts. The information in these files could have been added to httpd.conf but files are put here so that different packages can add their own configuration settings without having the RPM software package incorporate an automated method of adding their configuration information to the httpd.conf file.

Starting and Stopping the Server

The procedure for starting and stopping the Apache Web server is no different from that of many other daemons. You can use the chkconfig command to set the httpd service to start at boot time.

Cross-Reference

See Chapter 11 for detailed information on the inner workings of the shell scripts that control starting and stopping daemons and server processes. ■

The /etc/init.d/httpd shell script accepts any of a handful of command-line arguments. If it is called with the argument start, the httpd script will run one master daemon process (owned by root) that spawns other daemon processes (equal to the number specified by the StartServers directive) owned by the user apache (from the User and Group directives). These processes are responsible for responding to incoming HTTP requests. If called with stop, the server will be shut down as all httpd processes are terminated.

If given a command-line argument of restart, the script will simply execute stop and start procedures in sequence. Using reload as the argument will send the hangup signal (-HUP) to the master httpd daemon, which causes it to reread its configuration files and restart all the other `httpd` daemon processes. The shell script also supports an argument of `status`, which will report if the daemon is running and, if it is, the PIDs of the running processes. All other command-line arguments result in an error and cause a usage message to be printed.

The actual binary for Apache, `/usr/sbin/httpd`, supports several command-line arguments, although the default values are typically used. The possible command-line arguments are listed in Table 20-7.

TABLE 20-7

Command-Line Arguments to httpd

Argument	Description
`-c directive`	Reads the configuration files and then processes the *directive*. This may supersede a definition for the directive within the configuration files.
`-C directive`	Processes the *directive* and then reads the configuration files. The directive may alter the evaluation of the configuration file, but it may also be superseded by another definition within the configuration file.
`-d directory`	Uses *directory* as the `ServerRoot` directive, specifying where the module, configuration, and log file directories are located.
`-D parameter`	Defines the *parameter* to be used for conditional evaluation within the `IfDefine` directive.
`-f file`	Uses *file* as the `ServerConfigFile` directive, rather than the default of `/etc/httpd/conf/httpd.conf`.
`-h`	Displays a list of possible command-line arguments.
`-l`	Lists the modules linked into the executable at compile time.
`-L`	Prints a verbose list of directives that can be used in the configuration files, along with a short description and the module that contains each directive.
`-S`	Lists the configured settings for virtual hosts.
`-t`	Performs a syntax check on the configuration files. The results will be either `Syntax OK` or an error notification, such as: `Syntax error on line 118 of /etc/httpd/conf/httpd.conf.`
`-v`	Prints the version information: `Server version: Apache/2.2.13 (Unix) Server built: Aug 21 2009 10:14:11.`

continued

TABLE 20-7	(continued)
Argument	**Description**
-V	Lists the version information and any values defined during compilation:
	`Server version: Apache/2.2.16 (Unix)`
	`Server built: Jul 26 2010 09:13:03`
	`Server's Module Magic Number: 20051115:24`
	`Architecture:      32-bit`
	`.....`
	`Server compiled with....`
	`-D APACHE_MPM_DIR="server/mpm/prefork"`
	`-D APR_HAS_SENDFILE`
	`-D APR_HAS_MMAP`
	`.`
	`.`
	`.`
	`-D SERVER_CONFIG_FILE="conf/httpd.conf"`
-k *option*	Uses `-k` with the `start`, `stop`, `restart`, `graceful`, or `graceful-stop` options to change the current state of the Web server.

Monitoring Server Activities

An Apache Web server is a tempting target for someone with a desire to hijack a computer for bad purposes. This usually occurs because the server is placed on the public Internet to service client requests. Because of the open nature of the Internet, if you don't secure your Web server correctly you are likely to become a target for an attack.

You can use many techniques to secure your server (see Chapter 13), ranging from SELinux to certificates to controlling how scripts are run. Described here, however, are techniques for keeping an eye on the performance and security of your Apache Web server. Watching your server carefully can often stop an attack before it gets anywhere.

Caution

You can often stop an attack before it occurs by keeping a close eye on your server. Use the techniques shown here to provide a high-level view of your server's status and then delve into the log files to ensure that things are OK. Look for odd slowdowns, disks filling up, large numbers of requests, or odd patterns in the requests sent to your server. See Chapter 13 for more on system security. ■

Apache provides two unique built-in methods to check the performance and status of your Web server. The `server-status` handler can be configured to show information about server processes. The `server-info` handler can be configured to display a detailed summary of the Web server's configuration. You can activate these services by adding the following lines to the `/etc/httpd/conf/httpd.conf` file:

```
<Location /server-status>
    SetHandler server-status
    Order deny,allow
    Deny from all
    Allow from 127.0.0.1
</Location>
<Location /server-info>
    SetHandler server-info
    Order deny,allow
    Deny from all
    Allow from 127.0.0.1
</Location>
```

In this example, all users from the local computer can display the `server-info` and `server-status` pages. You can change 127.0.0.1 to the name of any domain or host that your Apache server is hosting.

Tip
If you want users to be able to put `localhost` in the URL, you need to add `localhost` as well as `127.0.0.1`. ■

Displaying server information

The Server Information (`server-info`) page contains server version information and various general configuration parameters, and organizes the rest of the data by module. Each loaded module is listed, with information about all directives supported by that module, and the current value of any defined directives from that module.

The server information is usually quite verbose, containing links to each module's section and the general Server Settings section.

Displaying server status

The contents of the `server-status` page include version information for the server, the current time, a timestamp of when the server was last started, and the server's uptime. The page also details the status of each server process, choosing from several possible states: waiting for a connection, just starting up, reading a request, sending a reply, waiting to read a request before reaching the number of seconds defined in the `KeepAliveTimeout`, performing a DNS lookup, logging a transaction, or gracefully exiting.

The bottom of the `server-status` page lists each server by process ID (PID) and indicates its state, using the same possible values. Figure 20-3 shows an example of this page.

The `server-status` page can also perform automatic updates to provide even closer monitoring of the server. If the URL `http://localhost/server-status?refresh=40` is specified, the `server-status` page displayed in your browser will be updated every 40 seconds. This enables a browser window to be entirely devoted to continually monitoring the activities of the Web server.

FIGURE 20-3

The Apache server-status page displays general Apache information and reports on individual server process activities.

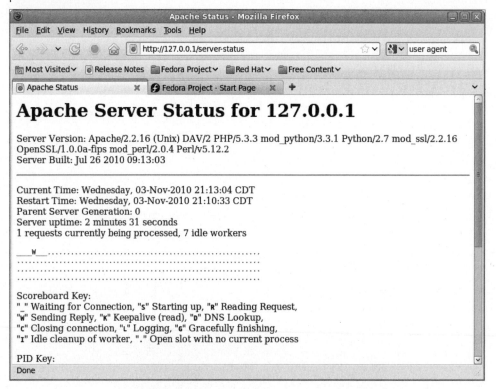

By default, only basic status information is generated. If you want to generate full status information, turn on the `ExtendedStatus` directive by uncommenting the last line in the following code:

```
#
# ExtendedStatus: controls whether Apache will generate "full" status
# information (ExtendedStatus On) or basic information (ExtendedStatus
# Off) when the "server-status" handler is called. The default is Off.
#
#ExtendedStatus On
```

Further security of server-info and server-status

Because both the server-info and server-status pages contain private information that should not be accessible to just anyone on the network, there are a few extra ways you can secure that information. You can restrict it to only the local host; however, in some environments that may not be practical.

If you must allow other machines or networks access to such detailed configuration information, allow only as many machines as necessary, and preferably only those machines on your local network. Also, be aware that, in the wrong hands, the information displayed by the server-info and server-status pages can make it much easier for the security of your entire machine to be compromised.

It may also be beneficial to change the URL used to reference both of the aforementioned pages. This is an example of "security through obscurity," which should not be relied on but which can make it just a little more difficult for unauthorized individuals to obtain information about your Web server's configuration (particularly if you cannot restrict such connections to the local network). To accomplish this, simply change the filename in the Location directive, as in the following lines:

```
<Location /server.information.page>
```

and

```
<Location /server.status.page>
```

Logging errors

The error log contains server-generated messages that describe various error conditions. The ErrorLog and LogLevel directives in the httpd.conf file (as described in the section on configuring HTTP logging) can modify the filename and the amount of information that is logged. The default file is /etc/httpd/logs/error_log (which is a link to /var/log/httpd/error_log). Here are a few sample lines from the error log:

```
[Wed Nov 03 19:49:43 2010] [notice]  Apache/2.2.16 (Unix) DAV/2 PHP/↵
5.3.3 mod_python/3.3.1 Python/2.7 mod_ssl/2.2.16 OpenSSL/↵
1.0.0a-fips mod_perl/2.0.4 Perl/v5.12.2
       configured -- resuming normal operations
[Wed Nov 03 19:49:43 2010] [error] [client 127.0.0.1] client denied by
       server configuration: /var/www/html/server-status
[Wed Nov 03 19:49:43 2010] [error] [client 127.0.0.1] File
       does not exist: /var/www/html/newfile.html
[Wed Nov 03 19:49:43 2010] [notice] caught SIGTERM, shutting down
```

The first line indicates that the server has just been started and will be logged regardless of the LogLevel directive. The second line indicates an error that was logged to demonstrate a denied request. The third line shows an error, which represents a request for a file that doesn't exist. The fourth line, also logged regardless of the LogLevel directive, indicates that the server is shutting down. The error log should also be monitored periodically because it will contain the error messages from CGI scripts that might need repair.

Logging hits

Every incoming HTTP request generates an entry in the transfer log (by default, /etc/httpd/logs/access_log, which is a link to /var/log/httpd/access_log). Statistics packages and log file analysis programs typically use this file because manually reading through it can be rather tedious. (See the information on the logwatch facility in Chapter 13.)

The format of the transfer log can be altered by the LogFormat and CustomLog directives in the httpd.conf file, as described in the "Configuring the Web Server (httpd.conf)" section. If you attempted to access http://localhost/ following the installation procedure (refer to Figure 20-1), the following lines (in the "common" format) would be written to the access_log:

```
127.0.0.1 - - [03/Nov/2010:21:10:51 -0500] "GET /server-info HTTP/1.1" 200 ↵
116115 "-" "Mozilla/5.0 (X11; U; Linux x86_64; en-US; rv:1.9.2.10)↵
Gecko/20101005 Fedora/3.6.10-1.fc14 Firefox/3.6.10"
127.0.0.1 - - [03/Nov/2010:21:12:20 -0500] "GET /server-status HTTP/1.1" 200 ↵
2575 "-" "Mozilla/5.0 (X11; U; Linux x86_64; en-US; rv:1.9.2.10)↵
Gecko/20101005 Fedora/3.6.10-1.fc14 Firefox/3.6.10"
```

The Apache Test Page actually is an error condition (403), which indicates that the Apache server is running but the server administrator hasn't added a home page yet. The next two lines show the Apache (apache_pb2.gif) and Fedora (poweredby.png) icons that appear on the test page, respectively, for Fedora.

Viewing the server-info and server-status pages generated the following entries:

```
127.0.0.1 - - [03/Nov/2010:21:10:51 -0500] "GET /server-info HTTP/1.1" 200 ↵
116115 "-" "Mozilla/5.0 (X11; U; Linux x86_64; en-US; rv:1.9.2.10)↵
Gecko/20101005 Fedora/3.6.10-1.fc14 Firefox/3.6.10"
127.0.0.1 - - [03/Nov/2010:21:12:20 -0500] "GET /server-status HTTP/1.1" 200 ↵
2575 "-" "Mozilla/5.0 (X11; U; Linux x86_64; en-US; rv:1.9.2.10)↵
Gecko/20101005 Fedora/3.6.10-1.fc14 Firefox/3.6.10"
```

The denied attempt to access the server-status page logged the following line (note the 404 server response code):

```
127.0.0.1 - - [03/Nov/2010:20:07:15 -0500] "GET /server-status HTTP/1.1" 404 ↵
270 "-" "Mozilla/5.0 (X11; U; Linux x86_64; en-US; rv:1.9.2.10) ↵
Gecko/20101005 Fedora/3.6.10-1.fc14 Firefox/3.6.10"
```

Analyzing Web-server traffic

The webalizer package can take Apache log files and produce usage reports for your server. Those reports are created in HTML format so you can read the information in your browser. Information is produced in both table and graph form.

To use the `webalizer` command, the webalizer package must be installed (`yum install webalizer`). You can run `webalizer` with no options to have it use the values in the `/etc/webalizer.conf` files to get the information it needs. As an alternative, you can use command-line options to override settings in the `webalizer.conf` file. To use the defaults, simply run the following:

```
# webalizer
```

Tip
If you see an error like "No valid records found!" this means your httpd server has not served any requests. ■

If all goes well, the command should run for a few moments and exit silently. Based on the information in the `/etc/webalizer.conf` file, the `/var/log/httpd/access_log` file is read and an `index.html` file is copied to the `/var/www/html/usage/` directory. You can view the output by opening the file in any browser window. For example, you could type the following in the location box:

```
http://localhost/usage
```

The output report shows a 12-month summary of Web server activity. On the bar chart, for each month a green bar represents the number of hits on the website, a dark blue bar shows the number of different file hits, and a light-blue bar shows the number of pages opened. It also shows, in the right column, data for the number of visits and the number of sites that were visited. The amount of data transferred, in kilobytes, is displayed as well.

Figure 20-4 shows an example of a webalizer output file for a Web server that has been running for only a short time.

The chart shows hits, files, and pages accessed, counting visits and the amount of data transferred. Below the chart, a table shows daily and monthly summaries for activity during each month. Users can click the name of a month to see detailed activity.

Tip
Because Webalizer supports both common log format (CLF) and combined log format, it can be used to display information for log files other than those produced for Apache. For example, you could display statistics for your FTP server or Squid server. ■

Several other software tools are available for analyzing transfer statistics. The accompanying sidebar on statistics packages available for Fedora describes some of these tools.

FIGURE 20-4

Webalizer displays Web data in chart and column formats.

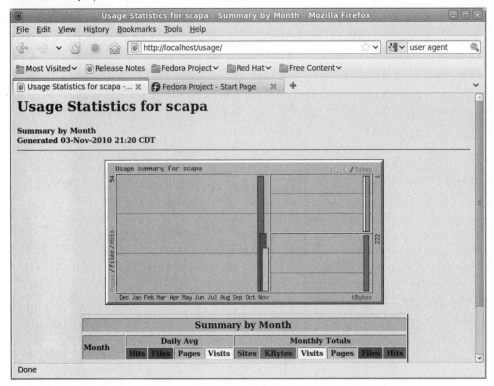

Statistics Packages Available for Fedora

Analyzing the transfer log manually isn't much fun. Several packages have been written to automate this task, including the following two:

- **Analog** — This free log-file analyzer is very fast and easily configurable, and it produces very detailed output (including bar graphs and hypertext links). More information can be found at www.analog.cx.

- **AWStats** — The Advanced Web Statistics tool (awstats package) produces graphical statistics representing Web-server access. AWStats can work with log files in the Apache common log format, as well as log files from sendmail, FTP, and other network servers. It can report statistics, such as the number of people who have visited, visits made per person, the domain and country of each visitor, and the number of visits made by bots. You can find more information at http://awstats.sourceforge.net.

Summary

Web servers are responsible for storing and delivering the vast amount of content available on the World Wide Web to clients all over the world. Although several Web-server software packages are available for Fedora systems, the most popular is by far the Apache Web server.

This chapter described how to install, configure, and run an Apache server in Fedora. The `httpd` daemon process handles requests for Web content (HTTP). Configuration files define what content is made available and how it can be accessed. In particular, the `/etc/httpd/conf/httpd.conf` file is used to configure the server.

The Apache httpd package also includes facilities for logging error and transfer messages. You can look for the `access_log` and `error_log` files in the `/etc/httpd/logs` directory. The `access_log` file contains information on content requests that have been serviced by the server. The `error_log` file lists error conditions that have occurred and times when service has been denied. You can use tools such as Webalizer to simplify the viewing of Apache log data.

Setting Up a DHCP Server

## 21

I f you are tasked with maintaining a network, you are probably interested in automating as much of the routine maintenance as possible. As your network grows, this becomes particularly important. When a new computer is added to your network or when a new employee joins your organization, you need to make configuration changes. You'd probably like a painless way to get the changes pushed out quickly, and preferably without having to touch each and every computer on your network. This is where DHCP (Dynamic Host Configuration Protocol) comes in.

The Internet Protocol (IP) has enabled network functionality that could scarcely be imagined when IP was first developed. In order for your network client and servers to take advantage of the numerous IP network services, software, and devices, each of your clients needs an IP address.

For all but the smallest networks, manually assigning and then tracking IP addresses can be a risky proposition. On top of the hassle of tracking who has which address, you could find yourself having to reconfigure every network client you have if you need to make a change in your IP addressing structure to accommodate new users or ISP services. Because DHCP can be used to dynamically assign IP addresses to DHCP clients, all of these pitfalls become irrelevant when DHCP is in use.

This chapter describes how to set up Fedora as a DHCP server. It then explains how to verify that the services are working and how to set up client computers to use those services.

Using Dynamic Host Configuration Protocol

Did you ever wonder why you can just plug your computer's Ethernet cable into a LAN jack at work, a hotel, or a DSL router in your home and immediately be on the Internet? In most cases, it's because that LAN is connected to a server that is set up for DHCP. Mac, Linux, and Windows systems are set up by default to look for a DHCP server on all Ethernet cards when the systems boot up. If your ISP or support staff has configured a DHCP server, you can be on the Internet faster than you can open your Web browser.

Setting up a DHCP server enables you to centrally manage the addresses and other network information for client computers on your private network. With DHCP configured on your network, a client computer can simply indicate that it wants to use DHCP, and the DHCP server can provide its IP address, network mask, DNS server, NetBIOS server, router (gateway), and other information needed to get up and running on the network.

With DHCP, you can greatly simplify the initial network configuration that each client computer on your network needs to do. Later, as your network evolves, you can easily update that information, having changes automatically picked up by clients when they restart their network interfaces.

Note

Although this chapter focuses on the configuration of DHCP client and server services on your Fedora systems, your Fedora DHCP client can use the services of other network devices. For example, you might have a Cisco router, a DSL/Cable device with DHCP services, or even a Windows-based DHCP server. DHCP clients for Fedora can work with any standards-compliant DHCP server. ∎

Setting Up a DHCP Server

To configure a DHCP server you need to install the dhcp package (yum install dhcp). Assuming you have already set up the physical connections between your DHCP server and the client computers on your network (presumably an Ethernet LAN), you need the following minimum tools to get the DHCP server working:

- A firewall and SELinux settings that allow requests for DHCP service
- A configured /etc/dhcp/dhcpd.conf file
- A running dhcpd server daemon (which can be started at boot time)

After the DHCP server is running, it listens to UDP port 67 for requests from DHCP clients on the LAN. A client simply boots up (with an Ethernet network interface turned on and DHCP identified as its method of getting network addresses). This causes the client to send out a DHCP discovery request to 255.255.255.255 (the global broadcast address). The DHCP server picks up that request and feeds the client the information it needs to get up and running on the network.

Note

The dhcpd.conf **file can serve a wide range of configuration information to DHCP clients. To see the full set of options and parameters you can set in that file, refer to the** dhcp-options **and** dhcpd.conf **man pages (type** man dhcp-options**). ■**

Opening your firewall and SELinux for DHCP

The firewall on your DHCP server must be configured to allow access to UDP ports 67 and 68. The easiest way to do this is to select System ➪ Administration ➪ Firewall from the GNOME desktop. From the Firewall Configuration window that appears, enable the firewall, and then select Other Ports and add UDP ports 67 and 68.

If you prefer to use iptables directly to change your firewall, you can add a new rule to iptables and then save the changes permanently. Type the following as root user:

```
# iptables -I INPUT -i eth0 -p udp --sport 67:68 --dport 67:68 -j ACCEPT
```

In this example, requests are allowed to and from source and destination ports 67 and 68 (--sport 67:68 and --dport 67:68) on the eth0 interface (which is your first Ethernet card). DHCP uses the User Datagram Protocol (UDP) (-p udp). If your DHCP server is also a routing firewall for your network, you should ensure that you are offering DHCP services only to your LAN, not to the Internet. (You need to figure out if eth0, eth1, or some other card is connected to your LAN.)

If the rule was accepted (type **iptables -L -n** to make sure), you can save your entire firewall configuration so that the new rule is included permanently. To change your firewall, type the following (as root user):

```
# service iptables save
```

This updates your /etc/sysconfig/iptables file so that all the current rules (including the one you just added) are included the next time iptables is restarted. To restore those firewall settings without rebooting, use the iptables-restore command:

```
# iptables-restore < /etc/sysconfig/iptables
```

SELinux should not block normal operations of the dhcpd daemon. SELinux does, however, enforce that particular file contexts be set on dhcp configuration files. For example, type:

```
# ls -lZ /etc/dhcp/dhcpd.conf
-rw-r--r--. root root system_u:object_r:dhcp_etc_t:s0    /etc/dhcp/dhcpd.conf
```

If you copied or moved your dhcpd.conf file from another location and it shows a context other than etc_t or dhcp_etc_t, you need to restore the proper context before the dhcpd service can start. To do so, type the following:

```
# restorecon -R /etc/dhcp
```

If you believe SELinux is still causing problems with your dhcpd service, and your environment does not require SELinux, consider setting SELinux to permissive. Open the SELinux Administration window (System ⇨ Administration ⇨ SELinux Management) and set enforcing mode to Permissive (both system default and current).

Configuring the /etc/dhcp/dhcpd.conf file

Suppose you have a single pool of IP addresses that you want to distribute to a set of computers that are all on the same subnetwork. In other words, all the computers are connected to one switch or cluster of switches with no routing between the devices. Here is an example of a simple dhcpd.conf file:

```
option domain-name              "handsonhistory.com";
option domain-name-servers   10.0.0.1, 10.0.0.2;
default-lease-time 21600;
ddns-update-style none;

subnet 10.0.0.0 netmask 255.255.255.0 {
    option routers          10.0.0.1;
    option subnet-mask      255.255.255.0;
    max-lease-time          43200;
    pool {
          range 10.0.0.150 10.0.0.225;
    }
}

# Set name server to appear at a fixed address
host ns {
next-server ns1.handsonhistory.com;
hardware ethernet 00:D0:B3:79:B5:35;
fixed-address 10.0.0.1;
}
```

In this example, the DHCP server provides IP addresses for client computers on a small LAN. The first line tells the DHCP server not to update DNS records for the local domain based on the IP addresses it assigns. (You can set ddns-update-style none; to either ad-hoc or interim if your DNS server is configured to have your DHCP server update host/address records for the host systems it serves.)

The DHCP server is serving a single LAN, represented by a 10.0.0.0 network address with a 255.255.255.0 netmask. Other data in this file defines what information the DHCP server will hand out to clients on this LAN.

A single server at address 10.0.0.1 is used as the router (or gateway) and DNS server for the LAN. A secondary DNS server is at 10.0.0.2. To ensure that the first server always gets the fixed address of 10.0.0.1, a host entry is set to the hardware ethernet address (00:D0:B3:79:B5:35) for the Ethernet card on the host named ns. (The hardware address is also called the MAC address.) If you specify the hardware address along with the option deny `unknown-clients`, you can allow only specified hardware addresses to obtain IP addresses from your DHCP server.

The pool of addresses handed out by this DHCP server is `10.0.0.150` to `10.0.0.225`, as set by the `range` line. Along with the IP address that each client is assigned, the client is also given the associated subnet mask and domain name.

The IP addresses that the DHCP server hands out are leased to each client for a particular time. The default-lease-time (set to 21,600 seconds here, or 6 hours) is the time assigned if the client doesn't request a particular lease period. The max-lease-time (43,200 seconds here, or 12 hours) is the longest amount of time the server will assign, if the client requests it. Clients can renew leases, so they don't have to lose an IP address while they are still using it.

Expanding the dhcpd.conf file

As noted earlier, this very simple example works well for a single network of client computers. The following are some examples of ways that you can expand your `dhcpd.conf` file:

- If you have multiple ranges of addresses on the same subnetwork, you can add multiple range options to a subnet declaration. Here is an example:

```
subnet 10.0.0.0 netmask 255.255.255.0 {
    range 10.0.0.10 10.0.0.100;
    range 10.0.0.200 10.0.0.250;
}
```

  This example causes the DHCP server to assign IP addresses between the ranges of 10 and 100 and between 200 and 250 on network 10.0.0.

- You can set fixed addresses for particular host computers, also called *address reservations*. In particular, you would want to do this for your server computers so that their addresses don't change. While you could simply omit the fixed IP addresses from your pool of DHCP assigned addresses, you would lose centralized management of IP configurations. The DHCP reservations enable you to centrally configure all IP address information. One way to do this is based on the Ethernet hardware address of the server's Ethernet card. All information for that computer can be contained in a host definition, such as the following:

```
host pine {
    hardware ethernet 00:04:5A:4F:8E:47;
    fixed-address 10.0.0.254;
}
```

  Here, when the DHCP server encounters the Ethernet address, the fixed address `10.0.0.254` is assigned to it. It's a good idea to statically assign server IP addresses. Type **ifconfig -a** on the server computer to see the address of its Ethernet hardware (while the interface is up). Within this host definition, you can add other options as well. For example, you could set the location of different routes (`routers` option).

- Many of the options enable you to define the locations of various server types. These options can be set globally or within particular host or subnet definitions. For example:

```
option netbios-name-servers 10.0.0.252;
option time-servers 10.0.0.253;
```

In these examples, the netbios-name-servers option defines the location of the WINS server (if you are doing Windows file and print server sharing using Samba). The time-servers option sets the location of a time server on your network.

- The DHCP server can be used to provide the information an X Terminal or diskless workstation could use to boot up on the network. The following example shows a definition you could use to start such a computer on your network:

```
host maple {
        filename "/dwboot/maple.nb";
        hardware ethernet 00:04:5A:4F:8E:47;
        fixed-address 10.0.0.150;
}
```

In the previous example, the boot file used by the diskless workstation from the DHCP server is located at /dwboot/maple.nb. The hardware ethernet value identifies the address of the Ethernet card on the client. The client's IP address is set to 10.0.0.150. All of those lines are contained within a host definition, where the hostname is defined as maple.

Another /etc/dhcp/dhcpd.conf example configuration file shipped with the DHCP server RPM can be found in /usr/share/doc/dhcp-*/dhcpd.conf.sample.

Adding options

There are dozens of options you can use in the /etc/dhcpd.conf file to pass information from the DHCP server to DHCP clients. Table 21-1 describes data types you can use. Table 21-2 describes options that are available.

Options contain values that are passed from the DHCP server to clients. Although Table 21-2 lists valid options, the client computer will not be able to use every value you could potentially pass to it. In other words, not all options are appropriate in all cases.

Table 21-2 is divided into the following categories:

- **Names, Addresses, and Time** — These options set values that are used by clients to have their hostnames, domain names, network numbers, and time zones (offset from GMT) defined.
- **Servers and Routers** — These options are used to tell DHCP clients where on the network to find routers and servers. Although more than a dozen server types are listed, typically you just indicate the address of the router and the DNS servers the client will use.

- **Routing** — These options indicate whether or not the client routes packets.
- **Thin Clients** — These options are useful if DHCP is being used as a boot server for thin clients. A thin client may be an X Terminal or diskless workstation that has processing power but no disk (or a very small disk), so it can't store a boot image and a file system itself.

TABLE 21-1

Data Types

Data Types	Description
ip-address	Enter *ip-address* as either an IP address number (11.111.111.11) or a fully qualified domain name (comp1.handsonhistory.com). To use a domain name, the name must be resolvable to an IP address number.
int32, int16, int8, uint32, uint16, uint8	Used to represent signed and unsigned 32-, 16-, and 8-bit integers.
"string"	Enter a string of characters, surrounded by double quotes.
boolean	Enter true or false when a boolean value is required.
data-string	Enter a string of characters in quotes ("client1") or a hexadecimal series of octets (00:04:5A:4F:8E:47).

Note

The Linux Terminal Server Project (LTSP) contains all the software you need to set up a server and thin clients. You can find a description of LTSP in *Linux Toys II* (Wiley, 2005). The Fedora K12Linux project (https://fedorahosted.org/k12linux) is an example of an LTSP-based project that provides educational tools to thousands of students in schools. ■

TABLE 21-2

DHCP Options

Options	Descriptions
Names, Addresses, and Time	
option hostname *string*;	Indicates the name that the client computer can use to identify itself. It can be either a simple hostname (e.g., pine) or a fully qualified domain name (e.g., pine.handsonhistory.com). You may use this in a host declaration, where a host computer is identified by an Ethernet address.

continued

TABLE 21-2 *(continued)*

Options	Descriptions
option domain-name *string*;	Identifies the default domain name the client should use to resolve DNS hostnames.
option *subnet-mask ip-address*;	Associates a subnetwork mask with an IP address; for example, `option 255.255.255.0 10.0.0.1;`
option time-offset *int32*;	Indicates the offset (in seconds) from Coordinated Universal Time (UTC). For example, a UTC offset for U.S. Eastern Standard Time is set as follows: `option time-offset -18000;`
Servers and Routers	
option routers *ip-address* [, *ip-address*...];	Lists, in order of preference, one or more routers connected to the local subnetwork. The client may refer to this value as the gateway.
option domain-name-servers *ip-address* [, *ip-address*...];	Lists one or more Domain Name System (DNS) servers that the client can use to resolve names into IP addresses. Lists servers in the order in which they should be tried.
option time-servers *ip-address* [, *ip-address*...];	Lists, in order of preference, one or more time servers that can be used by the DHCP client.
option ien116-name-servers *ip-address* [, *ip-address*...];	Lists, in order of preference, one or more IEN 116 name servers that can be used by the client. (IEN 116 name servers predate modern DNS servers and are considered obsolete.)
option log-servers *ip-address* [, *ip-address*...];	Lists one or more MIT-LCS UDP log servers. Lists servers in the order in which they should be tried.
option cookie-servers *ip-address* [, *ip-address*...];	Lists one or more Quote of the Day (cookie) servers (see RFC 865). Lists servers in the order in which they should be tried.
option lpr-servers *ip-address* [, *ip-address*...];	Lists one or more line printer servers that are available. Lists servers in the order in which they should be tried.
option impress-servers *ip-address* [, *ip-address*...];	Lists one or more Imagen Impress image servers. Lists servers in the order in which they should be tried.
option resource-location-servers *ip-address* [, *ip-address*...];	Lists one or more Resource Location servers (RFC 887). Lists servers in the order in which they should be tried.
option nis-domain *string*;	Indicates the name of the NIS domain, if an NIS server is available to the client.
option nis-servers *ip-address* [, *ip-address*...];	Lists addresses of NIS servers available to the client, in order of preference. You can also use `option nisplus-servers` to similarly define NIS+ servers as shown below.
option ntp-servers *ip-address* [, *ip-address*...];	Lists addresses of Network Time Protocol servers, in order of preference.

Options	Descriptions
option netbios-name-servers *ip-address* [, *ip-address*...];	Lists the addresses of WINS servers, used for NetBIOS name resolution (for Windows file and print sharing).
option netbios-dd-server *ip-address* [, *ip-address*...];	Lists the addresses of NetBIOS datagram distribution (NBDD) servers, in order of preference.
option netbios-node-type *uint8*;	Contains a number (a single octet) that indicates how NetBIOS names are determined (used with NetBIOS over TCP/IP). Acceptable values include: 1 (broadcast: no WINS), 2 (peer: WINS only), 4 (mixed: broadcast, then WINS), 8 (hybrid: WINS, then broadcast).
option font-servers *ip-address* [, *ip-address*...];	Indicates the location of one or more X Window font servers that can be used by the client, listed in order of preference.
option nisplus-domain *string*;	Indicates the NIS domain name for the NIS+ domain.
option nisplus-servers *ip-address* [, *ip-address*...];	Lists addresses of NIS+ servers available to the client, in order of preference.
option smtp-server *ip-address* [, *ip-* address...];	Lists addresses of SMTP servers available to the client, in order of preference.
option pop-server *ip-address* [, *ip-address*...];	Lists addresses of POP3 servers available to the client, in order of preference.
option nntp-server *ip-address* [, *ip-address*...];	Lists addresses of NNTP servers available to the client, in order of preference.
option www-server *ip-address* [, *ip-address*...];	Lists addresses of WWW servers available to the client, in order of preference.
option finger-server *ip-address* [, *ip-address*...];	Lists addresses of Finger servers available to the client, in order of preference.
option irc-server *ip-address* [, *ip-address*...];	Lists addresses of IRC servers available to the client, in order of preference.
Routing	
option ip-forwarding *flag*;	Indicates whether the client should allow (1) or not allow (0) IP forwarding. This would be allowed if the client were acting as a router.
option non-local-source-routing *flag*;	Indicates whether or not the client should allow (1) or disallow (0) datagrams with nonlocal source routes to be forwarded.
option static-routes *ip-address* *ip-address* [, *ip-address* *ip-address*...];	Specifies static routes that the client should use to reach specific hosts. (Lists multiple routes to the same location in descending priority order.)

continued

TABLE 21-2 *(continued)*

Options	Descriptions
option router-discovery *flag;*	Indicates whether the client should try to discover routers (1) or not (0) using the router discovery mechanism.
option router-solicitation-address *ip-address;*	Indicates an address the client should use to transmit router solicitation requests.
Thin Clients	
option boot-size *uint16;*	Indicates the size of the default boot image (in 512-octet blocks) that the client computer uses to boot.
option merit-dump *string;*	Indicates where the core image should be dumped if the client crashes.
option swap-server *ip-address;*	Indicates where the client computer's swap server is located.
option root-path *string;*	Indicates the location (path name) of the root disk used by the client.
option tftp-server-name *string;*	Indicates the name of the TFTP server that the client should use to transfer the boot image. Used more often with DHCP clients than with BOOTP clients.
option bootfile-name *string;*	Indicates the location of the bootstrap file that is used to boot the client. Used more often with DHCP clients than with BOOTP clients.
option x-display-manager *ip-address* [, *ip-address...*];	Indicates the locations of X Window System Display Manager servers that the client can use, in order of preference.

Starting the DHCP server

After the `/etc/dhcp/dhcpd.conf` file is configured, you can start the DHCP server immediately. As root user from a terminal window, type the following:

```
# service dhcpd start
```

Your DHCP server should now be available to distribute information to the computers on your LAN. If there are client computers on your LAN waiting on your DHCP server, their network interfaces should now be active.

Note

If you don't specify a subnet for every network interface card you have configured on your server, you need to edit `/etc/sysconfig/dhcpd` **and specify which interfaces it should listen on.** ∎

If everything is working properly, you can have your DHCP server start automatically each time your computer boots by turning on the `dhcpd` service as follows:

```
# chkconfig dhcpd on
```

You can verify that your DHCP server is working in a few ways:

- Check the /var/log/messages file. If the DHCP service has trouble starting, you will see messages in this file indicating what the problem is.

- Check the /var/lib/dhcpd/dhcpd.leases file. If a client has been assigned addresses successfully from the DHCP server, a lease line should appear in that file. There should be one set of information that looks like the following for each client that has leased an IP address:

```
lease 10.0.0.225 {
        starts 2 2009/05/04 03:48:12;
        ends 2 2009/05/04 15:48:12;
        hardware ethernet 00:50:ba:d8:03:9e;
        client-hostname "pine";
}
```

- Launch Wireshark (type **yum install wireshark** to install and **wireshark&** to run) and start capturing data (in promiscuous mode). Restart the DHCP server and restart the network interface on the client. You should see a series of DHCP packets that show a sequence like the following: DHCP Discover, DHCP Offer, DHCP Request, and DHCP ACK.

- From the client computer, you should be able to start communicating on the network. If the client is a Linux system, type the **ifconfig -a** command. Your Ethernet interface (probably eth0) should appear, with the IP address set to the address assigned by the DHCP server. If your client is a Windows system, open a command prompt and type **ipconfig /all**. You will see the configuration information for all your network interfaces.

When the server is running properly, you can continue to add DHCP clients to your network to draw on the pool of addresses you assign, up to the allotted amount.

Setting Up a DHCP Client

Most client computers (Linux, Windows, or Mac) are configured by default to boot up using DCHP to connect to the network. However, when that is not the case, you may need to indicate manually that DHCP be used.

Configuring a network client to get addresses from your DHCP server is fairly easy. Different types of operating systems, however, have different ways of using DHCP. Here are examples for setting up Linux, Windows, and Mac DHCP clients.

Fedora

While you are initially installing Linux, click Configure using DHCP on the Network Configuration screen. Your network client should automatically pick up its IP address from your DHCP server when it starts up.

To set up DHCP after installation using the Network Manager, follow these steps:

1. Right-click the Network Manager icon in the GNOME panel.
2. Select Edit Connections.
3. Highlight "System eth0" and press the Edit... button.
4. Select the IPv4 Settings tab.
5. Select Automatic (DHCP) from the Method drop-down box.
6. Click Apply and then click Close.
7. Click the Network Manager icon and select System `eth0` to reconnect.

There is also a traditional tool commonly used on Fedora servers that you can use instead of using the Network Manager. To set up DHCP after installation using the traditional Network Configuration tool, follow these steps:

1. Open the Network Configuration window (select System ⇨ Administration ⇨ Network or run the `system-config-network` command).
2. From the Network Configuration window:
   a. Click the Devices tab (on by default).
   b. Click your Ethernet device (probably `eth0`).
   c. Click Edit.
   d. Click the General tab.
   e. Click "Automatically obtain IP address settings with" and select dhcp.
   f. Click OK.
   g. Select File ⇨ Save.
3. From a terminal window, type the following:

```
# service network restart
```

Windows (Vista or 7)

To troubleshoot a modern Windows system's settings for DHCP, follow these steps.

1. From Windows Vista or Windows 7, select Start ⇨ Control Panel ⇨ Network and Internet ⇨ Network and Sharing Center ⇨ Manage Network Connections.
2. Select Local Area Connection.
3. Select Properties. The Properties window appears.
4. Select Internet Protocol Version 4 and click Properties.
5. On the General tab, make sure the Obtain an IP Address Automatically button is selected.

Windows (95, 98, 2000, or XP)

If you have a legacy Windows system, follow these steps:

1. From most older Windows operating systems (Windows 95, 98, and 2000), you open the Network window from the Control Panel (Start ➪ Settings ➪ Control Panel). For Windows XP systems, select Start ➪ Control Panel ➪ Network and Internet Connections ➪ Network Connections, and then select your Local Area Connection and choose Properties.

2. From the Configuration tab (or General tab in Windows XP), click the TCP/IP interface associated with your Ethernet card (something like TCP/IP ➪ 3Com EtherLink III).

3. Click Properties. The Properties window appears.

4. Click the IP Address tab (or General tab in Windows XP) and then select the Obtain an IP Address Automatically check box.

5. Click OK and reboot the computer so the client can use the new IP address.

Apple Mac OS X

On a Mac OS X system, follow these steps:

1. From the Mac OS X system, select Apple Menu ➪ System Preferences. From the Internet & Wireless section, open the Network window.

2. Select the appropriate network interface in which to configure DHCP.

3. In the Configure field, select Using DHCP.

4. Click the Advanced button to add your DHCP Client ID. You can also select Renew DHCP Lease to manually request an IP address with a new lease from the DHCP server. Click OK when complete.

5. Add any other pertinent information and click Apply.

By default, a Fedora client will not accept all information passed to it from the DHCP server. The Fedora client handles DHCP server input based on settings in the /etc/sysconfig/network-scripts/ifup script. If the client has DHCP turned on, when the system starts up networking, the ifup script runs the dhclient command. You can adjust the behavior of dhclient by creating the /etc/dhclient.conf file. (Type **man dhclient.conf** to find out how you can set your dhclient.conf file.)

Summary

DHCP provides a mechanism for centrally administering computers on your network, and can provide information that helps client computers get up and running quickly on the network.

DHCP is used to provide information about your network to Windows, Linux, Mac, or other client computers on your network. IP addresses can be assigned dynamically, meaning they are distributed from a pool of IP addresses; or specific addresses can be assigned to clients, based on specific Ethernet hardware addresses.

Setting Up a MySQL Database Server

MySQL is a popular Structured Query Language (SQL) relational database server. Like other database servers that use SQL, MySQL provides the means to access and manage SQL databases. However, MySQL also provides tools for creating database structures, as well as for adding data to those structures, modifying the data, and removing the data from those structures. Because MySQL is a relational database, data can be stored and controlled in small, manageable tables. Those tables can be used in combination to create flexible, complex data structures.

MySQL provides one of the most-used databases on the Internet, and it is especially used to provide data for Web applications. Nearly all Internet Service Providers (ISPs) provide MySQL if they provide a database.

A Swedish company called MySQL AB was responsible for developing MySQL (www.mysql.com). MySQL AB released MySQL as an open-source product several years ago, gaining revenue by offering a variety of MySQL support packages, commercial licenses, and MySQL-branded franchise products. In February 2008, Sun Microsystems Inc. acquired MySQL AB for about $1 billion. (Who says you can't make money with open-source software?) The following spring, Oracle acquired Sun and now has control of this and other open-source software projects.

Although not all the ramifications of Oracle's acquisition of MySQL have played out yet, for now MySQL is still available as open-source software. However, for the time being, you can also still purchase a range of MySQL Enterprise Server products directly from the Oracle site (www.oracle.com/us/products/mysql/).

IN THIS CHAPTER

Finding MySQL packages

Configuring the MySQL server

Working with MySQL databases

Displaying MySQL databases

Making changes to tables and records

Adding and removing user access

Checking and fixing databases

MySQL has been ported to several different operating systems (primarily Unix and Linux systems, although there are also Windows versions and a Mac OS X version). As you may have guessed, these include binary versions of MySQL that run on Fedora. This chapter contains descriptions of and procedures for the version of MySQL that is contained in Fedora.

The version of MySQL that comes with Fedora 14 is 5.1.50.

Finding MySQL Packages

You need at least the mysql and mysql-server packages installed to set up MySQL using the procedures described in this chapter. The following MySQL packages that come with Fedora are what you need to get started:

- **mysql** — This software package contains a lot of MySQL client programs (in /usr/bin) and documentation.
- **mysql-libs** — Contains several client shared libraries, the default MySQL configuration file (/etc/my.cnf), a few sample configuration files, and files to support different languages.
- **mysql-server** — This software package contains the MySQL server daemon (mysqld) and the mysqld startup script (/etc/rc.d/init.d/mysqld). The package also creates various administrative files and directories needed to set up MySQL databases.
- **mysql-devel** — This software package contains libraries and header files required for the development of MySQL applications.

Other packages available for adding functionality to your MySQL databases include php-mysql (contains a shared library to enable PHP applications access to MySQL databases), mod_auth_mysql (includes tools to authorize Apache Web server access from data in a MySQL database), and perl-Class-DBI-MySQL (provides a perl interface to MySQL databases). Among the packages including tools for using MySQL databases are mysql-bench (contains scripts for benchmarking MySQL databases), MySQL-python (contains a Python interface to MySQL), mysql-connector-java (contains a Java interface to MySQL), and qt-mysql (includes MySQL drivers for QT SQL classes).

If MySQL isn't installed yet, type the following:

```
# yum install mysql-server
```

If MySQL was installed during initial Fedora installation, update your MySQL packages (run yum update mysql*).

Starting the MySQL Server

For Fedora, the MySQL server is off by default. Turning it on is fairly simple. The `/etc/init.d/mysqld` startup script is delivered with the mysql-server package. To start the server, run the `mysqld` startup script to have it start immediately, and then set it to start each time your system boots.

To start the MySQL server immediately, type the following from a terminal window as root user:

```
# service mysqld Start
```

To set the MySQL server to start each time the computer boots, type the following (as root):

```
# chkconfig mysqld on
```

This sets `mysqld` to start during most multiuser run states (levels 2, 3, 4, and 5). To check that the service is turned on for those levels, type **chkconfig --list mysqld** from a terminal window.

Confirming That MySQL Server Is Working

You can use the `mysqladmin` or `mysqlshow` commands to confirm that the MySQL server is up and running. Here's an example of how to check information about the MySQL server using the `mysqladmin` command:

```
# mysqladmin -u root version proc
mysqladmin  Ver 8.42 Distrib 5.1.50, for redhat-linux-gnu on x86_64
Copyright 2000-2008 MySQL AB, 2008 Sun Microsystems, Inc.
This software comes with ABSOLUTELY NO WARRANTY. This is free software,
and you are welcome to modify and redistribute it under the GPL license

Server version        5.1.50
Protocol version      10
Connection            Localhost via UNIX socket
Uptime:               2 days 10 hours 47 min 35 sec

Threads: 2  Questions: 184  Slow queries: 0  Opens: 15  Flush tables: 1  Open
tables: 8  Queries per second avg: 0.25
+----+------+-----------+----+---------+------+-------+------------------+
| Id | User | Host      | db | Command | Time | State | Info             |
+----+------+-----------+----+---------+------+-------+------------------+
| 3  | root | localhost |    | Query   | 0    |       | show processlist |
+----+------+-----------+----+---------+------+-------+------------------+
```

If the server were not running at the moment, the `mysqladmin` command shown in the previous example would result in a failure message:

```
mysqladmin: connect to server at 'localhost' failed
error: 'Can't connect to local MySQL server through socket↵
'/var/lib/mysql/mysql.sock' (2)'
Check that mysqld is running and that the socket:
'/var/lib/mysql/mysql.sock' exists!
```

The recommended remedy is to try to restart the server (by typing **service mysqld restart**).

Getting MySQL GUI Tools

While most of this chapter focuses on using and administering a MySQL database from the command line, some graphical tools are available for working with MySQL databases. In particular, the `mysql-workbench` package contains GUI software for connecting to a MySQL server. This package replaces the earlier `mysql-administrator` package that came with previous versions of Fedora. To install the `mysql-workbench` package, type the following as the root user:

```
# yum install mysql-workbench
```

If you are familiar with MySQL, you can go ahead and use the MySQL Workbench to connect to your database (assuming it is already running). If MySQL is new to you, I recommend you run through the procedures in this chapter to become familiar with how MySQL works and how to use it from the command line.

Once installed, run the MySQL Workbench with the following command:

```
$ mysql-workbench
```

If your MySQL database is running, as described later in this chapter, click on New Connection. Enter the server hostname (such as localhost), user name (such as root), and password. You can now connect to your database and query data.

To administer your database, click on New Server Instance, enter the same connection information to the database, and click Next through all the initial tests. You can then click on the new server to administer that server.

Figure 22-1 shows the MySQL Workbench with a database connection set up for querying and another for administering.

Click on the new server you set up to administer that server. Figure 22-2 shows the administration window.

FIGURE 22-1

The MySQL Workbench provides a graphical tool for working with your databases.

FIGURE 22-2

Use the administration window to control your database server.

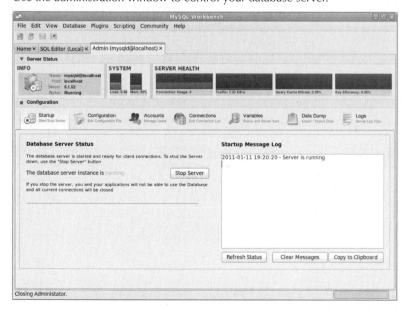

Configuring the MySQL Server

Like most server software in Fedora, the MySQL server relies on a startup script and a configuration file to provide the service. Server activities are logged to the `mysqld.log` file in the `/var/log` directory. There are also `mysql` user and group accounts for managing MySQL activities. The following sections describe how these components work together.

Using mysql user/group accounts

When the MySQL software is installed, it automatically creates a `mysql` user account and a `mysql` group account. These user and group accounts are assigned to MySQL files and activities. In this way, someone can manage the MySQL server without needing to have root permission.

The `mysql` user entry appears in the `/etc/passwd` file as follows:

```
mysql:x:27:27:MySQL Server:/var/lib/mysql:/bin/bash
```

This `mysql` entry indicates that both the UID is 27 and the GID for the `mysql` user is 27, which you can see in `/etc/groups`. The text string identifying this user account is `MySQL Server`. The home directory is `/var/lib/mysql` and the default shell is `/bin/bash`. The home directory identified will contain directories that hold each table of data you define for the MySQL server. Note that the user and group IDs may be different on your system.

If you care to check the ownership of files associated with MySQL, you will see that most of these files have `mysql` assigned as the user account and group account that own each file. This allows daemon processes that are run by the `mysql` user to access the database files.

Adding administrative users

To administer MySQL, you must have at least one administrative account. By default, the root user has full access to your MySQL server database and no password assigned. You can assign a password to the root user using the `mysqladmin` command, once the `mysqld` server is running. To add the root user as a MySQL administrator, type either of the following from a terminal window (substituting your own hostname and password):

```
$ mysqladmin -u root password 'myownpasswd'
$ mysqladmin -u root -h myhost.example.com password 'myownpasswd'
```

Tip

Enclose the password in quotes in case you have any characters in your password that are also interpreted as metacharacters by the shell. ∎

After this command is run, the MySQL root user can run any MySQL administrative commands using the password. If you forget or otherwise reset your MySQL password, refer to the information here: `http://dev.mysql.com/doc/refman/5.0/en/resetting-permissions.html`.

MySQL maintains a list of users and passwords that is separate from the list maintained by the operating system. If you don't provide a user name on the command line (as in -u root shown above), MySQL assumes you want to use your current Fedora user name to log in to MySQL. However, you will still need to provide the MySQL password (not the Fedora password) for that user to use the MySQL service.

To do MySQL administration, simply add the -u root argument to the command line of the MySQL command you are running. The Linux root user account has no connection to the MySQL root user account after the MySQL account is created. You would typically use different passwords for the two accounts.

Tip

To save yourself the trouble of typing the password each time you run a MySQL client command, you can add a password option under the [client] group in one of the option files. The most secure way to do that is to create a .my.cnf file in the root user's home directory that can be accessed only by root (chmod 600 /root/.my.cnf) and contains the following lines (substituting your password for the last argument shown):

```
[client]
password=myownpasswd
```

Setting MySQL options

You can set options that affect how the MySQL applications behave by using options files or command-line arguments. The MySQL server (as well as other administrative tools) reads the following options files when it starts up (if those files exist):

- **/etc/my.cnf** — Contains global options read by mysqld (server daemon) and mysql .server (script to start the server daemon).

- **--defaults-extra-file** — Contains options to be used by the server that you pass as a filename on the command line. For example, the following command would cause the file /home/jim/my.cnf to be read for options after the global options and before the user-specific options:

  ```
  # /usr/libexec/mysqld --defaults-extra-file=/home/jim/my.cnf
  ```

- **$HOME/.my.cnf** — Contains user-specific options. ($HOME refers to the user's home directory, such as /home/susyq).

Table 22-1 shows the MySQL commands that read the options files (in the order shown in the preceding bulleted list) and use those options in their processing. Options are contained within groups that are identified by single words within brackets. Group names that are read by each command are also shown in the table.

Although you can use any of the options files to set your MySQL options, begin by configuring the /etc/my.cnf file. Later, if you want to override any of the values set in that file, you can do so using the other options files or command-line arguments.

TABLE 22-1

Option Groups Associated with MySQL Commands

Command	Description	Group Names
mysqld (in /usr/libexec)	The MySQL server daemon	[mysqld] [server]
mysqld_safe	Run by the mysqld startup script to start the MySQL server	[mysql] [server] [mysql.server] [mysqld_safe]
mysql	Offers a command-line interface for displaying and working with MySQL databases	[mysql] [client]
mysqladmin	Used to create and maintain MySQL databases	[mysqladmin] [client]
myisamchk	Used to check, fix, and optimize MyISAM databases (.myi suffix)	[myisamchk]
myisampack	Used to compress MyISAM database tables	[myisampack]
mysqldump	Offers a text-based interface for backing up MySQL databases	[mysqldump] [client]
mysqlimport	Loads plain-text data files into MySQL databases	[mysqlimport] [client]
mysqlshow	Shows MySQL databases and tables you select	[mysqlshow] [client]

Creating the my.cnf configuration file

Global options that affect how the MySQL server and related client programs run are defined in the /etc/my.cnf file. The default my.cnf file contains only a few settings needed to get a small MySQL configuration going. The following is an example of the /etc/my.cnf file that comes with MySQL:

```
[mysqld]
datadir=/var/lib/mysql
socket=/var/lib/mysql/mysql.sock
user=mysql
# Disabling symbolic-links is recommended to prevent assorted security risks
symbolic-links=0

[mysqld_safe]
log-error=/var/log/mysqld.log
pid-file=/var/run/mysqld/mysqld.pid
```

Most of the settings in the default my.cnf file define the locations of files and directories needed by the mysqld server. Each option is associated with a particular group, with each group identified by a name in square brackets. The previous options are associated with the mysqld daemon ([mysqld]) and the safe_mysqld script that starts the mysqld daemon ([mysql_safe]). (Refer to Table 22-1 for a list of these groups.)

The default datadir value indicates that /var/lib/mysql is the directory that stores the MySQL databases you create. The socket option identifies /var/lib/mysql/mysql.sock as the socket that is used to create the MySQL communications end-point associated with the mysqld server. The user option identifies mysql as the user account that has permission to do administration of the MySQL service.

The log-error and pid-file options tell the safe_mysqld script the locations of the error log (/var/log/mysqld.log) and the file that stores the process ID of the mysqld daemon when it is running (/var/run/mysqld/mysqld.pid). The safe_mysqld script actually starts the mysqld daemon from the mysqld startup script.

Note
Each option that follows a group name is assigned to that group. Group assignments end when a new group begins or when the end of a file is reached. ■

Choosing options

Many values are used by the MySQL server but are not explicitly defined in the my.cnf file. The easiest way to see which options are available for MySQL server and clients is to run each command with the --help option. For example, to view the available mysqld options (as well as other information), type the following from a terminal window:

```
# /usr/libexec/mysqld --verbose --help | less
```

Then press the spacebar to step through the information one screen at a time. (An example of this output is shown in the next section.)

You can also use the man command to find which options are available. For example, to see which options are available to set for the mysqld daemon, type the following:

```
man mysqld
```

It's quite likely that you can try out your MySQL database server without changing any options at all. However, after you set up your MySQL database server in a production environment, you will almost certainly want to tune the server to match the way the server is used. For example, if it is a dedicated MySQL server, you will want to allow MySQL to consume more of the system resources than it would by default.

The following list describes a few additional options that you might want to set for MySQL:

- password = yourpwd — Adding this option to a [client] group in a user's $HOME/.my.cnf file allows the user to run MySQL client commands without having to enter a password each time. (Replace *yourpwd* with the user's password.) Note that this can be a security risk because your password is in plain text.

- `port = #` — Defines the port number to which the MySQL service listens for MySQL requests. (Replace # with the port number you want to use.) By default, MySQL listens to port number 3306 on TCP and UDP protocols.

- `safe-mode` — Tells the server to skip some optimization steps when the server starts.

- `tmpdir = path` — Identifies a directory, other than the default `/tmp`, for MySQL to use for writing temporary files. (Substitute a full path name for *path*.)

In addition to the options you can set, MySQL clients also have a number of variables you can set. Variables set such things as buffer sizes, timeout values, and acceptable packet lengths. These variables are also listed on the `--help` output. To change a variable value, list the variable name, an equals sign, and value. For example, to set the `sort_buffer_size` variable to 10MB, you could add the following option under your [`mysqld`] group:

```
[mysqld]
sort_buffer_size=10M
```

The following list identifies other variables you could set for your server. In general, raising the values of these variables improves performance, but it also consumes more system resources, so you need to be careful when raising these values on machines that are not dedicated to MySQL or that have limited memory resources.

Note

For variables that require you to enter a size, indicate megabytes using an M (e.g., 10M); or kilobytes using a K (e.g., 256K). ∎

- `key_buffer_size = size` — Sets the buffer size used for holding index blocks that are used by all threads. This is a key value to raise to improve MySQL performance.

- `max_allowed_packet = size` — Limits the maximum size of a single packet. Raise this limit if you require processing of very large columns.

- `myisam_sort_buffer_size = size` — Sets the buffer size used for sorting while repairing an index, creating an index, or altering a table.

- `sort_buffer_size = size` — Defines how much buffer size is allocated for each thread that needs to do a sort. Raising this value makes sorting threads go faster.

- `table_cache = #` — Limits the total number of tables that can be open at the same time for all threads. The number of this variable represents the total number of file descriptors that MySQL can have open at the same time.

- `thread_cache_size = size` — Sets the number of threads that are kept in cache, awaiting use by MySQL. When a thread is done being used, it is placed back in the cache. If all the threads are used, new threads must be created to service requests.

Checking options

In addition to seeing how options and variables are set in the options files, you can also view how all variables are set on your current system. You can view both the defaults and the current values being used by the MySQL server.

The `--help` command-line argument lets you see the options and variables as they are set for the server and for each MySQL client. Here is an example of the output showing this information for the `mysqld` server daemon:

```
# /usr/libexec/mysqld --verbose --help | less
      .
      .
      .
Variables (--variable-name=value)
and boolean options {FALSE|TRUE}  Value (after reading options)
--------------------------------  -----------------------------
abort-slave-event-count           0
allow-suspicious-udfs             FALSE
auto-increment-increment          1
auto-increment-offset             1
automatic-sp-privileges           TRUE
back_log                          50
basedir                           /usr/

...

tmp_table_size                    16777216
transaction_alloc_block_size      8192
transaction_prealloc_size         4096
updatable_views_with_limit        1
use-symbolic-links                FALSE
verbose                           TRUE
wait_timeout                      28800
warnings                          1

To see what values a running MySQL server is using, type
'mysqladmin variables' instead of 'mysqld --verbose --help'
```

After the server has been started, you can see the values that are actually in use by running the `mysqladmin` command with the `variables` option. (Pipe the output to the `less` command so you can page through the information.) Here is an example (if you haven't stored your password, you will be prompted to enter it before you see any output):

```
# mysqladmin -u root -p variables | less
+------------------------+----------------------------------------|
| Variable_name          | Value                                  |
+------------------------+----------------------------------------|
| auto_increment_increment| 1                                     |
```

```
| auto_increment_offset   | 1                  |
| autocommit              | ON                 |
| automatic_sp_privileges | ON                 |
| back_log                | 50                 |
| basedir                 | /usr/              |
                   .
                   .
                   .
| version                 | 5.1.50             |
| version_comment         | Source distribution |
| version_compile_machine | x86_64             |
| version_compile_os      | redhat-linux-gnu   |
| wait_timeout            | 28800              |
| warning_count           | 0                  |
+-------------------------+--------------------------------------------+
```

If you decide that the option and variable settings that come with the default MySQL system don't exactly suit you, you don't have to start from scratch. Sample my.cnf files that are included with the mysql package enable you to begin with a set of options and variables that are closer to the ones you need.

Using sample my.cnf files

Sample my.cnf files are available in the /usr/share/doc/mysql-server* directory. To use one of these files, do the following:

1. Keep a copy of the old my.cnf file:

```
# mv /etc/my.cnf /etc/my.cnf.old
```

2. Copy the sample my.cnf file you want to the /etc/my.cnf file. For example, to use the my-medium.cnf file, type the following:

```
# cp /usr/share/doc/mysql-server*/my-medium.cnf /etc/my.cnf
```

3. Edit the new /etc/my.cnf file (as root user), using any text editor, to further tune your MySQL variables and options.

The following list describes each of the sample my.cnf files.

- my-small.cnf — This options file is recommended for computer systems that have less than 64MB of memory and are used only occasionally for MySQL. With this options file, MySQL won't be able to handle a lot of usage, but it won't be a drag on your computer's performance.

For the `mysqld` server, buffer sizes are set low — only 64K for `sort_buffer_size` and 16K for `key_buffer_size`. The `thread_stack` is set to only 64K, and `net_buffer_length` is only 2K. The `table_open_cache` is set to 4.

● **my-medium.cnf** — Like the small options file, the `my-medium.cnf` file is intended for systems on which MySQL is not the only important application running. This system also has a small amount of total memory available — between 32MB and 64MB — but more consistent MySQL use is expected.

The `key_buffer_size` is set to 16M in this file, while the `sort_buffer_size` value is raised to 512K for the `mysqld` server. The `table_open_cache` is set to 64 (allowing more simultaneous threads to be active). The `net_buffer_length` is raised to 8K.

● **my-large.cnf** — The `my-large.cnf` sample file is intended for computers that are dedicated primarily to MySQL service. It assumes about 512M of available memory.

Server buffers allow more active threads and better sorting performance. Half of the system's assumed 512M of memory is assigned to the `key_buffer_size` variable (256M). The `sort_buffer_size` is raised to 1M. The `table_open_cache` allows more simultaneous users (up to 256 active threads).

● **my-huge.cnf** — Like the `my-large.cnf` file, the `my-huge.cnf` file is intended for use with a computer used primarily for MySQL. However, the system for which it is intended offers much more total memory (between 1G and 2G of memory).

Sort buffer size (`sort_buffer_size`) is raised to 2M, while the `key_buffer_size` is set to consume 384M of memory. The `table_open_cache` size is doubled to allow up to 512 active threads.

● **my-innodb-heavy-4G.cnf** — This sample configuration file is best suited for computers with 4GB of RAM that are expected to service complex queries without too many connections (using the InnoDB transaction storage engine). Special `innodb` options in this file allow MySQL to take advantage of a large buffer pool size (2G).

Tip

For more information on MySQL, see the online manual at `http://dev.mysql.com/doc/refman/5.1/en/index.html`. ■

Working with MySQL Databases

The first time you start the MySQL server (using the startup script described previously), the system creates the initial grant tables for the MySQL database. It does this by running the `mysql_install_db` command.

The `mysql_install_db` command starts you off with two databases: `mysql` and `test`. As you create data for these databases, that information is stored in the `/var/lib/mysql/mysql` and `/var/lib/mysql/test` directories, respectively.

Because the MySQL root user doesn't have to be the system's root user (provided you have the MySQL root user's password), you can be logged in to Fedora as any user you choose. In the following examples, be sure to provide the MySQL root user password when you run the commands shown.

Note

If you are using the old ISAM tables instead of MyISAM, note that support for ISAM tables was removed for MySQL 5.0. You need to convert your tables to MyISAM using a statement such as

```
ALTER TABLE table ENGINE=MYISAM
```

where `table` **is your table name. Refer to the MySQL Reference Manual for more on upgrading from older versions.** ∎

Starting the mysql command

To get started creating databases and tables, use the `mysql` command. From any terminal window, open the `mysql` database on your computer by typing the following:

```
$ mysql -u root -p mysql
Enter password: *********
Reading table information for completion of table and column names
You can turn off this feature to get a quicker startup with -A

Welcome to the MySQL monitor.  Commands end with ; or \g.
Your MySQL connection id is 10
Server version: 5.1.50 Source distribution

Copyright (c) 2000, 2010, Oracle and/or its affiliates. All rights reserved.
This software comes with ABSOLUTELY NO WARRANTY. This is free software,
and you are welcome to modify and redistribute it under the GPL v2 license

Type 'help;' or '\h' for help. Type '\c' to clear the current input statement.

mysql>
```

Type in the root user's MySQL password as prompted. (If no password has been set, you can skip the `-p` option.) The `mysql>` prompt appears, ready to accept commands for working with the MySQL database on the localhost, called *mysql*. If you are connecting to the MySQL server from another host computer, add `-h` *hostname* to the command line (where *hostname* is the name or IP address of the computer on which the MySQL server is running). Remember that you can also log in with any valid MySQL login you created, regardless of which Linux login account you are currently logged in under.

As the MySQL monitor welcome text notes, be sure to end each command that you type with a semicolon (;) or \g. If you type a command and it appears to be waiting for more input, it's probably because you forgot to put a semicolon at the end.

Before you begin using the `mysql` interface to create databases, try checking the status of the MySQL server using the `status` command. The following is an example of output from the `status` command:

```
mysql> status
--------------
mysql  Ver 14.14 Distrib 5.1.50, for redhat-linux-gnu (x86_64) ↵
using readline 5.1

Connection id:          10
Current database:       mysql
Current user:           root@localhost
SSL:                    Not in use
Current pager:          stdout
Using outfile:          ''
Using delimiter:        ;
Server version:         5.1.50 Source distribution
Protocol version:       10
Connection:             Localhost via UNIX socket
Server characterset:    latin1
Db      characterset:   latin1
Client characterset:    latin1
Conn.   characterset:   latin1
UNIX socket:            /var/lib/mysql/mysql.sock
Uptime:                 1 day 2 hours 57 min 19 sec

Threads: 2  Questions: 136  Slow queries: 0  Opens: 15
Flush tables: 1  Open tables: 8 Queries per second avg: 0.001
--------------
```

The `status` information tells you about the version of the MySQL server (14.14) and the distribution (5.1.50). You can see how long the server has been up (`Uptime`); and you can see how many threads are currently active and how many commands have been run to query this server (`Questions`).

Creating a database with mysql

Within an interactive `mysql` session, you can create and modify databases and tables. If you are not already connected to a `mysql` session, type the following command (assuming the `mysql` user name of root):

```
$ mysql -u root -p
Enter password: *********
mysql>
```

The general steps for creating a MySQL database include creating the database name, identifying the new database as the current database, creating tables, and adding data to the tables. While you are connected to a mysql session, you can run the following procedure to create a sample database.

1. To create a new database name, use the CREATE DATABASE command at the mysql> prompt. For example, to create a database named allusers, type the following:

   ```
   mysql> CREATE DATABASE allusers;
   ```

   This action creates a database called allusers in the /var/lib/mysql directory. (While you don't have to use capitals for the commands as shown, doing so makes it easier to distinguish the commands from the database entries.)

Note

Alternatively, you can create a database from the command line using the mysqladmin command. For example, to create the database named allusers with mysqladmin, you could type the following:

```
mysqladmin -u root -p create allusers ■
```

2. To see what databases are available for your mysql server, type the following at the mysql> command prompt. The databases shown are named information_schema, allusers, mysql, and test. The information_schema database contains metadata about information in other databases on your server (such as the types of data, columns, or tables used in each). The allusers database is the one created in the previous step. The mysql database contains user access data. The test database is created automatically for creating test mysql databases.

   ```
   mysql> SHOW DATABASES;
   +--------------------+
   | Database           |
   +--------------------+
   | information_schema |
   | allusers           |
   | mysql              |
   | test               |
   +--------------------+
   4 rows in set (0.00 sec)
   ```

3. To work with the database you just created (allusers), you need to make allusers the current database. To do that, type the following at the mysql> command prompt:

   ```
   mysql> USE allusers;
   Database changed
   ```

4. Creating a table for your database requires some planning and some understanding of table syntax. You can type the following commands and column information to try out creating a table. For more detailed information on creating tables and using different data types, refer to the section "Understanding MySQL Tables" later in this chapter.

To create a table called name, use the following CREATE TABLE command at the mysql> prompt:

```
mysql> CREATE TABLE name (
 -> firstname       varchar(20)      not null,
 -> lastname        varchar(20)      not null,
 -> streetaddr      varchar(30)      not null,
 -> city            varchar(20)      not null,
 -> state           varchar(20)      not null,
 -> zipcode         varchar(10)      not null
 -> );
Query OK, 0 rows affected (0.00 sec)
```

You have now created a table called name for a database named allusers. It contains columns called firstname, lastname, streetaddr, city, state, and zipcode. Each column allows record lengths of between 10 and 30 characters. MySQL supports several different database formats, but because none is specified here the default MyISAM database type is used.

With a database and one table created, you can now add data to the table.

Adding data to a MySQL database table

After the database has been created and the structure of a database table is in place, you can begin working with the database. You can add data to your MySQL database by manually entering each record during a mysql session or by adding the data to a plain-text file and loading that file into the database.

Note

While you are in a mysql session, keep in mind that you can use the up arrow key to retrieve and change previous commands. This is particularly useful if you are manually entering database records that contain similar information. ■

Manually entering data

To add data to an existing MySQL database, the following procedure describes how to view the available tables and load data into those tables manually.

1. To make the database you want to use your current database (in this case, allusers), type the following command from the mysql> prompt:

```
mysql> USE allusers;
Database changed
```

2. To see the tables associated with the current database, type the following command from the mysql> prompt:

```
mysql> SHOW tables;
```

```
+--------------------+
| Tables_in_allusers |
+--------------------+
| name               |
+--------------------+
1 row in set (0.00 sec)
```

You can see that the only table defined so far for the allusers database is the one called name.

3. To display the format of the name table, type the following command at the mysql> prompt:

```
mysql> DESCRIBE name;
+-----------+-------------+------+-----+---------+-------+
| Field     | Type        | Null | Key | Default | Extra |
+-----------+-------------+------+-----+---------+-------+
| firstname | varchar(20) | NO   |     | NULL    |       |
| lastname  | varchar(20) | NO   |     | NULL    |       |
| streetaddr| varchar(30) | NO   |     | NULL    |       |
| city      | varchar(20) | NO   |     | NULL    |       |
| state     | varchar(20) | NO   |     | NULL    |       |
| zipcode   | varchar(10) | NO   |     | NULL    |       |
+-----------+-------------+------+-----+---------+-------+
```

4. To add data to the new table, use the INSERT INTO command from the mysql> prompt. The following example shows how to add a person's name and address to the new table:

```
mysql> INSERT INTO name
    -> VALUES ('Jerry','Wingnut','167 E Street',
    -> 'Roy','UT','84103');
```

In this example, the INSERT INTO command identifies the name table. Then it indicates that values for a record in that table include the name Jerry Wingnut at the address 167 E Street, Roy, UT 84103.

5. To verify that the data has been properly entered into the new table, type the following command from the mysql> prompt:

```
mysql> SELECT * FROM name;
+-----------+----------+--------------+-------+-------+---------+
| firstname | lastname | streetaddr   | city  | state | zipcode |
+-----------+----------+--------------+-------+-------+---------+
| Jerry     | Wingnut  | 167 E Street | Roy   | UT    | 84103   |
+-----------+----------+--------------+-------+-------+---------+
```

The resulting output shows the data you just entered, displayed in the columns you defined for the name table. If you like, you can continue adding data in this way.

Typing each data item individually as an INSERT statement can be tedious. As an alternative, you can add your data to a plain-text file and load it into your MySQL database, as described in the following section.

Loading data from a file

Using the LOAD DATA command during a mysql session, you can load a file containing database records into your MySQL database. Here are a few things you need to know about creating a data file to be loaded into MySQL:

- You can create the file using any Linux text editor.

- Each record, consisting of all the columns in the table, must be on its own line. (A line feed indicates the start of the next record.)

- Separate each column with a tab character.

- You can leave a column blank for a particular record by placing \N in that column.

- Any blank lines you leave in the file result in blank lines in the database table.

In this example, the following text is added into a plain-text file. The text is in a format that can be loaded into the name table created earlier in this chapter. To try this out, type the following text into a file. Be sure to insert a tab character between each value.

```
Chris    Smith    175 Harrison Street    Gig Harbor    WA    98999
John     Jones    18 Talbot Road NW      Coventry      NJ    08759
Howard   Manty    1515 Broadway          New York      NY    10028
```

When you are done entering the data, save the text to any filename that is accessible to the mysql server daemon (e.g., /tmp/name.txt). Remember the filename so that you can use it later. If you are not already connected to a mysql session, type the following command (assuming mysql is the user name root):

```
$ mysql -u root -p
Enter password: *******
mysql>
```

Next, identify the database (allusers in this example) as the current database by typing the following:

```
mysql> USE allusers;
Database changed
```

To actually load the file into the name table in the allusers database, type the following command to load the file (in this case, /tmp/name.txt) from the mysql> prompt:

Note

Either enter the full path to the file or have it in the directory where the mysql command starts. In the latter case, you can type the filename without indicating its full path.

```
mysql> LOAD DATA LOCAL INFILE "/tmp/name.txt" INTO TABLE name;
Query OK, 3 rows affected (0.02 sec)
Records: 3  Deleted: 0 Skipped: 0 Warnings: 0 ■
```

Type the following at the mysql> prompt to ensure that the records have been added correctly:

```
mysql> SELECT * FROM name;
+----------+---------+--------------------+------------+-------+--------+
| firstname| lastname| streetaddr         | city       | state |zipcode |
+----------+---------+--------------------+------------+-------+--------+
| Jerry    | Wingnut | 167 E Street       | Roy        | UT    | 84103  |
| Chris    | Smith   | 175 Harrison Street| Gig Harbor | WA    | 98999  |
| John     | Jones   | 18 Talbot Road NW  | Coventry   | NJ    | 08759  |
| Howard   | Manty   | 1515 Broadway      | New York   | NY    | 10028  |
+----------+---------+--------------------+------------+-------+--------+
```

At this point, you have a database that includes some data that you can begin working with. If something went wrong, refer to the "Updating and Deleting MySQL Records" section later in this chapter. If you need more information than is provided in this chapter, refer to the MySQL documentation at http://dev.mysql.com/doc.

Note

Because some text editors (not including vi) don't use a hard tab character by default, it can be difficult to create a correctly formatted file. As an alternative, you can import a CSV-formatted text file (many spreadsheet programs can export to such a file). To include such a file that has comma-separated fields and text enclosed in quotes (e.g., named /tmp/name.csv), you could type the following (all on one line):

```
mysql> LOAD DATA LOCAL INFILE '/tmp/name.csv'
INTO TABLE allusers.name FIELDS TERMINATED BY ','
ENCLOSED BY '"' LINES TERMINATED BY '\n'; ■
```

Although MySQL doesn't support all of SQL, it does contain enough features for most users. If you find that MySQL doesn't meet your needs, try the PostgreSQL object-relational database management system (which also comes with Fedora systems). For further information on PostgreSQL, refer to www.postgresql.org. Firebird (www.firebirdsql.org) is another open-source relational database that might interest you.

Understanding MySQL Tables

You have a lot of flexibility when it comes to setting up MySQL tables. To have your MySQL database operate as efficiently as possible, you want to have the columns assigned to the most appropriate size and data type to hold the data you need to store.

Use the following tables as a reference to the different data types that can be assigned to your columns. Data types available for use in MySQL fall into these categories: numbers, time and date, and character strings. Here are a few things you need to know as you read these tables:

- The maximum display size for a column is 255 characters. An M data type option sets the number of characters that are displayed and, in most cases, stored for the column.

- There can be up to 30 digits following the decimal point for floating-point or fixed-point data types. A D option to a data type indicates the number of digits allowed for a number following the decimal point. (The value should be no more than two digits less than the value of the display size being used.)

- The UNSIGNED option (shown in brackets) indicates that only positive numbers are allowed in the column. This allows the column to hold larger positive numbers.

- The ZEROFILL option (shown in brackets) indicates that the data in the column will be padded with zeros. For example, the number 25 in a column with a data type of INTEGER(7) ZEROFILL would appear as 0000025. (Any ZEROFILL column automatically becomes UNSIGNED.)

- All values shown in brackets are optional.

- The parentheses around the (M) and (D) values are necessary if you enter either of those values. In other words, don't type the brackets, but do type the parentheses.

Table 22-2 shows numeric data types that you can use with MySQL.

TABLE 22-2

Numeric Data Types for Columns

Data Type	Description	Space Needed
BIGINT[(M)] [UNSIGNED] [ZEROFILL]	Can contain large integers with the following allowable values: –9223372036854775808 to 9223372036854775807 (signed)	Uses 8 bytes.
	0 to 18446744073709551615 (unsigned)	

continued

TABLE 22-2 *(continued)*

Data Type	Description	Space Needed
DECIMAL[(M[,D])] [ZEROFILL]	Contains an unpacked fixed-point number (signed only). Each digit is stored as a single character. When you choose the display value (M), decimal points and minus signs are not counted in that value. The value of (M) is 10 by default. Setting D to zero (the default) causes only whole numbers to be used.	Uses M+2 bytes if D is greater than 0. Uses M+1 bytes if D is equal to 0.
DOUBLE[(M,D)] [ZEROFILL]	Contains a double-precision, floating-point number of an average size. Values that are allowed include: $-1.7976931348623157E+308$ to $-2.2250738585072014E-308$ 0 $2.2250738585072014E-308$ to $1.7976931348623157E+308$.	Uses 8 bytes.
DOUBLE PRECISION	Same as DOUBLE.	Same as DOUBLE.
FLOAT(X) [ZEROFILL]	Contains a floating-point number. For a single-precision floating-point number, X can be less than or equal to 24. For a double-precision floating-point number, X can be between 25 and 53. The display size and number of decimals are undefined.	Uses 4 bytes if X is less than or equal to 24. Uses 8 bytes if X is greater than or equal to 25 and less than or equal to 53.
FLOAT[(M,D)] [ZEROFILL]	Contains a single-precision floating-point number. Values that are allowed include: $-3.402823466E+38$ to $-1.175494351E-38$ 0 $1.175494351E-38$ to $3.402823466E+38$. If the display value (M) is less than or equal to 24, the number is a single-precision floating-point number.	Uses 4 bytes.
INT[(M)] [UNSIGNED] [ZEROFILL]	Contains an integer of normal size. The range is -2147483648 to 2147483647 if signed, and 0 to 4294967295 if unsigned.	Uses 4 bytes.
INTEGER[(M)] [UNSIGNED] [ZEROFILL]	Same as INT.	Same as INT.

Data Type	Description	Space Needed
`MEDIUMINT[(M)]` `[UNSIGNED]` `[ZEROFILL]`	Contains an integer of medium size. The range is −8388608 to 8388607 if signed, and 0 to 16777215 if unsigned.	Uses 3 bytes.
`NUMERIC(M,D)` `[ZEROFILL]`	Same as `DECIMAL`.	Same as `DECIMAL`.
`REAL`	Same as `DOUBLE`.	Same as `DOUBLE`.
`SMALLINT[(M)]` `[UNSIGNED]` `[ZEROFILL]`	Contains an integer of small size. The range is −32768 to 32767 if signed, and 0 to 65535 if unsigned.	Uses 2 bytes.
`TINYINT[(M)]` `[UNSIGNED]` `[ZEROFILL]`	A very small integer, with a signed range of −128 to 127, and a 0 to 255 unsigned range.	Uses 1 byte.

The default format of dates in MySQL is YYYY-MM-DD, which stands for the year, month, and day. Any improperly formatted date or time values will be converted to zeros. Table 22-3 shows time and date data types that you can use with MySQL.

TABLE 22-3

Time/Date Data Types for Columns

Data Type	Description	Space Needed
`DATE`	Contains a date between January 1, 1000 (1000-01-01), and December 31, 9999 (9999-12-31).	Uses 3 bytes
`DATETIME`	Contains a combination of date and time between zero hour of January 1, 1000 (1000-01-01 00:00:00), and the last second of December 31, 9999 (9999-12-31 23:59:59).	Uses 8 bytes
`TIMESTAMP[(M)]`	Contains a timestamp from between zero hour of January 1, 1970 (1970-01-01 00:00:00), and a time in the year 2037. It is stored in the form YYYYMMDDHHMMSS. Using (M), you can reduce the size of the `TIMESTAMP` displayed to less than the full 14 characters (although the full 4-byte `TIMESTAMP` is still stored).	Uses 4 bytes
`TIME`	Contains a time between −838:59:59 and 838:59:59. The format of the field is in hours, minutes, and seconds (HH:MM:SS).	Uses 3 bytes
`YEAR[(2|4)]`	Contains a year, represented by either two or four digits. For a four-digit year, `YEAR` means 1901–2155 (0000 is also allowed). For a two-digit year, the digits 70-99 can represent 1970-1999 and 00-69 can represent 200-2069.	Uses 1 byte

Table 22-4 shows string data types that you can use with MYSQL.

TABLE 22-4

String Data Types for Columns

Data Type	Description	Space Needed
BLOB	Contains a binary large object (BLOB) that varies in size, based on the actual value of the data, rather than the maximum allowable size. Searches on a BLOB column are case-sensitive.	Uses up to L+2 bytes, where L is less than or equal to 65535.
[NATIONAL] CHAR(M) [BINARY]	Contains a character string of fixed length, with spaces padded to the right to meet the length. To display the value, spaces are deleted. The value of (M) determines the number of characters (from 1 to 255). If the BINARY keyword is used, sorting of values is case-sensitive (it is case-insensitive by default). The NATIONAL keyword indicates that the default character set should be used.	Uses between 1 and 255 bytes, based on the value of (M).
ENUM ('val1','val2',...)	Contains enumerated strings that are typically chosen from a list of values indicated when you create the column. For example, you set a column definition to ENUM('dog','cat','mouse'). Then, if you set the value of that column to "1", the value displayed would be "dog," "2" would be "cat," and "3" would be "mouse." It lets you take a number as input and have a string as output. Up to 65535 values are allowed.	Uses either 1 byte (for up to about 255 values) or 2 bytes, (for up to 65535 values).
LONGBLOB	Contains a binary large object (BLOB) that varies in size, based on the actual value of the data, rather than the maximum allowable size. LONGBLOB allows larger values than MEDIUMBLOB. Searches on a LONGBLOB column are case-sensitive.	Uses up to L+4 bytes, where L is less than or equal to 4294967295.
LONGTEXT	Same as LONGBLOB, except that searching is done on these columns in case-insensitive style.	Uses up to L+4 bytes, where L is less than or equal to 4294967295.
MEDIUMBLOB	Contains a binary large object (BLOB) that varies in size, based on the actual value of the data, rather than the maximum allowable size. MEDIUMBLOB allows larger values than BLOB. Searches on a MEDIUMBLOB column are case-sensitive.	Uses up to L+3 bytes, where L is less than or equal to 16777215.

Data Type	Description	Space Needed
`MEDIUMTEXT`	Same as `MEDIUMBLOB`, except that searching is done on these columns in case-insensitive style.	Uses up to L+3 bytes, where L is less than or equal to 16777215.
`SET ('val1','val2',...)`	Contains a set of values. A `SET` column can display zero or more values from the list of values contained in the `SET` column definition. Up to 64 members are allowed.	Uses 1, 2, 3, 4, or 8 bytes, based on how many of the up to 64 set members are used.
`TEXT`	Same as `BLOB`, except that searching is done on these columns in case-insensitive style.	Uses up to L+2 bytes, where L is less than or equal to 65535.
`TINYBLOB`	Contains a binary large object (`BLOB`) that varies in size, based on the actual value of the data, rather than the maximum allowable size. `TINYBLOB` allows smaller values than `BLOB`. Searches on a `TINYBLOB` column are case-sensitive.	Uses up to L+1 bytes, where L is less than or equal to 255.
`TINYTEXT`	Same as `TINYBLOB`, except that searching is done on these columns in case-insensitive style.	Uses up to L+1 bytes, where L is less than or equal to 255.
`[NATIONAL] VARCHAR(M) [BINARY]`	Contains a character string of variable length, with no padded spaces added. The value of (M) determines the number of characters (from 1 to 255). If the `BINARY` keyword is used, sorting of values is case-sensitive (it is case-insensitive by default). The `NATIONAL` keyword indicates that the default character set should be used.	Uses L+1 bytes, where L is less than or equal to M, and M is from 1 to 255 characters.

Displaying MySQL Databases

There are many different ways to sort and display database records during a `mysql` session. If you are not already connected to a `mysql` session, type the following command (assuming the `mysql` user name of root):

```
$ mysql -u root -p
Enter password: *******
mysql>
```

When you are in your `mysql` session (and have chosen a database), you can display all or selected table records, choose which columns are displayed, or choose how records are sorted.

Displaying all or selected records

Assuming that the current database is `allusers` (as shown in the previous examples), type the following command to choose (SELECT) all records (*) from the `name` table and display them in the order in which they were entered into the database:

```
mysql> SELECT * FROM name;
+-----------+---------+--------------------+------------+-------+--------+
| firstname |lastname|streetaddr          | city       | state | zipcode|
+-----------+---------+--------------------+------------+-------+--------+
| Jerry     |Wingnut |167 E Street        | Roy        | UT    | 84103  |
| Chris     |Smith   |175 Harrison Street | Gig Harbor | WA    | 98999  |
| John      |Jones   |18 Talbot Road NW   | Coventry   | NJ    | 08759  |
| Howard    |Manty   |1515 Broadway       | New York   | NY    | 10028  |
+-----------+---------+--------------------+------------+-------+--------+
```

The following command displays all records from the `name` table that have the `lastname` column set to Jones. Instead of using `lastname`, you could search for a value from any column name used in the table.

```
mysql> SELECT * FROM name WHERE lastname = 'Jones';
+-----------+---------+--------------------+------------+-------+--------+
| firstname |lastname |streetaddr         | city       | state | zipcode|
+-----------+---------+--------------------+------------+-------+--------+
| John      |Jones   |18 Talbot Road NW   | Coventry   | NJ    | 08759  |
+-----------+---------+--------------------+------------+-------+--------+
```

Note

If you are used to SQL, you will place data within single quotes, such as 'Jones'. MySQL supports either single quotes or double quotes, such as "Jones". ∎

Using the OR operator, you can select records that match several different values. In the following command, records that have either `Chris` or `Howard` as the `firstname` are matched and displayed:

```
mysql> SELECT * FROM name WHERE firstname = "Chris" OR firstname = "Howard";
+-----------+----------+--------------------+------------+-------+--------+
| firstname | lastname | streetaddr         | city       | state | zipcode|
+-----------+----------+--------------------+------------+-------+--------+
| Chris     | Smith    | 175 Harrison Street| Gig Harbor | WA    | 98999  |
| Howard    | Manty    | 1515 Broadway      | New York   | NY    | 10028  |
+-----------+----------+--------------------+------------+-------+--------+
```

To match and display a record based on the value of two columns in a record, use the AND operator. In the following command, any record that has `Chris` as the `firstname` and `Smith` as the `lastname` is matched:

```
mysql> SELECT * FROM name WHERE firstname = "Chris" AND lastname = "Smith";
+----------+---------+--------------------+------------+-------+---------+
| firstname| lastname| streetaddr         | city       | state | zipcode |
+----------+---------+--------------------+------------+-------+---------+
| Chris    | Smith   | 175 Harrison Street | Gig Harbor | WA   | 98999   |
+----------+---------+--------------------+------------+-------+---------+
```

Displaying selected columns

You don't need to display every column of data. Instead of using the asterisk (*) shown in the previous examples to match all columns, you can enter a comma-separated list of column names. The following command displays the firstname, lastname, and zipcode records for all records in the name table:

```
mysql> SELECT firstname,lastname,zipcode FROM name;
+-----------+----------+---------+
| firstname | lastname | zipcode |
+-----------+----------+---------+
| Jerry     | Wingnut  | 84103   |
| Chris     | Smith    | 98999   |
| John      | Jones    | 08759   |
| Howard    | Manty    | 10028   |
+-----------+----------+---------+
```

Likewise, you can sort columns in any order you choose. Type the following command to show the same three columns with the zipcode column displayed first:

```
mysql> SELECT zipcode,firstname,lastname FROM name;
+---------+-----------+----------+
| zipcode | firstname | lastname |
+---------+-----------+----------+
| 84103   | Jerry     | Wingnut  |
| 98999   | Chris     | Smith    |
| 08759   | John      | Jones    |
| 10028   | Howard    | Manty    |
+---------+-----------+----------+
```

You can also mix column selection with record selection as shown in the following example:

```
mysql> SELECT firstname,lastname,city FROM name WHERE firstname = "Chris";
+-----------+----------+-----------+
| firstname | lastname | city      |
+-----------+----------+-----------+
| Chris     | Smith    | Gig Harbor |
+-----------+----------+-----------+
```

Sorting data

You can sort records based on the values in any column you choose. For example, using the ORDER BY operator, you can display the records based on the lastname column:

```
mysql> SELECT * FROM name ORDER BY lastname;
+-----------+----------+------------------+-----------+-------+---------+
| firstname |lastname  |streetaddr        | city      | state | zipcode|
+-----------+----------+------------------+-----------+-------+---------+
| John      |Jones     |18 Talbot Road NW | Coventry  | NJ    | 08759   |
| Howard    |Manty     |1515 Broadway     | New York  | NY    | 10028   |
| Chris     |Smith     |167 Small Road    | Gig Harbor | WA    | 98999   |
| Jerry     |Wingnut   |167 E Street      | Roy       | UT    | 84103   |
+-----------+----------+------------------+-----------+-------+---------+
```

To sort records based on city name, use the following command:

```
mysql> SELECT * FROM name ORDER BY city;
+-----------+---------+------------------+------------+-------+--------+
| firstname |lastname |streetaddr        | city       | state | zipcode|
+-----------+---------+------------------+------------+-------+--------+
| John      |Jones    |18 Talbot Road NW | Coventry   | NJ    | 08759  |
| Chris     |Smith    |167 Small Road    | Gig Harbor | WA    | 98999  |
| Howard    |Manty    |1515 Broadway     | New York   | NY    | 10028  |
| Jerry     |Wingnut  |167 E Street      | Roy        | UT    | 84103  |
+-----------+---------+------------------+------------+-------+--------+
```

You can also add ASC or DESC to indicate the sorting order, because MySQL doesn't otherwise guarantee the order in which data are displayed. After entering and displaying the database records, you may find that you need to change some of them. The following section describes how to update database records during a mysql session.

Making Changes to Tables and Records

As you begin to use your MySQL database, you will find that you need to make changes to both the structure and content of the database tables. The following section describes how you can alter the structure of your MySQL tables and change the content of MySQL records. If you are not already connected to a mysql session, type the following command (assuming the mysql user name of root):

```
$ mysql -u root -p
Enter password: *******
mysql>
```

To use the examples shown in the following sections, identify the database (allusers in this example) as the current database by typing the following:

```
mysql> USE allusers;
Database changed
```

Altering the structure of MySQL tables

After you have created your database tables, you will inevitably want to make changes to them. This section describes how to use the ALTER command during a mysql session for the following tasks: adding a column, deleting a column, renaming a column, and changing the data type for a column.

To add a column to the end of your table that displays the current date, type the following:

```
mysql> ALTER TABLE name ADD curdate TIMESTAMP;
```

The previous line tells mysql to change the table in the current database called name (ALTER TABLE name), add a column named curdate (ADD curdate), and assign the value of that column to display the last edit date (TIMESTAMP). If you decide later that you want to remove that column, you can do so by typing the following:

```
mysql> ALTER TABLE name DROP COLUMN curdate;
```

If you want to change the name of an existing column, do so with the CHANGE option to ALTER. Here is an example:

```
mysql> ALTER TABLE name CHANGE city town varchar(20);
```

In the previous example, the name table is chosen (ALTER TABLE name) to change the name of the city column to town (CHANGE city town). The data type of the column must be entered as well (varchar(20)), even if you are not changing it. In fact, if you just want to change the data type of a column, use the same syntax as in the previous example but simply use the column name twice (in this case, zipcode). Here's an example:

```
mysql> ALTER TABLE name CHANGE zipcode zipcode INTEGER;
```

The previous example changes the data type of the zipcode column from its previous type (varchar) to the INTEGER type.

Note

Specifying a column when you first create a table (CREATE TABLE command) will change a column's default value. By running an ALTER TABLE statement, you can respecify the column default value, if you want to return to that value. ∎

Updating and deleting MySQL records

You can select records based on any value you choose and update any values in those records. When you are in your mysql session, use UPDATE to change the values in a selected table. Here is an example:

```
mysql> UPDATE name SET streetaddr = "933 3rd Avenue" WHERE firstname = "Chris";
Query OK, 1 row affected (0.00 sec)
Rows matched: 1 Changed: 1 Warnings: 0
```

This example attempts to update the name table (UPDATE name). In this case, each record that has the firstname column set to "Chris" will have the value of the streetaddr column for that record changed to "933 3rd Avenue" instead. Note that the query found one (1) row that matched. That one row matched was also changed, with no error warnings necessary. You can use any combination of values to match records (using WHERE) and change column values (using SET). After making a change, it is a good idea to display the results to ensure that the change was made as you expected.

To remove an entire row (i.e., one record), use the DELETE command. For example, if you want to delete any row where the value of the firstname column is "Chris", type the following:

```
mysql> DELETE FROM name WHERE firstname = "Chris";
Query OK, 1 row affected (0.00 sec)
```

The next time you display the table, there should be no records with the first name Chris.

Adding and Removing User Access

You can use several different methods to control user access to your MySQL databases. To begin with, assign a user name and password to every user who accesses your MySQL databases. Then use the GRANT and REVOKE commands of mysql to specifically indicate the databases and tables that users and host computers can access, as well as the rights they have to those databases and tables.

Caution

Database servers are common targets of attacks from crackers. While this chapter provides some direction for granting access to your MySQL server, you need to provide much more stringent protection for the server if you are allowing Internet access. Refer to the MySQL Reference manual (info mysql) for further information on securing your MySQL server. ■

Adding users and granting access

Although you have a user account defined to create databases (the root user, in this example), to make a database useful you might want to allow access to other users as well. The following procedure describes how to grant privileges for your MySQL database to other users.

Note

If you are upgrading your MySQL from a version previous to 3.22, run the mysql_fix_privilege_tables script. This script adds new GRANT features to your databases. If you don't run the script, you will be denied access to the databases. ■

This example adds a MySQL user named bobby who can log in to the MySQL server from the localhost. The password for bobby is i8yer2shuz. Note that bobby is just an account on the MySQL database — this is not a Fedora user account. Think of this as a login to an online system. Any user of your Fedora system could log in to the MySQL database with the name bobby and the correct password.

1. If you are not already connected to a mysql session, type the following command (assuming the mysql user name of root):

```
$ mysql -u root -p
Enter password: *******
mysql>
```

2. To create the user named bobby and a password i8yer2shuz, use the GRANT command as follows:

```
mysql> GRANT USAGE ON *.*
    -> TO bobby@localhost IDENTIFIED BY "i8yer2shuz";
```

At this point, someone could log in from the localhost using the name bobby and the password i8yer2shuz (mysql -u bobby -p); but the user wouldn't have the privileges to work with any of the databases. You still need to grant privileges.

3. To grant bobby privileges to work with the database called allusers, type the following:

```
mysql> GRANT DELETE,INSERT,SELECT,UPDATE ON allusers.*
    -> TO bobby@localhost;
```

In this example, the user named bobby is allowed to log in to the MySQL server on the localhost and access all tables from the allusers database (ON allusers). For that database, bobby can use the DELETE, INSERT, SELECT, and UPDATE commands.

4. To see the privileges you just granted, select mysql as your current database and then query the db table as follows:

```
mysql> USE mysql;
Database changed
mysql> SELECT host,db,user,select_priv as query,↵
insert_priv as ins,↵
update_priv as upd,↵
delete_priv as del FROM db ↵
WHERE db='allusers';
+-----------+----------+-------+-------+-----+-----+-----+
| host      | db       | user  | query | ins | upd | del |
+-----------+----------+-------+-------+-----+-----+-----+
| localhost | allusers | bobby | Y     | Y   | Y   | Y   |
+-----------+----------+-------+-------+-----+-----+-----+
```

The output here shows all users who are specifically granted privileges to the allusers database. Only a few of the columns are shown here because the output is very long. You can make a very wide terminal window to view all the columns if you don't like reading wrapped text. Other privileges on the line will be set to N (no access).

Revoking access

Using the REVOKE command, you can revoke privileges you've granted. To revoke all privileges for a user to a particular database, use the following procedure:

1. If you are not already connected to a mysql session, type the following command (assuming the mysql user name of root):

```
$ mysql -u root -p
```

```
Enter password: *******
mysql>
```

2. To revoke all privileges of a user named bobby to use a database named allusers on your MySQL server, type the following:

```
mysql> REVOKE ALL PRIVILEGES ON allusers.*
    -> FROM bobby@localhost;
```

At this point, bobby has no privileges to use any of the tables in the allusers databases.

3. To see the privileges you just granted, select mysql as your current database, then select the db table as follows:

```
mysql> USE mysql;
Database changed
mysql> SELECT * FROM db WHERE db="allusers";
```

The output should show that the user named bobby is no longer listed as having access to the allusers database. (The results might just say Empty set.)

Backing Up Databases

Use the mysqldump command to back up your MySQL databases. The following command backs up all your MySQL databases:

```
# mysqldump -u root -p --opt --all-databases \
> /home/chris/all-databases
```

In this case, all databases on the local system are copied to the file all-databases in the /home/chris directory. You can also use mysqldump to back up a single database, several databases, or tables within a database. Refer to the mysqldump man page for further information.

Checking and Fixing Databases

Over time, databases can become corrupted or store information inefficiently. MySQL includes commands you can use for checking and repairing your databases. The myisamchk command is available to check MyISAM database tables.

MyISAM tables are used by default with MySQL. (To use a different table type, assign it when you first create your MySQL table.) The tables are stored in the directory /var/lib/mysql/*dbname* by default, where *dbname* is replaced by the name of the database you are using. For each table, there are three files in this directory. Each file begins with the table name and ends with one of the following three suffixes:

- .frm — Contains the definition (or form) of the table
- .MYI — Contains the table's index
- .MYD — Contains the table's data

The following procedure describes how to use the myisamchk command to check your MyISAM tables.

Caution

Back up your database tables before running a repair with myisamchk. Although myisamchk is unlikely to damage your data, backups are still a good precaution. ■

1. Stop MySQL temporarily by typing the following from a terminal window as root user:

```
# /etc/rc.d/init.d/mysqld stop
```

2. You can check all or some of your database tables at once. The first example shows how to check a table called name in the allusers database:

```
# myisamchk /var/lib/mysql/allusers/name.MYI
Checking MyISAM file: /var/lib/mysql/allusers/name.MYI
Data records:        5    Deleted blocks:        0
- check file-size
- check key delete-chain
- check record delete-chain
- check index reference
- check record links
```

You could also check tables for all your databases at once as follows:

```
# myisamchk /var/lib/mysql/*/*.MYI
```

3. The preceding example shows a simple, five-record database in which no errors were encountered. If instead of the output shown in the previous example you see output like the following, you may need to repair the database:

```
Checking MyISAM file: /var/lib/mysql/allusers/name.MYI
Data records:        5    Deleted blocks:        0
- check file-size
myisamchk: warning: Size of datafile is: 89 Should be: 204
- check key delete-chain
- check record delete-chain
- check index reference
- check record links
```

```
myisamchk: error: Found wrong record at 0
MyISAM-table 'name.MYI' is corrupted
Fix it using switch "-r" or "-o"
```

4. To fix a corrupted database, run the following command:

```
# myisamchk -r /var/lib/mysql/allusers/name.MYI
- recovering (with keycache) MyISAM-table↵
'/var/lib/mysql/allusers/name.MYI'
Data records: 5
Found wrong stored record at 0
Data records: 4
```

5. If for some reason the -r option doesn't work, try running the myisamchk command with the -o option. This is a slower, older method of repair, but it can handle a few problems that the -r option cannot. Here is an example:

```
# myisamchk -o /var/lib/mysql/allusers/name.MYI
```

6. If your computer has a lot of memory, you can raise the key_buffer_size value on the myisamchk command line, which will shorten the time it takes to check the databases. For example, you could use the following command line:

```
myisamchk -r --key_buffer_size=64M *.MYI
```

This would set the key buffer size to 64MB.

Summary

MySQL is a structured query language (SQL) database server that runs on Fedora and other operating systems. Using a startup script (/etc/rc.d/init.d/mysqld) and a configuration file (/etc/my.cnf), you can quickly get a MySQL server up and running.

With tools such as the mysqladmin and mysql commands, you can administer the MySQL server and create databases and tables that are as simple or complex as you need. During mysql sessions, you can modify the structure of your database tables or add, update, and delete database records. You have a variety of options for querying data and sorting the output. You also have a lot of control over who can access your database tables and what privileges users have to modify, add to, or delete from the databases you control.

Setting Up
Virtual Servers

23

IN THIS CHAPTER

Preparing for virtualization

Creating virtual guests

Managing virtual guests

Working with virtualization commands such as virsh and virt-v2v

Using virtualization, you can have multiple operating systems, called *guest systems* or simply *guests*, running on your Fedora system. Those systems can be other Linux systems, Windows systems, or multiple instances of Fedora. As demands for those guests change over time, you can configure them to migrate to different machines on-the-fly, so they can instantly start running on other machines.

There are both GUI and command-line tools to create your virtual guests. You can create virtual guests by launching installers for your Linux system of choice and clicking through the installs or you can use kickstart files to fully automate the install process. Using operating system images on CD or DVD, or from your file system, you can boot up installers or simply boot and run those operating systems as live CDs. Linux supports a number of virtualization technologies, but the future of virtualization for Fedora can be spelled in three letters: KVM. The Kernel Virtualization Module (KVM) project drives development of a range of virtualization features that have made their way into Fedora. Instead of requiring a special kernel or proprietary software, as other virtualization solutions do, KVM is built right into the standard kernel that comes with Fedora.

Although virtualization features such as Xen are being phased out, some of the same tools you may have used in earlier versions of Fedora can still be used, but with KVM on the back end. For example, you can still create and manage virtual guests with the Virtual Machine Manager (`virt-manager`) GUI and launch and manage guests using QEMU tools.

This chapter describes KVM technology and how you can use it to run virtualized operating systems within your Fedora system.

793

Preparing for Virtualization

Before you start using KVM, you should understand the extra demands that are put on your system by running guest virtual machines. In particular, you should consider whether your computer has enough resources to run virtual guests, confirm that all the packages you need are installed, and ensure that the necessary services are running.

Checking computer resources for virtualization

When you run a guest virtual operating system, keep in mind that each instance might consume the same, or nearly the same, computing resources that the host system consumes. In other words, you must have enough processing power, disk space, and memory (RAM) available for all the guests you are running. Here are some things to check:

- **Memory** — Although some modern operating systems can run on less, most run best on at least 512MB of RAM. Therefore, ensure that you have that much available for your host system, as well as for each guest you are running.

- **Storage** — Check the disk space requirements for the operating systems you plan to install on your host computer (plus the applications you are installing with them). That storage area can come from a large raw file, a disk partition, a logical volume, or one of several different storage file formats. Storage images such as qcow or qcow2 have the advantage of being able to consume space from your hard disk only as the guest requires it. With inexpensive disk space these days, it's quite normal to create virtual guests with between 4GB and 8GB of disk space.

- **Virtualization support** — You need an Intel processor with VT (virtualization technology) or an AMD processor with SVM extensions to properly support virtualization in hardware. If your computer does not support hardware virtualization, KVM will rely on QEMU, which emulates computer hardware using software emulation, and can be slow. If your guest operating system supports Xen paravirtualization, I recommend that you use the Xen hypervisor instead of KVM. Once you have installed your guest virtual machines, you can improve their performance even further by installing KVM-specific drivers in the guest virtual machines for storage and network controllers.

Note

Fedora 13 added a number of features to improve the performance and stability of KVM and running guest systems, including VHostNet for speeding networking; stable PCI addresses, which especially help with Windows guests; and x2apic, which speeds systems using multiple virtual CPUs.

Fedora 14 adds Xenner, which enables the running of Xen paravirtualized kernels using KVM instead of the Xen hypervisor. ∎

Hardware virtualization is enabled by your computer via the BIOS. You can verify that hardware virtualization is available to Fedora by looking for the svm or vmx flags in /proc/cpuinfo. The rest of these instructions assume you are using KVM with hardware virtualization enabled.

Installing KVM packages

If you are starting with a fresh install of Fedora, you may not yet have all the packages installed that you need in order to do virtualization. To begin setting up the current Fedora to use KVM, install the Virtualization package group as follows:

```
# yum groupinstall Virtualization
```

This installs the following packages, along with about two dozen other packages needed to meet dependencies:

- **libvirt** — Contains the libvirt application programming interface (API) for abstracting away differences between Xen, KVM, and other virtualization technologies.

- **qemu-kvm** — Contains KVM components associated with QEMU utilities.

- **python-virtinst** — Contains commands such as virt-install (to create and manage virtual guests), virt-convert (to convert VMs into different formats), virt-image (to create VMs from image descriptors), and virt-clone (to create clone VMs from existing disk images).

- **virt-manager** — Contains the virt-manager Virtual Machine Manager application. It is used to start, stop, and otherwise manage virtual guest operating systems. It also can display summary information and statistics about your guest VMs.

- **virt-viewer** — Contains the virt-viewer Virtual Machine Viewer graphical client, which is used to connect to virtual machines via a VNC interface.

Starting the Virtualization Service (libvirtd)

Using virtualization requires that the libvirtd service be running. You can start it immediately with the service command and set it to start automatically on reboot by running the chkconfig command, as follows:

```
# chkconfig libvirtd on
```

Reboot your computer. With your computer rebooted and the libvirtd service running, you can use tools such as the Virtual Machine Manager (virt-manager) window or the virt-install command to begin creating your virtual guest operating systems.

Getting installation media

You need to get the installation media for the guest systems you want to install. To install another instance of Fedora, you can simply use the live CD or installation DVD that comes with this book. Then, once you have launched the install process as described in the next section, you can follow along with the Fedora installation process described in Chapter 2.

The following is a list of operating systems (from the drop-down list when you create a virtual guest) that you can install in Fedora. It's possible that other distributions derived from those systems would work as well:

- **Linux** — Listed distributions include Debian, Fedora, Red Hat Enterprise Linux, Mandriva, SUSE Linux Enterprise Server, and Ubuntu. There are also selections for Linux distributions with generic 2.4, 2.6, and 2.6.25 or later (with virtio) that you can choose.

- **Solaris** — Distributions include OpenSolaris, Solaris 10 and Solaris 9.

- **Unix** — FreeBSD 6–8, and OpenBSD 4 are listed as supported distributions.

- **Windows** — Microsoft Windows systems listed include 7, Vista, 2000, 2003, 2008, 7, XP (x86), and XP (x86_64).

You can get installation media for any of the Linux and Unix systems mentioned by visiting the project sites for those systems and downloading the installation media. You don't have to burn those media to CD or DVD. You can simply place copies of those media in your local file system. (Look for images ending in .iso that contain live CD/DVDs or installation images.)

Creating Virtual Guest Systems

If your Fedora system has enough resources (memory and storage), hardware support, the virtualization packages installed, and the libvirtd service running, you can begin installing virtual guests. The following procedure describes how to install a guest operating system from an Ubuntu live CD image:

1. **Open the Virtual Machine Manager window.** Select Applications ➪ System Tools ➪ Virtual Machine Manager. The Virtual Machine Manager window appears.

2. **Add a connection.** Select File ➪ Add Connection. The Add Connection pop-up appears.

3. **Start the connection.** From the Add Connection window, select QEMU/KVM as the hypervisor and the Connection as Local. Then select Connect.

4. **Set up storage.** If you simply want to create a raw storage volume from a disk partition or a file, you can skip this step and create the volume when you create each guest. For other types of storage, you can create volumes before creating a guest by selecting Edit ➪ Connection Details ➪ Storage and choosing a location for the image (/var/lib/libvirt/images by default). Next, select New Volume from the Host Details window to begin creating the new volume.

   The libvirt site (http://libvirt.org/storage.html) describes storage volume format options, which include the following:

   - **raw** — A raw disk image is the default type created by virt-manager. Although it doesn't make the most efficient use of disk space, it's a format that is easy to export to other formats so it can be used by other virtualization software.

- **bochs** — A disk image format used by Bochs, a portable x86 emulator.
- **cloop** — A loopback disk image format that can work with compressed CD images.
- **cow** — A disk image format used with User Mode Linux. At one time the only image format used by QEMU that was growable, it is now mostly supported for compatibility with older versions.
- **dmg** — A Mac disk image format.
- **iso** — A disk image format used with CDs and DVDs.
- **qcow** — The QEMU version 1 disk image format. This has largely been replaced by qcow2.
- **qcow2** — The QEMU version 2 disk image format. Images in this format are still substantially smaller than raw images. With a qcow image, you can store snapshots of the image's history. The image can also be compressed (using zlib compression) and encrypted (using AES encryption).
- **vmdk** — A disk image format used with VMware.
- **vpc** — A VirtualPC disk image format.

The qcow2 image format is popular because it only uses as much space as the guest operating system consumes, up to the maximum amount allocated. Therefore, with many guests installed, you can make much more efficient use of your disk space.

Choose the image Name, Format, Max Capacity, and Allocation, and click Finish. The new volume appears in the Host Details window under the Volumes Heading. Close the Host Details window.

5. **Create the new guest.** Right-click Localhost in the Virtual Machine Manager window, and then select New. The New VM window appears.

6. **Name the new guest**. Type any name you want to assign to the new guest VM. Choose where you are installing from (local media, network install, or PXE boot) and select Forward. A pop-up window asks for the location of your install media (CD, DVD, ISO image, Web server, FTP server, or PXE server).

7. **Select install media**. Depending on which type of media you selected, you can choose the location of that media. (In this example, I selected a live CD of Ubuntu.) After that, click Forward. You will be asked about CPU and RAM.

8. **Choose CPUs/RAM**. From the available RAM on your system, choose how much you want to allow the virtual guest to consume. Normally you want at least 512MB of RAM for each guest (although some can run with as little as 128MB for a low-volume server). You can also select to use one or more CPUs. If you have only one CPU, you can still select up to eight CPUs if your processor includes hardware virtualization support. This enables you to test how well applications can use the interfaces to multiple CPUs without having multiple CPUs on your hardware.

9. **Configure disk storage**. If you have already created a storage unit to use for your guest, select it here by browsing to the location of that storage unit. Otherwise, you can create a raw disk image on the computer's hard drive (selecting how big to make the storage image). Click Forward to review your options. Figure 23-1 shows the New VM storage settings window.

FIGURE 23-1

Setting up storage for your virtual machine.

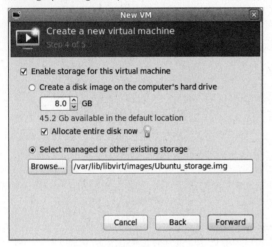

10. **Review and finish**. Review the options. Note that the name and location of the storage area is automatically selected if you didn't provide a specific device or filename. Selecting Advanced enables you to configure networking to do something other than use host device bridging, where the virtual machine uses the host physical network connection such as an Ethernet card. Click Finish if the settings look OK.

11. **Install the operating system**. What happens next varies according to the OS you are running or installing. In my example, the boot screen for the Ubuntu live CD appears in the Virtual Machine Manager window. Figure 23-2 shows an example of that window.

    Follow the installation procedure for the operating system you selected. I chose the Install Ubuntu selection. Then I followed along with the Ubuntu installation guide to complete the installation. Use the installation instruction for whatever operating system distribution you are installing.

12. **Shut down or reboot the guest.** Once the installation is complete, you can shut down or reboot the guest system as instructed. After that, you can use the Virtual Machine Manager or the virsh command to manage your virtual guest.

FIGURE 23-2

Begin the installation process for the guest system you choose to install (Ubuntu shown here).

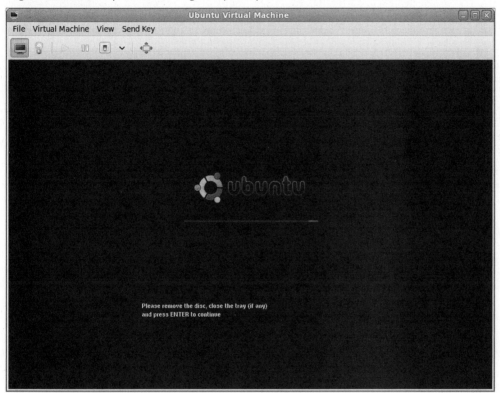

Managing Virtual Guest Systems

After you have installed a guest system, you can manage it through the same interface you used to create it: the Virtual Machine Manager window. Here are some of the things you can do from that window:

- **Start the guest** — Right-click on the guest you want to start and select Run. The guest boots up and displays in a window on your desktop.

- **Stop the guest** — Right-click on the guest you want to stop and select Shut Down ⇨ Shut Down. If the guest doesn't stop or if you are in a hurry, you can select Force Off instead, which effectively pulls the plug on the guest.

- **Reboot the guest** — Right-click on the guest you want to restart and select Shut Down ⇨ Reboot. The guest shuts down and boots back up as you watch it from your desktop.

- **View guest connection details** — To see details about a guest system, click on the host in the Virtual Machine Manager window and select Edit ⇨ Connection Details. From the Host details window, you can watch CPU and memory usage from the Overview tab. Select Virtual Networks to see details about your network device and IP addresses. Use the Storage tab to see the storage areas available to your guest.

- **Pause the guest** — Right-click on a guest entry and select Pause. All processing pauses on the guest until you select Pause again to resume.

- **Delete the guest** — You can permanently remove a virtual guest you no longer need. Make sure the guest is shut down, and then select Edit ⇨ Delete. You are then given the option to delete the guest, as well as its associated storage volume.

The actions just described can also be done as you display a text-based or graphical console of the guest. Opening and using the guest from your Fedora desktop is described in the next section.

Viewing and using guests

To open a guest, double-click on the guest's entry in the Virtual Machine Manager window. The window that appears displays a graphical or text-based console to use the guest. One of the first things you might want to do is view and change details about your guest.

Click the light bulb icon in the toolbar to see details about how the guest is configured. Figure 23-3 shows an overview of a virtual guest (e.g., name, run status, architecture, and so on).

More than a dozen options in the left column of this screen provide details about your guests. Here are descriptions of some of those options and where you have opportunities to configure your guests:

- **Performance** — Watch your CPU, memory, disk, and network usage live.

- **Processor** — See the number of allocated CPUs and possibly change that allocation.

- **Memory** — View how much memory is allocated to the guest and possibly change that.

- **Boot Options** — Specify whether the guest autostarts and where the guest boots from.

- **VirtIO Disk** — See details of your virtual hard disk. Each virtual disk is numbered, such as VirtIO Disk 1.

- **NIC** — View (and possibly change) your network interface card's device model.

- **Mouse** — See your mouse configuration.

- **Display VNC** — See the VNC server address and port for viewing the guest.

- **Sound, Serial, or Video** — See driver information for the virtual sound card, serial ports, and video card.

FIGURE 23-3

View and modify information about your virtual guest.

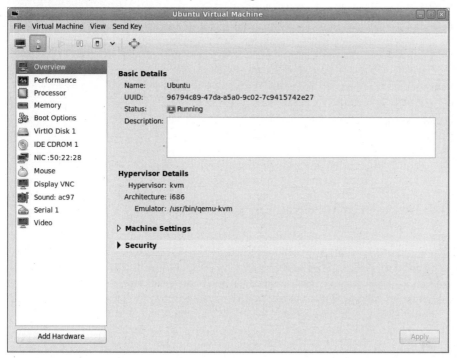

To use your virtual guest, you can simply click inside the Virtual Machine window for that guest once it is open and begin using it as you would any operating system from the system console. Because you are using the guest from a window, and not from the entire screen as you would normally, be aware of a few special features as you move around:

- **Grabbing the mouse pointer** — When you use a virtual guest, or any VNC client, clicking inside its window causes your mouse pointer to be trapped within that window. Press Ctrl+Alt to release the pointer back to your entire desktop. Note that you will see a prompt to click Control_L+Alt_L. Don't be fooled. These refer to the left side of the keyboard. Press Ctrl+Alt to release the pointer.

- **Using function keys** — If you need to do things such as view virtual windows within the console session to your guest, the functions keys won't work as expected. In other words, pressing Ctrl+Alt+F2 will show the second virtual terminal of your host system, not your guest system.

  To pass those and other key sequences to your guest system, select Send Key from the Virtual Machine window and choose the key sequence you want. For example, you could select Ctrl+Alt+F1 (to see the first virtual console on your guest),

Ctrl+Alt+Backspace (to kill your guest desktop session), Ctrl+Alt+Delete (to reboot the guest), or PrintScreen (to take a screenshot of the screen, the same effect as pressing the Print Scrn button).

- **Getting to the boot prompt** — If you are using Xen instead of KVM, when you go through VNC to view your guest, the view bypasses the boot loader when the system comes up. If you can't boot your guest properly, there's a way to get to the boot loader screen and change boot options. First, select Shutdown to turn off your guest. Then, from the command line, type the following line (replacing myguest with your guest system's name):

```
# xm create -c myguest
```

A text-based version of the bootloader should appear. You will probably have to press a key to prevent the system from booting the default boot entry. Edit the boot loader as needed (for example, you may want to add a 1 to the end of the kernel line to enter run level 1) and have the bootloader continue. After that, press Ctrl+] to close the console window and return to your regular VNC view of the guest.

Besides the issues just mentioned, you can use your virtual guest from within the VNC window as you would any operating system directly from the desktop. When you are done using it for the moment, just close the window. While this closes your view to the running system, it does not stop that system from running. Just double-click the guest's entry in the Virtual Machine Manager window to begin viewing it again.

Cloning guests

Once you have a virtual guest working the way you want it, why not repeat your fun? By cloning your virtual guest, you can have a copy of that guest that can run on your host system or another system. Here's how you clone a virtual guest:

1. **Pause or shut down the guest.** If the guest you want to clone is running, select Shut Down from the running guest. Then choose Shut Down or Force Off. If you prefer, you can simply pause the guest by selecting the Pause button.

2. **Select Clone.** From the guest's Virtual Machine window, select Virtual Machine ⇨ Clone. A Clone Virtual Machine window appears.

3. **Identify the clone.** Select or type in the following information:
   - **Name** — By default, the current guest name with "-clone" added is assigned to the clone. You can change that to any name you like.
   - **Networking** — If you are using bridging (the default) on the guest, the same type of networking is assigned to the clone. (Click Details to see more about the device.)
   - **Storage (disk image)** — A storage area of the same size and type used by the guest is created in the same directory (such as /var/lib/libvirt/images). The text

"-clone" is included in the image name just before the .img suffix. (Click Details in the storage box if you want to change the name or location of the image.)

- **Storage (removable media)** — If your machine has removable media, such as a CD drive, it will appear under the Storage heading and will be identified as being shareable from the clone.

4. **Start the cloning.** Select the Clone Virtual Machine button. A new storage area is created, along with the new virtual guest itself.

The cloned virtual guest should appear in the Virtual Machine manager window. You can run it from there alongside your other virtual guests. If you want to move the clone to another system or back it up, it is located under the /etc/libvirt directory structure. The storage area is under /var/lib/libvirt/images, unless you saved it to a different location.

With different guest names and clone names, the guests can both run on the same system without conflict. When they boot, they will use their own resources and, by default, have network interfaces with different IP addresses.

Using Command-Line Tools to Manage Virtual Guests

Even with the nice graphical interfaces available with KVM virtualization, many Linux experts prefer to work from the command line to build and manage virtualization. The following sections describe tools for creating virtual guests, building storage volumes, and managing your guest systems.

Creating and converting storage volumes

The qemu-img is a versatile tool for creating storage volumes, checking volumes, and converting them to different formats. To use the qemu-img command, you must have the qemu-img package installed.

Getting information about a storage volume

If you have some existing storage volumes (created by virt-manager or some other tools), you can get information about a volume using qemu-img with the info option. For example, type the following from the /var/lib/libvirt/images directory:

```
# qemu-img info Fedora14.img
image: Fedora12.img
file format: qcow2
virtual size: 4.9G (5242880000 bytes)
disk size: 136K
cluster_size: 65536
```

The output shows that the image (Fedora14.img) is a 4.9GB virtual disk that is currently consuming only 136KB of space (in other words, it's ready to be installed). The format of this volume is qcow2.

Creating a storage volume

To use `qemu-img` to make a new storage volume, you can use the `create` option. Here is an example that creates a 4GB image in qcow2 format:

```
$ qemu-img create -f qcow2 storage_volume.qcow2 4G
Formatting 'storage_volume.qcow2', fmt=qcow2 size=429496↵
 encryption=off cluster_size=0
```

This next command creates a raw image that is 4GB in size:

```
$ qemu-img create -f raw myraw.img 4G
  Formatting 'myraw.img', fmt=raw size=4294967296
```

Converting a storage volume

You can convert any supported storage format to any other supported format using the `convert` option to `qemu-img`. While you are converting, you can also add features such as compression and encryption.

The following is an example of a `qemu-img` command for converting a 100MB raw image to qcow2 format, while compressing it:

```
$ qemu-img convert big.img -O qcow2 -c big.qcow
$ du -sh big*
101M    big.img
16K     big.qcow2
```

This example shows the raw `big.img` file being reduced from 101MB to 16KB in size as it is being converted to qcow2 format. Keep in mind that compression is read-only. That means if you rewrite a compressed sector, then that sector is rewritten as uncompressed data. The compression used is 128-bit AES.

Creating virtual guests with virt-install

If you are more comfortable using commands than graphical tools, or if you just need more flexibility working with your virtual guests than is available through the Virtual Machine Manager window, you can use the `virt-install` command to create virtual guests in KVM.

When you create a virtual guest, you want to pass it the same information you entered when you used the Virtual Machine Manager window. Before you begin you need a few things in place. Here's what I did for the following example:

- Create a storage volume called `myfedora.qcow2` (making sure it is large enough to hold the operating system being installed).
- Get an install CD or DVD (or simply an ISO image of an install CD or DVD). In this example, I inserted a Fedora 14 installation DVD in the first DVD drive (`/dev/cdrom`).

The following example creates a system named `fedora14-01`. It uses 512MB of RAM and has the default networking configuration (default, virtio). It reads the installation medium from the first CD drive and enables you to watch the installation from a VNC window. Here's what the `virt-install` command looks like (divided over several lines for readability):

```
# virt-install --connect qemu:///system \
          --name fedora14-01  \
          --ram 512  \
          --disk path=/var/lib/libvirt/images/myfedora.qcow2  \
        --network network=default,model=virtio  \
        --vnc  \
        --cdrom /dev/cdrom
Starting install...
Creating domain...
```

A VNC window appears, enabling you to step through the installation process. Once the installation process is done, you can manage the new guest from the Virtual Machine Manager window or from the command line using `virsh` (as described later in this chapter).

There are several ways you can modify the `virt-install` command just shown, including the following few examples:

- **Installation media** — Instead of installing from CD or DVD (`--cdrom /dev/cdrom`), you can choose the location of the medium in other ways. If you can find an Internet site that has the operating system you want, simply point to its URL. Here are some examples:

  ```
  Install from dvd.iso in /root
  --location=/root/dvd.iso

  Install from NFS share from bighost
  --location=nfs:bighost:/var/ftp/pub/MYOS

  Install from a directory on a Web server
  --location=http://server10/MYOS

  Install from a directory on an FTP server
  --location=ftp://myftp/MYOS
  ```

- **Architecture** — Using `--arch=ARCH`, you can specify that the guest requires a non-native architecture. By default, the architecture of the host CPU is used.

- **Unique identifier** — You can specify a UUID to ensure that the guest is uniquely identified across your entire data center. The format is `--uuid=UUID`, where UUID is a 32-digit hexadecimal number. If you don't enter one, one is randomly generated.

- **Virtual CPUs** — To test operating systems that use multiple CPUs, or to use multiple CPUs explicitly from the guest, you can add the `vcpus` option. For example, `--vcpus=3` indicates that the guest can use three virtual CPUs.

For descriptions of other options, see the virt-install man page (man virt-install).

Managing virtual guests with virsh

Using the virsh command, you can manage your virtual guests from the command line. To start a guest that's not running (e.g., one called fedora14-01), you could type the following:

```
# virsh start fedora14-01
```

To shut down a guest in an orderly way, type the following:

```
# virsh shutdown fedora14-01
```

If the guest doesn't respond to the shutdown request, or if you want it to shut down immediately, you can effectively pull the plug on the guest using the destroy option:

```
# virsh destroy fedora14-01
```

To set a guest to start automatically when the system boots, you can use the autostart option:

```
# virsh autostart fedora14-01
```

To turn off the autostart feature, you can disable it:

```
# virsh autostart --disable fedora14-01
```

There are many more options you can use with virsh to manage your virtual guests (also referred to as *domains*). Refer to the virsh man page for details (man virsh).

Managing virtual machines with Spice

The Spice project, short for simple protocol for independent computing environments, aims to help you manage all your virtual desktops across your entire network. Starting with Fedora 14, Spice provides a remote desktop for QEMU virtual machines.

Note

Spice requires a 64-bit version of Linux. ■

Much like the X Window System, Spice includes server and client components. The server component runs in front of your remote virtual machine, acting as a display driver (called a QXL driver) for the system running under QEMU. The client runs on your local system. Together, these components enable the remote virtual machine to run graphics operations that Spice sends to your local system, in effect allowing remote access to a virtual machine desktop.

See www.spice-space.org and http://fedoraproject.org/wiki/Features/Spice for more information on Spice.

Converting Xen virtual machines with virt-v2v

Because Fedora has aligned with KVM for virtualization, Fedora 14 provides a command to help convert older Xen virtual machines to KVM. The `virt-v2v` command, part of the `virt-v2v` package, does this. To use `virt-v2v`, you need to generate a libvirt domain description for your Xen virtual machine with a command like the following:

```
# virsh dumpxml xen_domain > xen_domain.xml
```

Replace *xen_domain* with the name of the Xen domain you want to convert. Next, run a command like the following to convert the Xen virtual machine:

```
# virt-v2v -i libvirtxml -op pool_name xen_domain.xml
```

In this command, you need to pass the name of a storage pool to use for your new KVM virtual machine. Create this pool with the `virt-manager` command.

See the `virt-v2v` man page for more information about this command.

Summary

By including KVM features in the basic kernel delivered with Fedora, virtualization is available on every Fedora system with enough horsepower to use it. Graphical tools such as the Virtual Machine Manager make it easy to create and manage virtual guests. Command-line tools enable you to do the same steps separately, such as creating storage volumes (`qemu-img`) and installing guests (`virt-install`), giving you more flexibility when creating your guests.

Once virtual guests are created, there are a lot of things you can do to manage them. You can start, shut down, clone, or migrate a guest from the Virtual Machine Manager window. Using the `virsh` command, you can perform many of the same tasks to start and stop your virtual guests.

About the Media

If you have a CD-ROM or DVD drive on a standard PC (32-bit i386 architecture), you can install Fedora 14 from the media that came with this book. Those media include the following:

- **Fedora 14 Install DVD** — This is the official Fedora 14 Install DVD. It contains more than 3GB of software packages from the Fedora software repository.

- **Fedora 14 Desktop Edition Live CD** — This is an official live CD from the Fedora project. A live CD is useful for trying out Fedora without disrupting software installed on your hard disk and for testing how well Fedora works on your computer hardware.

  The live CD boots to a GNOME desktop with a nice variety of applications, regardless of what is installed on your computer's hard disk. You can install the contents of this CD to hard disk by starting the installer icon from the live CD's desktop. Once the software is installed, you can install any other software you need from online repositories.

If you have a drive that supports both DVDs and CDs, use the DVD to install Fedora. It provides more options for selecting software and does not require access to online repositories to go beyond a basic desktop system. However, for the average desktop user, the CD will work well as a starting point for a useable Fedora desktop system.

Note

The CD and DVD included with this book are for 32-bit PC architectures. They will not work on other computer architectures. However, you can download ISO images of Fedora live and installation CDs and DVDs for the X86 64-bit (x86_64) architecture from the Fedora download page (http://fedoraproject.org/en/get-fedora-all). ∎

To install Fedora 14 from the DVD or CD, follow the instructions provided in Chapter 2 in this book and the Installation Guide or User Guide at http://docs.fedoraproject.org.

If for some reason you don't have the media that came with the book handy, you can find information on how to download different live and install CDs and DVDs from the Fedora Project website at http://fedoraproject.org. If you have a DVD drive on another computer on your LAN, see Chapter 2 for information on setting up a Fedora install server.

Repositories such as http://rpmfusion.org can help you find extra, useful software packages that are not in Fedora (or any other Red Hat distribution). Some of these sites act as yum or apt repositories that allow you to download sets of dependent packages (see the descriptions of yum and useful third-party Fedora software repositories in Chapter 5).

Fedora Source Code

From time to time, you may want to recompile the Linux kernel or another software package that comes with Fedora. Like the binary software packages, the source code packages are available from the Fedora Project site (http://fedoraproject.org/en/get-fedora-all). To work with Fedora source code packages, here is what you need:

- **kernel-devel** — The kernel-devel package comes with the Fedora binary packages. Included in the package name is the version number of the kernel it contains. The source code for the current kernel is contained in the /usr/src/kernels directory, ready to be recompiled, if the kernel-devel package is installed.

- **SRPMS directory** — Source code for each binary package outside of the kernel that is included in Fedora is available from any Fedora repository. Install the source code package for the software that interests you (the name ends in .src.rpm) and a copy of that software in subdirectories of your local rpmbuild directory.

To do the actual compilations, you need to install at least the gcc package. As with the installation DVDs, if you want to download DVDs containing Fedora source code, you can get them from a Fedora download site, called a *mirror site*. Individual software packages for Fedora source code are available in source/SRPMS directories at the same Fedora mirror sites.

Index

SYMBOLS

F

WILEY PUBLISHING, INC.
END-USER LICENSE AGREEMENT

GNU General Public License

Version 2, June 1991

Copyright © 1989, 1991 Free Software Foundation, Inc.

59 Temple Place - Suite 330, Boston, MA 02111-1307, USA

Everyone is permitted to copy and distribute verbatim copies of this license document, but changing it is not allowed.

Preamble

The licenses for most software are designed to take away your freedom to share and change it. By contrast, the GNU General Public License is intended to guarantee your freedom to share and change free software — to make sure the software is free for all its users. This General Public License applies to most of the Free Software Foundation's software and to any other program whose authors commit to using it. (Some other Free Software Foundation software is covered by the GNU Library General Public License instead.) You can apply it to your programs, too.

When we speak of free software, we are referring to freedom, not price. Our General Public Licenses are designed to make sure that you have the freedom to distribute copies of free software (and charge for this service if you wish), that you receive source code or can get it if you want it, that you can change the software or use pieces of it in new free programs; and that you know you can do these things.

To protect your rights, we need to make restrictions that forbid anyone to deny you these rights or to ask you to surrender the rights. These restrictions translate to certain responsibilities for you if you distribute copies of the software, or if you modify it.

For example, if you distribute copies of such a program, whether gratis or for a fee, you must give the recipients all the rights that you have. You must make sure that they, too, receive or can get the source code. And you must show them these terms so they know their rights.

We protect your rights with two steps: (1) copyright the software, and (2) offer you this license which gives you legal permission to copy, distribute and/or modify the software.

Also, for each author's protection and ours, we want to make certain that everyone understands that there is no warranty for this free software. If the software is modified by someone else and passed on, we want its recipients to know that what they have is not the original, so that any problems introduced by others will not reflect on the original authors' reputations.

Finally, any free program is threatened constantly by software patents. We wish to avoid the danger that redistributors of a free program will individually obtain patent licenses, in effect making the program proprietary. To prevent this, we have made it clear that any patent must be licensed for everyone's free use or not licensed at all.

The precise terms and conditions for copying, distribution and modification follow.

Terms and Conditions for Copying, Distribution and Modification

0. This License applies to any program or other work which contains a notice placed by the copyright holder saying it may be distributed under the terms of this General Public License. The "Program", below, refers to any such program or work, and a "work based on the Program" means either the Program or any derivative work under copyright law: that is to say, a work containing the Program or a portion of it, either verbatim or with modifications and/or translated into another language. (Hereinafter, translation is included without limitation in the term "modification".) Each licensee is addressed as "you".

Activities other than copying, distribution and modification are not covered by this License; they are outside its scope. The act of running the Program is not restricted, and the output from the Program is covered only if its contents constitute a work based on the Program (independent of having been made by running the Program). Whether that is true depends on what the Program does.

1. You may copy and distribute verbatim copies of the Program's source code as you receive it, in any medium, provided that you conspicuously and appropriately publish on each copy an appropriate copyright notice and disclaimer of warranty; keep intact all the notices that refer to this License and to the absence of any warranty; and give any other recipients of the Program a copy of this License along with the Program.

You may charge a fee for the physical act of transferring a copy, and you may at your option offer warranty protection in exchange for a fee.

2. You may modify your copy or copies of the Program or any portion of it, thus forming a work based on the Program, and copy and distribute such modifications or work under the terms of Section 1 above, provided that you also meet all of these conditions:

a) You must cause the modified files to carry prominent notices stating that you changed the files and the date of any change.

b) You must cause any work that you distribute or publish, that in whole or in part contains or is derived from the Program or any part thereof, to be licensed as a whole at no charge to all third parties under the terms of this License.

c) If the modified program normally reads commands interactively when run, you must cause it, when started running for such interactive use in the most ordinary way, to print or display an announcement including an appropriate copyright notice and a notice that there is no warranty (or else, saying that you provide a warranty) and that users may redistribute the program under these conditions, and telling the user how to view a copy of this License. (Exception: if the Program itself is interactive but does not normally print such an announcement, your work based on the Program is not required to print an announcement.)

These requirements apply to the modified work as a whole. If identifiable sections of that work are not derived from the Program, and can be reasonably considered independent and separate works in themselves, then this License, and its terms, do not apply to those sections when you distribute them as separate works. But when you distribute the same sections as part of a whole which is a work based on the Program, the distribution of the whole must be on the terms of this License, whose permissions for other licensees extend to the entire whole, and thus to each and every part regardless of who wrote it.

Thus, it is not the intent of this section to claim rights or contest your rights to work written entirely by you; rather, the intent is to exercise the right to control the distribution of derivative or collective works based on the Program.

In addition, mere aggregation of another work not based on the Program with the Program (or with a work based on the Program) on a volume of a storage or distribution medium does not bring the other work under the scope of this License.

3. You may copy and distribute the Program (or a work based on it, under Section 2) in object code or executable form under the terms of Sections 1 and 2 above provided that you also do one of the following:

   a) Accompany it with the complete corresponding machine-readable source code, which must be distributed under the terms of Sections 1 and 2 above on a medium customarily used for software interchange; or,

   b) Accompany it with a written offer, valid for at least three years, to give any third party, for a charge no more than your cost of physically performing source distribution, a complete machine-readable copy of the corresponding source code, to be distributed under the terms of Sections 1 and 2 above on a medium customarily used for software interchange; or,

   c) Accompany it with the information you received as to the offer to distribute corresponding source code. (This alternative is allowed only for noncommercial distribution and only if you received the program in object code or executable form with such an offer, in accord with Subsection b above.)

The source code for a work means the preferred form of the work for making modifications to it. For an executable work, complete source code means all the source code for all modules it contains, plus any associated interface definition files, plus the scripts used to control compilation and installation of the executable. However, as a special exception, the source code distributed need not include anything that is normally distributed (in either source or binary form) with the major components (compiler, kernel, and so on) of the operating system on which the executable runs, unless that component itself accompanies the executable.

If distribution of executable or object code is made by offering access to copy from a designated place, then offering equivalent access to copy the source code from the same place counts as distribution of the source code, even though third parties are not compelled to copy the source along with the object code.

4. You may not copy, modify, sublicense, or distribute the Program except as expressly provided under this License. Any attempt otherwise to copy, modify, sublicense or distribute the Program is void, and will automatically terminate your rights under this License. However, parties who have received copies, or rights, from you under this License will not have their licenses terminated so long as such parties remain in full compliance.

5. You are not required to accept this License, since you have not signed it. However, nothing else grants you permission to modify or distribute the Program or its derivative works. These actions are prohibited by law if you do not accept this License. Therefore, by modifying or distributing the Program (or any work based on the Program), you indicate your acceptance of this License to do so, and all its terms and conditions for copying, distributing or modifying the Program or works based on it.

6. Each time you redistribute the Program (or any work based on the Program), the recipient automatically receives a license from the original licensor to copy, distribute or modify the Program subject to these terms and conditions. You may not impose any further restrictions on the recipients' exercise of the rights granted herein. You are not responsible for enforcing compliance by third parties to this License.

7. If, as a consequence of a court judgment or allegation of patent infringement or for any other reason (not limited to patent issues), conditions are imposed on you (whether by court order, agreement or otherwise) that contradict the conditions of this License, they do not excuse you from the conditions of this License. If you cannot distribute so as to satisfy simultaneously your obligations under this License and any other pertinent obligations, then as a consequence you may not distribute the Program at all. For example, if a patent license would not permit royalty-free redistribution of the Program by all those who receive copies directly or indirectly through you, then the only way you could satisfy both it and this License would be to refrain entirely from distribution of the Program.

If any portion of this section is held invalid or unenforceable under any particular circumstance, the balance of the section is intended to apply and the section as a whole is intended to apply in other circumstances.

It is not the purpose of this section to induce you to infringe any patents or other property right claims or to contest validity of any such claims; this section has the sole purpose of protecting the integrity of the free software distribution system, which is implemented by public license practices. Many people have made generous contributions to the wide range of software distributed through that system in reliance on consistent application of that system; it is up to the author/donor to decide if he or she is willing to distribute software through any other system and a licensee cannot impose that choice.

This section is intended to make thoroughly clear what is believed to be a consequence of the rest of this License.

8. If the distribution and/or use of the Program is restricted in certain countries either by patents or by copyrighted interfaces, the original copyright holder who places the Program under this License may add an explicit geographical distribution limitation excluding those countries, so that distribution is permitted only in or among countries not thus excluded. In such case, this License incorporates the limitation as if written in the body of this License.

9. The Free Software Foundation may publish revised and/or new versions of the General Public License from time to time. Such new versions will be similar in spirit to the present version, but may differ in detail to address new problems or concerns.

    Each version is given a distinguishing version number. If the Program specifies a version number of this License which applies to it and "any later version", you have the option of following the terms and conditions either of that version or of any later version published by the Free Software Foundation. If the Program does not specify a version number of this License, you may choose any version ever published by the Free Software Foundation.

10. If you wish to incorporate parts of the Program into other free programs whose distribution conditions are different, write to the author to ask for permission. For software which is copyrighted by the Free Software Foundation, write to the Free Software Foundation; we sometimes make exceptions for this. Our decision will be guided by the two goals of preserving the free status of all derivatives of our free software and of promoting the sharing and reuse of software generally.

NO WARRANTY

11. BECAUSE THE PROGRAM IS LICENSED FREE OF CHARGE, THERE IS NO WARRANTY FOR THE PROGRAM, TO THE EXTENT PERMITTED BY APPLICABLE LAW. EXCEPT WHEN OTHERWISE STATED IN WRITING THE COPYRIGHT HOLDERS AND/OR OTHER PARTIES PROVIDE THE PROGRAM "AS IS" WITHOUT WARRANTY OF ANY KIND, EITHER EXPRESSED OR IMPLIED, INCLUDING, BUT NOT LIMITED TO, THE IMPLIED WARRANTIES OF MERCHANTABILITY AND FITNESS FOR A PARTICULAR PURPOSE. THE ENTIRE RISK AS TO THE QUALITY AND PERFORMANCE OF THE PROGRAM IS WITH YOU. SHOULD THE PROGRAM PROVE DEFECTIVE, YOU ASSUME THE COST OF ALL NECESSARY SERVICING, REPAIR OR CORRECTION.

12. IN NO EVENT UNLESS REQUIRED BY APPLICABLE LAW OR AGREED TO IN WRITING WILL ANY COPYRIGHT HOLDER, OR ANY OTHER PARTY WHO MAY MODIFY AND/OR REDISTRIBUTE THE PROGRAM AS PERMITTED ABOVE, BE LIABLE TO YOU FOR DAMAGES, INCLUDING ANY GENERAL, SPECIAL, INCIDENTAL OR CONSEQUENTIAL DAMAGES ARISING OUT OF THE USE OR INABILITY TO USE THE PROGRAM (INCLUDING BUT NOT LIMITED TO LOSS

OF DATA OR DATA BEING RENDERED INACCURATE OR LOSSES SUSTAINED BY YOU OR THIRD PARTIES OR A FAILURE OF THE PROGRAM TO OPERATE WITH ANY OTHER PROGRAMS), EVEN IF SUCH HOLDER OR OTHER PARTY HAS BEEN ADVISED OF THE POSSIBILITY OF SUCH DAMAGES.

END OF TERMS AND CONDITIONS